The Rorschach: A Comprehensive System, in two volumes
by John E. Exner, Jr.
Theory and Practice in Behavior Therapy
by Aubrey J. Yates
Principles of Psychotherapy
by Irving B. Weiner
Psychoactive Drugs and Social Judgment: Theory and Research
edited by Kenneth Hammond and C. R. B. Joyce
Clinical Methods in Psychology
edited by Irving B. Weiner
Human Resources for Troubled Children
by Werner I. Halpern and Stanley Kissel
Hyperactivity
by Dorothea M. Ross and Sheila A. Ross
Heroin Addiction: Theory, Research and Treatment
by Jerome J. Platt and Christina Labate
Children's Rights and the Mental Health Profession
edited by Gerald P. Koocher
The Role of the Father in Child Development
edited by Michael E. Lamb
Handbook of Behavioral Assessment
edited by Anthony R. Ciminero, Karen S. Calhoun, and Henry E. Adams
Counseling and Psychotherapy: A Behavioral Approach
by E. Lakin Phillips
Dimensions of Personality
edited by Harvey London and John E. Exner, Jr.
The Mental Health Industry: A Cultural Phenomenon
by Peter A. Magaro, Robert Gripp, David McDowell, and Ivan W. Miller III
Nonverbal Communication: The State of the Art
by Robert G. Harper, Arthur N. Wiens, and Joseph D. Matarazzo
Alcoholism and Treatment
by David J. Armor, J. Michael Polich, and Harriet B. Stambul
A Biodevelopmental Approach to Clinical Child Psychology: Cognitive Controls and Cognitive Control Theory
by Sebastiano Santostefano
Handbook of Infant Development
edited by Joy D. Osofsky
Understanding the Rape Victim: A Synthesis of Research Findings
by Sedelle Katz and Mary Ann Mazur
Childhood Pathology and Later Adjustment: The Question of Prediction
by Loretta K. Cass and Carolyn B. Thomas
Intelligent Testing with the WISC-R
by Alan S. Kaufman
Adaptation in Schizophrenia: The Theory of Segmental Set
by David Shakow
Psychotherapy: An Eclectic Approach
by Sol L. Garfield
Handbook of Minimal Brain Dysfunctions
edited by Herbert E. Rie and Ellen D. Rie
Handbook of Behavioral Interventions: A Clinical Gu
edited by Alan Goldstein and Edna B. Foa
Art Psychotherapy
by Harriet Wadeson
Handbook of Adolescent Psychology
edited by Joseph Adelson
Psychotherapy Supervision: Theory, Research and Practice
edited by Allen K. Hess

Continued on back

LONELINESS

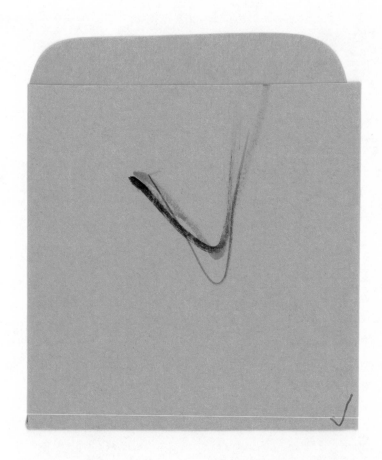

L O N E L I N E S S

A SOURCEBOOK OF CURRENT THEORY, RESEARCH AND THERAPY

Edited by
LETITIA ANNE PEPLAU
DANIEL PERLMAN

175 YEARS OF PUBLISHING
1807 1982

A WILEY-INTERSCIENCE PUBLICATION
JOHN WILEY & SONS
New York · Chichester · Brisbane · Toronto · Singapore

Library of Congress Cataloging in Publication Data:

Main entry under title:

Loneliness: A sourcebook of current theory,
    research, and therapy.

    (Wiley series on personality processes, ISSN
0195-4008)
    "A Wiley-Interscience publication."
    Includes index.
    1. Loneliness.   I. Peplau, Letitia Anne.
II. Perlman, Daniel.   III. Series.

BF575.L7L66   152.4   81-16272
ISBN 0-471-08028-4   AACR2

Printed in the United States of America

10 9 8 7 6 5 4

List of Contributors

CRAIG A. ANDERSON, PHD, *is Assistant Professor of Psychology at Rice University*

JOANNE BAUM, PHD, *founder of "Living is Learning," does therapy, training and teaching in the San Francisco area*

TORA KAY BIKSON, PHD, *is a Research Scientist at the Rand Corporation, Santa Monica, California*

TIM BRENNAN, PHD, *is Director of the Human Systems Institute in Boulder, Colorado*

MIHALY CSIKSZENTMIHALYI, PHD, *is Professor and Chair of the Committee on Human Development and Professor of Education at the University of Chicago*

CAROLYN E. CUTRONA, PHD, *is Assistant Professor of Psychology at the University of Iowa*

JENNY DE JONG-GIERVELD *is Professor of Sociology in the Department of Research Methods at the Free University of Amsterdam, The Netherlands*

VALERIAN J. DERLEGA, PHD, *is Associate Professor of Psychology at Old Dominion University*

CRAIG W. ELLISON, PHD, *is Professor of Psychology and Urban Studies at Simpson College, San Francisco*

CLAUDE S. FISCHER, PHD, *is Associate Professor of Sociology at the University of California, Berkeley*

JAMES P. FLANDERS, PHD, *is Associate Professor of Psychology at Florida International University*

RITA DE SALES FRENCH, PHD, *is a psychology intern in the Department of Psychiatry and a postdoctoral research affiliate of the Boys Town Center at Stanford University*

JACQUELINE D. GOODCHILDS, PHD, *is a Research Scientist at the Rand Corporation, Santa Monica and Adjunct Associate Professor of Psychology at the University of California, Los Angeles*

RONALD GRAEF, PhD, *is a clinical psychologist in private practice in Chicago*

GLORIA D. HEINEMANN, PhD, *is a Senior Research Sociologist, Division of Intramural Research, National Center for Health Services Research, Department of Health and Human Services, Hyattsville, Maryland*

LEONARD M. HOROWITZ, PhD, *is Professor of Psychology at Stanford University*

WARREN H. JONES, PhD, *is Associate Professor of Psychology at the University of Tulsa*

REED LARSON, PhD, *is Research Associate in the Committee on Human Development, University of Chicago, and Coordinator of the Clinical Research Training Program in Adolescence, Michael Reese Hospital and the University of Chicago*

HELENA Z. LOPATA, PhD, *is Professor of Sociology and Director of the Center for the Comparative Study of Social Roles at Loyola University of Chicago*

STEPHEN T. MARGULIS, PhD, *is Director of Research at the Buffalo Organization for Social and Technological Innovation, Buffalo, New York, and Adjunct Associate Professor of Man-Environment Relations in the College of Human Development at the Pennsylvania State University*

MARIA MICELI *is a Research Psychologist for the National Program on the Prevention of Mental Diseases of the Institute of Psychology of the Italian National Research Council*

BRUCE MORASCH, MA, *is a doctoral student in the Department of Psychology, University of California, Los Angeles*

RAYMOND F. PALOUTZIAN, PhD, *is Associate Professor of Psychology at Westmont College, Santa Barbara, California*

LETITIA ANNE PEPLAU, PhD, *is Associate Professor of Psychology at the University of California, Los Angeles*

DANIEL PERLMAN, PhD, *is Professor of Psychology at the University of Manitoba, Winnipeg, Canada*

SUSAN L. PHILLIPS *is a doctoral student in the Department of Sociology, University of California, Berkeley*

JOS RAADSCHELDERS *is a Research Sociologist in the Department of Research Methods at the Free University of Amsterdam, The Netherlands*

KAREN S. ROOK, PhD, *is Assistant Professor of Social Ecology at the University of California, Irvine*

CARIN M. RUBENSTEIN, PhD, *is an Associate Editor of Psychology Today magazine in New York*

ZICK RUBIN, PhD, *is Louis and Frances Salvage Professor of Social Psychology at Brandeis University*

DANIEL RUSSELL, PhD, *is an Assistant Professor in the Graduate Program in Hospital and Health Administration at the University of Iowa*

PHILLIP SHAVER, PhD, *is Associate Professor of Psychology at the University of Denver*

PETER SUEDFELD, PhD, *is Professor and Head of the Department of Psychology at the University of British Columbia, Vancouver, Canada*

ROBERT S. WEISS, PhD, *is Professor of Sociology at the University of Massachusetts in Boston and Lecturer in Sociology at Harvard Medical School*

JEFFREY E. YOUNG, PhD, *is Clinical Assistant Professor of Psychology in the Department of Psychiatry at the University of Pennsylvania*

Series Preface

This series of books is addressed to behavioral scientists interested in the nature of human personality. Its scope should prove pertinent to personality theorists and researchers as well as to clinicians concerned with applying an understanding of personality processes to the amelioration of emotional difficulties in living. To this end, the series provides a scholarly integration of theoretical formulations, empirical data, and practical recommendations.

Six major aspects of studying and learning about human personality can be designated: personality theory, personality structure and dynamics, personality development, personality assessment, personality change, and personality adjustments. In exploring these aspects of personality, the books in the series discuss a number of distinct but related subject areas: the nature and implications of various theories of personality; personality characteristics that account for consistencies and variations in human behavior; the emergence of personality processes in children and adolescents; the use of interviewing and testing procedures to evaluate individual differences in personality; efforts to modify personality styles through psychotherapy, counseling, behavior therapy, and other methods of influence; and patterns of abnormal personality functioning that impair individual competence.

IRVING B. WEINER

University of Denver
Denver, Colorado

Preface

Loneliness researchers are often asked, "How did you get interested in *that* topic?" From the inquirer's hushed voice and avoidance of eye contact, you sense that he or she expects an embarrassed answer revealing your own secret loneliness. Unabashedly, we admit that, like millions of other Americans, we have experienced the distress of loneliness. But that is not the source of this volume; rather its beginnings can be traced more directly to events of 1976, and its roots extend back at least another two decades.

In the fall of 1976, co-editor Dan Perlman had just arrived at UCLA for a sabbatical. Having for some time been interested in interpersonal attraction, he thought that one plausible way to gain a new perspective on friendship would be to focus on people who were lonely and without friends. As he was doing some writing at the time, Dan decided to include two pages—no more and no less—on social isolation. He mentioned this interest to colleagues he already knew at UCLA, who advised him: "Go talk to Anne Peplau, she knows about these things."

Even during childhood, Anne had been exposed to concern about social deficits. In 1955, Anne's aunt Hildegard Peplau had written an article entitled "Loneliness" for the *American Journal of Nursing*. Later, as a graduate student at Harvard, Anne heard Bob Weiss lecture on his important new book, *Loneliness: The Experience of Social and Emotional Isolation*. By 1976 Anne had joined the faculty at UCLA where she and a group of graduate students began a program of research on loneliness.

What started for the co-editors as a coffee break has now extended into a six-year collaboration. By the end of the 1976–1977 school year we had decided that a conference on loneliness would be productive, and were able to secure a grant from the National Institute of Mental Health to assist with expenses. With their help, the conference was held in May 1979. The ambience of the meeting, as well as many of the issues discussed, are nicely captured in Zick Rubin's award-winning article, "Seeking a Cure for Loneliness" (*Psychology Today*, October 1979).

The idea for this book crystallized at the time of the UCLA Loneliness Conference. We did *not* want to publish the conference proceedings; yet, from the papers given at that meeting, the form of the book took shape in our minds. We developed a blueprint of how specific conference papers could be developed into chapters and what additional contributions would be needed.

This book was designed as an up-to-date sourcebook on loneliness. It covers a broad range of topics including the nature of loneliness, the causes and consequences of loneliness, its assessment, its distribution in society, and loneliness across the life cycle. The book surveys basic research findings and theories about loneliness and considers interventions for helping lonely people. The chapters, written by leading experts in the field, integrate available information on key topics and provide overviews of major projects. They are written to be understood by readers with only modest statistical training. Collectively, the chapters place recent developments in historical perspective yet also bring the reader to the leading edge of loneliness work.

Loneliness is of interest to a broad spectrum of readers, and this book should appeal to several audiences. Professionals and advanced students in clinical, developmental, personality, and social psychology and in sociology should find the book relevant. The book will also be useful to practitioners in the fields of psychiatry, marriage and family counseling, social work, nursing, gerontology, and pastoral counseling. Researchers may be most interested in the descriptions of innovative methods for studying loneliness, the discussion of theoretical perspectives on loneliness, and the links between work on loneliness and such related areas as social networks, privacy, and interpersonal attraction. Clinicians may be most interested in gaining a better understanding of the characteristics and problems of lonely individuals and the suggested approaches to therapy. Even laypersons, curious about loneliness, should be able to gain insight from this anthology.

As anyone who has studied social relationships is well aware, most projects are accomplished only when the publicly visible players have the help and support of many other individuals. We have been very fortunate to have a wide and generous social network. We are grateful to the National Institute of Mental Health not only for their financial assistance but also for the enthusiasm of Joyce Lazar and Joel Goldstein for this project. Our work has also benefited from financial assistance from the Social Sciences and Humanities Research Council of Canada. Our universities and our department chairpersons (Seymour Feshbach and John McIntyre) have provided environments and teaching schedules conducive to the completion of this undertaking. Fellow loneliness researchers have shared their ideas and findings with us, and thus have facilitated our understanding and keeping abreast of work on loneliness. The authors who contributed to this volume have been a model group— they have cooperated with our requests and completed manuscripts relatively on schedule (an almost unheard-of practice in many academic enterprises). Several graduate students at both UCLA and the University of Manitoba have listened as we formulated ideas, shared their own insights with us, and collaborated in our research on loneliness. Our editor at Wiley, Herb Reich, provided just the right blend of nudging and compassion. The secretarial staff at the University of Manitoba typed various chapters of the manuscript. At

UCLA, Patricia Linton competently and cheerfully assumed responsibility for typing and a variety of editorial tasks. The author and subject indices were prepared with the help of Shelley Borys and Kathleen Boyle.

If our work on loneliness has provided a basic insight—a single idea worth cherishing—it is very simple: have the right balance of companionship and solitude. Our lives and our work on this project have been greatly enriched by having spouses with an uncanny ability to find this fulcrum point.

DANIEL PERLMAN
LETITIA ANNE PEPLAU

Winnipeg, Manitoba
Los Angeles, California
February 1982

Contents

Chapter 1

Perspectives on Loneliness

Letitia Anne Peplau and Daniel Perlman

To me, it is the strangest thing that in Western Christian society, founded on the love of God and the fellowship of mankind, loneliness has become one of the hallmarks. We are the only people who have had drummed into them from childhood the impossible commandment to love our neighbors like ourselves, and yet so many of us eke out an existence as loveless and unloved atoms—free individuals in an open society, condemned to form part of the great, grey subculture of the lonely.

ROBERT BRAIN, 1976, pp. 259–260

Few of us have escaped the painful experience of loneliness. In the natural course of growing up our social relationships begin, change, and end. In infancy we first experience the distressing anxiety of being separated, often only temporarily, from loving caretakers. As children, we venture into a wider world of social relations where we try, not always successfully, to gain acceptance and friendship from peers. As we grow older, the excitement of starting in a new school, going to summer camp, or moving to a new town is commonly mingled with feelings of loneliness and loss. For teenagers, the exhilarating prospect of first love may in reality include experiences of love spurned or gone sour. As adults, our web of social relations continues to shift. Marriages begun in love and hope do not always last; children are born but ultimately leave the family nest. Old social ties are lost through separation, neglect, or death. Social transitions are a basic fact of life in modern society, and so is loneliness. For most of us, intense feelings of loneliness are short-lived; for others, loneliness is a persistent aspect of daily life.

This book brings together social science findings and perspectives on loneliness. Perhaps because loneliness is so commonplace, it has attracted less attention from scientists than other more exotic social phenomena. In an attempt to correct this long-standing neglect, we and other contributors to this volume have taken loneliness as the direct focus of our scientific inquiry.

The results of this collective endeavor have shed light on the experiences of loneliness that we have all known in our lives.

In this first chapter we present an overview of key concepts and issues. Our hope is to help readers organize and integrate the many facts and theories presented in this book. We begin by noting the social and theoretical importance of the study of loneliness. We next attempt to go beyond an intuitive understanding of loneliness and consider formal definitions of the phenomenon. After a brief survey of the history of loneliness research, we present a general framework for the study of loneliness that examines the experience of loneliness, its antecedents, and the ways people cope with loneliness. Finally, we describe the general goals and organization of the book.

WHY STUDY LONELINESS?

The question "Why study loneliness?" has several answers. One of the simplest, yet most important, is that loneliness is interesting. Whether because of our own personal experiences or naive curiosity, many social scientists want to understand the loneliness puzzle. A second reason for studying loneliness is that it is so widespread. For instance, Cutrona (Chapter 18) reports that three-quarters of college students experience at least some loneliness during their first term. While the proportion of lonely people in this group is atypically high, it is safe to say that loneliness is a fact of life for millions of Americans. Third, loneliness is unpleasant and can even have life-threatening consequences. It has been linked to alcoholism, suicide, and physical illness. By helping people overcome loneliness, the incidence of such problems may be reduced.

Fourth, loneliness often creates concern about the health of our social institutions. Loneliness reflects a breakdown in social interactions. As Fischer and Phillips point out (Chapter 2),

> Sociology has always seen personal relations as the mortar of society. It is through such relations that people are taught norms that make for smooth social interaction, are assisted in times of trouble and become contributing members to a broader social life. When individuals are alone, they, by definition, do not benefit from social life; when a society has made isolated members it is prone to crumble.

Like alienation, high divorce rates, and widespread crime, loneliness is seen by some as a cause (or, if you prefer, a symptom) of social decay.

As a people, we are concerned—some might say obsessed—with the quality of our interpersonal relationships. Love and friendship are dominant American values. Not surprisingly, social psychologists have scrutinized the components of interpersonal attraction in some detail. Loneliness is, so to speak, the opposite side of this coin. Thus a fifth impetus for studying loneliness is that it may provide new insights about intimacy and friendship.

Sixth, loneliness research appears to be gaining momentum within the social sciences. Now is a good time to be doing loneliness research. Journals and even granting agencies appear to be receptive to this new topic. The field has to some extent been mapped out, some of the basic issues have been identified, and the tools of the search developed. Yet the literature is still small enough to be manageable. And the terminology is still fresh enough so that the investigator can leave his or her mark.

Given these half-dozen arguments for studying loneliness, and the many others that could be articulated, it may seem odd that social scientists have only recently begun to investigate loneliness. There are at least two factors that may have delayed attention to loneliness. First, many people are embarrassed by being lonely; it is awkward and not something they readily admit. This stigma may spill over to investigators studying loneliness. People sometimes look askance at loneliness researchers, perhaps wondering if their research is motivated by some unresolved "personal problem." Indeed we have both been asked such questions by reporters, students, and even colleagues. Second, research psychologists have often idealized the experimental method as the most valid approach to study reality. But there is no convenient and ethical way to manipulate loneliness in the laboratory, and so this topic requires the use of other, perhaps less fashionable methods.

Whatever the earlier barriers to loneliness research, the study of loneliness expanded rapidly in the 1970s. Loneliness is now a topic in good currency. And that in itself is a reason for studying it.

LONELINESS: WHAT IS IT?

When members of the general public are asked by pollsters about loneliness, they have no difficulty answering. Most people can unhesitatingly report whether or not they are presently lonely. Lay people may not all share exactly the same concept of loneliness, but intuitively they know what loneliness is. For everyday purposes, they have a satisfactory implicit referent for the concept.

Several more formal definitions of loneliness have been offered by social scientists. A dozen such definitions are shown in Table 1.1. There appear to be three very important points of agreement in the way scholars view loneliness. First, loneliness results from deficiencies in a person's social relationships. Second, loneliness is a subjective experience; it is not synonymous with objective social isolation. People can be alone without being lonely, or lonely in a crowd. Third, the experience of loneliness is unpleasant and distressing.

The varying definitions of loneliness given in Table 1.1 reflect differing theoretical orientations. These theoretical biases are related to some important aspects of the ways in which loneliness is conceptualized. In particular, these differences center around the nature of the social deficiency experienced by lonely individuals.

One approach emphasizes inherent human *needs for intimacy*. Sullivan

Table 1.1.   Twelve Definitions of Loneliness

I define loneliness as the absence or perceived absence of satisfying social relationships, accompanied by symptoms of psychological distress that are related to the actual or perceived absence. . . . I propose that social relationships can be treated as a particular class of reinforcement. . . . Therefore, loneliness can be viewed in part as. *a response to the absence of important social reinforcements* (Young, Chapter 22, p. 380, italics in original).

Loneliness is caused not by being alone but by being without some definite needed relationship or set of relationships. . . . Loneliness appears always to be a response to the absence of some particular type of relationship or, more accurately, a response to the absence of some particular relational provision (Weiss, 1973, p. 17).

Loneliness . . . is the exceedingly unpleasant and driving experience connected with inadequate discharge of the need for human intimacy, for interpersonal intimacy (Sullivan, 1953, p. 290).

Loneliness . . . is an experienced discrepancy between the kinds of interpersonal relationships the individual perceives himself as having at the time, and the kinds of relationships he would like to have, either in terms of his past experience or some ideal state that he has actually never experienced (Sermat, 1978, p. 274).

Loneliness is an experience involving a total and often acute feeling that constitutes a distinct form of self-awareness signaling a break in the basic network of the relational reality of self-world (Sadler & Johnson, 1980, p. 39).

Loneliness is the unpleasant experience that occurs when a person's network of social relations is deficient in some important way, either quantitatively or qualitatively (Perlman & Peplau, 1981, p. 31).

Loneliness is a sentiment felt by a person . . . [experiencing] a wish for a form or level of interaction different from one presently experienced (Lopata, 1969, p. 249–250).

Loneliness . . . refers to an affective state in which the individual is aware of the feeling of being apart from others, along with the experience of a vague need for other individuals (Leiderman, 1980, p. 387).

We define loneliness as: the experiencing of a lag between realized and desired interpersonal relationships as disagreeable or unacceptable, particularly when the person perceives a personal inability to realize the desired interpersonal relationships within a reasonable period of time (de Jong-Gierveld, 1978, p. 221).

Loneliness [is] a feeling of deprivation caused by the lack of certain kinds of human contact: the feeling that someone is missing. And since one has to have had some expectations of what it was that would be in this empty space, loneliness can further be characterized as the sense of deprivation that comes when certain *expected* human relationships are absent (Gordon, 1976, p. 26).

Loneliness is an adaptive feedback mechanism for bringing the individual from a current lack stress state to a more optimal range of human contact in quantity or form. "Lack stress" means too little of a given input, human contact in this instance (Flanders, Chapter 11, p. 170).

In our view, loneliness is caused by the absence of an appropriate social partner who could assist in achieving important other-contingent goals, and the continuing desire for such social contacts (Derlega & Margulis, Chapter 10, p. 155).

and Weiss represent this view. Fromm-Reichmann (1959, p. 3) belongs in the same camp. She maintained that a universal need for intimacy "stays with every human being from infancy throughout life." Weiss (1973) argued that vulnerability to loneliness may be part of our evolutionary heritage. He cited

Bowlby's (1973) work on attachment behavior, suggesting that "proximity-promoting mechanisms" may have survival value. Weiss (1974) has identified six essential provisions (e.g., social integration, guidance) of relationships. The implication of such an analysis is that one's relationships must adequately satisfy an inherent set of social needs, or the individual will experience loneliness.

A second approach to conceptualizing loneliness emphasizes *cognitive processes* concerning people's perception and evaluation of their social relations. From this perspective, loneliness results from perceived dissatisfaction with one's social relationships (Flanders, 1976; Sadler & Johnson, 1980). For example, Lopata (1969) defined loneliness as "a wish for a form or level of interaction different from the one presently experienced" (p. 250). Cognitive approaches (Peplau & Perlman, 1979; Sermat, 1978) propose that loneliness occurs when the individual perceives a discrepancy between two factors, the desired and the achieved pattern of social relations. Peplau and Perlman (1979) further suggest that loneliness can be seen as one endpoint of a continuum for evaluating social relations. In their view, each person has an optimal level of social interaction. When the person's social relations are suboptimal, he or she experiences the distress of loneliness; in contrast, when faced with excessive social contact, the person may experience the distress of "crowding" or feel an "invasion of privacy" (Altman, 1975). Evaluations of one's social relations are influenced by comparisons with one's own past experience and with the experiences of other people.

A third approach to loneliness identifies insufficient *social reinforcement* as the main deficiency experienced by lonely people. Young's chapter in this book takes such an approach. According to this view, social relations are a particular class of reinforcement. The quantity and type of contact a person finds satisfying are a product of his or her reinforcement history. One may learn, as Young points out, that confiding in a friend is rewarding. Relationships can assume secondary reinforcer status. Periods of isolation can cause deprivation, thus enhancing the subsequent reward value of social contacts.

The social needs and cognitive approaches to conceptualizing loneliness differ in two major ways. First, the needs approach emphasizes the affective aspects of loneliness; cognitive approaches emphasize the perception and evaluation of social relations and relational deficits. Thus proponents of the needs approach suggest a rather direct link between rational deficits and subjective reactions to these deficits. In Sullivan's (1953) words, "There is no way that I know of by which one can, all by oneself, satisfy the need for intimacy" (p. 271). In contrast, cognitive approaches (e.g., Peplau, Russell, & Heim, 1979) emphasize that cognitive processes play a central role in modulating the intensity of loneliness that results from deficits in sociability.

Second, advocates of the needs approach have suggested that people may experience loneliness without explicitly defining themselves as lonely or consciously recognizing the nature of their distress. Since people may have difficulty acknowledging loneliness to themselves or to others, it has been suggested (Fromm-Reichman, 1959; H. E. Peplau, 1955) that loneliness may be most recognizable to clinicians through the defensive behavior it triggers. In contrast, cognitive theorists emphasize the lonely person's perceptions and reports of relational inadequacies, and direct attention to those people who do label themselves as lonely. In this regard, the needs approach has been more closely tied to a psychodynamic tradition and to work with patient samples, while the cognitive view has been more closely tied to empirical survey research with students and members of the general public.

Young's reinforcement view of loneliness has not been emphasized in drawing these comparisons. His analysis is rooted in cognitive behaviorism rather than traditional reinforcement models. As a cognitive behaviorist, some of Young's views are closely akin to the purely cognitive approach to loneliness. For instance, with regard to our first comparative dimension, Young sees people's affective reaction to their social deficiencies as moderated by their automatic thoughts. However, with regard to our second comparative dimension, Young, like other clinicians, takes the view that symptoms without self-labeling are sufficient grounds for diagnosing an individual as lonely.

Up to this point we have been discussing loneliness as the aversive response to social deficits. This, in our view, is the dominant way loneliness has been used by social scientists. However, some writers, such as Moustakas (1961), believe that loneliness can lead to personal growth and creativity. Although this conceptualization of loneliness can be found in both philosophical and clinical discussions, it is of only secondary importance to the current research being done on loneliness. The contention that isolation can have positive results will be examined more closely in Part 1 of this volume.

EARLY WORK ON LONELINESS: WHERE HAVE WE BEEN?

The experience of loneliness may well be as old as the human race. Mijuskovic (1979) recently criticized those who suggest that loneliness is a recent product of modern society, arguing instead that "Man has always and everywhere suffered from feelings of acute loneliness" (p. 9). Certainly a concern about isolation and loneliness can be found in ancient writings. For example, the Book of Genesis emphasizes the pain of solitude, noting that after God created Adam he observed, "It is not good that the man should be alone: I will make him a help mate." Although the history of loneliness itself is long, the psychological study of loneliness is very young.

A comprehensive survey of the psychological literature on loneliness (Peplau, Russell, & Heim, 1978; see also the bibliography in this volume) documents the growth of psychological work on loneliness. Of the 208 publications available in English from 1932 to 1977, only 6% were published before 1960. These early works were almost exclusively commentaries by clinicians based on their observations of patients. Best known from this period are the theoretical writings of Sullivan (1953) and Fromm-Reichmann (1959). Other articles dealt with loneliness among special groups including children (Bakwin, 1942), adolescents (Collier & Lawrence, 1951), old people (Sheldon, 1948), wives of servicemen (Duvall, 1945), and alcoholics (Bell, 1956). A major emphasis among early theorists (e.g., H. E. Peplau, 1955; Von Witzleben, 1958) was the importance of distinguishing loneliness from such related states as solitude.

In the 1960s, 64 new publications on loneliness appeared. Although many continued to rely on clinical observations, empirical research became more prominent. For example, several major projects investigated loneliness and social isolation among older adults (Blau, 1961; Donson & Georges, 1967; Lopata, 1969; Lowenthal, 1964; Shanas et al., 1968; Tunstall, 1967). The 1960s also witnessed the publication of the *Lonely Crowd* (Riesman, Glazer, & Denney, 1961) and other sociological analyses of the impact of changing society on personal relations and loneliness. Early in the 1960s, Moustakas (1961) published the first of his popular books on existential loneliness, following an earlier tradition begun by Fromm (1955). Also noteworthy is the fact that three empirically based doctoral dissertations were completed in the 1960s (Bradley, 1969; Eddy, 1961; Sisenwein, 1964); these works all emphasized the need to develop measures to assess individual differences in loneliness.

Work on loneliness grew rapidly in the 1970s. An important early milestone was the publication of *Loneliness: The experience of emotional and social isolation* by Weiss (1973). This book did much to stimulate interest in loneliness and provided insights that have guided empirical investigations. Research was also fostered by the publication of a simple and reliable instrument to assess individual differences in loneliness—the UCLA Loneliness Scale (Russell, Peplau, & Ferguson, 1978; Chapter 6). Today research on loneliness is flourishing.

Several continuities between earlier work and current trends are noteworthy. The long-standing interest in clinical applications of work on loneliness can be seen in the development of systematic intervention programs to help lonely people. The measurement of individual differences in loneliness has become sophisticated, and has clarified conceptual distinctions between loneliness and related states. An early focus on the affective components of loneliness has been broadened to include studies of the cognition and social behavior of lonely people. Sociological interest in social integration has led to careful studies of social networks and a better understanding of who is socially isolated. Previous research has emphasized careful description and measurement. The time now seems ripe for the development and empirical testing of more complex theoretical models of loneliness and of the processes that produce and maintain it.

A FRAMEWORK FOR UNDERSTANDING LONELINESS

As the body of research and theory on loneliness increases, it becomes important to have a general framework for organizing and integrating concepts and findings. In this section we will briefly present such a framework; elsewhere (Perlman & Peplau, 1981) we have elaborated on these ideas in more detail. Two principles underlying this analysis are: (1) that loneliness is a response to a discrepancy between desired and achieved levels of social contact; and (2) that cognitive processes, especially attributions, have a moderating influence on loneliness experiences.

We find it useful to distinguish among antecedents of loneliness, characteristics of the experience of being lonely, and ways in which people cope with loneliness. However, in loneliness as in many similar phenomena, causality is complex and probably circular. For example, the extent to which low self-esteem is an antecedent cause of loneliness or a consequence of the experience of loneliness is unclear; it may well be both for some individuals.

Antecedents of Loneliness

Two distinct classes of causes of loneliness can be identified. The first concerns events or changes that precipitate the onset of loneliness. Thus the death of a loved one may trigger loneliness. A second class of causes concerns factors that predispose individuals to become lonely or to persist in remaining lonely over time. Thus a person's lack of social skills may make it difficult to develop or maintain satisfying social relationships.

Precipitating Events

Our general definition of loneliness as resulting from a relational deficit suggests two types of changes that may trigger loneliness. Perhaps most common are changes in the person's *actual social relations* that lead to relationships falling below an optimal level. The ending of a close relationship through death, divorce, or breakup often leads to loneliness. Physical separation from loved ones, as when children leave home to go to college or when a family moves to a new community, is a common antecedent of loneliness. Loneliness is affected not only by the presence or absence of relationships, but also by qualitative aspects of social relations. Thus decreases in satisfaction with relationships may lead to loneliness.

In addition to changes in actual social relations, loneliness can also be triggered by *changes in the person's social needs or desires*. Life-cycle changes in a person's capacities or desires for social relations may precipitate loneliness if they are not accompanied by correspondent changes in actual relations. Sullivan (1953) posited a developmental sequence in which children of different ages have different needs and social skills. In his view, loneliness first becomes possible during the preadolescent era, when a "need for intimacy" is added to earlier needs for tenderness and acceptance. Developmental changes undoubtedly occur after adolescence as well. Sheehy (1976) suggests that for many successful professional people, midlife brings a renewed interest in cultivating friendship—an increased desire to have a rich set of social relations in addition to work. Other experiences, such as psychotherapy or consciousness-raising groups, may also encourage individuals to reassess the importance and quality of their social relations. Finally, situational changes, such as periods of stress, may affect people's needs or desires for companionship and intimacy.

In summary, the onset of loneliness is triggered by a change in either actual social relations, or in the person's needs or desires for relationships. Theorists generally agree about the types of events that precipitate loneliness. But they differ in how they conceptualize the processes leading to loneliness. Thus the changed relationships may be seen as deficient because they fail to meet basic social needs, because they do not fulfill personal desires for relationships, or because the changed relationships lead to lower levels of social reinforcement.

Predisposing and Maintaining Factors

A variety of personal and situational factors increase an individual's vulnerability to loneliness. Such factors may increase the likelihood that a person will become lonely, and also make it more difficult for the lonely person to reestablish satisfying social relations.

As later chapters document, research is beginning to identify a set of *personal characteristics* that are consistently linked to loneliness. Lonely people are apt to be shy, introverted, and less willing to take social risks. Loneliness is often associated with self-deprecation and low self-esteem. For at least some people, inadequate social skills, perhaps stemming from childhood, contribute to loneliness. Personal characteristics such as these may contribute to loneliness in several related ways. First, such characteristics may reduce a person's social desirability and limit the person's opportunities for social relations. Second, personal qualities may influence a person's own behavior in social situations and contribute to unsatisfactory patterns of interaction. Third, personal qualities may affect how a person reacts to changes in his or her actual social relations, and so influence how effective the person is in avoiding, minimizing, or alleviating loneliness. Thus personal factors may predispose people to loneliness and make it harder for them to overcome loneliness when it does occur.

It is important to emphasize that *cultural and situational factors* also affect a person's chances of being lonely. Such an emphasis may help to correct a tendency (Peplau, Russell, & Heim, 1979) to overestimate the importance of personal factors in causing loneliness and so perhaps to unjustifiably "blame the victims" of loneliness for their social difficulties. Sociological theorists have long suggested that loneliness is exacerbated by cultural values and institutions. Slater (1970), for example, described a basic conflict between American values of competition, uninvolvement, and independence—and basic human needs for community, engagement, and dependence on others. To the extent that social institutions such as public schools and private corporations emphasize rugged individualism and success through competition, they may foster loneliness. By creating unrealistic expectations about relationships, the popular media may also contribute to feelings of social inadequacy and loneliness.

Features of a person's more immediate social situation can also influence the likelihood of loneliness. Research on interpersonal attraction (Berscheid & Walster, 1979) has documented a number of factors that increase social interaction, foster group cohesiveness, and so presumably influence loneliness. For example, a well-documented finding is that physical proximity fosters liking. As a result, the architecture of housing units affects social interaction and friendship formation. The individual who lives or works in a physically isolated location should be more vulnerable to loneliness. Most generally, loneliness is affected by the match between the individual's needs, desires or skills, and the realities of his or her social environment. For the outgoing social risk taker, physical isolation may be less of a problem than for the shy individual. The extent to which a person is similar to others in the environment in attitudes, values, and background may also play a role.

The Experience of Loneliness

Empirical research is beginning to identify typical signs and symptoms of loneliness. (See chapters by Horowitz et al.; Jones; Paloutzian & Ellison; Rubenstein & Shaver; Russell.) Our discussion of the manifestations and correlates of loneliness considers affective, motivational, cognitive, and behavioral factors as well as social problems. It is of course often difficult to draw the line between relatively changeable characteristics that accompany loneliness and more enduring factors that may have caused the loneliness to occur in the first place. Our emphasis here is on potentially transient features of the experience of loneliness.

Affective Manifestations

Loneliness is an unpleasant experience. Fromm-Reichmann (1959) described it as painful and frightening. Weiss characterized it as a "gnawing distress without redeeming features" (1973, p. 15). Empirical research adds detail to this depiction. Loneliness has consistently been linked to depression (Bragg, 1979; Russell, Peplau, & Cutrona, 1980; Weeks, Michela, Peplau, & Bragg, 1980). Lonely people report being less happy, less satisfied, more pessimistic, and more depressed (Bradburn, 1969; Perlman, Gerson, & Spinner, 1978). Despite the frequent co-occurrence of loneliness and depression, it appears useful to distinguish between the two concepts. Depression is a much broader phenomenon than loneliness; people can be depressed for a variety of reasons; hence depressed people are not invariably lonely.

Lonely people often feel anxious and describe themselves as tense, restless, and bored (Loucks, 1974; Perlman et al., 1978). Other affective correlates of loneliness have been less fully documented. There is some evidence that lonely people may feel hostile toward others (Moore & Sermat, 1974; Loucks, 1974). In one study (Russell et al., 1978) lonely college students were apt to feel angry, self-enclosed, empty, and awkward. Similar results were obtained among a sample of older adults studied by Perlman et al. (1978).

Motivational Manifestations

Two seemingly contradictory images of the motivational aspects of loneliness have been reported. On the one hand, some authors consider loneliness arousing. For instance, Sullivan (1953) believed loneliness was a "driving" force that motivates people to initiate social interactions despite the anxiety such interactions may hold for them. Weiss (1973) echoed this theme, indicating that "the lonely are driven to find others" (p. 15). In contrast, loneliness has also been described as decreasing motivation. For instance, Fromm-Reichmann (1959) contended that true loneliness creates a sense of "paralyzing hopelessness and unalterable futility." A study by Perlman (unpublished research) found that lonely people endorsed statements indicating apathy, such as, "At times I feel worn out for no special reason," and "My strength often seems to drain away from me," and they rejected the statement "I have a lot of energy."

Several factors may help resolve the apparently paradoxical motivational properties of loneliness. First, loneliness may arouse motivation for interpersonal contact but diminish motivation for nonsocial activities. Second, loneliness may be arousing yet interfere with the effective channeling of one's energies required to complete tasks successfully. Third, different types of loneliness may have different motivational properties. For example, nondepressed loneliness may be arousing, while depressed loneliness may involve decreased motivation. Fourth, loneliness may have different motivational properties over time. Whereas the onset of loneliness may be arousing, the persistence of loneliness over long periods of time may be debilitating (Gerson & Perlman, 1979). Fifth, cognitive factors may mediate the motivational force of loneliness. Perhaps the perception of personal control over one's loneliness motivates people to seek ways of alleviating their distress (Schulz, 1976). Last, but equally plausible, lonely people may fluctuate in their moods, alternating between periods of high and low motivational arousal.

Cognitive Factors

Recent research (see chapters by Jones; Peplau, Miceli, & Morasch; Young) has focused on the impact on loneliness of cognitive processes of attention and attribution. There is some evidence that lonely people may generally be less able to concentrate or focus their attention effectively (Perlman, unpublished research). Several studies suggest that lonely people are highly self-conscious or self-focused (Jones, Freemon, & Goswick, 1981). That is, they dwell on their own actions to a greater extent than do nonlonely people. This heightened self-focus may be reflected in subtle aspects of interpersonal behavior, such as asking fewer questions of others.

Weiss has suggested that lonely people are often highly vigilant about interpersonal relationships:

The individual is forever appraising others for their potential as providers of the needed relationships, and forever appraising situations in terms of their potential for making the needed relationships available . . . [Loneliness] produces an oversensitivity to minimal cues and a tendency to misinterpret or to exaggerate the hostile or affectionate intent of others. (1973, p. 21)

To date, however, evidence in support of this hypothesis has not been gathered.

Research by Peplau and her colleagues (Chapter 9) suggests that lonely people are typically eager to explain the reasons for their distress. Understanding the causes of loneliness may be seen as the first step toward predicting, controlling, and ultimately alleviating loneliness. The type of attributions that individuals make may have significant effects on their optimism about the future, their affective reactions to loneliness, their self-esteem, and their coping behavior. Thus the first-year college student who attributes her loneliness to temporary situational factors may feel more hopeful about improving her social life than another student who attributes his loneliness to relatively unchanging aspects of his personality. It has also been proposed that attributions may influence, in some measure, whether or not a lonely person becomes depressed. Believing that one's loneliness is due to stable features of one's personality may be especially likely to induce depression (Michela, Peplau, & Weeks, 1980). Attributions may also help explain the common finding that lonely people have lower self-esteem. For at least some people, blaming oneself for prolonged loneliness may lead to a decline in self-esteem.

Behavioral Correlates of Loneliness

In thinking about the behavioral manifestations of loneliness, it is at times difficult to distinguish among behavior that accompanies loneliness, behavior that leads to loneliness in the first place, and behavioral strategies for coping with loneliness. We have discussed social skill deficits in our earlier section on the antecedents of loneliness. Here we consider aspects of the affiliative behavior and interpersonal style of lonely adults.

Very few studies have attempted to document the actual behavior of lonely individuals (see review by Jones, Chapter 15), and this seems to be an especially important direction for future research. Available data suggest three possible behavioral manifestations of loneliness. First, lonely people may show different patterns of self-disclosure than nonlonely people. It may be that lonely individuals either pour out their hearts to listeners, or keep their personal lives extremely private. Second, the behavior of lonely people may reflect a greater self-focus than that of nonlonely people. Third, data linking loneliness to self-reports of shyness and low social risk-taking suggest that lonely people may be less assertive in their social interactions.

Social and Medical Problems

Loneliness has been linked to a variety of problems affecting not only individuals but also our society as a whole. Some evidence suggests that loneliness is related to adolescent truancy and behavior problems (Brennan & Auslander, 1979) and to suicide (Wenz, 1977). The possible negative implications of loneliness for mental health are suggested by findings that loneliness is correlated with depression and anxiety.

Also of interest are the possible effects of loneliness on physical health. Lynch (1977) has argued that loneliness makes people susceptible to serious illness and promotes the overuse of various medical services. However, most of the data cited by Lynch are based on measures of social isolation rather than loneliness. More direct evidence on the health consequences of loneliness is beginning to accumulate. First, to the extent that loneliness creates anxiety or depression, lonely people may exhibit some of the physical signs that frequently accompany these states, such as disturbances in eating or sleep patterns, headaches, or nausea. Some support for this has been presented by Paloutzian and Ellison (Chapter 14) and Rubenstein and Shaver (Chapter 13). Second, loneliness has been correlated with alcohol consumption. Perlman (unpublished research) found that lonely people may drink as a response to personal problems and feelings of stress, whereas nonlonely people drink more often to participate in group social activities. Third, there is some evidence that lonely people are more vulnerable to physical illness (Peplau, Russell, & Cutrona, unpublished research). Future research is needed to document more fully the relationship of loneliness and health, and to clarify the possible causal links involved. While in some cases loneliness may be detrimental to health, in other instances illness may precipitate loneliness.

Coping with Loneliness

Our framework suggests three general ways in which people can cope with loneliness. Coping strategies may seek to establish satisfying social relations by (1) changing the person's actual social relations, (2) changing the person's social needs or desires, or (3) reducing the perceived importance of the social deficiency.

Probably the most direct and satisfying way to overcome loneliness is to improve one's social relations. This can be done by forming new relationships, by using one's existing social network more fully, or by creating "surrogate" relationships with pets, TV personalities, radio talk show hosts, or the like. We are only beginning to understand ways in which lonely people try to improve their social relations (see chapters by Cutrona; Lopata et al.; Paloutzian & Ellison; Rook & Peplau). Since most lonely people cope without the benefit of professional guidance, research identifying the most effective self-help strategies would be especially useful.

A second general approach to coping with loneliness is to reduce one's desires for social contact. In the short run this might be accomplished by selecting tasks and activities that can enjoyably be done alone, rather than chosing activities that the person only enjoys with company. Lonely people may also reexamine their standards for social relations. Over time, adaptation may occur as lonely people develop new habitual levels of social relating. Weiss (1973) commented that persistent loneliness may lead people to "change their standards for appraising their situation and feelings, and, in particular, that standards might shrink to conform more closely to the shape of bleak reality" (p. 228). Weiss does not consider this an adequate solution to loneliness; research on the effectiveness of such coping efforts is needed.

A third way people may cope with loneliness is to try to reduce the importance of the social deficiency they are experiencing. Some people may deny feelings of dissatisfaction and loneliness, or may devalue the importance of social relations. More often, perhaps, lonely people may try to distract themselves from their painful feelings by throwing themselves into their work, drinking to "drown their sorrows," or other such activities. Some of the negative health consequences of loneliness may result from such maladaptive coping activities.

THE GOALS AND ORGANIZATION OF THIS VOLUME

Given the growth of work on loneliness at the beginning of the 1980s, the timing seemed excellent for developing a sourcebook on loneliness. The network of active scholars was still relatively small. Communication among loneliness scholars had begun through informal channels and at professional meetings. In May 1979, with the sponsorship of the National Institute of Mental Health, we organized at UCLA a research conference on loneliness (Rubin, 1979). The three days of meetings brought together scholars doing work on loneliness and closely related fields, and provided further encouragement to our idea of compiling a sourcebook of current research, theory, and therapeutic techniques.

The response from colleagues to our initial proposal for this volume was enthusiastic. By the fall of 1979 we had the necessary commitment from Wiley-Interscience as publisher and from potential contributors. Collectively, we began the process of transforming our blueprint for a book into reality. What we wanted to do was bring together the theoretical and empirical work of social scientists currently studying loneliness. We wanted both conceptual and empirical analyses because we are convinced that each enhances the other. We also believe that effective interventions to alleviate loneliness must be based on conceptual and empirical analysis of the phenomenon. Thus we wished to tie current perspectives on therapy for loneliness into the other two main elements of the volume.

We had several goals for the volume. We wanted to provide a relatively comprehensive perspective on contemporary work on loneliness. Thus we felt the volume should be eclectic with regard to theory and method. Second, we wanted chapters that would summarize and synthesize information. Given the large number of specific studies of loneliness, it would not be possible to publish even a representative sample of research reports in a single volume. Therefore we wanted chapters that would provide overviews of major research projects or integrations of available information on specific topics. Third, despite our respect for the importance of methodological rigor, we wanted the chapters written so they could be fully appreciated by readers with only modest research training.

This volume is organized into five major substantive sections. The first section focuses on aloneness. It is clear that loneliness is not the same as being alone. But it is equally clear that social isolation is often a key precursor to loneliness. The chapters in this section document who is alone in America and consider the consequences of solitude on people's moods and self-reported satisfaction. As noted earlier, an important question considered here is: Does solitude have positive effects?

The second section of the book presents methodological and conceptual issues in the study of loneliness. The first chapter by Weiss presents a distinguished scholar's view of where the field is and what issues it must face. The other two chapters provide accounts of efforts to measure loneliness and to identify types of loneliness.

The third section is on theoretical approaches to loneliness. The first chapter provides a brief overview of theoretical analyses. The next chapters provide statements of three contemporary conceptual frameworks.

The fourth section focuses on the experience of adult loneliness. It presents findings from four major research programs. Two chapters (Rubenstein & Shaver; Paloutzian & Ellison) provide information on such questions as: Who is lonely? What emotions are common among lonely adults? What do lonely people do to cope with their experiences? Jones discusses the social attitudes, skills, and behavior of lonely people. Horowitz, French, and Anderson attempt to uncover people's "prototype" or typical image of the lonely person. These researchers examine how such images of loneliness influence our judgments of loneliness in others, and how they relate to the social behavior and feelings of lonely individuals.

The fifth section considers loneliness throughout the life cycle. Rubin's chapter identifies three main reasons why young children lack friends. Brennan presents data and theory about loneliness among adolescents. Cutrona reports a longitudinal study of the course of loneliness during students' first year at college. Lopata and her associates look at another major transition point in life, widowhood. Finally, Peplau and her associates consider loneliness and aloneness among old people.

The final section is on therapy for loneliness. The first chapter by Rook and Peplau provides a general overview of issues and strategies for helping lonely people. Young's chapter is a detailed presentation of his cognitive behavioral therapy. His work represents one of the few well-developed therapeutic efforts addressed specifically toward combating loneliness.

In many subfields of psychology, the discrepancies in research findings outweigh the consistencies. Fortunately, loneliness is an area in which there has been a striking consistency in many of the major findings reported by different investigators using varying methods. There is also agreement on many of the issues worth addressing. Thus, throughout this volume, you will find what we consider a healthy cross referencing and overlap of ideas and results. Naturally, every question has not yet been answered, nor is there perfect agreement among investigators. Such tensions are crucial if the area is to grow and evolve.

Nonetheless, we are confident that by the end of your reading of this volume, you will have a clear, essential portrait of the lonely person. Along with the other contributors to this volume, we have spent several years coming to understand loneliness. For us, the effort has been both challenging and rewarding. We trust you will share in our enthusiasm, gain from our insights, and consider making your own contributions to loneliness research in the 1980s.

REFERENCES

Altman, I. *The environment and social behavior: Privacy, personal space, crowding.* Monterey, Calif.: Brooks-Cole, 1975.

Bakwin, H. Loneliness in infants. *American Journal of Diseases of Children,* 1942, *63,* 30–40.

Bell, R. G. Alcohol and loneliness. *Journal of Social Therapy,* 1956, *2,* 171–181.

Berscheid, E., & Walster, E. *Interpersonal attraction* (2nd ed.) Reading, Mass.: Addison-Wesley, 1979.

Blau, Z. Structural constraints of friendship in old age. *American Sociological Review,* 1961, *26,* 429–439.

Bowlby, J. *Attachment and loss. Separation: Anxiety and anger* (Vol. 2). New York: Basic Books, 1973.

Bradburn, N. *The structure of psychological well-being.* Chicago: Aldine, 1969.

Bradley, R. *Measuring loneliness.* Unpublished doctoral dissertation, Washington State University, 1969.

Bragg, M. *A comparative study of loneliness and depression.* Unpublished doctoral dissertation, University of California, Los Angeles, 1979.

Brain, R. *Friends and lovers.* New York: Basic Books, 1976.

Brennan, T., & Auslander, N. *Adolescent loneliness: An exploratory study of social and psychological predisposition and theory* (National Institute of Mental Health, Juvenile Problems Division, Grant No. R01-MH 289 12-01). Boulder, Colo.: Behavioral Research Institute, 1979.

Collier, R. M., & Lawrence, H. P. The adolescent feeling of psychological isolation. *Educational Theory,* 1951, *1,* 106–115.

Donson, C., & Georges, A. *Lonely-land and bedsitter-land.* Bala, North Wales: Chapples, 1967.

Duvall, E. M. Loneliness and the serviceman's wife. *Journal of Marriage and Family Living,* 1945, *7,* 77–81.

Eddy, P. D. *Loneliness: A discrepancy with the phenomenological self.* Unpublished doctoral dissertation, Adelphi College, 1961.

Flanders, J. P. From loneliness to intimacy. *Practical psychology.* New York: Harper & Row, 1976.

Fromm, E. *The sane society.* New York: Holt, Rinehart, & Winston, 1955.

Fromm-Reichmann, F. Loneliness. *Psychiatry,* 1959, *22,* 1–15.

Gerson, A. C., & Perlman, D. Loneliness and expressive communication. *Journal of Abnormal Psychology,* 1979, *88,* 258–261.

Gordon, S. *Lonely in America.* New York: Simon & Schuster, 1976.

Jones, W. H., Freemon, J. A., & Goswick, R. A. The persistence of loneliness: Self and other determinants. *Journal of Personality,* 1981, *49,* 27–48.

Jong-Gierveld, J. de. The construct of loneliness: Components and measurement. *Essence,* 1978, *2,* 221–238.

Leiderman, P. H. Pathological loneliness: A psychodynamic interpretation. In J. Hartog, J. R. Audy, & Y. A. Cohen (Eds.), *The anatomy of loneliness.* New York: International Universities Press, 1980.

Lopata, H. Z. Loneliness: Forms and components. *Social Problems,* 1969, *17,* 248–261.

Loucks, S. The dimensions of loneliness: A psychological study of affect, self-concept, and object-relations (Doctoral dissertation, University of Tennessee, 1974). *Dissertation Abstracts International,* 1974, *35,* 3024B. (University Microfilms No. 74–27, 221)

Lowenthal, M. F. Social isolation and mental illness in old age. *American Sociological Review,* 1964, *29,* 54–70.

Lynch, J. J. *The broken heart: The medical consequences of loneliness in America.* New York: Basic Books, 1977.

Michela, J. L., Peplau, L. A., & Weeks, D. G. *Perceived dimensions and consequences of attributions for loneliness.* Unpublished manuscript, July 1980. (Available from J. L. Michela, Box 6, Teachers College, Columbia University, New York, N.Y. 10027.)

Mijuskovic, B. L. *Loneliness in philosophy, psychology and literature.* Assen, Netherlands: Van Gorcum, 1979.

Moore, J. A., & Sermat, V. Relationship between self-actualization and self-reported loneliness. *Canadian Counsellor,* 1974, *8*(3), 84–89.

Moustakas, C. E. *Loneliness.* New York: Prentice-Hall, 1961.

Peplau, H. E. Loneliness. *American Journal of Nursing,* 1955, *55,* 1476–1481.

Peplau, L. A., & Perlman, D. Blueprint for a social psychological theory of loneliness. In M. Cook & G. Wilson (Eds.), *Love and attraction.* Oxford, England: Pergamon, 1979.

Peplau, L. A., Russell, D., & Cutrona, C. E. Unpublished research.

Peplau, L. A., Russell, D., & Heim, M. The experience of loneliness. In I. H.

Frieze, D. Bar-Tal, & J. S. Carroll (Eds.), *New approaches to social problems: Applications to attribution theory*. San Francisco, Calif.: Jossey-Bass, 1979.

Peplau, L. A., Russell, D., & Heim, M. Loneliness: A bibliography of research and theory. *JSAS Catalog of Selected Documents in Psychology*, 1978, *8*, 38. (Ms. No. 1682)

Perlman, D., Gerson, A. C., & Spinner, B. Loneliness among senior citizens: An empirical report. *Essence*, 1978, *2*, 239–248.

Perlman, D., & Peplau, L. A. Toward a social psychology of loneliness. In R. Gilmour & S. Duck (Eds.), *Personal relationships: 3. Personal relationships in disorder*. London: Academic Press, 1981.

Riesman, D., Glazer, N., & Denney, R. *The lonely crowd: A study of the changing American character*. New Haven: Yale University Press, 1961.

Rubin, Z. Seeking a cure for loneliness. *Psychology Today*, October 1979, pp. 82–90.

Russell, D., Peplau, L. A., & Cutrona, C. E. The revised UCLA loneliness scale: Concurrent and discriminant validity evidence. *Journal of Personality and Social Psychology*, 1980, *39*, 472–480.

Russell, D., Peplau, L. A., & Ferguson, M. L. Developing a measure of loneliness. *Journal of Personality Assessment*, 1978, *42*, 290–294.

Sadler, W. A., & Johnson, T. B. From loneliness to anomia. In R. Audy, J. Hartog, & Y. A. Cohen (Eds.), *The anatomy of loneliness*. New York: International Universities Press, 1980.

Schulz, R. Effects of control and predictability on the physical and psychological well-being of the institutionalized aged. *Journal of Personality and Social Psychology*, 1976, *33*, 563–573.

Sermat, V. Sources of loneliness. *Essence*, 1978, *2*, 271–276.

Shanas, E., Townsend, P., Wedderburn, D., Friis, H., Milhoj, P., & Stehouwer, J. *Old people in three industrial societies*. New York: Atherton, 1968.

Sheehy, G. *Passages: Predictable crises of adult life*. New York: Bantam, 1976.

Sheldon, J. H. *The social medicine of old age*. London: Oxford University Press, 1948.

Sisenwein, R. J. *Loneliness and the individual as viewed by himself and others*. Unpublished doctoral dissertation, Columbia University, 1964.

Slater, P. *The pursuit of loneliness: American culture at the breaking point*. Boston: Beacon Press, 1970.

Sullivan, H. S. *The interpersonal theory of psychiatry*. New York: Norton, 1953.

Tunstall, J. *Old and alone*. New York: Humanities Press, 1967.

Von Witzleben, H. D. On loneliness. *Psychiatry*, 1958, *21*, 37–43.

Weeks, D. G., Michela, J. L., Peplau, L. A. & Bragg, M. E. The relation between loneliness and depression: A structural equation analysis. *Journal of Personality and Social Psychology*, 1980, *39*, 1238–1244.

Weiss, R. S. *Loneliness: The experience of emotional and social isolation*. Cambridge, Mass.: MIT Press, 1973.

Weiss, R. S. The provisions of social relationships. In Z. Rubin (Ed.), *Doing unto others*. Englewood Cliffs, N.J.: Prentice-Hall, 1974.

Wenz, F. V. Seasonal suicide attempts and forms of loneliness. *Psychological Reports*, 1977, *40*, 807–810.

PART ONE

Aloneness

The topic of social isolation is a natural starting point for a volume on loneliness. While being alone and being lonely are not synonymous, a deficiency in social contacts is a key antecedent that can lead to loneliness. Thus, to know who is at risk for becoming lonely, it is helpful to know: "Who is alone?" In Chapter 2, Fischer and Phillips use data from a representative survey of Northern Californians to answer this question.

Being alone is also a topic in its own right. It has been a concern of social philosophers for many centuries. Aristotle, in his *Politics,* wrote "A man wholly solitary would be either a god or a brute." His remark is interesting because it anticipates the dual nature of contemporary reactions to aloneness.

On the one hand, there are many who see being alone as a sorry, unfortunate condition. In *The Inventor's Suffering,* Balzac identified the fear that isolation can generate:

Man has a horror of aloneness. . . . The first thought of man, be he a leper or a prisoner, a sinner or an invalid, is to have a companion of his fate. In order to satisfy this drive which is life itself, he applies all his strength, all his power, the energy of his whole life.

Stereotypes of single people as unhappy and unfulfilled are common in our society. It is widely believed that when one marital partner dies, the remaining spouse has an unusually high probability of dying shortly thereafter.

On the other hand, there are many who see being alone as a cherished, productive condition. For Moustakas (1972, p. 44): "In real solitude we are expansive, limitless, free. . . . We renew contact with ourselves and discover who we are . . . we see life as it really is." According to this view, solitude can be refreshing, can help in formulating one's values, promote personal growth, contribute to creativity and the like.

Chapters 3 and 4 address the issue of what role aloneness has in our lives. In Chapter 3, Larson, Csikszentmihalyi, and Graef use an innovative methodological technique: they equipped high school students and adults with electronic pagers. Thus they could signal these people at random times during the day. Each time the participants were signaled, they indicated whether they were alone or with others, and completed a short questionnaire. Using this information, Larson and his associates focus on several questions such as: At what times are people most apt to be alone? When people are alone, are they in a more positive mood than when they are with others? and Does isolation have a renewing effect that is manifest immediately following periods of aloneness?

In Chapter 4, Suedfeld explores aloneness as a healing experience. He notes that many great spiritual and political leaders from Christ to Gandhi had solitary experiences that helped them develop their philosophies. Suedfeld also advocates the use of Restricted Environmental Stimulation Therapy (REST) as a method for alleviating problems such a phobias, obesity, and smoking. REST combines aloneness with other forms of reduced sensory stimulation and often employs specific persuasive messages addressed to the client's problem.

None of the chapters in this section focuses on the medical consequences of isolation. The general conclusion we draw from this literature is that social isolation is detrimental to health and life expectancy. But the interested reader is referred to research (Berkman & Syme, 1979) and reviews (Cobb, 1976; Verbrugge, 1979) for a more comprehensive treatment of this matter.

REFERENCES

Berkman, L. F. & Syme, S. L. Social networks, host resistance, and mortality: A nine year follow-up study of Alameda County residents. *American Journal of Epidemiology,* 1979, *109,* 186–204.

Cobb, S. Social support as a moderator of life stress. *Psychosomatic Medicine,* 1976, *38,* 300–314.

Moustakas, C. E. *Loneliness and love.* Englewood Cliffs, N.J.: Prentice-Hall, 1972.

Verbrugge, L. M. Marital status and health. *Journal of Marriage and the Family,* 1979, *41,* 267–285.

Chapter 2

Who is Alone?
Social Characteristics
of People with Small Networks

Claude S. Fischer and Susan L. Phillips

The recently emerging interest among social psychologists in loneliness has brought with it a need to understand who is actually alone. For sociologists such as ourselves, however, concern with isolation is part of our profound and traditional interest in social integration. From de Tocqueville's (1836) essays on the role of mediating groups in American democracy to modern studies of political behavior (Bereleson, Lazarsfeld, & McPhee, 1954; Laumann & Pappi, 1976); from Durkheim's (1897) classic study of suicide to modern research on mental health (Horowitz, 1977; Kleiner & Parker, 1976); from Simmel's (1922) analysis of small group relations to contemporary studies of how large communities are integrated (Mitchell, 1969; Wellman, 1979); sociology has always seen personal relations as the mortar of society. It is through such relations that people are taught norms that make for smooth social interaction, are assisted in times of trouble, and become contributing members to a broader social life. When individuals are alone, they by definition do not benefit from social life; when a society has many isolated members, it is prone to crumble. For sociologists, isolation has significant consequences far beyond individuals' feelings of loneliness.

Although recent studies of loneliness carefully distinguish between loneliness and being alone, few actually examine the latter empirically. Amid the

The research reported here was funded by Grant # MH 26802 from the Center for Studies of Metropolitan Problems, National Institute of Mental Health. The senior author was supported during this work by a John Simon Guggenheim Memorial Foundation Fellowship while visiting the Center for Population Studies, Harvard University. Among our many co-workers on the Northern California Community Study we especially acknowledge Lynne McCallister and Kathleen Gerson for helping develop the network and psychological items, respectively.

The data described here are available from the Inter-University Consortium for Political and Social Research, Ann Arbor, Michigan.

new research exploring the psychological intricacies (Jones, Chapter 15; Peplau, Russell, & Heim, 1979; Weiss, 1973) and social correlates of loneliness (Rubenstein, Shaver, & Peplau, 1979; Wood, 1978), there is little parallel work on those who objectively lack sociable or intimate relations. Our data, describing in depth the social networks of over a thousand people, afford a unique opportunity to answer the question, who is alone? Our answer is divided into several parts. First, we simply describe the kinds of people, men and women separately, who reported the fewest social relations. Types of people—old versus young, rich versus poor, and so on—are contrasted in the extent to which they were isolated from all social relations, from nonkin, and from kin, using both a "moderate" and a "severe" definition of isolation. Second, we examine, through multiple regression analysis, which social characteristics seem to be the most important correlates of isolation. Third, we apply the same procedures to analyze a specific kind of isolation: having few or no intimate confidants. Fourth, we examine the subjective concomitants of isolation by assessing what the independent correlations are of various forms of isolation with respondents' perceptions of isolation and of their happiness. Before proceeding, however, two preliminary steps are necessary: defining "alone" and describing our study.

WHAT DOES "ALONE" MEAN?

A major task in studying isolation is to decide which particular *types of social relations* a person must lack in order to be considered isolated. The ambiguities of defining and measuring isolation match those of assessing loneliness. For example, should people who see others only X times a month be considered socially isolated? Or are people really isolated only if they have no one who really cares about them? Or no one to talk to? In designing the Northern California Community Study, we finally decided that the relevant relations that comprise a "social network" are those in which there is a high probability of alter providing ego with rewarding exchanges (for further discussion of our rationale and methodology, see Fischer, 1982; Jones & Fischer, 1978; McCallister & Fischer, 1978). Therefore, social isolation is defined here as knowing relatively few people who are probable sources of rewarding exchanges. From the thousands of exchanges we might have examined and the dozens we pretested, we settled on asking respondents to name people:

1. Who would care for their homes if they went out of town.
2. Who they talked to about decisions at work, if they worked.
3. Who had helped with household tasks in the last three months.
4. With whom they had engaged in social activities, such as having someone drop in or come over for dinner, or meeting someone in a bar or park.
5. With whom they discussed mutual spare-time activities.

6. If the respondents were not married, who were their fiancés or "best friends."
7. With whom they discussed personal worries.
8. Whose advice they considered in making important decisions.
9. From whom they would or could borrow a large sum of money.
10. Who over 15 years old lived in the same household (these persons were assumed to be involved in tacit exchanges).

For this paper, we restricted our definition of "network" to people who were "readily available" to the respondents, that is, *persons who lived within one hour's drive*. The average network, by this criterion, included 10.6 names.* By asking "How is this person related to you?" we were able to distinguish readily available kin from nonkin. One drawback to this method is that some psychologically important interactions can transcend long distances, notably discussing personal matters with confidants on the telephone. Consequently, we developed a *separate measure* of emotional isolation (Weiss, 1973), counting all named people with whom respondents discussed personal worries or from whom they sought advice (see questions 7 and 8 above), regardless of where the named people lived.

Once the overall measures of social and emotional ties were developed, the problem was to decide the criteria of isolation, that is, how small do their networks have to be for people to be "isolated"? There is little rationale for selecting some arbitrary absolute number as the dividing line between small and not small. Consequently, we chose two cutting points based on the distribution of respondents: the approximately lowest 10% and the approximately lowest 40% of respondents. The first is a relatively "severe" criterion, for we can assume that people in the lowest decile have considerably smaller networks than the general sample, and they may even be eccentrically "alone." The 40% line provides a more "moderate" criterion, subsuming most respondents with networks of below-average size. For the number of readily available nonkin, for example, the lowest decile—actually, lowest 7% —of respondents gave *one or no* names, and the lowest four deciles—actually, 33%—of respondents named five or fewer.**

* The counts of associates used here differ from those used in other reports of the Northern California Community Study in two ways. One is the exclusion of those living over an hour away. The other is the exclusion of the "anyone else" names. After asking the name-eliciting questions, we also asked, "Is there anyone else important to you?" Our reason for dropping the additional "anyone else" names for this paper is that we wished to be conservative in categorizing respondents, crediting them with social relations only where we were very confident that those relations were real, active, and available. The "anyone else" names tended disproportionately to represent wishful, lapsed, and distant relations. (See analysis in Jones and Fischer, 1978.) All told, we dropped 43% of the original 19,419 relations, leaving 11,087, or 10.6 per respondent.

** For our other measures, the cutting points are, kin: severe, 0 (15% of respondents) and moderate, 1 (39%); total: 6 (10%) and 10 (36%); and confidant: 0 (3%) and 1 (21%). Note carefully: the respondents in the lowest decile on one measure are not necessarily those who are lowest on another.

THE SAMPLE

In fall and winter 1977, we interviewed 1050 randomly selected adults in 50 Northern California communities, urban census tracts or small towns ranging from central San Francisco to agricultural regions over a hundred miles away. For reasons discussed elsewhere, the sample excluded towns under 2500 in size, neighborhoods that were 40% or more black, and people who did not speak English. The sample overdrew respondents from smaller places, but for the analysis reported here we *weighted the data* to approximate the English speaking population living in nonblack urban areas of Northern California in 1977.

WHO IS ALONE?

In this section we compare various types of respondents on their propensities to be isolated, showing, for example, that working women were less likely to be isolated than those who did not work for pay. The next section will consider which social characteristics were most important.

Tables 2.1 and 2.2 present in detail the basic descriptive results. They indicate the probability that respondents, differentiated in several ways, would be "isolated" on our six measures: severe and moderate isolation from nonkin, kin, and in total. The data are presented separately for men and women, because, as earlier studies suggest and our results bear out, the genders differ in their relations to kin and nonkin. For brevity's sake, we will focus our discussion on the results involving *nonkin,* making only brief references to the other network measures (and saving discussion of confidants for later). The reader will be readily able to determine the other results from Tables 2.1 and 2.2.

Two general features of the data are striking: the extent to which social background characteristics are strongly associated with isolation, and the contrast between kin and nonkin ties. The first finding implies that, while personality is no doubt a major determinant of isolation, so is position in the social structure (or at least personality types are distributed differentially in the social structure). For example, the difference between working and not working—17% of male nonworkers were severely isolated, compared to 3% of male workers (12 versus 3 for women)—underlines the way differential participation in social contexts affects network size.

The second set of findings, kin versus nonkin differences, alerts us to the fact that not all social involvements are the same. While women, for example, were more likely to be isolated from nonkin, men were more likely to be isolated from kin. More striking yet are the differential associations of background characteristics with each kind of isolation. Later we will also show that these two types of isolation, kin and nonkin, have different consequences.

Class and life-cycle stage are strong correlates of isolation. Respondents of

Table 2.1. Percentage of Males with Small Networks (defined two ways) by Respondent Characteristics

	N	Nonkin isolation		Kin isolation		Total isolation	
		Severe	Moderate	Severe	Moderate	Severe	Moderate
Household income							
0–$9,999	(97)	15	50	13	40	23	54
$10,000–$20,000	(162)	5	22	21	52	6	34
$20,000 and over	(189)	2**	20**	14	39+	4**	29**
Education							
Less than high school	(54)	15	59	6	28	19	38
High school graduate	(122)	9	31	18	42	10	62
College	(199)	4	24	15	42	9	67
Post grad	(96)	1**	14**	25**	60**	3**	73**
Length residence in city							
Less than 1 year	(49)	5	35	20	56	15	46
1–10 years	(233)	3	22	22	54	5	36
11+ years	(153)	9	34	10	32	14	37
All life	(37)	7+	27*	5**	18**	6*	25
Negative life events							
None	(167)	9	28	12	39	9	34
One	(183)	3	26	23	46	9	36
Two or more	(121)	5	30	13+	47	9	40
Labor force status							
Not working	(88)	16	56	8	41	27	59
Working	(383)	3**	21**	18*	45	5*	31**
Marital status							
Formerly married	(84)	4	30	31	61	17	49
Married	(245)	8	32	0	28	7	31
Never married	(148)	1**	19**	66**	62**	8**	37**
Age							
16–21 years old	(26)	0	18	15	31	0	18
22–35 years old	(228)	2	20	21	48	5	27
36–50 years old	(110)	6	25	18	45	7	46
51–64 years old	(58)	5	41	3	31	9	43
65+	(46)	22**	61**	8*	46*	33**	63**
Number of young children							
None	(364)	5	29	21	48	10	39
One or more	(108)	7	25	4**	21**	6	27+
Number of old children							
None	(410)	6	27	19	48	10	37
One or more	(61)	11	31	4**	16**	5	30
All men	(472)	6	28	17	44	9	36

χ^2 significant at: $+p \leq .10$ $*p \leq .05$ $**p \leq .01$

Table 2.2. Percentage of Females with Small Networks (defined two ways) by Respondent Characteristics

		Nonkin isolation		Kin isolation		Total isolation	
		Severe	Moderate	Severe	Moderate	Severe	Moderate
Household income	**N**						
0–$9,999	(189)	13	51	15	31	17	51
$10,000–$19,999	(188)	8	36	22	40	8	31
$20,000 and over	(184)	2**	24**	6*	33	3**	28**
Education							
Less than high school	(75)	31	74	4	17	23	60
High school graduate	(203)	7	43	9	26	10	39
College	(224)	3	29	17	38	6	32
Post grad	(74)	0**	11**	28**	61**	5**	23**
Length residence in city							
Less than 1 year	(74)	13	44	13	36	16	47
1–10 years	(239)	6	31	17	43	8	33
11 years or more	(209)	6	40	12	29	11	40
All life	(53)	13*	45*	8**	15**	5	28+
Negative life events							
None	(195)	6	33	15	35	7	34
One	(196)	4	36	15	37	12	33
Two or more	(183)	13**	43	12	30	9*	44+
Labor force status							
Not working	(264)	12	49	11	30	15	45
Working	(311)	3**	27**	16+	38*	5**	30**
Marital status							
Formerly married	(190)	8	48	22	45	33	55
Married	(261)	10	39	0	23	7	32
Never married	(123)	2**	16**	47**	40**	4**	20**
Age							
16–21 years old	(44)	6	44	10	17	8	26
22–35 years old	(231)	5	29	15	37	5	30
36–50 years old	(108)	7	33	11	40	8	34
51–64 years old	(111)	10	42	14	28	11	49
65+	(82)	12*	52**	15*	32*	23*	50**
Number of young children							
None	(409)	7	35	17	35	10	36
One or more	(166)	8	41	7*	32	8	38
Number of old children							
None	(487)	6	37	16	37	11	38
One or more	(88)	14	39	1**	17**	3	34
All women	(576)	7	37	14	34	12	37

χ^2 significant at: $+p \leq .10$ $*p \leq .05$ $**p \leq .01$

low occupational status, low income, and especially minimal educational attainment, were especially likely to name few nonkin. For instance, 31% of female respondents who had failed to graduate from high school (zero to 11 years) were severely isolated from nonkin compared to none of the women who had some training after a college B.A. (17 years). Although the opposite is true for kin networks—higher social position is connected with *fewer* kin —our measures of total isolation (having small networks of kin plus nonkin) still reveals that poor and uneducated respondents were more likely to be isolated than others.

Examination of various indicators of life-cycle stage suggests that older people, especially men, and married people, especially those with children, were most likely to be isolated from nonkin. Again the reverse tends to be roughly true if we ask about kin.

Other noteworthy results include these: Nonworking people were more isolated than respondents who were employed. This difference was somewhat greater among men, a finding, consistent with others, that testifies to the greater importance of extra-family contexts, especially work, for men in comparison to women. Widowed, divorced, and separated respondents were particularly isolated. Women were also slightly more isolated (from nonkin, not from kin) than men.

Two other social characteristics deserve special note: household structure and length of residence. Despite the suspicion raised recently that adults living alone are prone to isolation, our data show otherwise. Among men, 23% of those living alone were moderately isolated from nonkin, versus 29% of all other men; among women, it was 38% versus 37%; severe isolation from nonkin was *less* common among those living alone (data not shown). (To be sure, respondents living alone were much more likely to have small *kin* networks, but that was the result of being unmarried.)

Similarly, despite arguments that residential stability is a safeguard against isolation, our results show a more complex picture. Newcomers to their cities were indeed likelier to be isolated than other respondents, but only in the first year; after that first year, recent arrivals were actually slightly less likely to be isolated from nonkin than "oldtimers." This finding is all the more striking because our measure excludes associates living an hour or more away, that is, the newcomers' friends "back home." Had they been included, the first-year effect would have been yet weaker. The standard contention that mobility brings isolation is valid with respect to kin involvement; the more recently arrived the respondent, the greater the chance of having few kin in the vicinity. Here too, inclusion of distant relatives would have narrowed the differences.

Myths about residential mobility are persistent, in spite of such findings. Americans believe that mobility leads to isolation, when in fact there are, for most people, few effects after the initial adjustment period. And Americans believe that mobility has been increasing, when in fact it has been decreasing historically (for review, see Fischer et al., 1977, Chapters 9 and 10; Long, 1976).

In sum, the key characteristics of the person likely to be isolated from nonkin appear to be: low education, low income, being old, being married, not working, and being female. However, these are only simple descriptions of the correlates of small networks. A few difficulties must be dealt with before any conclusions are drawn from these results.

First, these characteristics are strongly interconnected: women tend to work less often than men, old people are less educated than the young, and so forth. To get a clear picture, we need to identify the key independent correlates of isolation. Second, there are noteworthy interaction effects in these results. In particular, some of the correlations are different for men and women, especially those with age and working status. While age and employment are strongly associated with being isolated among men, they are less strongly associated with being isolated among women. Third, another factor associated with network size is how cooperative the respondent was during the interview. Enthusiastic interviewees gave more names than did reluctant ones. This could have biased our results and should be taken into account.

To handle these issues we conducted multivariate regression analyses, incorporating several respondent characteristics simultaneously and including a measure of respondent cooperativeness. We conducted the analyses separately for men and for women.

WHAT ARE THE KEY CHARACTERISTICS?

Table 2.3 presents the results of multiple regression analyses, separately for men and women. These allow us to weigh the relative contributions of various characteristics to the probability of being isolated. The measures of isolation used here are dichotomies indicating the probability that the respondent was moderately isolated. (We could have employed a measure dichotomizing at the first decile mark, but statistical significance would be difficult to attain with a variable so skewed. Also it is likely that the substantive results would not have been much different.*) In addition to the characteristics discussed earlier, we included a scale measuring the cooperativeness of the respondents in the interview. Uncooperative respondents named notably fewer people than cooperative ones; using cooperativeness as a control provides a conservative test of the other variables.**

* The question might be raised: Why divide the sample at all? Why not simply use number named as a continuous dependent variable? The reason is that such a variable might reflect two different constructs, each with a different set of causes: isolation at the low end and gregariousness at the high end. Our purpose here is to understand who tended to be alone versus not alone, and we should avoid confusing that with the issue of who was especially popular versus not.

** This scale is composed of the *interviewer's* answers to three questions: (1) "What was the respondent's *initial* attitude about being interviewed?"; (2) "What was the respondent's attitude *during* the interview?"—each answered with a scale from "enthusiastic" to "very reluctant"; and (3) "How open do you think the respondent was about

Table 2.3. Multiple Regression Analyses of Network Isolation Measures: Beta-Weights

Respondent Characteristics	Moderate isolation from nonkin		Moderate isolation from kin		Moderate isolation total	
	Males	Females	Males	Females	Males	Females
Age in years	.18*		.30***		.29***	.14+
Respondent under 22					—.08+	
Married		.17*	—.45***	.14+	—.19**	
Formerly married		.17*				.20**
Number young children						
Number old children			—.16**	—.10*		
Years of education	—.13*	—.23***	.14*	.25***	—.11*	
Household income	—.18**				—.14**	—.12*
Respondent works	—.11+					
Years in city	—.10+		—.25***	—.18***	—.21***	—.12*
Negative life events		.09+		—.11*		
Uncooperativeness	.18***	.15***			.16***	.17***
R^2	.20	.21	.25	.16	.20	.17

β significant at: $+p \leq .10$ $*p \leq .05$ $**p \leq .01$ $***p \leq .001$

The details of the results can be examined by the reader; we focus on the highlights. The key predictor of moderate isolation from nonkin, for both men and women, is low social status, combining education and income. Other things being equal, a high-school graduate male earning $10,000 stood a .35 chance of being moderately isolated, compared to a .19 chance for a college graduate earning $25,000. For women, the figures are .43 and .23.*

Yet respondents of higher social status—at least, of higher educational attainment—had a *greater* chance of being isolated from *kin*. A woman with 16 years of education had a .37 greater chance, all else held constant, of being moderately isolated from kin than a woman with only 8 years of education. For isolation from nonkin, the difference was .35 in the other direction.

Stage in the life cycle is also important, but in different ways for men and women. For men, aging by itself increased the risk of isolation from nonkin, the risk almost tripling from age 20 to age 60. Women were hardly affected by age; all else being equal, 20-year-olds were as likely to be isolated as 60-

(his/her) personal problems and feelings—open, a little guarded, or basically not frank?" Controlling for this variable is conservative for two reasons: one, to some extent the interviewers' ratings could themselves be affected by the number of names respondents listed in their networks, rather than be indicators of an a priori artifact; two, this scale may index a personality dimension—say extraversion—that mediates the effect of background variables on isolation. We chose to employ this control despite its conservative effects because of our greater concern that situational conditions during the interview (e.g., the respondent's suspicion of polltakers, or rush to an appointment) not mislead us about the true correlates of isolation.

* These are approximations based on unstandardized regression coefficients for education and income (not shown in the table), and assume that all other variables are constant at their means.

year-olds. Marital status, however, was more significant for women than for men. Both married and formerly married women were about .17 likelier to be isolated than women who had never been married. (For more on differences between genders in the network consequences of life cycle stage, see Fischer and Oliker, 1980).

The most salient points to emerge from these results appear to be these: all else equal, (1) for both genders, high social status, especially more education, leads to less chance of moderate isolation from nonkin, but more chance of moderate isolation from kin; (2) for men, aging is strongly associated with isolation of all kinds (but being married protects them from kin isolation); (3) for women, a marriage, even if terminated, increases the risk of isolation from nonkin.

WHO LACKS CONFIDANTS?

So far, we have defined isolation as the relative absence of conveniently available associates who, together, interacted in a variety of ways with the individual. In this section we examine a second type of isolation: the absence of a confidant. Confidants are distinct from the other associates we have examined in that, first, they provide critical emotional support and guidance, and second, because of the telephone, they can provide such support and guidance even over long distances. A distinctly different population of people might lack confidants, people potentially vulnerable to "emotional loneliness."

In analyzing confidant relationships, we focus on the names respondents gave in answer to two specific questions: "Who do you talk with about personal matters?" and "Whose opinion do you consider[in making important decisions]?" Spouses were most commonly named in these answers (especially by men, to the first question); other close relatives were also overrepresented (but extended kin were underrepresented) in these lists.

This led us also to consider specifically the number of confidants respondents named who lived outside the household. Although we shall occasionally refer to this extra-household measure, our major index of having a small confidant network considers all possible confidants, spouses included. The most isolated respondents, in this sense, were the 3% who named *no one* in answer to either question. The next most isolated were the 18% who named only one confidant to either question. This single confidant tended to be a spouse.

The associations displayed in Table 2.4 show some consistency with our earlier findings on general isolation. Poorly educated people named fewer confidants: combining men and women, one-third of grade-school graduates were moderately isolated, one-fourth of college graduates, and one-tenth of postgraduates. Older people, especially older men, were at greater risk.

Other results differ from our earlier findings on network availability, those involving contrast between genders and marital status. Men were more likely than women to have no or only one confidant. Indeed 20% of men named

Table 2.4.   Percentage of Respondents with Few Confidants (defined in two ways) by Respondent Characteristics

Respondent Characteristics	Men's lack of confidants			Women's lack of confidants		
	N	Severe	Moderate	N	Severe	Moderate
Household income						
0–$9,999	(97)	8	30	(189)	5	20
$10,000–$19,999	(162)	2	21	(188)	1	17
$20,000 and over	(189)	4**	25**	(184)	0+	11+
Education						
Less than high school	(54)	12	44	(75)	6	29
High school graduate	(122)	5	28	(203)	1	17
College	(199)	4	28	(224)	2	13
Post grad	(96)	1**	11**	(74)	0**	9**
Length residence in city						
Less than 1 year	(49)	0	23	(74)	0	18
1–10 years	(233)	3	25	(239)	1	13
11 years or more	(153)	8	27	(209)	2	19
All life	(37)	6+	37	(53)	7*	18
Negative life events						
None	(167)	4	31	(195)	1	15
One	(183)	6	26	(196)	3	16
Two or more	(121)	4	21	(183)	2	17
Labor force status						
Not working	(88)	13	39	(264)	3	17
Working	(383)	3*	24**	(311)	1	15
Marital status						
Formerly married	(84)	11	24	(190)	3	21
Married	(245)	4	32	(261)	0	14
Never married	(142)	3**	19**	(123)	4	12
Age						
16–21 years old	(26)	0	14	(44)	0	13
22–35 years old	(228)	2	22	(231)	1	10
36–51 years old	(110)	2	24	(108)	0	17
51–64 years old	(50)	7	36	(111)	7	28
65+	(46)	20	46	(82)	0	20
Number of young children						
None	(364)	6	26	(409)	2	17
One or more	(88)	2	27	(116)	1	14
Number of old children						
None	(410)	5	26	(487)	2	15
One or more	(61)	0	34	(88)	3	20
Total	(472)	5	27	(476)	2	19

χ^2 significant at: $+p \leq .10$ $*p \leq .05$ $**p \leq .01$

no confidants outside their households, compared to only 9% of women (data not shown). There was a tendency for married men to name only one confidant—the spouse—and for unmarried men to name either more confidants (typically, the never-married men) or none at all (the older men). For women, the marital status differences were not as dramatic. Still, for both genders, being married meant a greater chance of lacking any *extra-household* confidants. These results suggest that, in acting as confidants, spouses often substitute for more than one other person. This is especially so for males, where the spouse also often substitutes for no confidant at all.

Again, many of the predictors of emotional isolation are themselves inter-correlated. Therefore, we performed multivariate analyses to uncover the unique contribution of each background characteristic to isolation from confidants (defined as having one or no confidant). We found only weak associations in these analyses (data not shown). The trends, such as they are, indicate that education and age were once again important: all else being equal, older people and less educated people were at greater risk of isolation. Also uncooperative respondents were likely to be isolated; women with young children were slightly more often isolated and women who worked slightly less often isolated than other women.

Despite our expectation that we might uncover a quite different set of predictors for emotional isolation, we actually found that the characteristics that predict emotional isolation overlap a good deal with those predicting general social isolation.

On another issue, our overall findings on networks and confidants are in keeping with the notion that feelings of loneliness and actual isolation, whether social or emotional isolation, may be two separate and perhaps independent conditions (Jones, Chapter 15). By comparing Wood's findings (1978) concerning the best predictors of loneliness and our best predictors of isolation, we find that we have identified two sets of people who are similar in some regards and different in others: for example, while Wood finds that *unmarried* people are likely to feel lonely, we find that *married* women are more at risk of being alone, at least of being isolated from nonkin. Similarly, Rubenstein, Shaver, and Peplau (1979) report that older people felt less lonely; but here the elderly were the most likely to be isolated. These differences may be due merely to the differences in the populations sampled; however, further evidence supporting the assumption that loneliness and isolation are two distinct conditions emerges from our findings that assessments of isolation were weakly associated with actual isolation.

WHAT ARE THE SUBJECTIVE CORRELATES OF ISOLATION?

Peplau, Russell, and Heim define "loneliness as occurring when there is a discrepancy between desired and achieved social relations" (1979, p. 55). Three questions included in our interview allow us to assess respondents' own appraisal of their networks' adequacy: questions asking whether they "wished to have more people to talk to," "more people to have fun with," and "more people to help."

Few respondents admitted that they wished they knew more people. Only about one-fifth said they wished they knew more people to talk to or to help them; two-fifths wished for more people to have fun with. And ironically, but perhaps not unexpectedly, the *kinds* of people who were most likely to say they wanted more tended to be the same *kinds* who already had more than average-sized networks. This does *not* mean that people with many friends typically wanted more, only that the two sets of respondents—those who had and those who wanted—came from the same groups. To see exactly what role isolation and background factors played in shaping such responses, we conducted regression analyses reported in Tables 2.5 and 2.6. In these analyses, we did not use interviewers' ratings of cooperativeness as a control because of the likelihood that such ratings were strongly affected by respondents' answers to psychological probes themselves. As a substitute check on validity, we replicated the regressions for only those respondents whom interviewers thought were "open" about their feelings.

The findings underline both the difficulties in measuring such subjective assessments and the tenuous connection between objective conditions and people's feelings about them. The isolation measures are barely correlated with respondents' saying they wanted more people (Equation 1 in Tables 2.5 and 2.6). The multiple R^2s range from .025 (isolated males wanted more people to talk to) down to .007 (isolated females wanting more help). The only constant tendency, if any, was for respondents isolated from kin to express the desire to know more people.

Even such marginal effects tend to disappear when individual characteristics are controlled (Equation 2 in Tables 2.5 and 2.6). In these equations, background characteristics might be interpreted as sources of standards for social contact, "desired relations" in Peplau's terms. A few of the interesting results from the many equations are these: higher income is generally associated with less expressed need for others; money may substitute for some social support. Older people expressed less need for "fun" companionship; this is consistent with the literature on lowered expectations with aging. Newcomers to the city expressed some greater desire for "fun" companions. Finally, married men tended to express the desire for more social contacts less often than unmarried ones, but this was not so for women. This finding appears to testify, again, to the extent to which wives substitute for a range of social contacts in men's lives, although husbands do not do the same for women.

In sum, having a small network does not greatly influence assessments of its adequacy. It may well be, as Weiss suggests (1973, p. 228), that isolated individuals adjust their standards regarding the adequacy of the number of available network members to conform to their actual situations. Yet even if this is the case, it may still be that small networks or lack of intimate ties influence feelings of well-being.

Table 2.5. Multiple Regression Analysis of Evaluation and Happiness Items on Isolation and Background Variables for Men [a]

	Wants more to talk to			Wants more to have fun with			Wants more for help			Happy	
	Eq. 1	Eq. 2	Frank	Eq. 1	Eq. 2	Frank	Eq. 1	Eq. 2	Frank	Eq. 2	Frank
Percent "Yes":	19%		22%	40%		44%	17%		19%	19%	
Isolated from nonkin	.14***	.09+					−.20***			−.12*	(−.11*)
Isolated from kin				.11*			.08+				(.17***)
Few confidants				−.13***			−.09+			−.08+	(−.10+)
Age					−.16*	(−.19*)					
Under 22 years old											
Married			(−.16*)		−.16*	(−.26***)			(−.21*)	.19**	(.20*)
Formerly married								−.15*	(−.19**)		
Number young children											
Number old children											
Years of education											
Household income		−.22***	(−.22***)		−.12*	(−.13*)				.12*	(.13*)
Respondent works										.20***	(.15*)
Years in the city		−.09+	(−.10+)		−.17***						
Negative events								.15**	(.12*)		
R^2	.025	.109	(.137)	.032	.184	(.178)	.056	.07	(.077)	.160	(.185)

[a] Equation 1 includes only the isolation measures; Equation 2 also includes background variables. "Frank" refers to only those respondents whom interviewers rated as being open about their problems and feelings and reports the results for that subsample of Equation 2.

Beta weight significant at: $+p \leq .10$ $*p \leq .05$ $**p \leq .01$ $***p \leq .001$.

Table 2.6. Multiple Regression Analysis of Evaluation and Happiness Items on Isolation and Background Variables for Women [a]

	Wants more to talk to			Wants more to have fun with			Wants more for help			Happy		
	Eq. 1	Eq. 2	Frank	Eq. 1	Eq. 2	Frank	Eq. 1	Eq. 2	Frank	Eq. 1	Eq. 2	Frank
Percent "Yes":	19%	19%	42%	43%	43%	18%	17%	17%				
Isolated from nonkin												
Isolated from kin	.11*	.09+	(.11*)	.09+		(.09+)	−.24***			−.24***	−.16**	(−.12*)
Few confidants								.08+	(.10*)			(−.12+)
Age												(−.09+)
Under 22 years					−.23**	(−.23**)						
Formerly married												
Married												(.15*)
Number young children												
Number old children												
Years education											−.11+	(−.08+)
Household income					−.13*	(−.12*)						
Respondent works								−.18**	(−.17**)		.24***	(.22***)
Years in city					−.10+							(−.09+)
Negative events									.058		−.11*	(−.10*)
R²	.015	.036	(.044)	.011	.104	(.103)	.007	.069	(.065)		.171	(.165)

[a] Equation 1 includes only the isolation measures; Equation 2 also includes background variables. "Frank" refers to only those respondents whom interviewers rated as being open about their problems and feelings and reports the results for that subsample of Equation 2.

Beta weight significant at: +p ≤ .10   *p ≤ .05   **p ≤ .01   ***p ≤ .001.

Happiness

Much research suggests that loneliness is typically associated with specific affective states such as low self-esteem (see Peplau, Miceli, & Morasch, Chapter 9) and being less happy (Russell, Peplau, & Ferguson, 1978). We included questions in our interview that can be combined into reliable indicators of feeling states, including feeling angry, upset, and pleased. We found that a low score on an index measuring positive affect, feeling pleased or happy, was most strongly associated with social isolation. See the far right column in Tables 2.5 and 2.6. That index is composed of the following items: (1) How often do you feel particularly excited or interested in something these days: a lot of the time; some of the time; only once in a while; never? (2) How often do you feel that things are going the way you want them to? (3) How often do you feel pleased with what you're doing these days? and (4) Thinking about your life as a whole, how happy would you rate the way you are these days; very happy, pretty happy, pretty unhappy, or very unhappy? (Note that this index also resembles, in part, measures of self-esteem.) Thus our results with isolation suggest some parallels to findings regarding the subjective correlates of loneliness: both conditions are associated with low scores on happiness.

Specifically, isolated respondents—notably, those isolated from nonkin—were less likely than others to express happiness. This difference holds up under controls, and for the "frank" respondents as well. Here, then, in contrast to the findings on the respondents' subjective assessments of their networks, is some evidence of an independent psychological consequence of social isolation.* Findings not reported here indicate that isolation may be detrimental even if an individual does not feel his or her network is inadequate, or perhaps even if he or she does not admit to being lonely. We plan further research exploring these findings.

This analysis of subjective consequences is just a beginning. Our impression —and at this stage of the analysis, it is only an impression—is that there are profound connections between network characteristics and psychological states, but they are complex and contingent associations. Not only are there varying standards of desired social involvement, there are complex situational circumstances. For example, sometimes social relations can be more of a burden than a support, as in the case of aging parents, psychologically disturbed kin, or friends going through life crises. Many of our interviewees faced circumstances such as these; alcoholic husbands were common. Social ties

---

* A perennial problem in the literature on mental health and social networks is the difficulty of assessing the causal direction between network size and well-being. While we suggest that network size affects well-being, the reverse may also be true; for example, depression may cause an individual to withdraw from others, or an individual with a low score on well-being may lack the social skills necessary for maintaining a wider network. It is quite likely that there are reciprocal effects between network size and well-being. Further research on these possible reciprocal effects is planned.

can be beneficial, neutral, or harmful, depending on what the individual's current needs are—help in finding a new job, or peace and quiet to finish a current one—and with whom one has a relationship. We expect to find in planned analyses complex patterns such as these, revealing certain conditions under which there are strong psychological effects of isolation.

CONCLUDING COMMENTS

In summary, we would stress three general themes: the complex structure of people's networks, the influence of social location on isolation, and the subjective consequences of isolation.

Even our method, let alone our results, testifies to the complexity of people's social networks. No simple question such as "How many friends do you have?" or "How often do you see your relatives?" can capture the various dimensions of personal milieux; we do different things with different people with different consequences. Our neighbors will water the plants, but distant relatives will lend us money. To ignore this complexity is to risk empirical errors.

Our findings underline the point: isolation from nonkin and from kin are somewhat different in character, cause, and consequence. Marriage, for example, isolates women (but not men) from nonkin; marriage protects women only slightly (and men much more) from kin isolation; and marriage hardly affects women's access to confidants, while reducing men's access greatly. Isolation from kin tends to be slightly associated with wanting to know more people, but it is isolation from nonkin that has a substantial association with not being happy. All friends are not the same; all isolation is not the same.

Who is isolated, in whatever form, tends to be socially patterned. The most significant patterns, from our findings, are those associated with class. Uneducated and poor people tend to be isolated from *nonkin* (and confidants). Their relatively low risk of *kin* isolation does not make up for the deficit, since they remain relatively isolated in terms of total network; these are the high-risk people. Stage in the life cycle reflects the other major pattern, albeit a complex one. For men, aging increases the risk of all kinds of isolation, partly because of retirement, perhaps also because of decreased mobility and the death of friends. Marriage, however, protects them against kin isolation, and provides at least one confidant. Aging has less effect on women, but marriage has more: it tends to isolate women from nonkin.

Most of the various correlations between background and isolation can be grouped together under a general principle: access to and participation in various social contexts determines isolation. Education provides cohorts of classmates and, indirectly, social skills. Income provides resources for keeping in touch. Aging, on the other hand, limits access in the various ways mentioned above. For women, marriage involves commitments and responsibilities that also limit access. All these constraints and opportunities affect the chances of being isolated from nonkin. Similarly, getting married introduces one to a new set of relatives, while moving to a new region removes one from an old set of relatives. These factors affect isolation from kin. Systematic, socially structured opportunities and constraints shape people's networks, above and beyond personality factors.

Because few data have previously been available on the subjective consequences of limited social networks, many unfounded assumptions have prevailed. It is often assumed that personality differences account in large measure for why some people with small networks seem to feel that they are adequate, while others may feel lonely. Our data suggest somewhat more complicated relations among isolation, standards for network size, and the possible adverse effects of small networks.

First, our results indicate that social background characteristics, as well as personality, affect the assessment of networks' adequacy. Second, though people with small networks may not necessarily desire more relations, they do seem to be adversely affected by their isolation.

Clearly, further research on social isolation, its subjective consequences, and loneliness is in order. New research in this area would benefit from more complex methods such as those used here. Specifically, if loneliness is to be defined as the discrepancy between one's current network and one's desired network, researchers would do well to assess the discrepancy between various types of relations; kin, nonkin, and confidants—and the various types of desired relations—people to talk to, help, or have fun with, among others. Isolation may be psychologically detrimental whether or not loneliness is reported.

REFERENCES

Berelson, B., Lazarsfeld, P. F., & McPhee, W. N. *Voting*. Chicago: University of Chicago Press, 1954.

Durkheim, E. *Suicide*. New York: Free Press, 1951 (Originally published, 1897).

Fischer, C. S. *To dwell among friends: Personal networks in town and city*. Chicago: University of Chicago Press, 1982.

Fischer, C. S., Jackson, R. M., Stueve, C. A., Gerson, K., & Jones, L. M., with M. Baldassare. *Networks and places: Social relations in the urban setting*. New York: Free Press, 1977.

Fischer, C. S., & Oliker, S. J. *Friendship, gender and the life cycle*. Paper presented at the annual meeting of the American Sociological Association, New York, 1980.

Horowitz, A. Social networks and pathways to psychiatric treatment. *Social Forces,* 1977, *56,* 86–105.

Jones, L. M., & Fischer, C. S. *Studying egocentric networks by mass survey* (Working Paper No. 284). Berkeley, California: University of California, Institute of Urban and Regional Development, 1978.

Kleiner, R. J., & Parker, S. Network participation and psychological impairment in an urban environment. In P. Meadows & E. Mizruchi (Eds.), *Urbanism, urbanization, and change* (2nd ed.). Reading, Mass.: Addison-Wesley, 1976.

Laumann, E. O., & Pappi, F. U. *Networks of collective action.* New York: Academic Press, 1976.

Long, L. J. *The geographical mobility of Americans.* (Current Population Reports, Special Studies, Series P-23, No. 64.) Washington: U.S. Government Printing Office, 1976.

McCallister, L., & Fischer, C. S. A method for surveying personal networks. *Sociological Methods and Research,* 1978, *7,* 131–148.

Mitchell, J. C. (Ed.). *Social networks in urban situations.* Manchester: Manchester University Press, 1969.

Peplau, L. A., Russell, D., & Heim, M. The experience of loneliness. In I. Frieze, D. Bar-Tal, & J. Carroll (Eds.), *New approaches to social problems: Applications of attribution theory.* San Francisco: Jossey-Bass, 1979.

Rubenstein, C., Shaver, P., & Peplau, L. A. Loneliness. *Human Nature,* February, 1979, pp. 58–65.

Russell, D., Peplau, L. A., & Ferguson, M. L. Developing a measure of loneliness. *Journal of Personality Assessment,* 1978, *42,* 290–294.

Simmel, G. *Conflict and the web of group affilations.* New York: Free Press, 1955. (Originally published, 1922.)

de Tocqueville, A. *Democracy in America.* Garden City, N.Y.: Anchor (Originally published, 1836).

Weiss, R. S. *Loneliness.* Cambridge, Mass.: MIT Press, 1973.

Wellman, B. The community question. *American Journal of Sociology,* 1979, *84,* 1201–1231.

Wood, L. Loneliness, social identity and social structure. *Essence,* 1978, *2,* 259–276.

Chapter 3

Time Alone in Daily Experience:
Loneliness or Renewal?

Reed Larson, Mihaly Csikszentmihalyi, and Ronald Graef

Virtually everyone in our society daily spends time alone. Over a lifetime this adds up to many years of solitude. We are predisposed to think of aloneness as undesirable and as necessarily leading to loneliness. However, solitude can also be a time of reflection, rest, and self-renewal. How typical Americans actually experience this part of their daily lives is the topic of this chapter.

In our research we have collected self-reports on over 9000 random moments in people's daily experience. Adolescents and adults carried electronic pagers for an ordinary week in their lives and responded to signals by filling out reports on their subjective states. These self-reports provide a representative sampling of their experiences throughout a week. In this chapter we examine people's self-descriptions at the times they were alone and contrast these with those obtained at times they were with others.

Perhaps the best way to conceptualize aloneness is to see it as the psychological equivalent of an "ecological niche" that offers various adaptive possibilities, while at the same time having peculiar disadvantages. A person who passes from the company of others to being alone enters this niche, and depending on his or her resources, will find opportunities for better adaptation in the state of solitude or, conversely, will suffer from its limitations.

The opportunities available in solitude are deeply rooted in the sociocultural system to which an individual belongs. In many preliterate societies, aloneness is shunned and being alone for extended periods of time is considered a fate worse than death. The dread of sorcery in many African societies keeps people close to their kin at all times. For example, among the Dobu, it is assumed that the only reason for being alone is to plot against the well-being of others (Fortune, 1963). In such cultures a person is alone only when survival demands for hunting or grazing make it necessary to choose solitude for short periods of time. Such cultures may not share our concept of loneliness, but they show constraints on being alone that are strikingly parallel to the ones present in our culture.

This research was done with partial assistance from the Spencer Foundation.

40

In contrast, in other preliterate societies aloneness has different and positive meanings. The Winnebago Indians, for instance, believed that a warrior must spend time fasting alone until he was visited by a spirit in a dream (Radin, 1923). Only after this event would he develop his adult identity. Such personal quests might last for weeks, or even years spent in solitude. In the great religious traditions, both of the East and the West, it is held that a person must periodically withdraw from the company of others if he or she wishes to find the path to salvation. In the case of Hindu sages or Trappist monks, the withdrawal might be permanent.

The limitations and opportunities of aloneness are no less prescriptive in our society. Being alone is assumed to be the occasion for painful loneliness. At the same time, poets, theologians, and others celebrate solitude as a unique occasion for reflection and serenity (Merton, 1955; Rilke, 1934; Thoreau, 1947). In this investigation we ask how these opportunities and limitations are manifest in daily American experience. How do they affect when and where people are alone, the way people feel when they are alone, the way they feel after being alone, and the experience of individuals whose time alone deviates from the prescribed normative patterns?

METHOD

The Adolescent Sample

A stratified random sample of adolescents was obtained through a large heterogeneous high school in an old, well-established suburb, bordering the city of Chicago. The 75 students who participated included roughly equal numbers of boys and girls from all four high school grades and roughly equal numbers of students from lower middle-class and upper-class areas of the community.

Data were obtained through the Experience Sampling Method (Csikszent-mihalyi, Larson, & Prescott, 1977). Student carried pagers and filled out self-reports for one week. Signals were sent to the pagers at random times between 7:30 a.m. and 10:30 p.m. On Friday and Saturday night the signals extended until 1:30 a.m. Receiving a signal cued students to fill out a self-report form, asking about their activity, their moods, and other aspects of their immediate situation.

During nonschool hours students received one signal at a random time within every two-hour block of time. During school hours signals were more frequent; however, for the analyses here those school reports have been downweighted, so that the total set of reports provide a representative sample of the waking hours of each person's week.

A total of 4489 reports were obtained (2734 with the weighting). The students responded to 69% of the signals by filling out self-reports. They were encouraged to turn off the pagers when they went to sleep and when they really did not want to be "bugged." Reports were also missed as a result of pager malfunction and a variety of other reasons. The evidence suggests that most of the missing reports were times when respondents were with other people (Larson, 1979).

The Adult Sample

A sample of 107 adults was obtained through five Chicago-area businesses. Participants included clerical workers, assembly line workers, managers, engineers, and railroad workers. The final sample included 67 women and 40 men, ranging in age from 19 to 65. Slightly over half (51%) of these participants were married.

Like the high school students, these adult workers carried pagers and filled out self-reports for a week. Signals were sent to them at random times, once within each two-hour period between 8:00 a.m. and 10:00 p.m. for all seven days of the week. The adults responded to 80% of the signals by completing a self-report and provided 4791 reports on their daily experience.

The Self-Report Form

The adolescents and the adults described their subjective states and activities on similar forms. There were three items common to both that inquired about the person's cognitive state at the moment before the signal. These asked for 10-point ratings of concentration, ease of concentration, and self-consciousness. Eight semantic differential items dealt with emotional dimensions such as happy-sad, sociable-lonely, and strong-weak. Additional items inquired about what the person was doing at the time of the signal and where they were.

Most pertinent for this chapter is the item asking whether the person was alone, with family, with friends, or with other consociates. We have accepted our subjects' definitions of when they were alone with two exceptions. We coded as "alone" time spent in public "with strangers"; we coded as "with others" time spent talking on the telephone.

RESULTS

When and Where Are People Alone?

The 9000 self-reports provided a sample of American daily life. We have reports from people in such ordinary activities as driving to work, sitting in class, reading a magazine, and eating supper with their families. We also have reports from individuals engaged in a fist fight, dancing around the house, smuggling whiskey into a rock concert, and pretending to be a famous cabaret singer.

This sample of self-reports indicates that both adolescents and adults spend about a quarter of their waking hours alone as a regular part of their daily round of activities. As shown in Table 3-1, most of the day is spent doing things with others: working, sitting in class, eating, and socializing. Periods of being alone happen at times least likely to be claimed by these social activities: late afternoons, evenings, and daytimes on weekends. Aloneness occurs, as if by default, in the spaces between primary involvements.

It follows that most aloneness occurs at home—the place of retreat. However, being alone is not associated only with undesirable or "default"

Table 3.1   What People Reported They Were Doing When Alone and With Others [a]

| | Percentage of all self-reports | | | |
| | Adolescents (N = 2,734; weighted) | | Adults (N = 4, 791) | |
Activity	Alone	With others	Alone	With others
Home				
Housework, other practical	6.7***	5.6	5.4**	8.6
Self care	2.1***	.5	2.2***	1.2
Studying (adolescents only)	3.5***	1.4	—	—
Eating	—	3.1***	.7	2.4***
Socializing (includes by phone)	.6	5.4	—	3.8***
Watching television	2.6	3.9	2.2	5.1
Personal reading	2.0*	1.4	1.5	1.4
Doing hobbies or art	.7	.5	.3*	.2
Idling, listening to music	1.8	2.5	2.4	3.3
Total home	20.0	24.3	14.7	26.0
Work and school				
Working at work	1.6	2.2	5.9	20.9***
In class (adolescents only)	.0	15.6***	—	—
Other at work or school	1.2	13.5***	3.6	11.5***
Total work and school	2.8	31.3***	9.5	32.3***
Public				
In transit	1.3	3.3	2.9	3.6
Other practical activities	1.2	6.2***	.8	1.1
Leisure	.6	9.0***	1.2	7.9***
Total public	3.1	18.6***	4.9	12.6***
Total	25.9	74.1	29.1	70.9

$*p \leq .05$ $**p \leq .01$ $***p \leq .001$

[a] The table shows the percentage of times people reported themselves to be doing each of the activities when alone and with others. The percentages are based on the entire pool of self-reports for each sample. The asterisks indicate whether an activity occurred at a higher rate alone or with others for a significant number of people.

activities. It occurs in conjunction with personal activities that require concentration, such as studying, reading, and working on hobbies. It also occurs
in conjunction with activities that require privacy, such as dressing and
bathing ("self-care"). While it may occur at times by default, it appears to
be chosen for the concentration and privacy it provides.

The strength of these associations between aloneness and certain activities
indicates its specific functions in American life. The rarity with which anyone
engages in leisure alone in public, for example, demonstrates the strength of
internalized constraints: one does not attempt to enjoy oneself in public without the companionship of others. Aloneness occurs as a natural part of everyday life, but it occurs within a context of cultural prescriptions.

Why People Are Alone

Our data provide two means for assessing why people are alone during their
daily activity: examination of the motivational states reported on the pager
questionnaires and consideration of the unique characteristics of people who
spend the most time alone.

On the pager questionnaire people responded to the question: "Do you
wish you were doing something else?" We compared people's responses to
this item when they were alone to when they were with their families, with
their friends, and with others at school or work. The adults reported a
significantly greater desire to be doing something else when they were alone
versus with others. Being alone is less voluntary than being with family or
friends. This was not, however, true for the adolescents (see Table 3.2).
Being alone is less voluntary than being with friends but not less than being
with family. Time alone is less often voluntary for adults, than for adolescents.

The same conclusions are apparent in consideration of who spends the most

Table 3.2. Self-Reported Motivation When Alone and with Others [a]

Context	Adolescents (N = 75)		Adults (N = 107)	
	Average wish	Significance from alone	Average wish	Significance from alone
Alone	4.15	—	3.35	—
With family	3.82	.33	2.15	.001
With friends	2.98	.001	2.33	.001
At work (adults) or in class (adolescents)	5.47	.001	3.99	.005
Total with others	4.00	.36	3.06	.05

[a] The table shows the mean of the average responses of individuals when alone and
with others to the question "Do you wish you had been doing something else?" Responses were made on a scale of 0–9, with 9 being "very much."

time alone. Among the adults, amount of time spent alone is strongly related to life-situational or social-role factors. The proportion of time each person reported being alone is related to an individual's marital status ($eta^2 = .03$, $p = .07$), household size ($eta^2 = .13$, $p = .03$), age ($eta^2 = .04$, $p = .10$), and occupational level ($eta^2 = .15$, $p = .001$). It makes sense that adults living with spouses and children spend substantially less time alone. Yet irrespective of marital and family status, adults in the 40–65 age group appear to spend 10% more of their waking hours alone than do adults in the 30–39 age group. More surprisingly, irrespective of marital status, people in semi-skilled jobs spend 14% more of their waking hours alone than do people with skilled jobs. They report more time alone at home, more time alone at work, and more time alone in public. Possibly companionship is a luxury more easily accessible to those with money and higher social status.

However, among the teenagers, none of these factors makes a difference. Furthermore, numerous other life-situational factors, such as number of friends, having a private bedroom, and family size, are unrelated to the proportion of time each teenager spends alone (Larson, 1979). Their amount of solitude appears to be impervious to situational pressures. Each seems to obtain his or her quantum of time alone regardless of circumstances.

The evidence provides additional indications that for the adolescents, solitude is a matter of choice. The proportion of time each teenager spends alone is related to his or her allotment of time to solitary activities. The ones with the most solitude are those who do the most reading, studying, and housework, and who spend the least amount of time at work, at school, and in public (Larson & Csikszentmihalyi, 1980). In other words, for them it appears to be part of a distinct solitary lifestyle, which is probably chosen. For the adults, proportion of time alone is related only to amount of time spent reading ($r = .17$, $p = .01$). For them solitude is less often chosen and more often appears to be imposed by social role such as marital status, socio-economic status, and type of occupation.

The Subjective Experience of Being Alone

Being alone is related to consistent patterns in self-reported cognitive and emotional state across the vast majority of people in the two studies. Solitude is related to positive changes in people's reported cognitive state. People report being significantly less self-conscious when they are alone (see Table 3.3). Furthermore, adults report that it is easier to concentrate when they are alone. And in certain activities, such as studying, playing sports, and working on hobbies, adolescents report better concentration when they are alone (Larson, 1979). Solitude appears to allow a more efficient use of attention.

However, although aloneness improves concentration, it also depresses a person's mood. As shown in Table 3.3, people report being significantly less

Table 3.3. Subjective State When Alone [a]

	Adolescents (N = 75)			Adults (N = 106)			Adolescents minus Adults
	Alone Mean	With others Mean	Difference in s.d. units	Alone Mean	With others Mean	Difference in s.d. units	Difference of differences
Attention (range 0–9)							
Concentration	4.84	4.66	.06	5.11	5.28	−.05	.10*
Ease of concentration	6.95	6.71	.10	7.71	7.54	.11*	−.01
Unself-consciousness	7.29	6.66	.28***	6.82	6.64	.12*	.16**
Mood state (range 1–7)							
Feelings							
Happy (sad)	4.74	5.15	−.32***	4.95	5.12	−.19***	−.13*
Cheerful (irritable)	4.57	4.88	−.23***	4.74	4.92	−.15***	−.07
Sociable (lonely)	4.22	5.23	−.78***	4.38	5.09	−.65***	−.14**
Activation							
Alert (drowsy)	4.57	5.04	−.29***	5.20	5.38	−.13*	−.16**
Strong (weak)	4.29	4.61	−.25***	4.68	4.85	−.19***	−.06
Active (passive)	4.08	4.51	−.25***	4.81	4.84	.04	−.21***
Excited (bored)	3.96	4.32	−.24***	4.29	4.43	−.14**	−.09
Other							
Free (constrained)	4.64	4.60	.04	4.72	4.69	.03	.01

*$p \leq .05$ **$p \leq .01$ ***$p \leq .001$

[a] The table is based on the average responses of each person when alone and with others. Standard deviation (s.d.) units have been used to control for differences in variance between the adolescents and the adults.

happy, cheerful, and sociable, and being less alert, strong, and excited when they are alone than when they are with people.

Those differences are substantial for the adults and even greater for the adolescents. For both, the most dramatic difference is in responses to the item lonely-sociable. The average adult responded two-thirds of a standard deviation lower on this item when alone than when with others. The average adolescent responded four-fifths of a standard deviation lower when alone. The average person reported feeling "very," "quite," or "somewhat" lonely three times as often when alone. Furthermore, in the entire group of 182 people, only 29 reported feeling lonely more often when they were with others than when alone. If we are to believe people's reports, being alone during daily life is associated not only with fewer positive states, but also with greater sadness, irritability, boredom, and loneliness.

Closer analyses reveal that the emotional effects of solitude exist regardless of a person's activity, environment, or prior mood. However, there is one situation when these effects are magnified. For adolescents, loneliness and other negative moods are higher when they are alone on a Friday or Saturday night than at other times (see Figure 3.1). During these times the average

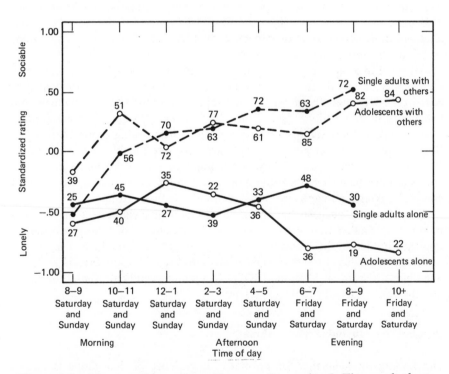

Figure 3.1. The experience of loneliness on the weekend. The graph shows mean "loneliness" reported for each time of day. The values have been standardized according to each person's mean and standard deviation. The numbers indicate the number of self reports for each mean.

teenager who is alone reports being "somewhat" lonely, and 24% report being "quite" or "very" lonely. Most teenagers are out with friends on Friday and Saturday nights. This magnified loneliness indicates the strong role played by sociocultural norms. Aloneness, at least in these circumstances, is heavily influenced by cultural prescriptions.

Whatever the combination of reasons, the subjective character of time alone is clear: It brings an improved cognitive state, but at the cost of greater loneliness and more negative moods. One might expect that these two sides of the experience represent separate occasions of being alone, but this is not the case. Across all the times people were alone, there are small negative correlations between reports of improved cognitive state and lower mood. Statistically, however, the effects on cognitive and emotional state are essentially independent. This means that those two sides of being alone are sometimes simultaneous aspects of the same experience.

Aftereffects of Being Alone

If emotions were governed by laws of inertia, we would expect people to feel worse after being alone than they felt before. The loneliness and lower moods of being alone would carry into the time with people afterwards. However, analyses indicate the relationship between time alone and time with others to be much more dynamic.

After solitude not only do moods return to their normal levels, but some dimensions of mood rise to levels higher than normal. This conclusion is based on an evaluation of all the self-reports with people following within two hours of being alone (see Table 3.4). These reports are compared to those at other times subjects are with people. After being alone there is no lingering trace of lower moods. People are not more lonely after being alone. In fact, several mood items show a net improvement. Both adolescents and adults report being significantly more alert after being alone; feelings of cheerfulness and strength are above normal for both groups.

These findings suggest that being alone has a renewing effect on people's mood state. Rather than creating inertia, the loneliness of time alone has an opposite influence. In laboratory experiments researchers have found that social isolation leads to increased social buoyancy (Oleson & Zubek, 1970; Suedfeld, Grissom, & Vernon, 1964). Our findings indicate that time alone has the same effect in daily experience.

People Who Maximize Time Alone

Our findings indicate that the normative experience of time alone is one of low moods and slightly improved cognitive state. In this section we consider people who deviate from this norm, either by feeling relatively good alone or by showing a substantially improved cognitive state. These are people for

Table 3.4. Mean Self-Ratings of Subjective State When with Others after Being Alone versus Other Times [a]

	Adolescents (N = 59)			Adults (N = 88)		
	After being alone (Mean Mean)	Other times (Mean Mean)	Difference (in s.d. units)	After being alone (Mean Mean)	Other times (Mean Mean)	Difference (in s.d. units)
Attention (range 0–9)						
Concentration	4.72	4.46	.11	5.11	4.94	.08
Ease of concentration	7.16	7.01	−.07	7.62	7.64	.01
Unself-consciousness	6.95	6.82	−.06	6.72	6.71	−.01
Mood state (range 1–7)						
Feelings:						
Happy	5.36	5.25	.09	5.33	5.19	.12
Cheerful	5.21	4.92	.21+	5.17	5.00	.13+
Sociable	5.41	5.30	.08	5.20	5.19	.01
Activation						
Alert	5.70	5.00	.43***	5.51	5.14	.27***
Strong	4.87	4.63	.19+	4.95	4.79	.18+
Active	4.80	4.55	.17	4.86	4.66	.16
Excited	4.70	4.61	.06	4.65	4.58	.07
Other						
Free	5.04	4.90	.09	4.85	4.83	.02

[a] The table is based on the average response of each person when with others. Self-ratings made within two hours of being alone are compared to self-ratings of other times the person was with others. Reports made during school and work have been excluded. Differences are reported in Standard Deviation (s.d.) units.
+ $p \leq .10$ *** $p \leq .001$

whom solitude is most positive. How does their unique experience of solitude affect the rest of their lives?

The top line of Table 3.5 shows the implications of experiencing positive moods when alone. In both studies, feeling relatively better alone is related to feeling worse with others. For the adolescents this is simply a trade-off: the overall mood of those who feel better alone is not significantly higher or lower. For the adults, however, there is a close to significant relationship between feeling relatively better alone and feeling worse overall. In sum, defying the norm appears to have a cost. Failing to experience the drop in moods that typifies most people's time alone appears to affect moods elsewhere.

Table 3.5.   The Correlation of Moods and the Quality of Time Alone Relative to Time with Others [a]

	Correlations to average mood ratings					
	Adolescents (N = 75)			Adults (N = 107)		
	Alone	With others	Overall	Alone	With others	Overall
Higher relative mood	.51***	—.30*	—.05	.38***	—.24**	—.18+
Better relative concentration	.30**	.06	.09	—.01	—.14	—.12
Greater relative ease of concentration	—.13	—.30**	—.28*	—.31**	—.26**	—.35**
Lower relative self-consciousness	—.43***	—.19	—.24*	.05**	—.18+	—.16

[a] The table shows the correlations between indexes of the quality and quantity of a person's time alone with the person's average moods for the week of study. Scores for average moods are the sum of a person's responses to all eight mood items.
+ $p \leq .10$
*$p \leq .05$
**$p \leq .01$
*** $p \leq .001$

This same trend is also evident for the cognitive variables. Among both the adolescents and adults, greater ease of concentration when alone is related to lower average moods both alone and with others (see Table 3.5). Having better attention alone appears to be related to lower overall moods. Elsewhere we have reported that the adolescents who feel relatively freer alone and those who report more choice over their activity show lower average moods and poorer school performance (Larson & Csikszentmihalyi, 1980). It is important to add that none of these correlations are due to overall differences in ease of concentration, self-consciousness, freedom, or choice. For example, relative ease of concentration alone is not related to overall ease of concentration ($r = .01$, adolescents; $r = —.13$, adults). Relative self-consciousness alone for the adolescents is not related to overall self-consciousness ($r = .06$). They are due simply to the relative balance in the quality of experience when alone and with others.

Of course the paths of causality in these relationships might go either way. However, what is important is the implicit trade-off. People who invest more of their emotion and attention in their time alone do not show higher well-being; rather that part of their experience shared with others seems to suffer not only in a relative but in an absolute way. Like the lonely people described by Warren Jones (Chapter 15), those individuals seem to shut themselves out from others. Ironically, it is these individuals who report being in the worse state when alone who show the highest overall moods.

DISCUSSION

In this chapter time alone was viewed as a constituent part of people's daily experiences. Aloneness can be viewed as an experiential niche, a situation or state of being that offers unique opportunities and imposes specific liabilities and constraints. Our first objective has been to identify the baseline properties of this niche, to outline the typical experience of time alone.

The findings indicate that time alone cannot be characterized exclusively as either renewal or as loneliness. The positive side is an improvement of attention processes: people report less self-consciousness and better concentration when they are alone. The process of renewal is suggested by the higher moods reported after being alone. Apparently the possibilities for relaxation and reflection available in this niche result in an improved emotional state after one rejoins the company of others. However, people also report feeling more depressed and lonely when alone (see also: Larson & Csikszentmihalyi, 1978). Teenagers appear to be more vulnerable to these emotions, especially if they are alone on Friday and Saturday night when most of their peers are out with friends. This painful side of aloneness is most evident in those individuals who appear to defy it: People who feel relatively better when they are alone than when they are with others experience greater loneliness and lower moods overall. Hence, while solitude may provide renewal, it is also governed by strong constraints. Being apart from others is both chilling and invigorating.

Our second objective in this chapter was to understand better the potentialities of time alone. The ritual seclusions, initiation procedures, and solitary quests prescribed in other cultures are suggestive of the possibilities this niche might provide within ours. In these canonized occasions of voluntary isolation from others, aloneness offers much beyond the narrow implications of our term "renewal" or Suedfeld's term "healing" (Chapter 4). Often aloneness occurs in association with significant life transitions and serves as a vehicle for the search, discovery, and crystallization of a new self, a new personal order, and a new relationship to others in the society.

Hence it may not be coincidental that within our sample it is those at a transitional stage of life—the adolescents—who appear to make the most use of their time alone. The findings show that they benefit from a larger reduction in self-consciousness when alone and show stronger positive aftereffects on their emotional state. More significantly, other research suggests that adolescents who spend more time alone show greater purposiveness and personal direction in their lives (McCormack, 1982).

At the broadest level, time alone can be thought of in terms of the opportunities it provides for individuation. When alone, a person has a chance to suspend the expectations of the cultural milieu and its feedback, and to reintegrate the beliefs, ideas, and values he or she has learned according to a personally meaningful pattern. Because adolescents are at a stage of life when pressures from peers are unusually strong (Costanzo, 1970) and there is a need to establish oneself independent of childhood parental bonds (Blos, 1961; Erikson, 1968), they may be more motivated to make use of the opportunities for individuation that aloneness provides. The weaker evidence for beneficial effects of aloneness in our older sample suggests that adults are either too deeply entrenched in set patterns or have found other means for generating and sustaining their individuality.

While creative solitude might be more common in adolescents, there is some indication that it is only the older and more intelligent teenagers who are able to make use of the opportunities (Larson & Csikszentmihalyi, 1980). This suggests that understanding the paradoxes of solitude and using solitude constructively may require a basic level of maturity and sophistication. An objective for future research is to determine the strategies adolescents employ to make use of these skills.

Perhaps the key to time alone involves the loneliness that it almost inevitably produces. This chapter has revealed that even people who do not (or will not) report a drop in moods when alone fail to escape loneliness and low moods elsewhere in their lives. To take advantage of the opportunities afforded by solitude, a person must be able to turn a basically terrifying state of being into a productive one. The issue may not be overcoming this loneliness, but being able to tolerate it (Winicott, 1958). Additional research could do much to clarify the opportunities and limitations of this experience as they are dictated by a person's culture, reference group, past history, and environmental constraints. For a person able to endure its painful effects, the potentials of aloneness are probably as rich and diverse as the individual person can be.

REFERENCES

Blos, P. *On adolescence.* New York: Free Press, 1961.

Costanzo, P. R. Conformity development as a function of self-blame. *Journal of Personality and Social Psychology,* 1970, *14,* 366–374.

Csikszentmihalyi, M., Larson, R., & Prescott, S. The ecology of adolescent activity and experience. *Journal of Youth and Adolescence,* 1977, *6,* 281–294.

Erikson, E. *Identity, youth and crisis.* New York: Norton, 1968.

Fortune, R. *Sorcerers of Dobu: The social anthropology of the Dobu islanders of the western Pacific.* New York: Dutton, 1963.

Larson, R. The significance of solitude in adolescents' lives, (Doctoral dissertation, University of Chicago, 1979.) *Dissertation Abstracts International, 1979, 40,* 169–A.

Larson, R., & Csikszentmihalyi, M. Experiential correlates of time alone in adolescence. *Journal of Personality, 1978, 46,* 677–693.

Larson, R., & Csikszentmihalyi, M. The significance of time alone in adolescent development. *Journal of Current Adolescent Medicine, 1980, 2(8),* 33–40.

McCormack, J. *Life influences and the development of purposive functioning in adolescents.* Unpublished doctoral dissertation, University of Chicago, 1982.

Merton, T. *No man is an island.* Garden City, N.Y.: Image Books, 1955.

Oleson, D., & Zubek, J. Effect of one day of sensory deprivation on a battery of open-ended cognitive tests. *Perceptual and Motor Skills, 1970, 31,* 919–923.

Radin, P. The Winnebago tribe. *U.S. Bureau of American Ethnology, 37th Annual Report,* No. 37, 1923.

Rilke, R. M. *Letters to a young poet* (M. D. Herton, trans.). New York: Norton, 1934.

Suedfeld, P., Grissom, R., & Vernon, J. The effects of sensory deprivation and social isolation on the performance of an unstructured cognitive task. *American Journal of Psychology, 1964, 77,* 111–115.

Thoreau, H. *Walden.* New York: Viking Press, 1947.

Winicott, D. The capacity to be alone. *International Journal of Psychoanalysis, 1958, 39,* 416–420.

Chapter 4

Aloneness as a Healing Experience

Peter Suedfeld

Human societies are by definition predicated upon the assumption that being together with other people is "good" in some universal sense. Togetherness not only facilitates solving the everyday problems of survival but is also generally accepted as one of the prerequisite conditions for happiness (Bowlby, 1973; Weiss, 1973). This philosophy is perhaps as pervasive in our own culture as it has been almost anywhere, with the possible exception of the highly collectivized and communally oriented systems that have occasionally arisen throughout history. Most people in modern Western society think of being alone as a generally undesirable state. When they themselves are solitary, they energetically attempt to find companionship, or failing that distract themselves from their misery by vicarious group activity such as watching other people on television. When they discover that someone else spends much of his or her time in solitude, they consider that person an appropriate object for pity, assistance, or even therapy (Fromm-Reichmann, 1959; Robertson, 1958; Varela, 1977; Stephens, 1974).

Social scientists, parents, teachers, and social critics see aloneness as aberrant. Being alone for a considerable proportion of one's time is sometimes characterized as a sign of the breakdown of society; sometimes as a symptom of individual maladjustment; and sometimes as a condition that is the precursor and cause of pathology (Solomon & Patch, 1974; Werner, 1978). At any rate, it certainly is not perceived as a healthy or acceptable way of life.

Psychologists have for the most part accepted this tradition unquestioningly, in the same way as we have gone along with most of the major societal norms of our environment. Adults worry about children who prefer to sit by themselves rather than participate in group activities (Lipsitt, 1979; Solomon & Patch, 1974); clinicians try to develop techniques for treating social isolates (Argyle, 1967; Gottman, Gonso, & Schuler, 1976; Oden & Asher, 1977); gerontological psychologists devise ways to overcome the tendency of old people to spend a lot of time alone (Schulz, 1976). The major theme of this book is the negative affective state that is aroused by solitude. Most personality theorists assume that attachment to other people is basic, and that when such attachments are disputed, loneliness results. Positive feelings about being alone have been described as reaction formation, or the outward signs of distrustfulness and defensiveness, or the atrophying of the normal attachment system in old age. Strong interpersonal bonds are assumed to be an optimal kind of affective tie (Argyle, 1967; Bowlby, 1951). Perhaps the most favorable thing that has been said about being alone is that people who are able to overcome its terrible effects may experience a strengthening and greater integration of their personality; the implication is that adversity is good for you and that solitude is necessarily a form of adversity.

These assumptions probably underlie the fact that, although loneliness research is in its toddlerhood, research on the positive effects of solitude is still in the fetal stage. Not much has been published, and a substantial proportion of the available literature is anecdotal and in some cases slightly off the beaten track of what psychologists typically read. Thus an overview of this literature lacks even that level of crispness and precision that social psychologists are accustomed to. Nevertheless, there are some common underlying themes and provocative hints that may induce scientifically minded researchers to undertake more controlled and systematic projects. For this to be accomplished, such individuals would have to read the material and overcome the cultural biases to which I have referred; I hope that the intrinsic challenges of the area and the possibility of entering a research field in its early stages will combine to motivate at least some investigators to follow up these leads.

LONELINESS AND ALONENESS

Loneliness is by definition a negative emotional state. But as many workers in the field have made abundantly clear, being alone is neither a necessary nor a sufficient condition for feeling lonely. In fact, a scanning of references to "Isolation" in *Psychological Abstracts* indicates a very heavy emphasis on alienation and lack of close emotional ties rather than an absence of other people in the immediate environment. Loneliness exists, and can be quite intense, among residents of large urban centers whose contacts with other people may not be as intimate, satisfying, or easy as they would wish—but who certainly have no absence of such contacts. While loneliness and solitude are often associated experientially, most of the relevant literature conceives of the lonely person as one who feels alone even in a crowd, one who has lost an important person in his or her life, or one who feels rejected and disliked (Weiss, 1973).

Let us look for the moment only at the externally observable, empirically defined, environmental condition of aloneness. The picture now becomes more complex. It is true that many people are alone; that many people feel lonely; and that some of those who are alone feel lonely. But the sets are overlapping, not redundant. The population of solitary people includes adventurers, sages, saints, sailors, and seekers. Many of them have found solitude to be pleasant, exciting, enlightening, and highly desirable. In fact, if we look at the literature carefully, we see that being alone can be a liberating situation in the sense that the individual finds the freedom to experience an unusually wide range of emotions, to have either stereotyped or wildly imaginative thoughts, to feel either hellishly miserable or ecstatically happy. Discussing profound experimental environmental restriction (lying for prolonged periods in a completely dark, soundproof room or being submerged in a tank of water), Zuckerman (1969, p. 47) described the situation as a "live-in ink-blot." In the sense that the situation itself is extremely amorphous, and the response to it is crucially influenced by the expectations, interpretations, and emotions of the individual himself, this description probably applies equally well to solitude (which, incidentally, is one component of experimental stimulus reduction).

Why is it, then, that people are differentially susceptible to feeling lonely, to some extent independent of the actual social environment? I would propose that we pay more attention to the state-trait distinction, just as researchers in the area of anxiety have had to do (Spielberger, Gorsuch, & Lushene, 1970). The two affects are obviously related. For one thing, anxiety is probably more basic, and is frequently one of the components of the more complex feeling of loneliness. There are individuals who occasionally feel lonely regardless of the environment, just as there are those who occasionally feel free-floating anxiety; others are chronically lonely, again regardless of the actual social circumstances, just as some people are chronically anxious even in safe environments; still others always feel lonely when they are by themselves—a counterpart to those people who react to any kind of risk with high anxiety; and another group has reasonable coping abilities but still occasionally feels lonely when they are solitary, the equivalent of realistic anxiety. There are probably also people who never feel lonely, just as there may be people who never feel anxious. But while this is conceptually possible, I doubt that one finds many such people in real life. Their theoretical existence, however, serves to remind us that all of these categories are overlapping and graded. We are talking about feeling more or less lonely for a greater or smaller proportion of the time, with higher or lower relationship to the actual observable environment, rather than about clearcut distinct categories.

As the title of this chapter implies, I shall emphasize instances in which solitude has had beneficial influences. There are three major sources of information on the effects of absolute isolation. One consists of dramatic tales of isolation in unusual circumstances, by unusual people, or in connection with some unusual activity. Examples are the accounts of solitary sailors or explorers, victims of shipwreck or plane crash, and isolated prisoners. A second category comprises religious and spiritual quests. Mystics wandering in the wilderness, adolescent tribesmen moving through their rites of passage, and meditators altering their state of consciousness are some of the people involved in this search. Some of them are deviants, in the sense of being unusual or even unique by the standards of their culture. They usually have a much less problem-oriented approach to the experience than do the members of the first category, for whom physical survival is a salient goal. The third line of evidence comes from specific attempts to use isolation, usually in conjunction with general stimulus reduction, as a therapeutic technique in somatic and behavioral medicine. The data here, while they still have a lot to be desired, are more objective and quantitative than in the first two situations.

Dramatic instances of solitude have had a great impact on the public mind. Singlehanded sailors could always count on fame, a bestseller, and sometimes a knighthood, at least until they became a glut on the market a few years ago. The sufferings of castaways (a term that I shall use, although inaccurately, for people who were isolated as a result of a wrecked ship or aircraft) have similarly attracted intrigued audiences. And prisoners in solitary confinement, no matter how odious their crime or personality, almost always found sympathetic supporters (Fox, 1974; Lucas, 1976; Suedfeld, 1980; Wyman, 1978; Zimbardo, 1974).

SOLITARY VOYAGERS AND PRISONERS

Lone circumnavigators have reported seeing imaginary people, animals, objects, and geographic features, and have experienced grotesque changes in body image, disorientation, labile affects, and vivid realistic dreams (Slocum, 1899/1970). But most students of this literature agree that the major causative factors are fatigue, especially sleep deprivation, and the need to perform a monotonous task such as steering the boat for hour after hour without relief. In fact, the occurrence of such phenomena has decreased markedly since the introduction of self-steering devices. Other contributing factors are the rhythmic motion of the waves, illness, dietary deficiencies, and food or drug poisoning (Henderson, 1976).

Most of the lone voyagers are well prepared, and are presumably self-selected as being able to stand isolation. Many have reduced aloneness by shipping a pet or, more recently, radios and tape recorders. According to one analyst of the solitary sailing experience, "loneliness only becomes significant when . . . the mind is already troubled" (Heaton, 1976, p. 181). The psychological detachment of solitary high-altitude fliers from the earth ("break-off") also does not appear to arise from loneliness, but rather from a lack of change, challenge, and orienting cues in the environment (Bennett, 1961). Among solitary adventurers who remained in one place, the most prominent is Byrd. He spent five months alone during the Antarctic winter of 1934. He too had some disturbing feelings and reactions, but they were apparently brought on by severe carbon monoxide poisoning (Byrd, 1938).

On the positive side, several of the people involved in this kind of event had deep and meaningful experiences. Some of these were religious in nature —a new relationship to God, a mystical feeling of oneness with the ocean, with the human species, or with the entire universe. Others could be characterized as new insights into the adventurer's own personality. In any case, they were perceived as having made a significant contribution to the individual's philosophy and style of life from then on (Heaton, 1976).

Aside from self-selection and preparation, the individuals in this group were in an environment where a series of tasks had to be competently performed for the sake of survival. This requirement not only increases the amount of stimulation in the situation, it also helps to structure and pass the time and to provide challenge and involvement. This, and the occasional episode of acute danger, may serve to distract the traveler from the monotony of the surroundings as well as from his own fears, fantasies, and memories.

Not so the castaway. Castaways may wind up as singlehanded sailors, or walkers, but they did not ask for it and usually are not prepared for it. As a result, they are much more vulnerable to physical and psychological danger. They may lack the necessary skills and supplies, and may also be injured and in shock. Their great need is not so much for companionship as for practical help and rescue. Some of the great stories of human endurance and ingenuity have come from such situations (Cooke, 1960; Critchley, 1943). Probably much more frequent, but less frequently published, are stories of withdrawal and death resulting from inability to cope with the situation. Apparently a high proportion of even uninjured survivors of such accidents die within a few days, the probable causes being physical and mental shock and helplessness (Bombard, 1953; Moore, 1978). Among those who do survive, both bizarre stressful experiences and spiritual cataclysms have occurred; but again, other causes of emotional and cognitive disruption appear to be intuitively more compelling than loneliness.

Solitary prisoners enter their cells with as little desire, and sometimes with as much surprise, uncertainty, and fear, as castaways board their life raft. Their survival is by no means assured. They may lack proper food, clothing, and medical care. Their confinement may be of unknown duration and in uncomfortable surroundings. They may not know whether they can expect help from other people, in or out of the prison. Perhaps worst of all, they are not merely the victims of misfortune and blind chance: they are in the hands of malign and powerful people.

Unlike the other situations mentioned so far, solitary confinement has been the focus of some systematic social science research. The available data indicate that the experience is not necessarily, nor even generally, deleterious or aversive (Ecclestone, Gendreau, & Knox, 1974; Walters, Callaghan, & Newman, 1963; Weinberg, 1967). Among isolated convicts in modern Western prisons, where the conditions of confinement are usually not inhumanely rigorous, many individuals have used the time to study, to think, to engage in personal problem solving, and even to plan self-rehabilitative activities (Glynn, 1957; Suedfeld, Ramirez, Clyne, & Deaton, 1976). Under other conditions, and after prolonged isolation, reverie, fantasy, and methodical self-scheduled activity patterns emerge (Deaton, Berg, Richlin, & Litrownik, 1977). Religious conversions and similar experiences also occur. Of course there are individuals who find the situation extremely unpleasant and damaging; and some extreme situations are likely to have that effect on most prisoners. The latter conditions, however, are probably those that add torture to isolation. It seems far-fetched to blame loneliness for their consequences, especially since it does not seem to be either a necessary or a sufficient factor (Suedfeld, 1980).

Solitary Quests

Another situation in which aloneness is an important factor is in the search for transcendental experiences. The use of wilderness in such quests has characterized many cultures all over the world and has lasted several millenia. Of the outstanding religious innovators in world history, those whose major vision and communion with God occurred in such settings include Zoroaster, Moses, Jesus, Mohammed, and the Buddha. Literally thousands of other mystics, monks, hermits, anchorites, mahatmas, and prophets have followed in these footsteps. At one time in the early centuries of Christianity, an estimated 5000 hermits were seeking solitude—probably without much success—in the deserts of the Near East (Waddell, 1942). The religious traditions of many societies have given honored roles to the contemplative or inspired individual who pursued enlightenment and insight far from the madding crowd.

It is also quite frequent among tribal cultures to incorporate a period of solitude in the life history of every individual, or at least of every male (I shall not speculate here on why this wide-spread sex discrimination may have developed and been so frequently the case). Adolescents passing into adulthood would, after appropriate purifications and ceremonies, leave the community to wander alone in the desert, mountains, forest, or prairie. This particular kind of puberty rite has been reported in scores of cultures in North and South America, Africa, Asia, and Australia. The specific details differ. In some groups, physical deprivation, pain, or fasting accompany the isolation procedure. The duration of aloneness may be only overnight or as long as several months. The explicit goal may be to search one's own soul, to dream a magic dream, to identify a totemic animal, to compose a powerful song, to communicate with one's ancestors or gods, or just to experience the oneness of the universe. But in all cases, the individual was expected to, himself expected to, and generally did, grow beyond his usual self to achieve some higher level of consciousness.

Frequently the actual phenomena that were experienced bore close similarity to those reported by the castaways and prisoners discussed previously. A modern Western psychologist would have seen hallucinations, illusions,

delusions, inappropriate affects, disorganized cognitions, and bizarre behavior. But the tribe saw only the manifestations of the supernatural, or perhaps the more deeply natural. And since the events were not categorized as
symptoms, no one realized that there was anything to worry about. As a
consequence, no one worried, and no one was damaged (Suedfeld, 1974).

We should not ignore the fact that such practices are still with us. There
are of course eremitic monastic orders in the United States and Canada, as
well as in the rest of the world. In her classic book on mysticism, Underhill
wrote: "Something equivalent to the solitude of the wilderness is an essential
part of mystical education" (1911/1961 p. 173). Merton, perhaps the most
lyrical writer on this topic, said in discussing the monastic life: "It is in
silence, and not in commotion, in solitude and not in crowds, that God best
likes to reveal Himself most intimately to men" (1957, p. 38). Is loneliness
a problem here? Probably, sometimes; but the writings and the sayings agree
that the search drives away the fears and the feelings of being lonely.

Clearly monks and mystics are very special people, deviant in the non-
pejorative sense to which I have already referred. But those adolescents out
there in the wilderness are not. And they're not all members of strange tribes,
either. From the German *Wandervögel* of the 1920s and 1930s to the back-
packers and Outward Bound adventurers of the United States today, our own
century and our own Western culture have had their share of people who
appreciate communion with nature instead of with man as an important part
of life. The "Solo" is an integral component of Outward Bound, as it is of
many camping programs, and participants sometimes describe transcendental
episodes that would do credit to any meditator or mystic.

Perhaps the most recent addition to this list is an outgrowth of laboratory
research in stimulus reduction. Lilly, one of the pioneers of this kind of ex-
perimentation, has moved during the past decade toward and into the use of
the restricted environmental stimulation technique (REST) in workshops
more related to the human potential/transpersonal psychology tradition than
the experimental one. In a book published in 1977, he recounts the stories of
more than 70 people who had spent time floating in an immersion tank in
darkness and silence. Obviously many of these individuals felt that they had
achieved unusual things. There were beautiful and exciting sensory experiences, vivid fantasies and memories, deep insights, relaxed and free emotions.
There were some negative reactions too, but these were rare and fleeting.
Once again, the anecdotes are selective; but they agree well with reports of
similar programs run by other people in other places. And of course the
participants had the "right" attitude: they expected and appreciated the
extraordinary environment and its equally extraordinary consequences.

A variant of this use of solitude has frequently been mentioned in autobi-
ography and biography. This is the fostering of creative thinking. The fact
that novel ideas frequently emerge and are developed during periods of isolation has been repeatedly verified by important contributors to philosophy, the
sciences, and the arts. Apparently there is a growing use of isolation and

reduced stimulation by people in creative professions. Although no data have been published, there have been reports of the use of water immersion tanks by scientists and artists. Some have found the experience so conducive to productivity that they have repeated it at regular intervals (Lilly, 1977).

These are the positive experiences to be savored in solitude. They are both beneficial and pleasant; and although they may not be "healing" in the strict sense—since there is no illness to be healed—they certainly are so in the wider sense. Aloneness in this context fills a need, removes a lack, impels growth. There seems to be no loneliness; rather the individual feels a freedom from distraction, from the usual restrictions imposed by social norms and the need to maintain face, and the benefits of reducing external stimulation to the point where the still, small internal voices can be heard.

RESTRICTED ENVIRONMENTAL STIMULATION THERAPY (REST)

Like the solitary quest, solitary therapy has a long history and varied locales. Descriptions of traditional practices in the treatment of the mentally ill have noted the use of isolation and stimulus reduction as far back as the oracles of ancient Greece and even today, north to the Arctic Circle and south to sub-Saharan Africa. I'm speaking here of treatment, not of punishment or quarantine, which is how these procedures are frequently reinterpreted by mental health professionals who, themselves coming from a bustling and crowded society, cannot imagine that silence and aloneness can be anything but aversive (Suedfeld, 1980).

In the tradition of scientific medicine as we know it, solitude has played a part that has never been abandoned. Psychiatric pioneers such as Rush, Mitchell, and Janet all recognized that overstimulation could be pathogenic, and prescribed rest and freedom from social intercourse for a variety of behavorial syndromes (Dercum, 1917). In Japan, Morita and others combined these ideas with traditions inherited from Zen Buddhism to develop therapeutic systems that are in wide current use (Reynolds, 1976). The seclusion of patients in mental hospitals, to reduce aggressive and otherwise violent behavior, grows directly out of some of the early uses of isolation as a calming environment. So does its application with agitated inmates in institutions that span the borders of mental health care and incarceration—for example, facilities for mentally disturbed juvenile or adult offenders (Suedfeld, 1980).

A more recent approach has been the adoption of techniques from the reduced stimulation laboratory to the psychiatric hospital, clinic, or office. Whereas the transfer in the case of transpersonal experiences relied upon the use of water immersion tanks, the equivalent application of basic research techniques to clinical settings has typically used the dark, silent room procedure. I shall not analyze this voluminous literature in detail (Suedfeld, 1980).

Even a summary, however, indicates the broad applicability of the technique, which involves not only social isolation but also profound sensory restriction. The most effective version tested so far requires the patient to lie on a bed quietly, in a dark and soundproof room, usually for a day or less. In cases of prolonged restriction, food, water, and a chemical toilet are typically made available in the room. Communication with the monitor is frequently possible through an intercom system, which in some studies is also used to present various kinds of therapeutic messages.

Two major lines of work have appeared, one dealing with psychotherapeutic treatment of institutionalized patients, and the other, more closely related to health psychology, directed toward the modification of health-dysfunctional habits and conditions. Among the former, the findings have included better rapport with the therapist and facilitation of desired regression (Azima, Vispo, & Azima, 1961); the reduction of hallucinations, repressive and inhibitory defenses, depression, hypochondriacal complaints, and general symptomatology among hospital psychiatric patients (Adams, 1980); a reduction in assaults, self-injuries, and bizarre behavior among individuals hospitalized for PCP or LSD psychosis (Adams, 1980); and improvements in ego strength, ego functioning, IQ scores, self-acceptance, self-concept, decision making, and internal control among inpatients (Adams et al., 1966). The use of solitude in the treatment of disturbed children has resulted in major symptom remission in cases of autism (Schechter et al., 1969) and in improved learning and decreases in disruptive behavior among retarded and delinquent children and adolescents (Glynn, 1957). This last body of work, which includes the use of "timeout" techniques, is closely related to the use of seclusion on psychiatric wards. Such applications of aloneness are less confounded with general stimulus restriction than most of the REST literature, but unfortunately have undergone less systematic testing.

With noninstitutionalized clients (Suedfeld, 1977; 1980), REST has been successfully used to induce weight gain in cases of anorexia nervosa and weight loss in cases of obesity. Pilot studies using REST have reported reductions in the alcohol intake of heavy social drinkers, improved speech fluency among stutterers, and reduced blood pressure in patients suffering from essential hypertension. Neuromuscular control was increased when standard eye exercises given to esophoric patients were combined with reduced stimulation, and a series of studies has shown reduced behavioral and verbal fear as well as associated psychophysiological changes among snake-phobic individuals. Other changes under conditions of isolation and reduced stimulation that appear to be therapeutically applicable, but have not been investigated in that context, include improvements in self-concept and optimism, increased ability to make decisions independently of external pressure, various alterations in the state of consciousness, and increased susceptibility to hypnosis.

One of the more systematic applications of REST in this context has been in smoking cessation. One study, using college students who were volunteers for an experiment rather than for smoking treatment, found that 24 hours of stimulus restriction, either with or without a 3-minute anticigarette message, resulted in an average 38% reduction in smoking rate three months later. A larger-scale project, using a cross-section of the population rather than only students and selecting psychologically addicted smokers who had been unsuccessfully trying to quit, retained the 24 hours of confinement but added approximately a dozen messages related to various aspects of smoking and smoking cessation. A 2-year follow-up showed that subjects who had gone through the REST procedure were smoking on the average less than half as many cigarettes as at baseline, compared to a reduction of between 15% and 20% for subjects who had received either only the messages in their home environment or no treatment at all except referral to other smoking clinics.

An even more recent study, combining REST and messages with a standard behavioral self-management package (self-monitoring, functional analysis, and satiation smoking) obtained one-year follow-up data showing that over half of the subjects were completely abstinent from cigarettes, and the average smoking rate for the group was about half of baseline. In contrast, success rate with clients who received either the self-management package only or the REST treatment only were in the neighborhood of around 25% abstinence. The important aspect of this last datum is that it is approximately equal to that previously reported to be as good as one could obtain by any single clinical procedure, even those that took several weeks or months of treatment and considerable effort on the part of both patient and therapist. The implication is that REST, which takes only one 24-hour session, can not only obtain results as good as any other technique that has been systematically investigated, but in combination with other techniques, it may have a potentiating effect that leads to a dramatic increase in success rates. (These studies are reported in more detail in Suedfeld, 1980.)

Thus it is obvious that Reduced Environmental Stimulation Therapy, which involves social isolation plus a global reduction in sensory input, is an effective clinical technique whose boundaries have not yet been fully explored. Neither has the degree to which solitude itself plays an important role in, or could substitute for, general environmental restriction. But there certainly seems to be no doubt that healing processes can be facilitated by such conditions. We may take note of the frequently observed phenomenon that ill or injured animals tend to seek isolation during the period of recovery. Again this is an observation that has not been thoroughly investigated and whose meaning has not been clarified. But it may be an important example of evolutionary adaptiveness, and may have its parallel in the frequently reported desire of hospitalized patients to seek less social and environmental stimulation than visitors and staff consider to be desirable (Suedfeld, 1979).

It may be important to say a word about the general acceptability of REST for clients. It appears that the stimulus reduced environment induces very little if any stress or anxiety in most participants, unless it is preceded by methodological components that arouse negative anticipations. When such effects are carefully avoided, however, attrition rates during the session are very low, and ratings of affect are essentially neutral. Occurrences of major disturbance among previously well-adjusted subjects have been extremely rare. In fact, there has only been one such case reported in the entire literature. This represents less than .0003 of experimental and clinical participants in REST studies. One would guess, although the data are not available, that equivalent periods of solitude would be even easier to tolerate. Thus social isolation therapy might be even more widely acceptable than REST. Whether this is in fact the case, and what differences in effectiveness would be found, is purely a matter for speculation at this time.

CONCLUSION

There is no disputing the fact that solitude and loneliness can sometimes be unpleasant, stressful, and injurious. In my opinion, this is to a great extent a result of cultural norms. Modern urbanites and dwellers in technologically advanced societies have been taught that isolation is a bad thing, and they react accordingly. Furthermore, they are seldom prepared to cope with its early effects. For example, the organism frequently begins to generate (or to perceive more sensitively) internal stimuli when the external level goes significantly below optimum, as it may during situations of low social and nonsocial input. This internal stimulation may include unusual (either novel or usually subthreshold) physical sensations, vivid fantasies and daydreams, distorted cognitions and perceptions, and labile emotional sequences. The individual who has been conditioned to interpret such phenomena as signs of an impending breakdown will react to them with negative feelings and fear, thus exacerbating the situation and possibly leading to actual psychological dysfunction. In some cases this destructive cycle has been reported as beginning when the isolate realized that he was talking to himself or herself, which he or she had been taught was a symptom of insanity (Suedfeld, 1974).

If the environment is approached in a different way, the expectations will be neutral or even positive, as they are in some other cultures. The altered states of consciousness that sometimes emerge are then perceived for what they are: a combination of lowered thresholds and adaptive attempts to increase inadequate input levels. People who take this view are much less likely to suffer in any of the situations I have discussed.

There are data supporting this argument. Experimental REST studies have found that tolerance of primary process experiences is a predictor of the subject's ability to endure and enjoy isolation and stimulus reduction. Similar relationships have been found between other personality characteristics—maturity, intelligence, conceptual complexity—and the ability to cope with REST. As Byrd wrote, "The ones who survive with a measure of happiness are those who can live profoundly off their intellectual resources" (1938, p. 19). That goes for a one-person sailing vessel going around the world, for a lifeboat, a prison cell, a water tank, an experimental chamber, or a desert hermitage.

After long resistance, we are at last coming to realize the aversiveness of the social and sensory overload that bombards us almost constantly. It has taken a long time. The fish is not aware of the water, as a general rule. But when the water becomes first dirty and then poisonous, and the fish gets sick, it will—if it is a thinking and self-aware fish—eventually recognize the existence of a problem. And piscine psychologists will start teaching their schools the facts, as human psychologists are beginning to pass the word about the effects of crowding, noise, information overload, future shock, lack of privacy, and the rest. The antidote is solitude, stillness, and time out. In an environment with fewer frantic distractions, we can learn once again to appreciate the important things that we have been driven to ignore.

No one would deny that loneliness can hurt. But it is equally certain that aloneness can heal. And solitude, properly structured, may even be used to heal and transcend loneliness, and to use it as a springboard for enjoyment, health, and growth.

REFERENCES

Adams, H. B., Robertson, M. H., & Cooper, G. D. Sensory deprivation and personality change. *Journal of Nervous and Mental Disease,* 1966, *143,* 256–265.

Adams, H. B. Effects of reduced stimulation in institutionalized adult patients. In P. Suedfeld, *Restricted environmental stimulation: Research and clinical applications.* New York: Wiley, 1980.

Argyle, M. *The psychology of interpersonal behaviour.* Harmondsworth, England: Penguin, 1967.

Azima, H., Vispo, R., & Azima, F. J. Observations on anaclitic therapy during sensory deprivation. In P. Solomon et al. (Eds.), *Sensory deprivation.* Cambridge, Mass.: Harvard University Press, 1961.

Bennett, A. M. H. Sensory deprivation in aviation. In P. Solomon et al. (Eds.), *Sensory deprivation.* Cambridge, Mass.: Harvard University Press, 1961.

Bombard, A. *The voyage of the Heretique.* New York: Simon & Schuster, 1953.

Bowlby, J. *Maternal care and mental health.* New York: Columbia University Press, 1951.

Bowlby, J. *Attachment and loss (Vol. 2.). Separation: Anxiety and anger.* New York: Basic Books, 1973.

Byrd, R. E. *Alone.* New York: Ace, 1938.

Cooke, K. *Man on a raft.* New York: Berkley, 1960.

Critchley, M. *Shipwreck survivors.* London: Churchill, 1943.

Deaton, J. E., Berg, S. W., Richlin, M., & Litrownik, A. J. Coping activities in solitary confinement of U.S. Navy POWs in Vietnam. *Journal of Applied Social Psychology,* 1977, *7,* 239–257.

Dercum, F. X. *Rest, suggestion and other therapeutic measures in nervous and mental diseases* (2nd ed.). Philadelphia: P. Blakiston's Son & Company, 1917.

Ecclestone, C., Gendreau, P., & Knox, C. Solitary confinement of prisoners: An assessment of its effects on inmates' personal constructs and adrenocortical activity. *Canadian Journal of Behavioural Science,* 1974, *6,* 178–191.

Fox, S. S. *Psychological and mental status examination report, US vs. Lopez and Miramon,* 74-S-C.R.3, November 7th, 1974.

Fromm-Reichmann, F. Loneliness. *Psychiatry,* 1959, *22,* 1–15.

Glynn, E. The therapeutic use of seclusion in an adolescent pavilion. *Journal of the Hillside Hospital,* 1957, *6,* 156–159.

Gottman, J., Gonso, J., & Schuler, P. Teaching social skills to isolated children. *Journal of Abnormal Child Psychology,* 1976, *4,* 179–197.

Heaton, P. *The single-handers.* New York: Hastings House, 1976.

Henderson, R. *Singlehanded sailing.* Camden, Me.: International Marine Publishing Company, 1976.

Lilly, J. C. *The deep self.* New York: Simon & Schuster, 1977.

Lipsitt, L. P. Critical conditions in infancy: A psychological perspective. *American Psychologist,* 1979, *34,* 973–980.

Lucas, W. E. Solitary confinement: Isolation as coercion to conform. *Australian and New Zealand Journal of Criminology,* 1976, *9,* 153–167.

Merton, T. *The silent life.* New York: Farrar, Straus & Giroux, 1957.

Moore, T. O. Personal communication, November 30th, 1978.

Oden, S., & Asher, S. R. Coaching children in social skills for friendship making. *Child Development,* 1977, *48,* 495–506.

Reynolds, D. K. *Morita psychotherapy.* Berkeley: University of California Press, 1976.

Robertson, J. *Young children in hospital.* London: Tavistock, 1958.

Schechter, M. D., Shurley, J. T., Sexauer, J. D., & Toussieng, P. W. Perceptual isolation therapy: A new experimental approach in the treatment of children using infantile autistic defenses. A preliminary report. *Journal of Child Psychiatry,* 1969, *8,* 97–139.

Schulz, R. Effects of control and predictability on the physical and psychological well-being of the institutionalized aged. *Journal of Personality and Social Psychology,* 1976, *33,* 563–573.

Slocum, J. *Sailing alone around the world.* New York: Blue Ribbon Books, 1899; republished, New York: Collier-Macmillan, 1970.

Solomon, P., & Patch, V. D. (Eds.) *Handbook of psychiatry* (3rd ed.). Los Altos, Calif.: Lange Medical Publications, 1974.

Spielberger, C. D., Gorsuch, R. L., & Lushene, R. E. *Manual for the State-Trait Anxiety Inventory.* Palo Alto, Calif.: Consulting Psychologist Press, 1970.

Stephens, J. *Society of the alone: Freedom, privacy, and utilitarianism as dominant norms in the SRO.* Mimeographed paper, Department of Anthropology and Sociology, University of Queensland, 1974.

Suedfeld, P. *The medical relevance of the hospital environment.* Paper read at the International Conference on Psychology and Medicine, Swansea, Great Britain, 1979.

Suedfeld, P. Social isolation: A case for interdisciplinary research. *Canadian Psychologist,* 1974, *15,* 1–15.

Suedfeld, P. Using environmental restriction to initiate long-term behavior change. In R. B. Stuart (Ed.), *Behavioral self-management: Strategies, techniques and outcomes.* New York: Brunner/Mazel, 1977.

Suedfeld, P. *Restricted environmental stimulation: Research and clinical applications.* New York: Wiley, 1980.

Suedfeld, P., Ramirez, C., Clyne, D., & Deaton, J. E. *The effects of involuntary social isolation on prisoners.* Paper read at the XVIth Interamerican Congress of Psychology, Miami Beach, 1976.

Underhill, E. *Mysticism.* New York: Dutton, 1961. Original publication 1911.

Varela, J. A. Social technology. *American Psychologist,* 1977, *32,* 914–923.

Waddell, H. *The desert fathers.* New York: Sheed & Ward, 1942.

Walters, R. H., Callaghan, J. E., & Newman, A. F. Effects of solitary confinement on prisoners. *American Journal of Psychiatry,* 1963, *119,* 771–773.

Weinberg, M. M. *The effects of partial sensory deprivation on involuntary subjects.* Unpublished doctoral dissertation, Michigan State University, 1967.

Weiss, R. S. (Ed.). *Loneliness: The experience of emotional and social isolation.* Cambridge, Mass.: MIT Press, 1973.

Werner, C. Lonely losers: Stereotypes of single dwellers. *Personality and Social Psychology Bulletin,* 1978, *4,* 292–295.

Wyman, M. Andy Bruce/Steinhauser play as raw as a new wound. Vancouver *Sun,* May 8th, 1978, p. C-3.

Zimbardo, P. G. *Statement in the case of J. L. Spain et al. vs. R. K. Procunier et al.,* C-431293AJZ, June 13th, 1974.

Zuckerman, M. Variables affecting deprivation results. In J. P. Zubek (Ed.), *Sensory deprivation: Fifteen years of research.* New York: Appleton-Century-Crofts, 1969.

PART TWO

Conceptual and Methodological Issues in Studying Loneliness

Loneliness is a complex phenomenon. Those who want to understand or study it are confronted with a number of knotty conceptual and methodological issues. The chapters in this section highlight three basic questions about loneliness and offer many practical guidelines.

How are we to identify the lonely? Loneliness is an intensely personal, subjective experience. There are no foolproof objective signs of loneliness. Researchers and clinicians cannot observe loneliness directly. Instead they must rely on people's statements about their internal experiences, or attempt to infer loneliness from clusters of symptoms. The task of identifying the lonely is further complicated by some people's unwillingness to acknowledge loneliness to themselves or to others. Believing that loneliness is a personal embarrassment, people may try to hide their inner pain.

How many kinds of loneliness are there? Workers in the field are divided on this important question. Some argue for a common core to all loneliness experiences; others have proposed typologies of loneliness. Yet all acknowledge the diversity of individual experiences of loneliness.

Where should we look for the causes of loneliness? Loneliness always stems in some measure from a painful mismatch of person and situation. Both situational and characterological factors contribute to loneliness. The danger is that we may emphasize one set of factors to the exclusion of others. In particular, researchers, clinicians, and lonely people themselves may be too quick to "blame the victim"—to focus on the faults or deficiencies of the lonely person and overlook social and situational factors in loneliness.

The chapters in this section discuss these and other issues. We begin with a chapter by Weiss, whose 1973 book on loneliness inspired much of the research described in this volume. Weiss reflects on recent developments in the field and lays out an agenda of unresolved issues and questions. In Chapter 6, Russell provides a comprehensive review of efforts to devise and validate instruments for measuring loneliness. In Chapter 7, de Jong-Gierveld and Raadschelders survey existing typologies of loneliness and identify basic dimensions underlying differences in the experience of loneliness.

Chapter 5

Issues in the
Study of Loneliness

Robert S. Weiss

When I surveyed the literature on loneliness, in preparation for my own book (Weiss, 1973), it seemed to me surprisingly limited. Sullivan (1953) had pointed out that loneliness seemed first to appear in adolescence, but that when it did appear, it did so with great force. This limited although acute observation had not been followed up. The standard text on loneliness was an article by Fromm-Reichmann (1959), in which loneliness was pictured as a state of profound isolation, a kind of Antarctica of the soul, experienced in pure form only by the most artistic and most disturbed. In another article, similar in perspective, loneliness was identified with recognition of the ultimately unbridgeable distance separating all of us (von Witzleben, 1968). On quite another tack, there were ventures in uplift in which readers were urged to treat their loneliness as opportunities for communion with self and the universe (Moustakas, 1961, 1972). Empirical studies of loneliness were scarce. A few PhD dissertations of value had been published, attracting, as is customary with PhD dissertations, no attention whatsoever (Bradley, 1969; Eddy, 1961; Francis, 1972; Sisenwein, 1964). Lopata (1969), working from interviews with widows, had categorized the ways in which these women had experienced loneliness. That was it; that was the literature.

Yet there was evidence that loneliness was by no means an unusual experience. Bradburn (1969) had asked in a survey study whether individuals had in the preceding few weeks felt "very lonely or remote from other people." Twenty-six percent of his respondents said that they had. I was puzzled that a phenomenon reported as a current experience by so large a proportion of the population, already identified, by Sullivan at least, as of psychiatric significance, should be so little written about. It seemed to me that defensive processes must be at work: that investigators who minimized or denied their own loneliness also directed their attention away from loneliness in others. In addition, investigators might shy away from studying loneliness because they didn't want to be thought of as afflicted with the condition, as people who study sexual aberrations risk being suspected of being a little odd themselves. But another, simpler explanation is just that loneliness was not a problem in good currency. Almost no one was working on it, and because almost no one was working on it, the issues were not defined, there were no colleagues whose work could be responded to or built on, there were no conferences, few journal articles, no field.

In the past seven years much has changed. There are now many serious investigators studying the nature of loneliness, its distribution, and its concomitants. The issues to which attention should be given can now be identified. It is to the question of what these issues are that I direct this paper.

CONCEPTUAL AND OPERATIONAL DEFINITIONS

In saying what we have in mind by "loneliness," we are in a better position than are the intelligence testers when they must say what they mean by "intelligence." The intelligence testers, when they characterize the referent for their concept, cannot do better than point out that some people seem better able to grasp ideas than do others. Intelligence is a quality of functioning that can only be assessed comparatively. Loneliness, on the other hand, is *there*. It has symptoms, expressions, a set of characteristics, just as does pellagra.

I point this out because it is so easy, when devising a measuring instrument that may help us identify the lonely, to act as if we could only measure loneliness comparatively. But while saying that someone is "intelligent" is ultimately only a statement of how he or she compares with others, saying that someone is "lonely" should mean that the person is experiencing a very special emotional state. Our work on measuring instruments should be directed to helping us identify the state, and perhaps its intensity, rather than to producing a distribution of scores in a normal population so that we can better identify the distinctly abnormal.

If we treat loneliness as a quality of functioning that can only be assessed comparatively, like intelligence, then any item that helps separate the lonely from the less lonely can find a place in our instrument. This is true even if the item deals only with a correlate of loneliness, such as introversion. But we should not proceed in this way. We should instead give our research energies to identifying just how loneliness expresses itself, and make these evidences of loneliness the basis for our measuring instrument.

How can we obtain good measurements of loneliness? It does not seem likely to me that we will ever find an objective correlate of loneliness that will tell us that loneliness is present without our having to ask, in the way that pupil dilation might tell us that receptive interest is present, or jaw clenching that anger is present. For better or worse, it seems that we are always going to have to rely on the reports of respondents. The question is, how best to do this.

We might rely on unstructured but extensive interviews. We might, for example, simply ask respondents to tell us about their lives, about times when they are with others and how they feel, about times when they are alone and how they feel. We might then infer from what they say whether they are lonely. I must confess that this has been my approach. It has meant that I have sometimes decided that people were lonely because they said they were, and other times decided they were lonely only because they described what I believed to be symptoms of loneliness. The discretion this approach gives to the investigator can raise problems, if not eyebrows. In its favor is its attempt to achieve valid characterization in every case, using all information available.

However, there is much to be said for structured instruments. We need not then puzzle over just how a particular characterization was arrived at, nor worry that one investigator is measuring something different from another. Nor need we develop extensive interview protocols and then subject them to careful study in order to decide whether someone is lonely; we can get the answer from responses to a fixed set of questions.

What would constitute a good instrument for measuring loneliness? A first thought might be to ask a single question, "Are you lonely?" An instrument of this sort would have high face validity, and would be easy to administer and easy to score. Indeed the single question instrument has been the basis of a number of studies, including the large-scale survey study conducted by Maisel (reported in Weiss, 1973) and the Bradburn and Caplovitz study (1965). But there are a number of reasons for preferring a multiple item test such as that developed by Russell, Peplau, and Ferguson (1978). The multiple item test would seem less vulnerable to idiosyncracies of interpretation and response and so more likely to be both reliable and valid. It would also facilitate discrimination of degrees of loneliness and make possible factor analytic search for components of loneliness. In addition, a scale that appears to have been carefully constructed may help bring an area of research into good currency. This last point, while having to do with the psychological functioning of investigators, rather than with that of subjects, is nevertheless worth noting.

I would again repeat, however, that we should be careful, in our scale construction, that our items, taken together, capture our concept of loneliness at least as well as does the single item, "Are you lonely?" A high correlation between scores on our scale and apparent loneliness would be reassuring but is not actually conclusive. The correlation may have been achieved by learning about phenomena only associated with loneliness, like introversion or spending time alone, while neglecting phenomena very much a part of loneliness, like pining for an emotional partner.

Worth considering as an approach to learning about loneliness may be presenting respondents with pictures intended to evoke situations of possible loneliness: someone staring out a window, for example. Respondents might be asked to describe what might be happening, and what the person might be feeling, and then asked to say whether they had felt that way, and how recently, and how often. Perhaps a way of coding such responses might be developed that could be systematically followed. The approach seems to me promising insofar as it might help respondents more effectively report feelings of loneliness while yet providing data that can be analyzed systematically. I hasten to say that I have no experience with this approach and have no assurance that it would be effective.

In any event, I would have us develop measuring instruments that are sensitive to the affective state we understand to be loneliness rather than to phenomena that are conducive to loneliness or associated with loneliness. A measuring instrument is, in effect, an operationalization. We have to be careful that it captures our concept.

ISSUES OF THEORY

What are the substantive questions we have to answer if we are to understand loneliness? Perhaps any list of such questions is arbitrary, but here is mine:

How many forms of loneliness are there? Is loneliness a single syndrome of definite character, or are there instead various types of loneliness? Or, a third alternative, is loneliness without definite character, so that one individual's loneliness is quite a different phenomenon from another individual's, except that each yearns for the presence of one or more other persons?

My own belief is that there are actually two affective states likely to be characterized as "loneliness" by those experiencing them. I have named these states, respectively, emotional isolation and social isolation (Weiss, 1973). The first, it seems to me, is produced by the absence of an attachment figure, the second by the absence of an accessible social network. The factor analytic results of Rubenstein and Shaver (Chapter 13) provide support for these ideas.

The issue does not seem entirely settled, however. In particular, it would be useful to work out what emotional states are being experienced when individuals describe themselves as lonely: are there just these two states, or are there others as well? If older parents are distressed by the inaccessibility of grown children who have moved away from home, how do they name their distress, and what seems to be its nature? (Perhaps they miss their children, but are not lonely for them.) In addition, it is not yet clear how much overlap there is between the states thus far identified as loneliness. It would be nice to think of them as entirely distinct, but they may not be.

Why does loneliness display its particular characteristics? Why is it that one element of the loneliness of emotional isolation so often is restless anxiety, and one element of the loneliness of social isolation is a feeling of intentional exclusion? There is a well-developed theory that can help us understand the loneliness of emotional isolation, insofar as we associate emotional isolation with the absence of an attachment figure (Bowlby, 1969, 1973, 1980; Parkes, 1972; Weiss, 1973). That social isolation should foster feelings of meaninglessness and marginality, as well as tension and boredom, seems almost obvious; and yet it is important to understand better whence the need for social participation, and how much social participation, under what circumstances, is necessary for symptoms to be allayed. Anne Peplau (personal correspondence) has suggested that there is promise in exploring the importance of social rewards, the gratifications mediated by social interchange, together with the cognitive reassurance provided by learning how others see things. These are indeed the two functions ascribed by Cooley to the primary group: the sustaining of morale and the provision of meaning. Perhaps we will find ourselves refurbishing early sociological theory.

What factors, both situational and characterological, foster loneliness? And how do situational and characterological factors interact? We have at present two lines of research on factors associated with loneliness. One considers *situations* in which loneliness is apt to occur: the life situations of the divorced and the widowed, the social situations of hospitalized individuals and of those who have recently moved into a neighborhood. The other line of research considers *personality characteristics:* introversion, shyness, low self-esteem. When we hold relatively constant the interpersonal situations of individuals, as we do when we study freshmen at a residential college, we move naturally toward consideration of characterological determinants. When we fail to obtain personality data, as generally is the case in large-scale surveys, we are left with situation as our only source of explanation.

Neither situational studies nor characterological studies have as yet attempted to identify just what it is that triggers loneliness. Situational studies have been content to note, for example, that about half of a sample of hospitalized patients report themselves as lonely. But they have not gone on to ask in just what respect the situation of the not-lonely hospitalized patient is different from that of the lonely hospitalized patient. Yet it is just this information that we need, not only to understand why it is that hospitals are lonely places, despite their utter absence of privacy, but also what might be done about it.

In a similar way, characterological studies have failed to consider which shy people are not lonely, and which extroverted people are. Early history may play a role in susceptibility to loneliness, or level of self-esteem may interact with outgoingness in some complex way. Better understanding of what kinds of people are susceptible to loneliness would contribute to an understanding of the nature of loneliness.

At some point we ought to study the interplay between situation and character as joint determinants of loneliness. There may be those who become lonely quickly, but only when among people they don't know; others may be intermittently lonely no matter what. Some individuals are likely to see any situation as interpersonally barren; others may be more optimistic and hold out against loneliness longer. Early loss or deprivation may play a role in the way any situation is interpreted, but there may also be a tendency for some individuals to deal well with some situations, badly with others.

Our aim in this work should be to reach the point of being able to predict which people will experience loneliness under what kinds of conditions. Being able to do this would not mean that we have solved the problem of loneliness, but it *would* mean that we were well on our way.

The epidemiology of loneliness. Closely related to questions of the situations and personal characterisics that are conducive to loneliness are questions of the demographic categories within which loneliness is especially frequent. These are the categories of individuals most "at risk."

We know that the unmarried are more likely to display loneliness than the married, and among the unmarried, those who were previously married are the most likely to experience loneliness. Undoubtedly what is determinative here is the absence of an attachment figure. It is regrettable that the usual survey study of well-being fails to distinguish between those unmarried individuals who nevertheless have attachments and those unmarried individuals who do not. In a survey study of loneliness it would seem reasonable to include items asking whether the respondent is currently going with or seeing someone, and whether there is any other adult, kin as well as friend, who the respondent feels shares his or her life.

Quite unclear is the relation between loneliness and gender. A number of studies have found a greater proportion of women than of men reporting loneliness. The differences in these studies are not large, but they appear consistent over various demographic groupings. Yet other studies, particularly those of Russell and Peplau (see Chapters 1, 6), fail to find any sex difference at all. The differences among findings may be due to differences in populations studied or in methods of study. Differences seem to be found in studies of general populations, absence of differences to be found in studies of student populations; but we do not have enough experience to be sure of very much as yet.

A perplexing finding is a correlation between loneliness and income level. The poor seem somewhat more lonely. Is this because low income makes for a restricted social life? Or because limited energy levels and social enterprise make both for lowered income and an inadequate social life? Or will the correlation disappear if statistical controls are imposed on marital status, numbers of children, kind of work, and similar matters?

What constitutes the natural history of loneliness, the succession of feeling states through which the experience of loneliness moves? We tend to think of loneliness as an acute episode of restlessness and tension associated with yearnings for companionship or intimacy. But it may be that loneliness undergoes modification if it becomes chronic: it may be that it gradually transmutes itself into hopeless apathy. Or it may be that individuals who are chronically lonely learn to avoid attending to their discomfort, as widows and widowers often learn not to attend to their feelings of loss. We need to know more about the changing nature of loneliness when it is a continuing state, and especially about whether chronic loneliness expresses itself differently from acute loneliness.

We also need to know more about changing vulnerabilities to loneliness as individuals age. Loneliness almost certainly is more common in adolescence than later in life, and possibly more intense as well, although we as yet lack the survey data that would provide conclusive evidence for this observation. We do have survey data that show that older divorced and widowed individuals are less likely to report themselves as lonely than are younger divorced and widowed individuals (Maisel, quoted in Weiss, 1973; Rubenstein & Shaver, Chapter 13). Is there a diminution of vulnerability to loneliness as individuals age? If there is, what does this mean for aging's effect on our capacity to form lasting bonds—or, at least, on our desire to do so?

What are the remote causes? How has it happened that humans are so constituted that we experience loneliness? To speak only of the loneliness of emotional isolation, what evolutionary processes have led to a sense of emotional isolation triggering the anxious and painful restlessness of loneliness? It seems to me that the capacity to experience this state must have been selected for because it produced individuals who sought not only to find someone of the other sex with whom to mate—sexual tensions alone would do this —but also to find someone with whom to share emotional life.

We find in our work with the divorced that loneliness fosters a search for something more than a companion or a sexual partner. Loneliness is allayed only by a relationship in which there is assurance of the continued accessibility of someone trusted. Lonely people often do look, at first, for someone, anyone, with whom to pass the time, but many soon learn that transitory relationships can make loneliness even worse. They become alert to indications that someone will remain with them, and that they will want that person to remain with them.

Loneliness may always have functioned to alert individuals to a relationship in which there would be mutual commitment; it may have been selected for because those who possessed the trait were more likely to choose as a mate someone with whom it would be possible to establish a persisting bond. Loneliness may have provided the incentive for forming a partnership that would eventually make more than one person available for child raising.

The evolutionary pressures that led to greater reproductive fitness among those individuals who possessed a capacity to experience loneliness is not the sort of issue that is easy to study empirically. We might, however, explore the occurrence of states similar to loneliness among other species, and if there are other species in which similar states occur, ask what sorts of bonds are formed in these species. Working out how we came to have a capacity for loneliness may have no direct application, but it may increase our acceptance of loneliness as a response as natural—and as valuable—as hunger.

LONELINESS AND ATTACHMENT

It may be that the best way to learn about the loneliness of emotional isolation is to study attachment. Insofar as this form of loneliness is produced by the absence of attachment figures, to understand it we would have to understand the attachment system. Perhaps that is what we should focus our attention on from the start. We would then consider not so much variations in individual propensity toward loneliness as variations in capacity for forming attachments, and variations in sensitivity to absences of attachment-providing relationships. We should try to learn how the attachment system develops over the life course, how relationships of attachment are established and with what sorts of figures, and what are the consequences, in addition to loneliness, of living without attachment figures. We would learn about the loneliness of emotional isolation, but only, as it were, in passing.

In a similar way, we might do well to focus our research attention on social integration if we hope to understand the loneliness of social isolation. In general, if we were directing a large-scale investigation of loneliness, we might want to divide our research energies, giving only a portion to the study of loneliness itself, while reserving some for the study of the socio-emotional systems with which loneliness is associated. Insofar as loneliness is only an alarm signaling a system in want, we have first to understand the system.

THEORIES IN USE

It is not possible for there to be a phenomenon as important as loneliness in everyday life without the society devising explanations for it. These culturally carried everyday explanations have enormous impact on how individuals are evaluated and on what prescriptions are offered for the management of loneliness. Scientific theories eventually become theories in use, but until they do, it is the theories in use rather than the scientific theories that guide individual behavior.

There have been a number of studies of theories in use regarding loneliness. Several of these are studies of attributions. It turns out that most among the lonely hold a multifactor theory of the etiology of their condition. They blame others, perhaps for the situation they are in, perhaps for having sponsored their vulnerabilities; they blame themselves, perhaps for choices that they made, perhaps for being the way they are; they blame their situations. And yet, even while they maintain a multifactor theory, people seem to underestimate the relative importance of situational causes and to overestimate the relative importance of their characters or actions.

There is much to be studied in relation to these theories in use. We might want to investigate still further the implications of attributing causation to self or to situation. Which of these attributions is more likely to be associated with effort to make changes, with capacity to maintain self-esteem, with recovery? How do theories in use affect the way in which people experience loneliness and what people do about loneliness? To paraphrase W. I. Thomas, even if what people believe isn't so, it is what they believe that they act on.

THERAPIES

Vello Sermat (1979) has referred to a master's thesis by Petryshen in which a loneliness scale was administered to patients going into psychotherapy. Some of the patients then received traditional psychotherapy while others received psychotherapy focused on issues of loneliness. Apparently those whose psychotherapy dealt with issues of loneliness stayed in the therapy and may have improved. The very lonely among those who received the traditional therapy dropped out of treatment. This suggests that in working with people who are lonely, we must acknowledge their loneliness if we are to be helpful. And, very likely, we must also help them reduce their loneliness or, at the least, learn to tolerate it.

How might people be aided to reduce loneliness? We might consider ways of helping them improve their capacities for establishing links with others. Perhaps shyness clinics might be useful. We might encourage the provision of settings within which bonds could be established, for example, activity groups for the unattached. It might be useful too for us to provide the lonely with some understanding of loneliness, perhaps through lectures, perhaps through written materials, so that they are not so dismayed by their experience.

It may be that the loneliness syndrome can be avoided or diminished in a variety of ways. We may find that loneliness can be mitigated to the extent that situations seem safe, and we may also find that this perception is a function not only of the objective characteristics of the situation but also of the extent to which the self can be trusted to function well in it. Heightening self-esteem may thus prove to be a means toward reducing loneliness, and support for self-esteem a way of providing help. Study of the situational and characterological determinants of loneliness may suggest both situational changes and personal therapies that can help the lonely.

We may discover that there are substances whose ingestion diminishes loneliness. These substances may act by changing perceptions of situations, by blocking anxious responses, or by inhibiting the formation of the loneliness syndrome. One candidate for such a substance is alcohol. The side effects of alcohol, needless to say, make it an inadvisable remedy. But it is conceivable that the study of loneliness may yet contribute to an understanding of alcohol's appeal.

In any event, it is important for those who do research on loneliness to give thought to application of their work. Concern for application can help ensure that the research does not become excessively academic. The condition we are studying is so disturbing that we surely have some responsibility to do what we can to be helpful to those who experience it.

REFERENCES

Bowlby, J. *Attachment and loss.* Vol. 1, *Attachment.* New York: Basic Books, 1969.

Bowlby, J. *Attachment and loss.* Vol. 2, *Separation.* New York: Basic Books, 1973.

Bowlby, J. *Attachment and loss.* Vol. 3, *Loss.* New York: Basic Books, 1980.

Bradburn, N. M. *The structure of psychological well-being.* Chicago: Aldine, 1969.

Bradburn, N. M., & Caplovitz, D. *Reports on happiness.* Chicago: Aldine, 1965.

Bradley, R. *Measuring loneliness.* Unpublished doctoral dissertation, Washington State University, 1969.

Eddy, P. D. *Loneliness: A discrepancy with the phenomenological self.* Unpublished doctoral dissertation, Adelphi College, 1961.

Francis, G. M. *Loneliness: A study of hospitalized adults.* Unpublished doctoral dissertation, University of Pennsylvania, 1972.

Fromm-Reichmann, F. Loneliness. *Psychiatry, 1959, 22,* 1–15.

Lopata, H. Z. Loneliness: Forms and components. *Social Problems, 1969, 17,* 248–261.

Moustakas, C. E. *Loneliness.* Englewood Cliffs, N.J.: Prentice-Hall, 1961.

Moustakas, C. E. *Loneliness and love.* Englewood Cliffs, N.J.: Prentice-Hall, 1972.

Parkes, C. M. *Bereavement: Studies of grief in adult life.* New York: International Universities Press, 1972.

Russell, D., Peplau, L. A., & Ferguson, M. L. Developing a measure of loneliness. *Journal of Personality Assessment, 1978, 42,* 290–294.

Sermat, V. Paper presented at the UCLA Research Conference on loneliness. Los Angeles, May 1979.

Sisenwein, R. J. *Loneliness and the individual as viewed by himself and others.* Unpublished doctoral dissertation, Columbia University, 1964.

Sullivan, H. S. *The interpersonal theory of psychiatry.* New York: Norton, 1953.

Von Witzleben, H. D. On loneliness. *Psychiatry, 1958, 21,* 37–43.

Weiss, R. S. *Loneliness: The experience of emotional and social isolation.* Cambridge, Mass.: M. I. T. Press, 1973.

Chapter 6

The Measurement of Loneliness

Daniel Russell

The "standard" introduction to a discussion of the measurement of loneliness includes two statements: (1) there has been very little empirical research concerning this important social problem; and (2) a major hindrance to empirical research in this area has been the absence of adequate instruments to assess loneliness. As the chapters in this volume clearly indicate, empirical research on loneliness has sharply increased in the past two to three years, calling the first statement into question. And as the present discussion of loneliness assessment will demonstrate, a number of measuring instruments have been developed, suggesting that inability to assess loneliness is no longer a hindrance to research.

This chapter examines how investigators have conceptualized and measured loneliness. Although a large number of measures have been devised, as of this writing only two scales, the UCLA Loneliness Scale (Russell, Peplau, & Cutrona, 1980; Russell, Peplau, & Ferguson, 1978) and the loneliness scale developed by de Jong-Gierveld and her associates (de Jong-Gierveld, 1979) have been published. This chapter begins with a review of existing loneliness measures, focusing on the reliability and validity of these scales. Next, an overview of work my colleagues and I have undertaken in developing the UCLA Loneliness Scale is presented. This scale has been widely used by other investigators, and some of the empirical findings from these studies will also be discussed. A final section examines a number of methodological and conceptual issues relevant to the assessment of loneliness and to our understanding of the causes and consequences of this important social phenomenon.

REVIEW OF LONELINESS MEASURES

Researchers have taken two different conceptual approaches to the problem of measuring loneliness. One, the *unidimensional* approach, views loneliness

The author would like to thank Letitia Anne Peplau, Daniel Perlman, and Carolyn Cutrona for their comments on earlier versions of this chapter.

as a single or unitary phenomenon that varies primarily in its experienced intensity. This approach assumes that there are common themes in the experience of loneliness, regardless of what the particular cause of loneliness is for the individual. Thus the same general loneliness scale should be sensitive to the loneliness experienced by a new college student who lacks friends and an older person whose lifetime mate has recently died. In contrast, the *multidimensional* approach conceptualizes loneliness as a multifaceted phenomenon that cannot be captured by a single global loneliness measure. Rather than focusing on the commonalities underlying the experience of loneliness for all individuals, this approach attempts instead to differentiate among various hypothesized types or manifestations of loneliness. The distinction between unidimensional and multidimensional conceptual approaches provides a useful framework for categorizing existing loneliness measures.

Unidimensional Loneliness Measures

Table 6.1 summarizes the reliability and validity data for unidimensional loneliness measures. The earliest global loneliness measure was developed by Eddy (1961), and consists of 24 statements describing different intensities of loneliness. Examples of these statements are "I feel abandoned" and "I have a feeling of emptiness." A Q-sort format is employed in which respondents use the statements to describe themselves. Based on data from students in a merchant marine academy, the measure was found to be internally consistent, although test-retest reliability was low (see Table 6.1). Citing the lack of external validity criteria for loneliness, Eddy presented no validity data for his measure. He did administer a Q-sort measure, on which the students rated themselves (self-ratings), how they thought they were perceived by others (reflected self-ratings), and how they would like to be ideally (ideal self-ratings). Eddy found quite substantial correlations between scores on his loneliness measure and differences between self-reflected self-ratings, self-ideal self-ratings, and ideal-reflected self-ratings (ranging from .63 to .71). No relationship was found between loneliness and a sociometric measure of popularity.

A scale developed by Sisenwein (1964) built upon Eddy's efforts. Sisenwein added additional statements thought to describe loneliness, yielding a 75-item measure. He abandoned the Q-sort response format in favor of asking respondents to rate on a 4-point scale how often they felt the way described in each statement (i.e., "often," "sometimes," "rarely," or "never"). Concerning reliability, test-retest correlations of .83 and .85 were reported by Sisenwein over a 1-week period, once again using students from a merchant marine academy. Sisenwein validated his measure by correlating loneliness scores with a single 6-point scale asking respondents to indicate how lonely they felt compared to other people. (The anchoring statements for the response scale ranged from "I am the most lonely person I know" to "I never

Table 6.1. Characteristics of the Global Loneliness Measures

Scale	Number of items	Response format	Reliability data	Validity data
Eddy (1961)	24	Q-sort	Split-half = .82 Test-retest (2-week interval): r = .52	None reported
Sisenwein (1964)	75	4-point rating scale	Test-retest (1-week interval): r = .83 and .85	Self-labeling questions: r = .72 and .70 [a]
Bradley (1969)	38	6-point Likert scale	Split-half = .95 Coefficient alpha = .90 [c] Test-retest (2-week interval): r = .89; (8-week interval): r = .83 [b]	Known groups: Emotionally disturbed inmates, students receiving counseling [b] Self-labeling question: Correlations range from .45 to .80 [b, c]
Ellison & Paloutzian (Chapter 14)	7	4-point rating scale	Test-retest (1-week interval): r = .85 Coefficient alpha = .67	Self-labeling question: r = .61
Young (1979, Chapter 22)	18	4 response options (scored 0 to 3)	Coefficient alpha = .78 to .84	Self-labeling questions concerning recent and long-term loneliness: r = .47 to .55; .50 and .66 [d] Known groups: Outpatients in a mood clinic
Rubenstein & Shaver (1979, Chapter 13)	8	Different formats for each item	Coefficient alpha = .88 and .89	None reported

[a] Data are from Moore (1972).
[b] Data are from Belcher (1973).
[c] Data are from Solano (1980).
[d] Data are from Primakoff (1980).

83

feel lonely".) A correlation of .72 was found between loneliness scores and this single item. Moore (1972) reported a correlation of .70 between scores on Sisenwein's scale and a similar single item self-rating of loneliness among a college student sample. Sisenwein examined the relationship between loneliness and discrepancies between self-descriptions and descriptions by others (e.g., roommates), but no systematic relationship was found. Moore (1972) found that students identified as lonely on Sisenwein's loneliness measure were more hostile and submissive on Leary's Interpersonal Checklist, and had a greater discrepancy between self and reflected self-concepts than did nonlonely students. Moore also found that lonely students retrospectively reported having fewer friends and engaging in more solitary activities while growing up, and having fathers with lower incomes.

A third general loneliness measure was developed by Bradley (1969). She based her measure on 38 statements describing both loneliness and "belonging." Thus her measure, in contrast to the previous scales, includes both negatively worded (lonely) and positively worded (nonlonely) items, such as "I have no one to depend upon but myself" and "I have friends who understand me." Individuals rate how self-descriptive each item is, using a 6-point Likert format. The measure appears to have good internal consistency. Bradley reported a split-half coefficient of .95, and Solano (1980) found an alpha coefficient of .90 for the measure. Test-retest reliability also appears to be quite high; Belcher (1973) reported test-retest reliabilities of .89 and .83 over 2- and 6-week intervals, respectively. All of the above reliability data were gathered from college student samples.

In validating her measure, Bradley used a "known groups" procedure, finding that a group of emotionally disturbed prison inmates scored significantly higher on her loneliness measure than did other inmates. Belcher (1973) reported that college students receiving counseling scored highly on Bradley's scale. Belcher also found correlations of .45 to .80 between loneliness scale scores and a single item asking students to indicate their current level of loneliness.

Several studies have examined empirical correlates of scores on Bradley's measure. Bradley (1969) found a significant relationship $(r = .37)$ between loneliness and the D scale of the MMPI, a measure of anxiety and depression. Belcher (1973) reported significant relationships between loneliness and scores on both the Taylor Manifest Anxiety Scale $(r = .69)$ and a Q-sort measure of self-ideal discrepancy $(r = .75)$. Finally, Nerviano and Gross (1976) correlated scores on Bradley's loneliness scale with Jackons's Personality Research Form (1967) and with Cattell's 16 PF (Form A; Cattell, Ebner, & Tatsuoka, 1970) for a sample of alcoholics. The pattern of relationships indicated that the lonely alcoholic was socially inhibited and highly anxious. Importantly, however, Nerviano and Gross found that the best predictor of loneliness was the Desirability scale from the Jackson measure, suggesting a confounding of loneliness scores with social desirability.

Ellison and Paloutzian (Chapter 14) have recently reported some preliminary data on another general loneliness measure, the Abbreviated Loneliness Scale. This measure consists of seven items, three of which are worded in a lonely or negative direction (e.g., "I feel emotionally distant from people in general") and four worded in a nonlonely or positive direction (e.g., "I have as many close relationships as I want"). It should be noted that two of the items on the scale ask respondents to indicate explicitly whether they are lonely or not (e.g., "I feel lonely"). Respondents indicate how often they feel the way described in each statement using a 4-point scale (ranging from "never" to "often"). Based on a sample of college students, Ellison and Paloutzian (1979a) reported a test-retest reliability of .85 over a 1-week interval and an alpha coefficient of .67. Concerning the validity of the measure, a correlation of .61 was found between scores on the scale and a single item asking respondents how lonely they felt. Finally, Ellison and Paloutzian (1979a, b) reported quite substantial relationships between loneliness scores and self-reported spiritual well-being ($r = -.41$), existential well-being ($r = -.64$), social skills ($r = -.55$), and self-esteem ($r = -.57$).

Another loneliness measure has recently been developed by Young (1979), and is presented in Chapter 22 in this volume. Young's scale is designed as a measure of chronic or long-term loneliness, with a format very similar to the Beck (1967) Depression Inventory. Concerning reliability, Young reported coefficient alphas ranging from .78 to .84 in college student samples and a clinic sample. Primakoff (1980) found a coefficient alpha of .79 for the Young measure, based on a sample of single adults. Validity for the measure was indicated by correlations with measures of recent and long-term loneliness (items 17 and 18 from the Young inventory); Young reported correlations ranging from .47 to .55, and Primakoff found comparable relationships. A form of "known groups" validity was indicated by the substantially higher loneliness scores found by Young for outpatients in a mood clinic.

The unidimensional loneliness measures that have been discussed to this point share one feature in common: for the most part, items on these scales make no mention of the term "loneliness." This avoidance of explicitly acknowledging the state being assessed is not unusual in mood assessment. For example, in measuring anxiety or depression psychologists typically do not limit themselves to asking the person "Are you anxious?" or "Are you depressed?", but instead ask respondents to indicate whether or not they are experiencing other emotions or feeling states related to the mood being measured. An advantage of such an assessment procedure is that it helps disguise what is being measured, thereby lessening the impact of social desirability on responses. Moreover, incorporating items that are negatively related to the construct being assessed (e.g., items reflecting social satisfaction or nonloneliness) serves to eliminate response sets or acquiescence biases in scores (Bentler, 1969).

A final approach to measuring unidimensional or global loneliness basically involves asking the respondent, "Are you lonely?" Note that for almost all the loneliness scales discussed above, such items have been employed as validity criteria. The procedure of asking respondents to make direct self-ratings of loneliness has been extensively used in large scale survey studies. For example, Bradburn (1969) included in his Affect Balance Scale an item asking respondents whether they had felt "very lonely or remote from other people" during the past few weeks. Similarly, Maisel (1969) asked respondents whether or not they had felt severely lonely during the past week. Other forms of these questions deal with the frequency of loneliness. For example, Lowenthal, Thurner, and Chirboga (1975) asked respondents to indicate how often they had felt lonely during the previous week, and a survey of older adults by Shanas, Townsend, Wedderburn, Friis, Milhoj, and Stehouwer (1968) simply asked respondents to indicate in general how often they were lonely. A final form of such self-labeling questions deals with social comparison, asking respondents to rate how their current loneliness compares to the loneliness of others (see Lopata, Heinemann, & Baum, Chapter 19).

The reliability of these measures has not been reported in survey studies. Indeed, since survey studies typically employ only single item measures of loneliness, the only form of reliability that could be determined is test-retest reliability. These explicit self-labeling questions obviously have content or face validity. However, social desirability concerns and response sets could seriously affect the findings based on these measures, as discussed above. Moreover, due to the variety of ways in which these self-labeling questions are asked, the comparability of findings from studies using different questions is difficult to determine.

A recent measure of loneliness developed by Rubenstein and Shaver (1979) has improved on these earlier survey measures. Their measure consists of eight explicit self-labeling questions, such as "How often do you feel lonely?" and "Other people think of me as a lonely person." The response format for the eight items varies, with 4- to 7-point response scales being used. (The exact wording of the items is given in Rubenstein & Shaver, Chapter 13.) These items were included in a questionnaire survey published in newspapers in New York City and Worcester, Massachusetts. Rubenstein and Shaver reported coefficient alphas of .88 and .89 for their scale. (A similar six-item "self-labeling loneliness index" has been used by this author and his colleagues in validating the revised UCLA Loneliness Scale and found to have a coefficient alpha of .88; see Russell et al., 1980). Content validity is of course evident for the Rubenstein and Shaver scale. Scores on this measure were also related strongly to low self-esteem ($r = .59$) and to the self-report of health problems ($r = .60$).

To summarize, most global loneliness measures appear to be very reliable. Validity evidence is, however, quite limited, being restricted to comparisons of "at risk" and normal samples, or correlations with questions eliciting explicit self-labels of loneliness. Although relationships between unidimensional loneliness measures and other variables have been reported that could be interpreted as indicating construct validity, no attempt has been made to demonstrate discriminant validity for these measures. Discriminant validity is

a serious issue for several of these measures, due to the extremely high correlations reported between loneliness scores and measures of self-esteem,
anxiety, and depression. Finally, only Bradley (1969) and Ellison and
Paloutzian (1979a) have attempted to counteract possible response set
problems by including reversed items in their measures.

Multidimensional Loneliness Measures

Reliability and validity data for multidimensional loneliness measures are
summarized in Table 6.2. The first of these scales was the Belcher Extended
Loneliness Scale (BELS; Belcher, 1973). Belcher modified the Bradley
measure, arguing that her global loneliness scale assessed only the "psychological" aspects of loneliness. To measure sociological components of loneliness, items were added to the Bradley scale from previously developed
measures of alienation (Keniston, 1960) and anomie (Srole, 1956). The final
measure consists of 60 items; respondents indicate how often they feel the
way described in each statement on a 6-point Likert scale. Concerning the
reliability of the scale, Belcher obtained test-retest correlations of .79 to .84
over a 9- to 11-week interval. Solano (1980) reported an alpha coefficient of
.93 for the total 60-item scale. These reliabilty data were gathered from
college student samples.

The validity of the total score of the BELS was supported by finding
significantly higher loneliness scores among students receiving counseling than
among a sample of "normal" college students (Belcher, 1973). Solano (1980)
reported a correlation of .59 between the total score on the BELS and a single
item question asking students how lonely they are. To demonstrate the dimen-
sional structure of the measure, Belcher factor analyzed the scale. He reported
eight overlapping factors: alienation, anomie, estrangement, existential loneliness, loneliness anxiety, loneliness depression, pathological loneliness, and
separateness.

Another multidimensional loneliness measure, the Differential Loneliness
Scale, was developed by Schmidt (1976). She attempted to assess loneliness
or social dissatisfaction within four types of relationships: romantic-sexual,
friendship, family, and community. Schmidt developed her measure based
on a sample of college students and a sample of adults, constructing separate
versions of her scale for students and for adults. Both scales consist of 60
statements, dealing with the four different types of relationships. Examples of
the statements for romantic relationships are "My romantic/marital partner
gives me much support and encouragement" and "I have never been able to
maintain a close romantic relationship over any length of time." Note that
the scale includes both positive and negative items. Respondents indicate
whether each statement is "true" or "false" in describing themselves. Both
the student and adult scales were found to be internally consistent, with K-R
20s of .90 and .92, respectively. Schmidt attempted to establish discriminant

Table 6.2. Characteristics of the Multidimensional Loneliness Measures

Scale	Number of items	Response format	Dimensions	Reliability data	Validity data
Belcher (1973)	60	6-point Likert scale	Global loneliness, alienation, and anomie	Coefficient alpha = .93 [a] Test-retest (9- to 11-week interval): r = .79 to .84	Known groups: students receiving counseling Self-labeling question: r = .59 [a]
Schmidt (1976)	60	True — False	Friendship, romantic-sexual, family and community relationships	K-R 20 = .90 and .92 for student and adult versions	None reported
de Jong-Gierveld (1978)	38	6-point Likert scale	Types of missing relationships, adjustment and defense mechanisms, future time perspective, and personal capabilities	Factors for the measure have coefficient alpha = .14 to .87	Self-reported loneliness: r = .49 Other-reported loneliness: r = .40

[a] Data are from Solano (1980).

88

validity for her scale by selecting items that had low correlations with measures of social desirability, self-esteem, anxiety, and depression. However, this effort was only partially successful; significant correlations were still found between total loneliness scores and social desirability ($r = -.38$ for students, $-.53$ for adults), self-esteem ($r = -.28$ and $-.50$), anxiety ($r = .29$ and .40), and depression ($r = .46$ and .62). Finally, concerning the multidimensional structure of Schmidt's measure, a factor analysis revealed that the largest factors concerned family, romantic-sexual relationships, and friendships, supporting Schmidt's distinction among these types of relationships.

A final multidimensional loneliness scale has been developed by de Jong-Gierveld and her colleagues (de Jong-Gierveld, 1978). Four components of loneliness are hypothesized to exist based on: (1) the types of relationships that are missing; (2) adjustment and defense mechanisms; (3) future time perspective concerning loneliness; and (4) personal capabilities to resolve loneliness. These components of loneliness are assessed by a 38-item loneliness scale, with separate items measuring each dimension. (The scale is described in Chapter 7.) A factor analysis of responses to this scale by a sample of adult men and women from the Netherlands generally confirmed the multidimensional structure of the measure. Results indicated that the factors corresponding to each of the four hypothesized components were generally reliable, with coefficient alphas ranging from .64 to .87. Exceptions here were the two factors corresponding to adjustment and defense mechanisms; the alpha coefficients for these two factors were only .47 and .14 (de Jong-Gierveld, 1978). De Jong-Gierveld has found significant correlations between her multidimensional loneliness scale and a unidimensional self-report measure of loneliness (consisting of items such as "I sometimes feel lonely" and "I sometimes find it difficult to develop lasting relationships"), as well as a rating of the person's loneliness by a close friend. Factors underlying the first loneliness component, concerning feelings of deprivation, were most strongly related to global loneliness, with the correlations ranging from .43 to .59 for self-rated loneliness and .21 to .49 for other-rated loneliness. An overall loneliness score, based on summing together responses to all the items on the multidimensional loneliness scale, correlated .49 with self-rated loneliness and .40 with other-rated loneliness.

At present, it is unclear whether multidimensional scales assess loneliness more adequately than global or unidimensional measures. More research is needed to develop such measures further. Multidimensional scales have the potential of identifying variations in the experience of loneliness that may be particularly useful in helping the lonely. There is, however, a need for greater clarity in the theoretical conceptualizations underlying multidimensional measures. The present scales appear to assess a wide array of factors, including antecedents of loneliness (e.g., satisfaction with different types of relationships), consequences of loneliness (e.g., future time perspective concerning loneliness), and variables related to but distinct from loneliness, (e.g., alienation and anomie). Future research needs to examine the relationship among these different aspects of loneliness as an important step in further developing theoretical models of loneliness. In addition, the relationship between unidimensional and multidimensional loneliness measures needs to be explored; understanding what each type of scale is measuring should advance our understanding of loneliness.

DEVELOPMENT OF THE UCLA LONELINESS SCALE

Having briefly reviewed the development of loneliness measures by other investigators, I would now like to review in some detail the development of the UCLA Loneliness Scale (Russell et al., 1980; Russell et al., 1978). When I and my colleagues began work on the measure in 1976, none of the loneliness measures discussed above had been published. We sought to create a psychometrically adequate, easily administered, and generally available scale that would serve as a stimulus for empirical research on loneliness. At present, the UCLA scale is the most widely used loneliness measure.

In assessing loneliness, my colleagues and I sought to identify several common themes that characterized the experience of loneliness for a broad spectrum of individuals. Thus we took a global or unidimensional approach to measuring loneliness. Our scale development work began with 25 items borrowed from Sisenwein's (1964) loneliness measure. Sampling of items from Sisenwein's scale was unsystematic; the only criterion was to eliminate very extreme statements (e.g., "The television is my only friend"). Examples of items that were selected are "I cannot tolerate being so alone" and "No one really knows me well." The response format (taken from Sisenwein) asked individuals to rate how frequently they felt the way described, from "never" to "often" on a 4-point scale.

This initial set of items was administered to two groups of young adults at UCLA. A *clinic sample* included volunteers recruited to participate in a discussion group on loneliness; a *student sample* included participants recruited from psychology courses in return for course credit. All participants responded to the set of 25 items and indicated how lonely they were compared to others on a 5-point Likert scale. Individuals also described their current affective state by making intensity ratings of such feelings as "restless," "empty," "depressed," and "bored."

The final loneliness scale, consisting of 20 items, was developed based on item-total correlations; selected items all had correlations above .50. The resulting scale had high internal consistency with a coefficient alpha of .96. Validity for the measure was assessed in three ways. First, a correlation of .79 was found between the total score on the loneliness scale and responses to the single item loneliness self-rating measure. A second test compared the loneliness scores of the clinic sample to scores of the student participants. The difference between these two groups was large and statistically significant; the mean of the clinic sample (60.1) was nearly two standard deviations higher than the mean for the student sample (39.1). Finally, loneliness scores were strongly related to the reported intensity of feelings one might associate with loneliness, such as depression, anxiety, dissatisfaction, unhappiness, and shyness; and scores were unrelated to feelings that appear to be conceptually distinct from the experience of loneliness, such as feeling "hardworking" or having "wide interests."

Subsequent research, both by ourselves and other investigators, has provided further evidence for the adequacy of the UCLA Loneliness Scale. Unpublished data from new samples of college students at UCLA have cross-validated the high internal consistency found initially for the measure; an alpha coefficient of .94 has been found in several different samples. Solano (1980) reported an alpha coefficient of .89 for a sample of students from Wake Forest University. Concerning test-retest reliability, Jones (cited in Russell et al., 1978) found a correlation of .73 over a 2-month period in a college student sample. Recent data gathered at UCLA (see Chapter 18 by Cutrona) indicated a test-retest correlation of .62 over a 7-month period for a group of first-year college students. These correlations indicate some stability in loneliness scores, but also indicate that variations do occur over time.

Concerning the validity of the UCLA Loneliness Scale, a number of investigations provide evidence of the measure's adequacy. Scores on the scale have correlated significantly with several other loneliness measures. Solano (1980) reported a correlation of .74 between the Bradley loneliness measure and the UCLA scale. Ellison and Paloutzian (1979a) found a correlation of .72 between their Abbreviated Loneliness Scale and the UCLA Loneliness Scale. Jones, Freemon, and Goswick (1981) reported a variety of personality correlates of scores on the UCLA loneliness measure. The lonely person indicated greater public self-consciousness and social anxiety, higher levels of shyness and normlessness, greater social isolation, lower self-esteem, less altruism, and less acceptance of others. Lonely students also felt less acceptance of themselves by others, scored lower in belief in a just world, and indicated a more external locus of control. Jones et al. also found that lonely individuals evaluated themselves and other people more negatively following brief social interactions. In a careful behavioral analysis of the interactions of lonely and nonlonely students, Jones and his colleagues found that lonely individuals made more self-statements, asked fewer questions of their partners, changed the topic of conversation more frequently, and responded more slowly to their partners (Jones, Chapter 15). Related to these findings, Horowitz and French (1979) have reported that lonely individuals experience greater feelings of inhibited sociability.

A limitation of the research just described is that it is based on college student samples, raising questions concerning the validity of the UCLA Loneliness Scale in assessing loneliness for other populations. Evidence on this important issue is still limited. Perlman, Gerson, and Spinner (1978) examined loneliness in a sample of senior citizens, using an 11-item version of the UCLA Loneliness Scale. They found that loneliness scores correlated significantly ($r = .72$) with an index of the frequency and intensity of the respondents' self-rated current loneliness. In addition, loneliness scores were highly related to experiencing such emotions as anxiety, depression, unhappiness, and dissatisfaction—affects that are associated with loneliness among college students (Russell et al., 1978). Finally, loneliness among senior citizens was associated with less frequent contact with peers and friends.

A comparison of the average loneliness scores for the older adults tested by Perlman et al. with the scores of students at UCLA (using the same 11-item version of the UCLA scale employed by Perlman et al.) indicates that the senior citizens scored significantly less lonely as a group than the college students (means of 18.44 and 22.63, respectively). While running counter to the stereotype of the lonely older person, this same pattern of findings has been reported in several survey studies of loneliness (Dyer, 1974; Lowenthal et al., 1975; Rosow, 1962; Rubenstein & Shaver, 1979; Shanas et al., 1968).

Data from other adult "at risk" groups also indicate that the UCLA Loneliness Scale validly assesses adult loneliness. Compared to the overall mean loneliness score for college student samples (M = 38.6), adult psychiatric inpatients (M = 51.8), divorced adults (M = 47.7), and adult participants in social skills workshops (M = 56.8) were all found to be significantly lonelier (Russell, 1978). Although there is a clear need for further systematic analyses of the validity of the UCLA Loneliness Scale in populations other than college students, the existing evidence is encouraging.

Several potential problems with the UCLA Loneliness Scale deserve comment. One issue concerns possible response biases. All of the items on the measure are worded in the same (lonely) direction; thus tendencies to respond in a certain fashion could systematically influence loneliness scores. A second potential problem is social desirability. Since a social stigma is attached to loneliness (Gordon, 1976), individuals may distort their responses in order to appear less lonely. A final problematic issue concerns discriminant validity. The relationships found between loneliness scores and measures of other constructs such as depression or self-esteem are intuitively quite reasonable, and therefore support the validity of the measure. However, the magnitude of these empirical relationships indicates a need to demonstrate that the UCLA Loneliness Scale is distinct from these other measures.

To address these issues, we have recently revised the UCLA Loneliness Scale. Two new studies using the revised scale provide clear evidence for the validity of the new measure (Russell et al., 1980). In a first study, a set of positively worded loneliness items was developed; items were written to reflect as nearly as possible the opposite of the original scale items (i.e., social satisfaction rather than social dissatisfaction). Examples of these positive items are "There are people I feel close to" and "I have a lot in common with the people around me." The original loneliness scale and the new positive items were administered to a group of 162 college students, along with a set of items asking students to indicate whether they were lonely or not (e.g., "During the past two weeks, how lonely have you felt?"). These latter items were summed together to form an index of self-labeled loneliness. In addition, several measures of affective states were included: the Beck Depression Inventory (Beck, 1967), the Costello-Comrey Anxiety and Depression Scales (Costello & Comrey, 1967), and intensity ratings of different feelings (e.g., bored, empty, hopeless).

A revised UCLA Loneliness Scale was developed (presented in Table 6.3), based on the correlations of individual items with the loneliness self-labeling index. The 10 positively worded and 10 negatively worded items with the highest correlations were chosen for the final measure. All of the item-criterion correlations were above .40. Coefficient alpha for the revised scale was .94, a figure comparable to that found for the original scale. Scores on the revised scale correlated in the expected fashion with the measures of emotional state. Substantial relationships were found with the Beck Depression Inventory ($r = .62$) and with the Costello-Comrey Anxiety ($r = .32$) and Depression ($r = .55$) scales. Significant relationships were also found between loneliness scores and feeling abandoned, depressed, empty, hopeless, isolated, and self-enclosed, and with *not* feeling sociable or satisfied; scores were unrelated to such conceptually distinct emotions as embarrassment or surprise.

A second study explored further the validity of the revised UCLA Loneliness Scale. Participants in this study were a heterogeneous sample of 237 college undergraduates from the University of Tulsa and from UCLA. Students completed the original loneliness scale, along with the 10 new positively worded items, and indicated how lonely they were on the loneliness self-labeling index from the earlier study. Other measures assessed aspects of the student's social and solitary activities during the past two weeks (e.g., "How often have you eaten dinner alone" and "How often have you done something with a friend") and social relationships (e.g., "How many close friends do you have?"). Finally, students completed several personality and mood inventories assessing depression, anxiety, self-esteem, introversion-extraversion, assertiveness, sensitivity to rejection, affiliative tendencies, lying, and social desirability.

Results from the second study further confirmed the internal consistency of the scale; a coefficient alpha of .94 was again found for the revised measure. Supporting the concurrent validity of the scale, loneliness scores were significantly related to social activities and relationships. Positive correlations were found between loneliness and the amount of time spent alone each day ($r = .41$), the number of times students had eaten dinner alone ($r = .34$), and the number of times students had spent a weekend evening alone ($r = .44$). Negative relationships were found between loneliness scores and the frequency of social activities with friends ($r = -.28$) and the number of close friends ($r = -.44$). Loneliness was also related to current marital or

Table 6.3.   The Revised UCLA Loneliness Scale [a]

Directions: Indicate how often you feel the way described in each of the following statements. *Circle* one number for each.

	Never	Rarely	Sometimes	Often
*1. I feel in tune with the people around me	1	2	3	4
2. I lack companionship	1	2	3	4
3. There is no one I can turn to	1	2	3	4
*4. I do not feel alone	1	2	3	4
*5. I feel part of a group of friends	1	2	3	4
*6. I have a lot in common with the people around me	1	2	3	4
7. I am no longer close to anyone	1	2	3	4
8. My interests and ideas are not shared by those around me	1	2	3	4
*9. I am an outgoing person	1	2	3	4
*10. There are people I feel close to	1	2	3	4
11. I feel left out	1	2	3	4
12. My social relationships are superficial	1	2	3	4
13. No one really knows me well	1	2	3	4
14. I feel isolated from others	1	2	3	4
*15. I can find companionship when I want it	1	2	3	4
*16. There are people who really understand me	1	2	3	4
17. I am unhappy being so withdrawn	1	2	3	4
18. People are around me but not with me	1	2	3	4
*19. There are people I can talk to	1	2	3	4
*20. There are people I can turn to	1	2	3	4

[a] The total score on the scale is the sum of all 20 items. Items with asterisks should be reversed (i.e., 1 = 4, 2 = 3, 3 = 2, 4 = 1) before scoring. The four item survey version of the UCLA Loneliness Scale consists of items 1, 13, 15 and 18. Reprinted from "The revised UCLA Loneliness Scale: Concurrent and discriminant validity evidence" by D. Russell, L. A. Peplau, and C. E. Cutrona, *Journal of Personality and Social Psychology,* 1980, *39*(3), p. 475. Copyright 1980 by the American Psychological Association. Reprinted by permission.

dating status; students who were not dating at all (M = 43.1) were much lonelier than students who were dating casually (M = 34.0) or who were dating regularly or married (M = 32.7).

An important goal of this second study was to examine the discriminant validity of the revised UCLA Loneliness Scale. The previous study indicated quite substantial relationships between scores on the revised loneliness scale and measures of depression. Previous research has also indicated strong relationships between loneliness scores and measures of anxiety and self-esteem. These relationships pose an important validity question: Does the loneliness scale actually measure loneliness, or is the measure so highly related to other constructs such as depression or low self-esteem that these latter constructs are actually being measured by the scale? (It is assumed here that loneliness is in fact a distinct concept; it is "more than" simply low self-esteem or depression.) To pursue this issue, a form of multitrait-multimethod analysis was performed (Campbell & Fiske, 1959; Magnusson, 1967). The general question examined was whether scores on the revised UCLA Loneliness Scale were more highly related to the self-labeling loneliness index (indicating convergent validity) than to scores on the other mood and personality measures (indicating discriminant validity).

The correlation between the revised loneliness scale and the self-labeling index ($r = .71$) was indeed higher than the correlation between loneliness scores and the mood and personality measures. However, several of these latter correlations were quite substantial, ranging as high as .51 with depression and $-.49$ with self-esteem. This raised the possibility that the mood and personality measures might, if combined, account for much of the reliable variance in loneliness scores. To explore this possibility, multiple regression analysis was used to combine the personality and mood measures in predicting loneliness scores. A factor analysis was first conducted on the mood and personality variables, to eliminate correlations among the predictors. From this analysis a four-factor structure emerged; the factors were labeled social risk taking, negative affect, social desirability, and affiliative motivation. These factors in combination were able to account for 43% of the variance in loneliness scores. The social desirability factor was unrelated to loneliness, while the affiliative motivation, social risk taking, and negative affect factors were all significant predictors, accounting for 12, 17, and 14% of the variance in loneliness scores, respectively.

To address the discriminant validity issue, it was necessary to examine whether the self-labeling loneliness index was still related to loneliness scores after controlling for the effects of the mood and personality measures. Results of this test supported the discriminant validity of the revised loneliness scale; the loneliness index explained an additional 18% of the variance in loneliness scores beyond that accounted for by the mood and personality measures. A final test of discriminant validity examined whether the concurrent validity evidence reported above was uniquely attributable to loneliness, or whether these relationships reflected the influence of mood and personality variables on loneliness scores. For example, does the relationship between loneliness scores and the number of close friends reflect the fact that lonely individuals are low in affiliative motivation and do not take social risks? Once again, the results were positive. After statistically controlling for the effects of the mood and personality variables, loneliness scores were still significantly related to the amount of time spent alone each day, the frequency of eating dinner alone and spending a weekend evening alone, the number of close friends, and the person's marital or dating status.

As part of our scale development efforts, my colleagues and I have also devised a short, four-item version of the UCLA Loneliness Scale, intended for use in survey research (the items are indicated in Table 6.3). Using optimal subset regression techniques, four items were selected (two positively worded and two negatively worded) that best predicted scores on the loneliness self-labeling index. This short loneliness measure was found to have a coefficient alpha of .75. We employed this loneliness scale in a telephone survey of working adults in Los Angeles (described in Gutek, Nakamura, Gahart, Handschumacher, & Russell, 1980). Table 6.4 presents the mean loneliness scores for different age groups from this sample. As can be seen, the general trend is for loneliness to decrease over the life span, with the oldest respondents having the lowest loneliness scores. Results from this survey also indicated a relationship between loneliness and socioeconomic status; respondents who reported having larger incomes and greater education were less lonely.

Table 6.4. Mean UCLA Loneliness Scores for Different Age Groups [a]

Age Group	Number of respondents	Mean loneliness	Standard deviation
18–30 year olds	149	8.31	2.02
31–40 year olds	94	8.17	1.97
41–50 year olds	53	7.51	1.88
51–60 year olds	52	7.86	2.32
Over 60 year olds	34	7.26	2.63

[a] The loneliness scores are based on the four-item survey version of the UCLA Loneliness Scale (see Table 6.3). Further details on the characteristics of the sample are given in Gutek et al. (1980). The one-way ANOVA comparing the mean loneliness scores of the age groups was significant, $F(4,377) = 2.80$, $p < .05$; the correlation between loneliness scores and age was also significant, $r(382) = -.17$, $p < .001$.

We believe that our efforts to develop an adequate loneliness scale have been very successful. The revised UCLA Loneliness Scale is relatively short, easily administered, highly reliable, and appears to be valid both in assessing loneliness and discriminating between loneliness and other related constructs. Of course, the validity of a measure is never "proven." Hopefully future research will continue to support the utility of this measure in assessing loneliness. Despite the success of these efforts, however, there remain important unresolved conceptual and methodological issues in the assessment of loneliness.

METHODOLOGICAL AND CONCEPTUAL ISSUES

In this final section, I consider some general issues of importance to the development of measures of loneliness. A basic point to be made is that theoretical conceptualizations and methodological issues are inseparable. Our judgments of the adequacy of loneliness measures are often dependent upon *how* we view loneliness theoretically. And conversely, the methodology we employ in studying loneliness may limit or constrain our theoretical view of the phenomenon. The relationship between theoretical conceptualizations of loneliness and the methodological problems of reliability and validity deserves special comment.

Reliability

Two forms of reliability have been examined in developing measures of loneliness: internal consistency and test-retest reliability. It is generally considered desirable to have internally consistent or homogeneous scales (Nunnally, 1978): a good measure should have high inter-item correlations. The implications for loneliness measures of this recommendation differ depending on one's theoretical conceptualization of loneliness. If loneliness is viewed as a unidimensional construct, then high inter-item correlations should be expected, since each item should be assessing the same thing (loneliness). For multidimensional measures of loneliness, however, high inter-item correlations would not necessarily be anticipated for the entire scale, since items are designed to assess different aspects or components of loneliness. Instead, internally consistent subscales should be developed, corresponding to the different components or dimensions of loneliness that the multidimensional scale is designed to assess (see Nunnally, 1978). If internally consistent subscales exist corresponding to the hypothesized dimensions of loneliness, then a factor analysis of the entire scale should reproduce these dimensions as separate factors, assuming that the loneliness dimensions are independent of one another. The scale development work of Schmidt (1976) and de Jong-Gierveld (1978, Chapter 7) illustrate this confirmatory factor analytic procedure.

Test-retest reliability also raises issues of a conceptual nature. These reliability correlations reflect the stability of scores on a measure over time. Generally speaking, high test-retest reliability is desirable, since variations in test scores over time are typically attributed to measurement error. However, this assumes that the construct being measured actually is stable over time. Although this may be a safe assumption for personality traits or abilities, it may be less reasonable for loneliness. Thus the issue of test-retest reliability raises questions concerning the state versus trait nature of loneliness.

Is loneliness a state or a trait? Undoubtedly, loneliness can have both characteristics. For example, the loneliness of a college student who is new on campus may be a short-lived state, lasting only until the student has become integrated into the new social situation. In contrast, another new student may suffer from chronic loneliness, having been socially maladjusted and lonely as an adolescent and continuing to be lonely in college. It may prove useful to distinguish both methodologically and conceptually between these two types or forms of loneliness. In the only study to examine this trait-state distinction directly, Gerson and Perlman (1979) administered the UCLA Loneliness Scale under both state (i.e., "How have you felt during the past two weeks") and trait (i.e., "How have you felt during your lifetime") conditions. They found that state-lonely individuals were better "senders" in a nonverbal communication task than trait-lonely individuals. Thus some interesting behavioral differences are suggested between state and trait loneliness (see also Young, Chapter 22).

The distinction between state and trait loneliness is analogous to the distinction between state and trait anxiety made by Spielberger (1975). It is informative that Spielberger, Gorsuch, and Lushene (1970) reported high levels of internal consistency for their measure of trait anxiety ($r = .73$ to $.86$) and low levels of test-retest reliability for their measure of state anxiety ($r = .16$ to $.54$). These reliability findings suggest that the level of test-retest reliability to be expected from loneliness measures should depend upon whether a scale assesses state or trait loneliness.

Validity

Three types of validity are important in psychological testing (see *Standards for Educational and Psychological Tests,* 1974): content validity, criterion validity (both concurrent and predictive), and construct validity.

Content Validity

One form of content validity is face validity, which concerns whether or not a measure appears to assess the construct. The most face valid loneliness measures are items asking for explicit self-ratings of loneliness (e.g., "Are you lonely?"). However, such undisguised measures may have problems of social desirability or acquiescence response set biases that could limit their validity.

More generally, content validity deals with how well the items on a test represent the construct that is being assessed. This issue is particularly relevant to multidimensional loneliness measures, where different components or dimensions of loneliness are hypothesized to exist. To have content validity, the items on such a scale should assess these different aspects of loneliness, thereby representing the multifaceted nature of the construct (loneliness) that is being assessed. Content validity is less crucial for unidimensional or global loneliness scales, since loneliness is viewed as a unitary construct and the representativeness of scale items is not an issue. So, once again, our theoretical perspective on loneliness dictates how we address issues of content validity.

Criterion Validity

A basic problem in constructing measures of loneliness is the lack of clear-cut external validity criteria for loneliness. Most researchers agree that loneliness represents a subjective reaction to deficiencies in social relationships. Loneliness is not synonymous with social isolation, and so measures of objective features of a person's social network (such as the number of friends or the frequency of social contact) are *not* foolproof validity criteria for loneliness measures. Faced with this problem, scale developers have typically relied on self-report questions (e.g., "Are you lonely?") as the most direct measure of a person's loneliness, despite the problems with such measures that were noted earlier.

Several other validity criteria have been employed by loneliness researchers. The "known groups" approach investigates individuals who are expected to be lonely on some a priori basis. Examples of such "at risk" groups used in validation studies have included participants in social skills workshops, divorced adults, psychiatric in-patients, students receiving counseling, and emotionally disturbed prisoners. A problem with this validation strategy is that these groups differ in many ways from "normal" comparison groups. For example, while these at risk groups may indeed be lonelier than a comparison group, the groups might also differ in depression, anxiety, or self-esteem. A loneliness measure could differentiate between the at risk and comparison groups, and still be highly confounded with these latter concepts. Indeed there is little doubt that measures of depression, anxiety, or self-esteem could also distinguish between the at risk and comparison groups used in previous loneliness research.

Another possible validity criterion would be ratings of a person's loneliness by others. Although this approach has been recommended (Ferguson & Taylor, 1979), only de Jong-Gierveld (1978) has used ratings of loneliness by others as a validation procedure. The usefulness of this validation strategy depends on the degree to which individuals communicate their loneliness to other people, either directly or indirectly. Psychodynamic theorists, particularly Fromm-Reichmann (1959), have suggested that loneliness is such an aversive experience that we strive to repress the memory of our own loneliness and avoid acknowledging the loneliness of others. Loneliness has a social stigma associated with it (Gordon, 1976) that could reduce a person's willingness to communicate his or her loneliness to others. Therefore, ratings of loneliness by others may not be a good indicator of loneliness. In this regard, it is interesting to note that de Jong-Gierveld (1978) found only a moderate relationship between self and other ratings of loneliness ($r = .39$).

In general, problems arise in the use of any single validity criterion for loneliness. Therefore, investigators are wise to use a number of validity criteria. Although each criterion has its limitations, the use of a wide variety of criterion variables that are indicative of loneliness can help overcome these individual shortcomings. The choice of validity criteria may also be dictated by an investigator's theoretical approach to loneliness. For example, in validating a global or unidimensional measure of loneliness, a person's general level of satisfaction with social relationships would be a suitable validity criterion. In contrast, validating a scale designed to differentiate among types of loneliness (e.g., based on different types of relational deficits, as in Weiss's (1973) distinction between social and emotional loneliness) might require more specific measures of a person's satisfaction with particular types of social relationships.

The discussion of criterion validity to this point has focused on concurrent validity, where loneliness measures are validated by demonstrating relationships with the person's current feelings of loneliness, satisfaction with social relationships, and so on. Another form of criterion validity is predictive validity, in which scores on a measure are related to validity criteria that are assessed at some future point in time. Unless loneliness is viewed as a trait or as enduring over time, it seems unlikely that scores on a loneliness measure would predict a person's future feelings of satisfaction with social relationships. Thus, our concern with the predictive validity of loneliness measures depends upon how loneliness is conceptualized.

Construct Validity

The most difficult and abstract form of validity involves construct validation. The concern here is not with the relationship between loneliness scores and any single validity criterion. Instead the focus is shifted to how the loneliness measure relates to a variety of other variables or constructs. This approach requires that the loneliness researcher have at least a tentative theory of loneliness from which to derive predictions linking loneliness to other measures. These predictions are then empirically tested. If the predictions are confirmed, then both the validity of the measure and the validity of the loneliness theory are supported. If the predictions are not confirmed, the interpretation is somewhat ambiguous—the problem could be with the measure or with the theory.

Attempts at construct validation of loneliness measures have been rare. One example comes from our work in developing the UCLA Loneliness Scale. Based on Weiss's (1973) ideas concerning the emotional concomitants of loneliness, we examined a variety of feeling states (such as feeling "bored," "empty," and "restless") that should be related to loneliness, as well as feeling states that should be unrelated to loneliness (such as feeling "surprised"). Empirical findings confirmed these hypothesized relationships. Another example of construct validation comes from a recent study by Cutrona (Chapter 18) employing the UCLA Loneliness Scale. Based on a social dissatisfaction model of loneliness (Peplau, Russell, & Heim, 1979), Cutrona predicted and found that loneliness scores were much more strongly related to measures of qualitative satisfaction with relationships than to quantitative measures of social contact (e.g., number of close friendships).

Establishing the discriminant validity of a measure can also be viewed as a form of construct validation (Campbell & Fiske, 1959; Magnusson, 1967). Discriminant validity is a particularly important issue for loneliness measures, since loneliness is strongly related to other constructs such as depression and low self-esteem. Our recent research using the revised UCLA Loneliness Scale illustrates discriminant validation, and provides clear evidence that the UCLA scale measures a construct that is distinct from other related constructs. The only other attempt to demonstrate discriminant validity for a loneliness measure (Schmidt, 1976) was less successful.

A further issue of discriminant validity concerns the possibility that relationships between loneliness and other variables are mediated by the impact of a third variable. For example, the general tendency of lonely individuals to evaluate themselves and other people negatively (see Jones, Chapter 15) may reflect the influence of depression on loneliness scores. This mediating effect could be tested by statistically controlling for the impact of depression on loneliness scores, and then examining whether the relationship between loneliness and this "negativity bias" persists. (For an example of this type of analysis, see Gerson & Perlman, 1979.) Given the extremely high correlations that have repeatedly been reported between loneliness measures and anxiety, depression, and self-esteem, discriminant validity should have a high priority in future loneliness research.

A final issue in the construct validation of loneliness measures concerns the nature of loneliness itself. As noted earlier, two different conceptual approaches to loneliness can be identified: the unidimensional and multidimensional approaches. Researchers who subscribe to each approach must provide support for their theoretical view of loneliness in validating their measures of loneliness. So, for example, developers of unidimensional measures must demonstrate that their scale is sensitive to loneliness in a wide range of individuals, varying in age, social class, and cause of social distress. Developers of multidimensional measures must substantiate that loneliness consists of the components or dimensions they propose, and that their scale adequately assesses these components. Although these two approaches to the assessment of loneliness appear contradictory, both approaches may prove to be correct. A general or common set of experiences could underlie loneliness as it is experienced by all people. Different components or dimensions of loneliness may also exist, reflecting different paths to this common experiential state (loneliness) or variations in how people respond to loneliness. An integration of these two conceptual approaches to loneliness may therefore be possible, and might yield a more general and comprehensive conception of loneliness.

As loneliness research leaves its infancy, there is a general need for greater theoretical development. As Kurt Lewin commented many years ago:

> The simple collection of facts is indispensable at certain stages of a science; it is a wholesome reaction against a philosophical and speculative building of theories. But it cannot give a satisfactory answer to questions about causes and conditions of events. Only with the help of theories can one determine causal interrelationships. (Lewin, 1936, p. 4)

At this point, it appears that we are able to assess loneliness with some confidence. And as the research summarized here and elsewhere in this volume demonstrates, a large number of empirical facts concerning loneliness have been gathered. For our understanding of loneliness to progress, we now need to develop theoretical models of loneliness that organize what is known about loneliness and serve to guide our search for further knowledge.

REFERENCES

Beck, A. T. *Depression.* New York: Hoeber, 1967.

Belcher, M. J. *The measurement of loneliness: A validation of the Belcher Extended Loneliness Scale (BELS.)* Unpublished doctoral dissertation, Illinois Institute of Technology, 1973.

Bentler, P. M. Semantic space is (approximately) bipolar. *Journal of Psychology,* 1969, *71,* 22–40.

Bradburn, N. *The structure of psychological well-being.* Chicago: Aldine, 1969.

Bradley, R. *Measuring loneliness.* Unpublished doctoral dissertation, Washington State University, 1969.

Campbell, D. T., & Fiske, D. W. Convergent and discriminant validation by the multitrait-multimethod matrix. *Psychological Bulletin,* 1959, *56,* 81–105.

Cattell, R. B., Ebner, H. W., & Tatsuoka, M. M. *Handbook for the Sixteen Personality Factor Questionnaire (16 PF).* Champaign, Ill.: Institute for Personality and Ability Testing, 1970.

Costello, C. G., & Comrey, A. L. Scales for measuring depression and anxiety. *Journal of Psychology,* 1967, *66,* 303–313.

de Jong-Gierveld, J. The construct of loneliness. Components and measurement. *Essence,* 1978, *2,* 221–238.

Dyer, B. M. Loneliness—there's no way to escape it. *Alpha Gamma Delta Quarterly,* Spring, 1974, 2–5.

Eddy, P. D. *Loneliness: A discrepancy with the phenomenological self.* Unpublished doctoral dissertation, Adelphi College, 1961.

Ellison, C. W., & Paloutzian, R. *Developing an abbreviated loneliness scale.* Paper presented at the UCLA Research Conference on Loneliness, Los Angeles, May 1979a.

Ellison, C. W., & Paloutzian, R. *Religious experience and quality of life.* Paper presented as part of the symposium "Spiritual Well-being, Loneliness, and Perceived Quality of Life," American Psychological Association Convention, New York City, September 1979b.

Ferguson, G., & Taylor, R. B. *The criterion problem and scale development: Loneliness, privacy, and self-disclosure.* Paper presented as part of the symposium "Social Psychology of Loneliness," American Psychological Association Convention, New York City, September 1979.

Fromm-Reichmann, F. Loneliness. *Psychiatry,* 1959, *22,* 1–15.

Gerson, A. C., & Perlman, D. Loneliness and expressive communication. *Journal of Abnormal Psychology,* 1979, *88,* 258–261.

Gordon, S. *Lonely in America.* New York: Simon & Schuster, 1976.

Gutek, B., Nakamura, C., Gahart, M., Handschumacher, I., & Russell, D. Sexuality and the workplace. *Basic and Applied Social Psychology,* 1980, *1,* 255–265.

Horowitz, L. M., & French, R. de S. Interpersonal problems of people who describe themselves as lonely. *Journal of Consulting and Clinical Psychology,* 1979, *47,* 762–764.

Jackson, D. N. *Personality Research Form Manual.* Goshen, N.Y.: Research Psychologists Press, 1967.

Jones, W. H., Freemon, J. E., & Goswick, R. A. The persistence of loneliness: Self and other rejection? *Journal of Personality,* 1981, *49,* 27–48.

Keniston, K. *The uncommitted.* New York: Harcourt, Brace, and World, 1960.

Lewin, K. *Principles of topological psychology.* New York: McGraw-Hill, 1936.

Lowenthal, M. F., Thurner, M., & Chirboga, D. *Four stages of life.* San Francisco: Jossey-Bass, 1975.

Magnusson, D. *Test theory.* Reading, Mass.: Addison-Wesley, 1967.

Maisel, R. *Report of the continuing audit of public attitudes and concerns.* Laboratory of Community Psychiatry, Harvard Medical School, 1969.

Moore, J. A. *Loneliness: Personality, self-discrepancy, and demographic variables.* Unpublished doctoral dissertation, York University, 1972.

Nerviano, V. J., & Gross, W. F. Loneliness and locus of control for alcoholic males: Validity against Murray need and Cattell trait dimensions. *Journal of Clinical Psychology,* 1976, *32,* 479–484.

Nunnally, J. C. *Psychometric theory.* New York: McGraw-Hill, 1978.

Peplau, L. A., Russell, D., & Heim, M. The experience of loneliness. In I. H. Frieze, D. Bar-Tal, & J. S. Carroll (Eds.), *New approaches to social problems: Applications of attribution theory.* San Francisco: Jossey-Bass, 1979.

Perlman, D., Gerson, A. C., & Spinner, B. Loneliness among senior citizens: An empirical report. *Essence,* 1978, *2,* 239–248.

Primakoff, L. Personal communication, May 1980.

Rosow, I. Retirement housing and social integration. In C. Tibbits & W. Donahue (Eds.), *Social and psychological aspects of aging.* New York: Columbia University Press, 1962.

Rubenstein, C. M., & Shaver, P. Loneliness in two northeastern cities. In J. Hartog & R. Audy (Eds.), *The anatomy of loneliness.* New York: International Universities Press, 1979.

Russell, D. *Conceptual and methodological issues in studying loneliness.* Paper presented as part of the symposium "Toward a Psychology of Loneliness," American Psychological Association Convention, Toronto, Canada, September 1978.

Russell, D., Peplau, L. A., & Cutrona, C. E. The revised UCLA Loneliness Scale: Concurrent and discriminant validity evidence. *Journal of Personality and Social Psychology,* 1980, *39*(3), 472–480.

Russell, D., Peplau, L. A., & Ferguson, M. L. Developing a measure of loneliness. *Journal of Personality Assessment,* 1978, *42,* 290–294.

Schmidt, N. *The construction of a scale for the measurement of loneliness.* Unpublished master's thesis, York University, 1976.

Shanas, E., Townsend, P., Wedderburn, D., Friis, H., Milhoj, P., & Stehouwer, J. *Old people in three industrial societies.* New York: Atherton, 1968.

Sisenwein, R. J. *Loneliness and the individual as viewed by himself and others.* Unpublished doctoral dissertation, Columbia University, 1964.

Solano, C. H. Two measures of loneliness: A comparison. *Psychological Reports,* 1980, *46,* 23–28.

Spielberger, C. D. Anxiety: State-trait-process. In C. D. Spielberger & I. G. Sarason (Eds.), *Stress and Anxiety* (Vol. 1). Washington, D.C.: Hemisphere, 1975.

Spielberger, C. D., Gorsuch, R. L., & Lushene, R. E. *Manual for the Strait-Trait Anxiety Inventory.* Palo Alto, Calif.: Consulting Psychologists Press, 1970.

Srole, L. Social integration and certain corollaries: An exploratory study. *American Sociological Review,* 1956, *21,* 709–716.

Standards for educational and psychological tests. Washington, D. C.: American Psychological Association, 1974.

Weiss, R. S. (Ed). *Loneliness: The experience of social and emotional isolation.* Cambridge, Mass.: MIT Press, 1973.

Young, J. *An instrument for measuring loneliness.* Paper presented as part of the symposium "Social Psychology of Loneliness," American Psychological Association Convention, New York City, September 1979.

Chapter 7

Types of Loneliness

Jenny de Jong-Gierveld and Jos Raadschelders

Loneliness, one of the more serious social problems of our time, is a complex phenomenon. "Knowing no limits of class, race, or age, loneliness is today a great leveler" (Gordon, 1976, p. 16). Writers of various disciplines have tried to capture the complexity of loneliness by distinguishing among such experiences as the loneliness of the poet, the religious hermit, the abandoned orphan, or the widow. This chapter begins with a brief review of existing typologies of loneliness. Then we present and discuss a new, empirically derived typology for adult loneliness.

TYPOLOGIES OF LONELINESS

The literature on loneliness offers many varied suggestions about possible typologies (e.g., Bragg, 1979; Gaev, 1976; Peplau & Perlman, Chapter 1). Underlying these diverse typologies are three major dimensions concerning how the person evaluates his or her social situation, the type of social deficit experienced, and the time perspective associated with loneliness. Each of these will be discussed briefly.

The Evaluative Dimension

Philosophers have often distinguished between positive and negative aspects of solitude and loneliness. Those in the German philosophical tradition have discussed the differences between positive and negative experiences of "Einsamkeit." Early writers (Parpert, 1955; Zimmerman, 1785/1786) emphasized the positive aspects of aloneness—when solitude provides an opportunity

This research project is subsidized by the National Mental Health Fund and the Fund for Social Welfare Research, which is supported by the National Council of Social Welfare, the Queen Juliana Foundation, and the Ministry of Cultural Affairs, Recreation and Social Welfare. The paper has benefited from a discussion of typologies during the UCLA Research Conference on Loneliness in May 1979 with Tim Brennan, Carin Rubenstein, and Linda Wood, and from the suggestions of Letitia Anne Peplau and Daniel Perlman.

for reflection, for communication with God and with oneself. In this context, "Einsamkeit" was seen as a means of realizing the strength of one's character through choosing to spend certain limited periods of time alone. The negative aspects of solitude have received greater attention in more recent writings; here emphasis has been given to a type of Einsamkeit (sometimes called "Vereinsamung") comparable in connotation to our concept of loneliness (Bitter, 1967; Carp, 1967; Van Oppen, 1967). For example, Kölbel (1960) has distinguished four types of Einsamkeit:

1. A positive, inner type ("splendid isolation"), experienced as a necessary means of discovering new forms of freedom or contact with other people.
2. A negative, inner type, experienced as an estrangement from oneself and from others, a feeling of alienation, even in the midst of others.
3. A positive, external type, present under circumstances of physical solitude, when one searches for new positive experiences.
4. A negative, external type, present when external circumstances (death of a partner, loss of contacts) lead to very negative feelings of loneliness.

A recurrent theme in such philosophical discussions is that the positive experience of solitude is the more basic or "true" form, and the negative experience of loneliness is a pseudo or pathological variant (Lotz, 1967).

Empirical studies have found cultural differences in the extent to which solitude is experienced as positive or negative. In 1947, Hofstätter (1957) compared experiences of Einsamkeit among Germans and Americans. The German sample perceived solitude as a positive phenomenon, associated with such words as "strong" and "healthy." In contrast, Americans perceived it as highly negative and associated with fear. Czernick and Steinmeyer (1974) replicated this study several years later, and reported that among Germans, Einsamkeit had taken on a more negative connotation.

Associated with the evaluative dimension is a common philosophical distinction (Moustakas, 1961) between loneliness as a basic fact of human existence and loneliness as a psychological reaction to relational deficits. Mijuskovic (1979) distinguishes metaphysical or existential loneliness from psychological loneliness:

I wish to claim that man is not only psychologically alone but metaphysically isolated as well. I am not maintaining that we *feel* or *think* we are alone all the time and at every moment. I am convinced that we *really* are, but are not always conscious of it. (p. 49)

Von Witzleben (1958) made a similar distinction between "primary" loneliness resulting from an awareness of being alone in the world, and "secondary" loneliness caused by the loss of a social object.

Most loneliness researchers have focused their energies on psychological loneliness. While not necessarily discounting the philosophical insight that individuals are ultimately alone in some existential sense, loneliness researchers have emphasized subjective responses to actual or perceived social deficits as the focus of their inquiry.

The Nature of the Relational Deficit

Many typologies have attempted to specify the nature of the missing relationship or the features of the lonely person's social situation that give rise to loneliness. Marital status appears to be an important factor. Widowhood, divorce, or the breakup of a relationship are common situations leading to loneliness. Lopata (1969) has pursued this issue and identified 11 types of loneliness among widows. Each type is directly related to the role of the deceased husband who is missed, such as the husband "as a person, as a love object or provider, as a companion."

Best known among relational deficit typologies is Weiss's (1973) fundamental distinction between emotional and social loneliness:

The *loneliness of emotional isolation* appears in the absence of a close emotional attachment and can only be remedied by the integration of another emotional attachment or the reintegration of the one that had been lost. Those experiencing this form of loneliness are apt to experience a sense of utter aloneness, whether or not the companionship of others is in fact accessible to them. The individual may describe the immediately available world as desolate, barren or devoid of others; or the sense of utter aloneness may be phrased in terms of an empty inner world, in which case the individual may say that he or she feels empty, dead or hollow.

The *loneliness of social isolation* . . . is associated with the absence of an engaging social network and this absence can only be remedied by access to such a network. For example, wives after moving to another region. Their partners, no matter how close the marriage, are of little help; the wives continue to be lonely for friends and acquaintances who would share their interests as their husbands did not. The dominant symptoms of this form of loneliness are feelings of boredom or aimlessness, together with feelings of marginality. (Weiss, 1973, pp. 18-19; italics added)

Empirical support for Weiss's typology has recently been provided in studies by Brennan and Auslander (1979), Cutrona (Chapter 18), and Rubenstein and Shaver (Chapter 13). It appears that further specification of different types of loneliness based on the kinds of relational deficits involved is a fruitful direction for future research.

Time Perspective

A final major dimension concerns the duration of loneliness. The therapeutically relevant distinction between chronic and short-term loneliness appears to be of considerable importance. Young and his colleagues (Chapter 22; Beck & Young, 1978) distinguish among three types of loneliness. *Chronic* loneliness evolves when, over a period of years, the person is not able to develop satisfying social relations. *Situational* loneliness often follows major life stress events, such as the death of a spouse or ending of a marriage. After a brief period of distress, the situationally lonely person typically accepts the loss and recovers from loneliness. *Transient* loneliness is the most common form and refers to shorter bouts of feeling lonely. Findings by Gerson and Perlman (1979) testify to the importance of this kind of typology for understanding the loneliness experience. They found that

The situationally lonely individuals and the chronically lonely individuals were significantly more depressed than the non-lonely individuals. And, situationally lonely persons proved to be more effective in sending emotional messages than chronically lonely persons . . . Perhaps chronically lonely persons are more self-focused in their interaction patterns. (p. 260)

In summary, we have presented a variety of loneliness typologies, emphasizing three fundamental aspects of loneliness: a negative evaluation of the situation, feelings of deprivation concerning the absence of certain relationships, and the time perspective associated with loneliness. Most typologies stress one of these aspects as the dominating principle. In this way, some focus on differences in situational or role characteristics, while others emphasize differences in time perspective. With the exception of the ideas of Weiss (1973), no typology has been widely accepted and utilized. To date, most typologies are theoretically derived speculations rather than empirically derived or empirically tested models.

In our opinion, a typology of forms of loneliness should be theoretically based. If we agree that loneliness concerns "being without some definite needed relationship(s)" (Weiss, 1973, p. 17), then the theoretical framework must refer to the nature and density of the network of social relationships as well as to the various characteristics of an intimate and meaningful relationship that may be absent. Differences in time perspective should also be taken into account. Thus we need a *multidimensional concept* of loneliness that can provide the basis for an empirically tested multivariate classification or typology. In the following sections, we describe an attempt to construct and empirically test such a typology of forms of loneliness.

THE MULTIDIMENSIONAL CONSTRUCT OF LONELINESS

The concept of loneliness concerns situations experienced by the person as involving a disagreeable or unacceptable lack of the quantity or quality of certain relationships. It is important to distinguish these subjective feelings of loneliness from objective social isolation. Objective social isolation refers to the lack of lasting interpersonal relationships. Loneliness concerns the manner in which the person perceives, experiences, and evaluates his or her isolation and lack of communication with other people. Our original theoretical notions concerning the complex nature of loneliness were influenced by the ideas of Weiss (1973), and by our own content analysis of the life histories of 114 lonely men and women. On the basis of these and further pilot data, we distinguished three dimensions of loneliness:

1. *Emotional characteristics* of loneliness refer to the absence of positive emotions such as happiness and affection, and the presence of negative emotions such as fear and uncertainty.

2. *Type of deprivation* refers to the nature of the missing relationships. In this regard it is crucial to collect information concerning those relationships that the person considers to be essential. This component obviously varies greatly according to the category of individuals being studied (Gordon, 1976; Weiss, 1973; Wood, 1953). This dimension can be further differentiated (de Jong-Gierveld, 1978) into three subcategories: feelings of deprivation associated with the absence of an *intimate attachment* (E_1), feelings of *emptiness* (E_2) and feelings of *abandonment* (E_3).

3. *Time perspective* is the third dimension. This can also be further differentiated into three subcomponents: the extent to which loneliness is experienced as being *unchangeable* (E_6), the extent to which loneliness is experienced as *temporary* (E_7), and the extent to which a person resigns himself or herself to loneliness by attributing the cause of the loneliness to *others* (E_9).

METHOD

Respondents

Data were obtained from a sample of single, married, divorced, and widowed adult men and women. Previous research has identified the important influence of sex and marital status on psychological well-being and loneliness (Bradburn, 1969; de Jong-Gierveld, 1971; Gove, 1972; Knupfer, Clark, & Room, 1966; Lopata, 1969; Lynch, 1977). Hence our sampling was *stratified* on these variables. Names and addresses of these subsamples were selected at random from the population registers of Haarlem, an older city (population about 175,000), Purmerend, a fast growing commuter city with many highrise apartments (population about 33,000), and Nieuwkoop (population about 9,000), a village in "the green heart" of Holland.

Of the married people, about 30% proved unavailable or simply refused to be interviewed. It was even more difficult to contact people living alone, especially divorced and unmarried men. People were called as many as three times if necessary, resulting in a sample of 129 unmarried, 128 divorced, 131 widowed, and 168 married adult individuals. There were roughly equal numbers of men and women. Interviews lasted from two to three hours, followed in most cases by an informal conversation about loneliness. The interviews were conducted between April and August 1978.

Questionnaire

Several loneliness measures were utilized in the survey, including a self-rating scale concerning perceived degree of loneliness at the present time, the six-item "Loneliness Scale 1965," a summary of stressful life events mentioned in relation to loneliness, and a 34-item multidimensional measuring instrument incorporating our three dimensions of loneliness. Other questions in the interview schedule concerned background characteristics, social contacts, measures of self-esteem (Brinkman, 1977), and a measure of depression (van Rooijen, 1979).

As a precursor to subsequent analysis, the first statistical procedures employed in the project examined the 34-item loneliness scale. Items had been written to capture three hypothesized dimensions of loneliness. Our initial analyses examined whether empirical results supported our prior speculations. Basically, the answer was yes. Mokken's (1970) nonmetric procedure for testing the homogeneity of scales was used. The Mokken scale is constructed as a general probabilistic multivariate scaling model, a special case of latent structure analysis. The homogeneity coefficients used are Loevinger's (1948) coefficient H.

An overview of the multidimensional structure of the loneliness scale, showing the items on each of the components and giving the internal consistency measures for each scale is presented in Table 7.1.

Procedures Used in Constructing a Typology of Loneliness

Once the dimensions of the loneliness scale had been confirmed, the pattern of respondents' scores on the various subscales could be used as the starting point for constructing a typology of loneliness. A large number of different response-profiles could occur in principle. Thus, the problem was to develop an adequate but limited set of response profiles.

First, we reasoned that feelings of deprivation are a necessary precondition for loneliness. Hence responses on the three deprivation scales (E_1, E_2, and E_3) were taken as a first criterion for identifying response profiles. Next we turned to the measure of time perspective, and specifically to the subscale (E_6) assessing whether or not loneliness is perceived as unchangeable and hopeless. Responses to each of these four subscales were dichotomized at the median. On the basis of these four dichotomous scales, 16 response profiles were possible. These are summarized in Table 7.2. Each of these 16 profiles relates to a specific combination of subjective feelings concerning important characteristics of loneliness. For example, profile #16 (see Table 7.2) includes people who score high on all four subscales, and hence suffer from the

Table 7.1. The 34 Items Used to Assess the Multidimensional Construct of Loneliness

Dimension	Items	H	Rho
1. Emotions			
Positive	Unique, beloved, useful, strong, happy, valued	.42	.70
Negative	Uncertain, frightened, sad, misunderstood, unsuccessful, failing, aimless, lacking feedback	.38	.77
2. Type of social deprivation			
E_1: Intimate partner	I miss a man/woman, especially mine	.54	.82
	You actually have no one you'd want to share your joy or sorrow with		
	I miss having a really good friend		
	I regret not having a mate		
E_2: Emptiness	I experience emptiness around me	.42	.70
	I miss having people around me		
	I miss good company around me		
E_3: Abandonment	I often feel deserted	.41	.55
	You can no longer expect any interest, · even from your closest kin		
	There's nobody who really cares for me		
3. Time perspective			
E_6: Hopelessness	Ultimately, there is no hope for a lonely person in our society	.36	.70
	The worst of all is that this situation is so endless		
	Once lonely, always lonely		
	There's no cure for loneliness		
	You can't resolve loneliness, not even in the long run		
	Loneliness can't be cured, you've got to learn to live with it		
E_7: Permanence	Speaking about loneliness, sooner or later you get yourself back on your feet	.36	.51
	Times of loneliness always go away		
E_9: Blaming others	People are by nature unwilling to rescue you from your loneliness	.42	.59
	As a lonely person, one is left to one's own fate		

lack of an intimate attachment, experience feelings of emptiness and abandonment, and perceive their loneliness as relatively unchanging over time.

The next step in our analysis was to reduce still further this rather complex set of 16 profiles. To do this, we used a statistical cluster analysis procedure*

* A hierarchical cluster analysis procedure was used, specifically Johnson's complete linkage cluster analysis (see Anderberg, 1973; Johnson, 1967; Overall & Klett, 1972). The measure of similarity employed was the two-dimensional Euclidian distance measure. Response profile #6 was deleted from the cluster analysis because there were only four cases in this group.

Table 7.2.   Summary of 16 Answer Profiles for the Loneliness Scales

	$E_1 (+) E_2 (+)$	$E_1(+)E_2(-)$	$E_1(-)E_2(+)$	$E_1(-)E_2(-)$
$E_3 (+) E_6 (+)$	Profile 16 $+ + + +$ ($N = 53$)	Profile 15 $+ - + +$ ($N = 16$)	Profile 14 $- + + +$ ($N = 9$)	Profile 13 $- - + +$ ($N = 22$)
$E_3 (-) E_6 (+)$	Profile 12 $+ + - +$ ($N = 41$)	Profile 11 $+ - - +$ ($N = 26$)	Profile 10 $- + - +$ ($N = 15$)	Profile 9 $- - - +$ ($N = 73$)
$E_3 (+) E_6 (-)$	Profile 8 $+ + + -$ ($N = 29$)	Profile 7 $+ - + -$ ($N = 13$)	Profile 6 $- + + -$ ($N = 4$)	Profile 5 $- - + -$ ($N = 27$)
$E_3 (-) E_6 (-)$	Profile 4 $+ + - -$ ($N = 28$)	Profile 3 $+ - - -$ ($N = 40$)	Profile 2 $- + - -$ ($N = 16$)	Profile 1 $- - - -$ ($N = 144$)

$+$ indicates that the respondent agrees with one or more of the statements of that scale.
$-$ indicates that the respondent disagrees with all the statements of that scale.

that attempted to create clusters or sets of profiles. The similarity between each possible pair of the original 16 profiles was assessed using criterion variables. Given their importance to loneliness, the criteria we used were measures of objective social isolation and social participation. Specifically, 12 criterion variables were selected that assessed the range and composition of the network of intimate relationships; relationships at work and in the neighborhood; participation in social organizations; and self-ratings of satisfaction/dissatisfaction with relationships in general.

The results of the cluster analysis using these twelve criterion variables are presented in Table 7.3. The table indicates the distribution of the 16 original response profiles into four basic cluster types. As can be seen, each of the four

Table 7.3.   The Distribution of the Original 16 Types into Four Major Loneliness Cluster Types

	$E_1 (+) E_2 (+)$	$E_1(+)E_2(-)$	$E_1(-)E_2(+)$	$E_1(-)E_2(-)$
$E_3 (+) E_6 (+)$	Type I Profile 16	Type I Profile 15	Type I Profile 14	Type IV Profile 13
$E_3 (-) E_6 (+)$	Type III Profile 12	Type III Profile 11	Type II Profile 10	Type IV Profile 9
$E_3 (+) E_6 (-)$	Type II Profile 8	Type II Profile 7	Type IV Profile 6	Type IV Profile 5
$E_3 (-) E_6 (-)$	Type II Profile 4	Type IV Profile 3	Type IV Profile 2	Type IV Profile 1

$+$ indicates that the respondent agrees with one or more of the statements of that scale.
$-$ indicates that the respondent disagrees with all the statements of that scale.
There are 78 respondents in Type I, 85 in Type II, 67 in Type III, and 326 in Type IV.

types is based on a set of related loneliness response profiles. For example, loneliness Type III combines profiles 11 and 12; the common features here are scoring high on lacking an intimate attachment (E_1), scoring low on abandonment (E_3), and scoring high on feeling that prospects for change in loneliness are small (E_6). Only on E_2 are there differences. In this way, the constructed typology of four loneliness types has a built-in control on content-validity concerning the subdimensions of feelings of loneliness.

In order to further clarify the interpretation of the four types, a discriminant analysis* was carried out using the same 12 criterion variables as used in the cluster analysis. Three dimensions were extracted. Figure 7.1 gives the location of the four types within this three-dimensional space.

Figure 7.1 illustrates how the typology may be characterized by one large Type IV ($n = 326$), located in a space opposing the three smaller Types I,

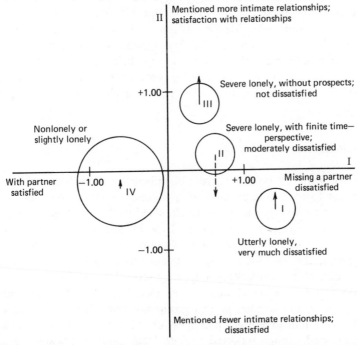

Figure 7.1. Geometrical representation of the location of the four types in the discriminant analysis space. Axis III is indicated by arrows: ↑ indicates few problems in the work situation; ↓ indicates a higher percentage of problems in the work situation.

* The discriminant analysis resulted in three significant functions:

	Eigenvalue	Canonical correlation
Function 1	.560	.599
Function 2	.134	.343
Function 3	.069	.254

II, and III ($n = 78$, $n = 85$, $n = 67$). Axis I seperate people who have an intimate partner from those who do not. The second dimension (Axis II) apparently relates to the number of good friends and other relationships described as intimate and the degree of (dis)satisfaction with this situation. A third dimension (Axis III), divides the groups into those with a relatively high percentage of problems in their work-situation versus those with a lower percentage of job problems.

RESULTS

Our data analyses identified four distinct groups. The largest group (Type IV, 59% of the sample) was either not lonely or only slightly lonely. The three other groups reflect variations in type of loneliness. Individuals in all three lonely groups lacked an intimate relationship (e.g., spouse) but differed in their relationships with friends and co-workers and in their feelings of deprivation. Table 7.4 compares the four groups on a variety of subscales. Because individuals in all three lonely groups lack an intimate relationship, it appears that they are all experiencing some form of emotional loneliness, as defined by Weiss. In the following section, each of these four groups is described.

The Nonlonely

Members of Type IV do not express dissatisfaction with their relationships. They appear to have a large number of intimate relationships. Most of the men and women we interviewed were classified in this nonlonely category. A relatively high percentage of people in Type IV are socially active and participate in a variety of organizations. Compared to members of the three lonely groups, the nonlonely people have a relatively extensive network of diverse relationships. Understandably, they score low on the three subscales measuring feelings of social deprivation (E_1, E_2, E_3). It is possible that among the men and women in this group are individuals who are experiencing feelings akin to Weiss's loneliness of social isolation. For example, a younger married woman reported, "Often I am alone, the whole day, alone at home—but I don't mind that." Further research designed explicitly to explore social loneliness is needed.

Type I: The Hopeless Lonely Who Are Very Dissatisfied with Their Relationships

Type I included 14% of the individuals in our sample. As with each of the types of loneliness, most of the people in Type I lack an intimate partner or spouse. They also have only a few non-intimate contacts, for instance with

Table 7.4. A Comparison of Individuals in the Four Major Types [a]

	Type I	Type II	Type III	Type IV
Multidimensional loneliness measure: Percentage agreeing with one or more items on each subscale				
E_1, deprivation concerning a partner	89	82	100	12
E_2, feelings of emptiness	80	85	61	5
E_3, feelings of abandonment	100	49	0	15
E_6, endless time perspective	100	18	100	(30)
E_7, loneliness is not temporary	31	8	18	13
E_9, attributes loneliness source to others	55	29	31	25
Negative emotions				
— core subscale: anxiety, sorrow	81	70	65	43
— disorientation—subscale	46	26	24	8
— feelings of failure (n.s.)	36	31	29	25
Positive emotions: Percentage disagreeing with one or more items of the subscale*	3	1	11	6
Self-reports of loneliness				
Percent scoring at or above median on Loneliness Scale 1965**	87	67	55	25
Percent saying they are one of "the lonely people in society"**	77	51	57	12
Mean number of stressful life events (range 0–21)**	4.7	3.7	3.2	1.2
Scores on 12 criterion variables				
Percent having strong feelings of dissatisfaction with relationships	42	20	12	3
Percent having less than five intimate relationships	59	32	40	32
Percent having an intimate partner relationship	21	24	13	66
Percent having intimate family relationships (n.s.)	72	85	76	79
Percent having intimate relationships with neighbors or colleagues (n.s.)	59	65	52	53
Percent of active people	40	52	24	58
Percent of disabled nonworkers	26	11	10	7
Percent with problems concerning the work-situation	13	31	9	18
Percent with no or only a few contacts in the "work"-situation (n.s.)	7	9	14	7
Percent nonactive in social organizations (n.s.)	24	22	37	26
Percent with no or only a few contacts with neighbors	62	52	37	31
Percent agreeing with "I have no good contacts in this neighborhood"	40	29	19	15

[a] All comparisons among four types are statistically significant at the $p < .001$ level unless otherwise indicated as *$p < .05$, **$p < .01$, n.s. = nonsignificant.

neighbors. What distinguishes this type is that they express strong feelings of dissatisfaction with their peer relations. Thus members of this type lack a close partner, feel empty and abandoned, and consider their situation relatively hopeless. They are more likely than people in other groups to blame others for their loneliness. They score high on measures of anxiety and sadness. This portrait contains elements of desolation—the loss of relationships—and it is not surprising that a high proportion of divorced men and women fall into this category. The major themes of Type I—lack of an intimate attachment, feelings of social deprivation, and hopelessness about the future—are illustrated by a 56-year-old woman in the sample: "I have no confidence in the willingness of other people to help me. You have to deal with it yourself. I lie down on the sofa and wait for the phone to ring. I'm certainly not the type of person that takes on something. There is no love, nothing at all. I feel as if I've been placed on a shelf." And a 52-year-old, married woman said: "I'm in desperation; my life is meaningless; I'm so disappointed in my friends. The essence of my loneliness is that I'm not important for anyone."

Type II: The Periodically and Temporarily Lonely

Although individuals in this group lack an intimate attachment or spouse, they have a moderate number of intimate relationships. In comparison to individuals in Types I and III, they are more often involved in social contacts at work, and in organizations or clubs. They are the most socially "active" of the lonely groups. This type, comprising 15% of the total sample, includes a higher proportion of never-married men and women than other types. What distinguishes this group most clearly from Type I is their time perspective; individuals in Type II believe that their loneliness is temporary and have less frequent feelings of abandonment. A never-married 45-year-old woman, a school teacher and vice-principal, told us: "As a single woman I am not by definition lonely. . . . Oh, now and then I am very lonely, especially in the evenings. But I have so many activities—schoolwork, watching T.V., planning my next vacation. . . . Feelings of loneliness always go away."

Type III: The Resigned, Hopelessly Lonely

Although individuals in Type III lack an intimate partner and have only a few other relationships, they do not express as much dissatisfaction as individuals in Types I or II. It appears that members of Type III may have become resigned to their situation. The majority of people in this group are widowed men and women, mostly over 55 years old, and many are unemployed. Such people appear to accept their social deprivations as unavoidable (cf. the disengagement theory of Tews, 1974). Although they feel severely lonely, respondents in Type III do not feel abandoned or blame others for their situation. Type III includes 12% of the total sample. The endless time perspective felt by individuals in this group is reflected in the statement of an unmarried, disabled man: "I cannot stand this situation. It's disgusting, I am bored. . . . I go to the pub to find company. I drink too much. I will die."

DISCUSSION

The results of this study indicate the usefulness of distinguishing among different types of loneliness. We believe that our efforts at typology construction have been quite successful. Our various data analyses have provided empirical evidence for the content, concurrent and external validity of our typology.* An examination of our typology indicates clearly that the experience of loneliness often varies across different groups in society. For example, married individuals were least likely to be lonely. Among the lonely, feelings of hopelessness and an endless time perspective were more characteristic of those who were divorced and widowed than of those who had never been married. Our typology thus provides support for the usefulness of distinguishing lonely individuals on the basis of their time perspective (Gerson & Perlman, 1979; Young, Chapter 22). More generally, our research provides strong support for the importance of employing a multidimensional concept of loneliness.

One surprising aspect of our results deserves further comment. We had anticipated that our typology might distinguish people experiencing emotional loneliness from those experiencing social loneliness (Weiss, 1973). Contrary to expectation, however, all of the types of loneliness in our typology appear to be forms of emotional loneliness. This issue should be a main topic for further research.

REFERENCES

Anderberg, M. R. *Clusteranalysis for applications.* New York: Academic Press, 1973.

Beck, A. T., & Young, J. E. College blues. *Psychology Today,* September, 1978.

Bitter, W. (Hrsg.), *Einsamkeit in medizinisch-psychologischer, theologischer und soziologischer Sicht.* Stuttgart, Germany: Klett, 1967.

*For a test of content validity, see de Jong-Gierveld, 1978. Concurrent validity is indicated in Table 7.2; self-reports of loneliness varied predictably among the four types of loneliness. External validity is also high. Consistent with findings of other researchers, the most severe types of loneliness occurred among widowed and divorced men and women. The four types are further validated by their significant ($p < .001$) relationships with depression and self-esteem:

	Type I	Type II	Type III	Type IV
Mean score on the depression scale: 0 (low) —16 (high)	11.8	8.9	8.5	6.1
Mean score on self-esteem: 0 (low) —11 (high)	3.3	3.6	3.8	3.9

Bradburn, N. *The structure of psychological well-being.* Chicago: Aldine, 1969.

Bragg, M. E. *A comparative study of loneliness and depression.* Unpublished doctoral dissertation, University of California, Los Angeles, 1979.

Brennan, T., & Auslander, N. *Adolescent loneliness: An exploratory study of social and psychological pre-dispositions and theory (Vol. 1).* Unpublished technical report, Behavioral Institute, Boulder, Colo., January 1979.

Brinkman, W. *Een assertiviteitsschaal II.* Rapport Psychologisch Laboratorium, Universiteit van Amsterdam, 1977.

Carp, E. A. D. E. Einsamkeit. In W. Bitter (Hrsg.), *Einsamkeit.* Stuttgart, Germany: Klett, 1967.

Czernick, A., & Steinmeyer, E. Experience of loneliness in normal and neurotic subjects. *Archiv für Psychiatrie und Nervenkrankheiten,* 1974, *218*(2), 141–159.

Gaev, D. M. *The psychology of loneliness.* Chicago: Adams Press, 1976.

Gerson, A., & Perlman, D. Loneliness and expressive communication. *Journal of Abnormal Psychology,* 1979, *88,* 258–261.

Gordon, S. *Lonely in America.* New York: Simon and Schuster, 1976.

Gove, W. R. The relationship between sex roles, marital roles and mental illness. *Social Forces,* 1972, *51,* 33–44.

Hofstätter, P. R. *Gruppendynamik- Kritik der Massenpsychologie.* Hamburg, Germany: Rowohlt, 1957.

Johnson, S. C. Hierarchical clustering schemes. *Psychometrika,* 1967, *32,* 241–254.

Jong-Gierveld, J. de. Social isolation and the image of the unmarried. *Sociologia Neerlandica,* 1971, *7,* 1–14.

Jong-Gierveld, J. de. The construct of loneliness: Components and measurements. *Essence,* 1978, *2*(4), 221–237.

Knupfer, G., Clark, W., & Room, R. The mental health of the unmarried. *American Journal of Psychiatry,* 1966, *122*(2), 841–851.

Kölbel, G. *Über die Einsamkeit. Vom Ursprung. Gestaltwandel und sinn des Einsamkeitserlebens.* München-Basel: Reinhart, 1960.

Loevinger, J. The technique of homogeneous tests compared with some aspects of "scale analysis" and factor analysis. *Psychological Bulletin,* 1948, *45,* 507–530.

Lopata, H. Z. Loneliness: Forms and components. *Social Problems,* 1969, *17,* 248–261.

Lotz, J. B. Das Phänomen der Einsamkeit im Lichte der personalen Anthropologie. In W. Bitter (Hrsg.), *Einsamkeit in medizinisch-psychologischer, theologischer und soziologischer Sicht.* Stuttgart, Germany: Klett, 1967.

Lynch, J. J. *The broken heart: The medical consequences of loneliness.* New York: Basic Books, 1977.

Mijuskovic, B. L. *Loneliness in philosophy, psychology and literature.* Assen: Van Gorcum Publishers, 1979.

Mokken, R. J. *A theory and procedure of scaling with applications in political research.* The Hague: Mouton, 1970.

Moustakas, C. E. *Loneliness*. Englewood-Cliffs, N.J.: Prentice-Hall, 1961.

Oppen, D. van. Einsamkeit als last und bedürfnis. In W. Bitter (Hrsg.), *Einsamkeit*. Stuttgart, Germany: Klett, 1967.

Overall, J. E., & Klett, J. C. *Applied multivariate statistics*. New York: McGraw-Hill, 1972.

Parpert, F. *Philosophie der einsamkeit*. München-Basel: Reinhardt, 1955.

Rooijen, L. van. Widows' bereavement: Stress and depression after one-and-a-half years. In I. G. Sarason & C. D. Spielberger (Eds.), *Stress and anxiety* (Vol. 6). Washington, D. C.: Hemisphere, 1979.

Tews, H. P. *Soziologie des alterns*. Heidelberg: Quelle & Meyer, 1974.

Weiss, R. S. *Loneliness: The experience of emotional and social isolation*. Cambridge, Mass.: MIT Press, 1973.

Witzleben, H. D. von. On loneliness. *Psychiatry*, 1958, *21*, 37–43.

Wood, M. *Paths of loneliness: The individual isolated in modern society*. New York: Columbia University Press, 1953.

Zimmermann, J. G. *Über die Einsamkeit*. Troppau. 1785/1786.

PART THREE

Theoretical Approaches to Loneliness

Theories are an essential part of any science. They help to simplify and organize knowledge, to explain, and to predict. At their best, they lead to the solution of practical problems. Conceptual analysis guides research by indicating what questions to ask and what relationships among variables to expect.

The four chapters in this section deal with "theories" of loneliness. In Chapter 8, the editors review existing conceptual frameworks. These views are briefly summarized, compared, and evaluated. In Chapter 9, Peplau, Miceli, and Morasch present a cognitive perspective on loneliness. This view grew out of the attribution theory tradition within social psychology, and has generated a number of studies done at UCLA and elsewhere.

The last two chapters in this section are efforts to develop new perspectives for understanding loneliness. The chapter by Derlega and Margulis offers a privacy analysis. Derlega and Margulis maintain that we try to regulate the amount of information others know about us and to avoid invasions of our privacy. In a sense, loneliness is the opposite of invasion of privacy; loneliness occurs when others know too little about us. Thus many of the factors influencing privacy should also influence loneliness.

In Chapter 11, Flanders puts loneliness in a broader perspective, that of general systems theory. This view stresses the interrelated nature of different spheres of life. Flanders applies this model to loneliness. To illustrate how social system forces can influence loneliness, he discusses how television viewing and keeping stores open on Sunday affect social relations and loneliness.

In the past 50 years, there has been much speculation about the nature of loneliness. In Chapter 10, Derlega and Margulis raise an interesting issue: Have the existing viewpoints been actual theories or have they merely been rudimentary conceptual precursors of theories? Whatever one's answer to this question (we have ours; see Chapter 8), conceptual analyses are at the heart of research and efforts to understand loneliness. Thus it is crucial that conceptual development keep pace with the growth of empirical work on loneliness. Each benefits the other.

Chapter 8

Theoretical Approaches to Loneliness

Daniel Perlman and Letitia Anne Peplau

Over the years, many psychologists and sociologists have offered theoretical remarks on loneliness. For didactic purposes, we will classify these speculations into eight different categories: psychodynamic, phenomenological, existential-humanistic, sociological, interactionist, cognitive, privacy, and systems theory. The purpose of this chapter is to present, compare, and evaluate these theoretical approaches.

Naturally, there are many dimensions on which to compare explanations of loneliness. We will focus on three main issues. First, what is the nature of loneliness itself? Is it a normal or abnormal condition? A positive or a negative experience? Second, what are the causes of loneliness? Do they reside within the person or within the environment? Do they stem from contemporary or historical/developmental influences on behavior? Third, and perhaps somewhat less important, on what evidence (i.e., case histories, systematic research, etc.) or intellectual traditions was the theory formulated?

These comparative presentations must of course be offered for what they are: brief, broad characterizations. The views themselves are not necessarily mutually exclusive. For instance, as we will see, Sermat takes positions consistent with at least two different viewpoints. Nor are the members within each camp always in complete agreement. Furthermore, comparative analysis is made difficult by the fragmentary nature of most of the "theoretical" statements about loneliness. In many cases, proponents of a particular school of psychology have only written a short article on loneliness or touched on it as part of a more general statement of their views.

In the introduction to Chapter 10, Derlega and Margulis note three stages of concept development. In Stage 1, the importance of a concept is justified. In Stage 2, the concept is explored and attempts are made to demonstrate its similarities and differences from other phenomena. Only in Stage 3 do theories emerge. Such theories involve a set of concepts plus a series of logically compatible statements about how the constructs are related to one another. As Derlega and Margulis note, most speculation on loneliness has been at

Stages 1 and 2. Most models for understanding loneliness have been neither fully nor systematically articulated at the level of a true theory.

EIGHT APPROACHES TO LONELINESS

Psychodynamic Models

Although Freud himself did not write about loneliness, several others following in the psychodynamic tradition did (Burton, 1961; Ferreira, 1962; Fromm-Reichmann, 1959; Leiderman, 1980; H. Peplau, 1955; Rubins, 1964; Sullivan, 1953; and Zilboorg, 1938).

Zilboorg (1938) published what is probably the first psychological analysis of loneliness. He distinguished being lonesome from being lonely. Being lonesome is a "normal" and "transient state of mind" resulting from missing somebody specific. Loneliness is an overwhelming, persistent experience. No matter what one does, loneliness is an "inner worm" that gnaws at the heart.

According to Zilboorg, loneliness reflects basic traits of narcissism, megalomania, and hostility. The lonely person retains infantile feelings of personal omnipotence, is egocentric, and wants to show off before an audience in order to "show others up." "The lonely individual seldom fails to display an ill-disguised or open hatred" (Zilboorg, 1938, p. 40) directed either inward or outward toward others.

Zilboorg traced the origins of loneliness to the crib. The infant learns the joys of being loved and admired, plus the shock of being a small, weak creature having to wait for others to gratify its needs. Here, says Zilboorg (1938, p. 53), "we have the quintessence of what later becomes a narcissistic orientation . . . . Here [too] is the nucleus of hostility, hatred, and impotent aggression of the lonely."

Sullivan (1953) also saw the roots of adult loneliness in childhood. He postulated a driving need for human intimacy. This need first appears in the infant's desire for contact. In preadolescence, it takes the form of needing a chum, someone with whom to exchange intimate information. Youngsters who lack social skills because of faulty interaction with their parents during childhood are apt to have difficulty forming a chumship. This inability to satisfy the preadolescent need for intimacy can lead to fully-blown loneliness.

Fromm-Reichmann's (1959) article is probably the most widely cited, early paper on loneliness. She acknowledged Sullivan's contribution to her thinking, and agreed with his view that loneliness is an "exceedingly unpleasant and driving experience." Based on her work with schizophrenics, Fromm-Reichmann (p. 3) claimed that loneliness is an extreme state: "The kind of loneliness I am discussing is nonconstructive . . . [and it] leads ultimately to the development of psychotic states. It renders people . . . emotionally paralyzed and helpless." Like Sullivan and Zilboorg, Fromm-Reichmann also traced the origins of loneliness to childhood experiences. In particular, she noted the harmful consequences of "premature weaning from mothering tenderness."

In terms of our three comparative concerns, the position of psychodynamic theorists is clear. Their observations on loneliness stemmed largely from their work in clinical settings. Perhaps because of this, they are prone to see loneliness as pathological. Probably more so than any other group, psychodynamically oriented theorists attribute loneliness to early influences. While these early experiences may have been interpersonal in nature, the focus of this tradition is on how factors within the individual (i.e., traits and intrapsychic conflicts) lead to loneliness.

Rogers' Phenomenological Perspective

Carl Rogers, who developed client-centered therapy, is the most noted proponent of a phenomenological perspective (see also Whitehorn, 1961). Rogers twice addressed the issue of loneliness (1961, 1970/1973), and his analysis reflects his "self theory" of personality. Rogers assumes that society pressures the individual to act in restricted, socially approved ways. This leads to a discrepancy between one's true inner self and the self manifested to others. Merely performing society's roles, no matter how adequately done, leads to an empty existence.

Loneliness occurs when individuals, having dropped their defenses to get in touch with their inner selves, nonetheless expect rejection from others. As expressed by Rogers (1970/1973, p. 119):

Loneliness . . . . is sharpest and most poignant in the individual who has, for one reason or another, found himself standing, without some of his customary defences, a vulnerable, frightened, lonely but *real* self, sure of rejection in a judgmental world.

According to Rogers (1970/1973, p. 121), the belief that their real selves are unlovable "keeps people locked in their loneliness." Fear of rejection leads people to persist in their social facades and so to continue feeling empty.

Based on such views, others (Moore, 1976) have derived the hypothesis that a discrepancy between one's actual and idealized self should result in loneliness. Eddy's (1961) doctoral dissertation supported this prediction.

Like the psychodynamically oriented theorists, Rogers' analysis of loneliness stems from his work with clinical clients. Rogers views loneliness as a manifestation of poor adjustment. For him, the cause of loneliness lies within the individual, in a phenomenological discrepancy in one's self-concept. Rogers differs from psychodynamic theorists in that he does not give much credence to childhood influences. Instead, current forces produce the experience.

The Existential Approach

Existentialists take as their starting point the "fact" that humans are ultimately alone. No one else can experience our thoughts and feelings; separateness is an essential condition of our existence. Those who accept this view often focus on the question of how people can live with their loneliness.

The leading spokesperson for this perspective has been Moustakas (1961, 1972), author of several popular books (see also Von Witzleben, 1958). Moustakas emphasizes the importance of distinguishing between loneliness anxiety and true loneliness. Loneliness anxiety is a system of defense mechanisms that distracts people from dealing with crucial life questions and that motivates them constantly to seek activity with others. True loneliness stems from the reality of being alone and of facing life's ultimate experiences (i.e., birth, death, change, tragedy) alone. From Moustakas' viewpoint, true loneliness can be a creative force:

> Every real experience of loneliness involves a confrontation or an encounter with oneself . . . The encounter . . . is a joyous experience . . . Both the encounter and the confrontation are ways of advancing life and coming alive in a relatively stagnant world; they are ways of breaking out of uniform cycles of behavior. (Moustakas, 1972, pp. 20–21)

Existentialists thus encourage people to overcome their fear of loneliness and learn to use loneliness positively.

Like the other theorists presented so far, Moustakas works with clinical clients. Other proponents of this position have of course derived their views largely from philosophical considerations. Unlike most theorists, Moustakas has a positive view of loneliness. Although he does not deny that it can be painful, he sees it as a productive, creative condition. Existentialists do not seek the causal roots of loneliness in the usual sense. They are not especially interested in the factors that increase or decrease the likelihood of loneliness; for them it is a given in human existence.

Sociological Explanations

Bowman (1955), Riesman (see Riesman, Glazer, & Denney, 1961), and Slater (1976) are representatives of the sociological approach to loneliness. In a short article, Bowman hypothesized three social forces leading to increased loneliness in contemporary society: (1) a decline in primary group relations; (2) an increase in family mobility; and (3) an increase in social mobility. Reisman and Slater have each linked their analysis of loneliness to the study of the American character and how society fails to meet its members' needs.

Riesman and his associates claimed that Americans have become "other-directed." Not only do other-directed individuals want to be liked, they also conform and continually monitor their interpersonal environment to determine how they should behave. Other-directed people are cut off from their inner selves, their feelings, and their aspirations. (Here, of course, Riesman's analysis complements Rogers'.) These traits are shaped by parents, teachers, and the mass media. The result, for an other-directed person, is a diffuse anxiety and an overconcern with peer popularity that is never really satisfied. As implied in the title of Riesman's book, the members of our other-directed society form "the lonely crowd."

For Slater (1976), America's problem is not other-direction but rather individualism. Slater believes we all have a desire for community, engagement, and dependence. We want to trust and cooperate with others, "to show responsibility for the control of one's impulses and the directions of one's life" (p. 9). However, these basic needs for community, engagement, and dependence are thwarted in American society because of a commitment to individualism, the belief that everyone should pursue his or her own destiny. The result is loneliness. Slater (1976, p. 34) argues:

Individualism is rooted in the attempt to deny the reality of human inter-dependence. One of the major goals of technology in America is to "free" us from the necessity of relating to, submitting to, depending upon, or controlling other people. Unfortunately, the more we have succeeded in doing this, the more we have felt disconnected, bored, [and] lonely.

Rather than classifying loneliness as a normal or abnormal behavior, it can be said that Riesman and Slater see loneliness as normative—a statistically common attribute of the population. While they discuss loneliness as a part of the American character, they explain this modal personality quality as the product of social forces. Thus for these sociologists the cause of loneliness is essentially outside the individual. In terms of time, these theories emphasize socialization (a historical type cause), but many of the forces (i.e., mass media effects) that contribute to socialization are in continuous, current operation. And of course Bowman, like many other sociologists, stresses events that happen in adulthood, such as divorce. In formulating their views, Reisman and Slater have relied on literature, social indicators, and the mass media as sources of their speculations.

The Interactionist View

Weiss (1973) is the leading spokesperson for the interactionist approach. His explanation of loneliness can be classified as interactionist for two reasons. First, he emphasizes that loneliness is not solely a function of personality factors, nor of situational factors. Instead loneliness is the product of their combined (or interactive) effect. (In this regard, Weiss's view is similar to Sermat's, 1975.) Second, Weiss (1973) has written on the pro-visions of social relationships—such things as attachment, guidance, and a sense of worth. Implicit in such an analysis is the view that loneliness results when one's social interactions are deficient in supplying crucial social requirements.

As noted elsewhere in this volume, Weiss postulated two types of loneli-ness, which he believes have different antecedents and different affective responses. Emotional loneliness results from the absence of a close, intimate attachment such as a lover or a spouse. An emotionally lonely person should feel something akin to the separation anxiety of a child: anxiety, restlessness, and emptiness. Social loneliness is a response to the absence of meaningful friendships or a sense of a community. A socially lonely person experiences boredom and feelings of being socially marginal.

Weiss has run seminars for the widowed and recently separated (see Chapter 21). Presumably, out of his efforts to help participants in these seminars, he has derived many of his insights. He is concerned with "ordinary" loneliness, a condition experienced by many if not most people during their lives. Thus he sees loneliness as a normal reaction. Obviously he considers both internal (characterological) and external (situational) causes of loneliness. However, he is clear that "of the two approaches, the situational would seem to have the greater attraction at this point" (Weiss, 1973, pp. 73–74). This being the case, he is emphasizing current conditions as the key factors in producing loneliness. With regard to causes, it is interesting to note that Weiss (see Chapter 5) entertains the possibility that even instinct plays a part in loneliness.

The Cognitive Approach

Peplau and her colleagues (see Chapter 9) have been leading advocates of a cognitive approach to loneliness. The most salient aspect of this approach is its emphasis on cognition as a mediating factor between deficits in sociability and the experience of loneliness. In articulating the role played by cognition, Peplau draws on attribution theory. She discusses, for example, how the perceived causes of one's loneliness can influence the intensity of the experience and the perceived likelihood of the loneliness persisting over time.

As indicated in Chapter 1, cognitive approaches propose that loneliness occurs when the individual perceives a discrepancy between two factors, the person's desired and achieved levels of social contact. In this regard, Peplau's view is akin to Sermat's (1978). This theme has been helpful in organizing the literature on loneliness and explaining findings that would otherwise be paradoxical (Perlman & Peplau, 1981).

Like Weiss, Peplau has been concerned with loneliness among "normal" populations. Empirical evidence from surveys and experiments has played an important role in Peplau's conceptual formulations. In her search for the causes of loneliness, Peplau has cast a broad net: she has examined both characterological and situational factors as well as both historical and current influences. Cognitive factors, the unique aspect of her theorizing, are processes within the individual operating in a contemporaneous manner.

A Privacy Approach

In Chapter 10, Derlega and Margulis use privacy and self-disclosure concepts as a way of understanding loneliness. Derlega and Margulis assume, somewhat akin to Weiss, that social relationships help the individual achieve various goals. Loneliness is caused by the absence of an appropriate social partner who could assist in achieving these goals. Loneliness is apt to occur when one's interpersonal relationships lack the privacy needed for honest communication.

Underlying the privacy approach is an assumption that the individual seeks to maintain an equilibrium between desired and achieved levels of social contact. Derlega and Margulis discuss how one's social networks, expectations, and personality can influence this balance.

The main source of Derlega and Margulis' ideas is previous theory rather than either clinical work or research. Implicitly they discuss loneliness as a normal experience encountered by a broad cross-section of society. Their attention to the continuous process of balancing desired and achieved levels of contact places emphasis on the contemporary determinants of loneliness. However, their analysis leaves room for the impact of past influences. They consider factors within both the individual and environmental as leading to loneliness.

General Systems Theory

Flanders, in Chapter 11 of this volume, articulates a general systems approach to loneliness. The basic assumption of this theory is that the behavior of living organisms reflects the intermeshed influence of several levels operating simultaneously as a system. The levels range from the cellular to the international. In this view loneliness is a feedback mechanism for helping the individual or society maintain a steady, optimal level of human contact.

Flanders' speculations on loneliness do not stem from an empirical source; instead they reflect an extension of Miller's systems theory. Flanders sees loneliness as potentially painful, but believes it is also a useful feedback mechanism that can contribute to the individual's or the society's well-being. Systems theory subsumes both individual and situational causes of behavior. The time span needed for certain variables to have their impact may be fairly long. Yet systems theory is essentially a model in which the causes of behavior are assigned to ongoing systems dynamics.

A Comparative Summary

Table 8.1 presents a summary of our comparisons among the eight theories. The majority of the theoretical speculation on loneliness has been tied to clinical work or stemmed from existing theory. Most commentators see loneliness as an aversive, unpleasant experience; yet only a minority of observers discuss loneliness as a pathological response. For most, it is a phenomenon experienced by a broad cross-section of the population. Only advocates of the psychodynamic tradition exclusively stress the childhood antecedents of loneliness. Most theoretical analyses emphasize the role of current factors in causing loneliness.

Table 8.1. Eight Approaches to Loneliness: A Comparative Summary [a]

	Psycho-dynamic	Phenome-nological	Existential	Socio-logical	Interac-tionist	Cognitive	Privacy	Systems
Views tied to	Clinical work	Clinical work	Clinical work	Social analysis	Clinical work	Research	Theory	Theory
Nature of loneliness								
Positive	No	No	Yes	No	No	No	No	Yes
Normal or pathological	Patho-logical	Patho-logical	Universal	Normative	Normal	Normal	Normal	Normal
Causes								
Within the person or the situation	Person	Person	Human condition	Society	Both	Both	Both	Both
Historical and childhood vs. current	Child-hood	Current	Perpetual	Both	Current	Current	Current	Current

[a] As a summary of trends and emphases, this table reflects judgments made by the present authors as well as a simplification of nuances and details.

CRITERIA FOR EVALUATING CONCEPTUALIZATIONS

Several criteria are commonly used for evaluating theories. These include parsimony, internal logical consistency, empirical support, breadth, and the like. At the present time, two criteria seem especially important to us, and two others warrant comment. Our two key criteria are completeness and stimulation of research. The other two are empirical support and practical usefulness.

Obviously the criteria one uses to evaluate theories influence the relative standing of different approaches. As social psychologists, we are perhaps more concerned than clinicians or philosophers with empirical research. We have also participated in the efforts to offer an adequate conceptualization of loneliness. Thus, in deciding how to evaluate theories, there may be a tendency on our part to select criteria favorable to our own perspective.

Completeness

As noted earlier, most perspectives on loneliness are little more than short articles or fragmentary observations. Riesman and Slater used the concept in the titles of their books; yet for them, loneliness is an implied aspect of American society rather than the focal point of their analysis. The chapters in this book by Derlega and Margulis and by Flanders show the usefulness of privacy and systems concepts. Yet these chapters represent initial efforts rather than fully developed analyses. Moustakas has written at length in popular books. But his concerns have been more with justifying and explaining the concept than systematically developing theoretical propositions.

In our opinion, the most developed treatments of loneliness are offered by psychodynamic theorists, Weiss and cognitive theorists. A number of psychodynamically oriented psychologists have written on loneliness, and this by itself has contributed to the more elaborate nature of their views. Weiss' 1973 volume is primarily at what we called Stage 2 conceptual development. He explores the concept of loneliness and its varieties. But he also discusses the causes of loneliness. Cognitive theorists such as Peplau and her associates have published extensively on loneliness; some of their writing achieves Stage 3 conceptualizing. In other words, they identify constructs and articulate the relationships among these factors.

Research Stimulation and Support

None of the conceptual viewpoints has stimulated a great deal of research. Obviously it is premature to evaluate the privacy and systems approaches on this criterion. The existential view maintains that loneliness is a fact of the human condition. It is not a predictive model in the usual sense, and as such, is unlikely to serve as the basis for much research.

Although research could be done to support their views, neither Riesman nor Slater have devoted their primary energies to empirical work. Demographic and sociological variables have been included in numerous research studies, but this has been done in an ad hoc basis. It is a source of mild embarrassment (but not a devastating blow) to sociologists that Rubenstein and Shaver (1980) failed to find a relationship between social mobility and loneliness.

Several theories have stimulated a modest amount of research. Weiss's notions of two kinds of loneliness and his provisions have been used in research by Rubenstein and Shaver (Chapter 13) and by Cutrona (Chapter 18). Rogers' position has stimulated several dissertation projects (see Eddy, 1961; Moore, 1976; Sisenwein, 1964) including work to show that a discrepancy between one's real and ideal self is associated with loneliness. Some evidence bearing on the psychodynamic viewpoint has emerged. For instance, Moore (1972) tested the predicted relationship between hostility and loneliness. But despite the longer history of the psychodynamic viewpoint, it has not led directly to programmatic efforts. While the body of evidence testing the interactionist, psychodynamic, and phenomenological viewpoints is small, the results have generally been consistent with theoretical expectations.

The cognitive approach stands out in terms of generating research. It has served as the basis for the number of studies (see Chapters 9 and 18). These have been of a programmatic nature and have demonstrated the important influence that attributions, perceived control, and the like have on loneliness.

Practical Usefulness

Theories of loneliness have had relatively little direct payoff for the treatment of loneliness (see Chapter 21). In seeing loneliness as inevitable or positive, existentialists and systems theorists are less concerned with alleviating it. Sociologists have not been concerned with the treatment of individual clients, although their views do have implications for the formulation of social policies. Similarly, Peplau's theorizing and research has implications for treatment, but this has not been the UCLA group's primary concern.

Several views of loneliness have been formulated by clinical practitioners. Naturally, these writers have their generally preferred approaches to therapy. Rogers has *not* spelled out how client-centered therapy should be specially applied to the problem of loneliness. Weiss has developed seminars for the separated, but the focus of these groups is only partially on loneliness. Psychodynamically oriented psychologists (see Chapter 21) have perhaps done the most to address the issue of how to treat loneliness.

With regard to treatment, we should call attention to Young's work (see Chapter 22). He draws on reinforcement theory and Beck's cognitive behavior therapy model. We have not treated Young's writing as a conceptual perspective because theory development was not Young's primary goal. However, his analysis contains the seeds of an important reinforcement analysis of loneliness, and in the present context, we would note he has developed a carefully articulated, theoretically grounded approach to treating lonely clients.

An Evaluative Summary

Using an absolute standard, one can identify faults in all the existing explanations of loneliness. Indeed these so-called "theories" aren't really theories in the most sophisticated sense of the term. Yet given the field's youthful stage of development, we would not be too critical. The existing speculations have without question justified the importance of the construct and helped to illuminate the phenomenon. Thus they have accomplished the goals of Stage 1 and 2 conceptualization.

Existing viewpoints have not yet stimulated a large, programmatic body of research nor resulted in a "cure" for loneliness, yet they have made contributions toward both. Certainly we are today in a better position to help alleviate loneliness than we were 50 years ago when Zilboorg wrote his first article.

In most cases existing formulations can be further elaborated and their potential more fully realized in the years ahead. As fairly recent statements, which reflect current trends in psychological thinking, we anticipate that the interactionist and cognitive models (or variations thereon) are apt to play a seminal role in guiding loneliness research in the early 1980s. We think reinforcement ideas could also play a more important role. Whatever perspectives become dominant, we hope this decade will see a shift from Stage 2 to Stage 3 conceptualizations: from exploring the nature of loneliness per se to developing more systematic sets of propositions about its relationships with other variables.

REFERENCES

Bowman, C. C. Loneliness and social change. *American Journal of Psychiatry,* 1955, *112,* 194–198.

Burton, A. On the nature of loneliness. *American Journal of Psychoanalysis,* 1961, *21,* 34–39.

Eddy, P. D. *Loneliness: A discrepancy with the phenomenological self.* Unpublished doctoral dissertation, Adelphi College, 1961.

Ferreira, A. J. Loneliness and psychopathology. *American Journal of Psychoanalysis,* 1962, *22,* 201–207.

Fromm-Reichmann, F. Loneliness. *Psychiatry,* 1959, *22,* 1–15.

Leiderman, P.H. Loneliness: A psychodynamic interpretation. In J. Hartog, J. R. Audy, & Y. A. Cohen (Eds.), *The anatomy of loneliness.* New York: International Universities Press, 1980.

Moore, J. A. *Loneliness: Personality, self-discrepancy and demographic variables.* Unpublished doctoral dissertation. York University, 1972.

Moore, J. A. Loneliness: Self-discrepancy and sociological variables. *Canadian Counsellor,* 1976, *10,* 133–135.

Moustakas, C. E. *Loneliness.* New York: Prentice-Hall, 1961.

Moustakas, C. E. *Loneliness and love.* Englewood Cliffs, N.J.: Prentice-Hall, 1972.

Peplau, H. E. Loneliness. *American Journal of Nursing,* 1955, *55,* 1476–1481.

Perlman, D., & Peplau, L. A. Toward a social psychology of loneliness. In S. W. Duck & R. Gilmour (Eds.), *Personal relationships: 3. Personal relationships in disorder.* London: Academic Press, 1981.

Riesman, D., Glazer, N., & Denney, R. *The lonely crowd: A study of the changing American character.* New Haven: Yale University Press, 1961.

Rogers, C. R. The loneliness of contemporary man as seen in "The case of Ellen West." *Annuals of Psychotherapy,* 1961, *2,* 22–27.

Rogers, C. R. The lonely person—and his experiences in an encounter group. In *Carl Rogers on encounter groups.* New York: Harper & Row, 1973 (Originally published, 1970).

Rubenstein, C. M., & Shaver, P. Loneliness in two northeastern cities. In J. Hartog, J. R. Audy, & Y. A. Cohen (Eds.), *The anatomy of loneliness.* New York: International Universities Press, 1980.

Rubins, J. L. On the psychopathology of loneliness. *American Journal of Psychoanalysis,* 1964, *24,* 153–166.

Sermat, V. *Loneliness and social isolation.* Unpublished manuscript, York University, Downsview, Canada, 1975.

Sermat, V. Sources of loneliness. *Essence,* 1978, *2,* 271–276.

Sisenwein, R. J. *Loneliness and the individual as viewed by himself and others.* Unpublished doctoral dissertation, Columbia University, 1964.

Slater, P. *The pursuit of loneliness.* Boston: Beacon Press, 1976.

Sullivan, H. S. *The interpersonal theory of psychiatry.* New York: Norton, 1953.

Von Witzleben, H. D. On loneliness. *Psychiatry,* 1958, *21,* 37–43.

Weiss, R. S. *Loneliness: The experience of emotional and social isolation.* Cambridge, Mass.: MIT Press, 1973.

Whitehorn, J.C. On loneliness and the incongruous self image. *Annuals of Psychotherapy,* 1961, *2,* 15–17.

Zilboorg, C. Loneliness. *Atlantic Monthly,* January 1938, pp. 45–54.

Chapter 9

Loneliness and Self-Evaluation

Letitia Anne Peplau, Maria Miceli, and Bruce Morasch

Emotional isolation is hard for anyone to endure; it becomes a calamity, however, if it coincides with apprehensions and uncertainties about one's self.

KAREN HORNEY, 1937, p. 286

A basic feature of human life is the desire to understand ourselves and to construct meaningful accounts of our experiences. Self-evaluation—the process of learning about and judging ourselves—is an important element in the experience of loneliness.

This chapter considers three ways in which self-evaluation processes influence loneliness. We look first at how people label themselves as lonely, and consider cognitive discrepancy models of loneliness. Such models emphasize that loneliness occurs when people perceive that their social relations are deficient in some important way. We next examine people's causal attributions for loneliness. The explanations people construct for their loneliness can influence the feelings and behaviors that accompany the experience of loneliness. Finally, we consider the reciprocal relationship of loneliness and self-esteem. Evidence suggests that low self-esteem puts people at risk for loneliness. Further, since social relations are a core component of our self-conception, persistent loneliness can lead to feelings of worthlessness and lowered self-esteem. A central theme in this chapter is that cognitive processes color the experience of loneliness, shaping our feelings and guiding our actions.

COGNITIVE APPRAISAL: PERCEIVING AND LABELING LONELINESS

It is often difficult to label subjective experiences accurately (Gordon, 1981; Pennebaker, 1980), to decide if one is really lonely, or to distinguish lone-

This chapter has benefited from the helpful comments of Steven Gordon, Daniel Perlman, and Karen Rook. The authors express their gratitude to Patricia Linton for her help in preparing this manuscript.

liness from other psychological states. Labeling ourself as lonely results from an inferential process by which we recognize or give meaning to our unique, personal experiences, and map them onto a more general category or concept.

The Self-Diagnosis of Loneliness

In arriving at the conclusion, "I am lonely," people use affective, behavioral, and cognitive cues. The affective signs of loneliness are often diffuse. Loneliness is a distressing emotional experience; severely lonely people are profoundly unhappy. It is unlikely, however, that affective cues alone are sufficient to identify an unpleasant experience as loneliness. There is no unique set of emotions associated with loneliness. Rubenstein and Shaver (Chapter 13), for example, identified four distinct clusters of feelings that can accompany loneliness. Although the experience of negative affect may alert people that "something is wrong" in their life, it will not invariably lead to a self-diagnosis of being lonely, rather than being depressed, overworked, or physically ill.

Behavioral cues, like affective ones, contribute to a self-diagnosis of loneliness, but are probably not sufficient for such a diagnosis. People may use a variety of behavioral cues to identify loneliness, including low levels of social contact, disruptions in established relationships, or unsatisfying patterns of social interaction. Spending time alone is not invariably associated with loneliness, however; people can be happy in solitude. But when people are unhappy because they are too often alone, then loneliness may be a plausible diagnosis.

It is unlikely that people label themselves as lonely unless cognitive cues are also present. Cognitive indicators of loneliness probably revolve around the theme of wanting a type of social relation that is currently lacking (see also Horowitz, French, & Anderson, Chapter 12). Common cognitions include the desire for more frequent or more intimate interaction, and the belief that improved social relations would alleviate one's distress.

People identify the experience of loneliness on the basis of a cluster of feelings, behaviors, and thoughts—not from a single defining feature. Horowitz and his associates refer to this set of characteristics as a "prototype" of the lonely person. Horowitz et al. have identified the major elements of the loneliness prototype in college students. They found much commonality in the meaning college students attach to loneliness, but also important individual variations. Not everyone uses the concept of loneliness in precisely the same way.

The meaning of loneliness may differ across social groups, life stages, historical periods, and cultural boundaries. An illustration of such variations comes from anthropological reports of the use of the term loneliness in different cultures. According to Levy's (1973) ethnography of the Tahitians, there exist "no . . . terms for loneliness in the sense of being depressed or sad because of the lack of friends, companionship, and so on" (p. 306). Levy noted that the absence of a specific word for loneliness would not necessarily prevent people from expressing the concept in other terms. Nonetheless, themes of loneliness were rare in his interviews. In contrast, Briggs (1970) described Eskimos as having several different words for loneliness. "Hujuujaq" is the most general term, meaning "to be unhappy because of the absence of other people." "Pai" refers more specifically to "being or feeling left behind; to miss a person who has gone." Finally, "tumak" indicates being "silent and withdrawn" in unhappiness, especially because of the absence of other people. The way in which linguistic categories and folk beliefs affect the individual's experience of loneliness is an important area for further investigation.

Cognitive Discrepancy Models of Loneliness

The importance of cognitive processes in the experience of loneliness has been emphasized in *cognitive discrepancy models*. While not denying that loneliness has affective and behavioral elements, cognitive models focus on subjective perceptions and standards. Cognitive discrepancy models define loneliness as a response to the perception that one's social relations fail to measure up to some internal yardstick (de Jong-Gierveld, 1978; Derlega & Margulis, Chapter 10; Lopata, 1969; Perlman & Peplau, 1981). Loneliness is affected not only by the person's actual social ties, but also by the person's desired pattern or standard for social relations. A discrepancy model thus examines loneliness from the "insider's" perspective, focusing on how the lonely person perceives and evaluates her or his social life, not on how outside observers might assess it. Although two people may have "objectively" similar patterns of social relations, one may feel lonely, and the other content. Loneliness can be heightened or reduced by changes in a person's subjective standards for relationships. For example, a person whose relationships remain constant might nonetheless start to feel lonely if her or his standards are raised.

Loneliness theorists have described relationship standards in quite general terms. For example, Peplau and Perlman (1979) referred to peoples' "desired or preferred" patterns of social relations. Gordon (1976) discussed a sense of being deprived of "certain expected human relationships." It is useful to take a closer look at how people assess the adequacy of their social relations and decide that they are lonely.

Personal Standards for Relationships

People are motivated to evaluate themselves, their experiences, and their relationships (Festinger, 1954; Pettigrew, 1967; Thibaut & Kelley, 1959). Subjective assessments of the quantity and quality of interpersonal ties are comparative, and involve judging oneself against a variety of standards. Such standards are not always explicit or consciously articulated. But they are reflected in common complaints of lonely people: "I wish I had more friends" or "No one really understands me."

Subjective standards for relationships are derived in two ways. First, *past experience* leads us to develop images of the kinds of social interactions and relationships that make us feel satisfied and happy, and those that do not. We learn about our social needs and how they can be adequately met. According to Thibaut and Kelley (1959):

> As a result of many experiences in many relationships, the person develops a general and relatively constant expectation of the satisfaction he can achieve in association with others—a generalized conception of his worth in interpersonal relationships. (p. 97)

We compare our social relations to this generalized standard or "comparison level," feeling unhappy if our current social life is worse than it used to be.

The importance of such standards is illustrated by several studies. For example, Cutrona and Peplau (1979; Chapter 18) asked college students to evaluate their current friendships and dating relationships, and to compare them to the relationships they had had in high school. The perception that present relationships were worse than previous ones was associated with current social dissatisfaction and loneliness. Similarly, Lowenthal and Robinson (1976) reported that for old people, "the concept of the former self" is a major reference point for evaluating current experiences (see also Townsend, 1957).

Second, *social comparisons* often influence our self-evaluations (see theoretical reviews by Pettigrew, 1967; Suls & Miller, 1977). We assess our interpersonal relations in comparison to those of other people. For example, Cutrona and Peplau (1979, Chapter 18) found that students' perception that their own relationships were worse than those of peers was significantly linked to social dissatisfaction and loneliness.

An important unresolved question in social comparison theory concerns how people select reference groups or standards. In the interpersonal domain, there has been some speculation about this matter, but little empirical research. For example, Townsend (1957) proposed that old people can experience different types of social isolation based on different comparisons: peer-contrasted isolation (comparison to age mates), generation-contrasted isolation (comparison to younger people), and preceding-cohort isolation (comparison to earlier generations of old people). Unfortunately, we have little information about the sorts of social comparisons that actually influence social dissatisfaction and loneliness.

Personal standards for social relations are not fixed, but can change over time. Many factors might cause such changes. First, there may be age-related development changes in a person's desires for social relations. Gail Sheehy (1976) noted that for many professionally successful people, "mid-life may be a time to relax . . . and put more . . . into cultivating friendships, being a companion" (p. 415). Second, experiences such as psychotherapy or consciousness-raising groups can lead individuals to reassess the quality of their social relations and to set new relationship goals. Third, processes of adaptation may also be at work, so that a person's current pattern of social relations influences his or her relationship standards. The person whose social life is extremely full and rewarding may come to expect high levels of satisfaction from relationships. Conversely, Weiss (1973) has suggested that when individuals are lonely for a long time, they might "change their standards for appraising their situations and their feelings, and, in particular, that standards might shrink to conform more closely to the shape of a bleak reality" (p. 228). These are just a few of the factors that can lead to changes in personal standards for social relations.

A useful direction for future loneliness research is to examine more closely the evaluative standards that people use in judging social relations. Research on judgments of psychological well-being (Campbell, Converse, & Rodgers, 1976) provides a helpful resource. For example, Andrews and Withey (1976) identified eight different "models for evaluation" that may influence assessments of personal happiness. They distinguished, for instance, an "ideal" standard versus a minimally "good enough" standard versus a standard of temporal improvement. Other standards might emphasize personal goals or aspirations for relationships, predictive experiences about the social relations a person is likely to have, or normative expectations about the social ties a person "should" have. At present there are no clear empirical or theoretical grounds for deciding how best to conceptualize the personal standards for social relations that affect loneliness. Andrews and Withey suggested that different standards may operate for different people or at different times, and that a comprehensive understanding of the dynamics of evaluation must await extensive basic research. An adequate cognitive analysis of loneliness will require a more precise specification of the nature of personal standards for social relations.

Implications for Helping the Lonely

What are the implications of a cognitive discrepancy model for helping the lonely? If loneliness occurs when people want more or better social relationships than they have, then it might seem that a sensible way to reduce loneliness is simply to lower one's personal standards. We urge caution in adopting such a strategy. For many people, the decision to lower one's standards might in itself be seen as an admission of failure and inadequacy.

It does seem useful for lonely people to scrutinize carefully their expectations and goals for social relationships. Unrealistic standards about friendship or marriage may create unnecessary difficulties (Lederer & Jackson, 1968). Zimbardo's (1977) advice to shy people may be equally applicable to the lonely: be careful in choosing models for comparison. In his words:

Some people are inappropriate comparison targets because they are uniquely gifted with looks or with brains, or with a desirable physique or other inherited qualities. I'd like to look like Robert Redford, think like Einstein, talk like Richard Burton, and write as prolifically and as well as Isaac Asimov. Ideals can be emulated, but should not be the established measures of success, status, or accomplishment. (p. 154)

Lonely people may do well to examine carefully their personal standards for relationships.

Loneliness may increase people's tendency to develop inaccurate or distorted standards for social relationships. Fearing that public comparisons would expose their failings, lonely people may conceal their feelings of dissatisfaction from others and avoid discussions about social matters (cf. Brickman & Bulman, 1977). As a result, lonely people may never learn about social problems experienced by their peers and so may erroneously assume that everyone else has a trouble-free social life. Further, lonely people may rely heavily on the media for social comparison standards, a source likely to foster unrealistic expectations for social relations.

Cognitive reassessment is not a foolproof remedy for loneliness. Many lonely people have standards for social relations that are "reasonable"—arising from basic social needs and consistent with their own past experience and with cultural norms. Not surprisingly, few of the college students we studied (see Chapter 21, Table 21.3) said that they coped with loneliness by lowering their goals for social relationships. For many people, overcoming loneliness requires improving social relationships, not changing subjective standards.

CAUSAL ATTRIBUTIONS FOR LONELINESS

The judgment that our social life is inadequate and that we are suffering from loneliness is seldom the end point in self-evaluation. Lonely people also seek to explain the causes of their plight. Discovering the reasons for one's loneliness helps make sense out of a distressing situation and is a first step toward alleviating the problem. A particularly important issue for lonely people may be self-blame—is the loneliness my own fault?

Personal Accounts of Loneliness

People attempt to construct an organized account of their loneliness, not merely a listing of possible reasons (cf. Schank & Abelson, 1977). This point is illustrated in Weiss's (1975) discussion of accounts of marital separation:

The account is of major psychological importance to the separated, not only because it settles the issue of who was responsible for what, but also because it imposes on the confused marital events . . . a plot structure with a beginning, middle and end, and so organizes the events in a conceptually manageable unity. (p. 15)

In analogous fashion, lonely people attempt to construct an organized explanation of their unsatisfactory social life.

Personal accounts of loneliness include three interrelated but distinct elements. First, lonely people can usually point to a *precipitating* event that led to the onset of their loneliness, such as the end of a love relationship. Second, in trying to explain why their loneliness persists over time and why they are unable to form satisfying social bonds, people explore the *maintaining causes* of their loneliness. These typically concern characteristics of the self (e.g., being too shy) or of the situation (e.g., being in a setting where it is hard to meet new people). Finally, lonely people typically have some idea of the sorts of changes in their social relations that would alleviate their loneliness. These *anticipated solutions* might include making new friends or developing greater intimacy in an existing relationship. The focus of research on attributions for loneliness has been on people's explanations for the maintaining causes of their loneliness.

Attributions for loneliness are not necessarily precise. People may be genuinely puzzled or confused about the reasons for their distress. And they may consider a number of casual factors. Initial attributions may lead to informal hypothesis testing behavior (cf. Wortman & Dintzner, 1978). For example, speculating that loneliness is due to one's appearance might lead to a new diet or hairstyle. If these changes make no difference, then the person may consider other causal attributions more plausible (Kelley, 1971). Thus explanations for loneliness may change with the passage of time.

Attributional analyses of loneliness (Anderson, 1980; Bragg, 1979; Peplau, Russell, & Heim, 1979) have been based largely on the theoretical work of Weiner and his associates (e.g., Weiner, 1974; Weiner, in press; Weiner, Russell, & Lerman, 1978). Weiner has demonstrated that causal attributions can be classified along two primary dimensions: locus of causality (internal or personal versus external or situational) and stability (constant versus changeable over time). More recently, Weiner has proposed the addition of a third dimension of controllability, concerning whether the person is believed to have control over their behavior or not.

Several studies conducted at UCLA (reviewed in Peplau et al., 1979) have demonstrated the applicability of Weiner's model to loneliness. For example, Michela, Peplau, and Weeks (1981) used multidimensional scaling to examine students' perceptions of common causes of loneliness. Results indicated that dimensions of internality and stability were salient in lay conceptions of the causes of loneliness. For instance, lack of effort was seen as an internal, unstable cause of loneliness; being physically unattractive as an internal, stable cause; and lack of opportunities as an external, unstable cause. Controllability did not emerge as a third dimension; rather, only causes such as effort that were both internal and unstable were seen as controllable. Available evidence suggests that people conceptualize the causes of loneliness on the basis of whether they reflect something about the self versus the setting, and whether they are relatively permanent or changeable.

The Consequences of Causal Attributions

Attributions for loneliness can have important implications for a person's future expectancies, emotions and behavior.

Loneliness is often depicted as accompanied by pessimism and hopelessness (low future expectancy). Fromm-Reichmann (1959) suggested that severe loneliness is characterized by "paralyzing hopelessness and unutterable futility" (p. 7). Attribution theory predicts that stable explanations for failure should lead to lower expectancies for future performance. At least one study (Michela, Peplau, & Weeks, 1981) supported this prediction for loneliness. Believing that loneliness was due to unchangeable features of the self or the situation was linked to pessimism and hopelessness.

Loneliness can be accompanied by a variety of emotions. One prediction from attribution theory is that depression should accompany attributions that are internal and stable. Preliminary support has been found for this idea (Peplau et al., 1979). For example, Bragg (1979) reported that among lonely college students, more severe depression was associated with attributing loneliness to one's physical appearance, personality, and fear of rejection.

Finally, causal attributions can influence the behavior and coping responses of lonely individuals. Anderson (1980; Chapter 12) provided evidence of this effect. He found that lonely college students tended to attribute interpersonal failures to unchangeable character defects (low ability, personality traits) rather than to changeable personal factors (lack of effort, use of ineffective strategies) or to situational factors. In a second study, Anderson demonstrated that this attributional style was associated with less effective behavior in an interpersonal persuasion task. Students who made ability or trait attributions showed lower success expectancies, lower motivation, and were actually less successful at the task than were students who made effort or strategy attributions. Similarly, Goetz and Dweck (1980) have shown that children who attribute social rejection to personal incompetence cope less effectively. Goetz and Dweck argued that even socially skilled children may misattribute social rebuffs to lack of ability and, as a result, respond less successfully. Finally, Cutrona (Chapter 18) presented data linking attributions to the persistence of loneliness over time. She compared attributions for loneliness made by students who subsequently recovered from loneliness and from students who remained lonely seven months later. The initial attributions of students who remained lonely were more internal and gave greater emphasis to their own personality, shyness, fear of rejection, and lack of knowledge about how to initiate relationships.

Research is accumulating to demonstrate the link between causal attributions and reactions to loneliness. Whether people respond to loneliness with depression or hostility, with passive withdrawal or active striving, may depend on their personal explanations for loneliness. We have discussed these results as though attributions are causal factors in determining expectancies, emotions, and behaviors. We are convinced that this does occur. But other causal links are also possible. For example, individuals who attribute their loneliness to lack of interpersonal skill may actually be inept; their poor social skills may cause both their attributions and their lack of success in social settings. Further research is needed to clarify the causal relationship of attributions and reactions to loneliness.

Implications for Helping the Lonely

Lonely people seek to understand their problem in order to alleviate it. Causal attributions can influence lonely people's motivation to improve their social life and guide their coping behavior. If attempts to overcome loneliness are misdirected at unimportant or inaccurate causes, they are unlikely to succeed and so may ultimately lead to feelings of lowered personal control. Thus a major goal of counseling or self-help for the lonely should be to identify accurately the important causes of an individual's loneliness and to assess correctly the potential changeability of these causes.

It may be especially helpful for the lonely person to sustain some sense of personal control over his or her social relations, and yet at the same time to avoid destructive tendencies toward self-derogation. In this regard, Janoff-Bulman's (1980) distinction between two types of self-blame is pertinent. *Behavioral self-blame* involves attributing results to changeable features of one's behavior, such as lack of effort or use of ineffective strategies. Such attributions should foster the belief that by modifying one's behavior, better results can be achieved in the future (see also Weiner, in press). In contrast, *characterological self-blame* involves attributions to relatively unmodifiable aspects of the self, such as one's personality or ability. Janoff-Bulman argued that characterological self-blame is associated with depression and with believing that one deserves one's fate. The question of how attributions for loneliness influence self-esteem is discussed further in the next section.

LONELINESS AND SELF-ESTEEM

Lonely people often feel worthless, incompetent, and unlovable. Indeed the link between severe loneliness and low self-esteem is one of the most consistent findings of loneliness research (Jones, Chapter 15; Moore & Sermat, 1974; Paloutzian & Ellison, Chapter 14; Wood, 1978). For example, Loucks (1980) found that loneliness was significantly correlated with self-criticism, low self-esteem, and "uncertainty of self-view." Russell, Peplau, and Cutrona (1980) found a correlation of —.49 between scores on the revised UCLA Loneliness Scale and the Texas Social Behavior Inventory, a measure of social self-esteem. In a large-scale survey, Rubenstein and Shaver (Chapter 13) found that self-depreciation, including feelings of being unattractive, stupid, and ashamed, was a common correlate of loneliness.

Although the link between loneliness and low self-esteem has been firmly established, the reasons for this association have not been precisely specified. We agree with Wood (1978) that the relationship of loneliness to self-esteem can reflect several different causal processes; low self-esteem may be both a cause and a consequence of loneliness. Although we acknowledge the reciprocal links between loneliness and self-esteem, we find it analytically useful to examine first ways in which low self-esteem can foster loneliness, and then ways in which loneliness can impair self-esteem.

Low Self-Esteem as a Cause of Loneliness

Two major views of how self-esteem affects loneliness can be distinguished. The first suggests that intrapsychic self-estrangement is a cause of loneliness. The second proposes that low self-esteem is accompanied by a set of attitudes and behaviors that hinder satisfying social interaction and so create the conditions for loneliness.

Loneliness as Self-Estrangement

Early psychological analyses of loneliness focused on the person's self-conception. Rogers (1961) discussed loneliness as an estrangement between the person and his or her true inner feelings. Rogers believed that in searching for acceptance and love, people often develop facades, and so become alienated from themselves. Whitehorn (1961) concurred in this position:

> Some substantial incongruity between the self as felt and the self as reacted to by others generates and accentuates a feeling of loneliness, and this process may become a vicious cycle of loneliness and estrangement. (p. 16)

Thus these theorists proposed that loneliness originates in the individual's perception of a discrepancy between his or her "real" self and the way others view them.

A few studies have tested this idea. Eddy (1961) hypothesized that loneliness is related to discrepancies among three aspects of self-concept: the person's self-view (actual self), the person's ideal self, and the person's view of how others see him or her (reflected self). Using a sample of students in the Merchant Marine Academy, Eddy found strong support for these predictions. Loneliness was correlated .71 with the discrepancy of actual and ideal self, .71 with the discrepancy of actual and reflected self, and .63 with the discrepancy of ideal and reflected self. In accord with Eddy's belief that perceptions are more important than objective features of social interaction, no relationship was found between loneliness and actual popularity ratings by classmates. In a later study, Sisenwein (1964) took a somewhat different perspective, hypothesizing that loneliness results from a discrepancy between how people view themselves and how others actually view them. Contrary to expectation, Sisenwein found no relationship between loneliness and discrepancies of self versus other ratings. In a more recent study, however, Lowenthal, Thurnher and Chiriboga (1976) reported greater loneliness among older men whose self-ratings differed from those of others (i.e., the interviewer). The importance of self-estrangement as a source of loneliness deserves further empirical investigation.

Self-Esteem and Social Competence

Low self-esteem is often part of a package of beliefs and behaviors that inter-fere with initiating or maintaining satisfying social relationships. People with low self-esteem may interpret social interactions in self-defeating ways. They may be more likely to attribute social failures to internal, self-blaming factors (Ickes & Layden, 1978; Weiner, in press). People who devalue themselves may assume that others will similarly find them undesirable (Jones, Chapter 15). They may also have more extreme reactions to social invitations and rebuffs (see review in Berscheid & Walster, 1978). In studies that have experimentally altered people's self-esteem, it appears that low self-esteem individuals are especially responsive to a friendly confederate, but feel espe-cially hostile toward a rejecting confederate. Perhaps most important, people low in self-esteem may interpret ambiguous social exchanges in more negative ways than do people with high self-esteem (Jacobs, Berscheid, & Walster, 1971).

Low self-esteem can also affect people's social behavior. Zimbardo (1977) argued that: "The person with low self-esteem . . . is likely to be more pas-sive, persuasible and less popular. These people are overly sensitive to criticism, thinking it confirms their inadequacy. They have difficulty accept-ing compliments" (p. 152). People with low self-esteem may be more socially anxious and less willing to take risks in social settings, hence less likely to start new relationships or deepen existing ones.

In some instances, low self-esteem reflects an inaccurate assessment of the person's social skills. It is not uncommon for attractive, competent individuals to perceive themselves and their behavior as inept (Zimbardo, 1977). But in other cases, low self-esteem reflects actual deficits in the skills necessary to begin or sustain social relations (Horowitz et al., Chapter 12).

In sum, low self-esteem is often embedded in an interrelated set of self-defeating cognitions and behaviors that impair social competence and so put people at risk for loneliness. Evidence that low self-esteem may be a causal factor in the persistence of loneliness comes from a longitudinal study by Cutrona, Russell, and Peplau (1979, Chapter 18). They found that self-esteem was an important factor in whether new college students experienced only transitory loneliness or continued to be lonely over a seven-month pe-riod. Those students scoring high in self-esteem at the beginning of the new school year were significantly more likely to overcome their loneliness and to make a successful social adjustment at college than were students with low self-esteem.

Loneliness as a Cause of Low Self-Esteem

Loneliness, especially when it is severe and prolonged, can lower a person's self-esteem. The consequences of loneliness for self-esteem are exacerbated if the loneliness is attributed to personal characteristics or defects. Further, when loneliness results from the loss of important relationships, as in divorce or widowhood, the person must create a new conception of herself or himself—a new "social self" to replace one that has been lost.

Loneliness as Social Failure

To be without a lover, friends, or family is to have failed in the eyes of society, and often in our own eyes as well (Gordon, 1976). Milner observed, "To say 'I'm lonely' is to admit you're essentially inadequate, that you have nobody who loves you" (1975, p. 3). The absence of social relationships is not only personally distressing but socially awkward as well. Stereotypes depict people who live alone as "lonely losers"—cold, unfriendly, and unattractive (Parmelee & Werner, 1978). People often find it uncomfortable to be the only "single" at a party of couples, to eat alone in a restaurant, or to go unescorted to a movie. In a gregarious culture, the lack of friends or a mate is a social failure. Perhaps less obvious but equally important, having unsatisfying relationships—an unhappy marriage or superficial friendships—may also be seen as a social failure.

Some years ago, William James (1908) proposed that self-esteem is "a fraction of which our pretensions are the denominator, and the numerator our success; thus self-esteem = success/pretensions" (p. 187). This and other discrepancy definitions of self-esteem (Cohen, 1959; Wells & Marwell, 1976) emphasize the correspondence between people's personal ideals or aspirations and their accomplishments. Thus the perception of a social deficit can both give rise to the experience of loneliness and also detract from a person's self-esteem. The more important and salient the social deficiency, the greater should be both the person's loneliness and the decrease in their sense of personal worth. Loneliness and low self-esteem are intimately and reciprocally interrelated.

Self-Blaming Attributions for Loneliness

If, as James and others suggest, self-esteem is based on the extent to which we attain our personal goals, then any failure should harm self-esteem. In actuality, however, the effect of failure on self-esteem is mediated by the person's causal attributions for the failure (Weiner, in press). In particular, failure attributed to personal inadequacies should have greater impact on self-esteem than outcomes attributed to situational constraints. In a study of achievement-related behavior, Weiner, Russell, and Lerman (1978) reported that the emotions accompanying failure differed significantly depending on the attribution made. Attributions to external causes led to feelings such as surprise and anger that were unrelated to self-esteem. Attributions to lack of effort led to feelings of shame and guilt, presumably because the person might have done better if he or she had tried harder. Failure attributed to personality or lack of ability was associated with feeling incompetent and inadequate; such attributions may be most damaging to self-esteem (see also Janoff-Bulman, 1980)

In research explicitly focused on loneliness, we (Miceli, Morasch, & Peplau, unpublished data) asked college students to evaluate a person who was lonely for one of several reasons. When the loneliness was experimentally attributed to internal causes, the person was perceived as more self-centered, less likeable, and less resourceful, and was expected to be lower in self-esteem than when the loneliness was due to external causes. Anderson (1980) presented evidence that many lonely students may adopt a self-blaming attributional style to explain their social outcomes, attributing failure to their own personality or low ability, and attributing social success to external circumstances outside their personal control.

The tendency to blame oneself for social failures may be influenced by the opinions of others. For example, Weiss (1975) suggested that in divorce, the individual's own self-condemnation may be augmented by accusations and disparagement from the former spouse. More generally, other people may blame the lonely person and so provide apparent corroboration for the individual's own feelings of personal inadequacy.

The Social Self

Our self-conception is largely based on our relationships to other people— as friend, lover, parent, child, neighbor, co-worker. "Specific persons and their behaviors get built into the contents of role-identities and become crucial to the legitimation and enactment of these identities" (McCall, 1970, p. 8). Both the loss and the absence of social relations can influence our self-conception.

The loss of important people from our lives, whether through separation, divorce, or death, often requires a reconstruction of our self-conception. Weiss (1975) observed that "with the end of their marriages, most among the separated suffer from the loss of some of the social scaffolding on which their self-definition rested" (p. 69). Widows apparently also experience a loss of self. Many of the bereaved women Parkes (1972) studied initially rejected the idea of being a widow in an effort to resist giving up their cherished identity as a wife for a new and uncertain one. The loss of important, long-established social ties has major ramifications for our self view. At least in the short run, such changes often lead to lowered self-esteem.

The absence of social relationships can also have important implications for our self-conception. Many of our life plans—to marry and live "happily ever after," to be a loyal and generous friend, to be surrounded in old age by loving grandchildren—require social relationships. For the young person on the brink of adulthood, the lack of a dating partner or spouse not only reduces current companionship, but can also thwart future dreams and goals (Schank & Abelson, 1977). Throughout life, important personal plans require "accomplices."

The Loss of Attachment in Childhood

The loss of an important relationship can be devastating at any age, but for young children the repercussions may be especially serious. In a provocative analysis, Shaver and Rubenstein (1980) argued that when children are deprived of secure attachments to their parents, they develop models of the self and the social world that are harmful to their self-esteem and to their later social adjustment. Shaver and Rubenstein suggested that children are likely to blame themselves for the loss of a parent, especially when the loss results from divorce rather than death. The child's level of cognitive maturity at the time of the divorce may be crucial. Younger children, prone to egocentrism, are more likely to believe that they were the cause of the marital separation. The result, Shaver and Rubenstein proposed, is a loss of self-esteem and a pessimism about social relations that are hard to overcome. Even as adults, such individuals may be at special risk for loneliness and may continue to blame themselves for their social problems. Thus early attachment losses may leave a legacy of loneliness and low self-esteem.

In this section we have examined the relationship between loneliness and low self-esteem. Low self-esteem may put people at risk for loneliness, which in turn may further impair their sense of self-worth. How to break this potentially vicious cycle is an important question for loneliness researchers and therapists. Two other unresolved issues are also noteworthy. First, it is unclear whether social desirability biases, the effort by some people to present a positive image to researchers, influence the observed relationship of measures of loneliness and self-esteem. People who want to present a favorable self-image may deny being lonely and also evaluate themselves positively. Some data (see Chapter 6) suggest that loneliness measures are not significantly affected by social desirability biases, but further evidence on this point is needed. Second, the possible role of depression in explaining why severe loneliness is accompanied by low self-esteem requires closer scrutiny. In at least some cases, major social losses may set in motion not only loneliness but also severe depression, which in turn may lead individuals to adopt a negative attitude toward themselves and their self-worth (Weiner & Litman-Adizes, 1978).

CONCLUSIONS

Loneliness is a complex experience encompassing the whole person—feelings thoughts, and actions. We believe that cognitions play an important part in this experience. We do not propose that loneliness is "only in your head," nor that loneliness can be magically cured by the power of "positive thinking." We do assert, however, that a comprehensive analysis of loneliness requires an understanding of the impact of cognitive processes.

REFERENCES .

Anderson, C. A. *Motivational and performance deficits as a function of attributional style.* Unpublished doctoral dissertation, Stanford University, 1980.

Andrews, F. M., & Withey, S. B. *Social indicators of well-being: Americans' perceptions of life quality*. New York: Plenum, 1976.

Berscheid, E., & Walster, E. H. *Interpersonal attraction* (2nd ed.). Menlo Park, Calif. Addison-Wesley, 1978.

Bragg, M. *A comparative study of loneliness and depression*. Unpublished doctoral dissertation, University of Cailfornia, Los Angeles, 1979.

Brickman, P., & Bulman, R. J. Pleasure and pain in social comparison. In J. M. Suls & R. L. Miller (Eds.), *Social comparison processes: Theoretical and empirical perspectives*. Washington, D. C.: Hemisphere, 1977.

Briggs, J. L. *Never in anger: Portrait of an Eskimo family*. Cambridge, Mass.: Harvard University Press, 1970.

Campbell, A., Converse, P. E., & Rogers, W. L. *The quality of American life: Perceptions, evaluations and satisfactions*. New York: Russell Sage Foundation, 1976.

Cohen, A. Some implications of self-esteem for social influence. In C. Hovland & I. Janis (Eds.), *Personality and persuasibility*. New Haven: Yale University Press 1959.

Cutrona, C. E., & Peplau, L. A. *A longitudinal study of loneliness*. Paper presented at the annual meeting of the Western Psychological Association, San Diego, April 1979.

Cutrona, C. E., Russell, D. W., & Peplau, L. A. *Loneliness and the process of social adjustment: A longitudinal study*. Paper presented at the annual meeting of the American Psychological Association, New York, September 1979.

De Jong-Gierveld, J. The construct of loneliness: Components and measurement. *Essence*, 1978, *2*(4), 221–238.

Eddy, P. D. *Loneliness: A discrepancy with the phenomenological self*. Unpublished doctoral dissertation, Adelphi College, 1961.

Festinger, L. A theory of social comparison processes. *Human Relations*, 1954, *7*, 117–140.

Fromm-Reichmann, F. Loneliness. *Psychiatry*, 1959, *22*, 1–15.

Goetz, T. E., & Dweck, C. S. Learned helplessness in social situations. *Journal of Personality and Social Psychology*, 1980, *39*, 246–255.

Gordon, S. L. The sociology of sentiments and emotion. In M. Rosenberg & R. H. Turner (Eds.), *Social psychology: Sociological perspectives*. New York: Basic Books, 1981.

Gordon, S. *Lonely in America*. New York: Simon and Schuster, 1976.

Horney, K. *The neurotic personality of our time*. New York: Norton, 1937.

Ickes, W., & Layden, M. A. Attributional styles. In J. H. Harvey, W. Ickes, & R. F. Kidd (Eds.). *New directions in attribution research* (Vol. 2). New York: Wiley, 1978.

Jacobs, L. E., Berscheid, E., & Walster, E. Self-esteem and attraction. *Journal of Personality and Social Psychology*, 1971, *17*, 84–91.

James, W. *Psychology*. New York: Henry Holt, 1908.

Janoff-Bulman, R. Characterological versus behavioral self-blame: Inquiries into depression and rape. *Journal of Personality and Social Psychology*, 1980, *37*, 1798–1809.

Kelley, H. H. *Attributions in social interaction*. New York: General Learning Press, 1971.

Lederer, W. J., & Jackson, D. D. False assumption 6: That loneliness will be cured by marriage. *The mirages of marriage*. New York: Norton, 1968.

Levy, R. I. *Tahitians: Mind and experience in the society islands*. Chicago: University of Chicago Press, 1973.

Lopata, H. Z. Loneliness: Forms and components. *Social Problems*, 1969, *17*, 248–261.

Loucks, S. Loneliness, affect and self-concept: Construct validity of the Bradley Loneliness Scale. *Journal of Personality Assessment*, 1980, *44*(2), 142–147.

Lowenthal, M., & Robinson, B. Social networks and isolation. In R. Binstock & E. Shanas (Eds.), *Handbook of aging and the social sciences*. New York: Van Nostrand Reinhold, 1976.

Lowenthal, M., Thurnher, M., & Chiriboga, D. *Four stages of life*. San Francisco: Jossey-Bass, 1976.

McCall, G. J. The social organization of relationships. In G. J. McCall, M. M. McCall, N. K. Denzin, G. D. Suttles, & S. B. Kurth (Eds.), *Social relationships*. Chicago: Aldine, 1970.

Michela, J. L., Peplau, L. A., & Weeks, D. G. *Perceived dimensions and consequences of attributions for loneliness*. Unpublished manuscript, Columbia University, New York, October 1981.

Milner, J. *Los Angeles Times*, April 27, 1975, Part II, page 3.

Moore, J. A., & Sermat, V. Relationship between loneliness and interpersonal relationships. *Canadian Counsellor*, 1974, *8*, 84–89.

Parkes, C. *Bereavement: Studies of grief in adult life*. New York: International Universities Press, 1972.

Parmelee, P., & Werner, C. Lonely losers: Stereotypes of single dwellers. *Personality and Social Psychology Bulletin*, 1978, *4*(2), 292–295.

Pennebaker, J. W. Self-perception of emotion and internal sensation. In D. M. Wegner & R. R. Vallacher (Eds.), *The self in social psychology*. New York: Oxford University Press, 1980.

Peplau, L. A., & Perlman, D. Blueprint for a social psychological theory of loneliness. In M. Cook & G. Wilson (Eds.), *Love and attraction*. New York: Pergamon, 1979.

Peplau, L. A., Russell, D., & Heim, M. The experience of loneliness. In I. H. Frieze, D. Bar-Tal, & J. S. Carroll (Eds.), *New approaches to social problems: Applications of attribution theory*. San Francisco: Jossey-Bass, 1979.

Perlman, D., & Peplau, L. A. Toward a social psychology of loneliness. In S. Duck & R. Gilmour (Eds.), *Personal relationships 3: Personal relationships in disorder*. New York: Academic Press, 1981.

Pettigrew, T. F. Social evaluation theory: Convergences and applications. In D. Levine (Ed.), *Nebraska symposium on motivation* (Vol. 15). Lincoln: University of Nebraska Press, 1967.

Rogers, C. R. The loneliness of contemporary man as seen in the "Case of Ellen West." *Annals of Psychotherapy*, 1961, *1*, 22–27.

Russell, D., Peplau, L. A., & Cutrona, C. E. The revised UCLA Loneliness Scale: Concurrent and discriminant validity evidence. *Journal of Personality and Social Psychology,* 1980, *39*(3), 472–480.

Schank, R., & Abelson, R. *Scripts, plans, goals and understanding.* New York: Wiley, 1977.

Sermat, V. Sources of loneliness. *Essence,* 1978, *2*(4), 271–276.

Shaver, P., & Rubenstein, C. Childhood attachment experience and adult loneliness. In L. Wheeler (Ed.), *Review of personality and social psychology* (Vol. 1). Beverly Hills, Calif.: Sage, 1980.

Sheehy, G. *Passages: Predictable crises of adult life.* New York: Bantam, 1976.

Sisenwein, R. *Loneliness and the individual as viewed by himself and others.* Unpublished doctoral dissertation, Columbia University, 1964.

Suls, J. M., & Miller, R. L. (Eds.). *Social comparison processes: Theoretical and empirical perspectives.* Washington, D. C.: Hemisphere, 1977.

Thibaut, J. W., & Kelley, H. H. *The social psychology of groups.* New York: Wiley, 1959.

Townsend, P. *The family life of old people.* London: Routledge and Kegan Paul, 1957.

Weiner, B. (Ed.). *Achievement motivation and attribution theory.* Morristown, N. J.: General Learning Press, 1974.

Weiner, B. An attributionally-based theory of motivation and emotion: Focus, range and issues. In N. T. Feather (Ed.), *Values, expectancy and incentives.* Hillsdale, N. J.: Erlbaum, in press.

Weiner, B., & Litman-Adizes, T. An attributional, expectancy-value analysis of learned helplessness and depression. In J. Garber & M. E. P. Seligman (Eds.), *Human helplessness: Theory and applications.* New York: Academic Press, 1978.

Weiner, B., Russell, D., & Lerman, D. Affective consequences of causal ascriptions. In J. Harvey, W. J. Ickes, & R. F. Kidd (Eds.), *New directions in attribution research* (Vol. 2). Hillsdale, N. J.: Erlbaum, 1978.

Weiss, R. S. *Loneliness: The experience of emotional and social isolation.* Cambridge, Mass.: MIT Press, 1973.

Weiss, R. S. *Marital separation.* New York: Basic Books, 1975.

Wells, L. E., & Marwell, G. *Self-esteem: Its conceptualization and measurement.* Beverly Hills, Calif.: Sage, 1976.

Whitehorn, J. C. On loneliness and the incongruous self image. *Annals of Psychotherapy,* 1961, *1*, 15–17.

Wood, L. A. Loneliness, social identity and social structure. *Essence,* 1978, *2*(4), 259–270.

Wortman, C. B., & Dintzer, L. Is an attributional analysis of the learned helplessness phenomenon viable? A critique of the Abramson-Seligman-Teasdale reformulation. *Journal of Abnormal Psychology,* 1978, *87*(1), 75–90.

Zimbardo, P. G. *Shyness.* Reading, Mass.: Addison-Wesley, 1977.

Chapter 10

Why Loneliness Occurs: The Interrelationship of Social-Psychological and Privacy Concepts

Valerian J. Derlega and Stephen T. Margulis

There are distinct but, in practice, overlapping stages in concept development (Margulis, 1977). The first stage justifies interest in a concept such as loneliness by presenting studies, observations, and cases that demonstrate the importance and viability of a behavioral concept of loneliness. This stage is now more or less complete. It includes the work of Bell (1956), Abrahams (1972), and Cottle (1974). The second stage accepts the importance of the concept and attempts to explore it further. This stage includes initial attempts at explication (Peplau & Caldwell, 1978; Weiss, 1973) and attempts to demonstrate similarities and differences between loneliness and cognate concepts (Zipris, 1979, Chapter 6). This stage characterizes most of the current work on loneliness, both conceptual and research. In the third stage, explication becomes systematic, and the whys and hows of loneliness are directly and fully addressed. This stage will build on Stage 2 analyses, and the results will be theories: systematically related sets of statements, some of whose logical implications are empirically testable. That is, in Stage 3, definitions of loneliness will be theoretical; loneliness will be defined in terms of the laws and lawlike statements in which it occurs. This set of interlocking statements will be a theory of loneliness (Cronbach & Meehl, 1956). There appears to be no serious evidence of Stage 3 theory construction as of the time of writing in 1980.

There have been examinations of how different theories address loneliness and attempts to explore the contribution of behavioral concepts to loneliness (Perlman & Peplau, 1981). These are important Stage 2 func-

Acknowledgments are gratefully extended to Barbara Z. Derlega, Letitia Anne Peplau, Daniel Perlman, and Arthur Zipris for their comments and helpful feedback on earlier drafts of this chapter. Thanks are also due to Didi McSwain and Monica Presser who typed the manuscript.

tions. This chapter also falls within Stage 2. It is an attempt, admittedly speculative, to explore the role of social-psychological and privacy-related concepts to explain when loneliness occurs. The perspective is somewhat narrow. We are not dealing with developmental, dispositional, sociological, or anthropological aspects of loneliness. We believe that a complete account would require considering these other perspectives. Nevertheless, this chapter will be justified if we can derive testable hypotheses and bring some order to the diverse research on loneliness that has already appeared. Our analysis mainly explores *why* loneliness occurs as opposed to *what* loneliness is. The latter approach to the study of loneliness is best illustrated by phenomenological psychologists who focus on the "experience-as-lived" of loneliness (Zipris, 1979). We will argue that the experience of loneliness may be the joint result of the unavailability or absence of someone appropriate who could assist in the attainment of certain socially mediated goals, the belief that the unavailability will endure, and the continued desire for such a relationship.

A PRIVACY FRAMEWORK

Social psychologist Irwin Altman (1975, 1976, 1977) has made notable contributions to developing a theory of privacy. He writes:

Privacy is conceived of as an interpersonal boundary process by which a person or group regulates interaction with others. By altering the degree of openness of the self to others, a hypothetical personal boundary is more or less receptive to social interaction with others. Privacy is, therefore, a dynamic process involving selective control over a self-boundary, either by an individual or by a group. (Altman, 1975, p. 6)

Altman's approach represents a general theory of social behavior based on how individuals regulate social contacts (Margulis, 1977). It integrates phenomena such as territorial behavior, personal space, crowding, verbal and nonverbal behavior. Questions have been raised about the comprehensiveness of Altman's theory of privacy. The theory may be too broad to handle adequately a wide range of behavior (Margulis, 1977). For present purposes our theoretical analysis of privacy is limited to how individuals exercise control over their communications to achieve certain other-contingent goals. We focus on an important class of communications represented by the phenomenon of self-disclosure, which is defined by what one person tells another about himself or herself. Self-disclosure is an example of privacy regulation, and the degree of control individuals maintain over this flow of personal information affects the kind of privacy they have in a relationship.

Privacy Regulation and Socially Mediated Goals

Privacy regulation contributes to the achievement of various goals. Johnson (1974) notes that "privacy does not in itself satisfy any fundamental need"

(p. 91). Individuals decide how to manage the flow of personal information between themselves and others according to the goals that they seek to attain in a relationship. When individuals interact with an appropriate person (i.e., someone who can assist them in goal achievement), a precondition for the satisfaction of certain socially mediated goals has been met. When these persons are not available, it may be difficult (if not impossible) to achieve the goals sought.

Privacy regulation describes how individuals seek to control the flow of information between themselves and others. The specific goals that persons seek to achieve in relationships are less clear. Sullivan (1953) points to a global need for intimacy, while Weiss (1974) has identified a longer list of six social provisions, including attachment, opportunity for nourishment, and the obtaining of guidance. Our analysis of privacy focuses on the transmission of personal information between individuals. Based on this focus, there are four major effects (or goals) that individuals may seek in their relationships that influence their decisions to disclose or not disclose. These socially mediated goals have been suggested by prior research on communication processes (Derlega & Grzelak, 1979).* These goals include:

1. *Expressive function,* whereby individuals seek to ventilate their feelings by talking with someone. For instance, anguish or grief associated with the death of a close friend may be ventilated by talking with a confidant.

2. *Self-clarification* involves talking about feelings and thoughts to increase understanding and reduce uncertainty. Individuals may express their thoughts in a letter or talk about a problem to a confidant to acquire greater insight about their own ideas.

3. *Social validation,* in which self-disclosure in a relationship serves to generate feedback from others. In Festinger's (1954) theory of social comparison, in the absence of objective standards, we look to social reality to gain feedback about our opinions, beliefs, and feelings. Feedback and advice from others may help us to understand ourselves better and to suggest ways to confront and deal with a difficult matter.**

4. *Relationship development,* in which social communication is a vehicle for developing close relationships. The development of friendships is based partly on an increase in mutual self-disclosure as individuals communicate increasingly more intimate information to one another (Altman & Taylor, 1973).

* Our privacy analysis suggests certain relationship-linked goals (or needs) associated with information management. There may be other types of relationship goals that are not described in our analysis (Weiss, 1974). We are concerned theoretically with social needs that are relational in nature and that can be spoken of in terms of the "quality of a relationship."

** Social validation can sometimes occur in the absence of social communication. For instance, in Schachter's (1959) studies on emotional arousal, some subjects were able to satisfy their social comparison needs by observing but not talking with others. Self-disclosure may contribute to social comparison, but it is not necessary for comparison (and ultimately social validation) to occur.

In our view, loneliness is caused by the absence of an appropriate social partner who could assist in achieving important other-contingent goals, the belief that unavailability will endure, and the continuing desire for such social contacts. In this analysis, the emergence of salient socially mediated goals sets the stage for the experience of loneliness. These goals include the four functions of self-disclosure we have identified: expressiveness, self-clarification, social validation, and relationship development. Thus loneliness is partly a consequence of not having an appropriate social partner or confidant with whom to communicate. As a result of this absence of an appropriate social partner, important socially mediated goals are beyond reach. (A persisting desire for positive social contacts is discussed in the next section.)

Recent work of phenomenological psychologists suggests that reactions to a partner's unavailability are linked to temporal factors. According to Arthur Zipris (personal communication, March 13, 1980), loneliness includes the belief that the future will be like the present—with ,no appropriate social partner in sight to mediate one's needs. The lonely person is at the boundary between what was, what is wanted or hoped for, and what will be for the foreseeable future, with the present being a prediction of what that future will be like. Zipris's notion of a temporal component of loneliness suggested this possible antecedent: Loneliness may occur only when individuals believe that the absence of a partner will be prolonged and that it will continue into the future. (The belief that the unavailability will endure is discussed further in the final section of the chapter.)

A sequence of events that may contribute to loneliness is represented in the following manner: a salient other-contingent goal + unavailability of an appropriate social partner + belief that the unavailability will endure + persisting desire for such a person(s) → experience of loneliness.

The psychological response that is loneliness has at least two aspects: (1) cognitive—perceived absence of an appropriate person who could assist in achieving socially mediated goals; and (2) affective—a negative emotional reaction brought on by the absence of an appropriate social partner.

Evaluating Relationships and Loneliness

Individuals seek certain types of relationships (so-called "desired social contacts") that may differ from their actual relationships with others ("achieved contact"). If the achieved contact does not match the desired contact, a series of acts may be initiated to establish a match between the achieved and desired type of relationship (Altman, 1975).

We do not define desired and achieved relationships in terms of how many social contacts an individual has (that is, too few, enough, or too many). In our view, the unavailability of others who can assist in achieving certain results bears on the quality of a relationship as a factor in producing loneliness. Social contacts are probably evaluated in terms of the quality of the relationship that individuals have with others, unless number of contacts per se is a sought-after outcome. Some support for our position derives from research by Cutrona and Peplau (1979; see also Chapter 18) who found that individuals' satisfaction with the quality of their relationships was more strongly related to loneliness than the number of social contacts.

It is important to clarify what is meant by "desired" social contact. In our view desire represents a psychologically based need for relationships with others. It should be distinguished from "expectancies" for social relationships that derive from individuals' beliefs about what types of relationships they do have with others. For instance, individuals who move from a large city to a physically isolated rural community may scale down their expectancies about the types of social relationships they have in the new setting. However, the desire for certain relationships may persist unabated. The desire may even operate at a level outside of the individual's cognitive awareness.

Expectancies may influence how individuals assess the effects of an absent social partner. A useful basis for examining people's expectancies for relationships is the notion of comparison level (CL) described by Thibaut and Kelley (1959; also see Kelley, Hastorf, Jones, Thibaut, & Usdane, 1960). The comparison level represents a level of results (that is, rewarding versus negative experiences) that is experienced as neutral in value. It reflects the quality of relationships that a person expects to have. A person with a high CL will expect a great deal from his or her relationships. A person is satisfied with a relationship to the extent that results are above CL. The height of CL may depend on one's past experiences in relationships as well as on comparisons with what kinds of successful relationships other people are believed or observed to have. Consider what happens when someone loses a partner who has helped achieve socially mediated goals in the past (e.g., through divorce, death of a friend, or physical separation). Experienced results have now dropped below CL. Our analysis assumes that the CL still remains relatively high immediately after the loss of the social partner, and that the person assesses the loss in results that have occurred. Thus an important antecedent for loneliness is a comparison with the past that shows that one's present interpersonal relationships are of an unsatisfactory quality. The magnitude of loneliness may be affected by the extent to which a person's level of results is below CL.

While it appears that a comparison between expected and achieved social contacts may be a critical element in loneliness, it is not sufficient to explain why loneliness occurs. The unavailability of an appropriate social partner, in the context of being unable to satisfy sought-after goals, could easily produce anger, frustration, and hostility. Why then does loneliness occur? Loneliness is also predicated on the desire for positive social relations with others that continues to operate when a needed partner is not available.

Social Networks, Centrality of Partner(s), and Loneliness

Humans are inherently social. By "social" we do not mean merely that our behavior is the product of social forces or that our behavior has others as important antecedents or consequences. Rather we wish to emphasize that relationships with others are a major aspect of human experience.

We can describe sociality in terms of networks of relationships. These networks are characterized by various kinds of social exchanges, for example, social communication or other social commodities, such as physical intimacy. These networks can be described sociometrically with the person (P) as the node:

1. Networks vary in their number (how many networks P belongs to) and in their size (how many members each of P's networks has). A small community, a club, or a number of individual friends each may constitute a network.

2. Network memberships vary in overlap from being completely independent to being totally nested. The relations among members of networks also can vary from all related only to P to all related to one another, as in a family.

3. Networks and their members vary in centrality, that is, in their association with satisfying certain goals that P seeks to satisfy. Centrality implies a high probability that a particular network or a particular network member (O) can satisfy, serve, or meet P's socially based needs.

We have emphasized how one important factor contributing to loneliness is the unavailability of an appropriate social partner who can assist P to achieve an other-contingent goal. Based on this unavailability notion, predictions can be generated about the effects of P's social network on when loneliness occurs.

The probability of loneliness is a direct function of the centrality of the unavailable social partner. The greater the centrality of the absent partner, the greater the likelihood of loneliness occurring. As a corollary to this prediction, note that vulnerability to loneliness is based on P's degree of dependency on certain others to assist in satisfying certain needs. If there is less dependency on O, there should be less reason for loneliness under conditions that would otherwise give rise to loneliness. For instance, Lowenthal and Haven (1968) report that "there are some life long isolates and near-isolates whose later-life adaptation apparently is not related to social resources" (p. 25). These persons presumably have developed their own inner resources to satisfy their needs.

The probability and duration of loneliness is an inverse function of the number of central others in the network, or of central networks. Assume that central members or central networks that serve the same need are substitutable. Thus loneliness is less likely, and should be shorter in duration, if there is more than one central other (or network) that can help satisfy a need and if substitution of social partners (or networks) is not otherwise precluded. Support for this prediction derives from research that finds that elderly widows are less susceptible to loneliness than widowers, partly because widows are more likely to have adequate substitutes for the loss of the spouse. Elderly widows are more likely than widowers to belong to organizations, maintain social ties, and have intimate contacts outside of the relationship with their spouse. In many cases the wife was the only central partner for the elderly husband, whereas the husband was just one of multiple social partners available to the elderly wife (Haas-Hawkings, 1978).

A curvilinear relationship is predicted between network characteristics and the probability of being lonely. A set of noncentralized members (or noncentralized networks) and a set of highly centralized members (or highly centralized networks) should both result in little loneliness. In the former case individuals are not dependent on one another for goal satisfaction, and there is nothing to lose by unavailability or "separation." In the latter case, with highly centralized members or highly centralized networks, partner substitution is possible and loneliness can be escaped or avoided. It is the person who has only one centralized partner or one centralized network who is most vulnerable to loneliness. (If there are multiple central members or networks, but other factors preclude substitution, then loneliness is also likely to occur.)

A Typology of Privacy

Westin (1970) identified four states of privacy based on how individuals manage the flow of information between themselves and others. In the state of *intimacy,* the individual is part of a small group (e.g., two close friends) who can converse honestly with one another. In intimacy, that is, in an intimate relationship, individuals have the opportunity to be alone together so they can talk freely. Examples include a husband and wife or a circle of close friends who exchange personal information with one another. In *anonymity* individuals communicate personal information about themselves but not about their identities. For instance, someone may call a telephone counseling service and speak openly about certain emotional problems without identifying himself or herself (Grumet, 1979). *Solitude* excludes others but it is not a turning away from others so much as a turning inwards and communicating with one's self. Examples include individuals who meditate or who are involved in an internal dialogue with themselves. According to Westin (1970, p. 32), *reserve* represents "the creation of a psychological barrier against unwanted intrusions," and it is respected by others' discretion and their willingness not to intrude. Reserve is based on the need to hold back information about the self that is too personal to reveal. For instance, individuals may honor a combat veteran's unwillingness to talk about wartime experiences that would be painful to discuss. It can also reflect the "silent type" who does not invite or breach intrusions. Our lives are spent mainly in situations of varying degrees of intimacy and not in solitude or anonymity. Individuals' claims to reserve and the extent to which this claim is honored represent a major means of controlling the flow of information between individuals and groups.

Westin's (1970) taxonomy of privacy may help us understand when loneliness is likely to occur. Intimacy is the *social* form of privacy that provides a setting in which socially mediated goals can be achieved through open communication. Individuals are unlikely to be lonely in an intimate relationship, that is, where one can speak honestly to a confidant. People who are lonely lack the privacy associated with intimacy, the privacy that *requires* others. On the other hand, lonely people may have access to other, *nonsocial* forms of privacy, including solitude, anonymity, and reserve. Intimacy is a social form of privacy in the sense that it brings individuals together in open communication. Reserve, solitude, and anonymity create barriers between individuals; hence they are nonsocial forms of privacy.

Privacy Regulation, Boundaries, and Loneliness

Terms such as *boundary* and *barrier* have been used to refer to privacy regulation (Altman, 1975; Margulis, 1979). Interpersonal boundaries may be more or less open according to the type of relationship we choose to have. Changes in self-disclosure output (what we reveal to others about ourselves) and input (what others reveal to us about themselves) are examples of boundary regulation. Privacy regulation may be represented as the opening and closing of a hypothetical boundary separating the person from others. Self-disclosure *is* boundary regulation, since it regulates the nature of our relationships with others. There are at least two major boundaries involved in regulating self-disclosure (Derlega & Chaikin, 1977; Margulis, 1979).

One boundary, the *dyadic boundary,* is for the discloser the boundary within which self-disclosure takes place and across which the self-disclosure must not cross. A secure dyadic boundary is a discloser's basis for believing there will be no leakage of information to excluded others. This boundary is based on the discloser's perception that conditions and circumstances make it safe to disclose to the recipient and that no information will cross the boundary. The second boundary, the *personal (or self) boundary,* is the barrier that each of us adjusts when we divulge information about ourselves to others. When this boundary is open, self-disclosure occurs. When this boundary is maintained, nondisclosure is the result.

Important rewards derive from establishing and maintaining intimate relationships in terms of the achievement of socially mediated needs. However, our disclosures, that is, an open personal boundary, make us vulnerable to influence, embarrassment, exploitation, and social invalidation. The more personal information others know about us, the more they are able to control and predict our behavior. A discloser becomes vulnerable to influence when the confidant has access to this information (Kelvin, 1977). If situational intimacy (that is, self-disclosure) depends on open self-boundaries, relationship intimacy (e.g., close friendships) also depends on consensually closed dyadic boundaries to insure confidentiality and mutual protection of shared information.

An example based on the experiences of cancer patients illustrates how problems with boundary regulation may contribute to loneliness. Cancer patients face terrible uncertainties associated with their illness (Wortman & Dunkel-Schetter, 1979). Cancer patients who seek to clarify their feelings may become isolated (i.e., blocked from having intimacy) because of their own and others' inability to talk about the illness. They may fear that they will be rejected by others if they discuss their illness (resulting in a closed self-boundary). Health professionals also may avoid talking with cancer patients about their illness because of their own anxieties about cancer, which in turn makes it even more difficult for patients to talk about their problems. These cancer patients may become lonely due to the absence of an appropriate person with whom to share and who will protect P's intimate disclosures. The presence of a true confidant would create the social condition favorable to the achievement of the cancer patient's social validation needs.

Inappropriate Personal Communications and Loneliness

The emergence of intimacy depends on self-disclosure, that is, on regulating the personal or self-boundary. However, individuals must be able and willing to divulge at a level that is appropriate to the sort of relationship they wish to maintain with others (Derlega & Grzelak, 1979). Research by Solano and Batten (1979) indicates that the social interaction styles of lonely persons may make it difficult for them to form intimate relationships. After a half hour of mutual disclosure, partners of lonely persons did not feel that they knew them as well as did partners of nonlonely persons. Also the lonely persons seemed to disclose inappropriately too much, in same-sex interaction and too little in opposite sex interaction, relative to nonlonely persons.

Inappropriateness of communications may assume other forms. Shy persons, for instance, have difficulty in regulating the personal (self) boundary according to situational requirements, which may contribute to their loneliness. They tend to avoid direct eye contact and to speak quietly when they interact at all. They tend to avoid others, and they have difficulty in being properly assertive in expressing their beliefs and opinions (Zimbardo, 1978). Shy individuals may be denied intimacy due to their lack of social skills, though they may have available other forms of privacy such as solitude, reserve, and anonymity.

Defensiveness and Loneliness

Some individuals may be susceptible to loneliness because of an excessive concern about the threat posed by intimate relationships, which prevents them from seeking intimacy when socially based needs are salient. (However, in Chapter 6, Russell notes that the revised UCLA Loneliness Scale does not correlate significantly with Marlowe-Crowne Social Desirability measure.) Highly defensive persons, as measured by high scores on the Marlowe-Crowne Social Desirability Scale, may worry about their inability to maintain a closed dyadic boundary; hence they tend to avoid intimacy (Brundage, Derlega, &

Cash, 1977; Crown & Marlowe, 1964; Dion & Dion, 1978). Nevertheless, individuals who are distrustful of intimacy could use anonymity as a basis for achieving socially mediated goals. Anonymity does not exclude others from being recipients of one's intimate disclosure, but it creates a special basis for sharing the information. The anonymous discloser conceals information about his or her personal identity. In anonymity, individuals maintain a partially closed self-boundary, withholding information about their personal identity, but keep an open self-boundary for the disclosure of other types of personal information. The popularity of telephone counseling services may be due partly to the anonymity given to callers who feel ashamed and embarrassed to discuss a problem in person (Grumet, 1979). Dating bars may also be popular because individuals can maintain anonymity or exercise reserve, that is, withhold certain critical information about themselves, while at the same time fulfilling various socially based needs. An extreme example is the school teacher, Theresa Dunn, in the novel *Looking for Mr. Goodbar,* who prowls bars at night looking for sex but fears intimacy.

Defensive persons and others who might be vulnerable to loneliness may learn to adapt to it. The prospect of loneliness may become a catalyst to loneliness-reducing action, such as reducing one's psychological dependence on others and developing inner resources to satisfy one's needs. An important area for study would be the "personal resources" that enable individuals to stave off loneliness when social partners are not available, such as diaries, pets, personality characteristics, attribution of responsibility for the partner's absence, and so forth.

ANTECEDENTS OF LONELINESS: FINAL THOUGHTS

A difference of opinion exists among loneliness researchers about what causes the phenomenon (Rubin, 1979). Weiss (1973) believes that loneliness is due to a deficiency of a necessary "relational provision." Peplau and Perlman see loneliness as a negative response to a discrepancy between a desired and achieved social relationship. The Peplau-Perlman position is somewhat similar to our own approach, since it emphasizes the absence of an appropriate partner with whom to have a relationship as well as the continuing desire for social contacts. However, they tend to reduce "desire" to "expectations" in deriving predictions about when loneliness is likely to occur (Peplau & Perlman, 1979; Perlman & Peplau, 1981).

Weiss (1973) views the inability to achieve a certain social provision (or goal) as *the* critical factor in accounting for loneliness. The failure to achieve a socially mediated goal could play a role in loneliness, but not in the manner that Weiss (1973) suggests. Imagine the case in which an other-contingent goal is salient and an appropriate social partner is unavailable. In this situation an individual might think about absent others who could have been suitable partners for an intimate relationship. The unfulfilled desire for these absent others may thus contribute to the loneliness experience.

A number of psychological theories address the consequences of commitment to the unavailability of a desirable alternative. These theories suggest possible effects of believing that a partner will remain unavailable (for some period of time) on the evaluation of that partner. Research by Festinger and Walster (Festinger & Walster, 1964; Walster, 1964) indicates that in the period immediately after making a decision, persons tend to direct their attention in particular to the good features of the now "unavailable" alternative. As a result, the "unavailable" alternative becomes increasingly attractive. This phenomenon is called regret. It results in an attempt to reverse or undo the decision, if this is possible (Festinger & Walster, 1964), or to reevaluate the alternatives so that the unavailable alternative becomes less attractive and the available (chosen) alternative becomes more attractive (Walster, 1964). This reevaluation illustrates dissonance reduction.

If the decision cannot be undone, and if the dissonance associated with a decision is difficult to reduce, the period of regret may last a long time. The regret about the unavailable partner may be labeled and experienced as loneliness, and it may continue so long as postdecisional regret is salient.

The dissonance theory analysis presumes that the person is responsible for the absence of the unavailable alternative (Wicklund & Brehm, 1976). However, we suggest that commitment to a loss might be sufficient to create regret and the consequent overvaluation of the lost partner (Margulis, 1967). Evidence for this proposition is indirect. One source is research on Brehm's (1966, 1967) theory of psychological reactance. According to Brehm, if an alternative is eliminated by personal or impersonal events, and if the impersonal elimination is unjustified in P's view, then P should experience reactance and consequently should regard the eliminated alternative as increasingly attractive. Furthermore, in Brehm's (1966) analysis, object attractiveness implies potential need satisfaction by the object, as previously mentioned. This is consistent with our position that social partners associated with need satisfaction will be sources of satisfaction and that their unavailability will be psychologically painful. In our view, the increased attractiveness of the unavailable partner, because of his or her absence, may not only signal loneliness but make the loneliness more painful to bear: the person has lost a partner who is more attractive than had earlier been imagined. Thus the longing for an absent or lost partner, experienced as loneliness, may have as preconditions feeling committed to the loss and cognitive reevaluations that heighten the sense of loss.

SUMMARY

We examined social-psychological and privacy concepts that affect loneliness. Critical antecedents of loneliness include the unavailability of an appropriate social partner who could assist in achieving salient socially mediated goals, the belief that the unavailability will endure, and the continued desire for such a relationship. The contribution of a number of variables to loneliness were discussed, including the role of "desired," "expected," and "achieved" social contacts, comparison level, social networks, partner centrality, and interpersonal boundaries. Applying Westin's (1970) taxonomy of privacy, we showed that lonely persons lack the privacy associated with intimacy, a state in which other-contingent goals can be satisfied through open communication. On the other hand, lonely persons may have available other kinds of privacy, including solitude, anonymity, and reserve. The framework is admittedly speculative; however, it provides a useful way to integrate existing research and to suggest directions for future research and theory development on loneliness.

REFERENCES

Abrahams, R. B. Mutual help for the widowed. *Social Work,* 1972, *17,* 55–61.

Altman, I. *The environment and social behavior: Privacy, personal space, territory, crowding.* Monterey, Calif.: Brooks/Cole, 1975.

Altman, I. Privacy: A conceptual analysis. *Environment and Behavior,* 1976, *8,* 7–29.

Altman, I. Privacy: Culturally universal or culturally specific? *Journal of Social Issues,* 1977, *33,* 66–84.

Altman, I., & Taylor, D. A. *Social penetration: The development of interpersonal relationships.* New York: Holt, Rinehart, & Winston, 1973.

Bell, G. R. Alcohol and loneliness. *Journal of Social Therapy,* 1956, *2,* 171–181.

Brehm, J. W. *A theory of psychological reactance.* New York: Academic Press, 1966.

Brehm, J. W. Responses to loss of freedom: A theory of psychological reactance. In J. W. Thibaut, J. T. Spence, & R. C. Carson (Eds.), *Contemporary topics in social psychology.* Morristown, N. J.: General Learning Press, 1976.

Brundage, L. D., Derlega, V. J., & Cash, T. F. The effects of physical attractiveness and need for approval on self-disclosure. *Personality and Social Psychology Bulletin,* 1977, *3,* 63–66.

Cottle, T. The felt sense of studentry. *Interchange,* 1974, *5,* 31–41.

Cronbach, J., & Meehl, P. E. Construct validity in psychological tests. In H. Feigel & M. Scriven (Eds.), *Minnesota studies in the philosophy of science* (Vol. 1). Minneapolis: University of Minnesota Press, 1956.

Crowne, D. P., & Marlowe, D. *The approval motive.* New York: Wiley, 1964.

Cutrona, C. E., & Peplau, L. A. *A longitudinal study of loneliness.* Paper presented at the meeting of the Western Psychological Association, San Diego, 1979.

Derlega, V. J., & Chaikin, A. L. Privacy and self-disclosure in social relationships. *Journal of Social Issues,* 1977, *33*(3), 102–115.

Derlega, V. J., & Grzelak, J. Appropriateness of self-disclosure. In G. Chelune (Ed.), *Self-disclosure.* San Francisco: Jossey-Bass, 1979.

Dion, K. K., & Dion, K. L. Defensiveness, intimacy, and heterosexual attraction. *Journal of Research in Personality,* 1978, *12,* 479–487.

Festinger, L. A theory of social comparison processes. *Human Relations,* 1954, *7,* 117–140.

Festinger, L., & Walster, E. Post-decision regret and decision reversal. In L. Festinger, *Conflict, decision, and dissonance.* Stanford, Calif: Stanford University Press, 1964.

Grumet, G. W. Telephone therapy: A review and case report. *American Journal of Orthopsychiatry,* 1979, *49,* 574–584.

Haas-Hawkings, G. Intimacy as a moderating influence on the stress of loneliness in widowhood. *Essence,* 1978, *2,* 249–258.

Johnson, C. A. Privacy as personal control. In D. H. Carson (Ed.), *Man-environment interactions: Evaluations and applications* (Part II, Vol. 6: S. T. Margulis, Vol. Ed.). Washington, D. C.: Environmental Design Research Association, 1974; and Stroudsburg, Pa.: Dowden, Hutchinson, & Ross, 1975.

Kelley, H. H., Hastorf, A. H., Jones, E. E., Thibaut, J. W., & Usdane, W. M. Some implications of social psychological theory for research on the handicapped. In L. H. Lofquist (Ed.), *Psychological research and rehabilitation.* Washington, D. C.: American Psychological Association, 1960.

Kelvin, P. Predictability, power, and vulnerability in interpersonal attraction. In S. Duck (Ed.), *Theory and practice in interpersonal attraction.* New York: Academic Press, 1977.

Lowenthal, M. F., & Haven, C. Interaction and adaptation: Intimacy as a critical variable. *American Sociological Review,* 1968, *33,* 20–30.

Margulis, S. T. *On the loss of a partner: The effects of responsibility on post-decisional re-evaluation processes.* Unpublished doctoral dissertation, University of Minnesota, 1967.

Margulis, S. T. Conceptions of privacy: Current status and next steps. *Journal of Social Issues,* 1977, *33*(3), 5–21.

Margulis, S. T. *Privacy as information management: A social psychological and environmental framework* (NBSIR 79-1793). Washington, D. C.: National Bureau of Standards, 1979.

Peplau, L. A., & Caldwell, M. A. Loneliness: A cognitive analysis. *Essence,* 1978, *2*(4), 207–220.

Peplau, L. A., & Perlman, D. Blueprint for a social psychological theory of loneliness. In M. Cook & G. Wilson (Eds.), *Love and attraction.* Oxford, England: Pergamon, 1979.

Perlman, D., & Peplau, L. A. Toward a social psychology of loneliness. In S. Duck & R. Gilmour (Eds.), *Personal relationships 3: Personal relationships in disorder.* New York: Academic Press, 1981.

Rubin, Z. Seeking a cure for loneliness. *Psychology Today,* October 1979, pp. 82ff.

Schachter, S. *The psychology of affiliation.* Stanford, Calif.: Stanford University Press, 1959.

Solano, C. H., & Batten, P. G. *Loneliness and objective self-disclosure in an acquaintanceship exercise.* Unpublished manuscript, Wake Forest University,

Sullivan, H. S. *The interpersonal theory of psychiatry.* New York: Norton, 1953. 1979.

Thibaut, J. & Kelley, H. H. *The social psychology of groups.* New York: Wiley, 1959.

Walster, E. The temporal sequence of post-decision processes. In L. Festinger, *Conflict, decision, and dissonance.* Stanford, Calif.: Stanford University Press, 1964.

Weiss, R. S. *Loneliness: The experience of emotional and social isolation.* Cambridge, Mass.: MIT Press, 1973.

Weiss, R. S. The provisions of social relationships. In Z. Rubin (Ed.), *Doing unto others: Joining, molding, conforming, helping.* Englewood Cliffs, N. J.: Prentice-Hall Spectrum, 1974.

Westin, A. *Privacy and freedom.* New York: Atheneum, 1970.

Wicklund, R. A., & Brehm, J. W. *Perspectives on cognitive dissonance.* New York: Lawrence Erlbaum Associates, 1976.

Wortman, C. B., & Dunkel-Schetter, C. Interpersonal relationships and cancer: A theoretical analysis. *Journal of Social Issues,* 1979, *35*(1), 120–155.

Zimbardo, P. G. *Shyness.* New York: Jove/HBJ, 1978.

Zipris, A. *Being lonely: An empirical-phenomenological investigation.* Unpublished doctoral dissertation proposal, Duquesne University, 1979.

Chapter 11

A General Systems
Approach to Loneliness

James P. Flanders

Loneliness research now stands in the toddler stage of development with a modicum of theory and research to its credit. A research beachhead has been established with the creation of measures to assess loneliness (see Russell, Chapter 6). Perhaps most of all, the field needs an encompassing theoretical framework to guide and integrate research so that the diversity of factors influencing loneliness does not produce a scattered morass of research findings. Both psychologists (Caplan & Nelson, 1973) and lay people (Peplau, Russell, & Heim, 1979) seem to underestimate substantially the importance of situational factors in loneliness; a broader theoretical framework should help in identifying such variables. Also needed are diverse, fine-grained empirical studies of individuals, because the specific variables associated with the onset and alleviation of loneliness distress await discovery.

This paper sketches a metaframework for integrating both theory and research based on Miller's (1978) *General Living Systems Theory* (GLS). Conceptualizations based on GLS are then derived for loneliness and for emotional intimacy, the critical referent of loneliness. It is hypothesized that two factors in society substantially increase loneliness in everyday life: first, the decline of a day of rest free of most commerce reduces emotional intimacy and increases loneliness; second, the process of household televiewing has become the single most time-consuming activity in one's lifetime other than sleep: it consumes 57 working years of time. Several researchable hypotheses are offered to help understand televiewing's unmatched massive intrusion into nearly everyone's leisure—time that could otherwise be used for interactions with other people. The chapter's research hypotheses have been selected mainly because they seemed to fill gaps not addressed in detail by others in this book.

GENERAL LIVING SYSTEMS THEORY

Let us examine a unique ecosystem that illustrates the general need for multiple levels of analysis in understanding living systems. If you visit Florida

you will have the opportunity to view a most fascinating ecosystem in minia-
ture. Wildlife in the Florida Everglades revolves around alligator holes. In
Fall the water table starts dropping in the Everglades, and every alligator
knows it. Bull alligators anticipate the onset of the dry season, so they begin
to stake out and defend a territory. From their summer lackadaisical mood
they suddenly turn into savage defenders of their chosen area. They claw out
a pond-size hole into raw coral rock. They mate. When the dry season ar-
rives, Everglades wildlife concentrates around alligator holes. The holes teem
with fish and swarm with egrets. Nighttime attracts rabbits, raccoons, foxes,
deer, and an occasional Florida panther. When the rains arrive once again,
the wildlife disperses; the fish spread across the sawgrass plains. Alligators
once again snooze peacefully side by side (May, 1969). What have alligator
holes to do with theoretical paradigms?

Suppose you want to study loneliness in bull alligators. Suppose further
that you employ some familiar theories and methods: cognitive theory, attribution theory, questionnaires, one-hour behavioral observations, and of course
your new alligator speech translator. However, you soon discover the limitations of such tools for explaining the alligators' drastic shifts in mood and
social behavior. Of course the problem lies with the tools themselves, which
focus mainly on the individual alligator. The sophisticated understanding of
alligator holes requires analysis of individual-environment interaction systems
at several levels of analysis. Meteorological systems cause the water level to
change. Political systems affect how much water flows into the Everglades
from Lake Okeechobee versus how much civilization siphons off. The legal
system has caused a decline of poachers, who no longer pick off the most
venturesome alligators, which has probably raised average aggressiveness of
alligators. Biochemical systems inside the alligator surely assist in adapting to
seasonal changes.

In short, the alligator hole provides a vivid example of the necessity for
using an approach with multiple levels of analysis for sophisticated understanding of all life process. Does such an approach exist? Yes it does, but only
in framework form, leaving the hard spadework for the future. We turn now
to examine some central concepts in GLS.

Miller's huge volume, *Living Systems* (1978), proposes a metaframework
for interrelating theory and research about living creatures. Its basic assumption is that all behavior occurs in intermeshed systems at seven levels of
analysis: the cell, the organ, the organism, the group, the organization, the
society, and the supranational system. At the various levels and between levels
of analysis, notions of cause and effect generally give way to a view of behavior
occurring in interlocking systems in which most factors comprise both cause
and effect over time. One accurately understands and predicts through the
study of system processes adjoining the phenomenon in question. Adjoining
systems can comprise *suprasystems* above, *infrasystems* below, or *parallel*
systems at the same level of analysis. The female alligator makes gestures of
submission prior to mating, which illustrates behavior in parallel systems at the
organism level of analysis. Two shy people who do not speak to each other

at a party may harbor similar fearful perceptions and emotions about meeting new people, which also illustrates parallel systems at the individual organism level of analysis. Weather systems comprise a suprasystem for the individual alligator. Loneliness may well produce increased risk of death from hypertensive heart disease (Lynch, 1977). In this example the person's circulatory system comprises an infrasystem at the organ level of analysis, one level below the organism level.

To survive, organisms try to maintain *steady states* of functioning largely through the use of *negative feedback,* which acts to restore the prior steady state by definition in the cybernetic sense. Individual body cells restore a prior level of oxygen supply using negative feedback to the heart and lungs. Positive feedback, in the cybernetic sense, acts to increase deviation from a prior steady state, oftentimes toward a new equilibrium. Clubs and other civic organizations often exert pressure on parents to increase time allocated to the group at the expense of family time, which, if it happens, would comprise positive feedback. GLS emphasizes the interplay of both negative and positive feedback, as have proponents of a dialectic view of psychology (Altman & Chemers, 1980) and of the opponent-process approach to motivation (Solomon & Corbit, 1974). GLS also emphasizes dynamic change over time, not static states. Life processes change by definition. Examples at four levels of analysis are now derived from Miller's (1978) Hypothesis 5.6-1 to illustrate the range of GLS.

"If a system's negative feedback discontinues and is not restored by that system or another on which it becomes parasitic or symbiotic, it decomposes into multiple components and its suprasystem assumes control of them" (Miller, 1978, p. 110, original italics deleted). At the *cell* level of analysis, the exceedingly lonely person may develop tissue damage from ulcers or alcoholism. Individual cells in an ulcerating duodenum may dissolve or be removed surgically. At the *organ* level of analysis, the exceeding lonely person can decompose physically. For example, the death rate from heart disease, cancer, stroke, cirrhosis of liver, hypertension, and pneumonia are each at least twice as high for divorced versus married U. S. males (Lynch, 1977, p. 41). At the *organism* level of analysis, similar death rates occur in males, and in widowed versus married females for death by suicide (Lynch, 1977, pp. 40–41), where the group of family survivors generally assume control of the remains. With psychological decomposition (e.g., schizophrenia), relatives usually assume control and then relinquish control to a mental institution. At the *group* level, loneliness may precipitate decomposition of a family. The individual members (components) then often go to live with relatives. The upper three levels of analysis are now illustrated using other loneliness-related phenomena.

At the *organizational* level, corporate steady states may paradoxically require that individual people be kept in a state of restless detachment from other people. Slater (1970) has noted that businesses would lose money and some would fail without the patronage of family members on evenings and weekends. Television networks would lose vast revenues without the enthralled prime-time captivation of multitudes. Single people ensconced in separate dwellings consume more of just about everything to the extent they do not make joint use of virtually all goods and services. Of course the "loneliness business" (Gordon, 1976) requires loneliness. The relationship of loneliness to the vitality of local church organizations awaits study.

At the *societal* level, widespread loneliness may comprise an early warning about the foundations of that society. The military security of a nation's boundaries may well require individuals connected enough and therefore committed enough to defend it. Also, at the *supranational* level, the policies of the OPEC oil-producing cartel may require Americans to stay home one day per week as Europeans have chosen to do (for longer than the current energy crunch). In addition, the availability of energy will certainly affect future housing, city life, and railroad planning around the world and comcomitant social behavior.

The organization level of analysis hurls an especially tantalizing paradox at loneliness researchers. How is it that, of all the seven levels, only systems at the organization level seem generally to flourish more as loneliness goes *up?* At all other levels the integrity of systems seems to increase with less loneliness. This is an intriguing problem for future research.

GLS does not generally differentiate the individual from his or her surroundings except as components of a system. Theory should parallel life, and life involves interactive systems. Thus one cannot properly study even one person's loneliness without also studying the reactions of others in that person's group or society with whom, for example, interactions might occur but do not. The notion of an "essence" of a phenomenon such as loneliness is also false, regardless of the cognitive or behavioral status of the essence. Rather one must use the syndrome or cluster notion with multiple components. A purely cognitive *or* behavioral *or* dyadic interaction notion of loneliness will produce the same deadends encountered by trait-paradigm-oriented researchers of personality and leadership, because the paradigm itself is fundamentally too narrow to address the object of study.

The sophisticated scientist routinely examines the suprasystem above, infrasystems below, and parallel systems adjacent to the phenomenon under study. The multilevel strategy is far more important than any given theory or finding about loneliness. It is defined as necessary for scientific sophistication in general. It is manifested by individual researchers who use theory and gather data from more than one level in the same article. It is manifested by scientific editors who include papers from differing levels of analysis in their journal or book, as Peplau and Perlman have in the present volume.

There exist three grades of theoretical sophistication in psychology. At the lowest grade resides person or individual centered approaches, and also situationism. On the second grade resides person-surroundings interactionism, the level to which clinical and social psychology are now moving. On the highest grade sits GLS, which has not only the advantages of the previous two, but also the unique capability of encompassing and interrelating more focused theories and research. Applications of systems approaches exist already in clinical psychology (Beavers, 1977; Minuchin, 1974), community psychology (Murrell, 1973), and organizational psychology (Katz & Kahn, 1978). While not deriving directly from GLS, these approaches embody many GLS attributes, and ultimately derive from the classic work of von Bertallanfy (1966, 1968). Loneliness researchers can now become the first group in the history of psychology to begin their research area at the highest grade of sophistication.

A GLS DEFINITION OF LONELINESS

A GLS approach provides a new definition of loneliness. *Loneliness is an adaptive feedback mechanism for bringing the individual from a current lack stress state to a more optimal range of human contact in quantity or form.* "Lack stress" means too little of a given input, human contact in this instance. Human contact refers to both superficial and deep social relations and will be discussed later. Several novel features stand out in this definition.

"Feedback mechanism" is more general than, say, a purely cognitive definition, because much more is involved in loneliness than human cognition. Words without behavior are generally unconvincing. The present definition is functional and not tied to one specific morphology of behavior or cognition. Rather it emphasizes functionally equivalent patterns that may differ radically among people. Thus the coping strategies following the poignant emotions of loneliness certainly count as loneliness phenomena. In fact, the adjustive processes following loneliness emotions may be the most critical external indicators of loneliness; momentary loneliness expressions followed by the total absence of even blocked dispositions toward change would not convince any jury that loneliness exists. The definition is not overly restrictive and thus does not overstep the methodological state of the art. It allows for the study of animal behavior. It emphasizes that the feedback mechanism comes into play at specific times and encourages study of the momentary antecedents of those times.

The present definition retains the achieved-desired distinction, while softening "desired level" to "optimal range" because (a) not all people may behaviorally seek what they cognitively desire, and (b) "optimal range" connotes a cluster of phenomena with a time dimension. The definition is purposive. The definition's time perspective matches the phenomenon itself. The definition is dynamic, emphasizing change and goals. Both "adaptive" and "optimal" connote survival value lying just below the surface of loneliness emotions. This adaptive approach is exactly what Bowlby (1969) advocated when he emphasized the survival value of attachment behavior.

The feedback mechanism of loneliness need not always function successfully, as all rejected suitors can testify. The present definition does not differentiate between individual and surroundings, although the purposive end state emphasizes the individual. This definition does not argue against alternative views but rather embraces them. For example, Altman (1975),

Derlega and Margulis (Chapter 10), and Suedfeld (Chapter 4) emphasized the need for privacy and the healing aspects of loneliness. The present definition casts these conceptions into a larger framework, in which the individual strives to stay inside an optimal range of human contact as a steady state. Too little human contact elicits poignant feelings of loneliness. Too much human contact produces social overload, a stressor that often afflicts psychologists and psychiatrists.

The current model likewise embraces the cognitive view of loneliness (see Chapter 9) as an essential component of the whole process, because the individual usually labels the current distress as loneliness and takes action based on that cognition. The individual's perceptions represent the kinds and amounts of social interaction that define the person's optimal range of emotional intimacy. In keeping with the multilevel GLS perspective, the present definition emphasizes the utility of both cognitive and behavioral data to study the truly multifaceted phenomenon of loneliness.

The present definition conceives of loneliness as ordinarily produced by factors from several different levels of analysis. Likewise, intervention to alleviate loneliness must occur at different levels for maximal effectiveness. For example, individual therapy may heal the majority who partake while failing to address the genesis of loneliness or its prevention, both of which may reside primarily in family and societal factors.

Finally, this definition highlights the importance of "human contact," a concept that must be defined in order to make sense out of loneliness. The following section contains my attempt at such a specification.

A CONCEPT OF HUMAN CONTACT

Everyone agrees that loneliness reflects a deficit condition, a lack of something. The antidote to loneliness is generally agreed to comprise human contact, human closeness, meaningful relationship, intimacy, or some other everyday language concept. For the full-fledged study of loneliness to get off the ground, a conceptualization of human contact is required that is precise enough to allow disconfirmation through empirical research.

Some prior attempts to conceptualize human contact have involved specifying features of emotional intimacy within the dyad. Thus for Jourard (1971) and Derlega and Chaikin (1975), intimacy is self-disclosure; confession and psychotherapy involve self-disclosure but not necessarily intimacy. For Montagu (1971) and Morris (1971), intimacy is touching; but the prostitute does not relieve loneliness for long. Levinger (1977b) and Raush (1977) argue for studying human contact using different levels of analysis. Levinger (1977a) describes deep relationships as characterized by mutuality: "The deep as opposed to the shallow relationship, then, is characterized by stronger commonality, heavier emotional investment and a more definite structure containing it" (p. 7). However, the referent of mutuality and commonality is clearly missing. Levinger accurately summarized,

"Yet, while blessed with case history and anecdotal material, we still lack systematic theory to guide empirical work" (1977a, p. 13).

The present conceptualization embodies self-disclosure, touching, and other features of human contact in a multidimensional framework first presented in Flanders' *Practical psychology* (1976, Chapters 3 and 4). Conceptual emphasis is laid on the exchange of scarce personal resources such as money, time, good looks, quick wit, and anything else the other person seeks. In GLS all systems are presumed to process or exchange information, matter, and energy, and so it is with the human dyad.

Human contact consists of seven essential features. Six concern the allocation of scarce personal resources, and the seventh is a cognitive conclusion. While the presence of any given feature is not necessary on any given interaction occasion, all seven must be present over months and years. For the first five, the forerunners can be found in childhood patterns of attachment (Bowlby, 1969). The overall dimension of human contact runs from the superficiality present in acquaintances to the great closeness or depth present in intimates of long standing.

Two features are necessary for human contact to exist at all. First, *time for frequent interactions* must exist, especially at the beginning of a relationship. Second, the individuals must have *informal interactions* free of pressing role demands that constrict action. These first two features highlight the dimension of time as it concerns both frequency of interaction occasions and duration of the dyadic relationship over months and years. Clearly implied is the need to study time budgets as necessary antecedents for human contact to exist at all (Robinson, 1977).

Other features are necessary for human contact to develop and to deepen. Third, *self-disclosure* must occur and increase substantially (Altman & Taylor, 1973; Flanders, 1976). Fourth, *touching* must occur, such as ritual handshakes or sexual touching.

Two other features are necessary for human contact to endure over time. A fifth feature of *favorable exchange of resources* must occur over months and years. "Favorable" means that the individual has decided that the other person has provided a more positive exchange of resources than otherwise available, that is, in the absence of this particular relationship. A favorable exchange must also contain a sufficient preponderance of the other person's scarce personal resources. Because this novel component lies at the heart of adult human intimacy, we shall explore it in some detail.

What is the special something that allows something you do or give or receive to count toward deepening an intimate relationship? Something personal must occur, but not all personal expressions count. Also, sometimes we give in vain. The other person displays the unspeakably poor judgment to reject our most worthy offering. I contend that a something special does exist and that we can indeed get a psychometric handle on it.

The something special that makes our offering eligible to count toward a human contact relationship is the *scarcity* of the resource we offer. To the degree that whatever resource you offer is in short supply for you personally, it can count all the more because there is so little of it. The millionaire's $1000 does not count much, but your loan of $25 does. Store-bought cookies do not count much, but your homemade goodies do. "I love you" said once in a lifetime counts, while "I love you" every weekend does not. And this brings us to the topics of determining scarcity and kinds of resources.

Personal resources consist mainly of time, money, and affection, but also include status, information, goods, and services in the Foa and Foa (1974) cognitive theory of resource exchange. To be useful, taxonomies of resources need not be independent, but they do need to be operational. Accordingly, loneliness researchers might well explore first the most easily measurable of scarce personal resources: time, money, and affectional exchanges.

Allocation of personal time may well be the missing gold standard of social interaction that has stifled social exchange field research thus far. Since time is scarce and since everyone gets a 24-hour ration of it daily, the time equivalent of personal resources may well serve as a handy gauge of scarcity in everyday life. To the degree that you allocate time to the other person or to resources you exchange, that other person will conclude that your true values are showing. Research with parametric variation in scarcity of otherwise constant resources exchanged should support this hypothesis. However, bear in mind that even supplying the other person with a resource of high time investment does not guarantee human contact, because all resources have limited substitutability. For instance, money can hardly be substituted for affection. You cannot send money to replace you at your own wedding, but you can bring flowers to a dinner to make amends when you are a little late.

Finally, on the topic of scarce resources, the present conception allows us to use economic theory, which may be the most sophisticated of the social sciences. For example, birth control technology, laxer social norms, and mate swapping do indeed lessen the potential value of sex, because greater supply per se lowers the value. For a free-wheeling application of economic supply and demand to psychology over topics from love to grade inflation, see McKenzie and Tullock (1978).

A sixth feature is also required for a relationship to endure over time. The exchange of resources over time must be reasonably reciprocal to assure a *fair relationship,* where a fair or equitable dyadic relationship yields each party results in proportion to inputs (Flanders, 1976, Chapters 3 and 4; Walster, Walster & Berscheid, 1978). I would apply this concept to everyday life in a somewhat novel manner.

Of course each party is attracted to a relationship by positive results or fun, but the key to maintaining a relationship lies in investment, which always equals cost and usually entails work. More specifically, costs such as time and effort put expressly into activities that directly benefit the dyadic system define the investment each party has in the relationship. No cost, no investment in the relationship. This reasoning has powerful implications for studying close relationships and loneliness today, because it implies that family bonds and later human contact require an investment of substantial cost to the individual. Modern Americans have been moving away from such a lifestyle since World War II, and the low work investment of children and adolescents in their families today comprises one of the most important factors in producing loneliness. Why? Because relationships without such an investment are fragile, lacking the resilience to withstand stress to the relationship system. Research linking prior investment in family activities to family stability should support this claim (Kanter, 1972).

Seventh, the individual must develop *feelings of closeness,* which is a cognitive conclusion. In adults, desired human contact may be even more important than currently attained human contact. While most people can render an accurate description of attained human contact, desires are subject to much social influence and distortion. This implies the need for careful study of how expectations about human contact are formed and altered developmentally throughout the life span.

These features are not independent or orthogonal, but neither is social life. Social life consists of clusters of related behavior, and so should our research methods if they are to mirror reality. Each feature is necessary over time but none is sufficient. Abundance of the first six will not guarantee intimacy if conclusion is denied. The genetic endowment and learning history of each person will produce a unique set of output capabilities and input desires for that person. However, cultural commonalities and individual patterns can be studied scientifically.

Be it inborn instinct or acquired behavior disposition, the need for human contact arises with such regularity (nearly everyone displays it) and strength (almost no true hermits exist) that we can truly conceive of it as a need. As such, it comprises a specific kind of stimulation that adult humans seek out, much as we seek out salt or suffer for the lack of it. Moreover, the specificity of human contact means that we can experience the paradox of general stimulus overload from job, pollution, or harried superficial interactions, while at the same time suffering from a deficit of human contact. This very state of affairs characterizes the modern urban condition as Gordon (1976), Milgram (1970), and Slater (1970) described it.

The considerations about human contact advanced in this section dictate the direct study of the exchange of scarce personal resources. Potential analysis might focus on time budgets, checkbooks, and self-disclosure. Clinical and social psychologists have much to gain from the study of family finances, which is now virtually ignored or left to social workers. The present approach sees household decisions about time and money allocations as today's crucible for showing personal values. Such decisions also comprise a research gold mine for studying the underlying dynamics of power and fairness in intimate relations (Benjamin, 1974; Haley, 1963).

SOCIAL SYSTEM FACTORS INFLUENCING LONELINESS

All loneliness researchers agree on the central importance of nonoptimal human contact as it affects the individual's thoughts and behavior. Most deep human contact of the kind that forestalls or alleviates loneliness occurs during the individual's free time. Free time means discretionary time not allocated to the physical necessities of life such as sleep and earning a living. The individual presumably has a good deal of freedom in deciding how free time is spent. If certain factors influence use of leisure time so as to cause massive reallocations of time and personal resources away from human contact, then loneliness researchers may profitably study them. As it happens, two such factors now exist.

The Day of Rest

The day of rest enhances human contact even apart from its effect on religious activities. It means closing nearly all commercial enterprises, not physical rest, because the day of rest has traditionally provided for doing work around one's dwelling. The day of rest has tremendous symbolic and behavioral import for close human relationships. When Europeans close up shop on Saturday afternoons or small towns in the United States roll up the streets on Sunday, the government has explicitly created a dramatic symbol endorsing personal resource exchange away from business and usually toward friends and family.

Eliminating the day of rest reduces human contact in at least three ways. First, the cognitive consequence of removing a time block signifying the preeminence of social institutions (friendships, family) over commercial institutions cannot be underestimated. At the very least one would expect lesser value attributed to the social institutions of family and friends, perhaps even to oneself. One would also expect greater value attributed to the social institutions of corporations and the national economic system. One would expect such attributions to turn up in research using standard attribution methodology, in which subjects would make judgments about fictional societies. Second, the pure work investment into personal relationships is probably diminished, thus diminishing commitment to the relationship, because activities now contain less work and more play. Thus dyadic and familial relationships should be judged more susceptible to loneliness and breakup by outside stress. Third, the personal time allocated directly to close relationships probably shrinks. Increased commercial exchanges are generally characterized by spending more money and less time, and money is not very substitutable for time in interpersonal relationships.

Process of Household Televiewing

Zimbardo (1977) hypothesized a direct link between the process of televiewing and shyness. "Curiously, the passive nature of the shy person may be a learned pattern of responding to a televised world" (p. 43). Flanders (1976) proposed another effect of televiewing, which directly affects loneliness. Televiewing stands "ready to take over your social functions by displacing the time given you by your intimates" (p. 223). These hypotheses warrant more detailed explication.

Televiewing has directly changed Americans' use of time more than any other development of the twentieth century, according to the best time budget data (Robinson, 1977, p. 31). If one assumes the average working year to consume 2000 hours, the average American who lives to age 75 will spend about 114,000 hours or 57 working years watching television (Comstock, Chafee, Katzman, McCombs, & Roberts, 1978, p. 85). Comstock et al. conclude that "television dominates the free time of children as well as adults" (1978, pp. 150–151). Incredibly, television owners report spending 10 to 15% more time televiewing than on conversation and social activities combined as a primary activity (Robinson, 1977, p. 31; Szalai, 1972, pp. 197–212). In short, televiewing looms far and away the most important factor influencing use of modern discretionary time.

Televiewing's major effects may well stem from the process of televiewing itself, not the content, which has largely distracted researchers. Televiewing's major effect probably consists of the alternate behavior foregone because of it. Economists call this the *opportunity costs,* namely the value of one's best foregone alternatives. Thus for American adults the opportunity cost of televiewing by definition comprises the value of those activities replaced by televiewing. Televiewing's other main effect is to degrade the prevailing expression of affect in the household. These effects must be studied directly and experimentally, which has not been done.

Flanders (1980) marshals empirical and observational support to propose a number of testable predictions about the televiewing process. In the realm of expressions of affect, household televiewing should draw household members into closer physical proximity, while decreasing nonverbal expressions of liking. Thus between members of any given dyad, we might expect more televiewing to produce less eye contact, less smiling, less forward lean toward the other person, less parallel body torsos, and less touching of all kinds including sexual. In the crucial area of self-disclosure and conversation, more televiewing should produce less self-disclosure (more superficial topics discussed), fewer different topics discussed, fewer total words of conversation, and less listening to the other person.

In the realm of opportunity cost, more televiewing should produce fewer outings, special occasions, and rituals of all kinds for the family. Rituals here include mealtimes, bedtime activities, holiday rituals, and so on. More televiewing should also result in less time spent with friends, less time spent outside the physical boundaries of the household, less total physical exercise, less time spent with pets, less reading, and less sleep time. Because household televiewing is largely a passive behavior, more televiewing should produce less curiosity and assertiveness. Curiosity can apply to physical exploration of novel but standardized physical settings, such as a new room or park, as well as to social exploration of new persons and visual exploration of novel visual stimuli.

Televiewing seems to possess the attributes of an addiction, which would make it the second most widespread kind of behavior—after gambling—to be recognized as an addiction. Household televiewing generally does not produce individual pathologies directly comparable to the compulsive gambler, but the enormous time allocated by a wide segment of the population may well render the opportunity cost of household televiewing far higher than that of gambling.

In short, televiewing effectively turns people away from each other and onto television. Televiewing's unmatched massive intrusiveness into the daily lives of nearly everyone makes it a prime candidate for loneliness research.

CONTROLLING LONELINESS

If we adopt the GLS conception of loneliness as an adaptive feedback mechanism, then we do not wish to eliminate loneliness any more than we wish to eliminate the experience of physical pain. To do so would deprive the individual of warning subsystems with important survival values. Loneliness may also comprise a positive feedback mechanism that spurs the individual on to a new, improved state of existence. Rather we hope to provide individuals the wherewithal to personally control loneliness in their own lives.

Individuals wish to reduce loneliness to a minimum. On the other hand, the growth and survival of organizations in the loneliness industry and of television networks may thrive upon capturing resources such as time that would otherwise be allocated to other people, thus promoting loneliness for the individual. Businesses in shopping malls thrive on evening and weekend shopping hours. The GLS view mandates interventions at various levels to match the factors that help cause loneliness. Therefore, those seriously interested in alleviating loneliness may soon find themselves embroiled in nasty confrontations of a legal and political sort. Glittering shopping malls and television networks do indeed compete directly with one's personal social world for one's free time, the very occasions so essential for human contact.

CONCLUSIONS

Widespread use of General Living Systems approach will facilitate integration of loneliness research results while not restricting the researchers from focusing on a specific domain. Loneliness is fruitfully conceptualized as an adaptive feedback mechanism for bringing the individual from a current lack stress to a more optimal range of human contact. Human contact is fruitfully defined in terms of (a) reciprocal exchange of scarce personal resources over time, and (b) the resulting cognitive conclusion of closeness. Personal values are convincingly displayed only through allocation of scarce personal resources. Two recent factors have invisibly but massively channeled Americans' use of free time away from people and toward commercial exchanges and televiewing. First, the disappearance of the day of rest has caused more commercial and less personal exchange for most people. Second, even average televiewing today may well replace many if not most of a lifetime's mellow moments of human contact, which illustrates the paradoxical benefits to organizations of increased individual loneliness. Finally, loneliness warrants control but not elimination, because loneliness is a valuable feedback mechanism with important survival value to both the individual and the nation.

REFERENCES

Altman, I. *The environment and social behavior.* Monterey, Calif.: Brooks/Cole, 1975.

Altman, I., & Chemers, M. M. *Culture and environment.* Monterey, Calif.: Brooks/Cole, 1980.

Altman, I., & Taylor, D. *Social penetration: The development of interpersonal relationships.* New York: Holt, 1973.

Beavers, W. R. *Psychotherapy and growth: A family systems approach.* New York: Bruner/Mazel, 1977.

Benjamin, L. S. Structural analysis of social behavior. *Psychological Review,* 1974, *81,* 392–425.

Bertallanfy, L. von. General systems theory and psychiatry. In S. Arieti (Ed.), *American handbook of psychiatry* (Vol. 3). New York: Basic Books, 1966.

Bertallanfy, L. von. *General systems theory.* New York: Braziller, 1968.

Bowlby, J. *Attachment and loss: Attachment.* New York: Basic Books, 1969.

Caplan, N., & Nelson, S. D. On being useful: The nature and consequences of psychological research on social problems. *American Psychologist,* 1973, *28,* 199–211.

Comstock, G., Chafee, S., Katzman, N., McCombs, M., & Roberts, D. *Television and human behavior.* New York: Columbia University Press, 1978.

Derlega, V., & Chaikin, A. *Sharing intimacy.* Englewood Cliffs, N. J.: Prentice-Hall, 1975.

Flanders, J. P. *Practical psychology.* New York: Harper & Row, 1976.

Flanders, J. P. *Televiewing behavior in households: A paradigm for study and modification.* Unpublished manuscript, Florida International University, 1980.

Foa, U. G., & Foa, E. B. *Societal structures of the mind.* Springfield, Ill.: Charles C. Thomas, 1974.

Gordon, S. *Lonely in America.* New York: Simon & Schuster, 1976.

Haley, J. *Strategies of psychotherapy.* New York: Grune & Stratton, 1963.

Jourard, S. M. *The transparent self* (2nd ed.). New York: Van Nostrand Reinhold, 1971.

Kanter, T. M. *Commitment and community*. Cambridge, Mass.: Harvard University Press, 1972.

Katz, D., & Kahn, R. L. *The social psychology of organizations* (2nd ed.). New York: Wiley, 1978.

Levinger, G. The embrace of lives: Changing and unchanging. In G. Levinger & H. L. Raush (Eds.), *Close relationships*. Amherst: University of Massachusetts Press, 1977 a.

Levinger, G. Re-Viewing the close relationship. In G. Levinger & H. L. Raush (Eds.), *Close relationships*. Amherst: University of Massachusetts Press, 1977 b.

Levinger, G., & Raush, H. L. *Close relationships*. Amherst: University of Massachusetts Press, 1977.

Lynch, J. J. *The broken heart: The medical consequences of loneliness*. New York: Basic Books, 1977.

McKenzie, R. B., & Tullock, G. *The new world of economics* (2nd ed.). Homewood, Ill.: Irwin, 1978.

May, J. *Alligator hole*. Chicago: Follett, 1969.

Milgram, S. The experience of living in cities. *Science*, 1970, *167*, 1461–1468.

Miller, J. G. *Living systems*. New York: McGraw-Hill, 1978.

Minuchin, S. *Families and family therapy*. Cambridge, Mass.: Harvard University Press, 1974.

Montagu, A. *Touching*. New York: Perennial, 1971.

Morris, D. *Intimate behavior*. New York: Bantam, 1971.

Murrell, S. A. *Community psychology and social systems: A conceptual framework and intervention guide*. New York: Behavioral Publications (now Human Sciences Press), 1973.

Peplau, L. A., Russell, D., & Heim, M. The experience of loneliness. In I. Frieze, D. Bar-Tal, & J. S. Carroll (Eds.), *New approaches to social problems: Applications of attribution theory*. San Francisco: Jossey-Bass, 1979.

Raush, H. L. Orientations to the close relations. In G. Levinger & H. L. Raush (Eds.), *Close relationships*. Amherst: University of Massachusetts Press, 1977.

Robinson, J. P. *How Americans use time: A social-psychological analysis of everyday behavior*. New York: Prager, 1977.

Slater, P. *The pursuit of loneliness: American culture at the breaking point*. Boston: Beacon Press, 1970.

Solomon, R. L., & Corbit, J. D. An opponent-process theory of motivation: Temporal dynamics of affect. *Psychological Review*, 1974, *81*, 119–145.

Szalai, A. (Ed.). *The use of time*. The Hague: Mouton, 1972.

Walster, E., Walster, W. G., & Berscheid, E. *Equity theory and research*. Boston: Allyn & Bacon, 1978.

Zimbardo, P. *Shyness: What it is and what to do about it*. Reading, Mass.: Addison-Wesley, 1977.

PART FOUR

Loneliness in Adulthood

The four chapters in this section all deal with loneliness among adults. The authors were not necessarily trying to identify midlife crises that lead to loneliness. Instead, for the most part, they were studying adults to form a more general picture of the nature of loneliness.

Though each of the chapters in this section is unique and makes a distinctive contribution, they cover some common ground. For instance, both Chapters 13 and 14 present short scales for measuring loneliness and describe the feelings associated with loneliness. Most of the chapters examine various correlates or predictors of loneliness. Chapters 12 and 15 consider the social behavior of lonely individuals.

Horowitz, French, and Anderson are innovative in their use of the "prototype" approach. A prototype is "a theoretical notion, consisting of the most common features or properties of members of that category." With regard to loneliness, a prototype consists of the composite of the most common features of a lonely person. All the attributes in the prototype characterize at least some lonely person, but no one attribute is either necessary or sufficient for loneliness. In other words, the prototype is a "fuzzy set" of properties. Thus any given person can vary in the number of prototypic qualities he or she manifests. This probabilistic approach contrasts with many earlier approaches to ideal types or syndromes of loneliness, which assumed that all qualities of the ideal type must be present for a positive classification. Horowitz and his associates first develop the prototype for loneliness. They then compare this with the prototype for depression, discuss interpersonal problems associated with loneliness, and examine the causal explanations lonely and nonlonely students make for interpersonal success and failure.

Rubenstein and Shaver's work is novel in that they capitalized on a neglected data collection technique: the newspaper survey. They placed an 84-item questionnaire in newspapers in six communities. The response was overwhelming: in one community alone, 22,000 readers returned questionnaires! Chapter 13 focuses on the feelings these people experienced when they were lonely as well as the reasons people cited for being lonely. Rubenstein and Shaver conclude that their data support Weiss's distinction of social versus emotional loneliness.

Another noteworthy feature of both Rubenstein and Shaver's chapter, and the next chapter by Paloutzian and Ellison, is an examination of what people do (e.g., try to meet new friends, watch television) in response to being lonely. A second distinctive aspect of Paloutzian and Ellison's contribution is their concern with the role of religious values and spiritual well-being in loneliness.

Jones's program of research on the social behavior of lonely people is praiseworthy in several regards. First, Jones carefully examines the available evidence on the relationship between social contact and loneliness. Much of the early work had shown virtually no impact of low social contact. Jones clarifies this matter and indicates the nature of the social contacts that are most closely associated with the experience of loneliness. Second, Jones describes his studies of the behavior of lonely students while they are interacting in groups. These studies serve as a basis for answering the interesting question "Do lonely people reject potential relationships?" Third, Jones has used his laboratory findings to develop a brief social skills training program to help alleviate loneliness. Collectively, Jones's studies shed light on the full range of factors involved in loneliness—those that cause it, those that lead to its persistence, and those that can reduce it.

Chapter 12

The Prototype of a Lonely Person

**Leonard M. Horowitz, Rita de S. French,
and Craig A. Anderson**

The concept of the lonely person is not well defined. Its meaning varies somewhat from person to person, and people seem to apply different standards when they judge loneliness in themselves and in others. Therefore, when people say "I feel lonely," their intended meanings are not precise. Three people beginning psychotherapy with a complaint of loneliness may have quite distinct problems in mind: One may be experiencing an awkwardness in initiating social contacts, another may be experiencing deep feelings of inferiority and inadequacy, a third may be experiencing existential feelings of separateness and alienation.

Because of this diversity in meaning, some method is needed that not only describes the "average" meaning but also allows us to describe variability in people's usage. Our goal in this chapter is to provide such a description. We will describe the major features of a lonely person and show how these features can be organized into a "cognitive structure." This organized set of features will comprise the prototype of a lonely person, which will describe the "average meaning" of the concept and also allow us to characterize variability in its usage.

OVERVIEW

Let us begin with five propositions about loneliness that we shall then develop more fully. The propositions are organized around the concept of a prototype, and after the overview has been presented, we shall systematically elaborate each of the propositions with supporting data.

The research reported in this chapter was supported in part by funds from the Boys Town Center for the Study of Youth Development at Stanford University. However, the opinions expressed and the policies advocated herein do not necessarily reflect those of Boys Town.

We would like to express our gratitude to Jean Amrhein, David Grandin, Betsy Lamson, Jeffrey Lapid, and Kathryn Tucker for their help in the collection and analysis of the data.

183

The Lonely Person as a Prototype

First, we propose that a lonely person should not be conceptualized in terms of a traditional *trait* or *type,* but rather in terms of the more contemporary concept of a "fuzzy set." This more modern conception can be used to describe a theoretically ideal "lonely person," or prototype, a standard against which real people can be evaluated. We know that lonely people in general feel cut off from others and unable to connect socially, but other characteristic feelings, thoughts, and behavior need to be examined that also contribute to the experience of loneliness and to different people's conceptions of a lonely person. We shall also ask whether lonely people and nonlonely people produce the same prototype when they describe their conceptions of a lonely person.

The Prototype and Judgments of Loneliness

Second, we propose that disagreements about loneliness (and unreliability in judging loneliness) can be clarified through the concept of a prototype. If a person is described by *many* prototypic features, then the person is easily judged to be lonely and different observers agree with each other about the loneliness. But *disagreement* (and lower reliability) seem to arise when the description of the person contains fewer prototypic features. We shall present empirical data to show that judges perceive an individual as lonelier—and agree with each other more—when the person is described by many prototypic features.

Relation Between Loneliness and Depression

Third, we propose that the prototype of a lonely person is itself nested within the prototype of a depressed person. That is, the major features of a lonely person are a subset of those of a depressed person. This relationship implies that it is more probable for a lonely person to complain of feeling depressed than for a depressed person to complain of feeling lonely.

Loneliness and Interpersonal Problems

Fourth, we propose that a symptom like loneliness implies specific interpersonal problems that are included in the prototype. Indeed the adjective "lonely" is part of a cluster of adjectives that seem to correspond to a cluster of interpersonal problems over socializing. We shall therefore examine the correspondence between these two classes of psychiatric complaint in an effort to articulate the interpersonal problems of people who feel lonely. We shall also consider misleading similarities that can exist between adjectives like "lonely" and "passive" that have very different interpersonal or behavioral origins.

The Meaning of "I Can't" in Interpersonal Problems

Fifth, we propose that interpersonal problems that are part of the prototype of a lonely person reflect a lack of interpersonal competence. Interpersonal problems often take the general form "I can't (do something interpersonal)," yet the phrase "I can't" is ambiguous. At times, "I can't" denotes a lack of competence, but at other times it denotes an inhibition over behaving in some way that means "I can't bring myself to." However, certain features of the prototype suggest that the lonely person's problems involve a lack of competence. If this interpretation is correct, then two consequences should follow. The person should attribute interpersonal failures to a lack of ability, and second, a lack of ability should be evident from the person's performance on a task of interpersonal ability. Data will be presented that support both of these hypotheses.

Let us now turn to the concept of a prototype as applied to these propositions about loneliness.

THE LONELY PERSON AS A PROTOTYPE

Recent research in cognitive psychology has focused on the "prototype" as a way of defining a concept or category. A prototype is a theoretical notion, consisting of the most common features or properties of members of that category. All of these properties characterize at least *some* members, but in actual practice, no one property is either necessary or sufficient for membership in that category.

At one time it was fashionable to define a category in terms of a discrete set of features that were individually necessary and jointly sufficient. The category "girls," for example, was defined by a set of critical features like: +animate, +human, +young, −male. Each feature was considered necessary, and together the features were sufficient for classifying any object as a member of the category or not.

In more recent years, however, psychologists have come to view certain important categories in more probabilistic terms. Members of the category "birds," for example, share many properties with each other: some birds are alike in being small, others are alike in being colorful, still others are alike in producing sweet songs. We could list all the features that people cite most often when they describe birds, and the composite of the most frequent features would define a kind of theoretical ideal, the prototype. No actual bird would have all these features, and very few features would apply to all birds. However, in practice, some birds have more features than others, and a bird with a large number of these features (or the more important ones) would generally be a good example of that category, while a bird with fewer (or less important) features would be a poorer example. Thus a sparrow (which has *many* features) is a good or prototypic example, while a penguin (which has fewer features) is a poorer or less prototypic example; an owl (with its intermediate number of features) is an intermediate example (Rosch, Mervis, Gray, Johnson, & Boyes-Braem, 1976). Concepts from the literature of personality and psychotherapy have also been subjected to this kind of analysis (Cantor & Mischel, 1979; 1979; Cantor, Smith, French, & Mezzich, 1980). In the work described below, we adapted procedures of these studies to examine the concept of the "lonely person."

Forty introductory psychology students at Stanford University were selected on the basis of their scores on the UCLA Loneliness Scale; 13 had obtained high scores (51 to 71), 14 had obtained moderate scores (36 to 41), and 13 had obtained low scores (22 to 28). First, these subjects were asked to think of the best example they could of a person that they knew to be lonely; they were also asked to state the approximate age and sex of the person they were describing. Then they were asked to describe the person—to write down the person's most usual feelings, thoughts, and behavior. The writers were encouraged to be as specific as they wished and to feel free to include descriptive statements, even if the statements could not be easily labeled as a feeling, thought, or behavior. They spent about half an hour describing the person's feelings, thoughts, and behavior.

It is interesting to note that 11 of the 13 lonely subjects described lonely people who were of the same sex and age as themselvs, while subjects of the other two groups were about equally divided in this respect (6 of 14 for the moderate subjects and 6 of 13 for the nonlonely subjects); χ^2 (2) $=$ 5.82, $p < .06$. Thus the lonely subjects more often described someone very much like themselves (perhaps themselves), while the other subjects more often described grandmothers, divorced parents, and other acquaintances.

Each subject's description was typed and then submitted to a panel of three judges. Each judge independently tabulated every feature, and the judges met to discuss the features they had identified. The group's consensus was then recorded to obtain separately for each group a final listing and frequency count for subjects in that group.

The three groups of subjects did not differ from each other in the number or nature of identified features. Therefore features from all 40 subjects were combined to derive a more stable summary. Features that had been supplied by 20% or more of the subjects (i.e., eight or more subjects) formed the final prototype. Eighteen features met this criterion. The most common features (and their relative frequencies) were: "avoids social contact and isolates self from others" (.55), "feels depressed" (.45), "thinks [I want a friend]" (.45). There were more feelings than thoughts or kinds of behavior in the prototype, and the most salient feelings were interpersonal ones (e.g., rejected, angry, isolated, inferior).

In order to determine the cognitive organization of the features of the lonely person, we performed a hierarchical clustering procedure (Johnson, 1967). In this procedure, 50 subjects were each given a stack of 18 cards that contained the 18 features, one to a card. The subjects were asked to sort the cards into categories, showing which features seemed to go together. We then computed a matrix showing how often each feature was categorized together with each other feature.

This matrix of proportions was then subjected to a hierarchical clustering procedure (Everitt, 1974; Johnson, 1967). The method identified major clusters within the set of features. The resulting clusters are shown in Figure 12.1. Features that are enclosed in the innermost rectangles were the most tightly clustered. As the rectangles become larger, the denoted cluster is weaker. The figure also shows the criterion for each cluster, that is, the proportion of subjects who placed the features in a common category.

These results showed that the features of the lonely person can be grouped into three major sets. The largest describes thoughts and feelings of being separated from other people, isolated, different, unloved, inferior. A second (smaller) set includes lonely people's actions that bring about this result—avoiding social contacts, isolating themselves from others. A third set concerns paranoid feelings, including feeling angry and depressed. In the clinical literature, a dimension ranging from depression to paranoia has been postulated (Schwartz, 1964), and it is interesting to observe that such a grouping has been captured by our empirical methods.

THE PROTOTYPE AND JUDGMENTS OF LONELINESS

According to our hypothesis, a person who possesses many features of the prototypic lonely person should be a better example of a lonely person than one who possesses fewer features. We expected such people to be seen as lonelier by naive raters. We therefore examined the original essays describing the lonely people in order to identify essays that contained one or two prototypic features, five or six prototypic features, or nine or 10 prototypic features. For each of these subsets, we randomly selected three essays—one written by a lonely person, one written by a not lonely person, and one written by an intermediate person. (The word "lonely" did not appear explicitly in any of the essays.) The resulting nine essays each described a lonely person, but those with one or two prototypic features did so through many idiosyncratic features that had not achieved prototype status.

Sets of three essays were presented to 39 naive subjects, students in a class in introductory psychology at Stanford University. The order of essays was varied systematically across subjects. The subjects were asked to read each essay and make several judgments. First, the subject was asked to rate the person along various dimensions—how likeable the person seemed, how depressed, how angry, how lonely, and how superior and inferior to others

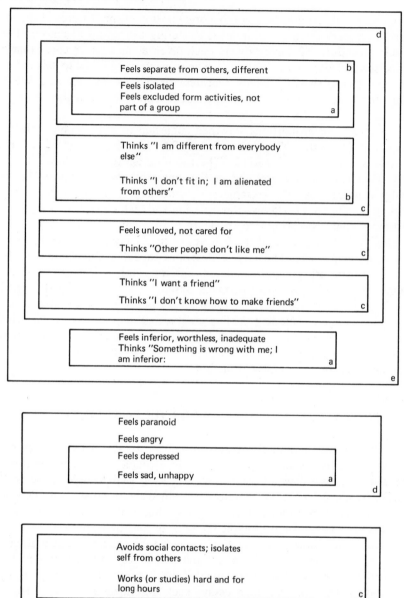

Figure 12.1. Prototype of a lonely person. Strength of cluster: (a) .71–.90; (b) .51–.70; (c) .31–.50; (d) .11–.30; (e) .01–.10.

the person seemed to feel. These ratings were made along a 5-point scale; loneliness, for example, was rated along a scale from 1 ("not lonely") to 5 ("very lonely"). Then the subject examined a list of 24 adjectives, selecting the five adjectives that best characterized the person. The list included the following adjectives: hostile, happy, introverted, uncomfortable, sensitive, clownish, easygoing, competitive, selfish, disturbed, arrogant, resentful, lonely, aggressive, shy, ineffective, mean, vulnerable, needy, ambitious, self-centered, anxious, depressed, angry.

We were especially interested in the subjects' ratings of the person's loneliness. Our results showed that these ratings varied significantly with the number of prototypic features; F $(2,76)$ $= 5.09$, $p < .01$. For essays with one or two features, the mean rating was 3.79; for essays with five or six features, the mean was 4.00; for essays with nine or 10 features, the mean was 4.47. This difference was also reflected by another measure, the proportion of times a subject rated the person's loneliness as 4 or higher. These proportions for the three groups of essays were .64, .79, and .95 respectively; χ^2 (2) $= 11.3$, $p < .005$.

We also examined the subjects' choice of adjectives for describing the person. The most commonly chosen adjective was "lonely," selected .68 of the time. The next most common choices and their relative frequencies were "introverted" (.49) and "depressed" (.46). Adjectives like hostile, happy, clownish, easy-going, aggressive, mean, and angry were rarely or never selected.

Furthermore, the probability of these three most popular descriptions increased as the number of prototypic features increased. "Lonely" was selected for the three sets (1–2, 5–6, and 9–10 features) with the following relative frequencies: .42, .71, and .89; "introverted," .18, .58, and .71; and "depressed," .37, .32, and .68. In all cases the increase was significant; all X^2 (2) ≥ 11.9, $p < .005$.

Thus the more prototypic features the essay contained, the greater the probability that the person was described as lonely. These essays of course, were all intended as descriptions of some lonely person, a good example of a lonely person that the writer knew. However, the essays were not all "diagnosed" as lonely by the judges with equal probabilities. The probability of the diagnosis "lonely" was highest only when the description contained nine or ten prototypic features.

RELATION BETWEEN LONELINESS AND DEPRESSION

A similar analysis has been applied to the concept of a depressed person. We asked 40 subjects to describe someone they knew to be depressed, and in the same way, we obtained the most common features of a depressed person. These features were far more numerous than those of a lonely person; approximately 40 features occurred with a probability of .20 or more. These features were also subjected to a hierarchical clustering procedure that yielded the results shown in Figure 12.2. The "depressed person" is a broader, more variegated concept that includes various subsets of features—feeling unenergetic, feeling pessimistic, eating too much, and so on.

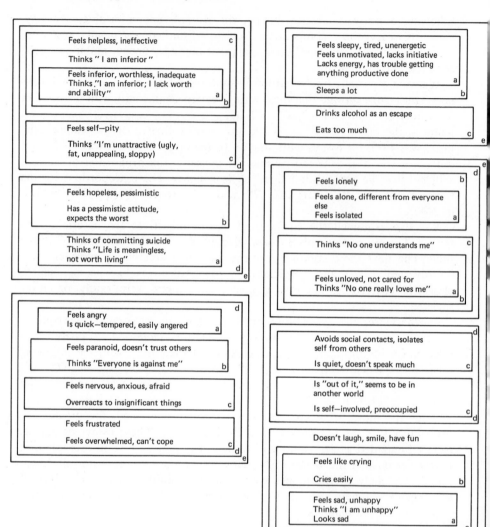

Figure 12.2. Prototype of a depressed person. Strength of cluster: (a) .71–.90; (b) .51–.70; (c) .31–.50; (d) .11–.30; (e) .01–.10.

Furthermore, the 18 features of the lonely person are almost entirely subsumed within those of the depressed prototype. In other words, the lonely prototype is nested within the depressed prototype. To know that a person is lonely is to know that the person possesses some major features of depression. The converse, however, is not true. Knowing that a person is depressed does not necessarily imply that the person possesses features of being lonely. There are other routes to depression besides the lonely route.

To be more precise, let us assume that *m* features of a prototype lead a judge to categorize a person into category c with a probability p. Because of the nesting, any individual with m features of the lonely prototype must possess m features of the depressed prototype as well. Thus the probability should be relatively high that a person labeled lonely would also be labeled depressed. However, a person who possesses m features of the *depressed* prototype would not necessarily be labeled lonely, since there are many subsets of depressed features that are not part of the lonely prototype. Therefore, the probability should be relatively lower that a person labeled depressed would also be labeled lonely. Indeed our data showed that the probability was .45 that a lonely person was described as depressed, while the probablity was only .29 that a depressed person was described as lonely; this difference, however, needs to be cross-validated on an independent sample of subjects.

LONELINESS AND INTERPERSONAL PROBLEMS

Features of the prototype of a lonely person, like all psychiatric complaints, fall into several conceptually distinct categories. If we examine psychiatric complaints that bring people to psychotherapy, we observe qualitatively different kinds of problems. One class consists of symptoms (typically self-descriptive adjectives), like feeling depressed, lonely, paranoid, or tense. Another consists of self-defeating perceptions, often about the self, such as "Something is wrong with me," "I am a failure," and "I am an ungiving person." Still another consists of specific behavioral disabilities, typically interpersonal, such as "I can't seem to make friends," or "I find it hard to say 'no' to my friends."

We would like to know how these categories of complaints are related. Does the symptom "loneliness" correspond to any particular set of interpersonal problems? If so, are they included among the prototypic features of a lonely person? The following section shows a way to relate self-descriptive adjectives to interpersonal problems. One previous study has shown that interpersonal problems can be arranged in a three-dimensional semantic space, and another study has shown that self-descriptive adjectives can also be arranged in a three-dimensional semantic space. Furthermore, these two spaces have similar dimensions that correspond in meaning. In addition, particular clusters of interpersonal problems in one space correspond in meaning to particular clusters of adjectives in the other space. Because of these correspondences, it has been possible to relate particular adjectives to particular interpersonal problems. The details are presented below.

In a previous study (Horowitz, 1979) we examined interpersonal problems that began "I can't (do something interpersonal)." Through a multidimensional scaling we found that the problem behaviors varied along three underlying dimensions. One of these dimensions, a dimension of friendliness, ranged from hostile to friendly; another, a control dimension, expressed the degree of control exerted over the other person; a third, a dimension of involvement, expressed the degree of psychological involvement with the other person. These dimensions corresponded to similar dimensions proposed by earlier investigators (Benjamin, 1974, 1977; Osgood, 1970; Wish, Deutsch & Kaplan, 1976).

The problematic interpersonal behavior was also organized into thematic clusters (intimacy, aggression, independence, socializing, compliance) that occupied different regions of the three-dimensional space. The major clusters of interpersonal problems are listed in Table 12.1 with examples. The prob-

Table 12.1.   Examples of Problem Statements in the Form *It's hard for me to . . .*

NOT BE AGGRESSIVE.   "I . . .
get annoyed by other people too easily.
talk back to other people too much.
criticize other people too much.
put too much pressure on other people.
BE INTIMATE.   "It's hard for me to . . .
commit myself to another person.
trust other people.
tell personal things to other people.
love another person.
BE AGGRESSIVE.   "It's hard for me to . . .
tell another person that I have a different opinion.
say "no" to other people.
make demands of other people.
criticize other people.
BE INDEPENDENT.   "It's hard for me to . . .
end a relationship when I want to.
"make it" without other people.
do as I please without feeling guilty toward other people.
go out to do my work and leave the other person at home alone.
BE SOCIABLE.   "It's hard for me to . . .
have fun at parties.
telephone other people and arrange to get together with them.
join in on groups.
make friends in a simple, natural way.
NOT BE COMPLIANT.   "I . . .
let myself be persuaded by other people too easily.
find myself joking and clowning around too much to get
    other people to like me.
care too much about other people's reactions.
always act like a helpless, little child in front of others.

lems in a thematic group were also described in terms of their three-dimensional location. For example, problems in being intimate reflected behavioral difficulties in being (a) friendly, (b) subjectively involved with the other person, but (c) uncontrolling. Problems in socializing were similar but reflected less subjective involvement with the other person.

We then wanted to determine how these interpersonal behavior problems are related to self-descriptive adjectives. If a person reports feeling lonely, can we make any inference as to his or her probable interpersonal problems? To clarify the relationship, we proposed (Horowitz & Post, 1980) that a statement like "I am depressed" or "I am lonely" be regarded as an abstraction that summarizes a set of more specific thoughts, feelings and behavior, like those listed in the corresponding prototype. Some of these thoughts, feelings, and behavior are themselves abstract summaries of still more specific observations about the self, including observations of particular interpersonal problems. Thus an original statement like "I am depressed" is regarded as an abstraction that can be expanded into increasingly specific thoughts, feelings, and behavior.

Therefore, when a person reports being depressed, an interviewer must unravel the meaning of the complaint by asking the person to tell more about being depressed. There is no sure way for the interviewer to help the person become less depressed other than to probe into the meaning (for that person) of being depressed, since one person's depression contains different ingredients from another person's depression. Figure 12.3 illustrates a hypothetical set of responses to the probe. This hypothetical person describes feeling *lonely* and *unloved*. The interviewer then probes further, and the person expands on each of these perceptions. Eventually "I feel lonely" is reduced to difficulties in making friends, participating in groups, relaxing on a date, and the like.

Successive probes eventually lead the person to describe specific interpersonal problems, which are then treated by psychotherapy. The interpersonal problems are thus pivotal—a kind of bottom line—in articulating the superordinate perceptions, since they explain why the person feels depressed, inferior, unloved, and lonely. In our view, many common symptoms and self-observations can be reduced in this way to forms that include significant interpersonal problems.

If self-descriptive adjectives are abstract summaries of interpersonal problems, then we might expect those adjectives to vary along a similar set of three dimensions and fall into clusters comparable to those of the interpersonal behavior. Horowitz and Post (1980) studied the self-descriptive adjectives that occurred in psychiatric interviews of people about to undergo psychotherapy. These adjectives were subjected to a multidimensional scaling procedure and to a hierarchical clustering procedure like that described for interpersonal problems. The results showed that the adjectives did vary in three dimensions that were comparable to those found for problematic interpersonal behavior. Furthermore, the adjective clusters appeared to correspond to the clusters of interpersonal behavior. For example, one major *adjective* cluster included such words as: lonely, introverted, inward, isolated, alone, separate, withdrawn, shy, and timid. This cluster occupied a region of the three-dimensional space comparable to that occupied previously by the problems of socializing (Horowitz, 1979).

To establish the correspondence more directly, we asked lonely people about their major interpersonal problems (Horowitz & French, 1979). We

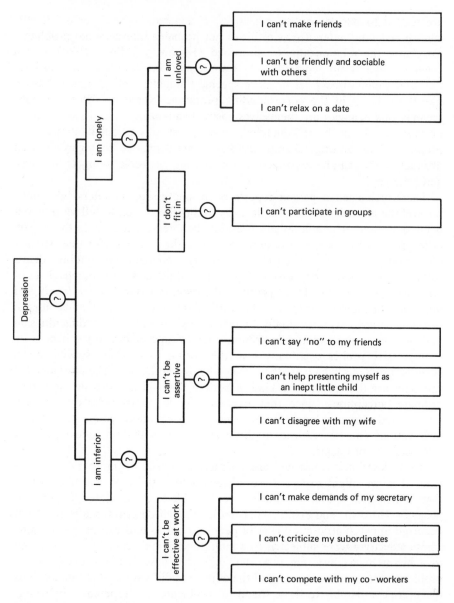

Figure 12.3. Hypothetical set of responses to probes in the form of "Tell me about. . . ."

administered the UCLA Loneliness Scale to undergraduate students at Stanford University and identified individuals who described themselves as lonely. We then administered a deck of 100 cards describing interpersonal problems drawn from Horowitz (1979). Each subject arranged the cards by the Q sort technique into nine categories, from Category 1 ("least familiar as a problem of mine") to Category 9 ("most familiar as a problem of mine").

We then determined which problems the subjects most often placed among their top problems. The most common type of problem for the lonely subjects were those describing difficulties in socializing. This category contained 13 different problems, which are shown in Table 12.2. We recorded the mean

Table 12.2. Problems of Inhibited Sociability

Problem: I find it hard to . . .	Probability of being among top five problems		Mean category placement	
	Lonely	Not lonely	Lonely	Not lonely
make friends in a simple, natural way.	.28	.00	6.16	2.84
introduce myself to O(s) at parties.	.24	.18	6.36	5.84
make phone calls to O to initiate social activity.	.20	.02	6.12	4.76
participate in groups.	.16	.04	5.12	4.60
get pleasure out of a party.	.16	.02	5.64	4.64
get into the swing of a party.	.12	.07	6.00	4.89
relax on a date and enjoy myself.	.12	.00	5.84	3.56
be friendly and sociable with O.	.08	.00	5.36	3.78
participate in playing games with O.	.04	.02	5.04	4.49
get buddy-buddy with O.	.04	.00	5.64	4.93
entertain O at my home.	.00	.04	4.84	4.56
get along with O.	.00	.02	6.08	5.04
extend myself to accept O's friendship.	.00	.00	4.48	3.33

number of times that each of these problems was placed in Category 9 by lonely and not-lonely subjects. The results in Table 12.2 showed that lonely people suffered significantly more often from problems of this type.

We also recorded the number of the category into which each problem of socializing was placed and averaged the category placements. As shown in Table 12.2, lonely subjects, on the average, placed every problem of socializing into a higher category. Thus lonely people can be characterized by a greater prominence of problems of socializing; however, other groups of problems, such as problems with intimacy, did not discriminate between lonely and not-lonely subjects. It is also worth noting that one problem of socializing does occur frequently enough to appear as a feature of the lonely prototype, namely, "I find it hard to make friends in a simple, natural way." This problem was the single most frequent problem in Table 12.2.

These results suggest that adjectives like "lonely" do have a meaning similar to that of problems of socializing. Other correspondences between adjective clusters and behavior clusters were also found. However, we cannot claim that simple relationships translate adjectives into problem behavior. Suppose a problematic behavior (e.g., telephoning a potential friend) has the coordinates x_B, y_B, z_B in the behavior space, and suppose some corresponding adjective, like lonely, has the coordinates x_A, y_A, z_A in the adjective space. We might expect corresponding coordinates of the two sets to bear a systematic contrast: If the problematic behavior connotes friendliness, for example, we might expect the self-descriptive adjective to connote unfriendliness.

However, a person who has difficulty acting friendly might behave in a neutral rather than in an unfriendly way. Thus, while people who have difficulty socializing do describe themselves as lonely, the adjective "lonely" connotes nonfriendliness, not unfriendliness. (This is one way in which a lonely person's behavior can be misunderstood.) Furthermore, the dimensions of contrast are not the same for all clusters of adjectives, so two clusters of adjectives in the three-dimensional space would not necessarily maintain the same intercluster distances that had held for the corresponding interpersonal behaviors.

For these reasons, we cannot state a simple relationship between coordinates of the adjectives and corresponding coordinates of the problem behaviors. As a result, two different adjectives can be closer in meaning to each other (in the adjective space) than the corresponding behavioral problems had been (in the behavior space). Indeed two behavioral clusters might be quite far apart in the behavioral space—for example, socializing and behaving independently—but the corresponding clusters of adjectives might be much closer together and seem rather similar. For example, a word like "lonely" and a word like "passive" seem to have quite different behavioral origins; problems of socializing for the one, problems of being assertive and independent for the other. Yet as adjectives, they seem fairly similar. These two adjective clusters were in fact quite close together, and their proximity might cause a lonely person to be viewed (incorrectly) as passive; in that case, problems of socializing might be confused with problems of being assertive and independent. Thus it is particularly important to determine the precise meaning of self-descriptive adjectives in terms of particular interpersonal problems, or else we may misunderstand the person's problems.

THE MEANING OF "I CAN'T" IN INTERPERSONAL PROBLEMS

To know that a lonely person "finds it hard to make friends" is useful for clarifying the meaning of "lonely," but another ambiguity arises over the wording of the interpersonal problem.

Expressions like "I find it hard to" and "I can't" are characteristic ways of introducing an interpersonal problem, but they are actually ambiguous. Sometimes they denote a lack of competence, meaning "I don't know how to" (e.g., "I can't swim"). At other times they denote an inhibition against executing the desired behavior: The speaker has the necessary skill, but a self-restraint checks the behavior, and "I can't" has the meaning "I can't bring myself to." At still other times "I can't" reflects the interfering effects of situational anxiety, masking the competence that would otherwise manifest itself.

We therefore need to understand the intended meaning of the problem statement if we are to formulate a proper treatment strategy. If the lonely person's problems imply a lack of competence over socializing, then an appropriate treatment should provide the person with relative skills. If the problems reflect an inhibition, then the treatment should clarify the conflict, reduce whatever conditions had caused the inhibition (e.g., guilt), and help the person choose freely among response options. And if the problems reflect the interfering effects of anxiety, then the treatment should desensitize the person to anxiety.

The top-rated problem "I find it hard to make friends in a simple, natural way" was the only problem that was frequent enough to achieve prototype status; it occurred in the prototypic thought "I don't know how to make friends." This prototypic thought implies that the lonely person's problem reflects a lack of know-how, a lack of competence. If this interpretation is correct, then two consequences should follow. First, when lonely people explain their failures in social situations, their account of what went wrong should reflect their lack of know-how. In the language of attributional theories, their attributional style should draw particularly upon *ability* attributions to explain failures in interpersonal situations (see, for example, Peplau, Russell, & Heim, 1979). Second, the observation that they lack ability in interpersonal situations should be valid. When their competence is assessed, even for benign social situations, their performance should be poorer. In the following sections we examine and test these hypotheses.

The Attributional Style of Lonely People

First, we composed 22 descriptions of situations that could end either in success or failure, situations in which college students might find themselves. Some of these situations described interpersonal activities (e.g., attending a party for new students) and others described noninterpersonal activities (e.g., working a crossword puzzle). To validate the interpersonal versus noninterpersonal distinction, we asked 20 judges to read each situation and rate it on a 9-point scale, ranging from 1 ("not at all interpersonal") to 9 ("very interpersonal"). The mean rating of the interpersonal situations ranged from 6.20 to 8.05, while the mean rating of the noninterpersonal situations ranged from 1.70 to 4.15.

Ten situations (five interpersonal and five noninterpersonal) were selected to form a questionnaire. Each situation was written in two forms. One described an outcome of success, the other described an outcome of failure, making 20 situations altogether—five of interpersonal success, five of interpersonal failure, five of noninterpersonal success, and five of noninterpersonal failure.

Six alternative reasons (or attributions) for the outcome were offered for each situation. These reasons, which were the most frequent responses that the subjects produced during a pretest, can be classified as follows: (1) the *effort* attribution explained the outcome in terms of how hard the person had tried; (2) the *ability* attribution explained the outcome in terms of the person's competence (or lack of competence); (3) the personality *trait* attribution explained the outcome in terms of some pervasive characteristic of the person other than ability; (4) the *strategy* attribution explained the outcome in terms of the person's particular approach, tactic, or method; (5) the *mood* attribution explained the outcome in terms of a transitory mood state; and (6) the *other circumstances* attribution explained the outcome in terms of any remaining external circumstances beyond the person's control.

Here is an example of an interpersonal failure item.

You have just attended a party for new students and failed to make any new friends.
1.   I did not try very hard to meet new people.
2.   I am not good at meeting people at parties.
3.   I do not have the personality traits necessary for meeting new people.
4.   I used the wrong strategy to meet people.
5.   I was not in the right mood for meeting new people.
6.   Other circumstances (people, situations, etc.) produced this outcome.

The subjects were asked to imagine themselves in each situation and to consider each possible reason that might explain why the situation had turned out as it did. They were asked to rate each reason to show how much, in their experience, it would have contributed toward the outcome if it had happened to them. A 7-point rating scale accompanied each alternative: "1" meant that that reason contributed little to the outcome, "7" meant that it contributed much. In addition, the subjects were asked to circle the one reason that best explained the outcome.

The questionnaire was administered to 298 students in an introductory psychology class at Stanford University. These students also completed the UCLA Loneliness Scale and the Beck Depression Inventory.

The subjects were categorized into five groups on the basis of their loneliness scores, with approximately 60 subjects in each group. One-way analyses of variance were performed on the importance ratings for each attributional factor. Table 12.3 shows the results of a priori contrasts, comparing the two extreme groups. (The lonely group had loneliness scores of 50 and above; the nonlonely group had scores of 30 and below.)

Table 12.3 shows that lonely and nonlonely subjects differed primarily in their use of ability and trait attributions. Lonely people attributed interpersonal failures to a lack of ability and to personal traits more than nonlonely people did. The opposite was true for interpersonal successes, where lonely people did not attribute success to these factors as often as nonlonely people. On noninterpersonal situations, however, the two groups did not differ very much.

Previous researchers have suggested that depressed and lonely people do not as readily attribute failures to factors like strategy and effort, that is, to unstable, controllable factors (see, for example, Anderson & Jennings, 1980; Seligman, Abramson & Semmel, 1979; Weiner, 1979). Although some

Table 12.3. Importance Ratings of the Causes of Interpersonal and Noninterpersonal Success and Failure

Reason or Cause	Interpersonal failure			Interpersonal success			Noninterpersonal failure			Noninterpersonal success		
	Lonely $n = 65$	Non-lonely $n = 56$	t	Lonely $n = 65$	Non-lonely $n = 56$	t	Lonely $n = 65$	Non-lonely $n = 56$	t	Lonely $n = 65$	Non-lonely $n = 56$	t
Ability	4.25	2.82	6.54**	3.80	4.98	6.03**	4.35	4.24	.54	5.04	5.36	1.63
Trait	3.64	2.45	5.59**	3.60	4.61	5.09**	2.68	2.37	1.68	3.54	3.38	.68
Strategy	4.51	4.67	.26	4.41	4.79	1.84	4.35	4.80	2.01*	4.83	5.30	2.13*
Effort	4.15	4.59	2.07*	5.00	5.09	.44	4.13	4.22	.35	5.72	5.94	1.42
Mood	4.38	4.59	1.03	5.02	5.26	1.21	4.27	4.42	.69	4.98	5.16	.91
Other	3.71	4.20	1.99*	4.34	4.08	1.11	3.32	3.62	1.31	3.33	3.36	.15

Pooled variance estimates from all 5 groups were used in all t tests, $df = 293$.

*$p < .05$, two-tailed
**$p < .001$, two-tailed.

differences in Table 12.3 supported that hypothesis, those differences were much weaker than the differences for ability and trait attributions.*

Table 12.4 presents the results of the forced choice attributions, showing the proportion of times that each reason was selected as the single best reason for explaining the outcome. Again the differences were significant only for the interpersonal situations shown in Table 12.4. As with the importance ratings, lonely people attributed their interpersonal failures to a lack of ability more than nonlonely people did. Furthermore, they did not attribute their interpersonal successes to ability as often. A similar pattern occurred for the use of personal traits, though the difference for interpersonal successes did not reach statistical significance.

The forced choice data also showed which attributions were avoided by lonely people. Among the four remaining reasons, lonely people did not attribute failures to the strategy choice as often as nonlonely people did. Furthermore, when asked to explain their successes, lonely people seemed to be at a loss and chose "other circumstances" more often as their explanation.

Table 12.4. Forced Choice Attributions of the Causes of Interpersonal Success and Failure: Proportion of Times Each Reason Was Selected as the Main Cause [a]

Reason or Cause	Interpersonal failure			Interpersonal success		
	Lonely $n = 65$	Non lonely $n = 56$	t	Lonely $n = 65$	Non lonely $n = 56$	t
Ability	.27	.05	6.57**	.09	.20	3.11*
Trait	.10	.01	4.21**	.04	.07	1.22
Strategy	.14	.26	2.84*	.12	.16	1.09
Effort	.17	.24	1.17	.26	.26	.09
Mood	.21	.28	1.76	.26	.25	1.30
Other	.12	.17	1.23	.22	.06	4.81**

[a] Pooled variance estimates from all 5 groups were used in all t tests, $df = 293$.
*$p < .05$, two-tailed
**$p < .001$, two-tailed

* Since the subjects had also completed the Beck Depression Inventory, we analyzed the data using depression scores in place of the loneliness scores. The value of r between the two sets of scores was .58 ($p < .001$), so the results for depression were practically identical to those for loneliness. Depressed subjects, like lonely subjects, differed from nondepressed (and nonlonely) subjects in ascribing interpersonal failures to their lack of ability and personal traits; they did not differ, however, in their attributions for noninterpersonal failures. Since the experimental literature on depression and learned helplessness has often relied on noninterpersonal experimental tasks (e.g., anagram solving), it seems unlikely that a depressed person's attributional style per se would produce the observed performance decrement.

These results show that interpersonal situations play a salient role in the lonely person's dilemma. Put simply, lonely people believe that they are interpersonally less competent. This attributional style clarifies their feeling of inferiority: they attribute interpersonal failures to social ineptness and do not believe, as nonlonely people do, that interpersonal failures reflect temporary conditions that can be remedied by trying harder or by trying other strategies. Moreover, people who regard themselves as interpersonally incompetent would come to feel that there is no use in trying. The person would thus give up more easily or, if possible, avoid interpersonal situations. Such self-imposed isolation would provide fewer opportunities to develop social skills, leading to more failure, more negative self-assessments, and more social withdrawal.

Assessing Competence

These results suggested that lonely people do regard themselves as less competent in social situations; they are more apt than nonlonely people to attribute interpersonal failures to their lack of ability. But the question still remains as to whether their attributions are valid. Are they in fact interpersonally "less able"? We wanted to compare lonely and nonlonely people on a simple test of interpersonal competence. However, many interpersonal tasks might arouse anxiety in lonely people, and a performance decrement could arise, not from lack of competence, but from the interfering effects of anxiety. Therefore, we searched for a test of competence that was relatively impersonal and nonthreatening, a task that the subject could approach in a relatively leisurely and nondefensive way, one that would test the limits of the subject's competence rather than assess the net performance observed under anxiety and interpersonal stress.

The task we selected was adapted from one developed by Platt and Spivack (1975). This task required the subject to consider hypothetical situations that posed different kinds of problems and to generate possible solutions. The subject was free to think about each situation and, in a leisurely way, to write a possible solution. The task was scored for the number and quality of methods, or "means," that the subject generated. Each situation was described in impersonal terms about some fictitious character, in order to further divert the subjects' attention from themselves and possibly reduce stress. The task was therefore benign in that the subjects (a) were under no time pressure, (b) focused their attention on a fictitious character, and (c) were not required to enact the behavior itself.

The subjects were presented with a set of 11 situations. Each situation described the problem and a successful outcome in which some fictitious person successfully fulfilled his or her needs. The subjects were asked to supply the means by which the successful end was achieved, telling how the person managed to solve the problem. Here is one example:

C. had just moved in that day and didn't know anyone. C. wanted to have friends in the neighborhood. The story ends with C. having many good friends and feeling at home in the neighborhood. You begin the story with C. in his (her) room immediately after arriving in the neighborhood.

Most of the situations were interpersonal and involved different themes, particularly ones concerned with socializing—making friends in a new neighborhood, getting to know a new roommate, meeting new people at a party, meeting someone of the opposite sex, participating in a neighborhood meeting. One situation, however, was different from the others in that it was not interpersonal; it concerned a person who lost and later recovered a watch. A separate group of judges read the situations and rated them along various dimensions—how interpersonal they seemed, what skills they called for—and the judges' ratings corroborated our judgment that this situation was different from the others. Lonely people were expected to perform more poorly on the interpersonal situations that called for skills at socializing, but not on this control item.

The UCLA Loneliness Scale was administered to a large class in introductory psychology at the beginning of the term. Subjects were selected from this pool to have high, medium, or low scores of loneliness, corresponding to the top, middle, and bottom fifth of the distribution. There were 39 subjects in all—15 nonlonely subjects (7 males, 8 females) who had scores below 30; 10 medium subjects (7 males, 3 females) who had scores between 40 and 45; and 14 lonely subjects (9 males, 5 females) who had scores above 55. The subjects were contacted by telephone several weeks after they completed the Loneliness Scale, and they were tested in groups of four. Each situation was presented at the top of a separate page, and the subjects wrote their responses on that page. Situations for male subjects were written about a male person, those for female subjects, about a female person. The entire procedure took about half an hour.

Three naive judges rated each response independently and blindly. To check that the three groups of subjects were comparable in verbal productivity, the judges first counted the total number of words in each response. The three groups of subjects did not differ; F (2, 36) < 1. The judges also examined other characteristics of the subjects' verbal style, such as the frequency with which positive and negative affect were expressed and the frequency with which personal names were used. The three groups of subjects did not differ significantly in any of these respects.

Then the judges counted the number of methods (or "means") that the subjects generated as a way of solving the problem. The scoring procedures of Platt and Spivack (1975) were adapted in order to identify and score the number of methods that the subjects generated. Corresponding scores of the three judges were then averaged to yield a single, stable index of each subject's performance.

First we examined the subjects' performance on the control item (methods of recovering a lost watch). The three groups did not differ significantly on this task in any way. For the total number of methods produced, F (2, 36) = .07, $p > .93$. This F was smaller than the corresponding F for any other item.

Having established the comparability of the groups on the control item, we then examined the number of methods produced. In each of these situations, the lonely subject produced fewer methods for solving the problem. The three groups differed significantly; F (2, 36) = 4.28, $p < .02$. The mean number of methods per item were 2.17, 2.95, and 2.74, respectively, for lonely, medium, and nonlonely subjects.

In addition, the judges rated the overall quality of each response as a way of solving the problem. These global ratings ranged from 1 ("poor") to 5 ("excellent"), and the three groups differed significantly in this respect as well; F (2, 36) = 4.85, $p < .01$. The mean ratings for the three groups were: 1.73, 2.24, and 2.07. Thus lonely subjects produced fewer methods of solving the problems, and their responses in general were judged to be of poorer overall quality. Subjects of the lonely group also used more fantasy in their responses, F (2, 36) = 3.52, $p < .05$, and they more often failed to generate any method at all, F (2, 36) = 3.32, $p < .05$.

To summarize, these results show that lonely people are less able to think of ways of solving the problems posed by interpersonal situations. Even though they were comparable to the other subjects in their performance on the control (impersonal) situation, they were less able to generate ways of solving the interpersonal problems. In this sense, lonely people do appear to be interpersonally less competent, thus validating their own self-description and attributional style.

COMMENT

This chapter has described our progress in studying the prototype of a lonely person. At times our work has focused on specific prototypic features as a way of clarifying the lonely person's struggle. The prototypic thought "I don't know how to make friends," for example, has led us to study the lonely person's attributional style and to test for possible behavorial deficits.

However, the prototype of a lonely person is more than a list of individual features. It is an *organized* list, and we have tried to portray this organization through a clustering procedure. Because of the organization, the concept of "a lonely person" is analogous to a gestalt: When a description of the person cites enough prototypic features, the prototype is activated; and once activated, the prototype suggests other features that were not included in the original description. Thus a person who is labeled "a lonely person" then seems to be characterized by other prototypic features such as "introspective" and "introverted."

The *similarity* between two concepts can also be expressed in terms of prototypic features. To determine whether "a lonely person" is conceptually similar, for example, to "a passive person," we would need to compare the two prototypes and determine their number of overlapping features. If they have few features in common (as we have hypothesized), then the concepts would be different.

Perhaps the most important aspect of a prototype is the variability that it implies among the features that characterize different people's concepts. Our prototype of a lonely person contained 18 features, but there was no one feature that occurred in all (or even most) essays describing lonely people. Indeed the probability of the single most common feature was only .55. Furthermore, the majority of prototypic features appeared in less than half the essays. For these reasons we cannot make specific predictions about individual cases; we can only make probabilistic statements about lonely people in general. The prototype does provide us with educated hunches and leads towards describing those individuals who call themselves lonely, but each person's unique meaning still needs to be determined through systematic questioning.

REFERENCES

Anderson, C. A., & Jennings, D. L. When experiences of failure promote expectations of success: The impact of attributing failure to ineffective strategies. *Journal of Personality,* 1980, *48,* 393–407.

Benjamin, L. S. Structural analysis of social behavior. *Psychological Review,* 1974, *81,* 392–425.

Benjamin, L. S. Structural analysis of a family in therapy. *Journal of Consulting and Clinical Psychology,* 1977, *45,* 391–406.

Cantor, N., & Mischel, W. Prototypicality and personality: Effects on free recall and personality impressions. *Journal of Research in Personality,* 1979, *13,* 187–205.

Cantor, N., & Mischel, W. Prototypes in person perception. In L. Berkowitz (Ed.), *Advances in experimental social psychology.* New York: Academic Press, 1979.

Cantor, N., Smith, E., French, R. de S., & Mezzich, J. Psychiatric diagnosis as prototype categorization, *Journal of Abnormal Psychology,* 1980, *89,* 181–193.

Everitt, B. *Cluster analysis.* New York: Wiley, 1974.

Horowitz, L. On the cognitive structure of interpersonal problems treated in psychotherapy. *Journal of Consulting and Clinical Psychology,* 1979, *47,* 5–15.

Horowitz, L. M., & French, R. de S. Interpersonal problems of people who describe themselves as lonely. *Journal of Consulting and Clinical Psychology,* 1979, *47,* 762–764.

Horowitz, L., & Post, D. The interpersonal meaning of adjectives appearing in psychiatric complaints. *Journal of Consulting and Clinical Psychology,* 1980, *48,* 409–411.

Johnson, S. C. Hierarchical clustering schemes. *Psychometrika,* 1967, *32,* 241–254.

Osgood, C. E. Interpersonal verbs and interpersonal behavior. In J. L. Cowan (Ed.), *Studies in thought and language.* Tucson: The University of Arizona Press, 1970.

Peplau, L. A., Russell, D., & Heim, M. The experience of loneliness. In I. Frieze, D. Bar-Tal, & J. Carroll (Eds.), *New approaches to social problems: Applications of attribution theory.* San Francisco: Jossey-Bass, 1979.

Platt, J. J., & Spivack, G. *Manual for the mean-ends problem-solving procedure (MEPS): A measure of interpersonal cognitive problem-solving skill.* Philadelphia: Hahnemann Medical College and Hospital, 1975.

Rosch, E., Mervis, C. B., Gray, W. D., Johnson, D. M., & Boyes-Braem, P. Basic objects in natural categories. *Cognitive Psychology,* 1976, *8,* 382–439.

Schwartz, D. A. The paranoid-depressive existential continuum. *The Psychiatric Quarterly,* 1964, *38,* 690–706.

Seligman, M. E. P., Abramson, L. Y., & Semmel, A. Depressive attributional style. *Journal of Abnormal Psychology,* 1979, *88,* 242–247.

Weiner, B. A theory of motivation for some classroom experiences. *Journal of Educational Psychology,* 1979, *71,* 3–25.

Wish, M., Deutsch, M., & Kaplan, S. J. Perceived dimensions of interpersonal relations. *Journal of Personality and Social Psychology,* 1976, *33,* 409–420.

Chapter 13

The Experience of Loneliness

Carin Rubenstein and Phillip Shaver

When social scientists study people's experience or feelings, they usually begin from one of two alternative points of view. The most common stance, at least in American psychology, is behavorial and mechanistic. According to this view, human beings are materialistic processes or mechanisms; their most interesting feature is their behavior, and internal dynamics matter only insofar as they help to offer a mechanistic explanation of behavior. In psychology this approach is epitomized by Skinner's (1953) behaviorism, but in modified forms it appeals to many nonbehaviorists as well. In sociology a similar emphasis can be seen in researchers' preference for objective, behavioral variables over self-reports of attitudes or feelings. An example is Chapter 2 in this book, by Fischer and Phillips, which reports a study of objective social isolation and size of social networks; subjective self-reports of feelings were considered only secondarily in this study.

An alternative starting point is the experience—or phenomenology, as it is technically called—of individuals. According to many phenomenologists (for overviews, see volumes edited by Kockelmans, 1967; Valle & King, 1978; and Wann, 1964), human experience cannot be adequately explained in mechanistic terms. Only a sympathetic, meaning-oriented analysis of self-reports can provide deeper insights into human psychology and social life.

The trouble with the phenomenological method, from the perspective of social scientists at any rate, is that it rarely leads to systematic, empirically testable psychological theories. The trouble with the objective, mechanistic approach, on the other hand, is that it often leaves people's most urgent questions about themselves unanswered. In principle, there seems to be no reason why the two kinds of data, behavioral and phenomenological, cannot be explained by a *single* theory. Miller, Galanter, and Pribram (1960) suggested the term "subjective behaviorist" for theorists who want to do justice to both aspects of human psychology, and parodoxical as the term may sound, this approach is rapidly becoming the dominant one in American psychology.* Peplau's attribution theory approach (see Chapter 9) is an

---

* The original statement by Miller et al. (1960, pp. 211-213) is worth the attention of a new generation of psychologists: "Deep in the middle of this dilemma it suddenly occurred to us that we were subjective behaviorists. When we stopped laughing we began

example. Perhaps the best evidence for the generality of this trend is the revised definition of psychology that appears in many recent introductory textbooks; what was once touted as the "science of behavior" is now generally called the "science of behavior and experience."

Loneliness is an ideal topic for the subjective or phenomenological behaviorist; in fact, it may in part have been neglected by psychologists until recently because it cannot be studied effectively either by exclusive behaviorists (since loneliness is not a behavior) or by exclusive phenomenologists, whose descriptions are often empirically untested, if not untestable, and rarely connected with analyses of behavior. Loneliness had been described by phenomenological writers (e.g., Moustakas, 1961, 1972, 1975), but until recently had not been assessed quantitatively or studied experimentally.

In the early phases of phenomenological-behaviorist research, it is valuable to listen carefully to people's accounts of their own experiences. These accounts can be gathered in interviews and open-ended questionnaires, and by combing through novels and poems. From these accounts, more systematic measures can be constructed that allow for the collection of reports from larger numbers of people. This is the research strategy we have adopted. In the present chapter we will briefly recount key excerpts from interviews, open-ended questionnaires, and imaginative literature, and then report the results of a series of large closed-ended questionnaire studies that systematically explored people's experiences of loneliness. At the end of the chapter we will examine recent theories of loneliness in light of our results and suggest possible refinements in current research strategies.

LONELINESS IN LITERATURE

Loneliness is a major theme in literature, perhaps because writers themselves are often lonely, but the word "loneliness" has not always been in vogue. It doesn't appear, for example, in the story of the most famous of all loners, *Robinson Crusoe* (Defoe, 1720/1960). Crusoe describes himself as a "solitaire, one banished from human society" who lives on an "island of despair." Although not one to talk about his feelings (and so not a good subject for phenomenology), Crusoe does at one point reveal feeling "so absolutely miserable, so without help, abandoned, so entirely depressed, that it could hardly be rational to be thankful for such a life."

Huck Finn, a famous fictional loner of the nineteenth century, suffered from loneliness and discovered a temporary cure for it. At one point he says,

---

to wonder seriously if that was not exactly the position we had argued ourselves into . . . Why not be subjective behaviorists? The objection, of course, is that 'subjective' and 'behaviorism' do not go together. We might as well talk about a black whiteness, or a square circle. But almost every behaviorist has smuggled into his system some kinds of invisible gimmicks . . . Everybody does it, for the simple reason that you cannot make any sense out of behavior unless you do."

"I felt so lonesome I most wished I was dead." His remedy was to distract himself by counting stars, or the drift logs on the Mississippi, until he fell asleep. "There ain't no better way to put in time when you are lonesome . . . " (Twain, 1885/1969). Decades later, Holden Caufield (*A Catcher in the Rye;* Salinger, 1961) echoed Huck's sentiment almost precisely: "I felt so lonesome, all of a sudden. I almost wished I was dead." Holden, unlike Huck, cannot shake the feeling easily and frequently winds up "very depressed." An even younger boy's viewpoint was expressed by Rufus in *A Death in the Family* (Agee, 1938) when he had to stay home while his friends went off to school: "He . . . always felt disconsolate and lonely . . . when he kept on walking away, he felt even more lonely and unhappy."

The connection between loneliness and meaninglessness, stressed in much of contemporary literature, was concretely noted by the narrator in Conrad's (1899/1966) *Heart of Darkness*: "I couldn't have felt more of lonely desolation somehow, had I been robbed of a belief or missed my destiny in life . . ." Holden Caufield too seemed to have no clear beliefs, causes, or meaningful destiny.

Most feelings of loneliness expressed by fictional characters are due either to abandonment or forced solitude. Robinson Crusoe, devoid of companionship, was "miserable . . . I have no soul to speak to, or relieve me." The blinded Mr. Rochester, in Brontë's (1847/1950) *Jane Eyre,* explained to Jane how he felt when she left him: "I was desolate and abandoned—my life dark, lonely, hopeless—my soul athirst and forbidden to drink—my heart famished and never to be fed." The tone of contemporary novels is less effusive—more world-wise, wry, even cynical—but the problem of loneliness is just as evident. The protagonist of Styron's (1979) *Sophie's Choice* puts it well:

> While I droned in the hive at McGraw-Hill there had been something sick, self-flagellating in my withdrawal from people into a world of fantasy and loneliness; on my terms it was unnatural, for I am a companionable person most of the time, impelled genuinely enough toward friendship but equally smitten by the same horror of solitude that causes human beings to get married or join the Rotarians. There in Brooklyn I had come to the point where I sorely needed friends, and I had found them, thus soothing my pent-up anxieties and allowing me to work.

Perusing fiction, we can thus come up with a host of adjectives that describe loneliness: desperate, abandoned, depressed, helpless, isolated, alienated, unhappy, hopeless. But we don't know how to organize these to form a coherent picture of loneliness and can't interrogate our fictional subjects further to be sure we understand what they are experiencing. In fact, we were surprised at the rarity of explicit descriptions of loneliness in literature. Many authors simply use the word "loneliness" or describe the lonely character's situation or behavior (e.g., walking along, head down, teary-eyed) without attempting to capture the character's experience in words. In any case, we have to be somewhat cautious about fictional accounts of loneliness, because they may not be accurate or representative. They are undoubtedly based on astute observations and introspection, but are also tailored to fit a particular story and to serve the artistic needs of an author, and so may be misleading in various ways. For these reasons, we have interviewed and surveyed flesh-and-blood lonely people.

INTERVIEWS

As part of our research on loneliness we have interviewed 50 adult Americans living in different parts of the United States—most for an hour, some for several hours—and have surveyed hundreds of students at New York University. As most clinical psychologists will attest, case studies are often more powerful and telling than fiction.

One of our interviewees, a 24-year-old black woman who lives with her mother and son in New York City, is frequently lonely. "I just feel afraid and angry. I feel like breaking down and crying or punching out at something. I sit by the window and look out at all the people having a good time. I feel like I'm going in a big circle, and I start feeling stupid and good-for-nothing." Divorced a few years before our interview, and then stunned by the murder of a new fiancé, she joined the Job Corps and was sent to Oregon.

That was the *loneliest* place! So quiet—no sirens or street noises. I dreamed about him all the time, like he was right there with me. He'd made me feel so good; I started dressing and wearing my hair the way he liked. I lost weight and was looking good . . . I really do miss him. I started eating and the next thing I know I was eating too much—like I was filling up an empty spot somewhere. But it never did get filled.

A 20-year-old man in Worcester, Massachusetts, lives with his parents and younger sister. He graduated from high school and lost contact with his classmates. He has no close friends, and his days consist of working and sleeping, in a monotonous, predictable cycle. "I would like to have a close friend; if I needed somebody I could call him up and talk. I could just dial a number and talk. I feel so bored and lonely, nothing seems worthwhile." To fill up his day, this young man goes to work early and reluctantly leaves late. In the evenings he listens to records, half-heartedly watches television, or drives his car aimlessly around town.

In an open-ended survey questionnaire, we asked New York University students how loneliness feels. Below are some typical responses, edited for brevity:

"I feel depressed, left out, unwanted."

"Sorry for myself, sad."

"My actions seem clumsy and inappropriate. Physically, I feel as though I am in the way."

"Bored, drowsy, down."

"I feel sort of empty inside."

"Like I'm evaporating or disintegrating, like maybe I don't really exist."

"I don't remember anymore why I'm working so hard, why life is supposed to be worthwhile."

From these accounts we begin to sense the texture and complexity of loneliness, but its structure and dynamics remain unclear. We need a method for placing the descriptions into categories and for relating these categories to possible causes and consequences of loneliness.

FACTOR ANALYSES OF FEELINGS, REASONS, AND REACTIONS

In order to explore loneliness more systematically and with a larger sample of subjects, we designed an 84-item questionnaire that could be printed in newspapers around the country. Readers were asked to complete the questionnaire, whether or not they were lonely, and to mail a precoded answer sheet to us for computer analysis. (Details of the studies have been reported elsewhere; see Rubenstein, 1979; Rubenstein & Shaver, 1980; Rubenstein, Shaver, & Peplau, 1979.) The questionnaire included three multiple-response items concerned with (1) how loneliness feels, (2) reasons for or causes of loneliness, and (3) reactions to loneliness. Each item consisted of a question (e.g., "How do you usually *feel* when you are lonely? Circle all that apply.") followed by a randomly ordered list of answer alternatives (e.g., down on myself, sad, unable to concentrate, bored) derived from the fictional accounts, interviews, and open-ended surveys discussed earlier.

The questionnaire was published during 1978 in six American newspapers.* The two largest returns, and the ones presented here, were from the New York *Daily News* ($N = 22,000$) and the Worcester (Massachusetts) *Telegram* ($N = 1500$). For purposes of analysis, a random subset of 2000 responses from the New York sample was used; all 1500 who responded in Worcester were included. Although newspaper surveys are subject to the biases of people who choose to fill out questionnaires, there are good reasons for believing that our results are generally valid. Comparison of the New York and Worcester samples with market surveys of representative samples of *Daily News* and *Telegram* readers reveal no substantial differences. Also, regardless of city size and geographic location, the findings within each of our six samples were virtually the same. When these findings are compared with the results of other recent studies, they prove consistent. Until a truly representative national survey is conducted, our results will provide the best available clues about the likely results of such a survey.

The answers to each of three multiple-response items (feelings, reasons,

---

* Besides New York and Worcester, these cities include Charlotte, North Carolina; Fort Myers, Florida; Wichita, Kansas; and Billings, Montana. While obviously not fully representative of the United States, this set of cities is heterogeneous enough to suggest that our main conclusions, borne out in each city, are generally replicable.

and reactions) were submitted to a principal components factor analysis with varimax rotation. This procedure identifies intercorrelated clusters of responses that can be viewed as independent (distinct) dimensions or factors.* Besides these factor analyses, correlational analyses were conducted to see how the factors related to loneliness and to other items on our questionnaire.

Loneliness was measured by an eight-item scale (here called the NYU Loneliness Scale to distinguish it from the UCLA Scale, described in Chapter 6). The items are shown in Table 13.1; to compute a loneliness score, each item is transformed into a standard score (z score) and added to the other standardized item scores. A score of zero indicates an average degree of loneliness; a high positive score indicates a high degree of loneliness. The reliability of this scale (Cronbach's alpha) was .88 for the New York sample and .89 for the Worcester sample. Later in this chapter we will discuss potentially important differences between the NYU and UCLA scales.

Table 13.1. NYU Loneliness Scale Items

1. When I am completely alone, I feel lonely. (5 points: almost never . . . most of the time)
2. How often do you feel lonely? (7 points: all the time . . . never)
3. When you feel lonely, how lonely do you feel? (6 points: extremely lonely . . . I never feel lonely)
4. Compared to people your own age, how lonely do you think you are? (5 points: much lonelier . . . much less lonely)

How much do you agree with each of the following (on a 4-point agree-disagree scale):

5. I am a lonely person.
6. I always was a lonely person.
7. I always will be a lonely person.
8. Other people think of me as a lonely person.

All scale points are labeled on the questionnaire. Here, to save space, we indicate only the end points.

FEELINGS ASSOCIATED WITH LONELINESS

Twenty-seven adjectives were offered as possible feelings associated with loneliness. When people label themselves "lonely," the feelings they mention having most often are: sadness (60% in New York, 56% in Worcester), depression (—, 60%),** boredom (55%, 46%), self-pity (50%, 49%), longing to be with one special person (56%, 45%).

* Varimax rotation was chosen to distinguish maximally between potentially different constructs. The same factors emerge, however, when oblique rotation is used. Also the factor structure is quite similar for males and females, so in this chapter we will discuss findings without mentioning gender.

** Due to a typographical error in the *Daily News,* the word "depression" was omitted from the answer alternatives to this question. Since the results were so similar for New York and Massachusetts, it seems justifiable to place "depression" on the factor where it loaded in the Massachusetts factor analysis.

The 27 responses were intercorrelated and factor analyzed; the results are shown in Table 13.2. Four reliable, interpretable factors emerged. We have called these Desperation, Depression, Impatient Boredom, and Self-Deprecation.

Table 13.2. Factor Analysis of Feelings When Lonely

Factor 1: Desperation	Factor 2: Depression	Factor 3: Impatient boredom	Factor 4: Self-deprecation
Desperate	Sad	Impatient	Unattractive
Panicked	Depressed	Bored	Down on self
Helpless	Empty	Desire to be	Stupid
Afraid	Isolated	elsewhere	Ashamed
Without hope	Sorry for self	Uneasy	Insecure
Abandoned	Melancholy	Angry	
Vulnerable	Alienated	Unable to	
	Longing to be	concentrate	
	with one special		
	person		

The first factor, Desperation, accounts for the largest share of the common variance (76.5%) and reminds us of theoretical discussions of loneliness that emphasize broken relationships, especially the separation of a child from its parents. Weiss (1973), for example, distinguishes *emotional* from *social* isolation, likening the former to the "distress of a small child who fears that he has been abandoned by his parents" (p. 20). This, according to Weiss, is the form of loneliness experienced by separated, divorced, and widowed marital partners—adults whose most intimate social ties have been severed. Our third factor, Impatient Boredom, is similar to Weiss's "social isolation," associated with a bored and restless feeling similar to that of "the small child whose friends are all away" (p. 20). Among adults these feelings commonly arise after moving to a new job, neighborhood, or city. (For a more detailed examination of childhood prototypes and antecedents of adult loneliness, see Shaver & Rubenstein, 1980.)

The two remaining factors, Depression and Self-Deprecation, are probably best conceptualized as *reactions* to loneliness. Although measures taken at a single point in time cannot establish a temporal relationship, it seems reasonable, given what is known about depression (Friedman & Katz, 1974), to suggest that prolonged loneliness or repeated rejection lead to self-blame and finally to depression. In our interview with the young mother quoted earlier, this pattern was evident: "I feel like I'm going in one big circle, and I start feeling stupid and good-for-nothing."

In order to conduct additional statistical analyses using the four "feeling factors," items loading on a particular factor were unit-weighted and summed to form an index. For example, a person who checked four of the seven items on the Desperation factor received a Desperation score of 4; a person who checked six of the seven received a score of 6. These factor indexes were correlated with other variables assessed by our questionnaire.

In line with Weiss's (1973) theorizing, Desperation scores were higher for adult respondents whose parents were divorced (t (1998) $=$ 3.72, $p <$ .001) and for respondents who were separated or divorced themselves (t (1990) $=$ 1.96, $p =$ .05). (Desperation correlates $r =$ .49 with the NYU Loneliness Scale, indicating that lonelier people are more likely to feel desperate when lonely.)* Of all four feeling indexes, Impatient Boredom has the largest negative correlation with age ($r = -.24$, $p <$ .001), suggesting that boredom as a component of loneliness is more characteristic of the young than of the old. (Our respondents ranged in age from 18 to 87.)

SELF-REPORTED REASONS FOR LONELINESS

On our questionnaire we said: "Listed below are some reasons that various people have given for feeling lonely. If you have been lonely during the past year or so, circle all the *major* reasons." Twenty reasons, most of them taken from our earlier open-ended questionnaire study, were provided. Loneliness is most often attributed to: having nothing to do, feeling bored (49%, 31%), being alone (49%, 36%), and having no spouse or lover (36%, 27%).

A factor analysis of the reasons yielded five replicable factors, shown in Table 13.3. Once again, two of the factors correspond well to Weiss's (1973) distinction between emotional and social isolation. Being Un-attached, accounting for 44.4% of the common variance, is similar to emotonal isolation. Alienation, accounting for 22.3% of the common variance, is comparable to social isolation.

Indexes based on these factors were constructed and correlated with other variables. If emotional isolation is parallel to Being Unattached and

Table 13.3.   Factor Analysis of Reasons for Being Lonely

Factor 1: Being unattached	Factor 2: Alienation	Factor 3: Being alone	Factor 4: Forced isolation	Factor 5: Dislocation
Having no spouse	Feeling different	Coming home to an empty house	Being house-bound	Being far from home
Having no sexual partner	Being mis-understood	Being alone	Being hospital-ized	In new job or school
Breaking up with spouse or lover	Not being needed		Having no trans-portation	Moving too often
	Having no close friends			Traveling often

* Most of the correlations reported in this chapter are presented in Table 13.6.

is associated with feeling Desperation, then these two unit-weighted indexes should be related, and they are ($r = .26$, $p < .001$). Similarly, if social isolation is comparable to what we call Alienation and is associated with Impatient Boredom, these two indexes should be related. In fact, the correlation between the two is .39 ($p < .001$). As we would expect, a large portion of the variance in Being Unattached (30%) is accounted for by marital status; see Table 13.4.

Table 13.4. Scores on the "Being Unattached" Factor for Various Marital Status Categories [a]

Reason factor	"Being unattached"
Marital Status:	(n)
Separated	1.47 (130)
Divorced	1.40 (213)
Single	1.29 (775)
Widowed	.88 (119)
Live with lover	.46 (95)
Remarried, more than once	.39 (18)
Remarried	.22 (82)
Married, first time	.16 (560)
$F\ (7,1984) = 121.78$, $p < .0001$	

[a] These results are for the New York sample only, but they were replicated in all of the other samples we studied.

The remaining third of the common variance in reasons for being lonely is due to three additional factors. Factor 3, Being Alone (acounting for 13.8%), describes simple situations in which the absence of other people (or another person) is noticed. The fourth factor, Forced Isolation (accounting for 11.9% of the variance), is an important reason for loneliness among the infirm and handicapped. Dislocation (accounting for only 7.6% of the common variance) identifies mobility and being in a new social setting as reasons for being lonely.

Forced isolation is a reason for loneliness among the elderly (ages 60 to 69 and 70 plus), who are significantly more likely than people in any other age group to say they are housebound, hospitalized, or without transportation. This does not mean that a disproportionate number of old people are lonely, however, since only a small minority are isolated in these ways (Harris et al., 1976; Rubenstein & Shaver, 1980).

Living situation accounts for 10% of the variance in Being Alone (one of the "reason" factors). For those who live alone, Being Alone is an important cause of loneliness. However, the effect of living alone is powerfully mediated by *how* a person responds to being alone (Shaver & Rubenstein, 1979). Lonely people (i.e., those with high scores on the NYU Loneliness Scale) tend to associate negative feelings with being alone—when alone they feel afraid ($r = .41, .42$), anxious ($r = .48, .50$), and angry ($r = .51, .47$).

In contrast, those who aren't often lonely think of solitude as a satisfying state. They feel calm ($r = -.34, -.38$), relaxed ($r = -.44, -.46$), creative ($r = -.34, -.38$), and happy ($r = -.60, -.57$).* Part of this difference is due to personality factors influenced by childhood experiences (Shaver & Rubenstein, 1980); part is due to recent adult experiences such as marital separation, divorce, widowhood, and living situation (Shaver & Rubenstein, 1979).

REACTIONS TO LONELINESS

We asked: "When you feel lonely, what do you usually do about it?" The question was followed by 24 responses to loneliness. The most common ones proved to be: reading (50%, 52%), listening to music (57%, 48%), and calling a friend (55%, 45%). A factor analysis of these yielded four factors (see Table 13.5). Sad Passivity, accounting for 46.6% of the common variance, is a characteristic reaction to loneliness among those who are severely lonely. Of the four unit-weighted reaction indexes, Sad Passivity is most highly correlated with loneliness ($r = .42, p < .001$). It is a state of lethargic self-pity that may well contribute to a vicious cycle of low self-esteem and social isolation. It is highly correlated with both Depression ($r = .49, p < .001$) and Self-Deprecation ($r = .46, p < .001$). (See Table 13.6.)

Table 13.5. Factor Analysis of Responses to Loneliness

Factor 1: Sad passivity	Factor 2: Active solitude	Factor 3: Spending money	Factor 4: Social contact
Cry	Study or work	Spend money	Call a friend
Sleep	Write	Go shopping	Visit someone
Sit and think	Listen to music		
Do nothing	Exercise		
Overeat	Walk		
Take tranquilizers	Work on a hobby		
Watch television	Go to a movie		
Drink or get "stoned"	Read		
	Play music		

Psychoanalytically trained readers will notice the similarity between this factor and the concept of "oral passivity." Overeating, taking tranquilizers, drinking, and passively "taking in" television images are all "oral" in the psychoanalytic sense. The items on this factor, taken together, say: "I am helpless and dejected; love me, take care of me." Sad Passivity is negatively correlated with age ($r = -.23, p < .001$), suggesting that this reaction to loneliness is especially characteristic of the young.

* All correlation coefficients reported in this paragraph are significant beyond the .001 level.

Table 13.6. Intercorrelations for Loneliness and 13 Unit-Weighted Factors, for the New York Sample [a]

	Feelings:				Reasons:					Reactions:				NYU Loneliness Scale
	2	3	4	5	6	7	8	9	10	11	12	13	
1	.56	.50	.60	.26	.46	.13	.28	.09	.39	.08	.08	−.02	.49
2		.48	.57	.26	.49	.09	.25	.12	.46	.08	.14	.00	.48
3			.50	.19	.39	.12	.25	.15	.41	.14	.12	.14	.38
4				.34	.51	.13	.36	.15	.49	.15	.17	.05	.55
5					.20	.04	.26	.05	.20	.14	.09	.05	.33
6						.14	.24	.15	.40	.15	.09	−.07	.51
7							.08	.11	.15	.15	.02	.04	.09
8								.11	.25	.08	.10	.07	.38
9									.10	.14	.05	.06	.10
10										.14	.14	.05	.42
11											.20	.22	.02
12												.19	.07
13													−.12

[a] 1 = Desperation; 2 = Self-deprecation; 3 = Impatient boredom; 4 = Depression; 5 = Being unattached; 6 = Alienation; 7 = Forced isolation; 8 = Being alone; 9 = Dislocation; 10 = Sad passivity; 11 = Active solitude; 12 = Spending money; 13 = Social contact.
The intercorrelations among the feeling indexes are high, indicating that the factors reported in earlier tables are orthogonal only due to weights derived from factor analyses. For most people, the feeling dimensions of loneliness are probably not distinct.

The remaining three factors represent solutions to loneliness chosen by people who are infrequently lonely. Active Solitude, accounting for 24.4% of the common variance, portrays a creative and rewarding use of time spent alone; it is an *alternative* to loneliness. The profligates, who react by Spending Money (accounting for 17.2% of the common variance), compensate themselves for negative feelings—or at least attempt to distract themselves (in a way more extravagant than Huck Finn's log counting). Not surprisingly, people with incomes over $30,000 circled significantly more of these items than did respondents with incomes below $5,000.

Social Contact, accounting for 12.0% of the common variance, deals with the problem of loneliness head-on, by "calling a friend" or "visiting someone." For people who use this strategy, loneliness is likely to be a transient state. In fact, the unit-weighted Social Contact index is slightly negatively correlated with loneliness ($r = -.11$, $p < .001$).

RELATIONSHIPS BETWEEN LONELINESS AND OTHER VARIABLES

We have now examined the experience of loneliness from what might be called a systematic phenomenological perspective. People's self-reports of feelings and reasons are highly structured, and these structures fit well with Weiss's (1973) distinction between social and emotional isolation. People's responses to loneliness, although not all part of their phenomenology (we assume that their behavioral descriptions are fairly accurate), are also meaningfully structured and related to phenomenology. (For example, feelings of self-deprecation and depression are associated with sad-passive reactions; see Table 13.6.) We are now ready to consider possible causes, correlates, and consequences of loneliness that may not be evident to respondents and are not therefore part of their phenomenology, although our evidence for them is based on self-reports and remains to be confirmed by other methods.

Our questionnaire asked about several potentially relevant features of childhood: parental death and divorce (and the respondent's age when such events occurred), and quality of relationships with mother and father. Adult loneliness was weakly but significantly related to most of these variables ($.15 < r < .25$, $p < .001$). That is, adults who reported having better relationships with their parents during childhood were less lonely at the time of our survey. Respondents whose parents were divorced before the respondent was 18 years of age were more lonely as adults, especially if the divorce occurred before the respondent was six years old. Surprisingly, parental death had no such lasting effect (Shaver & Rubenstein, 1980).

Contrary to popular expectation, age has been negatively correlated with loneliness in every city we have surveyed. This corroborates studies reported by Blau (1973), Harris and Associates (1976), Lowenthal (1968; Lowenthal, Thurner, & Chiriboga, 1976), Rosow (1962), Shanas (1968), and

Townsend (1957). According to our data, loneliness in old age is a result of poverty and poor health, not a characteristic of age per se.

Also contrary to popular expectations (Packard, 1972), geographic mobility was *not* related to adult loneliness. We inquired about both childhood and adult mobility, and found no relationship between number of moves and current loneliness. Evidently most mobile Americans learn to establish a new social network soon after arriving in an unfamiliar community (see also Fischer & Phillips in this volume).

Finally, loneliness and living alone turned out to be quite different in their relationship to other variables. For example, the NYU Loneliness Scale correlated $r = .60$ ($p < .001$) with a composite measure of psychosomatic symptoms, but living alone was unrelated to this index (Shaver & Rubenstein, 1979).*

THEORETICAL IMPLICATIONS

Weiss (1973) and Peplau and her colleagues (Peplau & Perlman, 1979; Peplau, Russell, & Heim, 1979) are responsible for the two major theoretical frameworks discussed in this book. In this section, we will explore possible implications of our results for those two theories.

Weiss (1973), as mentioned previously, distinguished between emotional and social isolation, basing this distinction on interviews with and observations of two groups of adults: members of an organization called Parents Without Partners and people who had recently moved from one community to another. Parents Without Partners provided many examples of emotional isolation: adults whose marital partner had died or departed but some of whose friends (social contacts) were still available. The recent resettlers displayed the opposite pattern—intact marriage combined with absence of a friendship network. Although Weiss's observations were provocative, he did not attempt to make operational the concepts of emotional and social isolation. Our results (and Brennan's; see Chapter 17) indicate that operationalization is both feasible and empirically warranted.

We created our lists of feelings, reasons, and reactions to loneliness without regard for existing theories. The list came from literary examples, unstructured interviews, and open-ended questionnaires. Yet the results offer substantial support for Weiss's distinction. Of the four feeling factors, two (Desperation and Impatient Boredom) are conceptually similar to emotional and social isolation. Of the five reason factors, Being Unattached and Alienation together account for two-thirds of the common variance. Being Unattached, being

---

* As mentioned earlier, living alone is slightly related to loneliness, but this is due mainly to the fact that many separated, divorced, and recently widowed respondents are unhappy about living alone. (Separated and divorced respondents are much lonelier, on the average, than widowed, single, or married respondents; and the married are least lonely of all.) Single people who choose to live alone are not especially lonely.

without a spouse or lover, is the phenomenon Weiss was studying when he conceptualized emotional isolation. Alienation—feeling different, not being needed, having no close friends—is very similar to the social isolation of the recent resettlers Weiss studied, although resettling is obviously not the only cause of alienation or social isolation.

The prominence of these dimensions in our data is strong evidence of their validity and a sign that separate scales could be constructed to measure emotional and social isolation. Our separation of potential item content into feelings and reasons should alert scale constructors to the difference between these two categories. Weiss (1973) derived the emotional-social distinction from simultaneous assessment of both feelings and situations. It is still unclear whether scales to measure emotional and social isolation should focus only on feelings, leaving situational variables in an explanatory rather than classificatory role, or should also include items that specify situations. It seems possible, despite our success in distinguishing between Desperation and Impatient Boredom using only questions about feelings, that the full meaning of Weiss's terms will require specification of the lonely person's situation. Certainly Impatient Boredom fails to capture all that Weiss intended by the term social isolation.

Our analysis of feelings produced two additional factors, Self-Deprecation and Depression. These do not correspond to either factor in Weiss's framework, not because they are incompatible, but because they are not *types* of loneliness in the same way that emotional and social isolation are. We said earlier that prolonged loneliness, especially loneliness that persists despite efforts to dispel it, may lead people to blame themselves for rejection or social isolation and consequently to feel hopeless and depressed. A natural consequence of this final feeling state is the set of behaviors we have called Sad Passivity—crying, overeating, watching television, taking drugs, and oversleeping. In this case phenomenology and behavior appear to be closely linked.

In a recent paper Bragg (1979) presented data linking loneliness and depression, and then showed that loneliness need not be associated with depression. People who are both lonely and depressed tend to be dissatisfied with both social and nonsocial aspects of their lives, whereas lonely non-depressed people are bothered only by social dissatisfaction. This makes sense, since there is obviously more than one reason for becoming depressed. Still it would be a mistake not to notice the well-worn path from loneliness to depression. Social losses or deficits that are blamed on the self lead naturally to depression; it is no accident that loneliness and depression are highly correlated.

Peplau's (Peplau, Russell, & Heim, 1979) attribution model helps to make sense of the connection between loneliness and depression, and between loneliness and the other reaction factors we identified—Active Solitude, Spending Money, and Social Contact. Peplau and her colleagues have shown that lonely people can explain their negative feelings in a variety of ways. The dimensions underlying the possible explanations of loneliness appear to be internality, stability, and controllability (Michela, Peplau, & Weeks, 1981). A person who chooses (or is forced to accept) internal, stable, uncontrollable attributions or explanations (e.g., "I am basically unlovable") is likely to give up trying to form satisfying relationships and is a good candidate for Depression and Sad Passivity. A person who believes that the causes of loneliness are internal and controllable is likely to exert effort toward change; a person who blames external conditions may lash out in anger.

The temporal course of loneliness and of attributions concerning loneliness deserve further study. There are likely to be individual differences in the perceived plausibility of various attributions: a person whose parents quarrel or separate may be more prone than others to believe that social relations are inherently uncontrollable and punishing (Shaver & Rubenstein, 1980). Despite perceptual biases, situational factors must eventually penetrate almost everyone's perceptions. Even a dispositional optimist, upon repeatedly experiencing rejection (say, after moving to a new community), is likely to accept a painful constellation of internal, stable, and uncontrollable attributions. ("What is wrong with me? Won't I ever be accepted and appreciated?")

Our factor analysis of reasons, one might think, should have produced evidence for Peplau's three attribution dimensions; after all, reasons and attributions are highly similar concepts. However, our list of reasons didn't contain all of the kinds of attributions discussed by Peplau, Russell, and Heim (1979). Our list was based mainly on an open-ended questionnaire study of college students, completed before we learned of Peplau's work. Our subjects provided mainly situational reasons for their own loneliness. They didn't refer to qualities of themselves, such as unlovability, shyness, or poor social skills, which might have allowed an internality factor to emerge. It is interesting that Peplau and her colleagues got their factor structure by asking subjects to explain *not* themselves, but a hypothetical lonely person, in a story constructed especially for the study.* The relationship between our two procedures remains to be explored, but subjects would probably attribute negative qualities to themselves more readily if they were invited to do so in a closed-ended questionnaire than if they were asked an open-ended question like ours: "For what reasons have you felt the most severe loneliness?"

Our neglect of dispositional reasons for loneliness prompted us to think about the importance of the disposition-versus-situation issue for designers of loneliness scales. The NYU Loneliness Scale was designed with a dispositional bias; it includes such items as "I am a lonely person" and "I always was a lonely person." Thus it is not surprising that loneliness, *as we measure it,* correlates highly with depression, low self-esteem, and psychosomatic symptoms. The UCLA Scale, on the other hand, seems to us to embody a situational

---

* The difference between our results and Peplau's may be due in part to the well-researched actor-observer dichotomy (Jones & Nisbett, 1972; Storms, 1973) and the more general "fundamental attribution error" (Ross, 1977), the "general tendency to overestimate the importance of personal or dispositional factors relative to environmental influences."

bias. Surprisingly, in 20 different items it never mentions the word "lonely" or "loneliness." (Each of our eight items explicitly mentions the concept.) This is natural, since Peplau and her colleagues define loneliness in terms of social deficit, which immediately implicates the social environment.

We are not arguing for our own operational definition, only pointing out that the results of future studies may depend on the way loneliness is measured. Before a single instrument is accepted as the best way to measure loneliness, if such a consensus is ever deemed appropriate, further psychometric exploration is called for. (See Weiss's related comments in Chapter 5.)

THE ENDURING CHALLENGE OF PHENOMENOLOGY

Like most social scientists, we know more than our numbers tell. Intensive interviews with dispositionally lonely people—those who have experienced loneliness many times and know that they are uncommonly susceptible to it—reveal phenomena that cannot yet be measured or fully understood. For example, in some of our longer interviews we asked people what loneliness feels like "in the body." A surprising proportion of people say, without much difficulty or hesitation, "a hole or space in my chest (or stomach, or near my diaphragm)." This answer elaborates on the more cryptic and common term "emptiness." We are so familiar with this notion (it appears in all of the popular books about loneliness) that we fail to question it. But why exactly does a lonely person feel empty? A "deficit in social relations" (Peplau & Perlman, 1979) might reasonably imply a "hole" in one's social world, but why is this experienced as a hole in the self?

Another example: When we ask people, in a supportive, nondirective way, to imagine a solution for their loneliness—if possible, a single visual scene in which their loneliness is completely assuaged—they do so without hesitation. And the image often startles both them and us. One 30-year-old woman imagined snuggling up against and "burrowing under" a vaguely defined older male figure who was lying down. When asked to discuss this image further, again in a nondirective way, she recalled, to her surprise, that when she was young, her father, who worked late during the week, would come home early on Friday evenings, change clothes, and lie down on the floor under an afghan and "let me snuggle up next to him while he watched TV." Most of the "solution images" we have recorded are reminiscent of parent-child relations, although not always in such a concrete way.

Are such metaphors and images worth taking seriously? We aren't sure. But we are convinced that it would be a mistake to restrict and quantify the study of loneliness prematurely, leaving potentially significant research avenues unexplored. Social psychology is, unfortunately, remarkable for its ability to reduce profound and fascinating human issues to rather superficial and uninteresting generalizations (Elms, 1975; Moscovici, 1972; Ring, 1967). We would hate to see loneliness suffer this fate. One safeguard would be to return regularly to the complexities of phenomenology.

REFERENCES

Agee, J. *A death in the family.* New York: Avon, 1938.

Blau, Z. *Old age in a changing society.* New York: New Viewpoints, 1973.

Bragg, M. *A comparative study of loneliness and depression.* Unpublished doctoral dissertation, University of California, Los Angeles, 1979.

Brontë, C. *Jane Eyre.* New York: Modern Library, 1950.

Conrad, J. *Heart of darkness.* In *Great short works of Joseph Conrad.* New York: Harper & Row, 1966.

Defoe, D. *Robinson Crusoe.* New York: Signet, 1960.

Elms, A. C. The crisis of confidence in social psychology. *American Psychologist,* 1975, *30,* 967–976.

Friedman, R., & Katz, M. (Eds.). *The psychology of depression: Contemporary theory and research.* New York: Wiley, 1974.

Harris, L., & Associates, Inc. *The myth and reality of aging in America.* A study for the National Council on the Aging. New York, July 1976.

Jones, E. E., & Nisbett, R. The actor and the observer: Divergent perceptions of the causes of behavior. In E. E. Jones et al. (Eds.), *Attribution: Perceiving the causes of behavior.* Morristown, N.J.: General Learning Press, 1972.

Kockelmans, J. J. (Ed.), *Phenomenology.* Garden City, N.Y.: Doubleday, 1967.

Lowenthal, M. F. Social isolation and mental illness in old age. In B. Neugarten (Ed.), *Middle age and aging.* Chicago: University of Chicago Press, 1968.

Lowenthal, M. F., Thurner, M., & Chiriboga, D. *Four stages of life.* San Francisco: Jossey-Bass, 1976.

Michela, J., Peplau, L. A., & Weeks, D. *Perceived dimensions and consequences of attributions for loneliness.* Unpublished manuscript, Columbia University, New York, October 1981.

Miller, G. A., Galanter, E. H., & Pribram, K. *Plans and the structure of behavior.* New York: Holt, 1960.

Moscovici, S. Society and theory in social psychology. In J. Israel & H. Tajfel (Eds.), *The context of social psychology: A critical assessment.* New York: Academic Press, 1972.

Moustakas, C. E. *Loneliness.* New York: Prentice-Hall, 1961.

Moustakas, C. E. *Loneliness and love.* Englewood Cliffs, N. J.: Prentice-Hall, 1972.

Moustakas, C. E. *Portraits of loneliness and love.* Englewood Cliffs, N. J.: Prentice-Hall, 1975.

Packard, V. *A nation of strangers.* New York: David McKay, 1972.

Peplau, L. A., Russell, D., & Heim, M. The experience of loneliness. In I. H. Frieze, D. Bar-Tal, & J. Carroll (Eds.), *New approaches to social problems: Applications of attribution theory.* San Francisco: Jossey-Bass, 1979.

Peplau, L. A., & Perlman, D. Blueprint for a social psychological theory of loneliness. In M. Cook & G. Wilson (Eds.), *Love and attraction.* Oxford, England: Pergamon, 1979.

Ring, K. Experimental social psychology: Some sober questions about frivolous values. *Journal of Experimental Social Psychology,* 1967, *3,* 113–123.

Rosow, I. Retirement housing and social integration. In C. Tibbitts & W. Donahue (Eds.), *Social psychological aspects of aging.* New York: Columbia University Press, 1962.

Ross, L. The intuitive psychologist and his shortcomings. In L. Berkowitz (Ed.), *Advances in experimental social psychology* (Vol. 10). New York: Academic Press, 1977.

Rubenstein, C. *A questionnaire study of adult loneliness in three U.S. cities.* Unpublished doctoral dissertation, New York University, 1979.

Rubenstein, C., & Shaver, P. Loneliness in two northeastern cities. In J. Hartog & J. Audy (Eds.), *The anatomy of loneliness.* New York: International Universities Press, 1980.

Rubenstein, C., Shaver, P., & Peplau, L. A. Loneliness. *Human Nature,* 1979, *2,* 59–65.

Salinger, J. D. *The catcher in the rye.* New York: Bantam, 1961.

Shanas, E. *Old people in three industrial societies.* New York: Atherton Press, 1968.

Shaver, P., & Rubenstein, C. Childhood attachment experience and adult loneliness. In L. Wheeler (Ed.), *Review of personality and social psychology.* (Vol. 1). Beverly Hills, Calif.: Sage, 1980.

Shaver, P. & Rubenstein, C. *Living alone, loneliness, and health.* Paper presented at the annual meeting of the American Psychological Association, New York City, 1979.

Skinner, B. F. *Science and human behavior.* New York: Macmillan, 1953.

Storms, M. Videotape and the attribution process: Reversing actors' and observers' points of view. *Journal of Personality and Social Psychology,* 1973, *27,* 165–175.

Styron, W. *Sophie's choice.* New York: Random House, 1979.

Townsend, P. *The family life of old people.* New York: Free Press, 1957.

Twain, M. *The adventures of Huckleberry Finn.* New York: Signet, 1969.

Valle, R. S., & King, M. (Eds.), *Existential-phenomenological alternatives for psychology.* New York: Oxford University Press, 1978.

Wann, T. W. (Ed.), *Behaviorism and phenomenology: Contrasting bases for modern psychology.* Chicago: University of Chicago Press, 1964.

Weiss, R. S. *Loneliness: The experience of emotional and social isolation.* Cambridge, Mass.: MIT Press, 1973.

Chapter 14

Loneliness, Spiritual Well-Being
and the Quality of Life

Raymond F. Paloutzian and Craig W. Ellison

Within the past ten years considerable interest has developed in assessing the emotional and social health of Americans. Those interested in social indicators have recently focused on the perceived quality of life, and have attempted to measure subjective impressions such as happiness and psychological well-being (Bradburn, 1969; Campbell, 1976). This chapter focuses on subjective measures of loneliness and spiritual-existential well-being. We believe that both of these conditions are facets of the more general concept of quality of life, and that loneliness is directly linked to the perceived quality of one's social life.

Measuring loneliness and well-being is an attempt to assess the quality of people's lives. Thus our work falls into what has been called the social indicators movement (Campbell, 1976; Moberg, 1979). This concept was developed within the American government to refer to statistics reflecting the goodness or badness of life quality in this country. The U. S. Department of Health, Education, and Welfare (1969) stated that a social indicator is "a direct measure of welfare and is subject to the interpretation that, if it changes in the 'right' direction . . . things have gotten better or people are 'better off'" (p. 97). Measures of suicide rate, crime, alcoholism, physical and mental health, and housing conditions are all examples of social indicators of the quality of life.

The quality of life concept has been given both objective and subjective meanings. The phrase was first used to refer to quality of life in a strictly objective sense, that is, to tangible or countable goods or events such as those mentioned above.

The problem with such indicators was that, though they did reveal people's objective circumstances, they did not reveal people's experience of how "well

The research reported in this chapter is fully collaborative. Order of authorship was randomly determined. The research was conducted while Paloutzian was at the University of Idaho. The article was written while he was Visiting Scholar, Psychology Department, Stanford University.

off" their lives were. It is an historical paradox that during the last 25 years, as things got physically and economically better, they apparently got psychologically worse (Campbell, 1976). If we assume, as Campbell does, that "the quality of life lies in the experience of life" (p. 118), then statistics based on our objective situation are only surrogate indicators. What is needed are subjective measures of the quality of life experience. The attempt to develop subjective measures is in part an attempt to assess people's interpretation of the things or events that affect them, as opposed to tabulating those things or events themselves. It is this subjective meaning of quality of life that sparked our concern with loneliness and spiritual well-being.

Our conceptual framework for loneliness has stemmed from the underlying assumption that one's history of intimate social interaction and one's current social experience both fundamentally affect perceived quality of life. Life satisfaction seems in large part to be related to the quality of our social relationships. Lonely people are often depressed and unhappy. Our inference was that one indicator of the quality of life is loneliness.

At the time that our investigations began, very little empirical work had been done on loneliness or on the quality of life. As a result, our research has been highly empirical and oriented toward information-gathering of a primary sort. Our studies called primarily on survey research methods. Various surveys contained the original UCLA Loneliness Scale (Russell, Peplau, & Ferguson, 1978), our own Abbreviated Loneliness Scale (Paloutzian & Ellison, 1979a), questions regarding developmental background, values, feelings and responses associated with loneliness, attributed causes of loneliness, effectiveness of a variety of responses in coping with loneliness, and quality of life measures designed to assess one's sense of spiritual well-being. Depending upon the specific study, additional questions were asked regarding campus and dormitory life (Ellison & Campise, 1978), marital satisfaction and living situation (Paloutzian & Ellison, 1979c), and religious commitment (Ellison & Paloutzian, 1979a).

The first section of this chapter outlines our research on the social variables influencing quality of life as reflected in loneliness. The second section includes our efforts at measuring quality of life. The Abbreviated Loneliness Scale, descriptive data on the emotional and behavioral correlates of loneliness, and the Spiritual Well-Being scale are presented. The third section reports findings on how loneliness and spiritual well-being relate to each other and to religious orientation.

SOCIAL FACTORS INFLUENCING QUALITY OF LIFE

Three types of social influences were hypothesized to relate to perceived quality of life as reflected in loneliness and spiritual well-being. These include social context variables, developmental background variables, and values.

Social Context Variables

A study of 115 middle-aged women (Paloutzian & Ellison, 1979c) assessed the relationships between quality of life and two situational variables: density of living environment and social roles. Living environment was assessed by collecting data in three cities, San Francisco, Santa Barbara, and Moscow (Idaho). These represented, respectively, a dense urban center, a medium sized city of 100,000, and a small farm town of 15,000. The rationale was that urban environments foster more surface contact and less intimacy between people (Moustakas, 1961), resulting in a lower experience of life quality and greater loneliness. Our second social context variable, social roles, was assessed by collecting data in all three cities from both full-time homemakers and full-time professional women. An often heard argument is that homemakers experience lower life quality and more loneliness because they are trapped at home with few interpersonal contacts, whereas employed women are less lonely because they have greater opportunity for contact with others.

As expected, spiritual well-being was lower for women living in large urban settings than in smaller cities. But results for loneliness contained some unexpected features. Loneliness was not related to city size nor to employment status. These findings run counter to both theorizing and popular opinion. It is commonly thought that city people experience less intimacy and more loneliness, and that homemakers are lonely (Middlebrook, 1980). Note, however, that both living environment and employment status are global situational variables. Additional analyses revealed that satisfaction in marriage and living situation were related to loneliness ($r = -.36$, $p < .01$, for marriage; $r = -.40$, $p < .01$, for living situation), suggesting that specific situational variables are more critical than general living or working environment. In other words, whether a woman was satisfied with her marriage and living situation was more important than what her situation happened to be.

Developmental Background

In addition to the influence of current interpersonal relations on loneliness and life quality, historical factors may also play a part. The degree of warmth, closeness, and love experienced with parents and peers during one's early years may affect how one learns to relate to others. As adults, our ability to relate intimately and to experience satisfying social relations may rest on the foundation of early experience (Ellison, 1978).

Questionnaire data pertinent to developmental issues were collected from 206 students at the University of Idaho, Westmont College, Biola College, and Pepperdine University. The students were single and married, male and female, religious and nonreligious, and evenly spread out within the 15 to 35 year age range. Nine questions were asked regarding early childhood experiences, three items in each of three categories. The three categories were parent-child relationships (e.g., I told my parents about my problems as I was growing up), family togetherness (e.g., We did a lot of fun things together as a family), and childhood peer relationships (e.g., I had very close friends while growing up).

Our findings indicate a moderate association between developmental factors and loneliness. As summarized in Table 14.1, the reported quality of parent-child relationships, the quality of remembered childhood peer relationships, and the degree of remembered family togetherness are all inversely related to loneliness. Greater intimacy during childhood is associated with less loneliness during adulthood. These results are very similar to independent findings by Shaver and Rubenstein (1980), which showed that people who had parents who were warm, helpful, and supportive were less lonely as adults. Our interpretation is that early life factors that foster a sense of intimacy and belonging have beneficial effects in later life by facilitating these same qualities.

Table 14.1. Correlations Between Developmental and Evaluational Variables and Loneliness [a]

Variable	UCLA Loneliness Scale	Abbreviated Loneliness Scale
Developmental		
Parent-child relationships	—.28***	—.34***
Childhood peer relationships	—.22**	—.14*
Family togetherness	—.24***	—.32***
Evaluational		
Social skills	—.47***	—.55***
Self-esteem	—.58***	—.58***

[a] All statistical tests are two-tailed. N for entire sample is 206, though some correlations are based on a slightly smaller N due to incomplete data.

  * $p < .05$
 ** $p < .01$
*** $p < .001$

Values

Our values shape how we approach interaction with others as well as how we interpret the actions of others toward us. Certain values may work against genuine, intimate interpersonal relations, and as a byproduct may facilitate a lower quality of life. Values that downplay interpersonal trust and undercut a sense of belonging and community may contribute to feelings of emotional isolation.

Our questionnaire given to the college student sample included four items designed to tap individualistic values. The items asked, for example, whether "people should try to get ahead even if it means hurting others," or whether "making sure one is a success is more important than making friends." Our results showed only a negligible tendency for individualistic values to be associated with loneliness. Individualistic values were, however, associated with lower levels of spiritual well-being, $r(174) = -.37$, $p < .001$. These results leave open the possibility that although individualistic values have positive effects such as independence and self-reliance, an overemphasis on individualism reduces quality of life by prompting people to be out for themselves first and by decreasing people's sense of community.

MEASURING QUALITY OF LIFE

In the course of our research, problems associated with measuring quality of life became clear. It became necessary to develop a brief measure of loneliness, to discover the emotional and behavioral correlates of loneliness, and to develop an instrument to measure spiritual well-being in both its religious and existential senses.

The Abbreviated Loneliness Scale

We initially used the UCLA Loneliness Scale, but three problems with this measure readily became apparent. First, in the original scale (Russell, Peplau, & Ferguson, 1978) all items were worded negatively and in the same direction, so that any response-set bias could influence loneliness scores. Second, for some subjects, responding to a long list of negative items was itself a negative experience, so that responses to later items may have been distorted. A third problem was scale length. We thought that a shorter version of a loneliness scale would be useful for some types of research.

Consequently we began to develop an Abbreviated Loneliness Scale. Our initial scale contained three items, scored in the often-to-never format of the UCLA Scale. These were: I feel lonely; I feel emotionally distant from people in general; I have felt very lonely during my life. Results obtained from our study of middle-aged women showed that these combined items correlated very highly with the UCLA Scale, r (111) $= .86$, $p < .001$. Furthermore,

Table 14.2. Abbreviated Loneliness Scale, Version 2: (ABLS) [a]

Please *circle* the choice that best indicates how often each of the following statements describes you in general:

0 = Often   S = Someimes   R = Rarely   N = Never

1. I feel like the people most important to me understand me.	O S R N
2. I feel lonely.	O S R N
3. I feel like I am wanted by the people/groups I value belonging to.	O S R N
4. I feel emotionally distant from people in general.	O S R N
5. I have as many close relationships as I want.	O S R N
6. I have felt lonely during my life.	O S R N
7. I feel emotionally satisfied in my relationship with people.	O S R N

Copyright © 1982 by Raymond F. Paloutzian and Craig W. Ellison.
[a] Items are scored 1 to 4 so that a higher number reflects greater loneliness. Odd-numbered items are positively worded. Reverse scoring for these items. The ABLS score is the sum of the seven responses.

the results obtained on practically all of the variables studied in relation to these two scales were the same. However, all of the items in this scale were worded negatively.

In order to remedy this problem, Version 2 of the Abbreviated Loneliness Scale (ABLS) was developed (Table 14.2) as part of our survey of college students. This improved ABLS contained seven items, four of which were stated in the positive direction. The correlation between the improved ABLS and the UCLA Scale was good, r (194) $= .73$, $p < .001$. The magnitude of this correlation suggests that the ABLS is tapping essentially the same dimension as the UCLA Scale. Test-retest reliability of the ABLS was $r = .85$ ($p < .001$) with 121 subjects and one week between testing. The index of internal consistency, coefficient alpha, was .68, indicating that the items cluster together fairly well. The validity of the ABLS is supported by the nearly parallel correlations between both the ABLS and the UCLA measures of loneliness and a variety of criterion variables. These include self-esteem, social skills, and developmental background variables (Table 14.1), as well as a list of emotional experiences when lonely (Table 14.3). Taken together, these findings suggest that the ABLS would be useful in subsequent research.

Table 14.3. Emotional Correlates of Loneliness

Emotion	Correlation of loneliness scores and frequency of experiencing specific emotions when lonely		Percentage responding to loneliness with specific emotions	
	UCLA Loneliness Scale	Abbreviated Loneliness Scale	Sometimes	Often
Helpless	.10	.17*	43.3	16.0
Depressed	.31**	.27**	81.0	44.2
Rejected	.31**	.30**	47.6	20.3
Misunderstood	.26**	.25**	50.7	16.5
Unwanted	.41**	.38**	38.1	16.5
Empty	.26**	.23**	52.0	24.7
Worthless	.32**	.31**	28.6	11.3
Frustrated	.22*	.21*	75.4	33.8
Isolated	.29**	.22*	63.6	29.0
Grieved	.21*	.11	36.8	12.1
Unloved	.41**	.40**	31.1	13.4
Anxious	—	—	51.9	22.5

* $p < .01$, two-tailed
** $p < .001$, two-tailed

Correlates of Loneliness

How do people feel and behave when they are lonely? What responses do they find effective in coping with loneliness? Answers to these questions contribute to a conceptual picture of the lonely person's quality of life.

Data pertinent to these issues were collected as part of our college student survey. The assessment devices included the UCLA Loneliness Scale, the ABLS, 12 items assessing people's emotional feelings when lonely, eight items assessing the likelihood of specific physical feelings when lonely, 23 items asking what subjects did when lonely, and 23 items asking how effective each of those actions was in coping with loneliness (Ellison & Paloutzian, 1979b).

Emotional Correlates

The data reveal that lonely people are likely to experience painful emotions. As summarized in Table 14.3, the frequency of loneliness was significantly correlated ($p < .01$) with feelings of depression, rejection, being misunderstood, being unwanted, emptiness, worthlessness, frustration, isolation, and being unloved. A sense of being rejected, unwanted, worthless, and unloved carried the strongest relationship to loneliness. These same emotions were also found to be predictive of low self-esteem, a result consistent with the inverse association between self-esteem and loneliness (Table 14.1).

The proportional data in Table 14.3 are also informative. Examination of the proportion of people who experience various emotions when they are lonely reveals that the greatest percentage of people often or sometimes experience depression, frustration, isolation, emptiness, anxiety, and feeling misunderstood. The picture of the lonely person that emerges from these data is similar to that obtained by Rubenstein and Shaver (Chapter 13). It is a picture of a poor quality of life in lonely people.

Behavioral Correlates

In order to detect which responses to loneliness cluster together, the 23 items used to assess what people were most likely to do when lonely were factor analyzed. Seven factors emerged: *Sensually oriented responses* such as drinking, taking drugs, and sexual involvement; *religiously oriented responses* such as praying and reading the Bible; *searching responses* including going to a dance, play, movie, or taking a drive; *nonsocial diversion* such as eating, doing anything to keep busy, reading a book or magazine, and studying or working; *reflective solitude,* represented by getting alone to think and walking anywhere by themselves; *intimacy contact responses* such as talking to a close friend about one's feelings, going someplace where friends will be, and spending time with a close friend just to be together; and *passivity* (sleep).

Which specific acts are the most common responses to loneliness? Examination of individual response items indicated that the greatest percentage of people are moderately to highly likely to do the following: get alone to think (65.7%), listen to music (67.1%), talk to a close friend (54.1%), read (52.4%), spend time with close friends (51%), and eat (50.2%). These findings for both factors and percentages are highly similar to independent findings by Rubenstein and Shaver (Chapter 13).

With regard to the effectiveness of specific behaviors in coping with loneliness, over two-thirds of our subjects, 68%, felt that talking to a close friend about their feelings was moderately to highly effective, and 57.5% said that spending time with a close friend just to be together was effective. Of the other most frequently chosen coping responses, 56.7% of subjects felt that getting alone to think was effective, 48.5% found listening to music likely to be effective, and 36.4% said that reading was at least moderately effective. Only 12.6% found eating to be effective. As part of the intimacy contact factor, 46.8% said that going someplace where friends are was moderately to highly effective. Finally, 42% said that they found prayer effective.

Together, these emotional and behavioral correlates of loneliness provide an empirical definition of the state of the lonely individual. They indicate the sorts of internal states that a counselor can expect in a lonely client, and the sorts of things lonely people use to cope.

The Spiritual Well-Being Scale

Another methodological challenge was to measure facets of quality of life other than loneliness. Many of the measures that were developed during the 1970s involved objective indicators, and didn't assess the internal feelings or perceptions of respondents. Also very few measures even mentioned the role of religion in perceived well-being, and none used religious experience as a central measure of well-being. This absence seemed strange in light of the recent upsurge of religious interest in America. According to a recent Gallup Poll, 86% of Americans say that their religious beliefs are fairly or very important, and 34% or 50 million Americans consider themselves to have been "born again" (Gallup, 1977–1978). Worldwide estimates indicate that over 2,000,000,000 people in the world have religious commitments. For most of these people, religious commitment plays an important role in how they live and experience life (Zimbardo, 1979, pp. 392–398). Campbell, Converse, and Rodgers (1976) found that religious faith was a highly important domain for understanding quality of life experience for 25% of the American population. Paradoxically, however, these authors treated religious influence as having only a secondary influence on life quality.

In pioneering work, Moberg and Brusek (1978) suggested that spiritual well-being is best conceived as having two dimensions. A vertical dimension refers to one's sense of well-being in relationship to God. A horizontal dimension connotes one's perception of life's purpose and satisfaction apart from any specifically religious reference. In the absence of any systematic quality of life measure that included both general life satisfaction (existential well-being) and religious well-being, we set about to develop such an instrument (Paloutzian & Ellison, 1979b).

The Spiritual Well-Being Scale (SWB) is presented in Table 14.4. In order to distinguish religious and existential items, all of the religious well-being (RWB) items contained a reference to God. The existential well-being (EWB) items contained no such reference. In order to control for response set problems, half of the items from each subscale were worded in positive and negative directions. After preliminary versions of the SWB Scale were tested and revised, the final version was constructed with 10 existential and 10 religious items. Factor analysis (using Varimax rotation) of the SWB Scale on data

Table 14.4. Spiritual Well-Being Scale [a]

For each of the following statements circle the choice that best indicates the extent of your agreement or disagreement as it describes your personal experience:

SA = Strongly Agree	D = Disagree
MA = Moderately Agree	MD = Moderately Disagree
A = Agree	SD = Strongly Disagree

1. I don't find much satisfaction in private prayer with God.   SA MA A D MD SD
2. I don't know who I am, where I came from, or where I'm going.   SA MA A D MD SD
3. I believe that God loves me and cares about me.   SA MA A D MD SD
4. I feel that life is a positive experience.   SA MA A D MD SD
5. I believe that God is impersonal and not interested in my daily situations.   SA MA A D MD SD
6. I feel unsettled about my future.   SA MA A D MD SD
7. I have a personally meaningful relationship with God.   SA MA A D MD SD
8. I feel very fulfilled and satisfied with life.   SA MA A D MD SD
9. I don't get much personal strength and support from my God.   SA MA A D MD SD
10. I feel a sense of well-being about the direction my life is headed in.   SA MA A D MD SD
11. I believe that God is concerned about my problems.   SA MA A D MD SD
12. I don't enjoy much about life.   SA MA A D MD SD
13. I don't have a personally satisfying relationship with God.   SA MA A D MD SD
14. I feel good about my future.   SA MA A D MD SD
15. My relationship with God helps me not to feel lonely.   SA MA A D MD SD
16. I feel that life is full of conflict and unhappiness.   SA MA A D MD SD
17. I feel most fulfilled when I'm in close communion with God.   SA MA A D MD SD
18. Life doesn't have much meaning.   SA MA A D MD SD
19. My relation with God contributes to my sense of well-being.   SA MA A D MD SD
20. I believe there is some real purpose for my life.   SA MA A D MD SD

Copyright © 1982 by Craig W. Ellison and Raymond F. Paloutzian.
[a] Items are scored from 1 to 6, with a higher number representing more well-being. Reverse scoring for negatively worded items. Odd-numbered items assess religious well-being; even-numbered items assess existential well-being.

obtained from 206 students at three religiously oriented colleges (Biola College, Westmont College, and Pepperdine University) and at the University of Idaho revealed that the items clustered together generally as expected. All of the religious items loaded on the RWB factor. Existential items appeared to load into two subfactors, one connoting life direction and one connoting life satisfaction. The correlation between the RWB and EWB subscales was $r = .32$ ($p < .001$).

The SWB Scale yields three scores: (1) a total SWB score; (2) a summed score for religious well-being items; (3) a summed score for existential well-being items. Test-retest reliability coefficients were .93 (SWB), .96 (RWB), and .86 (EWB). Alpha coefficients reflecting internal consistency, were .89 (SWB), .87 (RWB), and .78 (EWB). The magnitude of these coefficients suggests that the SWB Scale and subscales have high reliability and internal consistency.

The SWB Scale appears to have sufficient validity for use as a quality of life indicator. Face validity of the SWB Scale is suggested by examination of the item content. Also, SWB scores correlated in predicted ways with several other scales. People who scored high on SWB tended to be less lonely, more socially skilled, higher in self-esteem, and more intrinsic in their religious commitment. As expected, SWB, RWB, and EWB all correlated positively with the Purpose in Life Test (Crumbaugh & Maholick, 1969).

RELIGIOUS COMMITMENT, LONELINESS, AND QUALITY OF LIFE

Religious belief can be among the most potent influences in life. Its effects may include profound changes in subjective experience and social behavior. It can supply purpose and meaning (Frankl, 1975), facilitate intimate inter-personal contact and a sense of belonging (Ellison, 1978), and affect one's entire satisfaction with existence. Our findings indicate that it may also relate in important ways to loneliness.

We reasoned that there are different types of religious commitments that may be differentially related to quality of life and loneliness. As compared to casually religious persons, those whose religious commitment is very personal and intimate should have a greater sense of purpose in life, sense of belonging, satisfaction with existence, and less loneliness. This prediction of less loneliness in deeply religious people may be due to either the greater "personalness" of the commitment itself or the increased involvement in religious groups by such persons.

Assessment

Additional parts of our surveys were designed to explore these relationships. We had subjects answer a religious commitment item, the Intrinsic-Extrinsic Religious Orientation Scale (Allport & Ross, 1967), the UCLA Loneliness Scale, the ABLS, the Purpose in Life Test, and the SWB Scale.

The degree to which one's religious commitment was personal and intimate was assessed in two ways. The first procedure, borrowed from Paloutzian, Jackson, and Crandall (1978), attempted to separate those who saw their religious commitment as a personal relationship from those who saw it as an ethical orientation. Given the predominantly Christianized population that we were studying, subjects were first asked to indicate whether or not they considered themselves to be Christian. Those who did were then asked to choose only one of two statements, whichever most accurately reflected their own religious commitment. One emphasized the personal nature of the commitment and highlighted accepting Jesus as personal Saviour and Lord. The other emphasized adherence to the ethical and moral teachings of Jesus. The first group was labeled "born again" believers, and the second group was referred to as ethical believers.

The second procedure was based upon Allport and Ross's (1967) Intrinsic-Extrinsic Religious Orientation Scale. An intrinsic orientation connotes that which is genuine, personal, devout, and internalized. The religion is incorporated into the fabric of one's personality. Thus, for example, whenever there is a conflict between motives (e.g., between the religious motive and an economic or sexual one), the intrinsically religious person would behave in ways consistent with the religious motive. Such persons are said to live their faith. The extrinsic orientation, on the other hand, is best described as utilitarian. The extrinsic person participates in religion for self-serving ends, and is therefore more likely to compromise the religion in mixed motive situations. These persons are said to use their faith.

Results

The trends in the data are consistent with our notions about the relations among personal religious commitment, loneliness, and other indexes of the quality of life. Subjects who chose the personal commitment option scored lower on loneliness ($p < .06$). Item analysis revealed that the nonreligious were significantly more likely to feel a lack of companionship, not feel close to anyone, feel completely alone, feel unable to reach out and communicate, feel that nobody really knows them well, and feel emotionally distant from people. Subjects who espoused the personal religious commitment also scored significantly higher on SWB, EWB, and RWB ($p < .01$).

The correlations between these measures yield a similar picture of the relation between religion and loneliness. Lower loneliness was associated with higher SWB, RWB, EWB, purpose in life scores, and intrinsic religious orientation. These latter measures were all positively related to each other, a finding that is consistent with prior research (Bolt, 1975; Crandall & Rasmussen, 1975; Paloutzian et al., 1978; Soderstrom & Wright, 1977). The correlations between the well-being measures and loneliness were similar for both the ABLS and UCLA measures of loneliness (Table 14.5), a result that is to be expected given the previously noted high association between the ABLS and UCLA Scales.

Finally, one question pertinent here is whether the relationships obtained for the religious population are different than those for the nonreligious population. Could it be that the association between type of religious commitment and loneliness is present only in religious colleges? In order to explore this issue, data for the nonreligious population were analyzed separately. In nearly all cases, the strength of the relationships obtained with the nonreligious population were comparable to those obtained with the religious population. The implication is that a personal religious commitment is no more effective at combating loneliness in a religious social context than in a secular context.

Table 14.5   Correlations Between Spiritual Well-Being and Loneliness [a]

	UCLA Loneliness Scale	Abbreviated Loneliness Scale
Spiritual well-being	−.37***	−.41***
Religious well-being	−.20**	−.15*
Existential well-being	−.52***	−.65***

[a] All statistical tests are two-tailed. N for entire sample is 206; some correlations are based on a slightly smaller N due to incomplete data.
In a separate study of 115 middle-aged women (Paloutzian & Ellison, 1979c), loneliness correlated −.55 with SWB, −.48 with RWB and −.57 with EWB.

  * $p < .05$
 ** $p < .01$
*** $p < .001$

CONCLUSION

There are distinctive conceptual and methodological features in our approach to studying loneliness. Perhaps the most important conceptual contribution is the quality of life framework in which our work was cast. We interpreted quality of life in its subjective rather than objective sense, and we assumed that a person's sense of quality of life is intimately linked to satisfaction with his or her social relations. Hence the use of loneliness as an index of negative quality of life. Interpreting loneliness in this way appears to be valid, as evidenced by the list of negative emotions that are associated with loneliness. Our conceptual framework assumes that there are other facets of quality of life in addition to loneliness. The inverse association between spiritual well-being and loneliness is consistent with this notion. Consequently, loneliness itself may be best looked upon as an index of the perceived quality of *social* life.

The methodological contributions include the ABLS and the SWB scales. The results obtained with the ABLS were comparable to those obtained with the original UCLA Loneliness Scale. Therefore, the ABLS should be useful in future research, especially when a brief loneliness scale is needed. The SWB Scale is unique among the quality of life measures. No other scale exists to assess spiritual well-being in both the religious and existential dimensions.

Finally, the scope of our set of research questions has been wide. It has included developmental, social, methodological, emotional, behavioral, and religious issues. Few of these have been answered to our complete satisfaction. Unanswered questions remain regarding how early childhood factors affect adult loneliness, the possible role of values in determining loneliness, how religion influences quality of life, and the usefulness of the quality of life framework as a guide. Nevertheless, our approach serves as a complement to the other research in this volume.

REFERENCES

Allport, G.W., & Ross, J. M. Personal religious orientation and prejudice. *Journal of Personality and Social Psychology,* 1967, *5,* 432–443.

Bolt, M. Purpose in life and religious orientation. *Journal of Psychology and Theology,* 1975, *3,* 116–118.

Bradburn, N. *The structure of psychological well-being.* Chicago: Aldine, 1969.

Campbell, A. Subjective measures of well-being. *American Psychologist,* 1976, *31,* 117–124.

Campbell, A., Converse, P. E., & Rodgers, W. L. *The quality of American life.* New York: Russell Sage Foundation, 1976.

Crandall, J. E., & Rasmussen, R. D. Purpose in life as related to specific values. *Journal of Clinical Psychology,* 1975, *31,* 483–485.

Crumbaugh, J. C., & Maholick, L. T. *The Purpose in Life Test.* Munster, Ind.: Psychometric Affiliates, 1969.

Ellison, C. W. Loneliness: A social-developmental analysis. *Journal of Psychology and Theology,* 1978, *6,* 3–17.

Ellison, C. W., & Campise, R. *Developmental background, loneliness, and spiritual well-being.* Paper presented at the annual meeting of the Western Psychological Association, San Francisco, April 1978.

Ellison, C. W., & Paloutzian, R. F. Religious experience and quality of life. In R. F. Paloutzian (Chair), *Spiritual well-being, loneliness, and perceived quality of life.* Symposium presented at the annual meeting of the American Psychological Associaton, New York, September 1979 a.

Ellison, C. W., & Paloutzian, R. F. *Emotional, behavorial, and physical correlates of loneliness.* Paper presented at the UCLA Research Conference on Loneliness, Los Angeles, May 1979 b.

Frankl, V. *The unconscious god.* New York: Simon and Schuster, 1975.

Gallup, G. *Religion in America: The Gallup Opinion Index.* Princeton, N. J.: The Princeton Religion Research Center, 1977–78.

Middlebrook, P. N. *Social psychology and modern life* (2nd ed.). New York: Knopf/Random House, 1980.

Moberg, D. O. The development of social indicators of spiritual well-being for quality of life research. In D. O. Moberg (Ed.), *Spiritual well-being: Sociological perspectives.* Washington, D. C.: University Press of America, 1979.

Moberg, D. O., & Brusek, P. M. Spiritual well-being: A neglected subject in quality of life research. *Social Indicators Research,* 1978, *5,* 303–323.

Moustakas, C. E. *Loneliness.* New York: Prentice-Hall, 1961.

Paloutzian, R. F., & Ellison, C. W. *Developing an abbreviated loneliness scale.* Paper presented at the UCLA Research Conference on Loneliness, Los Angeles, May 1979 a.

Paloutzian, R. F., & Ellison, C. W. Developing a measure of spiritual well-being. In R. F. Paloutzian (Chair), *Spiritual well-being, loneliness, and perceived quality of life.* Symposium presented at the annual meeting of the American Psychological Association, New York, September 1979 b.

Paloutzian, R. F., & Ellison, C. W. Loneliness and spiritual well-being as functions of living environment and professional status in adult women. Paper presented at the meeting of the Western Psychological Association, San Diego, April 1979c (ERIC Document Reproduction Service No. ED 176145).

Paloutzian, R. F., Jackson, S. L., & Crandall, J. E. Conversion experience, belief system, and personal and ethical attitudes. *Journal of Psychology and Theology,* 1978, *6,* 266–275.

Russell, D., Peplau, L. A., & Ferguson, L. Developing a measure of loneliness. *Journal of Personality Assessment,* 1978, *42,* 290–294.

Shaver, P., & Rubenstein, C. Childhood attachment experience and adult loneliness. In L. Wheeler (Ed.), *The review of personality and social psychology* (Vol. 1). Beverly Hills, Calif.: Sage Publications, 1980.

Soderstrom, D., & Wright, E. W. Religious orientation and meaning in life. *Journal of Clinical Psychology,* 1977, *33,* 65–68.

U. S. Department of Health, Education, and Welfare. *Toward a social report.* Washington, D. C.: U. S. Government Printing Office, 1969.

Zimbardo, P. G. *Psychology and life* (10th ed.). Glenview, Ill.: Scott, Foresman, 1979.

Chapter 15

Loneliness and Social Behavior

Warren H. Jones

Loneliness is, by definition, a self-perceived interpersonal problem, and therefore one might expect to find divergence in the social behavior of lonely as compared to nonlonely people. Since investigations of the social behavior associated with loneliness have only recently begun, indirect evidence must also be examined to characterize its social implications. Available data does suggest that loneliness frequently involves an inability or disruption in the ability to relate to others in an effective and mutually satisfying manner. Therefore, the focus of this review will be on those studies that directly or indirectly address the phenomenon of loneliness and its relationship to interpersonal and social behavior, with particular emphasis on effectively relating to others.

The first section examines primarily self-report studies indicating associations between loneliness and variables that might influence the manifestation of social competence, for example, disruptive feelings, negative attitudes, dispositional measures of social skill, and so on. The implications of loneliness for the frequency of contact and satisfaction with one's relationships is also covered, as well as the question of how lonely people attempt to solve their loneliness. The second section describes studies that examine loneliness and judgments of self and others following actual interactions in group and dyadic contexts, and the third section reports on the few investigations that have explored differences in the social behavior of lonely people.

SOCIAL AND INTERPERSONAL CORRELATES OF LONELINESS

Dispositions and Feelings

Indirect evidence that loneliness might be associated with divergent patterns of social behavior and ineffective relating comes from several studies reporting comparisons between loneliness and problematic dispositions and feelings, particularly self-derogation and negative emotions (Jones, Freemon, & Goswick, 1981; Moore & Sermat, 1974; Russell, Peplau, & Ferguson, 1978;

238

Russell, Peplau, & Cutrona, 1980; Barrett & Becker, 1978; Jones, Hansson, & Smith, 1980). For example, among college students loneliness is related to anxiety and depression, as well as various negative feelings including hopelessness, alienation, being misunderstood, empty, unloved, abandoned, and so on. In an extensive survey among adolescents, Brennan and Auslander (1979) found that loneliness was related to such variables as self-pity, feeling rejected by one's parents, and unpopularity among peers. One of the most frequent and consistent correlates of loneliness has been poor self-esteem. Significant results have been reported among college students in a wide varity of locations as well as several other populations of interest including adolescents and widows. Among divorced adults, negative affect and feelings of being rejected or "left out" following a divorce correlate with loneliness. Among widows, loneliness is positively correlated with marital happiness and grief.

The fact that social self-concept is strongly related to loneliness supports the validity of conceptualizing loneliness as a self-perceived failure in the interpersonal sphere of behavior (Goswick & Jones, 1981). But correlation data reveal association and not directionality. Thus the frequent self-descriptions of lonely people, which indicate negative dispositions and feelings, may be interpreted as the affective concomitants of loneliness that result from repeated social failure. Alternatively, such states may occur independently and inhibit or interfere with successful social functioning, resulting in loneliness. In either case, loneliness appears to involve self-defeating emotions and dispositions that, regardless of their origin, might be expected to disrupt normal social interaction.

Social Attitudes

Loneliness is frequently associated with cynical and rejecting attitudes toward other people and life in general, as well as beliefs that imply pessimism and a sense of not being able to control one's destiny (Jones et al., 1981; Moore & Sermat, 1974; Solano, 1980). Among college students, for example, loneliness is related to various indexes of social alienation (e.g., anomie, powerlessness, normlessness) as well as external locus of control and generalized hostility. Loneliness correlates inversely with acceptance of others, just world beliefs, and belief in the trustworthiness, altruism, and favorability of human nature.

Attitudes toward marriage and divorce were specifically explored in one study conducted by Jones et al. (1980). Results indicated that lonely students held a more pessimistic view of matrimony; for example, lonely subjects were less likely to believe that most people marry for love. Regarding their own potential experiences with marriage and divorce, lonelier students, particularly women, were again pessimistic, for example, anticipating a lower probability of having married by age 30, a greater likelihood of their own divorce, and less of a probability or remarriage should their marriage end in divorce. If divorced, lonelier students also expected greater negative reactions such as hostility. The disenchantment of lonely students regarding marriage becomes more understandable in light of the motivations lonely students envision for their own marriage. The lonelier the student, the greater the likelihood that he or she anticipated getting married because of loneliness, parental pressure, or a need for security and dependency; and the less likely he or she imagined that they would marry for love. The actual correspondence between such attitudes and subsequent experiences is of course unknown.

Measures of hostility, pessimism, alienation, fatalism, and cynicism have been related to loneliness in other populations as well. Among adolescents, Brennan and Auslander (1979) found that loneliness was related to several such indicators including external control, pessimism regarding social affirmation, feelings of powerlessness in both family and peer relationships, social paranoia, mistrust of others, negative attitudes toward school and teachers, low educational and occupational aspirations, rejection of parents, and the feeling that others cannot be relied upon. In a sample of widows, generalized hostility was related to loneliness, whereas for divorced adults, loneliness was inversely related to items assessing the degree of perceived control and predictability during the divorce (Jones et al., 1980). In this study it was also found that loneliness was related to the tendency to attribute greater blame to the former spouse for the divorce.

Again the direction of causality in these relationships is not known. It may be that actual or perceived social inadequacy in the form of less frequent contact or less rewarding interactions create the impression that other people are not worth knowing and that one's interpersonal fate is being determined by a hostile and capricious social environment. Perhaps such attitudes constitute rationalizations for self-perceived social failure. If one believes that other people are not worth knowing and if there is little one can do to develop satisfying relationships, then feelings of rejection can be intellectualized and explained. On the other hand, negative attitudes toward others and externalized fate control may be acquired from experiences not directly related to loneliness. If so, low expectations of success in social situations may lead to fewer or less responsive attempts to engage others, eventuating in loneliness. It is also possible that the negative attitudes toward others stem from unrealistic and rigid expectations regarding relationships. Thus the cynicism and hostility of lonely people may represent disappointment over the failure of other available persons to live up to their standards for the ideal friend, lover, or spouse, standards that may be so high and exacting that no one could satisfy the criteria.

Social Skills

Psychometric and self-report assessments of the social skills of lonely students implicate a variey of social skill deficits and inadequacies in the experience of loneliness (Jones et al., 1981; Russell et al., 1980; Chelune, 1979; Solano & Parish, 1979). Among college students, loneliness is inversely correlated with general indexes of social skill and social functioning including lower social risk taking, affiliative tendency and sociability, less expressed inclusion of and affection for others, and less intimate self-disclosure. Loneliness is also strongly correlated with such personality traits as self-consciousness, introversion, and shyness.

One study (Goswick & Jones, 1981) found that lonely college students reported greater self-focused attention. Thus lonely students may be less empathic or less responsive to the needs, concerns, and feelings of others. Another study (Horowitz & French, 1979) found that lonely students report problems of inhibited sociability, such as problems with making friends, introducing oneself, participating in groups, enjoying a party, and difficulties in being friendly and in relinquishing control. Also lonely college students are more likely to use coercive power in attempts to influence others, which, although possibly effective in the short run, may prevent relationships from developing (Gerson, 1978).

It is likely that social skill deficits contribute to loneliness in adolescents as well, particularly in the area of heterosexual functioning, and there is evidence that lonely adolescents describe themselves as being shy, passive, and unpopular (Brennan & Auslander, 1979). However, there is also evidence that social skill problems are related to loneliness among older respondents including elderly (Perlman, Gerson, & Spinner, 1978) and divorced subjects (Jones et al., 1980).

Closely related to the social skills problems of lonely people is an apparent tendency to violate normative social expectations. As norm violations are ordinarily met with disapproval, they may contribute to the difficulty in restoring meaningful relationships that lonely people experience. For example, Solano and Batten (1979) found unusually high self-disclosures in same sex dyads and unusually low disclosures in opposite sex dyads among lonely college students. Hansson and Jones (1981) reported that lonely students were less confident of their own opinions on controversial topics and also less willing to have their opinions made publicly available to others. Also Hansson and Jones reported two studies in which college students were exposed to the influence of others. In both studies, lonely women modeled or conformed more than not lonely men and women, whereas lonely men conformed and modeled less. These results may suggest that the social skills problems of lonely people stem not so much from an inability to relate to others as from socially inappropriate applications of interpersonal skills. Thus, anormative disclosure patterns and too much or too little cooperation with others may put the lonely person in a position of social marginality from which it becomes even more difficult to develop relationships.

Relational Status

Several studies have now been reported that examine the connection between loneliness and the status and number of various kinds of personal relationships

(Weiss, 1973). Typically, results indicate greater loneliness in the absence of a mate.

For college students, dating partners and friends are more pertinent, and several studies have indicated that being without friends and dating partners is associated with greater loneliness. For example, students indicating that they have never had a steady dating partner are more lonely than students who have had steady partners (Jones et al., 1980). One study showed that the cessation of an intimate dating relationship was associated with greater loneliness, particularly if the subject's partner, as opposed to the subject, had been the one who desired and initiated the breakup (Hill, Rubin, & Peplau, 1976). Loneliness has been related to the degree of romantic involvement and the number of close friends (Russell et al., 1980).

On the other hand, some comparisons have failed to indicate a relationship between loneliness and relational status, particularly when global indexes of friendship are examined (Jones et al., 1980; McCormack & Kahn, 1980). For example, loneliness is typically not related to such variables as total number of friends. This diversity of findings probably occurs because only one or a few rewarding relationships within a particular relational domain such as family or dating may adequately satisfy the interpersonal needs associated with that domain. For many people a single, satisfying romantic relationship not only makes other love relationships unnecessary but impossible as well.

The availability of friends and lovers is of obvious and direct importance to the development of loneliness in terms of opportunities for social activity, conversation, companionship, and mutual help. Indirectly, in a society that values heterosexual partnership, being married or having a lover also may contribute to avoiding loneliness due to enhancement of self-esteem and a sense of social or romantic competence. However, again the direction of causality remains unclear. Individuals coping with new or unfamiliar social situations may lack friends and romantic partners because of their circumstances and therefore become lonely. Alternatively, it is also possible that lonely people are simply less likely to seek or achieve long-term platonic or romantic relationships, perhaps as a result of inhibiting emotions, low expectations, inadequate social skills, excessive self-focusing, or any combination of these. The chronically lonely may be less likely to ever become married, for example, but if they do they also may be vulnerable to the pressures and problems that often lead to divorce.

Social Contact, Activities, and Satisfaction

Another type of data that may be used to assess the social behavior of lonely individuals involves the frequency with which people engage in social activities and their perceived satisfaction with avaliable relationships. There are two general hypotheses. First, one might expect lonely people to have less social contact, either because of the effects of uncontrolled circumstances or because of the interference of negative emotions and attitudes. Alternatively, lonely people may have as much contact and hence social opportunities as do not lonely people, but may be less satisfied with available relationships.

There are some indications that lonely college students have less social contact than do not-lonely students (Russell et al., 1980; Jones et al., 1980; McCormack & Kahn, 1980). Lonely students have been found to date less frequently, to report fewer social activities, more time spent alone, and more weekend evenings spent alone. Among adolescents, loneliness has been associated with less participation in the social and extramural activities of one's school, less time spent with peers and parents, lower dating frequency, more time spent alone, and less frequent membership in social organizations and clubs (Brennan & Auslander, 1979). Among widows and divorced adults, lonelier subjects report fewer social activities (Jones et al., 1980), and elderly lonely people report less contact with friends (Perlman, Gerson, & Spinner, 1978).

On the other hand, several studies have failed to find a relationship between loneliness and social contact or activities. Other studies have indicated that satisfaction with contacts is more important than the actual frequency. Using a self-monitoring procedure in which college students recorded in a diary each interaction engaged in for two days, loneliness was not related to the total number of interactions, average length of interactions, proportion of interactions with the opposite sex, or perceived intimacy level of the interactions (Jones, 1981). However, lonely students reported more interactions with strangers and acquaintances and fewer interactions with family and friends, which might suggest that lonely students have or exercise fewer opportunities to spend time with others who are intimate. Alternatively, lonely students may be more apt to label someone they know at a given level of intimacy as a stranger or acquaintance rather than a friend. It is also interesting to note that although loneliness was not related to the total number of interactions recorded, it was significantly correlated with the diversity of subjects' social contacts, that is, number of interaction partners divided by number of interactions. Thus lonely subjects, on the average, had as many interactions as did not lonely subjects, but with more people. In a study using a similar interaction recording method (McCormack & Kahn, 1980), it was found that lonely subjects reported less time spent with others and, specifically, less time with others who were intimate, whereas no significant differences occurred for rated intimacy or satisfaction with the contact. In addition, this study found that lonely subjects of both genders reported significantly less time than nonlonely subjects with female close friends and mixed-sex groups of close friends.

Another study (Cutrona & Peplau, 1979; Cutrona, Chapter 18) compared objective measures such as frequency of contact with satisfaction ratings within three domains of relationships: friendship, dating, and family. Ratings were obtained from entering college freshmen at the beginning of a fall semester and again seven months later. Analyses indicated that not being satisfied with one's relationships in each of the three categories explained a greater proportion of the variance of loneliness scores than did the objective indicators for both the initial as well as the follow-up assessments. In other words, not being satisfied with one's friendships, dating partners, and family were better predictors of loneliness than such variables as frequency of contact with friends, number of friends, dating frequency, distance from home, or frequency of contact with family.

Thus available evidence suggests that it is important to distinguish qualitative versus quantitative features of the lonely person's relationships and social contact. The evidence is somewhat inconsistent, but suggests that the important issue may be the type of contact rather than the amount of contact per se and that lonely people may simply be dissatisfied with the friends they have, rather than having no friends. To the extent that these results may be generalized, they suggest that the reasons for loneliness are not to be found so much in the objective characteristics of the lonely person's social milieu (e.g., number of available friends or amount of social contact) as they are in the way in which lonely people perceive, evaluate, and respond to interpersonal reality.

Social Solutions for Loneliness

An important issue in the study of loneliness concerns the strategies that people adopt in order to cope with and solve their feelings of loneliness. Assuming that the development of satisfying friendships is the most effective solution for loneliness, the question arises as to how loneliness could continue given the availability of others as friends and companions. The answer may be that for many people loneliness leads to behavior that tends to reduce rather than increase human contact. For example, Paloutzian and Ellison (1979) reported that college students who held a favorable view of their own social skills were more likely to engage in intimate activities (e.g., talking to a friend) when lonely, whereas students who viewed their social skills less favorably tended to engage in sensually oriented (e.g., drinking, taking drugs) and diversionary activities (e.g., keeping busy, reading, working) when lonely. Thus the more favorable the view of one's social functioning, the more likely loneliness results in approaches to other people, a strategy that might be expected to reduce the feelings of loneliness, as opposed to activities that do not directly address such feelings.

LONELINESS AND INTERPERSONAL JUDGMENTS

The cognitive and affective responses of lonely people have been investigated in the context of specific interpersonal situations, and such studies help bridge the gap between global, self-reported correlates of loneliness and the social behavior of lonely people in ongoing and everyday interpersonal situations. Attempts have been made to extend the findings reported above with particular emphasis on how the lonely person responds to specific persons and how the lonely person is evaluated by others.

Jones et al (1981) examined the relationship between loneliness and interpersonal perceptions within a specific group situation. Subjects were college students enrolled in a psychology course involving considerable class participation. Subjects were tested at the beginning and end of the semester. For both test administrations, subjects rated themselves and each other member of the group on several dimensions, such as friendliness. Sociometric choice status data were also obtained for trust, leadership, and so on. The rating data yielded evaluations from four perspectives including: (1) self ratings; (2) reflected self ratings, that is, how the subject expected to be rated by the other members of the group; (3) ratings of others, that is, subjects' mean rating of fellow group members; and (4) ratings by others, that is, mean rating of the subject by the other members of the group. Data reflecting these four perspectives as well as choice status were compared to self-reported loneliness scores for both administrations.

Initial-test results indicated significant correlations between loneliness and negative ratings of self and reflected self. Thus lonely subjects not only perceived themselves more negatively, they also expected others to evaluate them negatively. Also lonely men rated their fellow group members more negatively, whereas lonely women did not. There was also some evidence that lonely participants were evaluated less favorably by others, for example, lonely males were chosen as leader less frequently. Posttest data indicated a similar pattern of correlations except that there was one important change. None of the other-generated variables were reliably associated with loneliness, suggesting that lonely and nonlonely subjects were not judged differently by the end of the semester.

A second study reported by Jones et al. (1981) examined judgments of others following brief "get acquainted" conversations among unacquainted heterosexual dyads. After the interaction each member of the dyad completed an inventory designed to measure: (1) subjects' assessment of the partner's personality; (2) the subject's "accuracy" in describing the partner's personality, as compared to the partner's self-description; (3) interpersonal attraction for the partner; and (4) judgments of the partner's behavior during the interaction. Judgments given (called observer effects) were crossed with judgments received (called actor effects) in order to assess the effects of loneliness on perceiving and being perceived.

Results indicated no main effects for actor on any of the dependent variables, suggesting that lonely subjects were not differentially rated on any of the dimensions included in the study. However, there were some observer main effects and observer-actor interactions. Results indicated that lonely subjects were less attracted to their partners, that they rated their partner's personality more negatively, that they rated their partner's behavior during the interaction more negatively, and that to some degree they were less accurate in describing their partner's personality. These effects were particularly pronounced when lonely men were rating lonely women. Also loneliness scores were unrelated to either subject or experimenter-rated physical attractiveness.

In another study (Jones, 1978) the dyadic paradigm was expanded to include same sex as well as opposite sex dyads, and again subjects were instructed to get acquainted. Following the interaction, ratings were obtained on evaluative dimensions for the perspectives of self, reflected self, rating of other, and rating by other. Also subjects were asked to indicate whether they would be willing to participate in this kind of experiment again, whether they would like to have the same partner, and whether they would like to interact with their partner again in another situation.

Results replicated earlier findings with lonely subjects yielding more negative evaluations for self, reflected self, and ratings of the other. As before, there were no main effects for ratings by the partner. In addition, although there were a few main effects due to the composition of the dyad and sex of subject, no significant loneliness by composition interactions emerged, suggesting that the negative self-and-other bias that lonely subjects manifest in such interactions is a more general effect than simply greater sensitivity of lonely subjects to heterosexual situations. Finally, lonely subjects less frequently indicated that they desired continued contact with their partners.

Judgments of Self

These results clearly support the idea that lonely people engage in extensive self-derogation, and that they expect to be rejected by others. In contrast to the previously cited studies (e.g., on self-esteem) the present data confirm that such negative expectations also occur in response to specific interactions with other people. Lonely people may lack positive feedback from their social environment, which leads them to devalue themselves as well as to expect rejection. Another possibility is that lonely people somehow fail to perceive or accept as genuine, actual instances of social reinforcement and attention, at least in initial interactions with strangers. In either case, self-derogation and expectations of rejection would be expected to result in fewer or less effective attempts to interact with others.

Judgments by Lonely People

Lonely subjects not only dislike themselves, they tend not to like other people as well, both collectively and individually. In particular this has been found to be the case for lonely males. Paradoxically, presumed remedies for loneliness, for example, becoming involved with someone or making a new friend, do not appear to be viable options for the lonely person, at least in the situations examined thus far. Lonely subjects indicated that they were less attracted to their classmates and dyadic partners, and less frequently indicated a desire for continued contact. Lonely people may express less interest in continued contact in order to avoid anticipated rejection. They may "project" their own self-perceived inadequacies onto others as a means of externalizing them. Perhaps, as suggested above, lonely people may expect too much from others, or are looking for perfect mates and friends, and therefore fail to take advantage of available interpersonal opportunities.

Whatever the reason, the implication of rejecting others first is clear; it reduces the likelihood of continued contact from which a satisfying relationship might emerge. To the extent that these laboratory results indicate the lonely person's actual behavior, loneliness appears to result in the failure to exercise or maximize interpersonal opportunities.

Judgments of Lonely People

Despite their expectation that they would be rejected by others, there has been only weak and inconsistent evidence that lonely subjects are differentially evaluated by others. The failure to find consistent judgmental correlates of loneliness is surprising but has been reported also by Chelune (1979).

In a recent experiment (Sansone, Jones, & Helm, 1979) the heterosexual dyadic paradigm was used with an additional rating perspective, others' self-view, that is, the subject's evaluation of how the partner would rate himself or herself. Generally the results replicated the previous studies, but it was also found that lonely subjects were rated as more likely to rate themselves negatively. Thus lonely subjects were judged differently, although this effect was found in the metaperception of other's self-view. Solano and Batten (1979) have also reported a study indicating that lonely subjects are more difficult to get to know. They found that the partners of lonely subjects indicated that they did not feel as well acquainted as did the partners of not lonely subjects following dyadic interactions. This was probably due to the tendency of lonely subjects to choose less intimate topics of discussion, which was also found.

Thus, despite inconsistencies, it may be that lonely as compared to not lonely persons are perceived differently, although it appears that this effect is circumscribed. However, even indirect judgments on the order of "this person is difficult to get to know" or "this person does not like himself/herself" could influence the probability that a friendship would develop from a given acquaintanceship. Perceptions by others of aloofness or self-perceived inadequacy in the lonely person may result in less active attempts by others to engage someone who is lonely. This could occur without overt rejection by the other person, since lonely people may be less likely themselves to actively pursue potential relationships, and because they are apparently more likely to perceive less-than-thorough social reinforcement as rejection. Thus the combination of perceiving and being perceived as lonely may be implicated in the persistence of loneliness.

SOCIAL BEHAVIOR

Very few studies have been reported that involve direct assessments of the social behavior of lonely individuals; however, the available evidence does suggest that lonely subjects tend to behave in a less responsive, less intimate, and more self-focused manner in interactions with others. For example, Solano and Batten (1979) had both same sex and opposite sex college student dyads alternately disclose personal information. Disclosure topics were selected by the subjects from a list of intimacy-scaled topics. Among opposite sex dyads, lonely as compared to nonlonely subjects chose less intimate topics on both their first topic choice and the average of all topic choices. Within same sex dyads, lonely subjects selected a more intimate first topic than did nonlonely subjects. The authors suggest that lonely individuals disclose information at inappropriate levels, which violates social expectations and eventually results in less disclosure from others. As self-disclosure is an important dimension along which friendships develop, such anormative and nonreciprocal disclosure patterns of lonely people would be expected to result in less intimate friendships.

More directly measured behavioral differences associated with loneliness have also been reported (Jones, Hobbs & Hockenbury, in press). Male and female college students were paired with an opposite sex stranger and their interactions were video-recorded and scored for various verbal behaviors and related variables. Lonely subjects differed from nonlonely subjects on four variables: they made fewer personal attention statements (i.e., statements focusing on the partner), they asked fewer questions, they changed the topic under discussion more frequently, and they responded more slowly to the previous statements of their partners. Thus the behavior of lonely subjects during interpersonal interactions with opposite sex strangers may be characterized as more self-focused and less responsive. The effect of such divergent behavior on friendship formation would tend to be inhibitory for two reasons. First, by focusing attention inward, lonely subjects may fail to notice verbal and nonverbal cues of friendship and affection. Second, lonely subjects appear to provide less reinforcement and attention to others, which might ultimately reduce their attractiveness as potential friends.

Most of the data linking the experience of loneliness to inadequate or inappropriately applied social skill has been correlational. In a recent experiment (Jones, Hobbs & Hockenbury, in press), the functional relationship between loneliness and social skill problems was explored. Very lonely male subjects (i.e., 2½ standard deviations above the mean) were randomly assigned to one of three conditions: treatment, assessment only, and no contact control. Prior to and following the experiment, subjects completed the UCLA Loneliness Scale (Russell, Peplau, & Ferguson, 1978). In addition, the treatment and assessment only groups participated in a baseline and posttest behavioral assessment in which subjects' conversations with each of four female interaction partners were recorded. Subjects in the treatment group were also given training designed to alter the verbal behavior of personal attention (i.e., statements focusing on the other individual by direct reference or indirect implication, e.g., references to the other person's feelings, beliefs, or behavior). The training package included an explanation of personal attention, modeling tapes, behavioral rehearsal, and practice instructions.

Results indicated that the treatment procedures altered the frequency of personal attention in that the treatment group yielded more personal attention statements than the assessment only group at posttreatment. Furthermore, behavior change was accompanied by reductions in the self-report of loneliness. For example, only the treatment group showed a significant reduction in loneliness between baseline and posttreatment assessments. It should be acknowledged however, that the treatment group loneliness mean at posttreatment was still one standard deviation above the normative mean for college men.

SUMMARY AND CONCLUSIONS

Converging lines of evidence suggest that the behavior of lonely people may be characterized as being more negativistic, rejecting, self-absorbed, self-deprecating, and less responsive. One way to summarize this pattern of behavior is to suggest that loneliness occurs when there has been a failure to learn or a temporary disruption in the ability to exercise the social skills required to relate to others effectively. Social skills or competence is a principle for organizing seemingly unrelated behavior under a single construct. Social skills problems may be relatively stable or not, depending on the contribution of both situational and individual difference variables. Also applying a social skills model to loneliness does not necessarily imply a causal linkage, although such may be the case for certain lonely individuals. Instead the social skills approach provides conceptual organization regarding the causes, experiences and kinds of intervention for loneliness. As such, loneliness is seen as caused by those factors that prevent or interfere with social competence, and as discussed above, loneliness is experienced primarily as interpersonal failure, rather than physical or social isolation. Similarly, preliminary evidence suggests that therapeutic strategies directed toward enhancing the lonely person's social skill result in significant reductions of self-reported loneliness.

There are several advantages to conceptualizing loneliness from the perspective of social competence. For example, although environmental and external social factors undoubtedly contribute to the development of loneliness, a social skills analysis emphasizes the lonely person's problems in relating to others, and thus is applicable across various environmental and social conditions. Second, social skills may influence the probability or severity of loneliness in various situations. For example, as a group, beginning college students report feeling lonely. However, it may be those students who lack the necessary social facility to initiate and maintain friendships who account for this finding. Thus unacquired social skills, restricted social experience, or anxiety that interferes with performance in interpersonal situations may predispose certain individuals to loneliness, given a precipitating condition such as facing a new social situation without friends.

The social skill analysis promises the possibility of identifying procedures that might be effective in reducing the severity or chronicity of loneliness. Situational contributors to loneliness, such as social mobility, urbanization, or depersonalization, would be difficult to control or influence. By contrast, social skills can be taught or improved with a variety of techniques. Therefore, to the extent that loneliness derives from problematic social skills, either initially or subsequent to the experience of lonely feelings, it may be possible to identify and put into practice economical and feasible strategies for therapeutic intervention. Whether inadequate social skills leads to or is caused by loneliness, or both, is not yet clear. However, preliminary data have documented the association between deficient interpersonal behavior and loneliness, as well as the potential usefulness of social skills training in reducing feelings of loneliness.

Despite a promising beginning, many questions remain unanswered with respect to the implications of loneliness for social behavior. Although it seems reasonable to conclude that loneliness involves behavior that is less than ideal, data regarding the extent to which loneliness actually impacts on general social functioning, friendship formation, or existing relationships are currently more suggestive than conclusive. Additional behavioral and experimental studies would be desirable to confirm the largely self-reported data reported thus far. Longitudinal and more naturalistic assessments of the behavioral correlates of loneliness would particularly strengthen the external validity and generality of present results. Additional research is also needed to determine to what extent the behavioral correlates discussed above derive from loneliness itself versus related conditions such as depression.

A clearer understanding of the social implications of loneliness also awaits a more detailed specification of several theoretical dimensions, including the origins of loneliness (e.g., situational vs. personal determinants, rejection by others vs. rejection of others), types of loneliness (e.g., state vs. trait), the correlates of loneliness across various response modes (e.g., verbal behavior, proximics), the time course of loneliness (e.g., acute vs. chronic), and severity. Different types of social skill problems may be related to these distinctions. For example, the failure to acquire sufficient social competence may increase the probability of chronic loneliness, whereas the suppression of social competence due to strong affective states may be associated with more transient forms of loneliness.

The social skills perspective is consistent with findings that loneliness is more closely associated with the cognitive and affective processes of the lonely person than the lonely person's social environment. Lonely people attribute a variety of negative and limiting characteristics to themselves and to both existing and potential relationships that are inconsistent with appraisals from other perspectives. Lonely subjects expect decisive rejection even when it does not occur. There is little evidence to support the idea that lonely college students are socially isolated, and yet they act as if they are. Indeed differences between lonely and nonlonely students in terms of the frequency and number of social contacts as well as interpersonal behavior are not as extensive and dramatic as one might expect from examining self-perceptions alone.

The social skills analysis is not necessarily incompatible with other explanations of loneliness such as a situational perspective. For example, objective situational factors may contribute to that type of loneliness that is occasionally experienced by almost everyone, whereas inadequate social skills may be implicated in the more clinically relevant forms of loneliness. Or social skills and environmental factors may be related sequentially. Perhaps situational determinants play a decisive role in the initial phases of loneliness, whereas poor social skills might determine the persistence of such feelings. Whatever the eventual mix of potential theoretical explanations, it nevertheless appears both empirically and theoretically sound to use a social skills analysis as one perspective from which to examine loneliness.

REFERENCES

Barrett, C. J., & Becker, R. M. *The prediction of adjustment to widowhood from social and demographic data.* Paper presented at the meeting of the Western Social Science Association, Denver, Colorado, April 1978.

Brennan, T., & Auslander, N. *Adolescent loneliness: An exploratory study of social and psychological pre-dispositions and theory.* Unpublished manuscript, Behavioral Research Institute, Boulder, Colorado, January 1979.

Chelune, G. J. *Disclosure flexibility and interpersonal functioning.* Paper presented at the annual meeting of the American Psychological Association, New York, September 1979.

Cutrona, C., & Peplau, L. A. *A longitudinal study of loneliness.* Paper presented at the annual meeting of the Western Psychological Association, San Diego, California, April 1979.

Gerson, A. C. *Loneliness and the social influence process.* In D. Perlman (Chair), *Toward a psychology of loneliness.* Symposium presented at the annual meeting of the American Psychological Association, Toronto, Canada, August, 1978.

Goswick, R. A., & Jones, W. H. Loneliness, self-concept and adjustments. *Journal of Psychology,* 1981, *107,* 237–240.

Hansson, R. O., & Jones, W. H. Loneliness, cooperation, and conformity among American undergraduates. *Journal of Social Psychology,* 1981, *115,* 103–108.

Hill, C. T., Rubin, Z., & Peplau, L. A. Breakups before marriage: The end of 102 affairs. *Journal of Social Issues,* 1976, 32 (1), 147–168.

Horowitz, L. M., & French, R. de S. Interpersonal problems of people who describe themselves as lonely. *Journal of Consulting and Clinical Psychology,* 1979, *47,* 762–764.

Jones, W. H. Loneliness and social contact. *Journal of Social Psychology,* 1981, *113,* 295–296.

Jones, W. H. *The persistence of loneliness.* In D. Perlman (Chair), *Toward a psychology of loneliness.* Symposium presented at the annual meeting of the American Psychological Association, Toronto, August 1978.

Jones, W. H., Freemon, J. A., & Goswick, R. A. The persistence of loneliness: Self and other determinants. *Journal of Personality,* 1981, *49,* 27–48.

Jones, W. H., Hansson, R. O., & Smith, T. G. *Loneliness and love: Implications for psychological and interpersonal functioning.* Unpublished manuscript. University of Tulsa, 1980.

Jones, W. H., Hobbs, S. A., & Hockenbury, D. Loneliness and social skills deficits. *Journal of Personality and Social Psychology,* in press.

McCormack, S. H., & Kahn, A. *Behavioral characteristics of lonely and non-lonely college students.* Paper presented at the annual meeting of the Midwestern Psychological Association, St. Louis, May 1980.

Moore, J. A., & Sermat, V. Relationship between loneliness and interpersonal relationships. *Canadian Counselor,* 1974, *8,* (2), 84–89.

Paloutzian, R. F., & Ellison, C. W. *Emotional, behavorial and physical correlates of loneliness.* Paper presented at the UCLA Research Conference on Loneliness. Los Angeles, May 1979.

Perlman, D., Gerson, A. C., & Spinner, B. Loneliness among senior citizens: An empirical report. *Essence,* 1978, *2,* 239–248.

Russell, D., Peplau, L. A., & Cutrona, C. The revised UCLA Loneliness Scale: Concurrent and discriminant validity evidence. *Journal of Personality and Social Psychology,* 1980, *39* (3), 472–480.

Russell, D., Peplau, L. A., & Ferguson, M. L. Developing a measure of loneliness. *Journal of Personality Assessment,* 1978, *42,* 290–294.

Sansone, C., Jones, W. H., & Helm, B. *Interpersonal perceptions of loneliness.* In S. A. Hobbs (Chair), *Social skills assessment and intervention.* Symposium presented at the annual meeting of the Southwestern Psychological Association, San Antonio, Texas, April 1979.

Solano, C. H. Two measures of loneliness: A comparison. *Psychological Reports,* 1980, *46,* 23–28.

Solano, C. H., & Batten, P. G. *Loneliness and objective self-disclosure in an acquaintanceship exercise.* Unpublished manuscript, Wake Forest University, 1979.

Solano, C. H., & Parish, E. *Loneliness and perceived level of self-disclosure.* Unpublished manuscript, Wake Forest University, 1979.

Weiss, R. S. *Loneliness: The experience of emotional and social isolation.* Cambridge, Mass.: MIT Press, 1973.

PART FIVE

Developmental
Perspectives on Loneliness

The difficult task of charting the life course of loneliness in America is well underway. We know much about age trends in the experience of loneliness and about common events throughout the life cycle that lead to loneliness.

Contrary to folk wisdom, loneliness appears to be most common among adolescents and declines with age. Many factors contribute to this pattern. First, as people age their desires and expectations for social relations change, along with their repertoire of social skills for making and keeping friends and for enjoying solitude. One explanation for the widespread loneliness of adolescence is that teenagers have unrealistically high expectations for their social life or incompletely developed interpersonal skills. Second, the social world we inhabit changes as we age. Many social transitions, such as leaving home for college, moving to a new community, losing a spouse, or retiring from work, are predictable causes of loneliness. Throughout the life cycle, we encounter changing social opportunities and social constraints. Third, it is possible that some age trends in loneliness are best explained as "cohort effects," differences due to the historical experiences of successive generations. Thus young people today may report greater loneliness than their elders because they are growing up in an era that encourages the expression of feelings and that regards romantic passion as essential to health and happiness. At present we can only speculate about the relative importance of these three factors in loneliness. Longitudinal studies that follow individuals throughout a part of their life cycle are needed to provide more definitive explanations for age-linked patterns in loneliness.

A question that has long intrigued theorists concerns the age at which loneliness first occurs. Such a discusson obviously depends in large measure on how one defines loneliness. Psychiatrist Sullivan (1953) proposed that the potential for loneliness develops only during preadolescence, with the emergence of a fully developed need for intimacy. Sullivan emphasized the loneliness that results from the absence of a special one-to-one relationship with a peer. In Chapter 16, however, Rubin takes a different view on this matter. Based on observational studies of young children, Rubin believes that children as young as three can experience loneliness resulting from social isolation—from the lack of friends.

The chapters in this section provide a broad overview of loneliness throughout the life cycle. In Chapter 17, Brennan reviews his own and others' research on loneliness among adolescents. He documents that loneliness is a pervasive problem for teenagers, and points to elements in our society that may exacerbate this situation. In Chapter 18, Cutrona looks at students' first year in college, a common transition period leading to loneliness for young adults. Her research shows that most students overcome their initial loneliness with time, and highlights factors that promote a successful recovery. In Chapter 19, Lopata, Heinemann, and Baum discuss loneliness among widowed women. They find that women use diverse strategies to cope with loneliness, but seldom turn to mental health professionals. A final chapter by Peplau, Bikson, Rook, and Goodchilds reviews research on loneliness in old age. Although many old people are alone, both in the sense of being widowed and living alone, this situation does not inevitably produce loneliness.

Chapter 16

Children without Friends

Zick Rubin

There are many varieties of children without friends, including children in isolated environments where no potential friends are available, and children with serious physical, intellectual, or emotional disabilities that cause them to be shunned by others. There may also be children who have little need or desire for friends at particular points in their development—who are, at least for the time being, more interested in painting or reading or music than in interacting with other children. My focus in this chapter is on three broad categories of "children without friends," each of which involves children who would like to have more or better friendships than they do. I will not be dealing with extreme cases of social isolation or with children who have no contact at all with their peers. Rather I will be discussing a much larger range of social difficulties that may in fact affect the majority of children at one time or another.

Three categories of children without friends will be discussed. First, children who find it hard to make or keep friends because they lack necessary social skills. Second, children who have lost friends because of a move from one neighborhood or school to another. And third, children whose friendships falter or end because they have grown apart psychologically. These three categories are not mutually exclusive. Thus, for example, a child who moves with her family to a new part of the country may also find herself lacking the social skills needed to make friends in her new setting. But the categories are useful cover terms that will enable us to consider a range of issues related to children's friendships and their absence or loss. In each case I will present some descriptions of children's experiences, hypotheses about the factors that may affect these experiences, and suggestions about how positive results might be facilitated. I will conclude the chapter with

The preparation of this chapter was aided by a grant from the Foundation for Child Development. I am grateful to Peggy Stubbs for sharing with me her observations of a preschool child's reaction to separation, as well as the logs about friendship that older children had written for her when she was their teacher. This chapter is adapted from a paper delivered at the UCLA Research Conference on Loneliness, May 1979. Portions of the paper are incorporated in my book *Children's Friendships* (Cambridge, Mass.: Harvard University Press, 1980).

some thoughts about what the study of children without friends may suggest about the origins of loneliness.

The tone of this chapter will be descriptive, pointing to issues and themes rather than attempting to document specific causes and effects. Such an approach is necessitated by the paucity of existing research on children's friendships. Systematic research on many of the issues to be discussed is badly needed. Most of the descriptions to be provided derive from my observation of a nursery school class of 3-year-olds at the Harold E. Jones Child Study Center in Berkeley, California, in 1977–1978. Some of the observations were made when I revisited the children a year later, when they were between four and five. The reports of older children's feelings about friendship and its loss were obtained from logs that they had written for their teachers, which were graciously provided to me by Peggy Stubbs. The children's names have been changed.

LACK OF SOCIAL SKILLS

Many children find it hard to make or keep friends because they lack the social skills needed to do so. Danny is one such child. He is a bright, alert 3-year-old who attended a preschool class five mornings a week. Danny was eager to have friends, but was not very successful in this enterprise. Early in the year he rarely approached other children, and much of the time could be found wandering about by himself. He came to the fore most conspicuously at song time, when he would go into extended renditions of songs he had learned at home. As the term progressed, Danny made regular attempts to join other children in their activity, but with little success. For example, he approaches Alison and Becky, who are playing with puzzles, and stands beside them. Alison says softly, "Move." "Why?" Danny asks. "Because I don't want you here." Danny goes off quietly. Another time Danny goes up to the table where Josh is working and says "Hi." Josh doesn't reply and Danny just drifts away. Since he was unable to engage other children, Danny turned to the teachers instead. While several other children are playing with colored plastic tubes, Danny takes some of the tubes and asks the head teacher, "Will you do this with me, Mrs. Benson?" When she suggests that he play with Dylan, Danny takes the tubes on his arm, sings a song to no one in particular, and goes off to a distant table by himself. On another occasion, Danny and Kevin are swinging on ropes together. Then Kevin runs off, calling to his best friend Jake to join him. Danny is left to swing by himself. He walks slowly over to the schoolyard fence and looks for a long time through a crack into the adjacent schoolyard where the unknown children from the other class are playing. When asked who his best friend in school is, Danny replies "Caleb." When asked why Caleb is his friend, he answers, "I want him to be."

In order to make and keep friends, children need to master several different skills. They must learn how to gain entry into group activities, to be approving and supportive to their peers, to manage conflicts appropriately, and to exercise sensitivity and tact (Putallaz & Gottman, 1981; Rubin, 1980, Chapter 4). Mastering such skills can be a difficult endeavor. As Danny's experience suggests, nursery school children who make direct attempts to enter ongoing group activities run the risk of being rebuffed. William Corsaro (1979) notes that once two or more children have structured and defined for themselves a particular activity, whether it is playing with puzzles or blasting off in a spaceship, they often "protect" their activity by excluding any outsiders who might dare to request entry. A "Hi" may be ignored, a "What ya doing?" responded to with "We're making cupcakes and you're not," and a direct "Can I play?" answered with an equally direct "No." To enter the activity, therefore, the child may have to be cautious, strategically subtle, and persistent in the face of an initial rebuff—abilities that Danny has not yet mastered.

The skills of friendship also include the ability to *be* a friend. The most popular nursery school children, those whom their classmates say they like to play with most, tend to be the ones who most often pay attention to other children, praise them, and willingly accede to their requests. In contrast, children who frequently ignore, ridicule, blame, threaten, or refuse to cooperate with others tend to be disliked by their classmates (Hartup, Glazer, & Charlesworth, 1967; Moore, 1967). For a child to be included and accepted, then, he or she must also include and accept. It should be recognized, however, that "friendly" behavior does not always win friendship. Whether an affectionate act is in fact rewarding to the other child depends on how the affection is expressed and how it is interpreted by the recipient. While some children must learn to be more outgoing, others must learn to stop "coming on too strong."

As children become more sensitive to the feelings of others, they also learn the subtle skills of interaction that are needed to manage conflict and maintain friendships. Even 4-year-olds may begin to display such tact, especially in the context of close friendships. For example, I listened in on the following conversation between David and Josh, who were walking together and pretending to be robots:

David.   I'm a missile robot who can shoot missiles out of my fingers. I can shoot them out of everywhere—even out of my legs. I'm a missile robot.

Josh.   (tauntingly): No, you're a fart robot.

David.   (protestingly): No, I'm a missile robot.

Josh.   No, you're a fart robot.

David.   (hurt, almost in tears): No, Josh!

Josh.   (recognizing that David is upset): And I'm a poo-poo robot.

David.   (in good spirits again): I'm a pee-pee robot.

In this encounter, Josh realized that he had said something ("You're a fart robot") that greatly distressed his friend. He handled the situation resourcefully, by putting himself down as well ("I'm a poo-poo robot"), thus demonstrating that his insult was not to be taken seriously. David's response to Josh's move ("I'm a pee-pee robot") indicates that Josh had appraised the situation accurately and had successfully saved his friend's feelings.

Acquiring the skills of friendship can be a difficult struggle for the pre-school child, especially if he or she has not had much previous experience in peer interaction without direct adult supervision. Nursery schools often serve as proving grounds for the development of such skills. The development of general communication skills through interaction with one's peers may itself be a prerequisite for the acquisition of skills specifically related to friendship. Danny, who had doting parents but little experience with age mates before entering nursery school, probably suffered in his attempts at friendship making because of his relatively undeveloped powers of communication. With additional experience, as it turned out, Danny became more successful at making friends. When I revisited him when he was four-and-a-half, he was interacting much more successfully and was sought out by several other children.

Children acquire social skills not so much from adults as from their interaction with one another. They are likely to discover through trial and error which strategies work and which do not. Children also learn social skills from direct tutelage or examples provided by their peers. When David whines, "Gary pushed me," for example, Josh firmly advises him, "Just say stop." In other instances, children introduce their friends to one another, help others to launch joint activities, or show others how to resolve their conflicts. One suspects that such advice and assistance from respected peers are often more effective than similar interventions by teachers or parents.

There are also cases, however, when children need help from adults in mastering particular skills of friendship. When children wish to make friends but lack the skills to do so, vicious cycles can be set in motion. Friendless children must interact with their peers in order to develop the self-confidence and skills needed for social success. But their lack of social skills—for example, their inability to approach other children or their tendency to scare them off—may cut them off from just such opportunities. In such cases intervention by parents or teachers may be necessary. One approach is to steer a friendless child to a particular other child—sometimes one who also lacks friends—whom the adult thinks the child might hit it off with. In at least some cases, such matchmaking helps to give two withdrawn children an initial and valuable experience of social acceptance. Another tactic is to pair an older child who is overly competitive or aggressive with a younger child to whom he can relate as a "big brother"—and, in the process, learn that he can win the acceptance of others without being a bully (Furman, Rahe, & Hartup, 1979; Rand, 1976).

Psychologists have also developed a variety of social skills training programs for both preschool and school-aged children. In such programs children who have been identified as isolates or outcasts are given a series of sessions that may include demonstrations of specific social skills, opportunities to practice them, and feedback on their performance. In one such program (Oden & Asher, 1977), unpopular third- and fourth-graders took part in pairs in a series of coaching sessions that focused on four sets of skills: participating in certain games, taking turns and sharing, communicating with other children by talking more, and supporting peers by paying attention and helping them. In at least some cases, such training programs have been notably successful in increasing the social acceptance of initially unpopular children (see reviews by Asher & Renfrew, 1981; Combs & Slaby, 1977).

Because social skills training programs tend to be focused on increasing social acceptance or popularity, they bring up some troublesome questions of values. Do the programs really help children develop the capacity for friendship, or are they geared to an American ideal of glib sociability and congeniality that has little to do with real friendship? (Peter Suedfeld, Chapter 4, comments on our society's "pro-togetherness" bias.) The answer to this question depends both on the details of the program and on the values of the adults who administer it. In the view of at least some leading practitioners, "The objective of social skills instruction is not to create 'popular' or 'outgoing' children, but to help youngsters, whatever their personality styles, to develop positive relationships . . . with at least one or two other children" (Stocking, Arezzo, & Leavitt, 1980, p. 19). One can also question the ethics of imposing social skills training on children who have little choice in the matter, and who in some instances, may not really want to be changed into "friendlier" people. In the last analysis, the most compelling defense for such programs is that they may be able to increase the child's degree of control over his or her own life:

A child who has the skills to initiate play and communicate with peers may still choose to spend a good deal of time alone. But that child will be able to interact effectively when she (he) wants to or when the situation requires it. On the other hand, a socially unskilled child may be alone or "isolated" out of necessity rather than by choice (Combs & Slaby, 1977, p. 165).

Even without instituting formal training, parents and teachers can make use of similar demonstrations, explanations, and feedback in order to teach the skills of friendship in school or home settings (see the useful guidebook by Stocking, Arezzo & Leavitt, 1980). Although adults have a role to play in teaching social skills to children, it is often best that they play it unobtrusively. In particular, adults must guard against embarrassing unskilled children by "correcting" them too publicly and against labeling children as "shy" in ways that may lead the children to see themselves in just that way (Zimbardo, 1977, Chapter 4).

Rather than "pushing" social skills indiscriminately, adults should respect the real differences between children that motivate some to establish friendly relations with many others, some to concentrate on one or two close friendships, and some to spend a good deal of time by themselves. Any of these patterns may be satisfying and appropriate for a particular child. In our efforts to help children make friends, we should be more concerned with the quality of their friendships than with their quantity.

MOVING TO A NEW SCHOOL OR NEIGHBORHOOD

When I revisited the preschool children whom I had been observing the previous year, I immediately noticed that Ricky, once the most outgoing and popular boy in the class, seemed unusually quiet and subdued. Although he was playing with other children, he was engaged in activities that were beneath his usual level of sophistication, such as jumping repeatedly on a plank, and he seemed to be playing with a lack of real involvement. When I returned to school the next day, Ricky came up to me and said sadly, "Buddy Josh, Buddy Tony, Buddy David." I asked Ricky why he was saying that. "Cause those are my buddies," he replied, "I miss them." Toward the end of the previous year, Ricky, Josh, Tony, and David had formed a close clique. They were among the most imaginative children in the class and would often build parking garages, rush to put out fires, or man a spaceship together. Two months before my visit, Josh, Tony, and David were transferred by their parents from the half-day nursery school to an all-day preschool. This left only Ricky of the original group in the old school. Although he seemed to understand the situation and to be adapting to it, his sense of loss was unmistakable.

Social scientists, who have long been concerned with the effects of children's short-term and long-term separations from their parents, have done virtually no systematic research on children's separations from their friends. Nevertheless, there has been no shortage of speculation about the effects of moving, and most of it has been highly cautionary. Writing about the early school years, Sullivan (1953, pp. 241–242) declared that frequent moves often prove to be "disastrous" influences on children's lives, and that any moves during this period may cause serious social handicaps. More recently, a noted child psychologist was quoted as suggesting that moving is likely to be traumatic both for preschoolers and for teenagers, whose "lives are shattered by leaving their home towns and their home-town friends" (Packard, 1972).

Severe reactions to moving may be understood in part as grief reactions to the loss of particularly close friends, people on whom one has come to depend for companionship and support. Feelings of loneliness, depression, irritability, and anger are all common reactions to such loss. These feelings can be experienced by the child whose friend has moved away, as well as by the child who has moved away. In at least some cases, like that of 12-year-old Andrea, the pain can be intense:

I've done so much thinking I have to write. I've said so much to myself and now it's got to come out. Sometimes I want to kill myself. Do I? Seriously, I've thought about it. My problem is that I want to go back to my old school and my real home.

An additional difficulty is that the child who moves must now become integrated into a new social setting, where, to make matters worse, "everyone acts as though they've known everyone for a long time." For children of all ages, such moves can resurrect all of the difficulties and anxieties of the first arrival into a preschool setting. Making new friends is sometimes especially difficult for older children, since by the later childhood years cliques are likely to be well-established and difficult to penetrate.

After a move, the opportunity to keep in touch with old friends may be rewarding, but such contacts may also remind the child of how much he or she misses them. Marlene, a 13-year-old who was transferred by her parents, with her own partial acquiescence, from one private school to another, reported on an encounter she had had with an old friend:

I really miss Bancroft so much sometimes. At lunch I saw a really close friend— at least he was last year—and he was so nice. I felt like just leaving school and going to talk to him for the rest of the day. It just makes me feel so sad each time I talk or see someone from there. I get so sad about not being there but at the same time I'm so glad I'm not. It's confusing and it hurts like hell.

Such ambivalence may be characteristic of children who have moved from one setting to another, as they attempt to cope both with their feelings of loss and their need to make the best of their new situation.

In addition to the immediate effects of having to leave old friends and make new ones, some writers have suggested that frequent moves are likely to have more lasting effects. In his book about mobility in the United States, *A Nation of Strangers,* Vance Packard (1972) reports on the prototypical case of a young man raised in a military family who had, since his boyhood, great difficulty in making close friendships: "He was certain it was because his close friends when he was growing up were inevitably from military families and they were usually rotated out every two years. The pain of losing friends repeatedly caused him unwittingly, he suspected, to start shunning close friendships."

But moving does not always have such severely negative effects on children. The limited evidence that exists indicates no systematic link between the number of times people moved during childhood and their feelings of loneliness as adults (Rubenstein & Shaver, Chapter 13). Children are likely to miss their old friends, to be sure, and often keep thinking and talking about them for a long time. Young children sometimes incorporate their old friends into their fantasy play ("That's Ronny's space ship and this is mine") as a way of adjusting to the loss. Some older children also manage to maintain friendships for many years through letters, phone calls, and occasional visits. At the same time many children look on their moves as a positive opportunity, and most succeed in gradually making friends in their new locale.

Although children's reactions to separations differ widely from case to case, I think that in general we can credit our children with a good deal of resilience. For example, 4-year-old Ricky managed to adjust to his new situation, in which his most valued companions were no longer available. Ricky gradually began to spend more time with other children in the class, including some he previously had ignored. He also discovered and came to enjoy new activities, such as playing "daddy" in family role play with some of the girls in the class. Thus Ricky's loss of friends had the hidden benefit of making new sorts of social relationships and experiences available to him. Parents and teachers should appreciate, however, that being forced to separate from one's friends and to enter a new social world is going to be stressful for children of any age, just as it is for adults. These are times when secure and supportive family relationships are likely to be especially important for the child.

Although social scientists have done very little research on children's separation from their friends, writers of books for children have frequently addressed this issue. For example, *Janey,* by Charlotte Zolotow (1973), is a book for 4-to-8-year-olds that takes the pain of separation seriously. The girl who narrates this picture book expresses her feelings eloquently:

> Janey it's lonely all day long since you moved away. When I walk in the rain and the leaves are wet and clinging to the sidewalk I remember how we used to walk home from school together. . . . I remember how we'd go home for dinner and I could hardly wait for dinner to end to call you. But sometimes you called me first. . . . I didn't want you to move away. You didn't want to either. Janey maybe some day we'll grow up and live near each other again.

Children's books such as these deserve serious attention by researchers seeking insights about children's reactions to separation from friends. They may also be useful as resources to help children cope with separation and loss. A valuable listing and discussion of such books is provided by Bernstein (1977).

WHEN FRIENDS GROW APART

Five-year-old Erik had been best friends with Peter for two and a half years at their day care center. Peter gradually came to be more interested in playing with a new boy, Curtis, who had joined the group. Their teacher, Peggy Stubbs, recalls:

> Finally Peter formed a relationship with Curtis which excluded Erik. Erik at first reacted to the change by expressing sadness and rage. For a time, he was unable to participate effectively in school activities. He seemed to need to show off in front of the group, even though he had never before sought attention so directly. He over-reacted to criticism, with prolonged fussing and arguing, whereas

previously he had been reasonable in his acceptance of his own misbehavior and pragmatic in serving out the accompanying punishment. He rigorously protested Peter's new exclusion of him and for a long time continued to interrupt Peter's new friendship with his presence.

Erik's loss was hard for him to bear. He had lost his best friend, one who had been his bosom buddy for half his life. Although Peter had not been callous or cruel in his rejection of Erik, it was still a clear case of abandonment. Even for a 5-year-old, questions of "Why doesn't he like me?" and its common sequel, "What's wrong with me?" are almost sure to arise in such circumstances. Erik's sadness, hostility, and attention-seeking can be understood as reactions both to his sense of loss and to his newly aroused feelings of doubt about his own worth.

Such endings of relationships that children themselves precipitate are probably even more frequent than the separations that result from moving. Children's friendships rarely seem to be disrupted permanently by a single dispute. Rather the breakups are likely to be the final result of a drifting apart, set in motion by one or both friends' gradual recognition that they no longer provide the same satisfactions to one another. As individual children grow up, their changing needs, abilities, and interests almost inevitably result in changing friendships. These changes are particularly striking as children progress, each at his or her own rate and in his or her own way, from childhood to adolescence. "Sometimes a kid grows up and sometimes the friend doesn't," an older girl explains. "So then all of a sudden you find out you don't have anything in common. You like boys and she's still interested in dolls" (Selman & Jaquette, 1977, p. 172).

In an account of four boys who were studied throughout their childhood and adolescent years, as part of a longitudinal study launched in the 1930s, Mary Cover Jones (1948) provided an extended description of such changes:

The four boys started out as close friends in elementary school. At the time, they were 10½ years old, with only four months difference between them in age. They were all above average in ability, with only 10 points difference in IQ. They were healthy, lively youngsters from good homes, doing well in school, and enjoying life in general. So firm were their bonds that even though they were separated in junior high school classrooms, they continued to mention each other as friends until the eighth grade.

Then came separations which appeared to result from differences in social maturity and in rate of physical development. Bob, the most advanced in skeletal build, was also socially most mature. For example, when observed at a dance in the eleventh grade, Bob was described as "poised, unself-conscious, competent in steering his partners around the floor, adultly inconspicuous." Bob pulled ahead of the group at this time in social status and remained at the top in this respect. How were the other boys affected? What adjustments did they make in the high school years?

One, Nelson, became a runner-up—something of a "fringe member" of Bob's prestige group, although they continued to be best friends throughout the school years. Nelson was slightly below average in physical maturity during this period and less sure of himself in social situations. At the high school dance, for example, Nelson danced in a strangely crab-like fashion, holding his partner at almost a right angle to himself. However, by dint of greater effort, which our observers often noted, he was able to keep up with Bob and to be included in his crowd.

Harry, the least physically mature of the clique, but as interested as Bob and Nelson in social activities, was not able to meet the social requirements of mixed-sex group situations with the same maturity as Bob or Nelson. At the high school dance, Harry, chewing gum, looking somewhat bravely worried, traded dances with other boys as the younger crowd usually do. His inexperience made him overly eager to conform to the accepted rituals; he covered up pauses in conversations by nervous giggles and "kiddish" tricks like shadow-boxing. He was dropped by his erstwhile friends, had a short period of disappointment over this rejection, but soon found an equally immature companion with whom he was happy. In fact, he probably functioned more easily in this new situation than his old friend, Nelson, who just managed to make the higher status group and had to work to stay there.

The last of the original four friends is Phil, whose physical development was slightly advanced and could have been a social asset. But Phil was not psychologically ready for the mixed-sex activities of his agemates. He selected as a friend a new boy who, like himself, might be described as relatively asocial. At a party in the eighth grade, "when the girls insisted upon dancing, Phil fled to the office and practiced typing, returning later to play a game of chess with his friend, Pierce." (Adapted from Jones, 1948)

Jones's chronicle emphasizes the close interplay of physical and psychological changes, on the one hand, and changes in friendship, on the other. Her account helps to make clear that the endings of friendships and their replacement with new ones should usually be taken as signs of normal development rather than of social inadequacy. As the world's most famous pediatrician writes, "The very fact that friendships wax and wane is evidence that at each phase of growth children are apt to need something different from their friends and, therefore, have to find a new one from time to time" (Spock, 1975, p. 31).

But although such endings are normal and necessary aspects of development, children often have great difficulty in dealing with breakups. Just as with the endings of marriages and love affairs, the endings of friendships are seldom completely mutual (Hill, Rubin, & Peplau, 1976). One child typically becomes disenchanted with the relationship sooner than the other and becomes the "breaker-upper," while the other child is "broken up with." Each of these roles can be very difficult to play. Especially among older children who have become sensitive toward others' feelings, deciding whether or not to end a friendship that one has outgrown can be an agonizing process. Twelve-year-old Naomi experienced such an inner struggle as she contemplated her friendship with Marcy:

She's such a phony, cutesy, show off, hypocrite. But I can't tell her that she bugs me, or why, because she gets defensive, confused, and hurt. I've tried, because we have a pact to tell each other our gripes instead of whispering to each other about them. But Marcy thinks I'm her friend, and I can't not be friends with her. Lately I haven't wanted to be around her.

Handling such a conflict sensitively is a difficult test for the child's developing social skills. In many such cases the best resolution—which was in fact accomplished by Naomi—is to continue the friendship, but at a lower level of intensity.

Coming to terms with rejection by a friend is even harder. For younger children, such as 5-year-old Erik, the discovery that your friend no longer wants to play with you may be almost totally incomprehensible and hence particularly hurtful. And even if the child can understand, in abstract terms, that he and his friend no longer have as much in common as they used to, the rejection is still likely to come as a devastating blow.

Especially as they approach adolescence, children sometimes become intensely preoccupied with changes in their friendships, as if to prepare themselves for the endings that may take place. In a mixed-age class of 11-, 12-, and 13-year-olds, some of the younger girls who were maturing more quickly sought to establish friendships with the older girls. As a result, others of the younger girls became acutely aware of the possibility of rejection. One of them, Sarah, wrote poignantly to her teachers: "Rachel is spending all her time with Paula Davis and deserting me. Rachel is conversing very loudly with two idiots in her cubby and I can't concentrate. Rachel is changing, she is not Rachel any more." Rachel herself was distressed by the same changing situation, although her perception of it differed somewhat from Sarah's:

Oh, I feel so horrible about friends. Everybody is deserting their best friend and everybody hates someone else and Paula Davis has been stranded with nobody— except me and Sarah, and Christine has run off with Liz, and Joan has moved up from being an 11-year-old to a 12- or 13-year-old and, oh, well, I suppose it happens every year.

Although these girls were upset by the changing friendships, their sensitivity to these fluctuations is likely to prove valuable in the long run. Such sensitivity can help children to identify accurately the emerging differences that may lead to endings, rather than hastily blaming these endings on other children's malice or on their own basic inadequacies. Children's assessments of the causes of a breakup play a critical role in determining their reactions to it. Whereas self-blame, for example, may discourage children from attempting to form new friendships (on the ground that "no one could ever like me"), a fuller understanding of the psychological differences that led to a breakup can help them to establish more satisfactory friendships in the future (Dweck & Goetz, 1979). There is reason to think, incidentally, that girls are more sensitive to the vicissitudes of intimate relationships than boys are (Rubin, 1980, Chapter 7). It may be in part for this reason that women seem to handle separation and loss more effectively than men in adulthood as well (Rubin, Peplau & Hill, 1981).

For most children, losing friends is a normal and necessary part of growing up. But these endings are also likely to represent crises of some proportion in the child's life. Parents often seem to underestimate the importance of these losses, especially when they are dealing with younger children. They tend to downplay the loss, assuring the child, "Don't worry, you'll find another friend," thus betraying the misconception that young friends are like standardized, replaceable parts. Parents would do better to take the situation more seriously and empathically (Brenton, 1979). In many cases, however, children are eventually able to turn these losses into gains—experiences that channel their interests and social networks in productive and satisfying ways. Behavioral scientists, for their part, need to learn more about such changes in children's friendships, and about how children can be helped to cope with them effectively.

CONCLUSION

We have looked at three categories of children without friends—those who lack the social skills needed for making and keeping friends, those who have moved (or whose friends have moved) to a new school or neighborhood, and those whose friendships have ended because the children have grown apart and no longer provide the rewards to one another that they used to. Children as young as three, and, I suspect, children even younger than that, can feel what Robert Weiss (1973) calls "the loneliness of social isolation." Although the loneliness of children may differ in its details from the loneliness of adolescents or adults, I believe that we are talking about the same basic experience. Like adults who lack a satisfying social network, children without friends can experience painful feelings of malaise, boredom, and alienation. This loneliness is often compounded by a feeling of being excluded, with resulting damage to the child's self-esteem. Loneliness, as experienced by young children like Danny, Ricky, and Erik, and by older children like Andrea, Marlene, Sarah, and Rachel, needs to be approached with the same understanding and compassion as the loneliness of adults.

The experience of children without friends takes on special importance because of its implications for later life. We have very little solid information about the impact of children's friendships on their psychological and social adjustment as adults. Although some longitudinal studies have found evidence for certain continuities between childhood and adult social experience (Cowen, Pederson, Babigian, Izzo, & Trost, 1973; Maas, 1968), there is no reason to believe that the lack of satisfactory peer relationships in early childhood will create deficits that cannot be reversed by later experience. However, the specific experiences of children without friends will probably influence the ways in which these children will experience separation and loss as adults. If a child learns that he or she can deal effectively with loneliness, he or she may well be better able to master similar situations 20, 40, or 60 years later. In this connection, it is especially important to make a clear distinction (as drawn by Suedfeld and others in this volume) between "aloneness" and "loneliness." Children who learn to equate being alone with being lonely and rejected may well carry a fear of loneliness with them as they grow up.

I believe that children without friends can help us to understand loneliness among adults. The friendships of young children tend to be played out over a shorter time scale than those of adults, in a more restrictive range of settings, and in ways that are typically more open and accessible to the outside observer. As a result, young children's friendships provide an extraordinary research opportunity for the student of social relationships, their absence, and their loss. In the preschool setting, in particular, the researcher can observe the comings and goings of friendships in microcosm, in ways that would be much more difficult, if not impossible, among adolescents or adults. The focus on developmental change that comes so naturally to us when we study children without friends can also provide a valuable perspective on the process of separation and loss among adults. Although we have not usually looked at them in this way, the strains and dissatisfactions of many close adult relationships may reflect normal processes of adult development, in which the two parties involved are developing at different rates or in different ways. Lonely adults have much in common with children without friends, as they face problems of engaging others in interaction, cope with physical separation and uprooting, and deal with individual changes in needs, interests, and values. Thus, students of loneliness can learn a great deal from children without friends.

REFERENCES

Asher, S. R., & Renfrew, P. D. Children without friends: Social knowledge and social skill training. In S. R. Asher & J. M. Gottman (Eds.), *The development of children's friendships.* New York: Cambridge University Press, 1981.

Bernstein, J. E. *Books to help children cope with separation and loss.* New York and London: R. B. Bowker, 1977.

Brenton, M. When best friends part. *Parents Magazine,* May 1979.

Combs, M. L., & Slaby, D. A. Social-skills training with children. In B. B. Lahey & A. E. Kazdin (Eds.), *Advances in clinical child psychology* (Vol. 1). New York: Plenum, 1977.

Corsaro, W. A. "We're friends, right?": Children's use of access rituals in a nursery school. *Language in Society,* 1979, *8,* 315–336.

Cowen, E. L., Pederson, A., Babigian, H., Izzo, L. D., & Trost, M. A. Long-term follow-up of early detected vulnerable children. *Journal of Consulting and Clinical Psychology,* 1973, *41,* 438–446.

Dweck, C. S., & Goetz, T. E. Attributions and learned helplessness. In J. H. Harvey, W. Ickes, & R. F. Kidd (Eds.), *New directions in attribution research* (Vol. 2). Hillsdale, N. J.: Lawrence Erlbaum Associates, 1979.

Furman, W., Rahe, D. F., & Hartup, W. W. Rehabilitation of socially-withdrawn preschool children through mixed-age and same-age socialization. *Child Development,* 1979, *50,* 915–922.

Hartup, W. W., Glazer, J. A., & Charlesworth, R. Peer reinforcement and sociometric status. *Child Development,* 1967, *38,* 1017–1024.

Hetherington, E. M., Cox, M., & Cox, R. Play and social interaction in children following divorce. *Journal of Social Issues,* 1979, *35* (4), 26–46.

Hill, C. T., Rubin, Z., & Peplau, L. A. Breakups before marriage: The end of 231 affairs. *Journal of Social Issues,* 1976, *32*(1), 147–168.

Jones, M. C. Studying the characteristics of friends. Paper presented at the annual meeting of the American Psychological Association, 1948.

Maas, H. S. Preadolescent peer relations and adult intimacy. *Psychiatry,* 1968, *31,* 161–172.

Moore, S. Correlates of peer acceptance in nursery school children. *Young Children,* 1967, *22,* 281–297.

Oden, S., & Asher, S. R. Coaching children in social skills for friendship making. *Child Development,* 1977, *48,* 495–506.

Packard, V. *A nation of strangers.* New York: David McKay, 1972.

Putallaz, M., & Gottman, J. Social skills and group acceptance. In S. R. Asher & J. M. Gottman (Eds.), *The development of children's friendships.* New York: Cambridge University Press, 1981.

Rand, H. Y. Multi-age groups: Let them reason together. *Day Care and Early Education,* March-April, 1976, 24–27.

Rubin, Z. *Children's friendships.* Cambridge, Mass.: Harvard University Press, 1980.

Rubin, Z., Peplau, L. A., & Hill, C. T. Loving and leaving: Sex differences in romantic attachments. *Sex Roles,* 1981, *7,* 821–835.

Selman, R. L., & Jaquette, D. *The development of interpersonal awareness.* Working draft of manual, Harvard-Judge Baker Social Reasoning Project, 1977.

Spock, B. How children make friends. *Redbook,* March 1975.

Stocking, S. H., Arezzo, D., & Leavitt, S. *Helping kids make friends.* Allen, Tex.: Argus Communications, 1980.

Sullivan, H. S. *The interpersonal theory of psychiatry.* New York: Norton, 1953.

Weiss, R. S. *Loneliness: The experience of emotional and social isolation.* Cambridge, Mass.: MIT Press, 1973.

Zimbardo, P. G. *Shyness.* Reading, Mass.: Addison-Wesley, 1977.

Zolotow, C. *Janey.* New York: Harper & Row, 1973.

Chapter 17

Loneliness at Adolescence

Tim Brennan

Adolescence is a particularly significant life stage for examining loneliness. Although there are no large-scale, systematic epidemiological studies of loneliness across different ages, the available evidence suggests that there is more loneliness among adolescents than among any other age group. Many writers claim that adolescence is a time of widespread and particularly intense loneliness (Buhler, 1969; Gaev, 1976; Ostrov & Offer, 1978; Robert, 1974; Rubenstein & Shaver, Chapter 13; Weiss, 1973; Wood & Hannell, 1977).

Adolescence seems to be the time of life when loneliness first emerges as an intense, recognizable phenomenon. Sullivan (1953) implies that, although loneliness may be present in the preadolescent stage, it is powerfully experienced at adolescence as a result of the development of new interpersonal needs for intimacy. Weiss (1973) agrees with this view. He states:

Insofar as the loneliness of emotional isolation represents the subjective response to the absence of not so much of a particular other but rather of a generalized attachment figure, it is a state that is probably not experienced until adolescence. . . . (p. 89)

Loneliness proper becomes a possible experience only when, in adolescence, parents are relinquished as attachment figures. (p. 90)

Why is this stage of the life cycle characterized by widespread intense loneliness? The evidence regarding the extent of loneliness during adolescence is examined below, and the particular processes of adolescent development that are responsible for such intense loneliness are reviewed. Specifically, the following issues are explored:

1. How widespread is the experience of loneliness among adolescents?
2. What developmental factors seem to be related to the emergence of loneliness?
3. What socio-structural and cultural processes seem to be responsible for the isolation and loneliness of many youth?
4. What personal factors relate to adolescent loneliness?
5. How do adolescents react to, and cope with, their loneliness?

The answers to these questions may have profound importance in the formulation of a theory of adolescent loneliness.

To date only a limited number of studies have empirically examined the nature of loneliness in adolescent populations. A few studies (Brennan & Auslander, 1979; Ostrov & Offer, 1978; Wood & Hannell, 1977) focus specifically on loneliness at adolescence and use large-scale samples, including lonely and nonlonely youth, and explicit measures of loneliness. More typically, the available data on adolescent loneliness stem from studies in which loneliness was not a central focus of the research. Useful information on loneliness has been gathered from studies of such diverse topics as adolescent suicide, exhibitionism, delinquent behavior, shyness, school failure, dropout, runaways, and social skill development.

THE EXTENT OF LONELINESS DURING ADOLESCENCE

Questions regarding the extent of loneliness inevitably have to deal with operational measurement and hence with definitions of what is meant by loneliness. Loneliness is multifaceted, both in its conceptual content and in the variety of measurement approaches. The present review adopts an eclectic position, drawing upon a variety of different conceptualizations and measurement approaches offered by different researchers. Many of these distinctions are discussed elsewhere in this volume and will not be reviewed here. In studying the extent of adolescent loneliness we have relied heavily upon self-reports of general loneliness, since this is the measure most commonly used. In our examination of the nature and development of loneliness at adolescence, however, some conceptual distinctions are quite important. The distinction between emotional and social dimensions of loneliness (Weiss, 1973) is critical in understanding the transformation in relations of the adolescent with parents and with peers. The concept of spiritual loneliness is useful in focusing attention on the adolescent search for meaning, identity, and worthwhile modes of participation (Buhler, 1969; Fabry, 1968; Frankl, 1959; Gaev, 1976). Failure in this search is seen as leading to spiritual loneliness. A final conceptualization that is useful in understanding adolescent loneliness is that of existential loneliness (Burton, 1961; Ferreira, 1962; Gaev, 1976). We will use this term to denote the kind of loneliness that emerges with the awareness of one's ultimate separateness from others and one's total personal responsibility for the decisions within one's own life.

Difficulties in Assessing the Incidence of Adolescent Loneliness

Currently there is no systematic, epidemiological study of loneliness among adolescents that has used normal probability sampling of the national adolescent population. Therefore, the available studies may be subject to various kinds of bias. In fact, a majority of published studies are based on small or highly unrepresentative samples. The findings of such studies cannot be generalized to other populations. Variations in the approach to sampling and operational measurement of loneliness may be partially responsible for variations in findings regarding prevalence.

Another general problem stems from the difficulty of operationalizing loneliness for measurement purposes. As a result of the absence of consensus regarding the meaning of loneliness, different research studies have used different approaches to measurement. Although new loneliness measures have been developed (Bradley, 1969; Russell, Peplau, & Cutrona, 1980), the task of integrating the findings to assess incidence levels from different measurement approaches is problematic.

In addition, it appears that adolescent loneliness is an extremely changeable and volatile phenomenon. Larson et al. (Chapter 3) found that adolescents show high variation in their self-reports of loneliness, depending partly on the time and place. As might be expected, adolescents reported being lonely most often on Friday and Saturday nights. Adolescents were also found to be far more volatile than older subjects in their levels of self-reported loneliness, showing much higher scores for intra-individual variation in loneliness.

The Extent of Loneliness at Adolescence

In spite of measurement difficulties, data from the available studies consistently suggest that loneliness is an acutely painful and widespread problem among adolescents. Findings from many small studies initially provided evidence that loneliness is a major social problem among youth. Saks (1974) and Bleach and Clairborn (1974) reported that loneliness, along with drug addiction, pregnancy, and family problems, was among the most frequently mentioned problems of youth seeking help via a crisis center hot-line.

Several studies point to the severe loneliness of college students. For example, Phillips and Pederson (1972) attempted to assess the "general mood" of students. They found that boredom, loneliness, and a sense of futility were the most prevalent problems. Examining student failure, Christiaans (1965) found that loneliness, in conjunction with certain critical interpersonal behavioral problems (i.e., romantic relationships and family), was extremely debilitating and related to a loss of motivation.

Four studies were based on larger samples and more explicit measurements of loneliness. In a study assessing self-reported loneliness across all age levels, Rubenstein and Shaver (Chapter 13) found that the incidence of loneliness peaked at adolescence and showed a decline with increasing age. Brennan and Auslander (1979) examined various scaled measures of loneliness including social and emotional isolation, spiritual loneliness (or meaninglessness), and self-reported loneliness in over 9000 adolescents, aged 10 to 18, sampled from 10 U.S. cities. This study estimated that about 10 to 15% of these adolescents were "seriously lonely," as defined by a pattern of simultaneously high scores on self-reported loneliness, emotional and social isolation, as well as other indicators of loneliness. Nearly 45% suffered from somewhat less severe levels of chronic loneliness. Fifty-four percent of those interviewed agreed with the statement "I often feel lonely."

Collier and Lawrence (1952) examined the feeling of "psychological isolation" in 150 high school students. This early and relatively small-scale study examined feelings of isolation of the adolescent from social objects toward whom feelings of relationship might be expressed, for example, parents, teachers, siblings, and peers. They concluded that this feeling of isolation is common enough—occurring in 65% of the adolescents studied—to be called a "typical experience" of adolescence. Their data also indicated that the experience was more typical of girls than boys, and that the social object of this feeling was more likely to be peers than either parents or teachers.

Finally, a study by Ostrov and Offer (1978) tested over 5000 youths between ages 12 and 18, including males and females; normal, disturbed and delinquent; and various ethnic groups. Separate samples were obtained from various metropolitan centers in the United States and from Australia and Ireland. This study used responses to the statement "I am so very lonely" as the primary measure of loneliness. Ostrov and Offer found that 22% of boys and 20% of girls aged 12 to 16, as well as 14% of boys and 12.3% of girls aged 16 to 20, agreed with the self-report loneliness statement.

Loneliness within Different Social Contexts

Brennan and Auslander (1979) examined variations in multiple indicators of loneliness within different social contexts.

Isolation from Parents

Ten percent of youths felt that their parents were "not interested in them," 19% agreed that their parents "did not spend sufficient time with them," 36% agreed that their parents "did not understand their problems," and 22% agreed that there was "no adult to talk to."

Isolation from Teachers

One third of the youths felt that their teachers "did not sufficiently understand them," 25% felt that their teachers were "not sufficiently interested," and 43% were uncertain whether their teachers and counselors "really cared" about them.

Isolation from Peers

Only 3% of these adolescents indicated that they had no close friends, 11% felt that there was no one to confide in, 12% felt that they could turn to no one for help, 54% indicated that they often felt "left out of things," 20% complained that they didn't feel free to talk about their personal problems with friends, 25% indicated that they spent virtually no time (less than one-half hour per day) with friends, 51% of those sampled acknowledged that boredom was a serious problem for them, and 27% indicated that they spent more than three hours per day alone.

Demographic Differences in Loneliness

The following findings also emerged from the study by Brennan and Auslander:

Sex Differences

In responding to the item "I often feel lonely", girls gave a substantially higher rate of agreement than boys, 61.3% versus 46.5% respectively. In other self-report questions indicating loneliness, girls also exceeded boys in the proportions of agreements. For example, 61% of girls reported boredom compared with 47% of boys. In questions dealing with isolation from teachers and from parents, girls scored higher than boys. This straightforward picture, however, did not recur when examining scaled measures of social and emotional isolation. There were no significant sex differences for these latter measures of loneliness. Wood and Hannell (1977) similarly found no clear differences between boys and girls in their study of loneliness.

Age Differences

In comparing youth in the three age categories of 10 to 12, 13 to 15, and 16+, no clear differences were found for most measures of loneliness. However, older youths felt more strongly that their parents did not understand them and lacked interest in them, that there was no adult to talk to, and that their teachers did not understand them. With increasing age there was also a steady decrease in the amount of time spent with parents and a decrease in the amount of time spent alone. Thus there is no unequivocal indication in this research that younger adolescents are any more lonely than older adolescents. The basic measures of self-reported loneliness and of social and emotional isolation showed no significant differences across the three age groups. These findings contrast with Ostrov and Offer (1976), who found that, for both boys and girls, self-reported loneliness was more widespread in the younger (under 16) age groups. However, the exact wording of the self-report question and the age groups used were different in these two studies.

Social Class and Ethnic Differences

The study by Brennan and Auslander (1979) compared loneliness among Black, Mexican-American, and Anglo youths, and among various social classes. Across the various scaled measures of loneliness, no significant differences linked to social class or ethnicity were found. Only in the case of self-reported loneliness was there a suggestion that loneliness was more widespread among adolescents of the lowest social classes.

In summary, it is difficult to integrate findings from studies using a variety of approaches in sampling, conceptualization of loneliness, and operational measures of loneliness. Nevertheless, the evidence, particularly from the large scale studies by Ostrov and Offer and by Brennan and Auslander. suggests that about 15 to 20% of the adolescent population experience painful levels of loneliness, with over 50% of youth experiencing recurrent feelings of loneliness.

FACTORS CONTRIBUTING TO ADOLESCENT LONELINESS

Various factors contribute to the loneliness of the adolescent. Many of these are developmental processes that introduce disruptive changes in the life of the adolescent. Such changes may create powerful new desires or expectations for social relations that cannot be readily satisfied. They may also precipitate loneliness by disrupting existing relationships, and affecting the social and personal adjustment of youths.

Two additional factors may also predispose adolescents toward loneliness. First, loneliness may be fostered by features of the sociocultural situation of adolescents, for example, a competitive milieu at high school, ill-defined or meaningless social roles, excessive stigmatization and negative labeling within major social institutions, social processes leading to powerlessness, and value confusions. Second, such personal characteristics as shyness, low self-esteem, inadequate social skills, and low social desirability may set the stage for loneliness.

Developmental Changes

At adolescence, a complex set of developmental changes appears to increase one's sense of isolation and need for affiliation, to introduce a sense of the ambiguity of future directions, and to disrupt the sense of personal identity. These processes are primarily related to the tasks of separation from parents, separation from the preadolescent identity, and the concomitant struggle for autonomy, individuation, and new modes of belonging. Although each of these processes is presented separately here, it is clear that they operate within a complex, dynamic relationship to each other. For any particular adolescent there may be a different "mix" of such factors operating at any one time.

Separation from Parents

The transformation of the attachment bond to parents has been pinpointed as a critical antecedent of loneliness in adolescence (Ostrov & Offer, 1978; Weiss, 1973). There is a reorganization of the attachment system of the youth, resulting in a separation from parents as the primary attachment figures and an increased emphasis upon relationships with the same sex, and perhaps the opposite sex. This readjustment almost certainly disrupts the important interpersonal relationships of the adolescent. There is much variation in the precise age at which this transformation begins. It also seems to be an uneven process, with frequent lapses into childhood dependencies and attachments. There may be times when the young adolescent is completely psychologically isolated. Weiss writes:

It is also possible for there to be intervals in which there is no accessible attachment figure at all: in which the world seems emptied, bereft of all possible attachment. The parents no longer serve in this way. Now it is possible to speak of loneliness as a condition of objectless pining, of pining for a kind of relationship rather than for a particular person. (1973, p. 93)

The role of parents in responding to the separation of their adolescent child is critical. Parental responses vary from supportive understanding, to attempts to undermine the separation by prolonging the preadolescent attachments, to premature rejection of the child (Stierlin, 1974). Inevitably the loss of an important attachment figure seems to be tinged with loneliness.

Cognitive Development

The emergence of the capacity for formal mental operations, the growth of cognitive and symbolization capacities, and the ability to think abstractly have been linked to the emergence of a new type of self-awareness (Elkind, 1968; Rappoport, 1972). The maturing adolescent is seen as being able to think in terms of "possibilities" rather than in the world of the "immediate realities" of the child. The world of the possible extends outward in space, time, successes, failures, and so on. There is an increase in the awareness of past and future, of separateness, and of mortality. Changes such as the emergence of new cognitive abilities and the drive for individuation may lead to a greater awareness of the self as "separate," and hence to existential loneliness and other forms of loneliness (May, 1953). Mijuskovic (1979) argues that the existence of a reflexive self-consciousness is a critical precondition for the experience of loneliness to be even possible.

Maturation

Physiological growth fosters emotional maturation. Emotional capacities for intimacy develop rapidly during adolescence. Konopka (1966), Collier and Lawrence (1951), and others indicate that such changes bring about strong needs for new and more varied interpersonal relations. This is coupled with normative expectations for cross-sex activity and social popularity. As adolescents struggle to acquire the confidence and social skills to successfully engage in such new kinds of relationships, and to satisfy new personal desires and socially induced expectations, they may face deficits in levels of emotional attachments.

Autonomy

Growth during adolescence is characterized by a striving for personal autonomy. The young person attempts to achieve behavioral, moral, ideological, and cognitive autonomy. The youth is then confronted with a large range of possibilities, with concomitant confusions and ambiguities. Physical, cognitive, and moral growth, in addition to social expectations, inexorably push the adolescent toward increased independence and autonomy. Ostrov and Offer state: "Every time we grow more autonomous, create our own thoughts, assert our own identity, we risk moving away from others and therefore risk loneliness." (1978, p. 34).

In facing the demands of personal decision-making and responsibility in areas such as daily time management, as well as moral, political, religious, and career choices, the young person is thrown back upon his or her own personal resources. He or she becomes the primary decision-maker, and such responsibilities can be frightening. The young person may feel lost, confused, and lonely. The components of loneliness emerging from this aspect of adolescent development may include feelings of aimlessness, frustration, and insecurity. Affiliation needs may escalate for relationships with peers that provide help in clarifying important decisions and that provide support, understanding, and information on how other teenage peers are dealing with these issues.

A common problem for lonely adolescents is a sense of boredom (Buhler, 1969; Lindenauer, 1970; Tanner, 1973). During childhood, parents take almost full responsibility for structuring the activities and time of the child. Tanner (1973) indicates that in early adolescence there is rapid reduction in parental control of time structuring. As adolescents assume personal control over their own time structuring, they become vulnerable to inadequate time management and boredom.

Disruption of Self-Concept

The self-concept of the child may become almost totally obsolete as he or she grows into adolescence. Rappoport (1972) states that "the teenager has to renovate, remodel, and reorganize the whole form; . . . his prior self-concept is no longer adequate" (p. 288). The basic argument here is that the developmental changes at adolescence, particularly the physiological changes, and the increased emotional, intellectual, and moral capacities, together with the loss of the child role, lead to disruption of the young person's self-concept.

It is not only the internal aspects of self-concept that require reorganization, but also the social position. Both Coleman (1974) and Rappoport (1972) point to the psychosocial reorganizations required in reference to morals and values, sex roles, achievement, religion, relations with teachers, peers, family, other adults, and aggression. The process of losing the self-conceptions of childhood inaugurates a major new task of adolescence, that is, the search to establish a satisfactory identity.

Ostrov and Offer (1978) note: "Characteristically, loneliness during adolescence is stamped with issues of mourning of one's own identity as a child and giving up certain forms of childhood attachments and beliefs" (p. 36). If the loss of such psychological and social reference points leaves the adolescent in a state of extreme uncertainty and confusion, it is not difficult to understand the escalation of needs for reassurance, guidance, and self-understanding among adolescents (Engel, 1959; Konopka, 1966; Marcia 1966; Rappoport, 1972).

The Struggle for Significance

During adolescence the emergence of a new profile of aptitudes, talents, and potentialities demands appropriate outlets and expression. Rollo May (1953) suggests:

> If any organism fails to fulfill its potentialities, it becomes sick. . . . If a man does not fulfill his potentialities as a person, he becomes to that extent constricted and ill. This is the essence of neurosis—the person's unused potentialities. (p. 95)

Further, he alludes to "the quiet joy when the adolescent can use his newly emerged power for the first time" (p. 96).

The emergence of new potentialities sets the scene for the struggle of the adolescent to find significant and appropriate outlets for them. If no such outlets are found, the adolescent may fall into the state of boredom, aimlessness, and restlessness that has often been identified as spiritual loneliness or meaninglessness (Buhler, 1969; May, 1953). The struggle for significance involves two separate challenges to the adolescent.

First, the young person must discover certain entities (other persons, causes, heroes, sports, values, or ideologies) about which he or she can feel enthusiastic, and which are important and valued. This process has been variously described as the development of emotional attachment bonds, sentiments, or normative integration (Brennan, Huizinga, & Elliot, 1976; Elliott et al., 1979; Hirschi, 1969; Kanter, 1972). In a similar vein, Allport (1961) used the term "self-extension" to refer to a person's struggle to find things that are important and valued. It is generally believed that if the person is unable to develop such attachments, his or her life will be empty, unchallenging, boring, and characterized by excessive preoccupation with self (Allport, 1961; DiCaprio, 1976).

Second, assuming that the young person has developed some internal attachment bonds, he or she needs to create or discover appropriate social roles, or modes of participation, to actualize his or her chosen attachment bonds. In Allport's terms the young person must then be successful in obtaining "worthwhile assignments." If such modes of participation are unavailable, or are not discovered by the youth, the results may include frustration, anger, a sense of loss, and perhaps the eventual erosion of the emotional sentiments and values that are being denied expression. Blocked participation in valued activities and roles has been explicitly related to a feeling of social isolation and loneliness (Brennan & Auslander, 1979).

Social Structural Factors that Induce Loneliness in Adolescents

Social structures and social processes provide an ongoing context within which the drama of adolescent development takes place. A large variety of social and cultural factors may contribute to the isolation and loneliness of many youth. These do not act as precipitators of any deficits in the social relations or attachments of the youth, but rather aggravate or undermine the youth's attempts to establish satisfactory attachments.

It is difficult to separate these social processes from each other and from the various psychological and personal factors that are also a part of the loneliness equation. It would require an enormous effort to elaborate all of the factors in the sociological analysis of aspects of social isolation, meaninglessness, and loneliness (Fabry, 1968; Frankl, 1959; Glasser, 1975; Klapp, 1969; Riesman et al., 1971; Seeman, 1975; Slater, 1970; Tournier, 1974; Wood, 1976). In this section we mention only a selected set of the main processes that affect the rejection and isolation of adolescents.

Inadequate and Marginal Social Roles

Rappoport (1972) writes, "The adolescent's social position is fairly clear, as compared with older and younger people, he hasn't got one." Rappoport describes the social role of adolescents as a sort of social "limbo" in which the adolescent enjoys neither the rights, privileges, and psychological supports of the child nor those of the adult, a status that Lewin (1939) has described as "marginal." This is probably an important part of the psychological isolation of adolescents. Role ambiguity, inadequate "role models," the absence of identification rituals and clearly understood "rites of passage," coupled with adult suspicion and mistrust, are among the features that deprive youth of a clear sense of belongingness, attachment sentiments, modes of participation, and a socially affirmed role in the society.

Excessive Rejection and Failure Roles

The ethic of competitive individualism implies that there may be a large number of potential failure or rejection roles within the society. A common reason given for the problematic nature of adolescence is that an inordinate number of adolescents fall into rejection and failure roles (Konopka, 1966; Stierlin, 1974). Competitive grading provides one source of failure roles. The early and continued absence of achievement experiences in school may make many youths feel inadequate and increase feelings of rejection and isolation (Konopka, 1966). Collier and Lawrence (1951) examined adolescents who could not compete successfully for desirable social roles, and found that these youths experienced a feeling of psychological isolation.

Excessive Expectations and Unrealistic Norms

Many commentators (e.g., Gordon, 1976) have argued that certain prevailing social norms and social expectations regarding youth may be inappropriately high, for example, that the teenager should always have dates, be popular, experience success, be beautiful, glamorous, or an athletic star. The mass media, parents, teachers, or peers may promote these values, and the adolescent somehow has to deal with such cultural expectations. If an adolescent does not keep pace with age-related expectations, he or she may feel left out, lonely, or inadequate (Klapp, 1969; Peplau & Perlman, 1979).

Social Comparisons within Adolescent Culture

The process of comparing one's social performance against others may magnify feelings of failure and rejection. The adolescent may assume that others are more popular, more successful, and less lonely. Such negative comparisons may lead the teenager to overestimate his or her own loneliness.

The Struggle for Independence

At least two additional family processes exist in which loneliness may emerge from the struggle for independence. First, if the adolescent is pushed by parents into premature independence, he or she may feel insecure and alone. The youth may not be ready for early or total independence (Konopka, 1966; Stierlin, 1974). Second, the struggle for independence may be thwarted or undermined by parents. Wood and Hannell (1977) stress that those youth who remain overly dependent on their parents may be susceptible to loneliness. Prolonged attachment to parents may undermine both the identity development process and the development of new kinds of peer and cross-sex social relationships (see Stierlin, 1974).

Bauer (1963) examined adult ambivalence and confusion regarding adolescent independence and argues that the behavior of parents and other adults may result in competition, anger, frustration, and misunderstanding on both sides. He argues that parents often frustrate the dependency needs of pre-adolescent youth, and that this process suddenly reverses itself in adolescence when the parents then undermine and frustrate the struggle for independence. Bauer sees many adolescents as being overprotected and overindulged. Thus their desire to strive for freedom, autonomy, and independence is perhaps weakened. An additional argument for this position is that the *whole* society, in various ways, is dedicated to the cultivation of dependency needs, not only of youth and adolescents, but of adults (Slater, 1970; May, 1953).

A widespread variation of this adult ambivalence is seen in the concept of the "foreclosed identity" (Marcia, 1966; Matteson, 1975). In this instance the adolescent's struggle to achieve an authentic self-chosen identity is undermined, usually by parents, who channel the youth toward commitments that are primarily chosen by the parents. Such commitments are adopted passively by the youth without the experience of exploration, discovery, and free decision-making.

In regard to loneliness, it may be argued that a foreclosed identity would obviate the natural development of personal sentiments, bonds, enthusiasms, and freely chosen commitments. Adolescents are channeled into a set of commitments and activities for which they may have no wholehearted feelings of enthusiasm. Deficits in affective internal bonding would likely arise from the process of foreclosure, and such adolescents might be hypothesized to suffer from feelings of meaninglessness or spiritual loneliness (Buhler, 1969; Fabry, 1968; Klapp, 1969).

Changing Family Structures

It has been argued, somewhat speculatively, that many changes in the American family lead to deficits in social relations. These changes include smaller families; increased levels of marital tension, divorce, and separation; parental role confusion; working mothers; family mobility; and separation of the nuclear family from an extended family. These have been implicated in arguments that children and youth find it increasingly difficult to obtain the warmth, protection, support, affirmation, and guidance that can satisfy their interpersonal needs. Feelings of loneliness and increased affiliation needs for a peer group are proposed as the likely result (Klapp, 1969; Konopka, 1966). The evidence for these assertions is, however, extremely mixed. Brennan and Auslander (1979) found no relationship between adolescent loneliness and the young person's number of siblings, whether the youth lived with one or both parents, and whether or not the family had moved frequently. The available evidence regarding family structure and loneliness is sufficiently inconsistent that assertions about the consequences of divorce, geographic mobility, etc. should be treated with caution.

Poor Parent-Child Relations

Lonely adolescents commonly report a complex pattern of negative, nonsupportive relationships with their parents (Brennan & Auslander, 1979; Rubenstein et al., 1979). Lonely youths report parental disinterest, limited nurturance, parental violence and rejection, low levels of encouragement for success, and negative labeling.

Blocked (Limited) Opportunity to Find Worthwhile Assignments

We argued earlier that a sense of belonging, commitment, and identity stems from the discovery of internal attachment bonds—enthusiastic sentiments, coupled with socially supported opportunities to actualize these sentiments. Social approval and encouragement, if provided, affirm the adolescent's sense of commitment and belongingness. However, the adult world may not provide anything significant for the adolescent to do (Henry, 1965). Although many youths have both energy and talent, they may face a society that seems incapable of creating adequate opportunities for them to use their talents. Konopka (1966) explores this issue in detail for teenage girls, pointing out the sense of emptiness, discouragement, and boredom that she believes results from this denial of opportunity. For example, jobs are simply not available for many teenagers. Where jobs are available, they are often characterized by limited future, trivial, menial, and repetitive tasks, low pay, and low intrinsic interest. New channels for social opportunity and personal achievement and social affirmation may be necessary. This problem and its solution appear to be located primarily in the world of social institutions rather than in youth themselves.

Some empirical evidence supports the connection between restricted social opportunity and high levels of loneliness. Brennan and Auslander (1979) found that lonely youths scored significantly higher on perceived blockage of access to educational, occupational, and recreational opportunities.

Personal Traits that Induce or Maintain Loneliness

A third and final class of variables that may profoundly influence the loneliness of adolescents consists of personal characteristics. Peplau and Perlman (1979) point out that the likelihood of loneliness is increased by personal characteristics that undermine either the initiation, maintenance, or quality of relationships, or that lead the person to adopt poor coping strategies in social situations or in response to deficient social relations. Personal characteristics related to social desirability can also result in the relative isolation and loneliness of certain adolescents.

The studies of adolescents by Brennan and Auslander (1979) and Wood and Hannell (1977) are consistent in finding that lonely adolescents are likely to have problems in all areas of interpersonal relationships (e.g., with peers, parents, and teachers) as well as in their feelings of personal success. The present review supports a suggestion made by Ostrov and Offer (1978) that most normal adolescents will have developed sufficient personal resources of self-esteem, trust, social skills and values to cope successfully with the challenges and possibilities of adolescence. Their strengths usually allow them to cope constructively with the emotional challenges of adolescence without the tendencies of escape, repression, denial, or other defensive tactics that seem to characterize lonelier youth. On the other hand, youth who lack such resources and psychological strengths may approach the challenge of adolescent life with lower feelings of competence, greater insecurity, anxiety, stronger feelings of vulnerability, and fears of rejection.

Low Self-Esteem and Powerlessness

Most available studies consistently find that the lonely adolescent has low self-esteem and stronger feelings of self-criticism (Wood & Hannell, 1977). Brennan and Auslander (1979) also found that lonely adolescents exhibit strong feelings of self-pity, unpopularity, and pessimism regarding being liked and respected by others. Both Ostrov and Offer (1978) and Middlebrook (1974) stress the relations between low self-esteem, feelings of vulnerability, fear of failure, and the tendency to withdraw from others. This withdrawal response would tend to increase the isolation of these youth. Feelings of powerlessness, external rather than internal control, passivity in regard to time management and in regard to control over both peer and family relations were found to be correlated with high scores on loneliness (Brennan & Auslander, 1979). Wood and Hannell (1977) found that feelings of low self-actualization were related to loneliness.

Apathy and Aimlessness

Earlier it was suggested that loneliness at adolescence would depend on the success or failure of the young person's struggle to develop internal commitment bonds. Apathy, aimlessness, and relative isolation might result from the inability to discover or develop such commitments. Brennan and Auslander found that lonely adolescents, to a much greater degree than non-lonely adolescents, were characterized by the following indicators of weak internal commitments and enthusiasms: disinterest in school activities, low educational and occupational aspirations, apathy regarding educational success, aimlessness, boredom, and confusion regarding personal values and commitments. Such apathy also extended to more general social relations, in which lonely youth showed a relative disinterest in gaining social popularity and in gaining social affirmation when compared with less lonely youth.

The lonely youth simply did not seem to care about other people or feel as strongly about certain goals to the same extent as the nonlonely youth. They exhibited less caring for their parents, teachers, peers, their schools, their educational and vocational futures, and even for themselves than most other youth. The profile of apathy, disinterest, and noncaring clearly suggests a state of emotional disconnectedness.

Shyness, Selfishness, and Poor Social Skills

Shyness, self-consciousness, inability to take social risks, and poor communication and social skills have been implicated in the loneliness of adolescents (Brennan & Auslander, 1979; Konopka, 1966; Weiss, 1973; Zimbardo, 1977). These characteristics may particularly interfere with the ability of the youth to initiate contacts with others. It has also been found that lonely adolescents are somewhat selfish, disinterested in others, mistrustful of others, and have higher scores for social paranoia than less lonely youth (Brennan & Auslander, 1979; Loucks, 1974). These characteristics can serve not only to isolate them but also to interfere with the quality and maintenance of their relationships.

This profile of the psychological characteristics of lonely adolescents is complex and multifaceted. These features would tend to push persons of any age toward social isolation and loneliness. The unique antecedents of the loneliness of adolescence seem to lie, not so much in personality predispositions (although these are clearly implicated), but in the novel set of developmental changes occurring at this stage of the life cycle and in the particularly vulnerable social position of the adolescent.

ADOLESCENT RESPONSES TO LONELINESS

An enormous variety of responses to loneliness are visible within the adolescent culture. The wish for popularity, acceptance, and a sense of belonging seems to drive many young persons into a frenzy of activities designed to establish a socially affirmed identity and to strengthen social affiliations. At first sight the range of adolescent activities that seem to fall under the general heading of coping and responding to loneliness appears chaotic. Adolescents join motorcycle gangs and religious cults; they bleach, dye, or grow their hair long, they wear ragged jeans, use drugs, indulge in sexual promiscuity, join communes, devote themselves enthusiastically to schoolwork, and practice all kinds of faddism. This variegated collection of behavior can be tentatively organized into a few general strategies. Cohen and Taylor (1978), Klapp (1969) and Peplau and Perlman (1979) have attempted to classify some general ways of dealing with loneliness. Klapp (1969) introduces the useful concept of "groping": "Groping . . . conveys the idea that a search is going on which is more or less in the dark, that what is being sought is not clear, that even having found it people are not quite sure what they have seized" (p. xi).

The behavior of adolescents in responding to the pain of loneliness, meaninglessness, and the task of identity building would appear to conform to this general concept. The analysis below conforms largely to the framework laid out by Peplau and Perlman (1979). It is acknowledged that the present section is speculative. To date there has been virtually no empirical research that has studied adolescent responses and coping strategies regarding loneliness.

Striving to Achieve Belonging

This general strategy has many variants. The basic goal, however, is to generate stronger attachments. Most adolescents participate enthusiastically in social activities (beach parties, picnics, high-school dances, discos, etc.) and also seem to have a strong motivation to join formal or semiformal groups (extramural school activities, organized sports, surfer groups, gangs of every kind, church groups, communes, fan clubs, etc.). Commentators (Coleman, 1974; Konopka, 1966) have repeatedly stressed the intense importance that teenagers place upon peer affiliations. Related to the high level of participation in social activities is a strong interest in maximizing social desirability. Enormous teenage markets have developed around the eradication of blemishes, teenage fashions, hair-styling, body-building, and so on.

Young persons, in their attempt to find a sense of belonging and meaning, often make mistakes. The pain of loneliness may make some adolescents vulnerable to the attractions of certain cults, fads, false gods, and superficial or vicious ideologies that demand mindless conformity or submission. In regard to such dangers Gardner (1963) writes: "There will never be a way of preventing fools from dedicating themselves to silly causes. There is no way to save some intense and unstable minds from a style of dedication that is in fact fanaticism" (p. 100). Thus the striving to achieve belonging contains dangers and involves some subtle decision-making. Adolescents who may not have the resources of patience, information or maturity to work through such difficult decisions may seize upon the first opportunity for belonging that comes along, no matter how superficial, shallow, hazardous, or damaging to their own developing sense of self.

Escape and belonging by means of romantic attachments is also a favored strategy. Teicher (1972) describes how certain lonely adolescent males desperately search and cling to intense romantic attachments. These attachments become the young man's major absorption, to the exclusion of almost every other person and activity. Teicher remarks on the clinging, dependent, passive aspects of this kind of relationship, and regards such relationships as pseudo-intimate, since they seem to be based largely on fear of isolation and loneliness. Presumably adolescents of both sexes may enter into such relations.

Surrogate relations are also clearly visible among adolescents. Television stars, sports heroes and rock stars may provide foci for the fantasy relations and attachments of many youth.

Lowering the Desired Level of Social Relations

Many adolescents use a second general strategy mentioned by Peplau and Perlman: they attempt to lower their desires for social relations. They may temporarily defer satisfaction of their desires, say for a romantic attachment, and instead devote their energy and time to education, vocational training, sports, or other tasks that are either highly valued or that they can enjoy alone.

Minimizing the Importance of Relational Deficits

Some adolescents will react to their loneliness by denial, or they may devalue social or emotional relations. Alternative gratifications such as sexual promiscuity, drugs, fun, alcohol, or rebellion may also provide a strategy for coping.

Adolescent Introspection and the "Turn Inward"

Excessive introspection and preoccupation with self are frequently noted as characteristics of adolescents. It may be hypothesized that this introspective tendency is a response to the various problems of adolescence, particularly those outlined earlier regarding the reorganization of self-concept and the discovery of identity.

Two forms of this self-preoccupation and aloneness may be delineated. One represents a positive and useful response to the confusion and loneliness of adolescence, while the other is less functional. On the positive side, the turn inward might be seen as a healthy withdrawal by the young person to explore, clarify, and question the confusions, challenges, and changes in his or her life. In this mode there is no dread of being alone. The intro-spection is useful in leading to increased understanding, awareness, and in-sights regarding his or her feelings about relationships, loneliness, identity, and commitments. This response to loneliness requires that the adolescent does in fact possess the ability to be alone, and that he or she can use soli-tude in these constructive ways. Many young people, however, may not have this capacity (Loucks, 1974; Winnicott, 1965).

The second and less functional kind of preoccupation with self involves a tendency toward narcissism, selfishness, inflation of self-evaluation, self-aggrandizement, and insensitivity to others. Since the motive in this instance seems to be self-bolstering, rather than a search for awareness and under-standing, this second strategy seems dysfunctional and may result in more pronounced isolation (Gardner, 1965; Lasch, 1979).

DISCUSSION

In considering the reasons for intense and widespread loneliness and the strong needs for affiliation at adolescence, we have examined three very general classes of background variables: developmental changes and their impact on affiliation needs and relationships; social structures and cultural processes; and personal predispositions. All of these are important in under-standing the loneliness of adolescence, and it is clear that they work in concert with each other. Different adolescents may therefore be lonely for quite different reasons.

The personal predispositions that have been identified as characteristics of lonely youth (shyness, low self-esteem, powerlessness, poor social skills, or disinterest in others) are obviously not unique to the adolescent life stage as causes of loneliness. Persons who have these personal characteristics would probably be isolated and lonely at any age. Therefore, although personal traits are important, the more unique reasons for adolescent loneliness are seen in the particular developmental changes and the unique social position of the person at this age.

Loneliness is often seen as emerging from changes that disrupt social rela-tions or create social deficits. The developmental changes that occur at adolescence appear to be particularly disruptive in this sense. There is both a loss of childhood ways of relating to peers, a transformation of the deep emotional attachment to parents, and a concomitant escalation of needs for relations, particularly with same age peers and with the opposite sex. The changes at adolescence therefore both disrupt existing patterns of attachments and soon produce powerful new needs for emotional attachments. These changes appear to lead directly to a deficit state in emotional relations. The emerging drives for independence, autonomy, and individuality as described earlier in this chapter would also be expected to lead to increased feelings of separateness and responsibility—and hence to stronger needs for affiliation and vulnerability to emotional and social loneliness. Existential loneliness, stemming from the new awareness of the self as a separate, finite being, combined with an increased sense of self-consciousness, seems to emerge at this age.

While developmental changes may be sufficient in themselves to propel a young person into a state of social and emotional isolation and existential loneliness, the analysis presented in this chapter implies that we cannot ignore the critical role of social structural processes. These in fact form a context within which the young person attempts to cope with the changes of adolescence and to build new relationships and find new modes of social participation. Some of the major social processes that negatively impinge upon the young person's task of developing attachments include inadequate and marginal social roles, inadequate role models, excessive provision of failure roles, prolonged dependency status, adult ambivalence regarding adolescent independence, unrealistic social expectations, and the loss or undermining of challenging and meaningful tasks. Earlier in the chapter it was argued that such social structural processes interfere with the development of internal commitment bonds, and that they may profoundly undermine the young person's attempts to find meaningful modes of participation. Many of these socially structured processes are particularly serious in the adolescent years. Some of them tend to diminish as the young person enters adulthood. Actually, social structures and cultural processes may have a profound impact on the loneliness of people of all ages (Cohen & Taylor, 1978; Klapp, 1969; Lasch, 1979; Novak, 1970; Slater, 1970). Adolescents, in particular, as they attempt to discover meaningful commitments and then to transform these into viable modes of social involvement and participation, are confronted with social processes that appear to undermine the search for meaning and that serve to block access to positive social roles. Isolation, confusion, anger, alienation, rebellion, and loneliness all are the multiple results of this situation (Clark, 1975; Coleman, 1974; Konopka, 1966).

Turning to the problem of the treatment of adolescent loneliness, we can make a few general observations. First, adolescents seem to be vulnerable to many different kinds of loneliness. It would be prudent to develop different intervention strategies to deal with each of the various forms of loneliness that occur for adolescents. Second, a certain amount of loneliness—particularly feelings of emotional isolation and existential loneliness—may be unavoidable at this time of life. Third, it is reasonable to suppose that the pain of loneliness may have a positive function in motivating the adolescent to upgrade and develop social and emotional relationships and to do something constructive about his or her needs for meaningful challenges, sentiments, and modes of belongingness.

A major goal for intervention seems to be the protection and strengthening of the internal commitment bonds of youth. The sense of apathy, meaninglessness, boredom, and disinterest is generally the result of ill-developed or deteriorated commitment bonds. Such apathy may be justified when held against the context of meaningless and ambiguous social roles, inadequate role models, rejection, and the relative powerlessness of youth. It would be mistaken to regard such apathy as simply a deficiency in the caring abilities of young persons, since it can so clearly be the result of social structural processes within the larger social context (Klapp, 1969). The situation is made more difficult by the fact that young persons, in their search for meaning and commitment, inevitably discover things to care about, for example, sports, heroes, rock stars, fashions, cults, or gurus. Some of these, unfortunately, operate to further erode the remaining bonds to conventional society and also perhaps to stultify or distort the continued intellectual and moral growth of the young person (Gardner, 1963). The discovery, support, and preservation of significant values, sentiments, and internal commitments seems to be a task of some urgency.

A second intervention at the social level is to strengthen social modes of participation for all youth. Certain youths are more vulnerable to the patterned rejection and stigmatization that occurs in many social institutions (Clark 1975). All processes that deny positive social roles to youth should be identified and modified wherever possible. Modes of positive participation and positive labeling should be found for those youths who currently occupy failing or peripheral roles.

At the psychological and behavioral level, conventional psychotherapies may have much to offer. These could be focused on the abilities of the young person to initiate and maintain satisfactory relationships. Problems such as shyness, poor social skills, assertiveness and aggression, dating behavior, and low self-esteem all seem to be amenable to specific psychotherapeutic approaches.

Turning to further research, we are only at the early stages of understanding adolescent loneliness. Epidemiological studies are required to more accurately map the age of onset, the extent, and severity of each of the major forms of loneliness across the adolescent years. Although a number of studies have examined the correlates of adolescent loneliness in areas such as personality traits and demographic features, there is a glaring lack of longitudinal studies that might unravel developmental sequences in background variables that precede the emergence of loneliness. Longitudinal data are required to fully describe and explicate the interactions between developmental changes and the various personal and social factors that have been linked to adolescent loneliness. The findings of such research would have important implications for the development of intervention strategies geared to the specific stage and type of loneliness of the particular youth.

A large number of more specific research questions also need to be addressed. These include the relation between adolescent loneliness and behaviors such as drug abuse, teenage alcoholism, and delinquency; loneliness and adolescent feelings of powerlessness; loneliness and parent-child relationships; loneliness and identity formation; and loneliness and the joining of cults. The development of better measures of loneliness, together with more appropriate cross-sectional and longitudinal samples of adolescents, should eventually lead to firmer understanding of this widespread problem of the adolescent life stage.

REFERENCES

Allport, G. W. *Pattern and growth in personality.* New York: Holt, Rinehart, & Winston, 1961.

Bauer, F. Problems of dependence and independence. In J. Bier (Ed.), *The adolescent: His search for understanding.* New York: Fordham University Press, 1963.

Bleach, G., & Claiborn, W. Initial evaluation of hot-line telephone crisis centers. *Community Mental Health Journal,* 1974, *10*(4), 387–394.

Bradley, R. *Measuring loneliness.* Unpublished doctral dissertation, Washington State University, 1969.

Brennan, T., & Auslander, N. *Adolescent loneliness: An exploratory study of social and psychological pre-dispositions and theory* (Vol. 1). Prepared for the National Institute of Mental Health, Juvenile Problems Division, Grant No. RO1-MH 289 12-01, Behavioral Research Institute, 1979.

Brennan, T., Huizinga, D., & Elliott, D. S. *The social psychology of runaways.* Lexington, Mass: Heath, 1976.

Buhler, C. Loneliness in maturity. *Journal of Humanistic Psychology,* 1969, *9*(2), 167–181.

Burton, A. On the nature of loneliness. *American Journal of Psychoanalysis,* 1961, *21, 34.*

Christiaans, X. Study of favorable and unfavorable influences on successful study in 200 students in a teacher's college. *Tijdschrift Voor Psychomedisch-Social Werk,* 1965, *12*(4), 155–163.

Clark, T. *The oppression of youth.* New York: Harper & Row, 1975.

Cohen, S., & Taylor, L. *Escape attempts.* New York: Penguin Books, 1978.

Coleman, J. S. *Youth: Transition to adulthood.* Chicago: University of Chicago Press, 1974.

Collier, R. M., & Lawrence, H. P. The adolescent feeling of psychological isolation. *Education Theory,* 1951, *1,* 106–115.

Di Caprio, S. *The good life, models for a healthy personality.* Englewood Cliffs, N. J.: Prentice-Hall, 1976.

Elkind, D. Cognitive development in adolescence. In J. F. Adams (Ed.), *Understanding adolescence.* Boston: Allyn and Bacon, 1968.

Elliott, D. S., Ageton, S. S., & Canter, R. C. An integrated theoretical perspective on delinquent behavior. *Journal of Research in Crime and Delinquency,* 1979, *16, 3–27.*

Elliott, D. S., & Voss L. *Delinquency and drop-out.* Lexington, Mass.: D. C. Heath, 1974.

Engel, M. The stability of the self-concept in adolescence. *Journal of Abnormal and Social Psychology,* 1959, *58,* 211–215.

Fabry, J. B. *The pursuit of meaning.* Boston: Beacon Press, 1968.

Ferreira, A. J. Loneliness and psychopathology. *American Journal of Psychoanalysis,* 1962, *22,* 201–207.

Frankl, V. *Man's search for meaning.* New York: Simon & Schuster, 1959.

Gaev, D. M. *The psychology of loneliness.* Chicago: Adams Press, 1976.

Gardner, J. W. *Self renewal—The individual and the innovative society.* New York: Harper & Row, 1963.

Glasser, W. *The identity society.* New York: Harper & Row, 1975.

Gordon, S. *Lonely in America.* New York: Simon & Schuster, 1976.

Henry, J. *Culture against man.* New York: Random House, 1965.

Hirschi, T. *Causes of delinquency.* Berkeley, Calif.: University of California Press, 1969.

Kanter, R. M. *Commitment and community.* Cambridge, Mass.: Harvard University Press, 1972.

Klapp, O. E. *Collective search for identity.* New York: Holt, Rinehart, & Winston, 1969.

Konopka, G. *The adolescent girl in conflict.* Englewood Cliffs, N. J.: Prentice-Hall, 1966.

Lasch, C. *The culture of narcissism.* New York: Warner Books, 1979.

Lewin, K. Field theory and experiment in social psychology. *The American Journal of Sociology,* 1939, *44,* 868–897.

Lindenauer, G. Loneliness. *Journal of Emotional Education,* 1970, *10*(3), 87–100.

Loucks, S. *The dimensions of loneliness: A psychological study of affect, self-concept and object-relations.* Unpublished doctoral dissertation, University of Tennessee, 1974.

Marcia, J. E. Development and validation of ego identity status. *Journal of Personality and Social Psychology,* 1966, *3,* 551–558.

Matteson, D. R. *Adolescence today: Sex roles and the search for identity.* Homewood, Ill.: Dorsey Press, 1975.

May, R. *Man's search for himself.* New York: Delta Books, 1953.

Middlebrook, P. N. *Social psychology and modern life.* New York: Knopf, 1974.

Mijuskovic, B. L. *Loneliness in philosophy, psychology, and literature.* The Netherlands: Van Gorcum, 1979.

Novak, M. *The experience of nothingness.* New York: Harper & Row, 1970.

Ostrov, E., & Offer, D. Loneliness and the adolescent. In S. Feinstein (Ed.), *Adolescent psychology.* Chicago: University of Chicago Press, 1978.

Peplau, L. A., & Perlman, D. Blueprint for a social psychological theory of loneliness. In M. Cook & G. Wilson (Eds.), *Love and attraction.* New York: Pergaman Press, 1979.

Phillips, M., & Pedersen, D. J. Unconsciousness IV: The new student mood. *Acta Symbolica,* 1972, *3*(1), 12–16.

Rappoport, L. *Personality development: The chronology of experience,* Glenview, Ill.: Scott, Foresman, 1972.

Riesman, D., Glazer, N., & Denney, R. *The lonely crowd.* New Haven, Conn.: Yale University Press, 1971.

Robert, M. *Loneliness in the schools, what to do about it.* Wiley, Ill.: Argus Communications, 1973.

Rubenstein, C., Shaver, P., & Peplau, L, A. Loneliness, *Human Nature,* 1979, *2,* 58–65.

Russell, D., Peplau, L. A., & Cutrona, C. The revised UCLA loneliness scale: Concurrent and discriminant validity evidence. *Journal of Personality and Social Psychology,* 1980, *39*(3), 472–480.

Saks, F. G. Current trends in youth service requests. *Social Casework,* 1974, *55*(7), 409–415.

Seeman, M. Alienation studies. In A. Inkeles (Ed.), *Annual Review of Sociology.* Palo Alto, Calif.: Annual Review, Inc., 1975.

Slater, P. E. *The pursuit of loneliness: American culture at the breaking point.* Boston: Beacon Press, 1970.

Stierlin, H. *Separating parents and adolescents.* New York: Harper & Row, 1974.

Stierlin, H., Levi, L. D., & Savard, R. J. *Centrifugal versus centripetal separation in adolescence: Two patterns and some of their implications.* U. S. Senate Hearings on runaway youth, 92nd Congress, 1st session, January 13–14, 1973, 193–210.

Sullivan, H. S. *The interpersonal theory of psychiatry.* New York: Norton, 1953.

Tanner, I. J. *Loneliness: The fear of love.* New York: Harper & Row, 1973.

Teicher, J. D. The alienated, older, isolated male adolescent. *American Journal of Psychotherapy,* 1972, *26,* 401–407.

Tournier, P. *Escape from loneliness.* Philadelphia: Westminster Press, 1974.

Weiss, R. S. *Loneliness: The experience of emotional and social isolation.* Cambridge, Mass.: MIT Press, 1973.

Winnicott, D. W. *The maturational processes and the facilitating environment.* New York: International Universities Press, 1965.

Wood, L. A., & Hannell, L. *Loneliness in adolescence.* Unpublished manuscript, University of Guelph, Ontario, Canada, 1977.

Wood, L. A. *Loneliness and social structure.* Unpublished doctoral dissertation, York University, Toronto, Canada, 1976.

Zimbardo, P. G. *Shyness.* Reading, Mass.: Addison-Wesley, 1977.

Chapter 18

Transition to College: Loneliness and the Process of Social Adjustment

Carolyn E. Cutrona

Coming to a large university such as this was a big change for me. After being voted in junior high and senior high school "Best Personality" and "Most Popular," I had to start over. Walking a long distance, seeing nothing but strangers was rather difficult at first, but I find myself getting used to it.

(UCLA Student, 7 months after arrival at college)

Leaving behind the familiar world of hometown and family to begin college requires starting over in many domains. As exemplified by the young woman quoted above, it is not possible to bring one's popularity or social standing from high school into the college environment. Distinctions earned in high school cannot aid in the process of finding a place for oneself in college. They are not only irrelevant but also commonplace. There may be a dozen merit scholars, and as many former student council presidents in a single dormitory wing. Especially if the student attends a college away from home, he or she is faced with the task of building a completely new set of social relationships. Friends known since childhood are often far away, beginning new lives in other parts of the country. As for romantic relationships, college students are faced with the problem of attracting the opposite sex in an unfamiliar arena, where they may or may not "have what it takes." Many individuals live away from their parents for the first time when they begin college. They are removed not only from the emotional support of their families but from the security

The author would like to thank Letitia Anne Peplau, Daniel Perlman, and Daniel Russell for their comments on earlier versions of this chapter, and Martin Bragg for permission to use his data in some of the analyses reported.

provided by familiar family routines. For some new college students, contact with family may be limited to an occasional phone call or letter.

It is not surprising, therefore, that loneliness is a serious problem among college students, especially during their first year. While loneliness can occur at any age, research suggests that late adolescence and early adulthood are times of especially high risk. A large-scale survey by Rubenstein and Shaver (Chapter 13) of adults between the ages of 18 and 87 found a significant *inverse* relationship between loneliness and age. That is, young respondents were the most lonely and older respondents the least. Other researchers have found similar results (Blau, 1973; Dyer, 1974; Lowenthal, Thurner, & Chiriboga, 1976; Russell, Chapter 6).

It is widely agreed that adolescence and early adulthood are particularly difficult transitional stages (Erikson, 1950, 1956; Freud, 1958; Sullivan, 1953). One important aspect of the transition to adulthood is establishing adult social relationships. Since college students all face relatively similar social situations, as contrasted with other 18-year-olds who take on a variety of jobs and living situations, they provide a unique research opportunity. In particular, studies of loneliness among college students may highlight individual differences in factors that contribute to successful social adjustment during an important developmental transitional stage.

Most new college students make a satisfactory adjustment by the end of their first year, but a significant proportion do not. Loneliness is not uncommon among advanced students, three and four years after the initial transition to college. Over one million students enter college in the United States each fall. One nationwide study found that over half drop out in two years and only a third complete four years (Newman, 1971). Loneliness is probably one important reason for this high dropout rate. Campus suicides and problems such as alcoholism have also been linked to feelings of extreme loneliness among college students (Lamont, 1979). Thus it is important clinically, as well as theoretically, to understand factors that enable some college students to make a satisfactory social adjustment, and factors that prevent others from doing so.

This chapter examines a wide range of factors related to loneliness among first year college students. One question concerns the causes of loneliness. Feelings of insecurity and isolation are probably experienced by most students when they first confront the college environment. However, for some individuals, certain circumstances or personal characteristics may make this initial adjustment more difficult and lead to prolonged feelings of loneliness. A second question is the impact of different kinds of social relationships on loneliness. For example, can a close group of friends compensate for the absence of a romantic relationship? A third issue concerns the type of relationship problems that are most likely to foster loneliness. For example, is loneliness more closely linked to problems of too few relationships, infrequent contact with others, or more subtle qualitative dissatisfactions with ongoing relationships? Finally, this chapter examines how students cope with and attempt to overcome their loneliness. What kinds of behavior or attitudes towards social relationships are particularly adaptive in adjusting to the university environment? The core of the following discussion is an analysis of the causes of loneliness among first-year college students, and the ways students use to avoid or overcome loneliness. This analysis draws on theory and on data from a longitudinal study of students during their first year of college.

THE UCLA NEW STUDENT STUDY

Sample and Methods

Participants in the study were students in their first year at UCLA. They were students in Introductory Psychology who received course credit for participation. A large sample of students ($N = 354$) was recruited to participate in two questionnaire sessions. The first session was 2 weeks after students arrived to begin classes in the fall, and the second session was 7 weeks after their arrival on campus. Data from these first two sessions were collected and analyzed by Martin Bragg (1979) for his doctoral dissertation. A follow-up study on a subset of this sample was conducted collaboratively by Daniel Russell, Letitia Anne Peplau, and myself. Seven months after their arrival on campus, we recontacted all of the original participants who could be located and asked them to participate in a third questionnaire session. A total of 162 students (46% of the original sample) participated in this follow-up study (64 males and 98 females). Students answered questions concerning both objective and qualitative aspects of their social lives. Loneliness was assessed at all three time points using the original UCLA Loneliness Scale (Russell, Peplau, & Ferguson, 1978), a 20-item self-report measure.

Loneliness

Two weeks after the school year began, 75% of the new students participating in the study had experienced at least occasional loneliness since their arrival on campus. Over 40% reported that their loneliness had been moderate to severe in intensity. The original large sample included approximately equal numbers of men and women from a mixture of ethnic backgrounds. No sex differences in loneliness were found. However, there was a relationship between ethnic background and loneliness, with Chicano students reporting somewhat greater loneliness than students from Anglo or other ethnic backgrounds (Bragg, 1979). About half the students in the sample lived in dormitories or other student housing. A third lived with their parents, and the rest in apartments or off-campus rooms. Two weeks after the beginning of school, loneliness was not affected significantly by living situation.

For the 162 students who were followed throughout the school year, the overall mean score on the UCLA Loneliness Scale at the first testing two weeks after classes began was 40.2. (Possible scores range from 20 to 80.)

This corresponds closely to the mean of 39.0 found in previous studies using college students (see Russell et al., 1978). At the second testing, 7 weeks after school began, mean loneliness scores had dropped significantly to 38.0 (t (161) $= 2.61, p < .01$). At the time of our 7-month follow-up, loneliness in the sample had dropped even more significantly to a mean of 34.0 (t (161) $= 5.75, p < .001$). By the end of spring term, only 25% of the sample reported having experienced loneliness in the previous two weeks. Thus, on the whole, students were quite resilient and made a good social adjustment by the end of the school year.

REASONS FOR LONELINESS

People are typically motivated to understand the causes of their loneliness (Peplau, Miceli, & Morasch, Chapter 9; Peplau, Russell, & Heim, 1979). Understanding the reasons for one's loneliness helps to make sense out of an unpleasant situation, and can be a first step towards correcting problems in one's social life. Attributions about the causes of loneliness provide important guides for coping with it.

At this point, an important distinction can be made between attributions for the onset of loneliness, and attributions for continuing loneliness. Lonely people can usually point to precipitating events that led to the onset of their loneliness. *Precipitating events* often involve changes in the person's social life, such as ending a love relationship or leaving home to attend college. Precipitating events initially cause a discrepancy between the person's actual and desired social relationships. However, when an unfavorable balance persists between the social life individuals want and the one they actually have, they may begin to consider *maintaining* causes of loneliness. Maintaining causes prevent people from adjusting to their altered social situation and achieving a satisfactory social life (e.g., shyness, lack of social skills, an inhospitable environment). Subjects in the New Student Study were asked to report both precipitating events and maintaining causes of their loneliness.

Precipitating Events

At spring testing, 7 months after their arrival on campus, students were asked open-ended questions regarding key events or situational factors that had triggered current or previous episodes of loneliness. Responses were coded into several different categories. As expected, most students cited leaving family and friends to begin college (40%) as the main precipitating event for their loneliness. However, others described a wide range of stressful events that triggered feelings of loneliness. These included the breakup of a romantic relationship (15%) and problems with a friend or roommate (11%). Family events, such as parental divorce, arguments with parents, or the marriage of a sibling were also cited as precipitating events for loneliness by some students (9%).

Somewhat more puzzling were statements that difficulties with schoolwork led to loneliness (11%). Students explained that sometimes the demands of schoolwork precluded social activities, or that after doing poorly on an exam, they simply felt isolated and lonely. One student described elements of both:

The fact that I was not used to studying [so] much caused me to be on probation . . . . There was no one to talk to me or encourage me to keep pressing on. I first felt that UCLA wanted to get rid of me and was totally uninterested in my unique problem. As a result, I withdrew myself and concentrated heavily on grades. School forced me to be antisocial.

Other reasons for loneliness were an isolated living situation (6%), rejection by a fraternity or sorority (3%), medical problems (2%), and having one's birthday forgotten (1%). Thus it appears that a wide variety of life events, some unrelated to social relationships, can trigger loneliness. One possible explanation for the link between stressful life events and loneliness comes from affiliation research. Schachter (1959) found that people seek companionship when they are anxious or frightened. That is, stress may increase the desire to affiliate. Entering college students must confront many unfamiliar and potentially threatening situations, such as the first final exam period. When facing such events, students' desires to be with others may be especially intense. The absence of a best friend or close-knit group may be felt most sharply at such times. Many of the stressful events mentioned above (e.g., parental divorce) may cause loneliness, both by disrupting the individual's accustomed social relationships and by creating a temporarily heightened need for contact with others. When this occurs, the discrepancy between desired and available social resources may be especially great, and loneliness may be particularly intense.

Maintaining Causes

While events that initially trigger loneliness may be easy to identify, factors that prolong or maintain loneliness may be more complex. Following a change in social environment, people try to adjust and remedy deficiencies in their social network. When these deficiencies persist and loneliness continues, the causal attributions people make for their loneliness may have a major impact both on their emotions and on their coping behavior. (For an overview of attribution theory, see Weiner, 1974, 1979.) For example, if students believe that their loneliness is caused by something beyond their control, they are likely to become discouraged and cease efforts to improve their situation. However, if they believe that their loneliness is caused by something within their control (e.g., not trying hard enough to be friendly), they are more likely to persist in efforts to remedy their social problems.

Our research examined whether there are differences in the causal attributions made by students who overcome loneliness and those who remain lonely throughout the year. (For related discussions of loneliness and causal attributions, see Bragg, 1979; Michela, Peplau, & Weeks, 1980; Peplau, Russell, & Heim, 1979; and Peplau, Miceli, & Morasch, Chapter 9). On the basis of free response data (Berke & Peplau, 1976), a list was compiled of 13 common reasons for loneliness frequently mentioned by college students. The list included both situational factors (e.g., few opportunities to meet people) and personal factors (e.g., shyness). Participants in the New Student Study rated how much each of these factors contributed to their own recent loneliness. Students rated the importance of these 13 causes at three time points (2 weeks, 7 weeks, and 7 months after their arrival on campus).

Loneliness may be prolonged when people misunderstand its causes. This misunderstanding may lead people to direct efforts at change to the wrong aspects of their social situation or to abandon all efforts at change. To examine the causal attributions of chronically lonely students, a subset of students was identified who labeled themselves as lonely at all three time points ($N = 22$, 13.5% of the sample). We compared this chronically lonely group to another subset of students who identified themselves as lonely in the fall, but not at the spring follow-up ($N = 84$, 52% of the sample). As shown

Table 18.1. Mean Importance Ratings of Causes for Loneliness [a]

	Chronically lonely (N = 22)	Transiently lonely (N = 84)	
	M	M	t [b]
My not trying hard enough to meet people	1.95	1.76	.68
Not enough opportunities to meet people	1.23	1.51	.82
My being too shy	2.45	1.51	3.06**
My belief that there's little chance of finding someone	.95	.73	.82
My personality	1.73	1.02	2.44*
Luck	1.14	1.02	.40
My fear of rejection	2.00	1.35	2.03*
My always being in impersonal situations with too many people	1.95	1.74	.72
My not knowing what to do to start a relationship	2.18	1.42	2.70*
Other people don't try to make friends	1.45	1.42	.13
My physical appearance	1.32	.95	1.33
Others are afraid to make friends	1.04	1.26	.80
Other people have their own groups and aren't interested in me	1.41	1.31	.36

[a] Students rated how important each factor was in causing them to be lonely in the past two weeks on a 5-point scale from 0 ("Not at all important") to 4 ("Very important"). Chronically lonely students defined themselves as lonely on a single self-report item at all three testings (2 weeks, 7 weeks, and 7 months after school began). Transiently lonely students defined themselves as lonely at the first testing but not the third testing on the same self-report item.

[b] df = 104.

*$p < .05$.

**$p < .01$.

in Table 18.1, there were significant differences between the chronically lonely and transiently lonely students' explanations for their loneliness. Table 18.1 presents data from the first questionnaire, given 2 weeks after school began. (Similar results were found at the second session 5 weeks later.) Students who remained lonely all year attributed their loneliness to their shyness, fear of rejection, lack of knowledge of how to initiate relationships, and their own personality more than did the transiently lonely. All of these causes refer to characteristics of the students themselves. Furthermore, with the possible exception of "lack of knowledge," all of these characteristics are relatively enduring or difficult to change.

Thus at the beginning of the school year, two distinct groups of lonely students could be identified. One group, who overcame their loneliness by the end of the year, blamed a wide range of both personal and situational factors for their loneliness. A second group, who tended to remain lonely throughout the year, blamed their loneliness on their own enduring traits. Students who remained lonely began the year with an attitude that may have inhibited active efforts to seek social relationships. They may have assumed too quickly that they were incapable of making and maintaining friendships. Efforts to help these students should examine their cognitions about the causes of their loneliness. Students should be helped towards a realistic understanding of their situation that will guide effective coping and encourage persistence in efforts to overcome their loneliness.

SOCIAL RELATIONS AND LONELINESS

Relationships with Family, Friends, and Lovers

At each stage in the life cycle, different kinds of relationships are important to people. For the young child, relations with parents are central. As children grow older, relations with peers become increasingly important. In adulthood, one's primary relationship is often with a spouse or romantic partner. Most individuals begin college during late adolescence, a time of transition between adolescence and adulthood. Thus the social relationships of college students may have features of both stages. What is the impact of different kinds of relationships on loneliness during college? Are bonds to family, friends, and romantic partners equally important in preventing loneliness, or does disruption of one type of relationship have greater impact than others?

In the New Student Study, satisfaction ratings of students' relationships with family, friends, and romantic partners were compared to see which best predicted loneliness. As shown in Table 18.2, degree of satisfaction with current friendships was a better predictor of Loneliness Scale scores than was satisfaction with either dating or family relationships. That is, dissatisfaction with friends was most closely linked to loneliness (see also Cutrona & Peplau, 1979 a).

Table 18.2. Impact on Loneliness of Family, Friend, and Dating Relationships: Stepwise Multiple Regression Predicting UCLA Loneliness Scale Scores [a]

Predictors	Standardized Beta
Satisfaction in relations with	
Friends	— .456
Dating partners	— .260
Family	— .182
Multiple R^2 = .42	
Frequency of contact with	
Friends	— .304
Dating partners	— .185
Family	— .013
Multiple R^2 = .15	

[a] Two separate stepwise regression analyses were conducted. In both analyses, both loneliness scores and predictors were assessed at the same time (2 weeks after school began). All subjects were included in the analyses who filled out questionnaires at all three time points. $N = 162$.

To obtain more objective, quantitative information about students' social lives, we asked students how often they had contact (phone calls, letters, and visits) with family, friends, and dating partners. Analyses determined whether frequency of contact with persons in a particular relationship category was most closely linked to loneliness. Once again, friendship emerged as particularly important. Infrequent contact with friends was a better predictor of loneliness than was contact with either family or dating partners.

Students' responses to open-ended questions concerning ways to overcome loneliness shed additional light on the issue of friendship, romance, and loneliness. Students who overcame their loneliness by springtime most often said that they became less lonely as the result of "gradually making friends with the people around me." Many of these students were not satisfied with their "love life" by the end of the year, but they were satisfied with their friendships. This suggests that for some students in this age group, making friends can compensate in some measure for the lack of a steady romantic relationship.

In contrast, students who remained lonely throughout the school year most often said that "finding a boyfriend/girlfriend" was the only way they would ever get over their loneliness. Students who remained lonely were dissatisfied with all kinds of relationships, but seemed to believe that their loneliness could be alleviated only through a romantic alliance. One possibility is that these students actually do require an intense dating relationship to meet their particular social needs. Another possibility is that they are simply overlooking the potential for overcoming loneliness through building friendships.

In summary, while first-year college students valued their relationships with family, friends, and romantic partners, friends were particularly important for avoiding loneliness. The distress that can result from feeling that one has no friends is illustrated by the following statement from a lonely male student: "I do not feel my interests and ideals are the same as other peoples'. I get especially lonely when I realize that I am an isolated person, alone even in a group. It's depressing because I might always feel this way."

The Social Provisions of Relationships

The previous section dealt with the impact on loneliness of relationships with family, friends, and lovers. This section takes a finer-grained look at the diverse psychological needs fulfilled by social relationships, and how each of these needs relates to loneliness. Robert S. Weiss (1974) proposed that there is a basic set of six "provisions" supplied by social relationships. According to Weiss, relationships tend to become "specialized" in their provisions. That is, different psychological needs are met by different kinds of social relationships, although a single relationship may offer more than one provision. Thus "social integration," a feeling of shared concerns and activities, is commonly provided by relationships with friends. For adults, "attachment," a sense of security and commitment, most often comes from intimate relations with a romantic partner or spouse. "A sense of reliable alliance," or assurance of continuing assistance, usually comes from relations with family and kin. Coworkers and colleagues can provide "reassurance of worth"; mentors and teachers may offer "guidance," and offspring provide an "opportunity for nurturance."

Although Weiss's typology is provocative, little empirical work has tested its usefulness. Our research group devised a measure to assess the extent to which a person's current relationships supply each of the six provisions. The Social Provisions Scale includes two items for each provision, one worded positively and the other negatively. For example, the attachment provision is assessed by the following two items: "I have a close relationship that provides me with a sense of emotional security and well-being" and "I lack a feeling of intimacy with one special person." Respondents rate on a 7-point scale the degree to which each statement is true for them at the current time. On separate rating scales, respondents also rate how *important* each provision is to them personally. The Social Provisions Scale was administered to all students who participated in our 7-month follow-up during spring term.

Turning first to importance ratings (see Table 18.3), students rated reliable alliance, social integration, attachment, and guidance as equally important. Reassurance of worth and opportunity for nurturance were rated as less important than the other provisions. Thus provisions associated with family, friends, lovers, and mentors were all very highly valued by students. At later stages of life, different provisions may become most important. For example, opportunity for nurturance may assume higher priority after marriage, when individuals are thinking of having children.

To understand the relationship between loneliness and each of the provi-

Table 18.3. Mean Ratings of Social Provisions [a]

	Personal importance	Extent supplied by current relationships
Reliable alliance	6.30	5.85
Guidance	6.31	5.77
Social integration	6.25	5.52
Attachment	6.10	4.65
Reassurance of worth	5.53	5.10
Opportunity for nurturance	4.30	4.08

[a] Ratings were made on 7-point scales. Means represent averages of two items for each provision. Data were collected 7 months after students' arrival on campus. $N = 162$. Copies of the Social Provisions Scale may be obtained from Daniel Russell, Graduate Program in Hospital and Health Administration, S-517 Westlawn, University of Iowa, Iowa City, Iowa 52242.

sions, students' ratings of how much their current relationships supplied them with each provision were entered into a stepwise multiple regression equation to predict Loneliness Scale Scores. Results showed that social integration was the best predictor of loneliness scores (standardized beta = .438). Second best was reassurance of worth (standardized beta = .289), followed by guidance (standardized beta = .197). None of the other provisions was a significant predictor of loneliness. In combination, the provisions accounted for 66% of the variance in loneliness scores.

Thus it appears that provisions associated with friends, lovers, and family are all highly valued, but that those associated with friends and colleagues are the best predictors of loneliness. It may be that the provisions associated with family relationships were not good predictors simply because they were generally well met in our sample (i.e., they had low variance). More difficult to explain is the finding that the provision associated with romantic bonds was not a good predictor of loneliness. Attachment had the highest variance of all the provisions. As discussed in the previous section it appears that for students in this developmental stage, it is more important that needs for friendship are met than needs for romantic affiliation. This appears to be true even though students themselves believe that these two kinds of relationships are equally important. There is evidence that later in college years loneliness is linked equally closely to romantic and friendship relations (Ferguson, 1977), suggesting that a developmental shift in social needs may take place during early adulthood.

Subjective Evaluations of Relationships

The cultural stereotype holds that when it comes to social relationships, "more is better"—more friends, more dates, more phone calls. However, we have taken a different position, arguing that loneliness is most directly related to satisfaction with relationships, not to frequency or number of social contacts.

This section presents data from the New Student Study concerning the relative contributions of quantitative and qualitative variables as predictors of loneliness.

Participants in the New Student Study were asked two general kinds of questions regarding their social relationships. Some concerned quantitative characteristics of their social lives such as number of relationships and frequency of social contact. Other questions concerned subjective feelings of satisfaction with current relationships. Separate analyses examined the relative impact on loneliness of quantitative and qualitative factors for relationships with friends, with dating partners, and with family members. For each type of relationship, quantitative and qualitative variables were used to predict loneliness scores. Results are summarized in Table 18.4.

Table 18.4. Impact on Loneliness of Subjective and Objective Variables: Stepwise Multiple Regression Predicting UCLA Loneliness Scale Scores [a]

Predictors	Standardized Beta
Friendship	
Satisfaction ratings	— .509
Frequency of contact	— .300
Number of close friends	.083
Multiple R^2 = .37	
Dating relationships	
Satisfaction ratings	— .310
Dating status	— .157
Frequency of dating	— .028
Multiple R^2 = .20	
Family relationships	
Satisfaction ratings	— .322
Distance from home	.120
Frequency of contact	— .074
Multiple R^2 = .12	

[a] Three separate regression analyses were conducted. In all three analyses loneliness scores and predictors were assessed at the same time (2 weeks after school began). All subjects were included in the analyses who completed questionnaires at all three time points. $N = 162$.

Subjective satisfaction with relationships was a better predictor of loneliness than any of the quantitative measures of social involvement (see also Cutrona & Peplau 1979a). Satisfaction with friendships was more closely linked to loneliness than either number of friends or frequency of contact with friends. Satisfaction with one's dating life was a better predictor of loneliness than frequency of dates or degree of romantic involvement (i.e. not dating; casually dating; serious involvement). Satisfaction with one's family relationships predicted loneliness better than frequency of contact with family or distance from home.

Because subjective satisfaction emerged as the most significant correlate of loneliness, further analyses were performed to examine what leads to satisfaction or dissatisfaction with relationships. Our data indicate that social comparisons, how favorably individuals felt their relationships compared to those of others, were of major importance. According to social comparison theory (see review by Pettigrew, 1967), people are motivated to assess the appropriateness or correctness of their opinions, abilities, and emotions. To the extent that objective standards of comparison are not available, people rely on social standards; that is, we compare ourselves to others in order to assess the adequacy of our own attributes and opinions. We are more confident that our own views are valid if they are shared by others. Particular kinds of people are most important in this self-validation process, namely, those who are similar to oneself in relevant characteristics. This perspective suggests that people may commonly compare their own social relationships to those of others, most centrally to those of peers. If an individual perceives his or her social relationships as deficient in comparison to those of peers, he or she is likely to feel dissatisfied and thus lonely.

In the New Student Study, undergraduates indicated how favorably they thought their own relationships compared to those of their peers. Social comparison appeared to play a major role in determining students' satisfaction with their relationships. The correlation between satisfaction with friendships and comparative ratings of friendships relative to those of peers was .64. In the domain of family relationships, the correlation was .70; for romantic relationships, the correlation was .77. Satisfaction with social relationships was more closely linked to social comparison than to number of relationships or frequency contact with others. Thus it appears that the cognitive process of comparing one's own social life to that of others plays a significant role in social satisfaction. Social satisfaction in turn has a major impact on loneliness. These findings suggest that people's standards for social relationships are a critical factor in social adjustment. Programs aimed at alleviating loneliness should recognize the importance of such cognitive factors. It may be that for some lonely people dysfunctional beliefs or unrealistic standards must be confronted before loneliness can be alleviated (see Young, Chapter 22).

PERSONALITY CHARACTERISTICS

Assessment of personality traits was not a major focus of the New Student Study, and few such measures were included. However, relevant data are available from a separate study of loneliness among UCLA students from all four college classes that was conducted by our research group (Russell, Peplau, & Cutrona, 1980). This study included measures of affiliative tendency and sensitivity to rejection (Mehrabian, 1970), introversion-extraversion (Eysenck & Eysenck, 1975), social self-esteem (Helmreich & Stapp, 1974), and assertiveness (Rathus, 1973). Lonely students had significantly lower self-esteem ($r = -.49$), were more introverted ($r = 46$), had lower affiliative tendencies ($r = -.45$), were less assertive ($r = -.34$), and were more sensitive to rejection ($r = .28$). A picture emerges of the lonely college student as an individual who lacks social self-confidence, is unassertive, and is sensitive to rejection. Clearly these characteristics impede the initiation of social relationships and may slow down the process of social adjustment.

ENVIRONMENTAL FACTORS

The environment in which people function can profoundly affect both their affective experience and their behavior (Barker, 1968; Moos, 1974). This section will discuss aspects of university environments that may bear on the ease with which interpersonal relationships are formed and the quality of these relationships.

During the 1970s, many universities increased their enrollments to meet rising costs, but did not adequately expand their housing facilities, which led to overcrowded conditions. Schools tended to build low-cost high-rise dormitories when they did expand. The result, according to a study of 12 major American universities (Lamont, 1979), was that students no longer felt that the dorms provided a homelike environment, and felt little involvement with their living places. Another consequence of expanding student bodies was very large classes, which do not promote the creation of bonds with faculty or classmates. Some observers believe that the psychosocial climates of many of today's highly competitive universities are highly detrimental to the creation of close cooperative relationships (Lamont, 1979). One student expressed his feelings about the university environment as follows:

This is a big impersonal school that treats people like numbers rather than people. . . . Here everybody cares about just one thing—grades. I like people. I like to be around them, and it was hard for me to realize that people don't really care for one another like high school, but for themselves and grades.

In the New Student Study, we obtained two kinds of information about environmental variables: the nature of students' living situations and their perceptions of the extent to which environmental factors had contributed to their loneliness. With respect to students' living arrangements, we compared loneliness scores of students who lived in group settings (dormitories, fraternities, co-ops) with those of students who did not. Surprisingly, loneliness scores were not significantly related to residence. This result is contradictory to findings by Ross (1979), who found significantly less loneliness among dorm dwellers than off-campus residents attending a Canadian university. The difference between the UCLA and Canadian samples appeared to be in the levels of loneliness among dorm dwellers. Dormitory residents at UCLA were lonelier than those in the Canadian sample; off-campus loneliness scores were comparable. Thus living in a dormitory at a large urban university like UCLA did not necessarily promote adequate social adjustment.

Students' perceptions of the role played by the environment in their loneliness was assessed as part of the attribution measure discussed earlier (see Table 18.1). An important difference was evident between students who recognized the impact of the environment and those who did not. Higher scores on the Beck Depression Inventory (Beck, 1967) were associated with personal rather than environmental attributions for loneliness (see also Bragg, 1979). At the end of the spring term, depressed students ascribed less importance to situational factors than did nondepressed students (t (160) = 2.81 p < .005). It may be that blaming themselves for their loneliness contributed to students' depression. These results suggest that college counselors should alert students to environmental factors that impede social relationships and avoid an exclusive focus on personal deficiencies. Students may require help in making realistic assessments of the extent to which they are responsible for their social difficulties, and the extent to which they are experiencing more situationally determined problems.

WHO OVERCOMES LONELINESS?

What enables some people to adjust to new social environments and overcome initial loneliness while others remain lonely? Participants in the New Student Study indicated steps they had taken to meet people, and various strategies they had used to overcome their loneliness. Data analysis examined two general questions: (1) What were the initial distinguishing characteristics of individuals who later overcame their loneliness as compared to those who did not? That is, how did these two groups differ at the beginning of the year? (2) What were the changes in social relationships and in attitudes toward relationships that occurred in conjunction with decreased loneliness? Discriminant function analysis was used to determine which variables best discriminated between students who overcame their initial loneliness and those who remained lonely at our seven-month follow-up (see also Cutrona & Peplau, 1979b).

Results showed that success in overcoming loneliness was not related to how far the student lived from his or her parents, nor to whether or not the student lived in a group residence such as a dormitory or fraternity. There were no differences between those who overcame loneliness and those who did not in number of social relationships at the beginning of the year. Two weeks after school began students in both categories said they knew an average of three to four people on campus well and five to seven people more casually.

Students were questioned about how they attempted to overcome their loneliness. Surprisingly, there were few significant differences between students who remained lonely and those who overcame their loneliness. Students who later recovered and those who did not reported about the same frequency of such activities as joining clubs, playing intramural sports, going to parties, and striking up conversations with strangers in classes. Both groups reported equally frequent attempts to attract others by improving their physical appearance or social skills. The two groups both reported that when they felt lonely, they tried harder to be friendly, or tried to find new ways to meet people. Yet for some students, these efforts did not pay off. A clue about why such strategies did not enable some students to overcome loneliness is provided by data on students' expectations and attitudes.

Students who later overcame their loneliness differed from those who did not in having higher expectations for future relationships, despite their initial loneliness (see Cutrona & Peplau, 1979b). In accordance with their low expectations for improvement in their social lives, students who remained lonely reported having changed or lowered their initial goals for desired relationships. (For example, they told themselves they don't really need a lot of friends, or that it's all right not to have a dating partner.) Students who were lonely at the end of the year said they had tried to cope with their feelings of loneliness by reminding themselves of other more positive aspects of their lives, such as work or creative efforts.

In general, students' attitudes were much better predictors of later recovery from loneliness than was their reported social behavior. To demonstrate this point, the best behavioral and attitudinal predictors were combined and contrasted, as shown in Table 18.5. Behavioral variables did not discriminate between students who overcame their loneliness and those who did not as accurately as did attitudinal variables. It should be noted, however, that our behavioral measures were quite limited. There may have been more subtle behavioral differences between students who made a good social adjustment by the end of the year and those who did not. For a discussion of observational data contrasting lonely and nonlonely individuals, see Chapter 15 by Jones.

Thus far, discussion has centered on predicting recovery from loneliness. But cognitive and social changes that accompany changes in loneliness were also of interest. Once again, the importance of friendship for individuals in this age group is apparent. Individuals who recovered from loneliness reported a very large increase in satisfaction with their friendships. The correlation between change in satisfaction and change in loneliness was .50. Increased number of friends also correlated significantly with decreased loneliness, but the correlation was lower ($r = .20$). Increased frequency of contact with friends did not correlate significantly with decreased loneliness, nor did changes in dating status. While the data suggest that making *more* friends was associated with recovery from loneliness, increased *satisfaction* with friends was more strongly linked to recovery. Thus one important process in overcoming feelings of loneliness may be deepening or enriching more casual friendships, so that they offer the relational provisions discussed earlier.

SUMMARY AND IMPLICATIONS

In the transition from high school to college, the entering student faces the task of adjusting to a completely new social environment. This transition can

Table 18.5.   Social and Cognitive Predictors of Recovery from Loneliness [a]

Predictors	Univariate F [c]
Social activities [b]: How often do you	
Go somewhere with a friend?	4.99*
Eat meals with a friend?	3.56
Telephone a friend?	2.51
Attend campus-related gatherings?	1.76
Go to parties?	1.52
Overall Wilks Lambda = .87; Cases correctly classified = 69%	
Cognitive variables [d]:	
Satisfaction with personality	7.66***
Believe that your personality is the cause of your loneliness	4.35*
When lonely, tend to think about your other personal assets	6.78**
Have lowered standards, goals for social relationships	9.33***
Expect social relationships to improve	5.34*
Overall Wilks Lambda = .71**; Cases correctly classified = 77%	

[a] Students who were above the sample median on the UCLA Loneliness Scale at time 1 (September) and below the sample median at time 3 (May) were termed "recovered." Students who were above the sample median at both time 1 and time 3 were considered "not recovered." Discriminant function analysis was used to predict membership in these two groups.
[b] Variables included in the analyses were the best five social behavioral predictors of recovery from loneliness.
[c] $df = 1,70$.
[d] Variables included in the analysis were the five best cognitive predictors of recovery from loneliness.
   * $p < .05$
   ** $p < .01$
   *** $p < .005$

be an exciting challenge that leads to significant personal growth. However, for some, the task is overwhelming. For these students, loneliness may be a dominant theme throughout their college years.

Findings from the New Student Study may be useful for people who seek to help college students going through this process of social adjustment. Our data suggest that certain dysfunctional attitudes play a significant role in maintaining loneliness.

One key finding from the New Student Study was the importance of subjective satisfaction with relationships. While number of relationships does have an impact on loneliness, people's qualitative assessments of their relationships have considerably greater impact. Thus it may be more fruitful to put effort into solidifying and deepening a few relationships than into pursuing a great number of more casual relationships.

Dissatisfaction with relationships can stem from many sources. One source may be unrealistic standards for social relationships. Our data suggest that students establish social standards through observing their peers. Students want their own social lives to be as exciting, busy, and full as those of the people around them. However, it is important to note that students' perceptions of peers' relationships may be quite distorted. The lonely students may not be aware of the evenings spent alone by admired peers. Thus one important task may be helping students develop realistic social goals for themselves, based in part on more realistic assessments of the relationships of their peers.

Another source of dissatisfaction with relationships may be unnecessarily narrow ideas about what is required for a gratifying social life. In the New Student Study, lonely students insisted that they needed a romantic attachment to overcome their loneliness. By contrast, students who recovered from initial loneliness were those who reported that they had built a satisfactory network of friends by the end of the year. Lonely students may overlook opportunities to befriend others because they are seeking romantic relationships. These students may not be aware of the "relational provisions" available through close relationships with friends.

An interesting finding from the New Student Study was that students who became chronically lonely believed that their loneliness was their own fault. Very early in the school year, these students blamed their loneliness on undesirable, unchangeable aspects of their personality. Thus they may have overlooked other reasons for their unsatisfactory social lives, such as environmental factors—large competitive lecture classes, or living in an impersonal dormitory. Recognition of such factors might help students use their energies successfully by changing their class schedule or moving to a more congenial residence, rather than wishing for a personality overhaul.

In recent years, behaviorally oriented assertiveness and social skills training programs have become increasingly popular in college counseling centers. However, as discussed in this chapter, students' beliefs about the causes of their loneliness, their standards for social relationships, and their perceptions of social norms can all serve to prolong feelings of loneliness. While it is important to help students acquire the behavioral skills necessary to initiate and maintain satisfying relationships, it is also important to address attitudes that impede social adjustment. This chapter has described a number of specific attitudinal factors that were empirically linked to loneliness and successful recovery from loneliness. These attitudinal factors were identified through studying how individuals actually coped over time with the transition to college. This kind of research has the advantage of yielding information that is directly applicable to a specific social problem. We hope that university personnel will find our data useful in helping students cope with the transition to college, and that other researchers will undertake similar studies of the process of social adjustment to other life transitions.

REFERENCES

Barker, R. *Ecological psychology.* Stanford, Calif.: Stanford University Press, 1968.

Beck, A. T. *Depression: Clinical, experimental and theoretical aspects.* New York: Harper & Row, 1967.

Berke, B., & Peplau, L. A. *Loneliness in the university.* Paper presented at the annual meeting of the Western Psychological Association, Los Angeles, 1976.

Blau, Z. *Old age in a changing society.* New York: New Viewpoints, 1973.

Bragg, M. *A comparative study of loneliness and depression.* Unpublished doctoral dissertation, University of California, Los Angeles, 1979.

Cutrona, C. E., & Peplau, L. A. *A longitudinal study of loneliness.* Paper presented at the annual meeting of the Western Psychological Association, San Diego, 1979a.

Cutrona, C. E., & Peplau, L. A. *Loneliness and the process of social adjustment.* Paper presented at the annual meeting of the American Psychological Association, Toronto, September 1979b.

Dyer, B. M. Loneliness—There's no way to escape it. *Alpha Gamma Delta Quarterly,* Spring 1974, 2–5.

Erikson, E. *Chidhood and society.* New York: Norton, 1950.

Erikson, E. The problem of ego identity. *Journal of the American Psychoanalytic Association,* 1956, *4,* 56–121.

Eysenck, H. J., & Eysenck, S. B. B. *Eysenck personality questionnaire.* San Diego, Calif.: Educational and Industrial Testing Service, 1975.

Ferguson, M. L. *Loneliness: Lack of romance or community?* Paper presented at the annual meeting of the Western Psychological Association, Seattle, April 1977.

Freud, A. Adolescence. *Psychoanalytic Study of the Child,* 1958, *13,* 255–278.

Helmreich, R., & Stapp, J. Short forms of the Texas Social Behavior Inventory (TSBI), an objective measure of self-esteem. *Bulletin of the Psychonomic Society,* 1974, *4,* 473–475.

Lamont, L. *Campus shock,* New York: Dutton, 1979.

Lowenthal, M. F., Thurner, M., & Chiriboga, D. *Four stages of life.* San Francisco: Jossey-Bass, 1976.

Mehrabian, A. The development and validation of measures of affiliative tendency and sensitivity to rejection. *Education and Psychological Measurement,* 1970, *30,* 417–428.

Michela, J. L., Peplau, L. A., & Weeks, D. G. *Perceived dimensions and consequences of attributions for loneliness.* Unpublished manuscript, University of California, Los Angeles, July 1980.

Moos, R. *Evaluating treatment environments: A social ecological approach.* New York: Wiley, 1974.

Newman, F. *Report on higher education.* Washington, D. C.: Department of Health, Education and Welfare. U.S. Government Printing Office, 1971.

Peplau, L. A., Russell, D., & Heim, M. The experience of loneliness. In I. Frieze, D. Bar-Tal, & J. Carroll (Eds.), *New approaches to social problems.* San Francisco: Jossey-Bass, 1979.

Pettigrew, T. F. Social evaluation theory: Convergences and applications. In D. Levine (Ed.), *Nebraska symposium on motivation.* Lincoln: University of Nebraska Press, 1967.

Rathus, S. A. A 30-item schedule for assessing assertive behavior. *Behavior Therapy,* 1973, *4,* 398–406.

Ross, A. *A cohort analysis of loneliness and friendship in the first year of uni-*

versity. Paper presented at the annual meeting of the American Psychological Association, Toronto, September 1979.

Russell, D., Peplau, L. A., & Ferguson, M. Developing a measure of loneliness. *Journal of Personality Assessment,* 1978, *42,* 290–294.

Russell, D., Peplau, L. A., & Cutrona, C. E. The revised UCLA loneliness scale: Concurrent and discriminant validity evidence. *Journal of Personality and Social Psychology,* 1980, *39*(3), 472–480.

Schachter, S. *The psychology of affiliation.* Stanford, Calif.: Stanford University Press, 1959.

Sullivan, H. S. *The interpersonal theory of psychiatry.* New York: Norton, 1953.

Weiner, B. (Ed.). *Achievement motivation and attribution theory.* Morristown, N. J.: General Learning Press, 1974.

Weiner, B. A theory of motivation for some classroom experiences. *Journal of Educational Psychology,* 1979, *71,* 3–25.

Weiss, R. The provisions of social relationships. In Z. Rubin (Ed.), *Doing unto others.* Englewood Cliffs, N. J.: Prentice-Hall, 1974.

Chapter 19

Loneliness: Antecedents
and Coping Strategies
in the Lives of Widows

Helena Z. Lopata, Gloria D. Heinemann, and Joanne Baum

This chapter examines factors contributing to the experience of loneliness in widowhood and strategies used by widows in American society to deal with this sentiment. The theoretical background comes from the current literature concerning loneliness and from Lopata's (1969, 1973a, 1979) studies of widows in metropolitan Chicago. Some of these ideas are then tested by Heinemann and Baum in two analyses of widows.

THEORETICAL BACKGROUND

Loneliness can be defined as the set of sentiments and emotions accompanying dissatisfaction with one's past, present, or future levels or forms of social relations, as the consequence of emotional or social isolation (Lopata, 1969, modified; Weiss, 1973). Loneliness is expected to be experienced by people who lose a spouse. This is especially true in American society, which assigns great emotional significance to marriage, to the extent of allowing its dissolution if the relation is not satisfactory to either partner, regardles of economic, parental, or kin disruptions. Although not totally isolated from the extended family, as suggested in the Parsonian (1943) model so frequently challenged by family sociologists (Stehouwer, 1968; Sussman, 1962), the family of procreation tends to live apart from other relatives and to function as an independent unit with high interdependence of members. Whether based on love or other positive sentiments, habit, need, or even conflictful interaction (or any combination of these), the formation of this unit and its continued existence involves at least some reconstruction of reality, self-identity, and support networks (Berger & Kellner, 1970; Berger & Luckman, 1966; Lopata, 1973b, 1975a). Because of the importance of the marital relation to those Americans who do not voluntarily separate, the society as a whole and we as

310

social researchers expect those who survive the death of a spouse to experience at least some loneliness. Of course many a spouse may actually have been lonely during marriage, but widowhood is generally seen as a major cause for loneliness in adulthood (Berardo, 1970; Buhler, 1969; Fromm-Reichmann, 1959; Riesman et al., 1950; Slater, 1970; Townsend, 1968; Tunstall, 1966; Weiss, 1973).

Previous research on widows indicates that loneliness is not a unidimensional experience, but rather includes a variety of different sentiments and feeling states (Lopata, 1969, 1973a, 1979). Weiss (1973, pp. 18–19) distinguishes two main types of loneliness, that of emotional isolation due to the loss of an important other person, and that of social isolation "in the absence of an engaging social network." Lopata (1969) concluded that widows can experience many levels and forms of loneliness, which combine into situational feelings or even a chronic state. Widows can experience loneliness not only in the present, but also as homesickness for the past and as "loneliness anxiety" for the future. Gordon (1976) found many lonely people in America so burdened by feelings of helplessness, failure, and worthlessness as to be too depressed to even try to alleviate this blanket of feelings (see also Peplau & Caldwell, 1978; Wood, 1978).

Lopata's (1969, 1973a, 1979) studies of Chicago area women found that these women expressed loneliness when they missed:

1. The main person who made them feel as a love object and as someone to whom they were important. This form of loneliness is especially devastating if women feel that there is no one else around who considers what they say and do to be important.

2. A love object, someone around whom they can focus a whole set of sentiments, providing the security of emotional attachment.

3. A companion with whom experiences and activities can be shared.

4. An escort in public encounters and events.

5. A team mate in couple companionate activities (see also Lopata, 1975a).

6. Another human being in the dwelling.

7. Another human being to share the work load in a domestic division of labor.

8. A style of life, resulting from being married, being married to that particular husband, living in a familiar neighborhood, being involved in activities through the husband, having a sufficient income to engage in many activities, having couple friends, and so on.

9. A comfortable relation with old friends, made difficult by the asymmetry due to the absence of the late husband.

10. The former support system, made partly dysfunctional by new needs and problems.

11. The former "self" that must now be restructured, in spite of feelings

of abandonment, of being rejected, of not being worthy of living or loving, lacking self-confidence in meeting new people or relating to old associates, and so on (see also Lopata, 1973b, 1975a).

In addition, grief work itself produces loneliness because it is so often accompanied by passivity-inducing depression, anger at associates or at societal resources over the failure to meet the sufferer's needs, and anger at the whole situation (Gordon, 1976; Lindemann, 1977; Marris, 1958). The future can also be visualized as bleak in terms of social relations, leading to loneliness anxiety (Parkes, 1973).

American society is aware of the high probability that its members will experience loneliness at certain times in their life or as a result of events, such as the death of a loved one, which disrupt social support. Society has built up an extensive and complex set of resources for social engagement, varying by community and region. Professional mental health personnel are trained for intervention in crises and for dealing with a variety of emotional problems. Medically trained people and hospitals care for the physically ill. Social workers, religious leaders, self-help groups, voluntary organizations including churches, and even commercial ventures can be used by lonely people to solve accompanying depression or to decrease social isolation (Bankoff, 1979; Barrett, 1977; Gordon, 1976; Lopata & Noel, 1967; Packard, 1972; Silverman, 1972; Silverman et al., 1974; Starr & Carnes, 1973).

Previous research indicates, however, that many widows do not utilize most of these resources in solving their loneliness problems. The use of professional mental health services is inhibited by a lack of familiarity with and willingness to use such resources, lack of connecting links, financial and time costs, and the fear of admitting to "mental problems," even loneliness (Lopata, 1978a; Riesman, 1973; Weiss, 1973). Most mental health practitioners do not specialize in the treatment of people going through bereavement as a natural process, and the stereotype of the mental patient is strong enough to push widows away (Schoenberg et al., 1975). Widows have to become severely disoriented or physically ill to come into contact with intensive intervention, and such cases are rare (Glassner, 1980). Organizations such as Parents without Partners or Widow-to-Widow programs are not available in many communities. Some widows do not wish to join such groups, feeling that they are depressing, too homogeneous, or composed of people unlike themselves in many ways. They feel stigmatized or oppressed by the need to "be a widow." At best, such groups cannot provide sufficient contact and activities to fill a lonely schedule.

Previous research by Lopata and others thus leads to the conclusion that American society has become so individualistic and voluntaristic as to require independent social engagement in its numerous resources. Many widows, especially the older ones, simply lack the knowledge, skills, and self-confidence needed to take advantage of such resources. Most are therefore dependent upon long-time associates, their family, especially their children, old friends, and neighbors in stable areas to serve as connecting links and alleviators of loneliness. However, widows vary considerably in the personal resources they have and are able to use. The more education a woman has, generally speaking, the more personal resources she has for social engagement on all levels and forms (Lopata, 1973a, 1973c). Educated women are better able to develop full and complex support networks—a variety of relations providing diverse emotional and social supports.

The importance of personal resources for alleviating loneliness in widowhood becomes apparent when we look at two specific samples of American urban widows.

TWO SAMPLES OF WIDOWS

Studies of two separate samples of women shed light on loneliness in widowhood. Baum (1979) investigated major problems encountered by widows in Madison, Wisconsin, and examined the strategies widows used to deal with loneliness. Heinemann (1979) conducted a secondary analysis of Lopata's 1974 widowhood data from a Chicago area sample. She focused on the relationship between loneliness and social supports. Although different measures of loneliness were used in each study, both researchers emphasized the extent and correlates of loneliness among widows, and the impact of family and friends on loneliness. Because of differences in the measures, the proportion of widows reporting loneliness varied considerably from one study to the other. Nonetheless, several similarities emerged with regard to the experience of loneliness in widowhood.

Sampling Procedures

The Wisconsin study used systematic, randomized sampling without replacement from the Madison City Directory to approximate a representative probability sample. A sample pool of 410 names was generated by copying the first widow's name and phone number on every third page of the Directory for the first half of the alphabet and on every fourth page for the second half of the alphabet to reflect in the sample the fact there are more people whose last names begin with A-M than N-Z. The list was numbered, and a table of random numbers was used to generate the 100 respondents. The researcher conducted telephone inquiries to set up personal interviews. (For further details see Baum, 1979.)

The Chicago sample was drawn by statisticians of the Social Security Administration from a master beneficiary record and from a less formally kept record of widowed women who had received a "lump sum" payment upon the death of the husband to help defray funeral costs. From these records, a stratified, random probability sample was drawn with systematic selection within five categories of social security recipients. Data were collected using structured personal interviews followed by a short self-administered form. Interviewers completed a total of 1,169 interviews. The subgroup under investigation in this study included only those 967 women who had remained widows after the husband's death. Data were weighted so that the number of widows in each of the five categories corresponded to their proportions in this particular universe of widows. In weighting these data, an attempt was made to approximate the original sample size so that tests of statistical significance could be used in the analysis. (For further details about this sample, see Lopata, 1979.)

Characteristics of the Widows

Age

The Madison sample had a mean age of 67 years; 8% were under 55 years of age and 50% were under the age of 65. Thirty percent of the widows were in the "old-old" age category of 75 or older as defined by Neugarten (1968). The median age for the Chicago area sample was 69 years, which approximates the median age for widowed women in this country (Carter & Glick, 1970). The average age of the widow at the time of her husband's death was 56 years. Overall, these women were long-term wives and widows. Their average length of marriage was 30 years; their average widowhood period was 10 years. The vast majority of the Chicago widows (92%) had been widowed only once. For those women who had been widowed more often, information was collected about their most recent widowhood experience.

Children and Living Arrangements

The Madison widows reported an average of 2.4 living children. Ten percent of this group had six or more children, while 12% were childless. Children's proximity to their widowed mothers ranged as follows: living in the same household (19% of the widows), living on the same block or immediate neighborhood (9%), living in the Madison area (65%), living outside the Madison area, but in Wisconsin (41% of the widows had at least one child here), or living in another state or country (65% of the widows had at least one child here.) More widows in this sample lived with sons than with daughters, which is contrary to the earlier findings of Lopata (1971, 1973a, 1979) and Shanas et al. (1968).

Almost half of the widows in the Chicago area sample had been residents of this area all their lives. The majority of them (82%) were household heads, and slightly over half of them owned their own homes. Forty-six percent were living alone at the time of the survey. All but 9% had at least one living child.

Education, Income, and Race

The Madison widows were better educated and better off financially than their Chicago area counterparts. Twenty-six percent of the Madison widows had completed less than a high school education, and 35% had a terminal degree from high school. An additional 38% had received a special diploma from a technical school or a Bachelor's, Master's, or PhD degree. Thus approximately 74% of these widows had obtained a high school education or better. As a result of their relatively high level of education, probably matched by a similarly high level among the late husbands, these widows were reasonably well off financially. Only 31% were living on less than $6,000 in 1976. This figure is balanced by 25% who reported incomes of at least $10,000. The median income for this group was approximately $8,000. Thirty-three percent of the respondents were employed at the time of the study. Ten percent had never worked for pay outside of the home.

The average number of years of schooling completed by the Chicago widows was 10; approximately 40% of the widows were high school graduates or went beyond that level. Their median total yearly household income was $4,000 in 1973. Slightly over a fourth were in the labor force at the time of the survey, and a similar proportion had never been employed.

All of the Madison widows were white, as were most (85%) of the Chicago area widows.

EXTENT OF LONELINESS: CORRELATES AND DETERMINANTS

Madison Widows

The Madison widows reported about loneliness in response to a list of 25 potential problems that might be encountered in widowhood (see Baum, 1979). Responses to a variety of open-ended questions also contained information about loneliness. Eighty-six percent of the Madison widows had encountered loneliness in widowhood, an amazingly similar proportion to that reported by Lopata (1969, 1973a) in response to a similar open-ended question. Seventy-five percent of the widows who had no living children reported loneliness, compared to 61% of widows with one or two children and 39% of those with three or more children. These findings suggest the importance of children's presence, since the more children one has, the higher the likelihood of contact with at least one child; and the greater the contact, the less lonely one feels. Shanas and her associates (1968) also reported that widows in contact with children were less apt to report loneliness than were women with other types of intimates in America, England, or Denmark.

Loneliness for the deceased husband was more frequently reported by widows whose late husbands had been ill for less than 6 months before death (63%) than by widows whose late husbands had been ill for longer periods of time (37%). These findings support Neugarten's (1968) and Parkes' (1975) conclusions that "unexpected and untimely" bereavement is more difficult for widows than is "expected, on time" bereavement. Widows who reported very positive characteristics of the late husband and of married life on the Lopata (1979) "husband sanctification scale" were more likely to be lonely (65%) than widows who felt less positively toward the late husband (35%).

The old adage that "time heals all wounds" was not true for these widows. Only 10% more of the women who had been widowed less than 6 years than those widowed at least 6 years reported loneliness (55% and 45%, respectively). These findings are similar to those reported by Shanas and associates (1968) that 55% of the British women widowed for 5 years or less were lonely, and that the proportion of lonely widows remained relatively high (38%) among British women widowed for 20 years or more.

Madison widows who reported more positive attitudes toward their life situations and toward other people on selected items of Lopata's (1973a) "relations-restrictive scale" were much less likely to report loneliness than were the widows with more negative attitudes (45% compared to 58%). This suggests the influence that a person's general attitudes and self-concept have upon subjective definitions of loneliness.

Religious preference was also significantly related to loneliness. More lonely widows tended to be Protestant (69%) than Catholic (31%). Perhaps this association is related to presence and contact with children, since Census data show that Catholic families have more children than do Protestant ones.

The last factor associated with loneliness among the Madison sample of widows was occupation. Seventy-five percent of the lonely widows had been employed in white collar occupations, while only 25% had been employed in blue collar occupations. This corroborates Lopata's (1973a) findings that women in white collar occupations seem to have better and closer relationships with their husbands, and are more lonely in widowhood because they miss the significant roles their husband had in their lives. There was an interaction between attitudes toward the late husband and type of employment; widows who had positive attitudes and were employed in white collar occupations were even more lonely than other widows.

Interestingly, a widow's age, education level, and income level were not associated with loneliness; however, widows who did not know their household income or did not choose to report income were lonely. This suggests that dependent women may experience more loneliness than independent ones in widowhood.

In summary, for widows in Madison, Wisconsin, loneliness was associated with: (1) having no or, at most, one or two children; (2) having had an unexpected bereavement; (3) having positive attitudes toward the late husband; (4) having been widowed for less than 6 years (although loneliness tends to persist over time as well); (5) having negative attitudes toward self and others in widowhood; (6) being Protestant; and (7) having been employed in a white collar occupation.

Chicago Area Widows

Chicago area widows were asked questions comparing their levels of loneliness to those of other people. A first composite measure included precoded questions about: (1) current level of felt loneliness (more lonely than most people, about as lonely as others, less lonely than others, or rarely or never lonely); (2) the desire for more friends (a 4-point scale ranging from strongly agree to strongly disagree); and (3) satisfaction with the way life is going presently (a 4-point scale ranging from strongly agree to strongly disagree). A second measure of loneliness—loneliness for the late husband himself—was measured from interviewers' perceptions of whether the widows were grieving or not on a 6-point scale.

Although various forms of loneliness were identified among Chicago area widows in previous studies, few of the women in this sample admitted loneliness in response to a direct question asking them to compare the level they experienced to that of other people. Sixty-one percent of these women believed they were less lonely than most people; slightly over half (56%) had no desire for more friends; and 79% were satisfied with the way their life was going. On a loneliness measure ranging from 1 (most lonely) to 12 (least lonely), the widows' average score was 8.3. This same pattern was evident with regard to grieving. On a scale from 1 (grieving) to 6 (nongrieving), the widows' average was 4. The majority of the Chicago area widows were not seen as heavily grieving mainly because they were long-term widows who had adapted to the loss of their spouse.

Loneliness was, however, a reality for a significant minority of the Chicago area widows. Approximately 20 to 25% of the total sample were lonely or grieving. Extreme loneliness was evident in a smaller proportion of the widows. Ten percent felt they were more lonely than most people. A strong desire for more friends was expressed by 16%, and 6% were strongly dissatisfied with life. Only 2% of the widows, however, scored in the lowest third of the distribution on both the composite measure of loneliness and grieving.

Among Chicago area widows, loneliness was related to age. Table 19.1 shows that loneliness and grieving were most prevalent among the young and middle-aged widows (under 60 years of age) and least prevalent among the old-old women (75 or over). A one-way analysis of variance showed that the differences among the means for each life stage with regard to loneliness and grieving were small, but statistically significant at the .001 level. For the

Table 19.1. Life Stage Trends in Experiencing Some Degree of Loneliness among Chicago Widows

Loneliness	Young and middle-aged	Young-old	Old-old	Total
Composite measure of				
loneliness (1–6)	27%	23%	15%	21%
N (weighted)	(262)	(457)	(301)	(1024)
Measure of grieving (1–3)	31%	28%	13%	25%
N (weighted)	(259)	(449)	(301)	(1012)

Chicago area widows, age and length of widowhood were positively correlated. Baum found no relationship between age and loneliness among the Madison widows, but she did report a negative relationship, although a low one, between length of widowhood and loneliness.

Regression analyses were used to examine the relationship between loneliness and other variables, most notably the strength of family and friendship support systems (measured by the availability of at least one role partner with whom interaction occurred within the year or who contributed to the economic, service, social, or emotional support systems). Taken together, these measures explained only 1% of the variance in loneliness and in grieving (see Heinemann, 1979, for details of the analysis). For loneliness, support from friends (but not from family) was a significant predictor. For the measure of grieving, support system strength involving family was a significant determinant. In this case, however, grieving widows had *stronger* family supports than nongrieving widows.

To improve predictive ability, several additional variables were added to the regression model. These included personal characteristics (age, number of children, health problems, length of widowhood), personal resources (employment history, education completed, yearly household income), social participation (religious involvement, number of social activities, and number of active organizational memberships), and social-psychological attributes (perceived hostility, idealization of the late husband). This expanded model explained 8% of the variance in the composite measure of loneliness and 11% of the variance in the measure of grieving.

For the composite measure of loneliness, physical health problems, friendship support system strength, number of social activities, and age were each significant ($p < .05$) determinants. The measure of grieving was significantly predicted by physical health problems, age, and scores on a sanctification of the husband scale. This later scale (Lopata, 1979) includes such items as "My husband had no irritating habits." Interestingly enough, family support system strength was no longer a significant determinant of grieving when additional variables were introduced into the regression model. These findings indicate that nonlonely widows tend to be healthy, elderly, socially active, and supported by friends. Grieving widows tend to have physical health problems and to idealize their late husband. It is important to note that these demographic and structural variables as a group were significant but weak predictors of loneliness.

Table 19.2 summarizes the characteristics of the lonely widows in the Madison and Chicago area studies. In both studies, loneliness was related to holding positive attitudes about the late husband. There was also a tendency (clearest in the Chicago data) for loneliness to decrease over time. Although these analyses shed light on demographic and structural characteristics of lonely widows, they also point to the importance of other determinants of loneliness that may be more elusive and difficult to measure.

Table 19.2. Characteristics of Lonely Widows

Madison, Wisconsin sample	Chicago area sample [a]
1. No or few children	1. Physical health problems
2. Unexpected bereavement	2. Idealization of late
3. Positive attitude toward	husband
late husband	3. Withdrawn from social
4. Short widowhood period	activities
(less than 6 years)	4. Young and middle-aged
5. Negative attitudes toward	5. Short widowhood period
self and others	(age correlated with
6. Protestant religious	length of widowhood .40)
preference	6. Weak friendship support
7. White collar occupation	system

[a] Characteristics associated with one or both loneliness measures (i.e., loneliness and grieving).

STRATEGIES FOR DEALING WITH LONELINESS

A central focus of analyses concerned possible ways in which widows might make use of formal community supports, of family and friends, and of themselves as resources for dealing with loneliness.

Formal Supports

Widows in Madison were more likely than widows in metropolitan Chicago to use formal, community-developed resources for dealing with loneliness. This difference may be due to the generally higher socioeconomic background and situation of Madison widows or to differences in the ease of social engagement in the two communities.

In Madison, approximately 31% of widows used churches, 27% used travel, 20% used voluntary associations, and 22% used "activities" outside of the home. Fifteen percent made efforts to meet new people, and 14% used work to cope with loneliness. This last resource was used relatively often when one considers that 76% of the widows were retired. Forty percent of these widows used at least two of these formal resources together, and 17% used three or more. Most of the women, however, were not dependent upon the secondary resources as their only strategy for alleviating loneliness, usually listing them in conjunction with more primary or personal ones. Thus 43% turned both to friendship and formal groups, 37% combined them with close family relations, 33% added extended family and friendships, 14% used extended family, friends and formal groups, and 9% combined both levels of family with the more formal resources.

The Chicago area widows who were socially active were not lonely, but they were involved in other, more personal social interactions. Thus women who were involved in roles away from home and friends tended also to have these primary resources. On the other hand, organizational involvement did not guarantee expressions of nonloneliness.

Although some widows are able to use "public" resources for social engagement, because of personal resources and community stability, neither sample of women utilized the helping professions and groups in order to alleviate feelings of loneliness. Thus the assumption stated in the theoretical introduction that such resources do not attract even those women who claim loneliness as a major problem of widowhood is born out by both studies. Churches are listed, but not church leaders such as priests, ministers, or rabbis. In fact, these people are most often listed as failing to assist the widow even at the time of the husband's illness and immediately after his death. They are definitely absent from the support systems of women already established as widows, and for the most part they are not turned to when loneliness is experienced either in Madison or in Chicago (see also Lopata, 1978a).

For widows, the main providers of support and alleviators of loneliness are family and friends, although women differ in which type of relation provides which type of support.

Family and Friends (Informal Supports)

Madison Widows

In her study of widows, Baum distinguished primarily resources (of children, siblings, and parents) from secondary resources (of other relatives and in-laws). Among widows experiencing loneliness, 55% identified their children as important resources in alleviating it. Approximately 40% of these widows identified at least one sibling as an important resource, and 30% used siblings in conjunction with children for alleviating loneliness.

Only 10% used parents, mainly because so many parents were no longer living or able to provide company. Other relatives and in-laws were utilized by 15% and 12%, respectively. In addition, 8% of the lonely widows used other relatives in conjunction with a child or a sibling, and 10% used in-laws with a child and a sibling. These findings indicate primary resources—children and siblings—were much more important in coping with loneliness than other relatives and in-laws. This finding supports Lopata's (1978a) research. When secondary family resources were utilized, they tended to be used in conjunction with a child or a sibling.

Turning to friendship, 61% of the Madison widows who defined loneliness as one of their problems used friends, and 33% used neighbors as resources in alleviating this feeling. Approximately one in four lonely widows turned to both friends and neighbors at such times. Thus the widows' resources involved friends as frequently as family in coping with loneliness. A large number of women, however, did not list friends, reminiscent of Lopata's (1979) finding that one in six widows claimed no friends before the husband's fatal illness or accident and made none since his death. Friendship of emotional significance is reported much more frequently among middle class women than among working class widows.

An examination of the relationship between the widows' friendship and family resources revealed that often widows used friends in conjunction with family members to cope with loneliness. Forty-four percent of the widows used friends in conjunction with a primary family resource, while 17% used friends with a secondary family resource. Neighbors were not used as often as friends in combination with family members to alleviate loneliness; 26% of the lonely widows used neighbors with primary family resources; and only 8% used neighbors with secondary family resources. Interestingly, in most cases where neighbors were used with primary or secondary family resources, the widows used friends as well. The strategies in these cases included friends, neighbors, and primary family resources (20% of the lonely widows) and friends, neighbors, and secondary family resources (8%).

The two most widely used resources to alleviate loneliness among the widows were friends or children, followed by siblings, neighbors, and children and siblings used together (see Table 19.3).

Table 19.3. Use of "Self" as a Resource in Conjunction with Family, Friends, and Formal Resources among Lonely Madison Widows

Resources utilized	Percent of utilization
Self	66
Self and primary family resources	48
Self and friendship resources	44
Self and formal resources	43
Self, friendship, and primary family resources	34
Self, formal, and friendship resources	29
Self, primary family, and formal resources	27
Self and secondary family resources	19
Self, friendship, primary and secondary family resources	17
Self, primary and secondary family resources	15
Self, friendship, primary or secondary family, and formal resources	10
Self, secondary family, and formal resources	10
Self, primary and secondary family, and formal resources	7

These findings reflect the importance of widows' informal support in strategies to alleviate loneliness. Such findings suggest that widows need to remain in contact with their families and friends beyond the immediate bereavement period, as these people provide valuable resources in coping with loneliness.

Chicago Area Widows

Overall, the relationships between the two measures of loneliness and the two types of support system strength were not strong in the Chicago sample. However, the directions of these relationships suggest that family and friendship support systems function differently for the widows with regard to loneliness. That is, while the relationships between family support system strength and the composite measure of loneliness were not statistically significant, the direction of the relationships suggests that family supportiveness does not alleviate loneliness. Conversely, the relationship between this loneliness measure and friendship support system strength indicates that friendship supports tend to be stronger for the nonlonely widow ($r = .11, p < .001$).

The relationships between both family and friendship support system strength and the measure of grieving were in the same direction; however, the former was significant, while the latter was not. The grieving widow tends to have stronger informal supports than does the nongrieving widow, especially among family members ($r = -.10, p < .01$).

The relationships between support system strength and the loneliness measures showed some interesting variations among the three life stage groups of widows. Among the young and middle-aged women (those under 60 years of age), neither type of support system strength was associated with the composite measure of loneliness. Among older widows, however, significant relationships were found between social support and loneliness. Among the young-old widows (ages 60 to 74), the nonlonely were most likely to have strong support systems of both types. Among the old-old widows (aged 75 and over), the lonely were most likely to have strong family supports and, the nonlonely, to have strong friendship supports.

Summary

The findings from both these studies support the importance and use of informal supports by widows in coping with loneliness. Baum showed that Madison widows used family, friends, and combinations of family and friends as strategies to alleviate loneliness. Heinemann found that those Chicago area widows who were lonely had stronger support systems among their family members than among their friends, although the relationship between loneliness and strong family supports was not always a significant one. Her findings suggest that family members tend to be more often involved with and more supportive of elderly widows than young and middle-age ones who suffer from loneliness. An alternative interpretation of these findings might be that Chicago area widows were able to alleviate loneliness through strong friendship support systems, and that while family members tend to be supportive of lonely widows, their support does not alleviate the loneliness.

The Self as a Resource

Widows often identified themselves as a resource for dealing with loneliness (see Table 19.3). In the Madison sample, 66% of widows mentioned the "self" as a resource for this purpose. In this sample, 48% of widows used the self as a resource in combination with other primary family resources as a strategy for coping with loneliness. Approximately 19% used the self with secondary family resources, and 15% combined self with both primary and secondary family resources. The self was used in conjunction with friendship resources by 44% of the Madison widows.

The Madison data support Lopata's (1979) conclusions as to the importance of the "self" as a resource upon which a widow can draw when facing loneliness. The self serves not only as a reservoir of memories, but as a definer of the situation. This fact came out clearly when the Chicago area widows were asked how lonely they were in comparison to other people. Women who had experienced the loneliness of "homesickness" for a prior lifestyle and for the late husband, in whatever form or component, were very likely to state that they were about "as lonely as other people" (29%). Others claimed to "very rarely" (24%) or "never" (15%) feel lonely (Lopata, 1980).

CONCLUSIONS

The studies discussed here shed light on the antecedents and strategies used to alleviate loneliness in widowhood. Many widows report loneliness when asked about the problems of widowhood, although few respond that they are the "most lonely person I know" or "more lonely than most people." Age, circumstances of their lives as wives, health problems, the severity and length of the husband's illness, length of widowhood, all influence whether or not a widow reports that she is lonely. Loneliness and husband sanctification or idealization to the point of converting the late husband into a saint go together. Loneliness is often experienced as relative deprivation, not in comparison to other people, but to one's own past, when the husband was well and life was moving along in an established way. Loneliness is particularly likely to occur among American widows because of this society's stress on marriage and on couple companionate relations.

American society has created numerous resources for the social integration of its citizens and for helping them through crises. However, the Madison and Chicago widows discussed in this chapter seldom utilize these resources to alleviate loneliness, being mainly dependent upon their children and friends. There are class differences in the use of these resources, and Madison women tend to mention siblings as part of their emotional support system more often than do the Chicago area widows. The church as an organization and voluntary associations provide companionship to some widows who use them to alleviate loneliness, but the "helping professions" and groups designed specifically to meet the needs of widows or other people who might be lonely are either unavailable in these two communities, or else the widows lack facilitating personal resources to use existing services.

The insistence of so many women (39% of the Chicago sample) that they are "rarely" or "never" lonely needs further comparative analysis. It relates to the tendency typical of Americans to block admission of anger and unhappiness. Of course it is also possible that women can become accustomed even to relative isolation, so that they really do not desire a more intensive set of social relations. Our findings indicate that social integration is not necessarily a guarantee of nonloneliness. Being linked to a system of mutual support does not necessarily prevent or alleviate loneliness, nor can we predict that isolation equals loneliness. The experience of aloneness and loneliness are not inevitably associated with one another. Loneliness can be experienced in terms of a specific other person who is no longer available as a love object (or even a hate object) even when other social and emotionally supportive relations are part of the support systems of a person.

REFERENCES

Bankoff, E. Widow groups as an alternative to informal social support. In M. Lieberman & L. D. Borman (Eds.), *Self-help groups for coping with crisis: Origins, members, processes and impact.* San Francisco: Jossey-Bass, 1979, 181–193.

Barrett, C. Review essay: Women in widowhood. *Signs,* 1977, *2*(1), 856–868.

Baum, J. *An exploration of widowhood: Coping patterns adopted by a population of widows.* Unpublished doctoral dissertation. University of Wisconsin, Madison, 1979.

Berardo, F. Survivorship and social isolation: The case of the aged widower. *The Family Coordinator,* 1970, *19,* 11–25.

Berger, P., & Kellner, H. Marriage and the construction of reality: An exercise in the microsociology of knowledge. In H. Dretzel (Ed.), *Patterns of communicative behavior, Recent sociology #2.* London: Collier-Macmillan, 1970, 50–73.

Berger, P., & Luckman, T. *The social construction of reality.* Garden City, N. Y.: Doubleday, 1966.

Buhler, C. Loneliness in maturity. *Journal of Humanistic Psychology,* 1969, *9* (2), 167–181.

Carter, H., & Glick, P. C. *Marriage and divorce: A social and economic study.* Cambridge, Mass.: Harvard University Press, 1970.

Fromm-Reichmann, F. Loneliness. *Psychiatry,* 1959, *22* (1), 1–15.

Glassner, B. Role discontinuity and manic depression. In H. Z. Lopata (Ed.), *Research in the interweave of roles: Women and men.* Greenwich, Conn.: JAI Press, 1980, 265–282.

Gordon, S. *Lonely in America.* New York: Simon and Schuster, 1976.

Heinemann, G. D. *Determinants of primary support system strength among urban, widowed women: Does life stage make a difference?* Unpublished doctoral dissertation. University of Illinois, Circle Campus, 1979.

Lindemann, E. Symptomology and management of acute grief. *American Journal of psychiatry,* 1977, *101*(1), 141–148.

Lopata, H. Z. Loneliness: Forms and components. *Social Problems,* 1969, *17*(2), 248–262.

Lopata, H. Z. Living arrangements of urban widows and their married children. *Sociological Focus,* 1971, *5,* 41–61.

Lopata, H. Z. Role changes in widowhood: A world perspective. In D. Cowgill & L. Holmes (Eds.), *Aging and modernization.* New York: Appleton-Century-Crofts, 1972.

Lopata, H. Z. *Widowhood in an American city.* Cambridge, Mass.: Schenkman Publishing Company, 1973a.

Lopata, H. Z. Self-identity in marriage and widowhood. *Sociological Quarterly,* 1973b, *14*(3), 407–418.

Lopata, H. Z. The effect of schooling on social contacts of urban women. *American Journal of Sociology,* 1973c, *79*(3), 604–619.

Lopata, H. Z. Grief work and identity reconstruction. *Journal of Geriatric Psychiatry,* 1975a, *8*(1), 41–45.

Lopata, H. Z. Couple-companionate relationships in marriage and widowhood. In N. Glazer-Malbin (Ed.), *Old families/New families.* New York: D. Van Nostrand, 1975b.

Lopata, H. Z. The absence of community resources in the support systems of urban widows. *The Family Coordinator,* 1978a, *26,* 383–388.

Lopata, H. Z. Contribution of extended families to the support systems of metropolitan area widows: Limitations of the modified kin network. *Journal of Marriage and the Family,* 1978b, *40,* 355–364.

Lopata, H. Z. *Women as widows: Support systems.* New York: Elsevier, 1979.

Lopata, H. Z. Loneliness in widowhood. In J. Hartog, J. R. Audy, & Y. A. Cohen (Eds.), *The anatomy of loneliness.* New York: International Universities Press, 1980.

Lopata, H. Z., & Noel, J. R. The dance studio: Style without sex. *Transaction/Society,* January/February, 1967, 24–34.

Marris, P. *Widows and their families.* London: Routledge and Kegan Paul, 1958.

Neugarten, B. L. The awareness of middle age. In B. L. Neugarten (Ed.), *Middle age and aging.* Chicago: University of Chicago Press, 1968.

Packard, V. *A nation of strangers.* New York: David McKay, 1972.

Parkes, C. M. Separation anxiety: An aspect of the search for a lost object. In R. Weiss (Ed.), *Loneliness: The experience of emotional and social isolation.* Cambridge, Mass.: MIT Press, 1973, 53–67.

Parkes, C. M. Unexpected and untimely bereavement: A statistical study of young Boston widows and widowers. In B. Schoenberg, I. Gerber, A. Weiner, A. H. Kutschner, D. Peretz, & A. C. Carr (Eds.), *Bereavement: Its psychological aspects.* New York: Columbia University Press, 1975, 119–138.

Parsons, T. The kinship system of the contemporary United States. *American Anthropologist,* 1943, *34,* 22–38.

Peplau, L. A., & Caldwell, M. A. Loneliness: A cognitive analysis. *Essence,* 1978, *2*(4), 207–220.

Riesman, D. Foreword. In R. Weiss (Ed.), *Loneliness: The experience of emotional and social isolation.* Cambridge, Mass.: MIT Press, 1973, ix–xxii.

Riesman, D., Glazer, N., & Denney, R. *The lonely crowd.* New Haven: Yale University Press, 1950.

Schoenberg, B., Gerber, I., Wiener, A., Kutschner, A. H., Peretz, D., & Carr, A. C. (Eds.), *Bereavement: Its psychological aspects.* New York: Columbia University Press, 1975.

Shanas, E., Townsend, P., Wedderburn, D., Friss, H., Milhoj, P., & Stehouwer, J. *Old People in three industrial societies.* New York: Atherton, 1968.

Silverman, P. The widow-to-widow program: An experiment in preventive intervention. In S. Sneidman (Ed.), *Death: Current perspectives.* Palo Alto, Calif.: Mayfield, 1972.

Silverman, P., Mackenzie, D., Pettipas, M., & Welson, E. (Eds.), *Helping each other in widowhood.* New York: Health Sciences Publishing Company, 1974.

Slater, P. *The pursuit of loneliness.* Boston: Beacon Press, 1970.

Starr, J. R., & Carns, D. E. Singles in the city. In H. Z. Lopata (Ed.), *Marriages and families.* New York: D. Van Nostrand, 1973, 154–161.

Stehouwer, J. The household and family relations of old people. In E. Shanas et al., *Old people in three industrial societies.* New York: Atherton Press, 1968, 177–226.

Sussman, M. The isolated nuclear family: Fact or fiction. In R. Winch et al. (Eds.), *Selected studies in marriage and the family.* New York: Holt, Rinehart and Winston, 1962, 49–57.

Townsend, P. Isolation, desolation and loneliness. In E. Shanas et al., (Eds.), *Old people in three industrial societies.* New York: Atherton Press, 1968.

Tunstall, J. *Old and alone.* London: Routledge and Kegan Paul, 1966.

Weiss, R. (Ed.). *Loneliness: The experience of emotional and social isolation.* Cambridge, Mass.: The MIT Press, 1973.

Wood, L. Loneliness, social identity and social structure. *Essence* 1978, 2(4), 259–270.

Chapter 20

Being Old and Living Alone

Letitia Anne Peplau, Tora K. Bikson,
Karen S. Rook, and Jacqueline D. Goodchilds

In the seventeenth century the English philosopher Thomas Hobbes (1961) characterized human life as "solitary, poor, nasty, brutish and *short*" (italics added). Cultural images depict old age in the twentieth century as equally gloomy, modifying the Hobbesian thesis only to acknowledge that for old people today, life is not only solitary, poor, and unpleasant, but also *long*. Americans are living considerably longer than their grandparents did, and are likely, with advancing age, to live alone (Glick, 1977). For many, growing old entails a substantial period of solitary living, a situation often viewed as severely negative. Stereotypes of people who live alone (Parmelee & Werner, 1978) characterize them as unfriendly, aloof, unattractive, and lonely. Researchers (Lynch, 1977) have sometimes used marital status as a proxy for measures of loneliness, assuming that the widowed, divorced, and never-married suffer from deficits in social relations not experienced by the currently married. Thus, being old and alone would seem to be a profoundly undesirable condition whose psychosocial consequences might temper the benefits of the extended life span of contemporary older Americans.

In this chapter we explore the soundness of the assumptions behind these negative images of those who are old and alone. We begin by examining the syllogism implicit in the line of reasoning just presented—that being old entails being alone, and that being alone entails being lonely, so that being old surely leads to being lonely. We next review evidence about factors that do contribute to loneliness among older adults. A third section discusses the effects of gender and marital status on loneliness, and presents evidence that marriage may be more beneficial to the well-being of older men than women. A final section considers some of the positive aspects of solitary living for old people, most notably the belief that living alone is a sign of personal independence.

The authors express their appreciation to Daniel Perlman for his helpful comments on an earlier version of this chapter.

A FAULTY SYLLOGISM: OLD = ALONE = LONELY

Evidence indicates that people are more likely to live alone as they grow old. However, there is little empirical support for the claim that this status is necessarily accompanied by increased loneliness.

Does Being Old Entail Being Alone?

The average life span of Americans has increased steadily. There are currently about 23.5 million individuals over age 65 in the United States, representing more than 11% of the population (1977 census update: Glick, 1977). Moreover, the number of individuals in the older age group is expected to increase by a third before the year 2000, with the proportion of old people increasing even more dramatically. These changes in the age composition of the American population reflect stable long-term trends toward lower birth rates and increased longevity (Shanas & Hauser, 1974).

Related trends converge to produce an older age group increasingly comprised of widowed women (Bikson & Goodchilds, 1978a). Since the turn of the century in the United States, the death rate for women has been substantially lower than the rate for men, and this differential itself is increasing (Berkman & Syme, 1979; Cutler & Harootyan, 1975; Retherford, 1975; Spiegelman & Erhardt, 1974). Because of this sex difference, the population of older women is growing faster than the population of older men. Among young-old adults (those in their late 60s and early 70s), the ratio of women to men is about 125 to 100; for old-old adults (those in their late 70s or older), the ratio is about 200 to 100.

Among adults over age 65, women are much more likely than men to be widowed. In 1975, only 14% of older men were widowed, compared to 52% of older women (Marquis, 1979). This difference reflects both the higher mortality rate of men and the fact that husbands are typically several years older than their wives. Another factor contributing to the disproportionate number of single older women is the differential remarriage rates of widows and widowers. Widowed women are much less likely to remarry than are widowed men, in part because of differences in the availability of age-appropriate partners.

Many older adults, particularly those who are widowed, live alone. Despite prevailing myths, a surprisingly small proportion of older adults live in group settings; in 1975 only 5% of those over age 65 were living in an institution (Marquis, 1979). Most older adults live in either one-person or two-person households. Census data (Marquis, 1979) show that both age and gender have a strong impact on living situations. Among men 80% of the young-old and 63% of the old-old live with a spouse. In contrast, among women only 46% of the young-old and 20% of the old-old live with a spouse. Those who are not currently married typically live alone. In 1975, 12% of young-old men and 18% of the old-old men lived alone. Among women 33% of the young-old and 41% of the old-old lived alone. Greater economic independence and improved health are enabling current cohorts of older adults to maintain individual households in greater numbers than ever before, and this trend is likely to continue.

Taken together, these data indicate that the first part of the syllogism is accurate: being old is frequently associated with being alone, both in the sense of being without a spouse and of living in a one-person household. The old and alone status is being occupied by larger and larger numbers of adults, especially older women.

Does Being Alone Entail Being Lonely?

Having corroborated the first premise, investigating the second takes on more importance. That is, in view of marked increases in the number of individuals who are old and alone, the psychosocial concomitants of this status deserve careful attention.

It is commonly assumed that older people who live alone have been rejected by their families, lead impoverished social lives, and lack close relationships. Although these beliefs are widely held, evidence is accumulating that they are "mythic" in the sense in which Baltes and Schaie (1976) use that term. That is to say, while these views undoubtedly have some basis in reality and may be true of some segments of the older adult population, they do not represent the modal or typical case.

First, it should be underscored that older adults who live alone are typically not cut off from or rejected by their families. While across age groups unmarried persons report having relatively less contact with relatives than their married counterparts, research indicates that most older adults do have regular family contact. Among the people 65 and over studied by Fischer and Phillips (Chapter 2), only 8% of men and 15% of women were severely isolated from their kin. In a study of inner city aged (Cantor, 1975), a group usually regarded as extremely vulnerable to social isolation, two-thirds of respondents reported at least monthly contact with relatives. The recent extensive work of Shanas (1979) indicates that older people living alone typically reside in the same city as their adult children, often not more than 10 minutes away from them. These older adults engage in regular telephone and face-to-face interactions with their children. Shanas concluded that old people perceive these forms of contact as preferable to living with adult children and as more conducive to maintaining good family relationships (cf. Kutner, Fanshel, Togo, & Langner, 1956). Older adults, like young adults, tend to value privacy and independence, and view living alone as an achievement rather than a sign of rejection by others.

Second, older adults who live alone do not ordinarily lead solitary or socially isolated lives. Cantor's (1975) study of inner city adults found that over 80% regularly socialized on steps or benches, in parks and other open spaces; many ate together regularly. An investigation of 11 midtown Manhattan single-room-occupancy dwellings (Cohen & Sokolovsky, 1977), thought to house an especially marginal population, also found viable and complex social networks among residents. Older residents reported networks of 0 to 26 people, with a mean of 7.5; over 70% of residents named at least five people with whom they interacted. Finally, Fischer and Phillip's (Chapter 2) study of a representative sample of adults clearly indicated that people who lived alone were not more isolated from friends and associates than those living with another person; in fact, severe isolation from friends was actually *less* common among men and women who lived alone. They conclude, "Despite the suspicion raised recently that adults living alone are prone to isolation, our data show otherwise."

Third, it should be emphasized that marital status and household composition per se are not good indicators of the quality of social interaction. More generally, measures of objective features of social relations are poor indicators of the subjective quality of these relations. As Lowenthal and Robinson (1976) remind us, aloneness is not the same as loneliness. Research indicates that quantitative aspects of relationships such as frequency of contact and number of friends are only modestly associated with subjective well-being (see reviews by Conner, Powers, & Bultena, 1979; Larson, 1978; Lowenthal & Robinson, 1976; Rook, 1980). For example, in 17 studies reviewed by Larson (1978), correlations between objective features of social contact and measures of morale or life satisfaction ranged from .01 to .46. In studies that controlled for socioeconomic status and health, the effects of frequent social contact were often reduced and in some cases disappeared (Lemon, Bengtson & Peterson, 1972; Smith & Lipman, 1972).

The finding that quantitative aspects of social relationships are only modestly predictive of well-being or loneliness among older adults is similar to findings for younger adults (see Cutrona, Chapter 18)—the assumption that "more is better" is too simplistic. Thus Conner et al. (1979) have urged gerontological researchers to shift "from questions of 'how many' and 'how often' to the meaning of social relationships and the interactional process" (p. 120). Likewise, researchers who study social support lament how little we know about factors that lead people to experience their social relations as emotionally supportive (House & Wells, 1977).

In this context, it becomes clear why living arrangements should not be taken as a proxy for loneliness or social satisfaction in later life. Although loneliness among old people has been linked to low social contact with friends and children (Perlman, Gerson, & Spinner, 1978), most old people living alone interact fairly regularly with other people. Further, living with another or others is no guarantee that social relations will be satisfying. Perlman et al. (1978) actually found greater loneliness among single old people who lived with relatives than among either those who lived alone or those who lived with friends. In that study, loneliness was much more closely linked to contact with friends ($r = -.51$) than with children ($r = -.18$) and was unrelated to contact with other relatives.

Results from a growing number of studies suggest that social contact with friends and neighbors has greater impact on well-being than does contact with grown children or other relatives (Arling, 1976; Edwards & Klemmack, 1973; Kutner et al., 1956; Lee & Ihinger-Tallman, 1980; Martin, 1973; Pihlblad & McNamara, 1965; Wood & Robertson, 1978). In an illustrative study, Arling (1976) asked 409 elderly widows about their frequency of contact with children or other relatives, and with friends or neighbors. He found that contact with family members, particularly children, was unrelated to measures of morale; but friendship-neighboring was related to decreased loneliness and a greater sense of usefulness and respect within the community. This outcome is consistent with the observation (Kutner et al., 1956) that one of the most frequent complaints of old people living with their grown children is a feeling of isolation within the family group.

Similarly, a study of "Golden Wedding" couples by Parron and Troll (1978) found that, while many older couples had happy marriages, a few experienced conflict and hostility. "Some people feel that their husbands or wives are the cause of all their troubles, and they often wish they could somehow terminate their marriages" (p. 459). Frequent but unpleasant social contact is unlikely to reduce loneliness or to contribute to psychological well-being. Tunstall (1967) found that 27% of the severely lonely old people he studied were currently married; their loneliness stemmed from being separated from the spouse, feeling neglected by a very "busy" spouse, being housebound, or missing someone other than the spouse.

Conversely, it should not be surprising that in Tunstall's sample most old people who lived alone were *not* lonely. Among the men and women living alone, only 15% reported that they were often lonely. Although this percentage is higher than that reported by those who lived with others (4%), it nonetheless indicates that the typical old person living alone seldom feels lonely. In sum, the second part of the syllogism—that living alone necessarily entails being lonely—is not supported by empirical research.

ARE OLD PEOPLE ESPECIALLY VULNERABLE TO LONELINESS?

We have indicated that for old people, being alone does not invariably produce loneliness. It is still useful to ask, however, whether there are age trends in loneliness. Although popular culture depicts youth as a time of sociability and old age as a time of loneliness, several large-scale surveys have found the opposite to be true (Parlee, 1979; Fidler, 1976; Rubenstein & Shaver, Chapter 13; Woodward & Visser, 1977). As shown in Table 20.1, self-reports of loneliness are highest among adolescents, and then decline among older groups. For example, in one survey (Parlee, 1979), 79% of respondents under age 18 said they were sometimes or often lonely, com-

Table 20.1.   Age Trends in Loneliness

| *Survey by Rubenstein and Shaver* [a] | | | | | | | |
Age in Years	18-25	26-30	31-39	40-49	50-59	60-69	70 +
Mean loneli- ness score (max. = +20)	+12.8	+ 9.5	+ 8.9	+ 2.9	− 3.8	− 9.4	−22.5

| *Survey by Parlee* [b] | | | | | | |
Age in Years	Under 18	18-24	25-34	35-44	45-54	55 +
Percent saying they feel lonely sometimes or often	79%	71%	69%	60%	53%	37%

| *Study by Dean* [c] | | | | | |
Age in Years	50-59	60-69	70-79	80+	Total
Percent saying they feel lonely "sometimes" or "more often"	26%	35%	29%	53%	32%

[a] Adapted from Rubenstein, Shaver, and Peplau (1979)
[b] Adapted from Parlee (1979)
[c] Adapted from Dean (1962)

pared to only 53% of 45 through 54 year olds, and 37% of those 55 and older. A nationwide British survey (Fidler, 1976) found that 20% of old people said they were occasionally lonely, and only 7% said they felt lonely most of the time; the remaining three-quarters of the older sample said they never felt lonely.

Survey data lead to two conclusions. First, self-reported loneliness is less common among older persons. Second, only a small minority of old people reports suffering from severe and prolonged loneliness.

One possible exception to this pattern should be noted. Two studies suggest that at very advanced ages, loneliness may be more common. Within Tunstall's (1967) sample of old people, loneliness was most often reported by the oldest respondents; this appeared to reflect increases in both widowhood and physical incapacity for that group. As shown in Table 20.1, Dean (1962) found fairly similar levels of loneliness among adults ages 50 to 79, but a sharp increase in loneliness among those 80 and older. Dean speculated that the meaning of the term loneliness may be somewhat different among the oldest (80+ years) adults in her sample. She argued that for the old-old, loneliness was closely linked to reduced activity due to physical incapacity and to lack of money or transportation, rather than to an absence of social contact.

The reasons for the general pattern of decreased self-reports of loneliness by respondents from successive stages in the life cycle are not well understood (cf. Campbell, Converse, & Rodgers, 1976). One possibility is that old people are genuinely more satisfied with their social relations than are young adults. Although young people typically have many more social opportunities, they may also have high and perhaps unrealistic expectations about social relations. With age, individuals may establish more reasonable expectations and standards for social relations. A second possibility is that these trends reflect a difference in willingness to acknowledge feelings of loneliness, rather than in the experience itself. Young adults may be more influenced by the contemporary ethic of "openness" and emotional expressiveness (Rubin et al., 1980) than are older adults. Finally, we do not know whether observed patterns represent developmental trends linked to aging or life stage, or rather reflect cohort effects due to historical differences in the experiences of various age groups.

SOURCES OF LONELINESS AND SOCIAL SATISFACTION IN OLD AGE

Although the majority of old people perceive their social relations as satisfying and do not feel lonely, some old people do experience painful feelings of loneliness. At any age, loneliness is a response to a deficit in the quantity or quality of one's social life. Proximal causes of loneliness, then, are to be found in the nature of a person's social relationships. For example, Perlman et al. (1978) found that loneliness was associated with a desire to receive more personal information from other people. Research is needed to identify specific social and psychological factors that contribute to social satisfaction in older adults. We review here three proximal factors that, on the basis of somewhat limited information, appear to be important determinants of loneliness and social satisfaction.

Availability of a Confidant

One of the earliest longitudinal studies of psychological health in later adulthood (Clark & Anderson, 1967) found the availability of a confidant to be the strongest single predictor of well-being. For older people, as for younger adults, the presence of an intimate relationship in which personal concerns can be shared is an important source of emotional well-being. For married old people, a spouse often provides this sort of relationship (Parron & Troll, 1978). Although little is known about the quality of interaction among older spouses, available evidence suggests that many older couples have positive views of their marriages, and some report increasing marital satisfaction with age (Lowenthal & Robinson, 1976). Perlman et al. (1978) found that among married old people, loneliness was significantly correlated with low marital satisfaction.

For those who are widowed or who remain in unhappy marriages, the availability of other confidants may be important (Blau, 1961). Lowenthal and Haven (1968) suggested that the presence of an intimate relationship serves as a buffer against both age-related losses in social interaction and role involvement, and against the more traumatic losses accompanying widowhood and retirement. In a 2-year study of 280 elderly San Franciscans, they found that individuals who had suffered reductions in social interaction or role losses reported considerably higher morale if they had a confidant than if they did not have a confidant. In perhaps a more dramatic comparison, Lowenthal and Haven found that widowed individuals who had a confidant reported higher morale than individuals who were married but lacked a confidant. Lowenthal and Robinson (1976) emphasized that intimacy and the capacity for mutuality are vital factors in the well-being of older adults.

These studies suggest an explanation for the common finding (cited above) that contact with kin does not reduce loneliness and enhance psychological well-being among older adults, while contact with peers often does. A study by Arling (cited in Blehar, 1979) suggests that older adults engage in rather different activities with friends than with grown children, and that relations with friends may involve more reciprocal exchanges of assistance than those with kin. Arling also found that the more people with whom an old person engaged in *reciprocal* exchanges, the lower the person scored on a measure of "lonely dissatisfaction." Further research is needed to clarify the reasons for the differential effects of relationships with friends versus kin. In such efforts it would be well to take into account the potential role of mutuality or sharing of information, problems, and assistance. On the basis of studies reviewed here, we would expect social relationships with kin (whether with a grown child, sibling, or spouse) to be perceived as satisfying to the extent that they are characterized by the positive qualities found in relationships with friends and confidants.

Personal Control

Evidence is accumulating that documents the importance of perceiving one's environment as predictable and controllable. Feelings of personal control may reduce stress (Averill, 1973). In contrast, loss of control may lead to feelings of helplessness and hopelessness (Schulz, 1976a; Seligman, 1975).

Perceptions of control over the social environment may have special significance for older people. It has been argued that age-related events, such as mandatory retirement, death of friends and relatives, and declining health can reduce the old person's sense of personal control (Lowenthal & Robinson, 1976; Schulz, 1976b). In a study of older adults in nursing homes, Langer and Rodin (1976) found that increased choice and personal responsibility, even in small matters such as the selection of a plant to care for, improved social participation and general well-being. Lowenthal and Robinson (1976) emphasized the importance of control over one's social life: "One of the serious and little studied problems of aging is the extent to which the individual . . . loses control of this chosen pattern and is forced to be alone when he would like company" (p. 432). In an empirical demonstration of the importance of control over social contact, Schulz (1976b) had college students visit residents of a retirement home for a 2-month period. Residents who could choose or predict the frequency and duration of these visits were significantly more active, and rated themselves higher in hope and happiness and lower in loneliness than did residents whose visitor just dropped in, even though actual interaction time was the same.

Perceptions of personal control may be useful in helping to understand why contact with kin does little to elevate the morale of old people while contact with friends does. Friendships develop voluntarily and are based on common interests and lifestyles. Family involvement, in contrast, arises more often from formal obligations. Older adults thus may experience greater control in relations with peers than in relations with family. Because grown children often have more constrained work schedules and other family obligations as well, they may determine the timing of visits with aging parents. Further, since older parents may lack mobility due to poor health or transportation difficulties, grown children may also control how a visit takes place. Finally, interaction with adult children may also result in a reversal of roles that produces unpleasant feelings of dependence in the older parent (Arling, 1976). In contrast, visits with neighbors and friends tend to be scheduled at mutual convenience and to afford greater parity of roles.

More generally, perceptions of control may be important in sustaining hope about improving relationship deficits. The pain of loneliness is compounded if people can foresee no possibility of change. The optimism of youth may decline with age. For example, while college students (Cutrona, Chapter 18) believe that new friendships can be established relatively easily, old people do not. One study of widows over age 50 (Lopata, 1969) found that 71% of these women felt that old friends could not be replaced, no matter how much one tried to make new friends. With age, the events that typically precipitate loneliness tend to become more aversive and less voluntary. Among young adults, the termination of a love relationship typically involves the breakup of a dating relationship; for older people, termination more often results from divorce or death. Similarly, for younger people, separation from family and friends is often motivated by a personal desire to pursue educational or career goals; for old people, separation more often results from others moving away, or because the old person is housebound or hospitalized. Finally, whereas young people often attribute their loneliness to changeable factors such as moving to a new city or being shy (Peplau et al., 1979), old people may more often attribute their problems to irreversible factors. In his study of old people, Tunstall (1967) found that "the lonely attribute being lonely . . . to increasing age. Nine in ten of those who answered think they are more lonely now than when they were young" (p. 93). Although evidence clearly shows that loneliness is not an inevitable part of aging, the *belief* that loneliness is inescapable may become a self-fulfilling prophecy preventing some lonely old people from taking steps to alleviate their predicament.

Social Comparison Processes

Social psychologists (see review by Pettigrew, 1967) have long recognized that individuals evaluate their current lives in large part by comparisons to their own past experiences and to those of other people. Gerontologists have invoked the concept of social comparison to help understand the psychological well-being of older adults.

Widowhood researchers (Gubrium, 1974; Townsend, 1968) who have distinguished between desolation and isolation emphasize the importance of comparisons with one's own past experiences. Gubrium argued that

It is not a certain absolute degree of isolation that makes for feelings of loneliness in old age, but rather *becoming* socially isolated relative to a prior degree of social engagement. This change or discontinuity in social engagement is referred to as desolation. (1974, p. 107)

Support for this interpretation of the effects of widowhood comes from several studies. Shanas et al. (1968) found that older persons who had been single all their lives complained of loneliness less than persons who were separated, divorced, or widowed. Similarly, Gubrium (1974) found that divorced and widowed old people rated their present lives as worse than they had been at age 45 and evaluated their lives more negatively than did never-married or currently married old people. Unfavorable comparisons between past and present experiences may be a major source of social dissatisfaction in later life (Lowenthal & Robinson, 1976).

The importance of comparisons with other people is also suggested, at least implicitly, in Blau's (1961) analysis of the effects of widowhood on social relations. Blau proposed that widowhood has adverse effects on social participation only when it places the individual in a position that differs from most of his or her age and sex peers. In a survey of 468 old people, Blau found that among those under age 70, widowed individuals were less socially active than married individuals. But among those over age 70, no differences were found between the friendship participation of the widowed and married. Blau explained this finding in terms of the proportion of widowed women and men in the two age groups.

People tend to form friendships with others in their own age group, and to the extent that this occurs, the widowed person under 70 is likely to be an odd person at social gatherings since most of [his or her] associates are probably still married and participating with their spouse in social activities. (p. 431)

We might add that these differences may also lead younger and older widows to use different standards against which to evaluate their own social lives.

Research that more explicitly examines the types of comparison standards used by older adults and their impact on loneliness is needed (cf., Cutrona, Chapter 18).

Distal Causes of Loneliness

Loneliness is most directly a result of deficits in a person's social relations. But social relations are in turn influenced by a broad range of distal factors that may assume considerable importance in later life. Very important among these influences for older adults is health (see review by Larson, 1978). Old people who are sick or physically disabled are less likely to be satisfied with their lives. For instance, among the old men and women studied by Tunstall (1967), 19% of those with severe physical incapacity said they were "often lonely," compared to only 5% of those with no or slight incapacity. Similarly, Perlman et al. (1978) found that old people who rated their health as poor reported greater loneliness.

Well-being is also affected by housing, transportation, and income. Psychological well-being is related to satisfaction with one's housing, but not with the frequency of residential moves nor with living in urban versus rural areas (Larson, 1978). Research specifically directed toward loneliness by Woodward et al. (1974) found no differences between old people living in urban versus rural Nebraska; nor was loneliness related to type of housing. Loneliness was, however, affected by the person's happiness with his or her current housing situation; those who liked their residence were less lonely. Perlman et al. (1978) found that loneliness was higher among old people who had moved to their present residence because of circumstances rather than personal choice. Access to transportation also enhances well-being in old people (Larson, 1978). In contrast, being "housebound" was a frequent source of loneliness among Tunstall's (1967) sample of older Britains. Obviously, financial resources are another important factor that can affect health care, housing, and transportation. Perlman et al. (1978) found that loneliness was higher among old people with lower incomes.

This review has highlighted a number of personal and social factors that contribute to loneliness among older adults. The next section considers in greater detail the impact of marriage on loneliness in older adults and finds that the implications of marital status differ for women and men.

MEN, WOMEN, AND MARRIAGE

Considerable evidence suggests that being married typically contributes to physical and mental health. Lynch (1977) reviewed extensive data indicating that married individuals enjoy greater health and longevity than do the single, divorced, or widowed. Studies consistently find that the married have lower rates of mental illness than the nonmarried (Bernard, 1972; Gove, 1972; Knupfer, Clark, & Room, 1966; Pearlin & Johnson, 1977). Married individuals report greater happiness (Bradburn, 1969; Glenn, 1975; Gurin, Veroff, & Feld, 1960) and greater psychological well-being (Larson, 1978). Most pertinent to our discussion is evidence that among older adults, the married are less likely to report loneliness than the nonmarried (Parlee, 1979; de Jong-Gierveld & Raadschelders, Chapter 7; Rubenstein & Shaver, Chapter 13; Tunstall, 1967). However, the benefits of marriage may be greater for men than for women in old age.

While public attention tends to focus on the plight of the lonely aging widow, there is reason to believe that the effects of being single, divorced, or widowed are more negative for old men than for old women. An early research review concluded:

> In several recent studies of mental health, a higher proportion of single men than of single women have shown indication of maladjustment. In accordance with the popular view of marriage as a triumph for women and a defeat for men . . . we would expect to find those men who have escaped marriage to be better adjusted than those women who have failed to marry. That their data suggest the opposite has been greeted by the authors of the studies concerned with varying degrees of surprise and disbelief. (Knupfer, Clark, & Room, 1966, p. 841)

Put simply, evidence suggests that marriage is more of an advantage for men than for women, and that being without a spouse is more of a liability for men than for women (Bernard, 1972; Eisenson, 1980).

Two recent studies investigating loneliness in older adults illustrate this pattern. Perlman et al. (1978) found that widowed men were significantly lonelier than married men; among women, no significant difference was found between those who were married and widowed. Bikson and Good-childs (1978a) found that members of older couples reported less loneliness than did single older adults. But again, this effect was strongest among men. Single men were the loneliest group, while married men reported the least loneliness; married and single women scored in the middle. Bikson and Good-childs suggested that this outcome might reflect in part differences in the leisure activities of older men and women. Results indicated that during their free time over two-thirds of the single men pursued solitary activities, whereas over two-thirds of the single women pursued social activities. The reasons for the differential effect of marriage for women and men are not well understood, although several possible explanations have been offered.

Are the Results Artifactual?

It is sometimes suggested that women are more willing than men to admit to various problems including loneliness. As Gove (1979) points out, however, this response bias explanation cannot account for the occurrence of highest reports of distress and unhappiness among unmarried men; if sex differences in responding were at work, they should appear regardless of marital status (see also Weissman & Klerman, 1979). A second artifact might be the differential selection of women and men into marriage—an explanation offered by Bernard (1972) in her discussion of younger adults. Bernard proposed that the most competent women and the least competent men are the ones likely to remain unmarried. This explanation is inadequate, however, to explain the effects of marital status in older samples, since for this cohort the great majority of currently "single" individuals were formerly married and became widowed later in life. Thus the observed interaction of gender and marital status is, we believe, "real."

Sex Differences in Social Activities

It has frequently been conjectured that women are better able to initiate and maintain relations with friends and relatives than are men. For example, based on qualitative observations, Knupfer, Clark, and Room (1966) speculated that "Man's lesser ability to form and maintain personal relationships creates a need for a wife, as the expressive expert, to perform this function for him" (p. 848). As a consequence, unmarried men experience an "expressive hardship." Troll and Turner (1979) echoed this theme, noting that "most older men have relied on their wives for intimacy . . . and for linkages with family, friends, and social life in general" (p. 128). Others (Brown & Fox, 1979; Lowenthal & Robinson, 1976) have emphasized that sex-role socialization discourages men from learning intimacy skills and from developing close same-sex friendships that might ease the loneliness of being widowed or unmarried.

Although direct evidence concerning the social skills of older men and women does not exist, available research does show sex differences in the patterning of social relations among older men and women. For example, in a recent survey, Fischer and Phillips (Chapter 2, see also Fischer, 1978) found that among people over age 65, women had 38% more friends than did men. Fischer speculated that women are generally more sociable than men, but that at younger ages this difference is not evident in patterns of friendship. Younger women are constrained in friendship formation by homemaking and childbearing responsibilities; younger men are aided by participation in contexts such as work that provide friends with little effort. In later life, both the constraints and supports for friendship diminish (e.g., as children leave home and workers retire). As a consequence, the friendships that old people have and maintain are more directly a result of their own initiative. Support for women's relative advantage in old age is shown by evidence that older women continue to make new friends, whereas older men are less likely to do so. Whether older men are less able or merely less interested in replacing friends who are lost through geographic mobility or death is not clear.

Sex Differences in Domestic Activities

A second explanation for the differential impact of marriage on men and women focuses on sex differences in instrumental behavior. Sex-role socialization encourages men and women to develop different skills. Women learn homemaking skills, whereas men acquire occupational skills. During much of adult life, these sex differences form the basis for traditional role differentiation in marriage. Time-budget studies (Robinson 1977; Walker, 1970) document that the behavior of most Americans shows a high degree of traditional role differentiation by gender. Some tasks are clearly considered to be "women's work" and others to be "men's work." Even in families in which the wife is employed full time for pay, she continues to perform most homemaking and childcare activities for the household.

Research concerning age-related trends in household task performance is sparse. Blood and Wolfe (1960), using a cross-sectional design, found that task specialization by sex increased over the life span and was greatest during retirement. Ballweg (1967) found that retired husbands did no more housework than employed husbands of the same age. Lipman (1961), however, reported that retired husbands tended to engage in such tasks as dishwashing and grocery shopping that required little in specialized skill and that could be done jointly with their wives. In any case, there is no evidence that retired husbands typically take over a major share of housework. An exception may occur among very old couples in which the wife's ability to perform household tasks is seriously impaired (Troll, 1971).

During much of adult life, role differentiation in marriage may be an efficient and comfortable pattern. In later life, however, rigid role differentiation by gender may create unexpected problems. Older adults who lose a spouse through death or divorce may find it difficult to assume tasks and responsibilities formerly performed by the partner. This may be especially problematic for men who have never acquired basic personal maintenance skills and who may reject such activities as "feminine." In contrast, older women are typically skilled at homemaking, having had years of practice. Thus older women alone may be at less of a disadvantage than older men alone.

Evidence supporting this view comes from a study of older adults conducted by Bikson and Goodchilds (1978a). They found that marital status had a striking impact on the health and eating practices of older men and women. Women living with a husband and women living alone were about equally likely to see a doctor regularly; in contrast, men living alone were much less likely to see a doctor than those living with a wife. Similarly, married women virtually always prepared their own meals, as did most women living alone. Married men generally ate meals prepared by their wife, while men alone were likely to eat out. There is little doubt that older women typically have greater experience than older men in basic maintenance tasks. This factor may contribute to the differential effects of living alone for women and for men. What is not clear is the extent to which men actually lack domestic skills such as the ability to cook, or rather avoid performing or learning to perform "women's work."

A sex-role analysis may also help explain why on some measures of psychological well-being, married women fare less well than married men (Gove, 1979). After a man retires, the work demands placed on him decline, but those on his wife may actually increase. While men can retire from their role as breadwinner, women never retire from the homemaker role. Following the husband's retirement, women may have reduced financial resources for homemaking, and may find that their own health and energy are declining (Kerckhoff, 1966). Yet as time budget studies indicate, older women typically receive minimal assistance for maintenance activities from their husbands.

The burdens that fall on older wives may be further exacerbated by the traditional age differential between spouses. In addition to caring for herself, many older wives may also need to take care of a husband of even more advanced age. Troll and Turner (1979) speculate that

> If a wife is in good health, and her husband is showing dangerous symptoms which he is ignoring, she can easily be drawn back into a repetition of the mother-nurse role. . . . It becomes her responsibility to see that he goes to the doctor, watches his diet, takes his medication, and alters his activities as indicated. (p. 126)

Although good data on this point do not currently exist, it seems reasonable to hypothesize that many older married women suffer from work and worry overload. Bikson and Goodchilds' data (1978b), for example, indicate that married older women experience greater decision-making problems than their unmarried counterparts. This finding may be analogous to data indicating that younger working wives often feel "rushed" and have very little leisure time (Robinson, 1977). Such a view suggests that although older women living alone may miss some of the benefits of a spouse, they also avoid high demands on their time and energy.

Further research is needed to untangle the complex ways in which gender and marital status affect loneliness among older adults. The finding that marriage is more advantageous for older men than women may be one reason why aging widowers are more eager to remarry than are their female peers. An intriguing implication of the preceding discussion concerns the possible impact of trends towards decreased sex-typing in socialization. We can speculate that as younger men and women become more androgynous—developing competence in both social and instrumental activities, and viewing daily living tasks as more equally the responsibility of both sexes—they may be better equipped as individuals for old age, whether time and chance leave them coupled or alone.

THE PURSUIT OF INDEPENDENCE

For those who survive to old age, a certain degree of aloneness is inevitable (Goodchilds & Bikson, 1980). Aging adults watch as their cohort dwindles;

old friends, relatives, former classmates, business associates die. Other relationships are lost through geographical moves, retirement, or physical incapacity. But it is also important to emphasize that for some old people, reductions in social involvement may be voluntary and rewarding. Retirement and the privileges of age may offer the possibility of being selective about one's associates, and of ignoring people who are boring or unpleasant. "Many roles and responsibilities are shed with relief and the supposed normlessness of late life enhances the role of personal preference concerning the kinds of social relations to maintain" (Stueve & Fischer, 1978, p. 22).

Widowhood is often a part of old age, and it too can be a powerful experience of loss and aloneness (see Lopata et al., Chapter 19). But as we have seen in this chapter, widowhood does not mark the end of social involvement. Most widowed individuals reconstruct their social lives, although men and women may find different solutions to creating a satisfying social world:

> The modal older man is bereft when his wife dies because she is his chief and probably only confidant, but . . . he should have little difficulty replacing her. . . . The modal older woman, when she is singled, has little chance of remarrying, but . . . she has personality and housekeeping skills to survive on her own, to make friends easily, and to take care of herself. (Troll & Turner, 1979, p. 152)

Although the social relations of older Americans may depart from cultural ideals of "coupled bliss," they are often personally satisfying. Perhaps especially for women, widowhood may bring new opportunities for independence. Many widows comment that following bereavement they experience positive feelings of self-sufficiency, and enjoy greater freedom than they have had in their adult lives (Lopata, 1979).

For those old people who are not currently married, living alone is a common pattern. But whereas stereotypes depict this as an unhappy necessity, old people are more likely to view living alone as a preferred lifestyle (Goodchilds & Bikson, 1980). For the unmarried, alternatives to living alone—living with children or relatives, moving to a communal residence, sharing a home with someone—are often unattractive. For example, although old people want to be in geographical proximity to their children, they do not want to share the same household (Brown, 1960; Shanas et al, 1968). Many an exasperated adult son or daughter worn out from continued pleading with an aging parent to "move in with us" or "let us arrange for someone to move in with you" can testify that keeping one's own place and keeping it to oneself is a matter of pride, fiercely defended. Old people often view living alone as a valued achievement, a sign of independence (Rabushka & Jacobs, 1980).

It is obvious that most people benefit from companionship, involvement in the world of people, and care from others. For those who are ill or disabled, living with others may be requisite for survival (Clark & Anderson, 1980). But for healthy single older adults, the available alternatives to living alone may be much less appealing. This should be no surprise. Throughout history, it has been the able, rich, and powerful who could attain privacy and personal space. For contemporary Americans, the desire for a "room of one's own" can be felt at any age. The pain of social isolation must be viewed against the pain of lost privacy or feelings of psychological "crowding" associated with forced togetherness.

Why then do we worry about the "plight" of those who are old and alone? Most of us feel ambivalence about aloneness: it can be a symbol of independence and autonomy, or a sign of social failure and loneliness. Both possibilities are real. The consequences of togetherness can also be mixed: living with others can be associated with feelings of love and acceptance, or with feelings of dependency and "being a burden." Certainly in our society it is considered desirable to live with a person with whom one is compatible; few would deny or doubt that. For older people especially, living with a companion can be a boon—someone to share the financial burdens, someone to help with the daily tasks of living, someone to talk to, lean on, care about. But the essential ingredient is compatibility and companionship; just anyone won't do. And old people know this.

Given adequate physical and financial means, going it alone is often preferable in light of presently available alternatives. The "plight" of the old and alone may be less social-psychological than economic and sociological. Those who are old and alone may be most appreciative of social policies that permit them to stay in their homes by providing assistance with the costs of housing, or by providing home help in health care and housekeeping (Rabushka & Jacobs, 1980). Contrary to myth, most old people are satisfied with their social relations; their worries are more often about safety, transportation, or finances. For many, the experience of being old and living alone is less lonely and more rewarding than we imagine.

REFERENCES

Arling, G. The elderly widow and her family, neighbors and friends. *Journal of Marriage and the Family,* 1976, *38,* 757–767.

Averill, J. R. Personal control over aversive stimuli and its relationship to stress. *Psychological Bulletin,* 1973, *80,* 286–303.

Ballweg, J. A. Resolution of conjugal role adjustment after retirement. *Journal of Marriage and the Family,* 1967, *29*(2), 277–281.

Baltes, P. B., & Schaie, K. W. On the plasticity of intelligence in adulthood and old age. *American Psychologist,* 1976, *31,* 720–725.

Bensman, J., & Lilienfeld, R. Friendship and alienation. *Psychology Today,* October, 1979.

Berkman, L. F., & Syme, S. L. Social networks, host resistance, and mortality: A nine-year follow-up study of Alameda County residents. *American Journal of Epidemiology,* 1979, *109*(2), 186–203.

Bernard, J. *The future of marriage.* New York: Bantam, 1972.

Bikson, T. K., & Goodchilds, J. D. *Old and alone.* Paper presented at the annual meeting of the American Psychological Association, Toronto, August, 1978a.

Bikson, T. K., & Goodchilds, J. D. *Product decision processes among older adults.* Research report R-2361-NSF, The Rand Corporation, Santa Monica, Calif., 1978b.

Blau, Z. Structural constraints on friendship in old age. *American Sociological Review,* 1961, *26,* 429–439.

Blehar, M. Family and friendship in old age. In E. Corfman (Ed.), *Families today—A research sampler on families and children.* NIMH Science Monograph 1. DHEW Publication No. (ADM) 79–815. Washington, D. C.: U. S. Government Printing Office, 1979.

Blood, R. O., & Wolfe, D. M. *Husbands and wives.* New York: Free Press, 1960.

Bradburn, N. *The structure of psychological well-being.* Chicago: Aldine, 1969.

Brown, R. G. Family structure and social isolation of older persons. *Journal of Gerontology,* 1960, *15,* 170–174.

Brown, P., & Fox. H. Sex differences in divorce. In E. S. Gomberg & V. Franks (Eds.), *Gender and disordered behavior.* New York: Brunner-Mazel, 1979.

Campbell, A., Converse, P. E., & Rodgers, W. *The quality of American life.* New York: Russell Sage, 1976.

Cantor, M. Life space and the social support system of the inner city elderly of New York. *Gerontologist,* 1975, *15,* 23–27.

Clark, M., & Anderson, B. *Culture and aging.* Springfield, Ill.: Charles C. Thomas, 1967.

Clark, M., & Anderson, B. Loneliness and old age. In J. Hartog, J. R. Audy, & Y. A. Cohen (Eds.), *The anatomy of loneliness.* New York: International Universities Press, 1980.

Cohen, C. I., & Sokolovsky, J. *Isolation of the inner city elderly: Myth or method?* Paper presented at the annual meeting of the Gerontological Society, San Francisco, 1977.

Conner, K. A., Powers, E. A., & Bultena, G. L. Social interaction and life satisfaction: An empirical assessment of late-life patterns. *Journal of Gerontology,* 1979, *34,* 116–121.

Cutler, N. E., & Harootyan, R. A. Demography of the aged. In D. S. Woodruff & J. E. Birren (Eds.), *Aging: Scientific perspectives and social issues.* New York: Van Nostrand, 1975.

Dean, L. R. Aging and the decline of affect. *Journal of Gerontology,* 1962, *17,* 440–446.

Edwards, J., & Klemmack, D. Correlates of life satisfaction: A re-examination. *Journal of Gerontology,* 1973, *28,* 497–502.

Eisenson, J. Loneliness and the divorced post-middle-aged male. In J. Hartog, J. R. Audy, & Y. A. Cohen (Eds.), *The anatomy of loneliness.* New York: International Universities Press, 1980.

Fidler, J. Loneliness: The problems of the elderly and retired. *Royal Society of Health Journal,* 1976, *96,* 39–44.

Fischer, C. S. *Friendship, gender, and the lifecycle.* Unpublished manuscript, Institute of Urban and Regional Development, University of California, Berkeley, 1978.

Glenn, N. D. Psychological well-being in the post-parental stage: Some evidence from national surveys. *Journal of Marriage and the Family,* 1975, *37,* 15–27.

Glick, P. *Perspectives on the living arrangements of the elderly.* Paper presented at the annual meeting of the Gerontological Society, San Francisco, 1977.

Goodchilds, J. D., & Bikson, T. K. The older woman living alone. *Generation,* 1980, *4*(4), 16–37.

Gove, W. The relationship between sex roles, mental illness and marital status. *Social Forces,* 1972, *51,* 34–44.

Gove, W. Sex differences in the epidemiology of mental disorder: Evidence and explanations. In E. S. Gomberg & V. Franks (Eds.), *Gender and disordered behavior.* New York: Brunner-Mazel, 1979.

Gubrium, J. F. Marital desolation and the evaluation of everyday life in old age. *Journal of Marriage and the Family,* 1974, *36,* 107–113.

Gurin, G., Veroff, J., & Feld, S. *Americans view their mental health.* New York: Basic Books, 1960.

Hobbes, T. *The English works of Thomas Hobbes, 1839–1845.* Edited by W. Molesworth. London: Oxford Press, 1961.

House, J. S., & Wells, J. A. *Occupational stress, social support and health.* Paper presented at a conference on Reducing Occupational Stress, New York Hospital-Cornell Medical Center, May 1977. (DHEW (N10SH) Publication No. 78–140)

Kerckhoff, A. C. Husband-wife expectations and reactions to retirement. In I. H. Simpson & J. C. McKinney (Eds.), *Social aspects of aging.* Durham, N. C.: Duke University Press, 1966.

Knupfer, G., Clark, W., & Room, R. The mental health of the unmarried. *American Journal of Psychiatry,* 1966, *122,* 841–851.

Kutner, B., Fanshel, D., Togo, A., & Langner, T. *Five hundred over sixty.* New York: Russell Sage, 1956.

Langer, E. J., & Rodin, J. The effects of choice and enhanced personal responsibility for the aged: A field experiment in an institutional setting. *Journal of Personality and Social Psychology,* 1976, *34,* 191–198.

Larson, R. Thirty years of research on the subjective well-being of older Americans. *Journal of Gerontology,* 1978, *33,* 109–125.

Lee, G. R., & Ihinger-Tallman, M. Sibling interaction and morale. *Research on Aging,* 1980, *2*(3), 367–391.

Lemon, B., Bengtson, V., & Peterson, J. An exploration of the activity theory of aging: Activity types and life satisfaction among in-movers to a retirement community. *Journal of Gerontology,* 1972, *27,* 511–523.

Lipman, A. Role conception and morale of couples in retirement. *Journal of Gerontology,* 1961, *16,* 267–271.

Lopata, H. Z. Loneliness: Forms and components. *Social Problems,* 1969, *17* (2), 248–261.

Lopata, H. Z. *Women as widows: Support systems.* New York: Elsevier, 1979.

Lowenthal, M., & Haven, C. Interaction and adaptation: Intimacy as a critical variable. *American Sociological Review,* 1968, *33,* 20–30.

Lowenthal, M., & Robinson, B. Social networks and isolation. In R. Binstock & E. Shanas (Eds.), *Handbook of aging and the social sciences*. New York: Van Nostrand Reinhold, 1976.

Lynch, J. J. *The broken heart: The medical consequences of loneliness.* New York: Basic Books, 1977.

Marquis Academic Media. *Sourcebook on aging* (2nd ed.). Chicago: Marquis Who's Who, Inc., 1979.

Martin, W. C. Activity and disengagement: Life satisfaction of in-movers into a retirement community. *Gerontologist,* 1973, *13,* 224–227.

Parlee, M. B. The friendship bond: PT's survey report on friendship in America. *Psychology Today,* October 1979.

Parmelee, P., & Werner, C. Lonely losers: Stereotypes of single dwellers. *Personality and Social Psychology Bulletin,* 1978, *4*(2), 292–295.

Parron, E. M., & Troll, L. E. Golden wedding couples. *Alternative Lifestyles,* 1978, *1*(4), 447–464.

Pearlin, L., & Johnson, J. Marital status, life-strains and depression. *American Sociological Review,* 1977, *42,* 704–715.

Peplau, L. A., Russell, D., & Heim, M. The experience of loneliness. In I. H. Frieze, D. Bar-Tal, & J. S. Carroll (Eds.), *New approaches to social problems: Applications of attribution theory.* San Francisco: Jossey-Bass, 1979.

Perlman, D., Gerson, A. C., & Spinner, B. Loneliness among senior citizens: An empirical report. *Essence,* 1978, *2*(4), 239–248.

Pettigrew, T. F. Social evaluation theory: Convergences and applications. In D. Levine (Eds.), *Nebraska Symposium on Motivation* (Vol. 15). Lincoln: University of Nebraska Press, 1967.

Pihlblad, C., & McNamara, R. Social adjustment of elderly people in three small towns. In A. Ross & W. Peterson (Eds.), *Older people and their social worlds.* Philadelphia: F. A. Davis, 1965.

Rabushka, A., & Jacobs, B. *Old folks at home.* New York: Free Press, 1980.

Retherford, R. D. *The changing sex differential in mortality.* Westport, Conn.: Greenwood, 1975.

Robinson, J. P. *How Americans use time: A social-psychological analysis of everyday behavior.* New York: Praeger, 1977.

Rook, K. S. *Social networks and well-being of elderly widowed women.* Unpublished doctoral dissertation, University of California, Los Angeles, 1980.

Rubenstein, C., Shaver, P., & Peplau, L. A. Loneliness. *Human Nature,* February 1979, 58–65.

Rubin, Z., Hill, C. T., Peplau, L. A., & Dunkel-Schetter, C. Self-disclosure in dating couples: Sex roles and the ethic of openness. *Journal of Marriage and the Family,* 1980, *42*(2), 305–318.

Schulz, R. Some life and death consequences of perceived control. In J. S. Carroll & J. W. Payne (Eds.), *Cognition and social behavior.* New York: Wiley, 1976a.

Schulz, R. The effects of control and predictability on the physical and psychological well-being of the institutionalized aged. *Journal of Personality and Social Psychology,* 1976b, *33,* 563–573.

Seligman, M. E. P. *Helplessness: On depression, development and death.* San Francisco: Freeman, 1975.

Shanas, E. Social myth as hypothesis: The case of the family relations of old people. *Gerontologist,* 1979, *19,* 3–10.

Shanas, E., & Hauser, P. M. Zero population growth and the family life of old people. *Journal of Social Issues,* 1974, *30*(4), 79–92.

Shanas, E., Townsend, P., Wedderburn, D., Friis, H., Miljoh, P., & Stehouwer, J. *Older people in three industrial societies.* New York: Atherton Press, 1968.

Smith, K., & Lipman. A. Constraint and life satisfaction. *Journal of Gerontology,* 1972, *27,* 77–82.

Spiegelman, M., & Erhardt, C. International comparisons of mortality and longevity. In C. Erhardt & J. E. Berlin (Eds.), *Mortality and morbidity in the United States.* Cambridge, Mass.: Harvard University Press, 1974.

Stueve, A., & Fischer, C. S. *Social networks and older women.* Working paper 292, Institute of Urban and Regional Development, University of California, Berkeley, 1978.

Townsend, P. Isolation, desolation and loneliness. In E. Shanas et al. (Eds.), *Older people in three industrial societies.* New York: Atherton, 1968.

Troll, L. E. The family of later life: A decade review. *Journal of Marriage and the Family,* 1971, *33,* 263–290.

Troll, L. E. & Turner, B. F. Sex differences in problems of aging. In E. S. Gomberg & V. Franks (Eds.), *Gender and disordered behavior: Sex differences in psychopathology.* New York: Brunner-Mazel, 1979.

Tunstall, J. *Old and alone.* London: Routledge & Kegan Paul, 1967.

Walker, K. Time spent by husbands in household work. *Family Economics Review,* 1970, 8–11.

Weissman, M. M., & Klerman, G. L. Sex differences in the epidemiology of depression. In E. S. Gomberg & V. Franks (Eds.), *Gender and disordered behavior.* New York: Brunner-Mazel, 1979.

Wood, V., & Robertson, J. Friendship and kinship interaction: Differential effect on the morale of the elderly. *Journal of Marriage and the Family,* 1978, *40,* 367–375.

Woodward, H., Gingles, R., & Woodward, J. C. Loneliness and the elderly as related to housing. *Gerontologist,* 1974, *14*(4), 349–351.

Woodward, J. C., & Visser, M. J. Loneliness. *Farm, Ranch and Home Quarterly,* Fall 1977, 5–6.

PART SIX

Therapy for Loneliness

It is probably no accident that the first psychologists to write about loneliness were clinicians. Fromm-Reichmann, Sullivan, and others who saw the pain of loneliness in the lives of their patients were quick to recognize the importance of this experience. For those who want to help, the basic question is what to do.

We have learned much about loneliness in the past 20 years that is useful to clinicians treating lonely clients. Chapter 21 by Rook and Peplau surveys information pertinent to clinical intervention for loneliness. This chapter discusses fundamental issues that affect the therapist's choice of goals for the treatment of loneliness, offers guidelines for the clinical assessment of loneliness, and reviews several specific intervention programs. Chapter 22 by Young details a promising new program for the treatment of loneliness. Young's combination of cognitive and behavioral approaches is the most comprehensive treatment program for loneliness now available.

There is still much that we need to know about alleviating loneliness. First, although specific treatment models have been proposed, research on the effectiveness of various kinds of intervention is needed. Second, we know that most people overcome loneliness on their own without professional assistance. Yet we know little about how people try to alleviate loneliness or about which coping strategies are most effective. Third, we know that it will never be possible to prevent loneliness entirely; major changes such as the death of a loved one are unavoidable. Yet other sources of loneliness may be amenable to change. We need to learn more about community and institutional intervention designed to reduce the general level of loneliness among the population. The research and theory about loneliness presented in this volume provide many suggestions about ways to help the lonely.

Chapter 21

Perspectives on Helping the Lonely

Karen S. Rook and Letitia Anne Peplau

As interpersonal and systems theories have gained popularity within the psychological community, therapists have increasingly focused on the social relations of individuals seeking help. Family therapists have developed strategies for helping marriages suffering from conflict and poor communication. Specific interpersonal problems such as sexual dysfunction and lack of assertion have similarly been a focus of clinical intervention and research. But other, perhaps less obvious, relational problems have received little attention from clinicians. Loneliness, the painful experience of deficits in one's social relations, has been a neglected problem.

Several factors may have contributed to the neglect of loneliness as a focus of clinical investigation. First, loneliness has not always been regarded as a separate entity; rather it has been seen as overlapping with other forms of psychological distress. Only recently has research begun to identify the unique aspects of loneliness that distinguish it from other phenomena, most notably depression and anxiety (Bragg, 1979a; Russell, Peplau, & Cutrona, 1980; Weeks, Michela, Peplau, & Bragg, 1980). Second, loneliness may not have seemed "exotic" enough to attract the attention of those more interested in psychopathology than in problems of personal adjustment. Professional prejudice against commonplace disorders may be increased by the fact that most people develop ways of coping with loneliness without professional intervention (Lopata, Heinemann, & Baum, Chapter 19). Third, early sociological analyses (Riesman, Glazer, & Denney, 1961; Slater, 1970) located the causes of loneliness in problems of the society, such as geographic mobility and the American ethic of individualism, rather than in the personality of lonely individuals. From the sociological perspective, reducing loneliness requires societal changes rather than psychotherapy.

As this volume attests, the neglect of loneliness as a focus for clinical

---

We gratefully acknowledge the helpful comments of Steve Alkus, Christine Padesky, and Daniel Perlman.

investigation is beginning to change. This chapter reviews research and theory relevant to helping lonely people. We stress "relevant to" because little work has directly attempted to develop or assess interventions for loneliness. The major goal of this chapter is to provide an organizing "road map" for researchers and practitioners interested in reducing loneliness. The chapter does not present a specific model of intervention for loneliness but rather discusses theoretical and pragmatic issues that arise in undertaking intervention as a goal. The chapter is organized in six sections: We first discuss characteristics of lonely individuals that clinicians may want to evaluate. The second section addresses several basic questions about the nature of social deficits and discusses implications for defining the goal of treatment. We next discuss problems that lead to social deficits. The fourth section reviews research on specific treatment strategies. The fifth section explores how people cope with their loneliness, and a final section addresses prevention of loneliness through community-based intervention and social change.

CHARACTERISTICS OF LONELY CLIENTS

To be most helpful to lonely individuals, it is important to know what the experience of loneliness is typically like and which individuals are most apt to feel lonely. This task is complicated by the fact that loneliness is not a unitary phenomenon. For many individuals, loneliness occurs in response to disruptive life changes, including widowhood, divorce, and moving, each of which raises unique treatment issues. For example, the alleviation of loneliness that follows the death of a spouse or close friend often entails resolution of grief as a prerequisite to formation of new social bonds (Lopata et al., Chapter 19). Loneliness in response to divorce, in contrast, may require attention to feelings of interpersonal inadequacy and insecurity about re-entering the social "marketplace" (Weiss, 1975). For other individuals, loneliness may be a lifelong problem not precipitated by recent social loss or disruption. An example is the painfully shy student who was friendless in high school and remains socially isolated in college.

Young (Chapter 22) suggests that chronicity is an important dimension on which lonely people differ. *Chronic loneliness,* in his view, results from long-term deficits in the individual's ability to relate to others, whereas *situational loneliness* results from a major disruption of the individual's pattern of social relationships. *Transient loneliness* refers to the occasional feelings of loneliness that most people seem to experience from time to time. Chronicity is an important diagnostic dimension, since it has direct implications for etiology and intervention. Chronically lonely individuals, for example, may benefit most from desensitization of social anxiety or from social skills training. Situationally lonely individuals, in contrast, may benefit most from reassurance and assistance in identifying social contexts in which new relationships can be explored.

Lonely individuals also differ in the extent to which they use the *self-label* of loneliness. Loneliness researchers have primarily studied people who identify themselves as lonely on self-report questions or loneliness scales (Russell, Chapter 6). In clinical settings, however, even severely lonely individuals may not necessarily recognize or discuss loneliness as a problem. Feared stigma may lead some clients to avoid the label "lonely" even with their therapists. Fromm-Reichmann suggested that "Even mild . . . states of loneliness do not seem to be easy to talk about" (1959, p. 6). Early clinical papers on loneliness emphasized that individuals may guard themselves against the pain of loneliness by denying the experience. "Often loneliness is not felt; instead the person has a feeling of unexplained dread, or desperation, or of extreme restlessness. These feelings [precipitate] automatic actions that force other persons to come into contact with the lonely individual" (H. E. Peplau, 1955, p. 67). For example, H. E. Peplau (1955) described one patient whose severe drinking required nursing care—thus providing the social contact he actually needed. It has been suggested that loneliness leads some individuals to abuse alcohol or drugs even though they may not recognize or describe themselves as lonely. The astute clinician must therefore be prepared to infer the presence of loneliness from other signs and cues.

In addition to differences in the duration and recognition of loneliness, lonely individuals also differ in specific affective, cognitive, and behavioral characteristics highlighted briefly below.

Affective Patterns

Loneliness is almost always an aversive experience, although research has identified considerable variation in the specific emotions associated with loneliness. For example, Rubenstein and Shaver (Chapter 13) identified four clusters of feelings: desperation, depression, impatient boredom (which included anger), and self-deprecation. Although these feelings were common among lonely adults, no single feeling was reported by more than 60% of the individuals in the study. Young (Chapter 22) suggested that variations in how people cope with loneliness influence whether they feel sad and depressed, or anxious and afraid, or angry and bitter.

Probably of greatest importance for clinicians is the common association of loneliness and depression. Empirical investigations have frequently found significant and substantial correlations between loneliness and depression (Bradburn, 1969; Bragg, 1979a; Young, Chapter 22). Conceptually, depression is a more general and global experience than loneliness (Horowitz, French, & Anderson, Chapter 12). Depression can be triggered by the sorts of changes in one's social relations that often lead to loneliness (e.g., divorce or widowhood), but depression can also result from nonsocial events (e.g., loss of one's job, flunking out of school, illness) that may be unrelated to loneliness.

Recent studies conducted at UCLA have examined loneliness and depression among college students. Results demonstrate empirically that loneliness and depression are overlapping but distinct experiences (Russell, Peplau, &

Cutrona, 1980; Weeks, Michela, Peplau, & Bragg, 1980). Bragg (1979a and b) has proposed what appears to be a useful distinction between the *depressed lonely* and the *nondepressed lonely*. He compared groups of lonely students matched on the severity of their loneliness, but differing in depression as measured by Beck's (1961) inventory. Results supported the view that depression reflects a more global pattern of negativity and dissatisfaction. Whereas the depressed lonely and nondepressed lonely were equally dissatisfied with their social relationships, the depressed lonely were significantly more dissatisfied with nonsocial aspects of their lives such as their schoolwork, employment, finances, or health. The depressed lonely also felt significantly greater anxiety and anger than did the nondepressed lonely. Bragg concluded that different types of intervention may be appropriate for these two types of loneliness. With severely depressed lonely patients, psychotherapy or psychopharmacological treatment aimed specifically at reducing depression may need to precede efforts to deal directly with loneliness as a problem.

In light of evidence linking risk of suicide to severe depression (Pokorny, 1964) and to social isolation (Becker, 1974; Colson, 1973), practitioners should be especially careful to monitor indications of suicidal intent among depressed lonely clients. It may be helpful to note in this regard that severely depressed patients are more likely to attempt suicide after they have begun to improve (Keith-Spiegel & Spiegel, 1967).

Cognitive Patterns

Cognitive processes that cause or accompany loneliness have been the subject of considerable research and speculation. Three issues seem most relevant to clinical intervention.

In helping lonely clients, it is useful to know how lonely individuals interpret their social situation. Peplau and her co-workers (Peplau, Miceli, & Morasch, Chapter 9; Peplau, Russell, & Heim, 1979) have stressed the importance of personal accounts or explanations that lonely people develop to interpret their social problems. Peplau speculated that as loneliness persists over time, lonely people often start to blame themselves for their social failure, thus increasing the risk of depression and perhaps decreasing efforts to improve their social relations. Young (1978) also believes that to understand why lonely people feel and act as they do, we must learn about their view of themselves and their relationships. His cognitive therapy for loneliness (detailed in Chapter 22) emphasizes the distortions, automatic thoughts, and assumptions of lonely people.

Another common pattern may be for lonely people to focus excessively on themselves and their internal experiences. Weiss (1973) proposed that lonely people are hyperalert and vigilant to threat. Thus they may be anxious in social settings and oversensitive to minimal social cues, resulting in a "tendency to misinterpret or exaggerate the hostile or affectionate intent of others" (p. 21). Jones (Chapter 15) reviewed evidence that lonely people interact in more self-focused ways, making more self-statements during conversations, asking fewer questions of their partner, changing the topic more often and responding more slowly. Perlman and his associates (Florentine, Perlman, & McIntyre, 1979; Gerson & Perlman, 1979) found that lonely people show difficulty in concentrating on tasks, and may actually perform more poorly than nonlonely people in situations requiring focused attention.

Finally, clinicians should be aware that lonely people often evaluate themselves and other people negatively. Jones (Chapter 15) suggests that attitudes of cynicism and interpersonal mistrust, along with a tendency to devalue new acquaintances, may contribute to the persistence of loneliness among individuals. There is also strong evidence that loneliness is often accompanied by low self-esteem (Peplau et al., Chapter 9). Given the cultural emphasis on having successful social relationships, it is understandable that lonely people who have recently gone through a divorce or who have not developed close friendships may think of themselves as "failures" (Gordon, 1976). Research is needed to clarify whether these negative perceptions are a direct result of loneliness or whether they stem from the depression and anxiety that frequently accompany loneliness. In either case, effective approaches to helping the lonely may need to address not only the painful emotions of loneliness, but also cognitive patterns that can exacerbate the experience of loneliness.

Behavior Patterns

Little research has focused on the actual behavior of lonely individuals, and most of the available studies (reviewed in Jones, Chapter 15) have been limited to college students. Data suggest, however, that for some lonely people, poor social skills are an issue. What is less clear is whether faulty social skills are the initial cause of loneliness or whether they are a result of being lonely, reflecting perhaps a lack of motivation or lack of opportunities to interact socially.

Three patterns have been tentatively identified. First, as mentioned earlier, Jones (Chapter 15) found that the verbal interactions of lonely people were self-focused and unresponsive. Second, Solano and Batten (1979) found that lonely students were more extreme than nonlonely students in their disclosure of personal information; in some instances the lonely students disclosed significantly more information, in other situations they disclosed significantly less. Third, loneliness is related to self-reports of being shy and reluctant to take social risks (Jones, Freemon, & Goswick, 1981).

Implications for Assessment

We have described characteristics of lonely individuals that clinicians may wish to assess, including the client's history of loneliness (chronic or situational), emotions associated with loneliness (anger, sadness, etc.), thoughts associated with loneliness (beliefs about the causes of loneliness, cognitive distortions, negativity), self-esteem, social skills, and means of coping with loneliness (particularly denial or substance abuse). Clinicians should also be alert for signs of coexisting clinical disorders, such as depression or anxiety.

Although we have emphasized dimensions along which lonely clients may differ, the one feature common to all lonely individuals is the experience of a deficit in their social relations. In the next section we examine how clinicians' conceptual perspectives on social deficit affect the goals and methods of intervention.

UNDERSTANDING SOCIAL DEFICITS

If the common denominator in the experience of loneliness is a perceived deficit in social contact, then the antidote to loneliness might seem relatively straightforward—increase social contact. Yet the implementation of this very general recommendation rests on implicit assumptions and value judgments about the functions of social contact and the desirability of various types of social relationships. In order to be helpful to lonely clients, it is useful to have a framework for conceptualizing social deficit. In this section we examine social deficits by asking a set of very basic questions: What is the nature of social deficit? What kinds of social contact alleviate loneliness? Can nonsocial activities help alleviate loneliness?

What Is the Nature of Social Deficit?

When a person is lonely, just what is it that he or she is actually missing— what is the nature of the social deficit? Three different answers to this question have been proposed.

One of the earliest answers, provided by Sullivan (1953), emphasized *human needs*. Sullivan viewed loneliness as a response to the "inadequate discharge of the need for human intimacy" (1953, p. 290). He went on to explain rather generally that intimate relations provide, among other things, an opportunity for consensual validation of personal worth. Sullivan used a biologically oriented language of human needs.

More recent analyses of social contact have borrowed the language of social exchange theory (Homans, 1974) and have attempted to specify more precisely important classes of *social exchanges* or *rewards*. Table 21.1 summarizes some of the taxonomies of social exchanges that have been proposed by different theorists. Most of these taxonomies have not been validated empirically, yet they represent important attempts to make operational the significant rewards or provisions derived from social contact and, by implication, to specify what it is that lonely people miss.

An unanswered question is whether all exchange deficits are related to loneliness. For example, lacking someone to turn to for guidance or for tangible assistance may not be related to feeling lonely, whereas lacking someone with whom to engage in informal interactions or to exchange reas-

Table 21.1.   Theoretical Taxonomies of Social "Exchanges" or "Rewards"

Theorist	Term	Taxonomy
Brim (1974)	Social relationship content	Assistance, value similarity, concern, trust, desired interactions
Caplan (1974)	Social support	Mobilization of personal resources, sharing of tasks, provision of tangible aid (e.g., money, materials, skills) and cognitive guidance
Cobb (1976, 1979)	Social support	Communicated caring (emotional support, esteem support, network support), instrumental support or counseling, active support or mothering, material support
Fischer (1978)	Social exchanges	Instrumental exchange (aid), social exchange (sociable interaction), personal exchange (advice, consolation)
Flanders (1976)	Features of emotional intimacy	Frequent interactions, informal interactions, self-disclosure, touching, favorable accumulation of rewards over time, reciprocity, feelings of closeness
Foa and Foa (1974)	Interpersonal resources	Love, status, information, money, goods, services
Kahn (1979)	Social support	Expression of positive affect, affirmation of another's behavior or views, symbolic or material aid
Lopata (1978, 1979)	Social support	Economic support, service support, social support (social activities), emotional support (relational sentiments, self-feeling states)
Weiss (1969, 1974)	Social provisions	Attachment, social integration, opportunity for nurturance, reassurance of worth, reliable alliance, guidance

surances of worth may be strongly related to feeling lonely. Loneliness researchers have seldom specified essential social exchanges or provisions and therefore offer few guidelines for inferring which among a set of possible provisions are actually related to loneliness. An exception in this regard is Weiss's work. Weiss (1973) distinguished two kinds of loneliness: emotional loneliness based on the lack of an intimate partner, and social loneliness based on the lack of ties to a social community. Thus, although Weiss (1974) identifies a set of six social provisions, he hypothesizes that two (attachment and social integration) are most important in producing loneliness.

A third approach to the question of what lonely people lack emphasizes the *status* associated with valued *social roles*. The idea here is that people may want certain social statuses for their own sake. Gordon (1976) argued that we live in a "couple culture," in which success is measured not only in terms of material possessions but also in terms of achieving certain types of relationships. For the young adolescent this may mean having a "best friend";

for the teenage girl it may entail having a "boyfriend." For adult Americans, considerable social status has traditionally been attached to marriage. Stein (1976) discussed the "cultural imperative" of marriage and cited such novels as *Sheila Levine Is Dead and Living in New York* by Gail Parent and *Looking for Mr. Goodbar* by Judith Rossner as reinforcing the cultural stereotype that unmarried people are failures in the marriage market. Because of social pressures and rewards associated with certain roles, individuals who fail to measure up to cultural expectations may feel dissatisfied and lonely, even if they derive many essential relational provisions from other types of relationships. Stein (1976) suggested that social scientists may share the bias that everyone "should" be married. It may be important in helping the lonely for therapists to examine both their own values about social roles and those of the client.

What Kinds of Social Contact Can Alleviate Loneliness?

Another issue concerns the desirability of different approaches to overcoming social deficits. For example, even if two therapists agreed on the importance of a particular social exchange, such as confiding personal problems, they might recommend different strategies for overcoming this deficit. One strategy might involve increasing the frequency of confiding in other people, regardless of who the others are, whereas a very different strategy might involve developing a confidant relationship with one particular person. In this section we contrast two theoretical positions on this issue, each of which has somewhat different implications for treatment.

One perspective, grounded in behavioral theory, emphasizes the benefits of rewarding *social events* or outcomes (e.g., going to a movie with someone, having a conversation), independent of the type of relationship in which they occur. Young (1978) suggested that people experience loneliness when they fall below a "threshold level" of social reinforcement based on prior experiences. One treatment implication of this perspective is that lonely clients may be helped by encouraging them to increase their frequencies of positive social events, whether the events involve a relationship with one other person or multiple relationships. Another implication is that having numerous social experiences of one type may compensate for the lack of others. For example, from this perspective, a high level of social recreation might compensate for a low level of intimate self-disclosure.

In contrast to this view, some theorists argue that certain types of *social relationships* are essential for psychological well-being. In fact, the capacity to develop and maintain an intimate relationship is in itself often considered an index of psychological health. Brain (1976) suggested that friendships should be elevated to a status similar to that ascribed to love relationships. Lowenthal and Haven (1968) have documented the importance of confidant relationships for psychological well-being. The treatment implication of this perspective clearly differs from the social event perspective; treatment should focus on helping the client to establish particular types of social relationships, such as love relationships, friendships, or confidant relationships. An extension of this perspective asserts not only that particular types of relationships should be established but also that they should be expressed through specific social roles, such as boyfriend-girlfriend or spouse. Treatment guided by this perspective would thus encourage lonely clients to establish social ties likely to culminate in culturally sanctioned role relationships.

From this relationship perspective, different types of social contact are not interchangeable. Weiss (1973), for example, argued, "It is not possible for an individual to compensate for the absence of one relational provision by increased acquisition of others" (p. 227). No single relationship can supply all essential social provisions, and so each individual must have both an attachment figure and a network of friends for optimal adjustment. Deficiencies in these different types of relationships will result in either emotional or social loneliness. Treatment in some cases may thus focus not only on particular dyadic relationships but also on the lonely client's *social network*.

Can Nonsocial Activities Help Alleviate Loneliness?

While this idea might intuitively seem far removed from the concerns of the lonely client, several potential benefits of rewarding solitary activities can be identified. First, the capacity to be alone is thought to enhance the capacity for intimacy. Improving one's capacity to be alone should thus improve one's capacity to be intimate with others. Young (Chapter 22) suggested that many lonely people are actually afraid of being alone and that, paradoxically, once they overcome their fears of aloneness they can often initiate friendships more easily. Moreover, the act of initiating activities that do not depend upon the availability or cooperation of others might increase lonely clients' sense of personal control (Peplau et al., 1979).

Second, preliminary research supports the value of increasing the frequency of enjoyable activities, including nonsocial activities, as a component of the treatment of depression (Lewinsohn, Biglan, & Zeiss, 1976). Activity-oriented approaches are based on the view that mood and activity are causally related, and on evidence that depressed individuals typically engage in low levels of reinforcing activities (MacPhillamy & Lewinsohn, 1974). Increasing the frequency of satisfying solitary activities may be a particularly helpful supplementary strategy for improving the morale of clients who are both lonely and depressed.

Finally, if encouraging lonely clients to develop enjoyable solitary activities seems only "second best," it should be remembered that social contact entails personal costs as well as rewards (Homans, 1974). Establishing a love relationship is not always the panacea that some individuals expect (Lederer & Jackson, 1968). A realistic appraisal of the costs as well as the rewards associated with social interaction may offer lonely clients a more balanced perspective on the relative merits of social and nonsocial activities.

Implications for Treatment

We recommend caution in defining relationship formation as *the* goal of intervention with lonely clients. We wish to underscore the potential value of conceptualizing social deficits in terms of specific social rewards or exchanges that are lacking. From the standpoint of treatment, such a conceptualization expands the range of acceptable treatment goals to include a focus on social events as well as on social relationships.

While lonely individuals are most likely to say that they need "one special person" (Rubenstein & Shaver, Chapter 13) or "a romantic partner" (Cutrona, Chapter 18), their views do not necessarily represent psychologically sound treatment goals. For example, even though Weiss (1973) believes that the only way to relieve loneliness is to form new relationships, he cautions that the "campaign for an attachment figure" is difficult and fraught with risks, including the risks of social embarrassment and of making hasty or troublesome partner choices. Moreover, having such relationships does not necessarily protect one against feeling lonely, particularly when important social exchanges are not provided through the relationship. For example, some lonely people may not take the time to plan satisfying activities with their friends or partners.

Young (Chapter 22) has recently developed a model of treatment that begins by having the lonely client engage in enjoyable solitary activities, followed by having the client develop casual social relationships and later working toward the development of an intimate, long-term relationship. A *succession* of different goals within treatment may represent a viable alternative to defining "finding someone special" as the only goal of treatment. This idea is consistent with several of the specific models of intervention described later.

PROBLEMS IN DEVELOPING SATISFYING RELATIONSHIPS

The preceding section examined essential elements of satisfying social relationships that if lacking can lead to loneliness. This section considers specific problems that lead to social deficits.

There is no single universal problem leading to loneliness; many potential problems can cause social deficits. It is useful to distinguish problems concerning the initiation of new relationships, the maintenance of satisfying relationships over time, and the dissolution of relationships (Levinger, in press).

Initiating Relationships

For many lonely people, a central problem is how to develop new relationships—how to find a confidant, make new friends, fall in love. Anthropologists suggest that this problem may be greater for Americans than for members of other cultures, in which there is less freedom of choice about social relations. Brain (1976) discussed cultures in which arranged marriages and even arranged friendships guarantee that everyone has those social ties considered essential by the culture. He commented:

We have overrated the necessity of choosing our friends and wives. We decry arranged marriages . . . Choice is the thing! However, this freedom of choice often means that it is never made—hence the frustrated spinsters, the friendless and the lonely. (p. 19)

Several specific problems may arise in initiating new relationships.

Social Opportunities

Although Americans are allegedly free in their choice of companions, many constraints affect the initiation of new relationships. Some constraints are very basic—time, distance, and money. The impoverished student who carries a full course load and a heavy employment schedule may have little time for sleep, let alone making friends. The firespotter who lives in a remote part of the forest has few opportunities to meet people. The single parent on a tight budget may not be able to afford the babysitters who would permit time to socialize.

Constraints can also limit a person's "pool of eligibles"—the set of people whom we consider appropriate as friends or lovers. We tend to be attracted to people who are similar to us in interests, values, and background (Rubin, 1973). Hence the match between a person and his or her social environment is important. People who are "different" from those around them—the only Black family in a neighborhood, the one old person in the apartment building—may have fewer opportunities to start relationships (cf., Blau, 1961). An example of such constraints comes from studies of the impact of sex ratios on remarriage among older adults. Because men tend to die at considerably younger ages than women, the older population is composed disproportionately of women (see Chapter 20 by Peplau, Bikson, Rook, & Goodchilds). Not surprisingly, older widowers are much more likely to remarry than are older widows. In understanding the roots of loneliness, it is essential to acknowledge the impact of social opportunities. Sometimes the most effective intervention for loneliness may be to encourage individuals to change their social environment—change jobs, move to a new area, join a new group—rather than to change themselves.

Personal Problems

Successful initiation of relationships may be hampered by poor social skills, social anxiety, and self-defeating perceptions. For some individuals, the lack of social skills is a serious problem. Among the relevant skills may be self-presentation (both appearance and demeanor), social assertiveness (overcoming shyness, taking the initiative), dating roles (as prescribed in various communities and age groups), and communication skills. A second problem may arise because lonely people are often anxious. For some people anxiety may lead to the avoidance of social interactions. But probably more often, lonely people seek companionship despite their fears (Sullivan, 1953). In such cases anxiety may interfere with effective social functioning. Finally, cognitive factors may be important. Individuals may have unrealistic standards for "eligible" companions, distorted perceptions of themselves and their interactions, or low self-esteem.

Maintaining Satisfactory Relationships

People can be lonely even with relationships. Just as being alone does not necessarily imply being lonely, so too being married or having friends is no certain guarantee of avoiding loneliness. We know relatively little about the loneliness that occurs *within* the context of relationships. Three possible problems include separation, restricted networks, and the quality of relationships.

Separation

Physical separation from family and friends is a fairly common occurrence in American society. Such events as moving to a new community, going away to summer camp or to college, or spending extended periods in such institutions as hospitals or the military all affect social relationships. Separation reduces the frequency of interaction, makes the satisfactions provided by relationships less available, and may raise concerns that the relationship will be weakened by absence. Evidence that physical separation puts people at risk for loneliness is readily available. For example, Weiss (1973) and Weissman and Paykel (1974) described the difficulties experienced by corporate wives forced to move by their husband's work. Duvall (1945) discussed the loneliness of servicemen's wives during wartime.

Restricted Networks

People may benefit most from having a fairly rich and diverse social network, including ties to friends, a loved partner, and family (Weiss, 1974). From this perspective, a person can be lonely despite having some relationships if other important relations are lacking. Thus the lonely housewife may be very satisfied with her marriage, but miss the companionship of female friends. In such cases it would be important for a therapist to explore deficiencies in a person's entire social network, and not assume that a lonely married person necessarily has a troubled marriage.

The Quality of Relationships

Loneliness can result not only from the absence of relationships, but from dissatisfaction with the quality of existing relationships. Indeed beyond some nominal threshold for the quantity of a person's social relations, qualitative dissatisfactions appear to be the more important determinant of loneliness (Cutrona, Chapter 18). We know little about those features of relationships that are critical in preventing feelings of loneliness. Issues of communication, empathy, and "feeling understood" may be of central importance. To the extent that competition and conflict inhibit open self-disclosure, they may be linked to loneliness as well. Goode (1961) described such a family relationship: "The atmosphere is without laughter or fun, and a sullen gloom pervades the household. Members do not discuss their problems or experiences with each other, and communication is kept to a minimum" (p. 441). This situation illustrates what Levinger (1979) called "empty shell" marriages—relationships that provide few satisfactions to the marital partners but persist because of children or other barriers to divorce.

Termination of Relationships

Ultimately all social relationships end, either through the death of one partner or through breakup or divorce. When relationships end, people often experience not only loneliness, but grief as well. Weiss (1973) distinguished between these two experiences. Grief is "the syndrome of shock, protest, anger, and painful, searing sadness, which is produced by traumatic loss" (p. 16). In contrast, loneliness is a reaction to the absence rather than the loss of the loved person. Studies of reactions to relationship dissolution have focused on family relationships, especially marriage, rather than on friendship. This reflects the assumption that the loss of close kin is more traumatic, and the fact that the ending of friendships is not marked by formal transitions as in widowhood or divorce. Several discussions of the special problems of divorce (Goode, 1961; Levinger & Moles, 1979; Weiss, 1975) and widowhood (Lopata, 1979, Chapter 19; Parkes, 1972) are available.

INTERVENTION STRATEGIES

Given the many factors that can cause a person to feel lonely, loneliness may become an issue in any psychotherapy context. Discussion in this section is limited to those instances in which some form of social deficit is a primary presenting problem. The treatment of social deficits that are secondary to such serious psychopathology as schizophrenia (Schein, 1974) is not addressed, although some of the intervention strategies described here may have broad application. Furthermore, this section focuses only on treatment strategies that attempt to increase or improve social contact; strategies for increasing involvement in enjoyable solitary activities are not discussed, although they may often be beneficial to lonely clients.

The design of systematic interventions for loneliness is new. Early writings by clinicians such as Fromm-Reichmann (1959) and Sullivan (1953) were intended primarily to sensitize therapists to loneliness as a significant and neglected clinical problem. These authors recommended that therapists take the initiative in acknowledging their clients' loneliness. Therapists were also encouraged to be alert for traces of their own loneliness. Since the publication of these early papers, additional books and articles have analyzed loneliness from a psychodynamic framework.

Most psychodynamic analyses suggest that loneliness can only be treated successfully through an intensive therapist-client relationship. One task of therapy from this viewpoint is for the clinician to understand the meaning of the client's communications by sharing the client's experience of loneliness (Burton, 1961; Fromm-Reichmann, 1959; Hobson, 1974). Leiderman (1969) suggested that self-object differentiation is a crucial treatment issue, since the yearning for another individual that is experienced as loneliness reflects incomplete or undifferentiated self-object representations. Other psychodynamic formulations emphasized fear of intimacy or fear of rejection (Gaev, 1976), and such defenses against loneliness as overeating (Fromm-Reichmann, 1959) and substance abuse (Bell, 1956; Gaev, 1976). The psychodynamic approaches have thus far generated little research. Systematic description and evaluation of psychodynamically based treatments are needed.

The remainder of this section discusses the few intervention strategies relevant to loneliness that are available. Much of this work is behaviorally oriented and problem-focused. The discussion is organized around the problems of initiating relationships, maintaining satisfying relationships, and ending relationships.

Initiating Relationships

Approaches aimed at helping people to form new relationships include social skills training, cognitive-behavioral therapy, and shyness groups.

Social Skills Training

Research described earlier suggests that some lonely people lack skills needed to initiate and maintain social interaction (Jones, Chapter 15). Social skills deficits have also been cited as a cause of heterosexual dating anxiety, a significant problem, particularly among adolescents and young adults (Martinson & Zerface, 1970). According to the skills deficit hypothesis, socially anxious individuals may have never learned appropriate behaviors or may have learned inappropriate behaviors (Bandura, 1969).

Considerable research has focused on programs to improve social skills. In a recent review Curran (1977) concluded that experimental investigations support the effectiveness of social skills training as a treatment for dating anxiety. These training programs draw upon behavioral techniques such as modeling, role playing, self-observation (using videotape methods), and homework assignments. Clients are taught skills such as initiating conversations, speaking fluently on the telephone, giving and receiving compliments, handling periods of silence, enhancing physical attractiveness, nonverbal methods of communication, and approaches to physical intimacy. Training is usually conducted in groups and lasts less than 10 weeks.

In a typical session, the therapist might show a group of clients a videotape of a model starting a conversation inappropriately. The group would then discuss ways in which the model could have performed better. Following this, another videotape would be shown in which the model performed more effectively. Each client might then role play starting a conversation while other group members observed. Such role plays are sometimes videotaped so that clients can see exactly what they did. The session might conclude with the therapist giving homework assignments, such as starting a conversation with a stranger, to be done before the next session.

In a recent therapy analogue study, Jones, Hobbs, and Hockenbury (1980) evaluated an intervention to increase personal attention among lonely college students. A group of lonely students was taught to increase personal attention (e.g., topic continuation, questions, references to the other person) shown to a stranger in a series of dyadic interaction tasks. Training consisted of modeling, practice interaction, and feedback. Compared with two control groups of lonely students who did not receive instruction in personal attention, these trained students reported less loneliness, less self-consciousness, and less shyness at the end of the study.

Research indicates that social skills training is also helpful for socially isolated children (Asher & Renshaw, 1980; Gottman, Gonso, & Schuler, 1976; Keller & Carlson, 1974; Oden & Asher, 1977). Such programs use behavioral techniques comparable to those employed with adults. Many of these programs have been developed for use in school settings. Oden and Asher (1977) cautioned researchers and practitioners to conduct interventions in ways that do not stigmatize children, for instance, by inviting non-isolated as well as isolated children to participate.

The particular skills emphasized in social skills training programs have been chosen largely on the basis of their face validity, rather than on the basis of empirical studies identifying important skill components in social relationships. The importance of various skills is likely to be a function of the duration of the relationship (Curran, 1977) and the type of relationship, such as friend, co-worker, or intimate partner (Oden & Asher, 1977). Existing social skills training programs appear to place greatest emphasis on skills needed to initiate relationships. This is a necessary starting point for socially anxious or isolated individuals; yet skills for "deepening" relationships and for managing problems that arise in relationships are also important. Assertion, conflict resolution, and appropriate self-disclosure may be particularly important in this regard. Future research might seek to identify specific skills that facilitate the transition to more intimate relationships (Levinger & Snoek, 1972).

Cognitive-Behavioral Therapy

Recently a number of cognitively oriented therapies have been developed to help clients recognize and correct self-defeating thought patterns (Beck, Rush, Shaw, & Emery, 1979; Mahoney, 1974; Meichenbaum, 1977). In a particularly promising development, Young (Chapter 22) has recently designed a cognitive-behavioral model for treatment of loneliness. Since this therapy model is described in detail in the next chapter, only its key features will be discussed here. It should be noted that cognitive-behavioral techniques have relevance to problems of improving and ending relationships as well as initiating relationships.

A critical feature of the cognitive-behavioral model is teaching clients to recognize automatic thoughts and to regard them as hypotheses to be tested rather than as facts. For example, in new situations, socially anxious lonely clients may automatically think "I'll make a fool of myself" and as a result may avoid such situations. The therapist would encourage the client to test this thought empirically by inquiring how many times the client has actually behaved foolishly in the past, by asking the client to estimate how many people would actually bother to evaluate the client's behavior, by having the client keep a record of "foolish behavior" for a specific period, and so forth. Through this process of testing automatic thoughts, clients often discover inconsistencies in their assumptions and alternative interpretations that may have been overlooked.

Peplau et al. (1979) emphasized that lonely individuals' self-defeating thoughts can result from common errors in evaluating the causes of behavior. People may underestimate the role of situational causes of loneliness and overestimate the importance of personal factors. People may also underestimate the changeability of causes of loneliness, leading to feelings of hopelessness and self-blame. For example, Peplau et al. suggested that physical appearance and social skills can be improved to a greater extent than most lonely people assume. Thus clinicians may want to help lonely clients reexamine beliefs about the factors that led to their loneliness.

Glass, Gottman, and Shmurak (1976) successfully used cognitive-behavioral techniques in conjunction with social skills training for socially anxious college men. Participants first observed a model who verbalized self-critical thoughts in a difficult social situation, such as a man handling a telephone conversation with a woman who did not remember his name. The model was then coached by the therapist and reenacted the situation making positive self-statements. In comparison with subjects who received only social skills training, those who received cognitive modification as well were significantly more skillful in novel social situations—that is, those in which they had not been trained. Learning how to cope with negative self-evaluations is a technique that individuals can practice on their own and apply in new situations.

Shyness Groups

A link has frequently been suggested between loneliness, shyness, and the inhibition of social risk-taking. Pilkonis and his colleagues (Pilkonis & Zimbardo, 1979; Pilkonis, Heape, & Klein, 1980) recommend small-group therapy as the preferred treatment for shyness. They draw upon social skills training techniques and recommend having two co-therapists who can model interpersonal behavior for group members. Pilkonis and Zimbardo (1979) suggest that shy people need to develop more adequate general response styles in addition to specific social skills. In particular, they argue that shy people need to learn to "restructure" social encounters that arouse anxiety because of their ambiguity. As an example of such restructuring, they suggest that shy people develop their "own agendas" for social interactions, such as getting to know as much as possible about another person in a conversation. Presumably having a specific agenda distracts the shy person from her or his anxiety.

Maintaining Satisfying Relationships

Virtually no research has addressed loneliness that occurs in the context of ongoing relationships. Our discussion is designed primarily to call attention to this problem.

Certain qualities of social relationships, such as conflict or poor communication, that may be associated with loneliness seem best treated within marital or couples therapies (Gurman & Rice, 1975; Jacobson & Margolin, 1979; Stuart, 1980). Marital enrichment programs (Olson, 1976; Otto, 1976; Patterson, Hops, & Weiss, 1975) may also be useful in enhancing primary relationships. Psychodynamic formulations that stress fear of intimacy, fear of commitment, and overdependency represent an alternative way to conceptualize the sources of loneliness in ongoing relationships.

For some individuals who have a satisfying primary relationship, loneliness may be linked to having a limited network of social relations. Given the widespread belief that a mate should satisfy most of one's social needs (Gaev, 1976; Lederer & Jackson, 1968), it may be easy to assume that married or "coupled" individuals are never lonely. Thus, while we recommend that clinicians always evaluate the primary relationship of a lonely client, we also urge attention to social network deficiencies that may cause or exacerbate loneliness.

Ending Relationships

Loneliness that results when a significant social relationship ends differs from loneliness due to the lack of relationships or to problems in existing relationships. Weiss and his colleagues (1975; 1976) have developed programs to deal with loneliness due to marital separation and bereavement.

Seminars for the Separated

This program (Weiss, 1976) was developed to alleviate feelings of marginality, confusion, and self-doubt that follow marital separation. Seminars for the Separated involve eight weekly meetings of approximately 30 men and women who have recently separated from their spouses. Each meeting begins with a 45-minute lecture given by a staff member, followed by small group discussions of five to eight people. The lectures cover such topics as the emotional reactions accompanying separation, the impact of separation on relationships with children, and starting to date again. Each meeting concludes with an opportunity for participants to socialize over refreshments.

While there are no published studies evaluating the effectiveness of this treatment approach, participants' evaluations of the program are reported to have been positive. Benefits of the program are attributed to several factors. First, the information provided through the lectures reportedly helped participants to understand puzzling and sometimes disturbing emotional reactions. Weiss gives the example of a woman who was disturbed by her impulse to attempt a reunion with her former husband and who reported relief when she learned through the seminar that such feelings are common and reflect the persistence of attachment feelings despite hostility toward the former spouse. Contact with a group of similar, supportive others apparently reduced participants' feelings of marginality and also provided an opportunity to practice socializing with members of the opposite sex. Finally, Weiss stresses the group's value in simply getting members moving again and initiating steps to improve their lives.

Seminars for the Bereaved

In attempting to generalize his group treatment approach to the recently bereaved, Weiss (1976) encountered unexpected problems. For example, whereas explanations of the nature of separation distress were comforting to the newly separated, comparable explanations of grief were experienced by the bereaved as painful. In contrast to the separated, the bereaved were more ambivalent about overcoming their distress, since they saw their pain as testifying to the intensity of their feelings for the deceased spouse. Weiss reports that the bereaved were also less self-doubting than the separated, and as a result were quick to resent clumsy or awkward attempts to help. Thus the bereaved were less tolerant of fellow group members whose mode of participation in the group differed from their own (e.g., who were more talkative), suggesting a need for careful screening of group members to ensure compatibility. Finally, whereas contact between the sexes had been an important benefit for the separated, Weiss found that the mourning process of widows and widowers differed enough that having both sexes together in one group was detrimental.

Weiss's (1976) description of the working assumptions that guided development of the two programs and the problems encountered in their implementation is useful to practitioners who anticipate developing similar group interventions. Weiss concludes that "any program intended to help people in transition will have to be responsive both in content and in format to the characteristics of the particular transition with which it deals" (p. 225).

SELF-HELP STRATEGIES OF LONELY PEOPLE

The discussion up to this point has focused on how professionals might help lonely people. Yet most lonely individuals do not seek professional help. For example, among a sample of new college students (Cutrona, Chapter 18), only 9% said they had ever talked to a counselor or therapist about ways to overcome their loneliness during the first year at college. Similarly, Lopata, Heinemann, and Baum (Chapter 19) report that few widows turned to the clergy for guidance, and even fewer consulted doctors or therapists. In a large-scale survey of Americans (Gurin, Veroff, & Feld, 1960), only 2% of respondents said they would seek professional help to handle "worries" or "periods of unhappiness." This section reviews research on how people cope with loneliness.

What Lonely People Say They Do

Available data about typical coping strategies for loneliness are based exclusively on self-reports. Two studies (Paloutzian & Ellison, Chapter 14; Rubenstein & Shaver, Chapter 13) asked people what they do when they "feel lonely." The most common responses included reading, watching television, listening to music, eating, and calling a friend. In interpreting these findings, it should be noted that the wording of the questions emphasized immediate responses that people might use to alleviate or divert attention from feelings of loneliness. A complete analysis of naturally occurring responses to loneliness ought to consider not only immediate responses to feelings of loneliness, but also longer-range strategies people use to improve their social life. In addition, it may prove useful to examine not only behavioral responses, but also cognitive strategies that are used to cope with loneliness.

More comprehensive information about coping strategies is provided by a study of new students at college conducted by Cutrona, Peplau, and Russell (described in Chapter 18). Toward the end of their first year at college, 162 students were asked about a diverse set of cognitive and behavioral strategies that they might have used to cope with loneliness during the school year. As can be seen in Table 21.2, students used a wide range of behaviors when they felt lonely. Students commonly tried behaviors that might improve their social life such as being friendlier to others, helping someone else, or improving their physical appearance. Students may also have tried to counteract the potentially negative impact of loneliness on self-esteem by engaging in nonsocial activities in which they were skilled. Many students reported that when they were feeling lonely they worked hard to succeed at some activity or did something they were good at. Students said they were more likely to distract themselves by mental and physical activities than by using drugs or alcohol.

Students also used cognitive strategies for alleviating loneliness (See Table 21.3). Cognitive approaches were used for problem solving (e.g., thinking about the causes of their loneliness and what they could do to overcome it), and for distraction (deliberately thinking about other things). Students also bolstered self-esteem by thinking about good aspects of themselves and their social relationships. Least popular were changing one's goals for social relationships or thinking about the benefits of loneliness.

Table 21.2. Behavioral Strategies College Students Used to Cope with Loneliness [a]

Strategy	Never	Sometimes	Often
Tried harder to be friendly to other people (such as making an effort to talk to people in your classes, etc.)	2%	62%	36%
Taken your mind off feeling lonely through some mental activity (such as reading a novel, watching TV, going to a movie, etc.)	6%	60%	34%
Worked particularly hard to succeed at some activity (such as studying extra hard for an exam, putting extra effort into practicing an instrument, pushing yourself on an athletic skill, etc.)	7%	53%	40%
Done something helpful for someone else (such as helping a classmate with homework, doing volunteer work, etc.)	7%	64%	29%
Done something you are very good at (schoolwork, athletics, artwork, etc.)	7%	66%	27%
Taken your mind off feeling lonely through some physical activity (such as jogging, playing basketball, shopping, washing the car, etc.)	12%	51%	37%
Tried to find new ways to meet people (such as joining a club, moving into a dorm, going to dances, etc.)	18%	64%	18%
Done something to make yourself more physically attractive to others (going on a diet, buying new clothes, changing your hairstyle, etc.)	20%	61%	19%
Done something to improve your social skills (such as learning to dance, learning to be more assertive, improving conversational skills, etc.)	25%	66%	9%
Talked to a friend or relative about ways to overcome your loneliness	40%	45%	15%
Taken your mind off feeling lonely by using drugs or alcohol	74%	25%	1%
Talked to a counselor or therapist about ways to overcome your loneliness	91%	6%	3%

[a] Strategies are listed in order of frequency.

The New Student Study also asked students about things they had done "in order to meet other people" during their first year at college. Many students (61%) reported that they selected a group living situation such as a dorm or sorority at least in part as a way of meeting people, and 31% said they had joined a club or organization for this purpose. Other popular ways to meet people included starting a conversation with a stranger on campus ("for example, in a class, in the library or waiting in lines"), used by 90% of students, and going regularly to a particular place or "hangout" on campus (82%). Most students also went to campus social gatherings such as dances (83%), and many joined organized recreational activities (40%). These results suggest that college students use a variety of tactics for improving their social life; most students appear to use many strategies in combination. Little is currently known about the factors that predispose in-

Table 21.3. Cognitive Strategies College Students Used to Cope with Loneliness [a]

Strategy	Never	Sometimes	Often
Thought about things you could do to overcome your loneliness	4%	52%	44%
Reminded yourself that you actually do have good relationships with other people	7%	33%	60%
Tried to figure out why you were lonely	7%	54%	39%
Thought about good qualities that you possess (such as being warm, intelligent, sensitive, self-sufficient, etc.)	7%	68%	25%
Told yourself that your loneliness would not last forever, that things would get better	10%	38%	52%
Thought about things you can do extremely well (excelling at schoolwork, athletics, artwork, gourmet cooking, etc.)	10%	47%	23%
Told yourself that most other people are lonely at one time or another	11%	56%	33%
Taken your mind off feeling lonely by deliberately thinking about other things (anything other than your loneliness)	13%	61%	26%
Told yourself that you were over-reacting, that you shouldn't be so upset	14%	62%	24%
Thought about possible benefits of your experience of loneliness (such as telling yourself that you were learning to be self-reliant, that you would grow from the experience, etc.)	21%	42%	37%
Changed your goals for social relationships (such as telling yourself that it is not that important to be popular; that at this point in your life it's all right not to have a boyfriend or girlfriend, etc.)	22%	55%	23%

[a] Strategies are listed in order of reported frequency.

dividuals to use some coping strategies rather than others; this appears to be an important direction for future research.

Effectiveness of Coping Responses

The question of greatest concern to lonely people themselves is undoubtedly which coping activities are most successful. Paloutzian and Ellison (Chapter 14) asked college students to rate the effectiveness of 23 coping responses. The activities perceived as most effective were talking to or spending time with a friend, thinking alone, listening to music and (among their highly religious sample) praying. In considering the effectiveness of coping responses, it is again useful to distinguish between tactics aimed at short-term distractions and those that lead to increased satisfaction with one's social life. Whereas reading a mystery novel may effectively blot out the pain of loneliness for an evening, it is not likely to improve a deficient social network.

The New Student Study addressed this issue by comparing students who continued to be lonely throughout their first year at college with students who overcame their loneliness during the school year (see Cutrona, Chapter 18). Students who were no longer lonely in May had not merely reconciled themselves to impoverished social relations; rather they reported that they had developed more satisfying relationships. The greatest benefits seemed to come from developing friendships, rather than dating relationships, although both contributed to decreasing loneliness. Students who remained lonely continued to be dissatisfied with their social relations. Analyses comparing factors that distinguished students who were successful versus unsuccessful led to some surprising results. No clear pattern was found linking reduction of loneliness to any of the behavioral or cognitive strategies listed in Tables 21.2 and 21.3. Students who continued to be lonely reported doing many of the same activities as students who recovered from loneliness. What did distinguish the two groups were initial differences in attitudes and self-views. When they first arrived at college, students who were ultimately successful in developing satisfying relations had higher self-esteem and higher expectations for future relationships, and were less likely to attribute their loneliness exclusively to themselves.

Available information about self-help strategies does not provide a clear set of guidelines for effective coping with loneliness. Several issues deserve further research attention. First, we need to know more about how people actually cope with loneliness. Self-report data may provide only a partial picture of what lonely people actually do; in some cases people may be unaware of the patterning of their own responses to loneliness. Second, we need to know more about the combination of different coping responses. For example, watching television may be ineffective as a sole solution to loneliness, but individuals who are actively engaged in the sometimes risky business of meeting new people may find that a distracting evening of TV renews their energies. Third, we need to know more about how and where individuals can best meet other people. College students can "hang out" in the library or cafeteria and bump into other young people who are likely to share at least some of their interests and concerns. But where can isolated homemakers, middle-aged singles, or elderly widows turn to meet friends and lovers? Studies of the relative effectiveness of established organizations with goals not directly related to friendship (e.g., churches, the Sierra Club, adult education classes) versus the "singles business" (e.g., dating bars, photo dating services, singles apartment complexes) would be useful. Fourth, data suggest the central importance of friends in alleviating loneliness. Although Americans tend to idealize "love" relationships as the solution to all problems, it may be that the single-minded search for a romantic partner to the exclusion of developing friendships is a particularly risky self-help approach. Finally, most people are successful in overcoming occasional bouts of loneliness. Hopefully future research will shed light on this process of adjusting to changes in our social lives, so that we can all make social transitions more easily.

PREVENTION OF LONELINESS

In thinking about the prevention of loneliness, it is important to beware of common but fallacious beliefs. It is frequently asserted, for example, that the increased geographic mobility of modern society has made loneliness epidemic. In fact, empirical evidence indicates that rates of mobility have remained relatively stable from 1800 to present (Fischer, 1977; Thernstrom, 1973). And Rubenstein and Shaver's (Chapter 13) survey of Americans of all ages found no relationship between current loneliness and how frequently an individual had moved during his or her lifetime. Although the immediate impact of moving is often to disrupt social relations and produce loneliness, these effects are typically short-lived. Loneliness caused by geographic mobility is probably no more common today than it was a century ago. Similarly, it is wise to be wary of nostalgic beliefs in the alleged "decline in community" attributed to modern urban living (Fischer, 1977). The point is that prescriptions for loneliness cures must be based on accurate diagnosis of the problems, rather than on cultural myths.

Among the sociocultural factors that we suspect contribute to loneliness are the social stigma associated with being alone (either spending time by oneself or being unmarried) and the cultural preoccupation with love relationships (Brain, 1976; Gordon, 1976). We would call for greater acceptance of lifestyles other than traditional marriage. We urge that the pressure to "achieve" love relationships be relaxed and that other forms of social relationships, particularly friendships, be given greater status.

Changes in specific social institutions, such as schools or college dormitories, might also reduce the incidence of loneliness. Hallinan (1979) found, for example, that structural characteristics of elementary school classrooms affected children's friendliness and popularity. Social psychology provides many clues about ways to promote friendly relations by changing the structure of social interactions, rather than by changing individuals. Research on interpersonal attraction (Huston & Levinger, 1978; Rubin, 1973) and on social contact theory (Amir, 1969) emphasizes that opportunities for informal social contacts—chatting in the laundromat of an apartment building, having a common lunch room at work—can set the stage for the beginning of new relationships. The development of relationships is further fostered when people, sometimes out of necessity rather than choice, work together to accomplish important, shared goals. Such cooperative interdependence presumably characterizes satisfying relationships with family and friends. In contrast, competition is often a barrier to satisfying relationships.

These general principles have many practical implications. For example, the transition to college should be easier for students assigned to live in small, cooperative housing units where they work together to prepare meals and care for the residence, than for students assigned to large impersonal buildings. An innovative intervention for school children based on these principles was developed by Aronson and his associates (1978). Aronson argued that elementary schools are often competitive, unfriendly places. Concerned especially about the impact of such an environment on minority children, Aronson suggested that "It would be valuable if the basic process could be changed so that children could learn to like and trust each other not as an extracurricular activity but in the course of learning their reading, writing, and arithmetic" (p. 23). To this end, he and his colleagues developed a new instructional method, the "Jigsaw Classroom" technique, in which children form small learning groups. In the groups each child has a different piece of information about the lesson; mastering the material requires learning from other children and in return teaching them about your own part of the assignment. Thus cooperation is the rewarded pattern. Evaluation studies indicated that children in the Jigsaw Classrooms showed greater liking for each other and greater self-esteem than children in traditional classrooms. Although the intervention was not designed to reduce loneliness, a consequence of the restructuring of classroom instruction was to reduce social isolation and increase friendliness.

Other kinds of community-based intervention could be developed, ranging from preventive social skills training for children (Sugai, 1978) to programs for groups known to be at high risk for development of loneliness, such as children of divorced parents (Shaver & Rubenstein, 1980).

CONCLUSION

This chapter has raised many issues concerning the nature of loneliness and strategies for intervention. Three themes from this discussion are worth highlighting.

First, the diversity of factors that lead to loneliness should be matched by a diversity of intervention strategies. We have suggested that strategies for reducing loneliness are based on implicit assumptions about the important provisions of social contact. In particular, the common assumption that securing a primary relationship (e.g., love relationship) provides an antidote to loneliness should be carefully examined. We have suggested that friendships, social networks, and solitary activities provide alternative foci for intervention.

Second, controlled investigations of the effectiveness of intervention strategies for loneliness are sorely needed. Such research should be extended to include evaluation of the self-help "interventions" employed by lonely people.

Third, helping the lonely sometimes involves changing the situation rather than the person. Loneliness may often represent a mismatch between the person and the environment. In working with lonely people we should guard against the tendency to blame them for their loneliness. The design of environmental intervention techniques that do not stigmatize the lonely individual provides a creative challenge to loneliness researchers.

REFERENCES

Amir, Y. Contact hypothesis in ethnic relations. *Psychological Bulletin,* 1969, *71,* 319–342.

Aronson, E., Blancy, N., Stephan, C., Sikes, J., & Snapp, M. *The jigsaw classroom*. Beverly Hills, Calif.: Sage, 1978.

Asher, S. R., & Renshaw, P. D. In S. R. Asher & J. M. Gottman (Eds.), *The development of children's friendships*. New York: Cambridge University Press, 1980.

Bandura, A. *Principles of behavior modification*. New York: Holt, Rinehart & Winston, 1969.

Beck, A. T., Ward, C. H., Mendelson, M., Mock, J., & Erbaugh, J. An inventory for measuring depression. *Archives of General Psychiatry*, 1961, *4*, 53–63.

Beck, A. T., Rush, A. J., Shaw, B. F., & Emery, G. *Cognitive therapy of depression*. New York: Guilford Press, 1979.

Becker, J. *Depression: Theory and research*. New York: Wiley, 1974.

Bell, R. G. Alcohol and loneliness. *Journal of Social Therapy*, 1956, *2*, 171–181.

Blau, Z. Structural constraints on friendships in old age. *American Sociological Review*, 1961, *26*, 429–439.

Bradburn, N. *The structure of psychological well-being*. Chicago: Aldine, 1969.

Bragg, M. E. A comparative study of loneliness and depression. (Doctoral dissertation, University of California, Los Angeles, 1979). *Dissertation Abstracts International*, 1979a, *39*, 79–13710.

Bragg, M. E. *A comparison of nondepressed and depressed loneliness*. Paper presented at the UCLA Research Conference on Loneliness, Los Angeles, May 1979b.

Brain, R. *Friends and lovers*. New York: Basic Books, 1976.

Brim, J. Social network correlates of avowed happiness. *Journal of Nervous and Mental Disease*, 1974, *138*, 432–439.

Burton, A. On the nature of loneliness. *American Journal of Psychoanalysis*, 1961, *21*, 34–39.

Caplan, G. *Support systems and community mental health*. New York: Behavioral Publications, 1974.

Cobb, S. Social support as a moderator of life stress. *Psychosomatic Medicine*, 1976, *38*, 300–314.

Cobb, S. Social support and health through the life course. In M. W. Riley (Ed.), *Aging from birth to death: Interdisciplinary perspectives*. Boulder, Colo.: Westview Press, 1979.

Colson, C. An objective-analytic approach to the classification of suicidal motivation. *Acta Psychiatrica Scandinavica*, 1973, *49*, 105–113.

Curran, J. P. Skills training as an approach to the treatment of heterosexual-social anxiety: A review. *Psychological Bulletin*, 1977, *84*, 140–157.

Duvall, E. M. Loneliness and the serviceman's wife. *Journal of Marriage and Family Living*, 1945, *7*, 77–81.

Fischer, C. S. *The contexts of personal relations: An exploratory network analysis*. Working paper 281, Institute of Urban and Regional Development, University of California, Berkeley, 1978.

Fischer, C. S. *Networks and places: Social relations in the urban setting*. New York: Fress Press, 1977.

Flanders, J. P. *Practical psychology*. New York: Harper & Row, 1976.

Florentine, N., Perlman, D., & McIntyre, J. *Loneliness, distraction and learning.* Unpublished manuscript, Univeristy of Manitoba, Winnipeg, Canada, 1979.

Foa, U., & Foa, E. *Societal structures of the mind.* Springfield, Ill.: Charles Thomas, 1974.

Fromm-Reichmann, F. Loneliness. *Psychiatry,* 1959, *22,* 1–15.

Gaev, D. M. *The psychology of loneliness.* Chicago: Adams Press, 1976.

Gerson, A. C., & Perlman, D. Loneliness and expressive communication. *Journal of Abnormal Psychology,* 1979, *88*(3), 258–261.

Glass, C. R., Gottman, J. M., & Shmurak, S. H. Response acquisition and cognitive self-statement modification approaches to dating skill training. *Journal of Counseling Psychology,* 1976, *23,* 520–526.

Goode, W. J. Family disorganization. In R. K. Merton & R. A. Nisbet (Eds.), *Contemporary social problems.* New York: Harcourt, Brace, 1961.

Gordon, S. *Lonely in America.* New York: Simon & Schuster, 1976.

Gottman, J., Gonso, J., & Schuler, P. Teaching social skills to isolated children. *Journal of Abnormal Child Psychology,* 1976, *4*(2), 170–197.

Gurin, G., Veroff, J., & Feld, S. *Americans view their mental health.* New York: Basic Books, 1960.

Gurman, A. S., & Rice, D. G. *Couples in conflict: New directions in marital therapy.* New York: Jason Aronson, 1975.

Hallinan, M. T. Structural effects on children's friendships and cliques. *Social Psychology Quarterly,* 1979, *1,* 43–54.

Hobson, R. F. Loneliness. *Journal of Analytical Psychology,* 1974, *19,* 71–89.

Homans, G. G. *Social behavior* (2nd ed.). New York: Harcourt, Brace, Jovanovich, 1974.

Huston, T. L., & Levinger, G. Interpersonal attraction and relationships. *Annual Review of Psychology,* 1978, *29,* 115–156.

Jacobson, N. S., & Margolin, G. *Marital therapy: Strategies based on social learning and behavior exchange principles.* New York: Brunner/Mazel, 1979.

Jones, W. H., Freemon, J. R., & Goswick, R. A. The persistence of loneliness: Self and other rejection? *Journal of Personality,* 1981, *49,* 27–48.

Jones, W. H., Hobbs, S. A., & Hockenbury, D. *Loneliness and social skill.* Unpublished manuscript, University of Tulsa, July 1980.

Kahn, R. L. Aging and social support. In M. W. Riley (Ed.), *Aging from birth to death: Interdisciplinary perspectives.* Boulder, Colo.: Westview Press, 1979.

Keith-Spiegel, P., & Spiegel, D. E. Affective states of patients immediately preceding suicide. *Journal of Psychiatric Research,* 1967, *5,* 89–93.

Keller, M. F., & Carlson, P. M. The use of symbolic modeling to promote social skills in children with low levels of social responsiveness. *Child Development,* 1974, *45,* 912–919.

Lederer, W. J., & Jackson, D. S. *The mirages of marriage.* New York: Norton, 1968.

Leiderman, P. H. Loneliness: A psychodynamic interpretation. In E. S. Shneidman & M. J. Ortega (Eds.), *Aspects of depression.* Boston: Little, Brown, 1969.

Levinger, G. A social psychological perspective on marital dissolution. In G. Levinger & O. C. Moles (Eds.), *Divorce and separation*. New York: Basic Books, 1979.

Levinger, G. Toward the analysis of close relationships. *Journal of Experimental Social Psychology*, in press.

Levinger, G., & Moles, O. C. (Eds.), *Divorce and separation*. New York: Basic Books, 1979.

Levinger, G., & Snoek, J. D. *Attraction in relationships: A new look at interpersonal attraction*. Morristown, N. J.: General Learning Press, 1972.

Lewinsohn, P. M., Biglan, A., & Zeiss, A. M. Behavioral treatment of depression. In P. O. Davison (Ed.), *The behavorial management of anxiety, depresison and pain*. New York: Brunner/Mazel, 1976.

Lopata, H. Z. Contributions of extended families to the support systems of metropolitan area widows: Limitations of the modified kin network. *Journal of Marriage and the Family*, 1978, *40*, 355–364.

Lopata, H. Z. *Women as widows: Support systems*. New York: Elsevier, 1979.

Lowenthal, J., & Haven, C. Interaction and adaptation: Intimacy as a critical variable. *American Sociological Review*, 1968, *33*, 20–30.

MacPhillamy, D. J., & Lewinsohn, P. M. Depression as a function of levels of desired and obtained pleasure. *Journal of Abnormal Psychology*, 1974, *83*, 651–657.

Mahoney, M. J. *Cognition and behavior modification*. Cambridge, Mass.: Ballinger, 1974.

Martinson, W. D., & Zerface, J. P. Comparison of individual counseling and a social program with nondaters. *Journal of Counseling Psychology*, 1970, *17*, 36–40.

Meichenbaum, D. *Cognitive behavior modification: An integrative approach*. New York: Plenum Press, 1977.

Oden, S., & Asher, S.R. Coaching children in social skills for friendship-making. *Child Development*, 1977, *48*, 495–506.

Olson, D. H. (Ed.), *Treating relationships*. Lake Mills, Ia.: Graphic, 1976.

Otto, H. A. (Ed.), *Marriage and family enrichment: New perspectives and programs*. Nashville, Tenn.: Abingdon, 1976.

Parkes, C. M. *Bereavement: Studies of grief in adult life*. New York: International Universities Press, 1972.

Patterson, G. R., Hops, H., & Weiss, R. L. Interpersonal skills training for couples in early stages of conflict. *Journal of Marriage and the Family*, 1975, *37*, 295–303.

Peplau, H. E. Loneliness. *American Journal of Nursing*, 1955, *55*(12), 1476–1481.

Peplau, L. A., Russell, D., & Heim, M. The experience of loneliness. In I. Frieze, D. Bar-Tal, & J. Carroll (Eds.), *New approaches to social problems: Applications of attribution theory*. San Francisco: Jossey-Bass, 1979.

Pilkonis, P. A., & Zimbardo, P. G. The personal and social dynamics of shyness. In C. E. Izard (Ed.), *Emotions in personality and psychopathology*. New York: Plenum Press, 1979.

Pilkonis, P. A., Heape, C., & Klein, R. H. Treating shyness and other relationship difficulties in psychiatric outpatients. *Communication Education*, 1980, *29*, 250–255.

Pokorny, A. D. Suicide rates in various psychiatric disorders. *Journal of Nervous and Mental Disease,* 1964, *139,* 499–506.

Riesman, D., Glazer, N., & Denney, R. *The lonely crowd: A study of the changing American character.* New Haven: Yale University Press, 1961.

Rubin, Z. *Liking and loving: An invitation to social psychology.* New York: Holt, Rinehart & Winston, 1973.

Russell, D., Peplau, L. A., & Cutrona, C. E. The revised UCLA Loneliness Scale: Concurrent and discriminant validity evidence. *Journal of Personality and Social Psychology,* 1980, *39* (3), 472–480.

Schein, H. M. Loneliness and interpersonal isolation: Focus for therapy with schizophrenic patients. *American Journal of Psychotherapy,* 1974, *28,* 95–107.

Shaver, P., & Rubenstein, C. Childhood attachment experience and adult loneliness. In L. Wheeler (Ed.), *Review of personality and social psychology* (Vol. 1). Beverly Hills, Calif.: Sage, 1980.

Slater, P. *The pursuit of loneliness: American culture at the breaking point.* Boston: Beacon Press, 1970.

Solano, C. H., & Batten, P. G. *Loneliness and objective self-disclosure in an acquaintanceship exercise.* Unpublished manuscript, Wake Forest University, 1979.

Stein, P. J. *Single.* Englewood Cliffs, N. J.: Prentice-Hall, 1976.

Stuart, R. B. *Helping couples change: A social learning approach to marital therapy.* New York: Guilford, 1980.

Sugai, D. P. The implementation and evaluation of a social skills training program for preadolescents. (Doctoral dissertation, University of Massachusetts, 1978). *Dissertation Abstracts International,* 1978, *39,* 2529.

Sullivan, H. S. *The interpersonal theory of psychiatry.* New York: Norton, 1953.

Thernstrom, S. *The other Bostonians.* Cambridge, Mass.: Harvard University Press, 1973.

Weeks, D. G., Michela, J. L., Peplau, L. A., & Bragg, M. E. The relation between loneliness and depression: A structural equation analysis. *Journal of Personality and Social Psychology,* 1980, *39,* 1238–1244.

Weiss, R. S. The fund of sociability. *Transaction/Society,* 1969, *6,* 36–43.

Weiss, R. S. (Ed.), *Loneliness: The experience of emotional and social isolation.* Cambridge, Mass.: MIT Press, 1973.

Weiss, R. S. The provisions of social relationships. In Z. Rubin (Eds.), *Doing unto others.* Englewood Cliffs, N. J.: Prentice-Hall, 1974.

Weiss, R. S. *Marital separation.* New York: Basic Books, 1975.

Weiss, R. S. Transition states and other stressful situations: Their nature and programs for their management. In G. Caplan & M. Killilea (Eds.), *Support systems and mutual help: Multidisciplinary explorations.* New York: Grune and Stratton, 1976.

Weissman, M. M., & Paykel, E. S. *The depressed woman: A study of social relationships.* Chicago: University of Chicago Press, 1974.

Young, J. E. *Loneliness in college students: A cognitive approach.* Unpublished doctoral dissertation, University of Pennsylvania, 1978.

Chapter 22

Loneliness, Depression and Cognitive Therapy: Theory and Application

Jeffrey E. Young

There have been no published systematic approaches to the treatment of loneliness. Many authors offer general advice. Weiss (1973) recommends that a lonely individual "direct one's energy to projects, friendships, groups one cares about" (p. 235). Tanner (1973) suggests that, even though loving carries a great risk of being hurt, "the more we assume personal responsibility for the consequences of loving, the less lonely we become" (p. 80). Rosenbaum and Rosenbaum (1973) advise lonely people to get to know themselves better, cleanse their minds of resentments, and "extend yourself to some other person" (p. 172). And Schultz (1976) counsels lonely individuals to experience themselves fully, get in touch with their emotions, and take chances with new activities until they reach the point where "our aloneness and uniqueness can be cherished and appreciated but, at the same time, our need for human contact fulfilled" (p. 181).

Most of this advice seems too general to be of much help to the lonely. This chapter presents a comprehensive approach to the treatment of loneliness. This approach rests on the premise that loneliness, like depression, is in large part a cognitive phenomenon; that is, the way individuals view relationships is perhaps the most important determinant of how satisfying their friendships are and therefore of how lonely they feel.

Several therapeutic approaches have been developed that emphasize the cognitive domain (Cautela, 1969; Ellis & Grieger, 1977; Goldfried & Davison, 1976; Meichenbaum, 1977). The approach to loneliness described in this paper is based primarily on Beck's cognitive therapy (Beck, Rush, Shaw, & Emery, 1979). The rationale for adopting this system of psychotherapy is based, first, on carefully controlled studies showing that Beck's approach is highly effective with depressed outpatients (Rush, Beck, Kovacs, & Hollon, 1977; Taylor & Marshall, 1977). Second, Beck's therapy seems (in the author's view) to be more comprehensive in the structure it provides for therapists and more easily adapted to a broad range of clinical problems. Third, our clinical experience thus far at the University of Pennsylvania suggests that these therapeutic principles are effective in treating lonely clients, although we have not yet done outcome research to substantiate these impressions.

In this paper I will outline a theory of loneliness based on cognitive-behavioral principles. I will then summarize Beck's approach briefly, since it forms a framework through which the techniques of the loneliness therapy can be understood. I will also discuss the relationship between loneliness and depression, phenomena which I believe are distinct yet closely intertwined in many populations.

A COGNITIVE-BEHAVIORAL THEORY OF LONELINESS

Definition

I define loneliness as the absence or perceived absence of satisfying social relationships, accompanied by symptoms of psychological distress that are related to the actual or perceived absence. According to this definition, I would not label as lonely someone who seems socially deprived to other people but does not manifest any signs of psychological distress. He or she might be enjoying the solitude. Furthermore, individuals might not be aware that there is a discrepancy between their desired and actual relationships, yet I would tentatively diagnose them as "lonely" if they showed one or more symptoms of psychological distress (e.g., anxiety, dysphoria, drug abuse) that seemed to be clearly related to a pattern of unsatisfying social contacts. Finally, people who are sad because their friendships do not meet their expectations I would label as lonely, even though their relationships objectively may seem adequate.

Deprivation and Reinforcement

Several important ideas underlie this definition. First, loneliness is not an entirely cognitive phenomenon. I propose that social relationships can be treated as a particular class of reinforcement and that the "laws" applying to other reinforcements can be applied in the same way to relationships (Young, 1979a). Just as one may learn that swimming is pleasant and enjoyable, one may also learn that confiding in a friend is rewarding. (Of course social relationships are far more complex, since they involve interdependence and mutuality.) As with other reinforcements, individuals manifest changes in behavior and in emotional response following deprivations in social relationships.

Under certain circumstances, therefore, loneliness can be viewed in part as *a response to the absence of important social reinforcements* even when there is no evidence of a discrepancy at the *cognitive* level between expectations and reality. Conversely, loneliness may persist because an individual perceives an absence of social reinforcements, even when there is no actual deprivation.

Negative Affect and Attribution

Even when the individual is aware of a discrepancy between desired and actual relationships, this recognition alone is not sufficient for me to apply the label of loneliness. According to this definition of loneliness, the discrepancy must be accompanied by one or more symptoms of psychological distress. Most often these "symptoms" include some sort of negatively tinged affective state. The specific *type* of affect will vary across lonely individuals. For example, while lonely people most often seem to report feeling sad or depressed (Young, 1979a), some say they feel anxious or afraid while others report anger and bitterness. I do not believe that any one symptom or pattern of symptoms uniquely characterizes loneliness. Rather it seems that individuals cope with loneliness in different ways and therefore evidence a variety of symptoms.

I would hypothesize that individuals come to associate different affective states with aloneness, depending on how each person interprets "aloneness." When there is a gap between desired and actual relationships, individuals can react in many ways. If they believe that they cannot function safely without the help of other people, they will experience anxiety. Attribution theory (Michela, Peplau, & Weeks, 1980; Peplau, Miceli & Morasch, Chapter 9) is useful in further explaining this concept. If individuals blame *others* for their aloneness (external attribution), for example, by telling themselves that everyone else is selfish, they will feel angry or bitter. If they believe that *they* are responsible for not having close friendships because they are dull and boring (internal attribution) and that they cannot change their personality (stable attribution), then they will probably feel sad and may even become clinically depressed. If they view the problems as a challenge and believe they can readily close the gap by taking steps to develop closer relationships, then they may not feel any negative emotion and therefore would not be labeled as lonely. According to this analysis, changing attributions about why one is lonely could change the specific affective state (e.g., from sadness to anger) without actually alleviating loneliness.

The important point here is that loneliness is defined in part by the presence of some negatively tinged emotion, and that the particular emotion is often a function of the attributions an individual makes in explaining his or her unsatisfying social relationships.

Loneliness and Depression

When I have discussed loneliness with other clinicians, they frequently express the opinion that loneliness is a subset of depression and not a distinct concept worthy of separate study. We cannot ignore clinical observations that there is a substantial overlap between loneliness and depression. These observations are supported by research showing correlations between loneliness and depression ranging from .38 (Jones, cited in Russell, Peplau, & Ferguson, 1978) to .71 (Young 1979b), depending on the populations examined and instruments used.

I believe that the overlap can be explained largely by cognitive theory. As I suggested above, when individuals attribute deficiencies in their social relationships to unchangeable personal faults, they are more likely to feel both lonely and depressed. Because it is probably far more common for people to blame themselves than to blame others for aloneness, and to see their social deficiencies as relatively unchangeable personality traits than as easily corrected behavior, it is not surprising to find that sadness and depression seem to be the most common affective states associated with loneliness. Furthermore, depression is often characterized by a global tendency to view life in a negative way (Bragg, 1979). Thus depressed people might be more likely to exaggerate the negative aspects of their relationships and thus feel lonely.

This overlap need not hinder the recognition of loneliness as a separate clinical entity. In fact, the overlap underscores the importance of understanding loneliness if we are to deal effectively with many depressed clients. Events such as the breakup of an important relationship are probably major contributors to both depression and loneliness. Weeks, Michela, Peplau, and Bragg (1980) report a structural equation analysis that suggests that loneliness and depression are distinct phenomena though correlated; that neither is the cause of the other; and that they seem to share some common casual origins.

Ideally, this chapter will demonstrate that research into loneliness can improve our ability to treat depression, and research into depression provides important insights that can be applied to lonely clients.

Chronicity

I have made a distinction (Beck & Young, 1978) between *transient* loneliness, *situational* loneliness, and *chronic* loneliness. This distinction primarily reflects the length of time an individual has been lonely. Chronic loneliness refers to people who have not been satisfied with their relationships for a period of two or more consecutive years. Situational or transitional loneliness involves individuals who had satisfying relationships until they were confronted either with a specific crisis such as death or divorce, or with a predictable developmental change like leaving home for college. As a result of the transition, they feel lonely frequently and for substantial durations of time. Individuals may initially fall into the situational category and, if they have not adjusted to the change within two years, they would then be recategorized as chronically lonely. Transient or everyday loneliness includes brief and occasional lonely moods.

The chronicity dimension is a critical one in understanding loneliness, even though it has generally been overlooked. It is apparent to clinicians that an adult client who has been lonely and isolated for 12 years and is severely depressed is unlike a college student who has been lonely for five months since he or she left home. Even though they may report equally strong beliefs about being unloved, different, friendless, and so on, the underlying reasons for their holding these beliefs are very different.

Chronic loneliness probably involves long-term cognitive and behavioral deficits in relating to other people rather than a temporary response to a new environment. The chronically lonely typically have had fewer close and intimate relationships than the situationally lonely. These differences were partially supported by a study (Young, 1979b) comparing college students with adult outpatients. Another study (Spitzberg, n.d.) revealed that chronically lonely individuals rated higher than situationally lonely people in communication apprehension.

In contrast, I would expect that people who are situationally lonely can reasonably be expected to develop satisfying new relationships within a period of several months (or longer if the opportunities in the new situation are limited).

I will discuss strategies for assessing chronicity later in this paper.

BECK'S COGNITIVE THEORY

Beck (1976) emphasizes the impact of cognition on behavior and emotion. He asserts that the way an individual structures his experiences is significantly related to how a person feels and acts. These personal meanings—views of the self and the environment—form the basis for an individual's "internal reality" (p. 50).

For example, a male client who believes that he is ugly and that women will reject him may *feel* sad and may *behave* in such a way that he avoids situations where he might be called upon to approach women. These feelings and kinds of behavior may persist in spite of the fact that in reality a majority of women find him attractive. When an individual's "internal reality" does not correspond to "external reality" in significant respects, he may experience emotional distress such as depression, anxiety, or loneliness.

Beck (1976) discusses a variety of cognitive phenomena that comprise each person's internal reality, including images, verbalized thoughts, automatic thoughts, and underlying assumptions. I will briefly describe the last two, since they figure prominently in the loneliness therapy.

Beck (1976) observed early in his work that many depressed clients often had two streams of thought occurring at about the same time. One stream was verbalized to the therapist; the second stream, however, was rarely reported and seemed more difficult for clients to focus on. These automatic thoughts seemed to emerge rapidly and were almost subliminal. Furthermore, these thoughts frequently represented departures from reality and logic; Beck labeled such thoughts "cognitive distortions."

Beck invokes an additional construct—the underlying assumption—to explain how clients come to have particular automatic thoughts and distorted thinking patterns. Underlying assumptions are rules, values, and standards that serve to steer behavior and determine how individuals evaluate themselves and others. In Piagetian terms, they are the schemata underlying the entire cognitive structure. Some of these assumptions are maladaptive for the patient, for example: "If someone rejects me, there must be something wrong with me."

In the next section, I will briefly outline the principles of cognitive therapy and explain the role of automatic thoughts and assumptions in the treatment approach.

BECK'S COGNITIVE THERAPY

Overview

Cognitive therapy is problem oriented. The therapist and client work together to reduce the client's distress into a set of problems (psychological, situational, and interpersonal) that can be corrected. The label "cognitive therapy" is applied because psychological disturbances frequently seem to stem from specific, habitual errors or deficits in thinking. For example, clients may judge themselves too harshly, jump to inaccurate conclusions, incorrectly interpret life stresses, or reason on the basis of self-defeating assumptions. Furthermore, they often cannot develop adequate plans or strategies to deal with external stresses.

The cognitive therapist works with clients collaboratively in a structured format to correct these errors in thinking and problem solving. He or she uses a graduated, step-by-step approach that incorporates both cognitive and behavioral techniques.

One of the primary characteristics of cognitive therapy is the collaborative relationship between the therapist and client. Unlike other behaviorally oriented therapies that downplay the relationship between the therapist and client, cognitive therapy places considerable emphasis on the interpersonal qualities of the clinician.

The cognitive therapist attempts to involve the client as an active participant. This process begins when the client and therapist initially develop a list of problems to address in treatment. The client and therapist then set priorities based on which problems are most distressing and which are most amenable to change at a particular point in treatment. The therapist explains the rationale for each therapeutic intervention, asks for the client's reactions periodically during each session, offers choices about alternative courses of action, and invites the client to summarize his or her understanding of the major points covered each week.

Because cognitive therapy is relatively short-term, the brief time allocated to each interview must be used efficiently. To accomplish this, each therapy session is highly structured. At the beginning of each session, the client and therapist develop an agenda together which incorporates the most pertinent issues to be addressed during the therapy hour. It is the responsibility of the therapist to follow the agenda and remain problem oriented, even when this involves gently interrupting clients who wander off track or who become too "abstract." For example, when clients make vague, untestable interpretations about the sources of their problems, the therapist can refocus on concrete thoughts, behavior, and feelings and can insist on staying with one problem at a time.

The assignment and completion of self-help work at home is critical to the success of cognitive therapy. We have found that unless clients systematically apply the concepts learned in session to their daily lives, progress is severely hampered. Homework promotes transfer of learning and encourages self-control.

Guided Discovery and Empiricism

As collaboration and structure are being established, the client and therapist first try to conceptualize the errors in thought, emotion, or behavior that might be interfering with solving the client's problems. This can be accomplished initially by training the client to *monitor* his or her own emotions and behavior on a daily basis, especially in situations in which the client seems to experience the greatest distress. The client and therapist can usually agree on new behaviors or emotions that would be more adaptive than the ones the client is presently engaging in.

The next task is to *change* the maladaptive behavior or emotions. Consider, for example, a male client who is lonely and stays at home alone every night. The client and therapist could agree to work on helping him meet more people. Sometimes the client is simply unaware of the dysfunctional behavior he has been engaging in. In these instances he can often correct the problem himself in a very brief time by making more effort to go out. Alternatively, he may be aware of the maladaptive behavior but has never learned how to act differently. The therapist can then help him practice new behavior, for example, by role playing how to approach a stranger.

Most often, however, we find that clients have particular automatic thoughts that inhibit their performance when they try to engage in new behavior. The client may think to himself, "I'm dull," when he imagines approaching a potential friend. For this reason, the cognitive therapist helps clients monitor and verbalize interfering thoughts that affect how they act and feel. These thoughts can usually be uncovered through several techniques. The therapist can ask the client to imagine himself in the problem situation, a singles' bar. As the client describes the setting and events in detail, and as the therapist asks a series of probing questions, they can probably approximate the automatic thoughts that the client was having at the time. Sometimes the thoughts can be elicited by having the therapist and client role play the encounter, thus recreating the situation in the therapist's office.

Generally, these thoughts seem plausible to the client even though they often appear illogical to the therapist. The cognitive therapist asks the client to suspend temporarily his conviction that the thought is unquestionably true and instead to treat it as a hypothesis to be tested. The therapist and client collaborate in assembling evidence that supports and contradicts the thought, in evaluating this evidence, and in drawing conclusions. In effect, the client is learning the experimental method.

Through this process of thinking, the client may discover that the *perception* of reality is not the same as reality itself. As he designs experiments to test the validity of his own automatic thoughts, he may find that he has ignored important conflicting information; has never even obtained data regarding some of his beliefs; has ignored logical contradictions within his own system of thinking; has blamed himself for mistakes when others were actually responsible; and has overlooked workable solutions to his problems. The client may also recognize that he has been operating according to assumptions about the way life "should" be that are self-defeating.

Stylistically, the therapist uses questions rather than didactic statements the vast majority of the time. Through questioning, the therapist shows the client how to apply the scientific method. "What evidence do I have?" "Is it sufficient to support my conclusion?" "Are there alternative explanations?" Thus clients "discover" the inconsistencies for themselves instead of having them pointed out. This process of guided discovery through inductive questioning is a widely accepted educational method and is an essential element of cognitive therapy.

As clients' cognitive structures change, their behavior and emotions change concurrently. The process is a gradual one, and the therapist should have modest expectations initially. It is helpful to view therapy as a systematic, step-by-step progression from the least difficult to most difficult changes. Typically the process begins to accelerate as the three components—emotional, behavioral, and cognitive—interact.

In the section that follows, we shall see how this general model of cognitive therapy can be applied to specific problems of lonely clients.

COGNITIVE THERAPY FOR LONELINESS

Before describing the therapy, I would like to emphasize that this approach is based primarily on my clinical experience and that of other therapists at our center. The therapy has been applied to adult outpatients varying widely in age; most are white and middle class, with diagnoses of depressive neurosis. In most instances the loneliness has been present for several years, and therefore the clients as a group can be labeled chronically lonely. It is difficult to anticipate how the therapy outlined below would be modified for situationally lonely individuals. Furthermore, I would stress that the hierarchical stages and loneliness clusters that follow have not been empirically validated. I developed them on the basis of our clinical experience, not from experimental research or some a priori theoretical model. It is too early to predict how long a full course of treatment for loneliness will require; some clients have overcome loneliness in 12 weeks, while others have remained in therapy for over a year.

Diagnosis and Baseline Data

To diagnose loneliness, I have developed a 19-item self-report inventory (Young, 1979b; Table 22.1), based on the types of relationships lonely clients often view as missing in their lives. In a clinical setting, the Loneliness Inventory should be administered in conjunction with a standard mental status examination, general history, and other psychometric instruments like the Beck Depression Inventory and the SCL-90 (Derogatis, Rickels, & Rock, 1976). The clinician should attempt to determine during the diagnostic phase whether loneliness seems to be a primary or a secondary problem and whether other clinical disorders like depression or anxiety are prominent. In doing so, it is important to ascertain for how long the client has felt lonely and what events, if any, triggered the most recent period of loneliness. As a result of this diagnostic process, it should be possible to determine whether therapy should focus on the problem of loneliness, and if so, whether the loneliness is chronic or situational.

With clients who have been diagnosed as having primary chronic or situational loneliness, the next step is to obtain detailed baseline data showing the pattern of the client's social relationships over the past two years. The Friendship Chart (Table 22.2) has proved to be a useful format for obtaining this information.

Consider again the male client referred to earlier. The therapist would ask him to list the names of all his friends and close family members during the past two years across the top of the chart. He then rates each friend on a scale from 0 (low) to 10 (high) for frequency of contact, disclosure, caring, and physical intimacy. The *frequency* scale measures the amount of time

Table 22.2. Sample Friendship Chart

| | Friends' names (1977–1978) | |
	John	Judy
Frequency rating (0–10)	8	5
Disclosure rating (0–10)	8	1
"Caring" rating (0–10)	9	5
Physical intimacy rating (0–10)	0	0
Date relationship began	Jan. 1975	March 1978
Date relationship ended or weakened	June 1978	May 1978
Reason for ending or weakening	He moved away	I lost interest

Table 22.1. Young Loneliness Inventory

On this questionnaire are groups of statements. Please read each group of statements carefully. Then pick out the one statement in each group which best describes you. Circle the number beside the statement you picked. If several statements in the group seem to apply equally well, circle each one. *Be sure to read all the statements in each group before making your choice.*

1. 0 When I want to do something for enjoyment, I can usually find someone to join me.
   1 Sometimes I end up doing things alone even though I'd like to have someone join me.
   2 It often bothers me that there is no one I can go out and do things with.
   3 I'm extremely disturbed that there is no one I can go out and do things with.

2. 0 I have a close group of friends nearby that I feel part of.
   1 I'm not sure that I really belong to any close group of friends nearby.
   2 It often bothers me that I don't feel part of any close group of friends nearby.
   3 I'm extremely disturbed that I don't have a close group of friends.

3. 0 I almost always have someone to be with when I do not want to be alone.
   1 I am sometimes alone when I would prefer to be with other people.
   2 It bothers me that I am often alone when I would prefer to be with other people.
   3 I'm extremely disturbed that I am alone so often.

4. 0 I have a lot in common with other people I know.
   1 I wish my values and interests, and those of other people I know, were more similar.
   2 It often bothers me that I'm different from other people I know.
   3 I'm extremely disturbed that I'm so different from other people.

5. 0 I feel that I generally fit in with people around me.
   1 I sometimes feel that I don't fit in with the people around me.
   2 I am often bothered that I feel isolated from the people around me.
   3 I'm extremely disturbed by how isolated I feel from other people.

6. 0 There is someone nearby who really understands me.
   1 I'm not sure there's anyone nearby who really understands me.
   2 It often bothers me that no one nearby understands me.
   3 I'm extremely disturbed that no one really understands me.

7. 0 I have someone nearby who is really interested in hearing about my private feelings.
   1 I'm not sure that anyone nearby is really interested in hearing about my private feelings.
   2 It often bothers me that no one nearby is really interested in hearing about my private feelings.
   3 I'm extremely disturbed that no one is really interested in hearing about my private feelings.

8. 0 I can usually talk freely to close friends about my thoughts and feelings.
   1 I have some difficulty talking to close friends about my thoughts and feelings.
   2 It often bothers me that I can't seem to communicate my thoughts and feelings to anyone.
   3 I'm extremely disturbed that my thoughts and feelings are so bottled up inside.

9. 0 I have someone nearby I can really depend on when I need help and support.
   1 I'm not sure there's anyone nearby I can really depend on when I need help and support.

2 It often bothers me that there is no one nearby I can really depend on when I need help and support.

3 I'm extremely disturbed that there is no one I can depend on when I need help and support.

10. 0 There is someone nearby who really cares about me.
    1 I'm not sure there's anyone nearby who really cares about me.
    2 It often bothers me that there is no one nearby who really cares about me.
    3 I'm extremely disturbed that no one really cares about me.

11. 0 The important people in my life have not let me down.
    1 Sometimes I feel disappointed at someone I thought I could trust.
    2 I often think about the important people in my life I trusted who have let me down.
    3 I can't trust anyone anymore.

12. 0 There is someone nearby who really needs me.
    1 I'm not sure anyone nearby really needs me.
    2 It often bothers me that there is no one nearby who really needs me.
    3 I'm extremely disturbed that no one really needs me.

13. 0 I have a partner I love who loves me.
    1 I'm not sure I have a partner nearby I love who also loves me.
    2 It often bothers me that I do not have a partner nearby I love who loves me.
    3 I'm extremely disturbed that I do not have a partner I love who loves me.

14. 0 I have a satisfying sexual relationship with someone now on a regular basis.
    1 I sometimes wish that I had a satisfying sexual relationship on a regular basis.
    2 It often bothers me that I do not have a satisfying sexual relationship with anyone.
    3 I am extremely disturbed that I do not have a satisfying sexual relationship with anyone.

15. 0 I rarely think about particular times in my life when my relationships seemed better.
    1 I sometimes wish my relationships now could be more like they were at another time in my life.
    2 I am often bothered by how unsatisfactory my relationships now are compared with another time in my life.
    3 I am extremely disturbed by how poor my relationships now are compared with another time in my life.

16. 0 I rarely wish that my relationships could be more like other people's.
    1 I sometimes wish that I could have relationships that satisfied me the way other people's relationships seem to satisfy them.
    2 I often compare the satisfaction other people seem to get from their relationships with my own lack of satisfaction.
    3 I cannot stop comparing the satisfaction other people get from their relationships with my own lack of satisfaction.

17. 0 I am confident about the way I relate to men and women.
    1 I sometimes question whether there is something wrong with the way I relate to men or women.
    2 I often criticize myself for faults that seem to turn men or women off.
    3 I'm extremely disturbed that I am so undesirable to other people.

18. 0 I am confident that I will have close, satisfying relationships in the future.
    1 I sometimes question whether I will have close, satisfying relationships in the future.
    2 I am often pessimistic about my chances of having close, satisfying relationships in the future.

    3   I feel hopeless about ever having close, satisfying relationships.

19. 0   I haven't felt lonely during the past week (including today).
    1   I've sometimes felt lonely during the past week (including today).
    2   I've often felt lonely during the past week (including today).
    3   I could barely stand the loneliness during the past week (including today).

---

the client and friend spent together during a typical month at the peak of the relationship. One (1) would indicate being together about an evening a month while ten (10) would represent living and spending almost all evenings together. The *disclosure* dimension reflects the extent to which the client was able to discuss his private thoughts and feelings with the friend. Low scores would indicate a friendship where only obvious, superficial topics were discussed like favorite movies or plans for the weekend; high scores are appropriate in relationships where very intimate problems could be discussed. The *caring* score represents the client's assessment of how much he and the friend trusted and could depend on each other at times of crisis. A low score signifies that neither the client nor the friend would go "out of his way" for the other; a high score means that both would be willing to make large sacrifices for each other. The *physical intimacy* rating includes both the regularity of sexual contact and the satisfaction the client reported obtaining from it at the peak of the relationship. Zero (0) scores indicate no sexual component to the relationship while a ten (10) signifies regular and gratifying sexual intercourse. Finally, the client notes for each friend the approximate dates of the relationship, and his explanation for why the friendship ended or weakened.

By examining the Friendship Chart, the therapist can make a preliminary determination about whether the client is lonely primarily because of difficulties in *initiating* relationships or problems in *deepening* them. The clinician can further classify the client into more specific categories such as the following common ones:

1. Client has had few friends of either sex, none close, suggesting an overall pattern of social isolation.

2. Client has had several friends of both sexes, but none of them involving significant disclosure or intimacy.

3. Client has had friends of both sexes involving self-disclosure, but no physical intimacy.

4. Client has had frequent contact and disclosure with same-sex friends, but infrequent contact, low disclosure, and low physical intimacy with the opposite sex.

5. Client has had intense, sexually satisfying relationships with the opposite sex, but for short periods of time.

6. Client had a long-term intimate relationship with someone of the opposite sex until the friend met someone else or one of them moved away.

Hierarchical Stages in Relationships

In working with chronically lonely clients, I have become aware of several stages in establishing relationships and overcoming loneliness. In order to reach a higher stage, it generally seems necessary to have successfully mastered the previous level (although these stages are certainly not invariant). The use of the term "hierarchy" does not mean that higher levels are more desirable than lower levels, nor does it mean that the end goal with every lonely client is emotional commitment to a partner. Rather I have used the term "hierarchy" because the higher levels seem more *complex* than the lower levels, and because clients who want to reach higher levels often need to master lower levels before they are able to succeed.

It has been therapeutically useful to view loneliness as a developmental process. Each client enters treatment having already reached a particular point in the hierarchy. The major objectives for the six stages are:

1. To overcome anxiety and sadness about spending time alone.
2. To engage in activities with a few casual friends.
3. To engage in mutual self-disclosure with a trustworthy friend.
4. To meet a potentially intimate, appropriate partner (usually of the opposite sex).
5. To begin to develop intimacy with an appropriate partner, usually through disclosure and sexual contact.
6. To make an emotional commitment to an appropriate partner for a relatively long period of time.

After completing the diagnosis and obtaining baseline data, it should be possible to determine where the client is on this hierarchy. Once the present level of social functioning has been established, the therapist and client begin the process of identifying the cognitive, behavioral, and emotional blocks that prevent the client from mastering the next stage in the hierarchy.

Loneliness Clusters

In working with lonely clients, we have observed several clusters of cognition, behavior, and emotion (Table 22.3). These clusters do not *define* loneliness, but rather they seem to predispose the individual to feel lonely and maintain the loneliness. The clusters differentiate one lonely client from another, and appropriate treatment strategies are being developed for each cluster.

Let me contrast a loneliness cluster with a core lonely thought. A core lonely thought is a statement endorsed by a high percentage of lonely clients, and reflects the individual's perception that a particular type of social relationship is missing. Examples are:

1. There's no one I can really depend on.

Table 22.3. Loneliness Clusters

Name of Cluster	Typical automatic thoughts	Typical maladaptive assumptions	Typical behavior	Typical emotions
1. Discontented being alone	1. I have nothing to do alone. 2. I don't want to go out by myself. 3. I can't stand being alone. 4. I feel cut off when I'm alone. 5. I'll always be alone. 6. It's scary being alone.	1. Life has no meaning without someone to share it. 2. There must be something wrong with me if I'm alone. 3. I'm better off doing nothing than doing things alone. 4. I cannot cope with problems without help.	Spends time alone with a low level of activity	Bored, hopeless, empty, sad, anxious, isolated
2. Low self-concept	1. I'm undesirable. 2. I'm ugly. 3. I'm dull and boring. 4. I can't change the way I am.	1. People are completely intolerant of other people's faults. 2. It's essential to be attractive, intelligent, lively, witty, etc. to have any friends.	Avoidance of other people	Sad, hopeless, worthless
3. Social anxiety	1. I don't know how to act in this situation. 2. I feel uncomfortable with people. 3. I'll make a fool of myself. 4. I feel detached from conversations.	1. Other people are judging me all the time. 2. If I make any mistakes, people will ridicule or reject me.	Avoidance of other people	Anxious, shy, isolated

4. Social awkwardness	1. No one seems to like me and I don't know why. 2. People make fun of me and avoid me.	[None]	Ineptitude in social situations; low empathy for others	Excluded, sad, frustrated
5. Mistrust	1. I'm better off by myself. 2. I don't like most people. 3. I don't trust anyone.	1. Most people only care about themselves. 2. People will take advantage of you if they can.	Avoidance of friendships	Bitter, isolated
6. Constriction	1. I can't communicate with other people. 2. I'm different from other people. No one can understand me. 3. I don't want to burden people with my problems. 4. My thoughts and feelings are bottled up inside.	1. If people knew what I was thinking, they'd reject me or ridicule me. 2. People do not want to hear other people's problems.	Low self-disclosure	Psychologically isolated
7. Problems in partner selection	1. There's no place to meet the opposite sex. 2. The men/women I get involved with always end up hurting me. 3. There are very few men/women I find desirable. 4. No one can measure up to my last lover. 5. The partners I find attractive will not be acceptable to my friends or to society.	1. I must find the perfect man/woman and not settle for less. 2. I should continue to pursue people I am strongly attracted to, regardless of whether we are well suited in other respects. 3. If I just try hard enough I can always get the man/woman I want to love me. 4. Meeting new people should be fun or I should not bother.	Low rate of initiating potentially intimate relationships *or* pattern of selecting inappropriate partners	Frustrated, hopeless, emotionally empty, bitter

393

Table 22.3 (continued)

Name of Cluster	Typical automatic thoughts	Typical maladaptive assumptions	Typical behavior	Typical emotions
8. Intimate rejection	1. I won't risk being hurt again. 2. There's something wrong with me. 3. I'd screw up any relationship. 4. He/she really let me down.	1. If someone leaves you, there must be something wrong with you. 2. I can't possibly correct mistakes I made in the past. 3. If people really care they have no right to leave me. 4. I'm better off being alone than risking being hurt again.	Avoidance of potentially intimate relationships	Worthless, guilty, bitter, hopeless, emotionally empty
9. Sexual anxiety	1. I'm not a good lover. 2. I can't relax, be spontaneous, and enjoy sex.	1. Sex is a performance that the other person is evaluating. 2. If he/she doesn't respond, there must be something wrong with me.	Avoidance of sexual activity	Sexually frustrated, emotionally distant, ashamed, anxious
10. Anxiety about emotional commitment	1. I can't give enough to satisfy him/her. 2. I feel overwhelmed by his/her feelings. 3. She wants me more than I want her. 4. I feel trapped.	1. I should be able to meet my partner's emotional expectations of me always. 2. It's dishonest to have a relationship where two people are not	Avoidance of intimate long-term relationships; difficulty expressing emotions	Anxious, trapped, ambivalent

	I get too close.	there's no way to get out. 4. I'll lose my independence and have no time for myself if I get too close.		
11. Insecure passivity	1. The problems in this relationship are all my fault. 2. I can't seem to get what I want from this relationship. 3. I can't say how I feel or he/she might leave me. 4. I'm always being criticized.	1. If someone criticizes me, he/she must be right. 2. People should give me what I want without having to ask them. 3. When someone criticizes me, it means he/she is preparing to leave me.	Lack of assertiveness in relationships	Frustrated, helpless, anxious, insecure, angry, ambivalent
12. Unrealistic expectations	1. My partner will not do certain things the right way even though I have asked him/her to change. 2. My partner is not the person I thought he/she was when we first got involved.	1. There are right and wrong ways of doing almost everything, and I know what they are. 2. I should not have to tolerate any faults in my partner. 3. People should live up to my expectations of them or they are letting me down. 4. It's better to live alone than to have other people disappoint me.	Unnecessary termination of relationships	Angry, frustrated, impatient, hostile

2. No one loves me.
3. I'm different from other people.
4. I'm not physically intimate with anyone right now.

Statements such as these are currently being used to measure the presence and and extent of loneliness and are not intended to differentiate various forms of loneliness. Furthermore, they are too general to suggest specific treatment maneuvers.

Loneliness clusters, in contrast, are more specific. They help explain why individuals cannot develop satisfying relationships. They organize sets of cognition, behavior, and emotion together, as they commonly seem to occur based on our clinical experience with lonely clients. Lonely clients generally exhibit several of these clusters simultaneously, and there is considerable overlap in the behavior and emotions associated with them. (These clusters may also include one or more of the core lonely thoughts within them.)

To illustrate the cluster concept, consider the "intimate rejection" cluster. Characteristic *automatic thoughts* are:

1. I won't risk being hurt again.
2. There's something wrong with me.
3. I'd screw up any relationship.
4. He/she really let me down.

A lonely client with the rejection cluster will spontaneously report thoughts that approximate one or more of the four above.

Lonely clients, after more extensive probing, will often show indications that their automatic thoughts follow logically from a more basic set of *underlying assumptions* they hold about why events happen and how people "should" be (Primakoff, 1980). They may never have verbalized these assumptions before, but will probably admit that one or more of them seems reasonable. In the rejection cluster, these assumptions could include:

1. If someone leaves me, there must be something wrong with me.
2. I can't possibly correct mistakes I made in the past.
3. If people really care, they have no right to leave me.
4. I'm better off being alone than risking being hurt again.

Lonely clients with these "automatic thoughts" and "underlying assumptions" often manifest behavior patterns of avoiding potentially intimate relationships. Furthermore, clients with the rejection cluster report similar emotions including worthlessness, guilt, bitterness, hopelessness, and a sense of loss. The entire cluster is generally triggered by a lover breaking off a relationship with the client.

Particular clusters seem to be associated with specific stages in the hierarchy, although many of the clusters cut across several stages. For example, the "intimate rejection" cluster seems to arise most commonly at the fifth stage of development, when the client is faced with the desirability of deepening a relationship with someone of the opposite sex to achieve intimacy.

The remainder of this chapter will be devoted to specifying the loneliness clusters associated with each of the six stages in the hierarchy of overcoming loneliness, and to discussing ways in which the therapist can help the client by applying the strategies of cognitive therapy.

Stage 1: Being Alone

Lonely clients often find being alone an intensely aversive experience. It is often useful in therapy to help clients become more comfortable with being alone before, or concurrent with, initiating friendships. Otherwise clients may overwhelm potential friends with their "neediness" out of a desperate fear of being alone.

"Discontented Being Alone" Cluster

Often lonely clients are depressed, inactive, unstructured, and lack energy. Some fear that something terrible will happen that they will not be able to handle. In order to determine exactly why clients are discontented, it is essential to elicit their automatic thoughts while they are alone. An example is the thought, "I don't want to go out by myself." We ask clients expressing this belief to test out their notion that they are actually happier staying home alone ruminating than they would be going out by themselves. To help isolated clients become more active, we often use the techniques of *activity scheduling* and *pleasure therapy,* described in detail elsewhere (Beck, Rush, Shaw, & Emery, 1979).

Low Self-Concept Cluster

Many lonely clients are blocked from pursuing relationships and from deepening them because they consider themselves undesirable in many respects. The "low self-concept" cluster affects clients at all stages of the hierarchy. They report automatic thoughts that they are, for example, unattractive, unlikable, dull, boring, stupid, cold, or selfish. Clients also tend to believe that these faults are basic to their personality and therefore unchangeable.

Assuming these clients are not terribly awkward in social situations, the therapist can help them examine their relationships in the past to test the hypothesis that other people have avoided them because they are dull, ugly, and so on. With the clinician's guidance, lonely clients can often recognize that they have had friends in the past who liked them, and that they may be overgeneralizing from a few instances of rejection. These clients can also be asked to list their positive qualities. The therapist can sometimes identify underlying assumptions, such as the notion that "It is essential to be beautiful, brilliant, lively, and witty in order to have friends." Through questioning, clients often realize that they themselves would not insist on these qualities in selecting friends, and therefore other people may not either. Finally, if serious faults do exist, the client can be shown that most personal characteristics are not innate but can be learned and unlearned.

Stage 2: Casual Friendships

Before initiating intimate relationships, it has proven exceptionally important for the lonely client to build up a solid base of casual friends first. These casual friendships often serve to counteract the boredom, inactivity, and low self-concept that are so prevalent among isolated clients.

Social Anxiety Cluster

One of the most common blocks to making friends is a set of thoughts expressing a fear of embarrassing oneself in front of other people and of not knowing what to do or say. These thoughts lead to a social phobia, accompanied by many symptoms of anxiety. Sometimes clients interpret these anxiety symptoms as indications that they will lose control, go crazy, or have a heart attack. Other socially phobic clients engage in "spectatoring" behavior, a concept drawn from sex therapy (Kaplan, 1974). Spectatoring refers to a process in which clients cannot stop observing themselves while they are with others. They are so focused on how poorly they are "performing" and so self-conscious that they cannot participate in or enjoy social encounters.

It is often effective to ask clients for evidence that other people are constantly examining and evaluating their behavior. Furthermore, the therapist can assist clients in questioning the assumption that they would be rejected or ridiculed if they made a social faux pas. Would they stop being friends with someone who acted in an awkward manner?

Another strategy for dealing with social anxiety is for the therapist and client to rehearse the feared social situation and videotape it. After viewing the tape, clients are often surprised that they appear more relaxed and appropriate than they had thought. Finally, it is often possible to interrupt spectatoring behavior by showing clients ways of distracting themselves from their self-monitoring by refocusing on some external object or person.

Social Awkwardness Cluster

Some lonely clients do not have appropriate social skills in their repertoire for handling certain situations. They may report being ridiculed and rejected by others yet not know why.

In these cases the therapist can model more desirable types of behavior and ask the client to try to incorporate them in the context of a role play. Through practice, the client will begin to get more positive feedback from others. Some lonely people seem to have difficulty relating to others because they do not understand how other people think—their own thinking is often very idiosyncratic. The therapist can educate these clients regarding conventional attitudes towards many areas of life and train the clients to listen more carefully to what other people are saying. Empathy can be learned, although the process is often difficult.

Mistrust Cluster

A significant number of long-term, chronically lonely people suffer from a profound mistrust of other people. They are often bitter about the world, yet feel painfully isolated. These clients often share maladaptive assumptions about other people being selfish, only caring about themselves, and taking advantage of everyone else.

The therapist can help in two major ways. First, he or she can review the factors in the individual's life that support the client's view that people are uncaring. The therapist can then inquire whether these few examples are adequate evidence to generalize about the rest of the world. He or she can suggest that the client "try out" a few more people to see if the client's assumption is truly accurate. A second important strategy is for the clinician to probe continually for the client's thoughts about whether the therapist can be trusted. Ideally the lonely client will come to recognize that he or she is placing the worst possible interpretation on many of the therapist's actions and that alternative explanations are more plausible. If the client can come to trust the therapist, then his or her view of the world at large may begin to change as well.

Stage 3: Mutual Self-Disclosure

Once the lonely client can develop a solid base of satisfying casual friends, the next step is to select the most trustworthy among them and begin the process of self-disclosure. We place a great deal of emphasis on self-disclosure because the first step toward intimacy is often the sharing of private thoughts and feelings with another person. The therapist usually encourages the client to begin this process with a friend who is safe and comfortable, often of the same sex, and who has already expressed an obvious interest in becoming closer friends. Generally the clinician discourages self-disclosure with a potentially intimate partner of the opposite sex in these early stages because the "threat" of emotional involvement may create too much anxiety and because the other person might misinterpret the client's intentions.

Constriction Cluster

Lonely clients often have difficulty with self-disclosure. They frequently have a stream of thoughts about their inability to communicate because they are different from others, no one can understand them, and people would reject them if they disclosed their weaknesses or "shameful" thoughts. Constricted clients may also express the opinion that they have no right to burden other people with their problems.

To test these thoughts, the therapist can play the role of the client while the client plays the role of a friend. As the therapist discloses some of the client's "secrets," the client listens and responds. Almost inevitably, clients report that they felt a great deal of understanding and caring for the therapist during the disclosure, not disgust. They often conclude from the role playing that their private fears are not so terrible after all and that they can probably enhance intimacy through such self-disclosure. The client also begins to recognize that other people are not so different and are able to understand and empathize.

Stage 4: Meeting a Potentially Intimate Partner

After the client has successfully established a relationship involving mutual self-disclosure with a "safe" friend, therapy is directed toward meeting someone who might be suitable for an intimate relationship. This usually involves partners of the opposite sex, but the same strategies would apply to homosexual clients. Often the obstacle to meeting someone of the opposite sex is the client's belief that he or she is undesirable. Strategies for handling this have already been discussed in connection with the "low self-concept" cluster. However, there are additional problems that arise in initiating opposite-sex relationships.

"Problems in Partner Selection" Cluster

Some lonely clients believe that there are no places to meet suitable partners. The therapist can work with such clients to develop a list of possible ways of getting acquainted. These include: contacting desirable friends or acquaintances from the past; asking friends to arrange a date; going to parties; approaching "candidates" at work or in the neighborhood; becoming involved in organizations with members who share the client's interests; and as a last resort, attending singles' functions.

Most people find the process of initiating opposite-sex relationships to be somewhat uncomfortable, especially when the setting or circumstances are unfamiliar. The possibility of being rejected is always "lurking" in the background, so of course it feels safer to be with someone who has previously demonstrated acceptance. Lonely clients often have to be encouraged to weigh the discomfort of the unfamiliar encounter with the potential advantages of meeting a desirable, accepting partner to become intimate with. A helpful perspective is that the more people one meets, the greater the odds of finding a suitable partner. This is true no matter how small a percentage of people they consider suitable.

A second set of problems in partner selection involves excessive or unnecessary restrictions on the choice of partner. Some lonely clients set unrealistically high standards before they will go out on a date. Each potential person is not attractive enough, intelligent enough, successful enough. The therapist can guide the client to the recognition that setting such high standards is self-defeating, because the client closes off so many opportunities for intimacy that might be preferable to "aloneness." The same logic applies when the client compares every new person to a wonderful person from the past who is no longer available. Another maladaptive restriction is when the client would like to go out with someone but does not because he or she does not feel other people will approve. (Homosexuals who have not "come out of the closet" are good examples of this problem.) With such clients, the therapist and client together can examine the consequences of making important decisions on the basis of other people's potential approval or disapproval.

A final obstacle to meeting an appropriate partner is illustrated by the client who consistently selects people who turn out to be unsatisfactory. In these instances it often seems that individuals, through some inexplicable emotional conditioning, are very attracted to particular types of partners who do not meet their needs. These partners are sometimes cruel, act in a rejecting way, prove to be disturbed, or are excessively dependent. When the therapist and client identify such a pattern, they can try to find clues to identify these inappropriate people in advance. The client will have to conclude that the long-run negative effects of continuing with a partner like this will outweigh the initial infatuation.

Stage 5: Developing Intimacy

Once the client has established contact with a desirable and interested partner, and they seem reasonably comfortable going out together, the focus of treatment turns to deepening the relationship. Intimacy is usually reached through a combination of self-disclosure, sexual contact, and other expressions of affection and caring.

Intimate Rejection Cluster

This cluster was discussed earlier in this chapter and represents a common reaction on the part of clients who have recently been rejected in intimate relationships. They may be comfortable with casual friends, especially of the same sex, but frequently avoid self-disclosure and sexual contact with the opposite sex. Divorced and separated clients are frequently blocked by thoughts in this cluster.

The most common thoughts concern guilt about what they did wrong to deserve rejection, and bitterness that someone they trusted hurt them so much. With lonely clients like these, it is often helpful to review the entire relationship to understand why the relationship ended. The client is usually able to reattribute the breakup either to (1) a fundamental incompatibility between the partners or (2) changes in one or both of them that made it difficult for them to readjust and function happily. Even when clients remain convinced that they are to blame, the therapist can suggest ways of changing their behavior so that they do not repeat the same mistake in other relationships. In general, then, the strategy is to stop the client from drawing any conclusions about future relationships on the basis of a past one. If this is successful, the risk in becoming intimate again will not seem so great.

Sexual Anxiety Cluster

Sexual intimacy is often a problem for lonely clients. Techniques for treating sexual dysfunction have been presented elsewhere (Kaplan, 1974), but I will elaborate on some of the problems we have most commonly encountered in conjunction with loneliness.

The first is related to the "spectatoring" I mentioned previously. Just as lonely clients frequently are worried that they will embarrass themselves or perform unsatisfactorily in social contacts, they also believe that they will prove to be incompetent lovers. The therapist can inquire whether there are other ways to view sexual contact rather than as a performance. Clients can generally recognize that it is more reasonable to concentrate on feeling close and obtaining pleasure than on evaluating each other. Furthermore, it is often valuable to ask clients to generate alternative reasons why someone might not be sexually responsive at a particular time.

In some other cases of sexual problems, lonely clients feel psychologically isolated. Frequently they have not shared doubts or fears about themselves or the relationship with their partner, and thus feel distant. This distance can seriously affect the level of satisfaction they derive from the sexual contact. By encouraging self-disclosure, the therapist can lead clients to overcome their sense of isolation.

Stage 6: Long-Term Emotional Commitment

The final stage in overcoming loneliness is to maintain an intimate relationship for a relatively long period of time. Some clients have few difficulties in the early stages of an intimate relationship, as defined by self-disclosure, caring, and sexual contact. However, their relationships either end quickly or are characterized by increasing insecurity, anger, or ambivalence.

"Anxiety about Emotional Commitment" Cluster

Some lonely clients achieve a certain level of intimacy but then begin to feel they are "holding back." They recognize that they have not fully committed themselves to their partner and are afraid to do so. They soon may want to run away and escape or at least withdraw from intimacy. These clients have a variety of automatic thoughts concerning feeling trapped, overwhelmed by their partner's feelings, afraid they will not be able to reciprocate the love they receive, convinced they will lose their freedom, and frightened that they will "lose themselves" if they get too close.

The therapist can suggest to the client that there is tremendous variation among individuals in the time it takes before they feel ready to make an emotional commitment. Some people are ready for "total involvement" in a matter of days or weeks, while others require months or even years. The ideal of equal commitment and total reciprocation is rarely achieved in the early stages of a relationship. If the partners openly discuss their readiness to become more involved and accept each other's feelings as valid, then neither partner need feel trapped or rejected. Entrapment only exists when one partner feels *obligated* to meet the other's demands. The degree of intimacy, dependence, time commitment, and freedom can usually be negotiated through mutual discussion and sensitivity.

Insecure Passivity Cluster

Some lonely clients are reluctant to express dissatisfaction directly to their partners. This fear of asserting themselves by making reasonable requests generally stems from one or both of these beliefs: "If I'm dissatisfied, it must be my fault" and "I can't say how I feel or my partner will leave me." Because they do not express their desires directly, the partner often has no way of knowing that something is wrong. Such clients, nevertheless, feel angry because they believe their partners should know what they want without having to be asked. Thus passive lonely clients are trapped. If they express themselves, they will either find out it is their own fault or be rejected; if they say nothing, they feel increasingly angry and eventually may decide to leave the relationship.

The solution is to help clients recognize that they can legitimately ask to have their desires met without having to fear abandonment from their partners. The therapist can point out that expressing dissatisfaction, criticism, and anger are all normal components of a long-term relationship and need not signal a breakup. Finally, the client and clinician can rehearse assertive behavior through role playing and modeling procedures.

Unrealistic Expectations Cluster

A significant number of chronically lonely clients set unrealistic expectations for their friends and partners. Often these clients are viewed by others as rigid, uncompromising, stubborn, inflexible, demanding, or moralistic. Such clients, however, rarely view themselves this way; they often see themselves as asking other people to do only what "everyone would agree is right." When friends fail to do what is "obviously" correct, clients with this cluster feel angry, insulted, frustrated, and disappointed in their friends. Sometimes these clients overlook weaknesses in their partners during the "infatuation stage" of relationships, or else anticipate that the partner will change as time goes on. When the partner does not meet their expectations later, they feel the other person has betrayed them or is stubbornly refusing to change, and they begin to harp and criticize.

When the underlying assumptions of such clients are uncovered, we sometimes find that they strongly believe in certain absolute standards of right and wrong and therefore are intolerant, or totally unaware, of differing views held by their partners. Other clients in this cluster recognize differences of opinion as valid, but still feel they should not have to tolerate behavior they dislike; they often believe that their partners should make adjustments just to show they care. Some clients with unrealistic expectations will actually choose to be alone rather than accept faults in their partner.

With lonely clients in this category, the therapist can follow two paths. The first is to help the person see that there are rarely absolute standards of right and wrong, and that other people are validly entitled to live according to different rules. The second path is to have the client contrast the disadvantages of continually demanding that expectations be met and becoming frustrated with the benefits of tolerating faults and accepting other people's points of view. Most clients can eventually accept certain flaws as a reasonable price to pay for achieving intimacy and companionship.

SUMMARY

I have outlined a systematic framework for understanding loneliness and for treating lonely clients. I have emphasized the importance of three components—cognition, behavior, and emotion—in defining and treating loneliness. I have stressed the notion that the particular behaviors and emotions that accompany loneliness are often a function of the individual's thoughts, attributions, and assumptions. If we can ascertain how lonely clients view themselves and their relationships, we can generally understand why they are acting and feeling as they do. Once we have reached this understanding, we can apply cognitive behavioral techniques to help clients overcome their loneliness.

REFERENCES

Beck, A. T. Cognitive therapy and the emotional disorders. New York: International Universities Press, 1976.

Beck, A. T., Rush, A. J., Shaw, B. F., & Emery, G. Cognitive therapy of depression. New York: Guilford Press, 1979.

Beck, A. T., & Young, J. E. College blues. Psychology Today, September 1978.

Bragg, M. A comparison of nondepressed and depressed loneliness. Paper presented at the UCLA Research Conference on Loneliness, Los Angeles, May 1979.

Cautela, J. R. Behavior therapy and self-control: Techniques and implications. In C. M. Franks (Ed.), Behavior therapy: Appraisal and status. New York: McGraw-Hill, 1969.

Derogatis, L., Rickels, K., & Rock, A. The SCL-90 and the MMPI: A step in the validation of a new self-report scale. British Journal of Psychiatry, 1976, 128, 280–289.

Ellis, A., & Greiger, R. Handbook of rational emotive therapy. New York: Springer Publishing Company, 1977.

Goldfried, M. R., & Davison, G. C. Clinical behavior therapy. New York: Holt, Rinehart, and Wintson, 1976.

Kaplan, H. S. The new sex therapy. New York: Brunner/Mazel, 1974.

Meichenbaum, D. B. Cognitive-behavior modification: An integrative approach. New York: Plenum, 1977.

Michela, J., Peplau, L. A., & Weeks, D. G. *Perceived dimensions and consequences of attributions for loneliness.* Unpublished manuscript, University of California, Los Angeles, July 1980.

Primakoff, L. *Patterns of living alone: A cognitive behavioral ethology.* Doctoral dissertation. University of Texas at Austin, 1980.

Rosenbaum, J., & Rosenbaum, V. *Conquering loneliness.* New York: Hawthorn Books, 1973.

Rush, A. J., Beck, A. T., Kovacs, M., & Hollon, S. D. Comparative efficacy of cognitive therapy and pharmacotherapy in the treatment of depressed outpatients. *Cognitive Therapy and Research,* 1977, *1,* 17–37.

Russell, D., Peplau, L. A., & Ferguson, M. Developing a measure of loneliness. *Journal of Personality Assessment,* 1978, *42,* 290–294.

Schultz, T. *Bittersweet: Surviving and growing from loneliness.* New York: Crowell, 1976.

Spitzberg, B. H. *Loneliness and communication apprehension.* Unpublished manuscript, Department of Communication Arts and Sciences, University of Southern California, Los Angeles, California.

Tanner, I. *Loneliness: The fear of love.* New York: Harper & Row, 1973.

Taylor, F. G., & Marshall, W. L. Experimental analysis of a cognitive-behavioral therapy for depression. *Cognitive Therapy and Research,* 1977, *1,* 59–72.

Weeks, D. G., Michela, J. C., Peplau, L. A., & Bragg, M. E. The relation between loneliness and depression: A structural equation analysis. *Journal of Personality and Social Psychology,* 1980, *39,* 1238–1244.

Weiss, R. *Loneliness: The experience of emotional and social isolation.* Cambridge, Mass.: MIT Press, 1975.

Young, J. E. Loneliness in college students: A cognitive approach (Doctoral dissertation, University of Pennsylvania.) *Dissertation Abstracts International,* 1979a.

Young, J. E. *An instrument for measuring loneliness.* Paper presented at the annual meeting of the American Psychological Association, New York, September 1979b.

A Bibliography on Loneliness: 1932-1981

Letitia Anne Peplau and Daniel Perlman

Anderson, C. A. *Motivational and performance deficits as a function of attributional style.* Unpublished doctoral dissertation, Stanford University, 1980.

Anderson, C. A., Horowitz, L. M. & French, R. deS. Attributional style in lonely and depressed people. *Journal of Personality and Social Psychology,* in press.

Applebaum, F. Loneliness: A taxonomy and psychodynamic view. *Clinical Social Work Journal,* 1978, *6*(1), 13–20.

Arling, G. The elderly widow and her family, neighbors and friends. *Journal of Marriage and the Family,* 1976, *38,* 757–768.

Arling, G. Resistance to isolation among elderly widows. *International Journal of Aging and Human Development,* 1976, *7*(1), 67–86.

Bahr, H. M., & Harvey, C. D. Correlates of loneliness among widows bereaved in a mining disaster. *Psychological Reports,* 1979, *44,* 367–385.

Bakwin, H. Loneliness in infants. *American Journal of Diseases of Children,* 1942, *63,* 30–40.

Balkwell, C. Transition to widowhood: A review of the literature. *Family Relations,* 1981, *30,* 117–127.

Barkas, J. L. *Single in America.* New York: Atheneum, 1980.

Barnett, J. On the dynamics of interpersonal isolation. *Journal of the American Academy of Psychoanalysis,* 1978, *6*(1), 59–70.

Barry, M. J. Depression, shame, loneliness and the psychiatrist's position. *American Journal of Psychotherapy,* 1962, *16*(4), 580–590.

Bart, P. The loneliness of the long-distance mother. In J. Freeman (Ed.), *Women: A feminist perspective.* Palo Alto: Mayfield, 1974.

Beck, A. T., & Young, J. E. College blues. *Psychology Today,* September 1978, 80–92.

Becker, E. The spectrum of loneliness. *Humanitas,* 1974, *10*(3), 237–246.

Belcher, M. J. *The measurement of loneliness: A validation of the Belcher Extended Loneliness Scale (BELS).* Unpublished doctoral dissertation, Illinois Institute of Technology, 1973.

Bell, R. G. Alcohol and loneliness. *Journal of Social Therapy,* 1956, *2,* 171–181.

Bennett, R. Social isolation and isolation-reducing programs. *Bulletin of the New York Academy of Medicine,* 1973, *49*(12), 1143–1163.

Berblinger, K. W. A psychiatrist looks at loneliness. *Psychosomatics,* 1968, *9*(2), 96–102.

Berblinger, K. W. Loneliness and the depressive perspective: The chronically depressed patient. In A. J. Enelow (Ed.), *Depression in medical practice*. West Point, Pa.: Merck, Sharp, & Dohme, 1970.

Berg, S., Mellstrom, D., Persson, G., & Svanborg, A. Loneliness in the Swedish aged. *Journal of Gerontology*, 1981, *36*, 342–349.

Bitter, W. *Loneliness from a medical, psychological, theological and sociological point of view*. Stuttgart, Germany: Ernst Klett, 1967.

Bowman, C. C. Loneliness and social change. *American Journal of Psychiatry*, 1955, *112*, 194–198.

Bowstill, D. *All the lonely people*. Indianapolis: Bobbs-Merrill Co., 1974.

Bradburn, N. *The structure of psychological well-being*. Chicago: Aldine, 1969.

Bradley, R. *Measuring loneliness*. Unpublished doctoral dissertation, Washington State University, 1969.

Bragg, M. E. A comparative study of loneliness and depression. (Doctoral dissertation, University of California, Los Angeles, 1979). *Dissertation Abstracts International*, 1979, *39*, 79–13710.

Brain, R. *Friends and lovers*. New York Basic Books, 1976.

Brown, R. W. *Lonely Americans*. Freeport, N.J.: Books for Libraries Press, 1970.

Bugbee, H. G. Loneliness, solitude, and the twofold way in which concern seems to be claimed. *Humanitas*, 1974, *10*(3), 313–328.

Buhler, C. Loneliness in maturity. *Journal of Humanistic Psychology*, 1969, *9*(2), 167–181.

Burke, C., & Provost, N. (Eds.), *Loneliness*. Winona, Minn.: St. Mary's, 1970.

Burnside, I. M. Loneliness in old age. *Mental Hygiene*, 1971, *55*(3), 391–397.

Burton, A. On the nature of loneliness. *American Journal of Psychoanalysis*, 1961, *21*(1), 34–39.

Byrd, R. E. *Alone*. New York: Ace, 1938.

Cargan, L. *Singleness and the problem of loneliness*. Unpublished doctoral dissertation, Wright State University, 1977.

Chandler, M. J. Relativism and the problem of epistemological loneliness. *Human Development*, 1975, *18*, 171–180.

Chapman, R. *The loneliness of man*. Philadelphia: Fortress Press, 1963.

Cheek, J. M., & Busch, C. M. The influence of shyness on loneliness in a new situation. *Personality and Social Psychology Bulletin*, in press.

Chelune, G. J., Sultan, F. E., & Williams, C. L. Loneliness, self-disclosure, and interpersonal effectiveness. *Journal of Counseling Psychology*, 1980, *27*, 462–468.

Christensen, J. A. Fiction of loneliness. *Media and Methods*, 1972, *8*, 24–28.

Clark, M., & Anderson, B. G. Loneliness and old age. In J. Hartog, J. R. Audy, & Y. A. Cohen (Eds.), *The anatomy of loneliness*. New York: International Universities Press, 1980.

Collier, R. M., & Lawrence, H. P. The adolescent feeling of psychological isolation. *Educational Theory*, 1951, *1*, 106–115.

Colligan, D. Biology of loneliness: Isolation vs. our brains. *Science Digest*, 1973, *74*, 36–41.

Colton, H. Loneliness—it's rough. *Forum Magazine*, December 1979, 31–35.

Conti, M. L. The loneliness of old age. *Nursing Outlook*, 1970, *18*(8), 28–30.

Curtin, S. R. In praise of old people: In outrage at their loneliness. *Bulletin of the New York Academy of Medicine*, 1973, *49*(12), 1143–1163.

Czernik, A., & Steinmeyer, E. Experience of loneliness in normal and in neurotic subjects. *Archiv für Psychiatrie und Nervenkranheiten,* 1974, *218*(2), 141–159.

D'Aboy, J. E. *Loneliness: An investigation of terminology.* Unpublished doctoral dissertation, Arizona State University, 1972.

Dasberg, H. Belonging and loneliness in relation to mental breakdown in battle: With some remarks on treatment. *Israel Annals of Psychiatry and Related Disciplines,* 1976, *14*(4), 307–321.

Davis, T. N. *The loneliness of man.* Chicago: Claretian Publications, 1968.

Dean, L. R. Aging and the decline of affect. *Journal of Gerontology,* 1962, *17,* 440–446.

DeJanos, S. *Loneliness and communication.* Toronto: New Press, 1971.

DeJong-Gierveld, J. Social isolation and the image of the unmarried. *Sociologia Neerlandica,* 1971, *7,* 1–14.

DeJong-Gierveld, J. The construct of loneliness: Components and measurement. *Essence,* 1978, *2*(4), 221–237.

DeJong-Gierveld, J., & Aalberts, M. Singlehood: A creative or lonely experience? *Alternative Lifestyles,* 1980, *3,* 350–368.

DeLaczay, E. *Loneliness.* New York: Hawthorne Books, 1972.

Denés, Z. Loneliness and old age. *Zeitschrift für Alternsforschung,* 1975, *29*(3), 305–310.

Donson, C., & Georgés, A. *Lonely-land and bedsitter-land.* Bala, North Wales: Chapples, 1967.

Dubrey, R. J., & Terrill, L. A. The loneliness of the dying person: An exploratory study. *Omega: Journal of Death and Dying,* 1975, *6*(4), 357–371.

Dunn, E. F., & Dunn, P. C. Loneliness and the black experience. In J. Hartog, J. R. Audy, & Y. A. Cohen (Eds.), *The anatomy of loneliness.* New York: International Universities Press, 1980.

Dusenburg, W. L. *The theme of loneliness in modern American drama.* Gainesville: University of Florida Press, 1960.

Duvall, E. M. Loneliness and the serviceman's wife. *Journal of Marriage and Family Living,* 1945, *7,* 77–81.

Dyer, B. M. Loneliness—There's no way to escape it. *Alpha Gamma Delta Quarterly,* Spring 1974, 2–5.

Eddy, P. D. *Loneliness: A discrepancy with the phenomenological self.* Unpublished doctoral dissertation, Adelphi College, 1961.

Eisenson, J. Loneliness and the divorced post-middle-aged male. In J. Hartog, J. R. Audy, & Y. A. Cohen (Eds.), *The anatomy of loneliness.* New York: International Universities Press, 1980.

Ellison, C. W. Loneliness: A social developmental analysis. *Journal of Psychology and Theology,* 1978, *6*(1), 3–17.

Ellison, C. W. *Loneliness.* Chappaqua, N.Y.: Christian Herald Books, 1980.

Farrell, J. T. *Lonely for the future.* Garden City, N.Y.: Doubleday, 1966.

Favazza, A. Feral and isolated children. *British Journal of Medical Psychology,* 1977, *50*(1), 105–111.

Ferreira, A. J. Loneliness and psychopathology. *American Journal of Psychoanalysis,* 1962, *22*(2), 201–207.

Fidler, J. Loneliness: The problems of the elderly and retired. *Royal Society of Health Journal,* 1976, *96,* 39–41, 44.

Flanders, J. P. From loneliness to intimacy. *Practical Psychology.* New York: Harper & Row, 1976.

Ford, E. E., & Zorn, R. L. *Why be lonely?* Niles, Ill.: Argus Communications, 1975.

Francel, C. G. Loneliness. In S. F. Burd & M. A. Marshall (Eds.), *Some clinical approaches to psychiatric nursing.* New York: Macmillan, 1963.

Francis, G. M. *Loneliness: A study of hospitalized adults.* Unpublished doctoral dissertation, University of Pennsylvania, 1972.

Francis, G. M. Loneliness: Measuring the abstract. *International Journal of Nursing Study,* 1976, *13,* 153–160.

Francis, G. M., & Odell, S. H. Longterm residence and loneliness: Myth or reality? *Journal of Gerontologic Nursing,* 1979, *5,* 9–11.

Frank, R. M. America's major diseases: Loneliness, anxiety, boredom. *Rehabilitation Record,* 1972, *13,* 5–8.

Frazao, V. A. *Emergence from loneliness.* Unpublished doctoral dissertation, California School of Professional Psychology, 1978.

Fromm, E. *The sane society.* New York: Holt, Rinehart, & Winston, 1955.

Fromm-Reichmann, F. Loneliness: *Psychiatry,* 1959, *22,* 1–15.

Gaev, D. *The psychology of loneliness.* Chicago: Adams, 1976.

Galassi, J. P., & Galassi, M. D. Alienation in college students: A comparison of counseling seekers and nonseekers. *Journal of Counseling Psychology,* 1973, *20,* 44–49.

Gallico, P. *The lonely.* New York: Knopf, 1949.

Gerson, A. C. *The relationship of chronic and situational loneliness to social skills and social sensitivity.* Unpublished doctoral dissertation, University of Manitoba, Canada, 1978.

Gerson, A. C., & Perlman, D. Loneliness and expressive communication. *Journal of Abnormal Psychology,* 1979, *88*(3), 258–261.

Gibson, J. E. You don't have to be lonely. *Science Digest,* 1967, *62,* 33–36.

Glasser, W. Loneliness and failure. *The identity society.* New York: Harper & Row, 1972.

Goldman, G. D. Group psychotherapy and the lonely person in our changing times. *Group Psychotherapy,* 1955, *8,* 247–253.

Gordon, S. *Lonely in America.* New York: Simon & Schuster, 1976.

Goswick, R. A., & Jones, W. H. Loneliness, self concept, and adjustment. *Journal of Psychology,* 1981, *107,* 237–240.

Gotesky, R. Aloneness, loneliness, isolation, solitude. In J. M. Edie (Ed.), *An invitation to phenomenology.* Chicago: Quadrangle Books, 1965.

Gotz, I. L. Loneliness. *Humanitas,* 1974, *10*(3), 289–300.

Gratton, C. Summaries of selected works on loneliness and solitude. *Humanitas,* 1974, *10*(3), 329–334.

Gratton, C. Selected subject bibliography on loneliness (covering the past 10 years). *Humanitas,* 1974, *10*(3), 335–340.

Green, M., & Kaplan, B. L. Aspects of loneliness in the therapeutic situation. *International Review of Psychoanalysis.* 1978, *5,* 321–330.

Greenwald, J. A. Self-induced loneliness. *Voices,* 1972, *8,* 14–23.

Greenwald, J. A. *Breaking out of loneliness.* New York: Rawson & Wade, 1980.

Greer, I. M. Roots of loneliness. *Journal of Pastoral Psychology,* 1955, *9*(35), 27–31.

Gunn, A. D. Vulnerable groups: Lives of loneliness. The medical-social problems of divorce and widowhood. *Nursing Times,* 1968, *64,* 391–392.

Haas-Hawkings, G. Intimacy as a moderating influence on the stress of loneliness in widowhood. *Essence,* 1978, *2*(4), 249–258.

Hammer, M. A therapy for loneliness. *Voices,* 1972, *8*(1), 24–29.

Hansson, R. O., & Jones, W. H. Loneliness, cooperation and conformity among American undergraduates. *Journal of Social Psychology,* 1981, *115,* 103–108.

Harper, R. The concentric circles of loneliness. *Humanitas,* 1974, *10*(3), 247–254.

Hartog, J., Audy, J. R., & Cohen, Y. A. (Eds.) *The anatomy of loneliness.* New York: International Universities Press, 1980.

Hau, T. F. von. Psychology and psychopathology of loneliness. *Zeitschrift für Psychosomatische Medizin und Psychoanalyse,* 1973, *19,* 265–271.

Hendrix, M. J. *Toward an operational definition of loneliness.* Unpublished doctoral dissertation, Boston University School of Nursing, 1971.

Hobson, R. F. Loneliness. *Journal of Analytic Psychology,* 1974, *19*(1), 71–89.

Hoover, S., Skuja, A., & Cosper, J. Correlates of college students' loneliness. *Psychological Reports,* 1979, *44,* 1116.

Horowitz, L. M., & French, R. de S. Interpersonal problems of people who describe themselves as lonely. *Journal of Consulting and Clinical Psychology,* 1979, *47*(4), 762–764.

Hoskisson, J. B. *Loneliness: An explanation, a cure.* New York: Citadel Press, 1963.

Howard, J. A. *The flesh-colored cage: The impact of man's essential aloneness on his attitudes and behavior.* New York: Hawthorn Books, 1975.

Hulme, W. E. *Creative loneliness.* Minneapolis, Minn.: Augsburg, 1977.

Johnson, J. *Loneliness is not forever.* Evanston, Ill.: Moody Press, 1979.

Jones, W. H. Loneliness and social contact. *Journal of Social Psychology,* 1981, *113,* 295–296.

Jones, W. H., Freemon, J. A., & Goswick, R. A. The persistence of loneliness: Self and other determinants. *Journal of Personality,* 1981, *49,* 27–48.

Jones, W. H., Hobbs, S. A., & Hockenbury, D. Loneliness and social skill deficits. *Journal of Personality and Social Psychology,* in press.

Kaufman, B. *Solitudes crowded with loneliness.* New York: New Directions, 1965.

Kennedy, E. *Living with loneliness.* Chicago: Thomas More Press, 1973.

Kennedy, E. *Loneliness.* Chicago: Thomas More Press, 1977.

Kerken, L. V. *Loneliness and love.* New York: Sheed and Ward, 1967.

Kersten, F. Loneliness and solitude. *Humanitas,* 1974, *10*(3), 301–312.

Keyes, R. *We, the lonely people: Searching for community.* New York: Harper & Row, 1973.

Kiefer, C. W. Loneliness and Japanese social structure. In J. Hartog, J. R. Audy, & Y. A. Cohen (Eds.), *The anatomy of loneliness.* New York: International Universities Press, 1980.

Killinger, J. *The loneliness of children.* New York: Vanguard Press, 1980.

Kivett, V. R. Loneliness and the rural widow. *Family Coordinator,* 1978, *27*(4), 389–394.

Kivett, V. R. Discriminators of loneliness among the rural elderly: Implications for intervention. *Gerontologist,* 1979, *19*(1), 108–115.

Klein, M. On the sense of loneliness. *Our adult world and other essays.* New York: Basic Books, 1963. Reprinted in J. Hartog, J. R. Audy, & Y. A. Cohen (Eds.), *The anatomy of loneliness.* New York: International Universities Press, 1980.

Knoblock, P. *The lonely teacher.* Boston: Allyn and Bacon, 1971.

Konopka, G. Friends-loneliness. *Young girls: A portrait of adolescence.* Englewood Cliffs, N.J.: Prentice-Hall, 1976.

Kosten, A. *How you can conquer loneliness.* New York: Twayne Press, 1961.

Krebs, J. S. The infinite spaceship: A phenomenological analysis of the experience of loneliness. (Doctoral dissertation, The George Washington University, 1974). *Dissertation Abstracts International*, 1974, *35*, 1052B. (University Microfilms No. 74-17, 406)

Krulik, T. Loneliness in school age children with chronic life-threatening illness. (Doctoral dissertation, University of California, San Francisco, 1978). *Dissertation Abstracts International*, 1978, *39*(10-B).

Kubistant, T. M. *A synthesis of the aloneness/loneliness phenomenon: A counseling perspective.* Unpublished doctoral dissertation, University of Northern Illinois, 1977.

Landefeld, R. E. *A study of the intrapsychic experience of loneliness in widowhood.* Unpublished doctoral dissertation, University of Pittsburgh, 1976.

Leal, F. The syndrome of the lonely woman. *Acta Psychiatrica Belgica*, 1973, *73*(7), 437–447.

Lederer, W. J., & Jackson, D. D. False assumption 6: That loneliness will be cured by marriage. *The mirages of marriage.* New York: Norton, 1968.

Leiderman, P. H. Loneliness: A psychodynamic interpretation. In E. S. Shneidman & M. J. Ortega (Eds.), *Aspects of depression.* Boston: Little Brown, 1969.

Lindenauer, G. G. Loneliness. *Journal of Emotional Education*, 1970, *10*(3), 87–100.

Lopata, H. Z. Loneliness: Forms and components. *Social Problems*, 1969, *17*, 248–261.

Lopata, H. Z. Loneliness in widowhood. In J. Hartog, J. R. Audy, & Y. A. Cohen (Eds.), *The anatomy of loneliness.* New York: International Universities Press, 1980.

Lotz, J. B. *The problem of loneliness.* New York: Alba House, 1967.

Loucks, S. The dimensions of loneliness: A psychological study of affect, self-concept, and object-relations. (Doctoral dissertation, The University of Tennessee, 1974.) *Dissertation Abstracts International*, 1974, *35*, 3024B. (University Microfilms No. 74-27, 221.)

Loucks, S. Loneliness, affect and self-concept: Construct validity of the Bradley Loneliness Scale. *Journal of Personality Assessment*, 1980, *44*(2), 142–147.

Lowenthal, M. F. Social isolation and mental illness in old age. *American Sociological Review*, 1964, *29*, 54–70.

Lynch, J. J. *The broken heart: The medical consequences of loneliness in America.* New York: Basic Books, 1976.

Lynch, J. J., & Convey, W. H. Loneliness, disease, and death: Alternative approaches. *Psychosomatics*, 1979, *20*(10), 702–708.

Madden, J. P. (Ed.), *Loneliness: Issues of emotional living in an age of stress for clergy and religious.* Whitinsville, Mass.: Affirmation, 1977.

Mannin, E. E. *Loneliness: A study of the human condition.* London: Hutchinson, 1966.

Mark, F. R. America's major diseases: Loneliness, anxiety and boredom. *Rehabilitation Record*, 1972, *13*, 5–8.

May, R. The loneliness and anxiety of modern man. *Man's search for himself.* New York: Norton, 1953.

Mead, M. Loneliness, autonomy, and independence in cultural context. In J. Hartog, J. R. Audy, & Y. A. Cohen (Eds.), *The anatomy of loneliness.* New York: International Universities Press, 1980.

Melzer, M. Group treatment to combat loneliness and mistrust in chronic schizophrenics. *Hospital and Community Psychiatry*, 1979, *30*(1), 18–20.

Meredith, C. P. *A comparative examination of anxiety, guilt, prejudice and loneliness in selected scriptural and psychological writings.* Unpublished doctoral dissertation, Florida State University, 1970.

Middlebrook, P. N. Loneliness. In P. N. Middlebrook, *Social psychology and modern life* (2nd ed.). New York: Knopf, 1980.

Mijuskovic, B. Loneliness and a theory of consciousness. *Review of Existential Psychology and Psychiatry*, 1977, *15*(1), 19–31.

Mijuskovic, B. Types of loneliness. *Psychology*, 1977, *14*, 25–29.

Mijuskovic, B. Loneliness and the reflexivity of consciousness. *Psychocultural Review*, 1977, *1*, 202–215.

Mijuskovic, B. Loneliness: An interdisciplinary approach. *Psychiatry*, 1977, *40*, 113–132.

Mijuskovic, B. Loneliness and the possiblity of a "Private Language." *The Journal of Thought*, 1978, *13*, 14–21.

Mijuskovic, B. Loneliness and time-consciousness. *Philosophy Today*, 1978, *22*, 276–286.

Mijuskovic, B. *Loneliness in philosophy, psychology and literature*. Assen, The Netherlands: Van Gorcum, 1979.

Mijuskovic, B. Loneliness and personal identity. *Psychology: A quarterly of human behavior*, 1979, *16*(3), 11–20.

Mijuskovic, B. Loneliness and narcissism. *Psychoanalytic Review*, in press.

Mishara, T. T. A social self approach to loneliness among college students. (Doctoral dissertation, University of Maine, 1974). *Dissertation Abstracts International*, 1975, *36*, 1446B. (University Microfilms No. 75–20, 267.)

Moore, J. A. *Loneliness: Personality, self-discrepancy and demographic variables*. Unpublished doctoral dissertation, York University, Canada, 1972.

Moore, J. A. Relationship between loneliness and interpersonal relationships. *Canadian Counsellor*, 1974, *8*(2), 84–89.

Moore, J. A. Loneliness: Self-discrepancy and sociological variables. *Canadian Counsellor*, 1976, *10*(3), 133–135.

Moore, J. A., & Sermat, V. Relationship between self-actualization and self-reported loneliness. *Canadian Counsellor*, 1974, *8*(3), 194–196.

Mosse, E. P. *The conquest of loneliness*. New York: Random House, 1957.

Moustakas, C. E. *Loneliness*. New York: Prentice-Hall, 1961.

Moustakas, C. E. *Loneliness and love*. Englewood Cliffs, N.J.: Prentice-Hall, 1972.

Moustakas, C. E. *The touch of loneliness*. Englewood Cliffs, N.J.: Prentice-Hall, 1975

Moustakas, C. E. *Portraits of loneliness and love*. Englewood Cliffs, N.J.: Prentice-Hall, 1975.

Munnichs, J. M. A. Loneliness, isolation and social relations in old age. *Vita Humana*, 1964, *7*, 228–238.

National Council of Social Service (London). *Loneliness: A new study*. London: International Publishing Service, 1973.

Neal, A. G., Ivoska, W. J., & Groat, H. T. Dimensions of family alienation in the marital dyad. *Sociometry*, 1976, *39*(4), 396–405.

Nerviano, V. J., & Gross, W. F. Loneliness and locus of control for alcoholic males: Validity against Murray Need and Cattell trait dimensions. *Journal of Clinical Psychology*, 1976, *32*, 479–484.

Nevils, R. S. *A study of loneliness: Selected interpersonal, historical, situational and experiential aspects*. Unpublished doctoral dissertation, University of Tennessee, 1978.

Niemi, T. Effect of loneliness on mortality after retirement. *Scandinavian Journal of Social Medicine*, 1979, *7*(2), 63–65.

Ochiai, Y. The structure of loneliness in current adolescents. *Japanese Journal of Educational Psychology*, 1974, *22*(3), 162–170.

Oles, C. *The loneliness factor.* Lubbock, Tex.: Texas Technological Press, 1979.

Olford, S. F. *Encounter with loneliness.* Kalamazoo, Mich.: Masters Press, 1977.

Olson, S. F. *The lonely land.* New York: Knopf, 1961.

Ortega, M. J. Depression, loneliness and unhappiness. In E. S. Shneidman & M. J. Ortega (Eds.), *Aspects of depression.* Boston: Little, Brown, 1969.

Ostrov, E. Loneliness and the adolescent. *Adolescent Psychiatry,* 1978, *6,* 34–50.

Ostrov, E., & Offer, D. Loneliness and the adolescent. In J. Hartog, J. R. Audy, & Y. A. Cohen (Eds.), *The anatomy of loneliness.* New York: International Universities Press, 1980.

Packard, V. *A nation of strangers.* New York: David McKay, 1972.

Paloutzian, R. F., & Ellison, C. W. Loneliness and spiritual well-being as functions of living environment and professional status in adult women. Paper presented at the annual meeting of the Western Psychological Association, San Diego, April 1979. (ERIC Document Reproduction Service No. ED 176145.)

Park, J. *Loneliness and existential freedom.* Minneapolis, Minn.: Existential Books, 1974.

Parmelee, P., & Werner, C. Lonely losers: Stereotypes of single dwellers. *Personality and Social Psychology Bulletin,* 1978, *4*(2), 292–295.

Paull, H. Rx for loneliness: A plan for establishing a social network of individualized caring. *Crisis Intervention,* 1972, *4*(3), 63–83.

Peplau, H. E. Loneliness. *American Journal of Nursing,* 1955, *55*(12), 1476–1481.

Peplau, L. A., & Caldwell, M. A. Loneliness: A cognitive analysis. *Essence,* 1978, *2*(4), 207–220.

Peplau, L. A., & Perlman, D. Blueprint for a social psychological theory of loneliness. In M. Cook & G. Wilson (Eds.), *Love and attraction.* Oxford, England: Pergamon, 1979.

Peplau, L. A., Russell, D., & Heim, M. The experience of loneliness. In I. H. Frieze, D. Bar-Tal, & J. S. Carroll (Eds.), *New approaches to social problems: Applications of attribution theory.* San Francisco, Calif.: Jossey-Bass, 1979.

Perlman, D., Gerson, A. C., & Spinner, B. Loneliness among senior citizens: An empirical report. *Essence,* 1978, *2*(4), 239–248.

Perlman, D., & Peplau, L. A. Toward a social psychology of loneliness. In S. Duck & R. Gilmour (Eds.), *Personal relationships 3: Personal relationships in disorder.* London: Academic Press, 1981.

Pittman, W. M. The relative effectiveness of three group counseling approaches in reducing loneliness among college students. (Doctoral dissertation, University of Georgia, 1977.) *Dissertation Abstracts International,* 1977, *37,* 77–4152.

Ponzetti, J. J., & Cate, R. M. Sex differences in the relationship between loneliness and academic performance. *Psychological Reports,* 1981, *48,* 75–77.

Portnoff, G. *The experience of loneliness.* Unpublished doctoral dissertation, City University of New York, 1976.

Potthoff, H. H. *Understanding loneliness.* New York: Harper and Row, 1976.

Potts, N. *Loneliness: Living between the times.* Wheaton, Ill.: Victor Books, 1978.

Powell, C. H. *Lonely hearts: The answer to the problem of loneliness through life.* New York: Abingdon Press, 1961.

Riesman, D. "The lonely crowd" 20 years after. *Encounter,* October 1969, pp. 1–5.

Riesman, D., Glazer, N., & Denny, R. *The lonely crowd: A study of the changing American character.* New Haven: Yale University Press, 1961.

Riley, L. Loneliness—A consideration in community health. *Imprint,* 1975, *22,* 17, 38–39.

Robert, M. *Loneliness in the schools (What to do about it).* Niles, Ill.: Argus Communications, 1973.

Roberts, J. M. Loneliness is. *Perspectives in Psychiatric Care,* 1972, *10*(5), 226–231.

Robinson, A. M. Loneliness. *Journal of Practical Nursing,* 1971, *21,* 18–20.

Rogers, C. R. The loneliness of contemporary man as seen in "the case of Ellen West." *Annals of Psychotherapy,* 1961, *3,* 22–27.

Rogers, C. R. The lonely person—and his experiences in an encounter group. In C. R. Rogers, *Carl Rogers on encounter groups.* New York: Harper & Row, 1973.

Rosenbaum, J., & Rosenbaum, V. *Conquering loneliness.* New York: Hawthorn Books, 1973.

Rubenstein, C. *A questionnaire study of adult loneliness in three U.S. cities.* Unpublished doctoral dissertation, New York University, 1979.

Rubenstein, C., & Shaver, P. Loneliness in two northeastern cities. In J. Hartog, J. R. Audy, & Y. A. Cohen (Eds.), *The anatomy of loneliness.* New York: International Universities Press, 1980.

Rubenstein, C., Shaver, P., & Peplau, L. A. Loneliness. *Human Nature,* 1979, *2,* 59–65.

Rubin, Z. Seeking a cure for loneliness. *Psychology Today,* 1979, *13*(4) 82–90.

Rubins, J. L. On the psychopathology of loneliness. *American Journal of Psychoanalysis,* 1964, *24*(2), 153–166.

Russell, D., Peplau, L. A., & Cutrona, C. E. The revised UCLA loneliness scale: Concurrent and discriminant validity evidence. *Journal of Personality and Social Psychology,* 1980, *39*(3), 472–480.

Russell, D., Peplau, L. A. & Ferguson, M. Developing a measure of loneliness. *Journal of Personality Assessment,* 1978, *42*(3), 290–294.

Sadler, W. A. The causes of loneliness. *Science Digest,* July 1975, pp. 58–66.

Sadler, W. A. On the verge of a lonely life. *Humanitas,* 1974, *10*(3), 255–276.

Sadler, W. A. Dimensions in the problem of loneliness: A phenomenological approach in social psychology. *Journal of Phenomenological Psychology,* 1978, *9,* 157–187.

Sadler, W. A., & Johnson, T. B. From loneliness to anomia. In J. Hartog, J. R. Audy, & Y. A. Cohen (Eds.), *The anatomy of loneliness.* New York: International Universities Press, 1980.

Sangster, J. K., & Ellison, C. W. Mental illness, loneliness and helplessness: A challenge for research and therapy. *Mental Health and Society,* 1978, *5,* 284–295.

Satran, G. Notes on loneliness. *Journal of the American Academy of Psychoanalysis,* 1978, *6*(3), 281–300.

Schmidt, J. H., & Niemark, P. *Good-bye loneliness.* Briarcliff Manor, N.Y.: Stein & Day, 1979.

Schultz, T. *Bittersweet: Surviving and growing from loneliness.* New York: Crowell, 1976.

Schulz, R. Effects of control and predictability on the physical and psychological well-being of the institutionalized aged. *Journal of Personality and Social Psychology,* 1976, *33,* 563–573.

Schwarzrock, S., & Wrenn, C. G. *Living with loneliness.* Circle Pines, Minn.: American Guidance Service, Inc., 1970.

Seabrook, J. *Loneliness.* London: Trinity Press, 1973.

Sermat, V. Sources of loneliness. *Essence,* 1978, *2*(4), 271–276.

Sermat, V. Some situational and personality correlates of loneliness. In J. Hartog, J. R. Audy, & Y. A. Cohen (Eds.), *The anatomy of loneliness.* New York: International Universities Press, 1980.

Shanas, E., Townsend, P., Wedderburn, D., Friis, H., Milhoj, P., & Stehouwer, J. *Old people in three industrial societies.* New York: Atherton, 1968.

Shapiro, J. Single room occupancy: Community of the alone. *Social Work,* 1966, *11,* 24–33.

Shaver, P., & Rubenstein, C. Childhood attachment experience and adult loneliness. In L. Wheeler (Ed.), *Review of personality and social psychology* (Vol. 1). Beverly Hills, Calif.: Sage, 1980.

Shein, H. M. Loneliness and interpersonal isolation: Focus for therapy with schizophrenic patients. *American Journal of Psychotherapy,* 1974, *28*(1), 95–107.

Sheldon, J. H. *The social medicine of old age.* London: Oxford University Press, 1948.

Shoben, E. J. Love, loneliness and logic. *Journal of Individual Psychology,* 1960, *16*, 11–24.

Siassi, I., Crocetti, G., & Spiro, H. R. Loneliness and dissatisfaction in a blue collar population. *Archives of General Psychiatry,* 1974, *30*(2), 261–265.

Siegel, E. *Help for the lonely child: Strengthening social perceptions.* New York: Dutton, 1978.

Sisenwein, R. J. *Loneliness and the individual as viewed by himself and others.* Unpublished doctoral dissertation, Columbia University, 1964.

Skoglund, E. *Loneliness.* Dawners Grove, Ill.: Inter-Varsity, 1975.

Slater, P. *The pursuit of loneliness: American culture at the breaking point.* Boston: Beacon Press, 1970.

Sobosan, J. G. Loneliness and faith. *Journal of Psychology and Theology,* 1978, *6*(2), 104–109.

Solano, C. H. Two measures of loneliness: A comparison. *Psychological Reports,* 1980, *46*, 23–28.

Solano, C. H., Batten, P. G., & Parish, E. A. Loneliness and patterns of self-disclosure. *Journal of Personality and Social Psychology,* in press.

Spence, I. *Coping with loneliness.* Grand Rapids, Mich.: Baker, 1975.

Sperber, M. *Masks of loneliness: Alfred Adler in perspective.* New York: Macmillan, 1974.

Steig, W. *The lonely ones.* New York: Duell, Sloan, and Pearce, 1942.

Stierlin, H. The dialectic of related loneliness. *Psychoanalytic Review,* 1965–66, *52*(4), 26–40.

Stoddard, T. L. *Lonely America.* Garden City, N.Y.: Doubleday, Doran, 1932.

Sullivan, H. S. *The interpersonal theory of psychiatry.* New York: Norton, 1953.

Tanner, I. J. *Loneliness: The fear of love.* New York: Harper and Row, 1973.

Taves, I. *Women alone.* New York: Funk and Wagnalls, 1968.

Thauberger, P. Avoidance of ontological confrontation of loneliness and some epidemiological indices of social behavior and health. *Perceptual Motor Skills,* 1979, *48*(3), 1219–1224.

Tournier, P. *Escape from loneliness.* Philadelphia: Westminster Press, 1962.

Townsend, P. Isolation, loneliness, and the hold on life. In E. Josephson & M. Josephson (Eds.), *Man alone: Alienation in modern society.* New York: Dell, 1962.

Tunstall, J. *Old and alone.* New York: Humanities Press, Inc., 1967.

Von Witzleben, H. D. On loneliness. *Psychiatry,* 1958, *21*, 37–43.

Wallerstein, J. S., & Kelly, J. B. The effects of parental divorce: Experiences of the child in later latency. *American Journal of Orthopsychiatry,* 1976, *46*, 256–259. Reprinted in J. Hartog, J. R. Audy, & Y. A. Cohen (Eds.), *The anatomy of loneliness.* New York: International Universities Press, 1980.

Wayne, D. The lonely school child. *American Journal of Nursing,* 1968, *68*, 774–777.

Weeks, D. G., Michela, J. L., Peplau, L. A., & Bragg, M. E. The relation between loneliness and depression: A structural equation analysis. *Journal of Personality and Social Psychology,* 1980, *39*, 1238–1244.

Weigert, E. Loneliness and trust: Basic factors of human existence. *Psychiatry,* 1960, *23,* 121–131.

Weinberg, A. A. Mental ill-health, consequent to migration and loneliness, and its prevention. *Psychotherapy and Psychosomatics,* 1964, *15*(1), 69.

Weiss, R. S. *Loneliness: The experience of emotional and social isolation.* Cambridge, Mass.: MIT Press, 1973.

Weiss, R. S. The provisions of social relationships. In Z. Rubin (Ed.), *Doing unto others.* Englewood Cliffs, N.J.: Prentice-Hall, 1974.

Wenz, F. V. Seasonal suicide attempts and forms of loneliness. *Psychological Reports,* 1977, *40,* 807–810.

Wenz, F. V. Marital status, anomie, and forms of social isolation: A case of high suicide rate among the widowed in an urban sub-area. *Journal of Clinical Psychiatry,* 1977, *38*(11), 891–895.

Whitehorn, J. C. On loneliness and the incongruous self image. *Annals of Psychotherapy,* 1961, *2,* 15–17.

Whitney, E. D. *The lonely sickness.* Boston: Beacon Press, 1965.

Wilkerson, R. *Loneliness: The world's number one killer.* Anaheim, Calif.: Melodyland, 1978.

Williams, L. M. A concept of loneliness in the elderly. *Journal of the American Geriatrics Society,* 1978, *26*(4), 183–187.

Women's Group on Public Welfare. *Loneliness: An enquiry into causes and possible remedies.* London: National Council of Social Service, 1964.

Women's Group on Public Welfare. *Loneliness: A new study.* London: Bedford Square Press, 1972.

Wood, L. A. *Loneliness and social structure.* Unpublished doctoral dissertation, York University, Canada, 1976.

Wood, L. A. Loneliness, social identity and social structure. *Essence,* 1978, *2*(4), 259–270.

Wood, M. M. *Paths of loneliness: The individual isolated in modern society.* New York: Columbia University Press, 1953.

Wood, R. S. *Goodbye loneliness.* New York: Dell, 1976.

Woodward, H., Gingles, R., & Woodward, J. C. Loneliness and the elderly as related to housing. *The Gerontologist,* 1974, *14,* 349–351.

Woodward, J. C. Loneliness and the rural female adolescent. *Nebraska Medical Journal,* 1977, *62*(10), 361–363.

Woodward, J. C., Zabel, J., & Decosta, C. Loneliness and divorce. *Journal of Divorce,* 1980, *4,* 73–82.

Woulff, N. Homesickness in college freshmen. (Doctoral dissertation, University of Maine, 1976.) *Dissertation Abstracts International,* 1976, *36*(10-B).

Wright, L. M. A symbolic tree: Loneliness is the root; delusions are the leaves. *Journal of Psychiatric Nursing,* 1975, *13,* 30–35.

Young, J. E. Loneliness in college students: A cognitive approach. (Doctoral dissertation). *Dissertation Abstracts International,* 1979, *40,* 1392-B. (University Microfilms No. 7919535).

Young, J. E. Cognitive therapy and loneliness. In R. Bedrosian, G. Emery, & S. Hollon (Eds.), *New directions in cognitive therapy: A case book.* New York: Guilford Press, 1980.

Zilboorg, G. Loneliness. *Atlantic Monthly,* January 1938, pp. 45–54.

Author Index

Subject Index

Psychology and Psychiatry in Courts and Corrections: Controversy and Change
  by Ellsworth A. Fersch, Jr.
Restricted Environmental Stimulation: Research and Clinical Applications
  by Peter Suedfeld
Personal Construct Psychology: Psychotherapy and Personality
  edited by Alvin W. Landfield and Larry M. Leitner
Mothers, Grandmothers, and Daughters: Personality and Child Care in
Three-Generation Families
  by Bertram J. Cohler and Henry U. Grunebaum
Further Explorations in Personality
  edited by A. I. Rabin, Joel Aronoff, Andrew M. Barclay, and Robert A. Zucker
Hypnosis and Relaxation: Modern Verification of an Old Equation
  by William E. Edmonston, Jr.
Handbook of Clinical Behavior Therapy
  edited by Samuel M. Turner, Karen S. Calhoun, and Henry E. Adams
Handbook of Clinical Neuropsychology
  edited by Susan B. Filskov and Thomas J. Boll
The Course of Alcoholism: Four Years After Treatment
  by J. Michael Polich, David J. Armor, and Harriet B. Braiker
Handbook of Innovative Psychotherapies
  edited by Raymond J. Corsini
The Role of the Father in Child Development (Second Edition)
  edited by Michael E. Lamb
Behavioral Medicine: Clinical Applications
  by Susan S. Pinkerton, Howard Hughes, and W. W. Wenrich
Handbook for the Practice of Pediatric Psychology
  edited by June M. Tuma
Change Through Interaction: Social Psychological Processes of Counseling and Psychotherapy
  by Stanley R. Strong and Charles D. Claiborn
Drugs and Behavior (Second Edition)
  by Fred Leavitt
Handbook of Research Methods in Clinical Psychology
  edited by Philip C. Kendall and James N. Butcher
A Social Psychology of Developing Adults
  by Thomas O. Blank
Women in the Middle Years: Current Knowledge and Directions for Research and Policy
  edited by Janet Zollinger Giele
Loneliness: A Sourcebook of Current Theory, Research and Therapy
  edited by Letitia Anne Peplau and Daniel Perlman